W9-BXX-474

Microsoft® Exchange Server 2010

Administrator's Pocket Consultant

William R. Stanek

PUBLISHED BY
Microsoft Press
A Division of Microsoft Corporation
One Microsoft Way
Redmond, Washington 98052-6399

Library of Congress Control Number: 2009938146

Printed and bound in the United States of America.

2 3 4 5 6 7 8 9   WCE   4 3 2 1 0

Distributed in Canada by H.B. Fenn and Company Ltd.

A CIP catalogue record for this book is available from the British Library.

Microsoft Press books are available through booksellers and distributors worldwide. For further information about international editions, contact your local Microsoft Corporation office or contact Microsoft Press International directly at fax (425) 936-7329. Visit our Web site at www.microsoft.com/mspress. Send comments to mspinput@microsoft.com

Acquisitions Editor: Martin DelRe
Developmental Editor: Karen Szall
Project Editor: Carol Vu
Editorial Production: Macmillan Publishing Solutions
Technical Reviewer: Todd Meister; Technical Review services provided by Content Master, a member of CM Group, Ltd.
Cover: Tom Draper Design

Body Part No. X16-03279

Contents

What do you think of this book? We want to hear from you!

Microsoft is interested in hearing your feedback so we can continually improve our
books and learning resources for you. To participate in a brief online survey, please visit:

microsoft.com/learning/booksurvey

What do you think of this book? We want to hear from you!

Microsoft is interested in hearing your feedback so we can continually improve our
books and learning resources for you. To participate in a brief online survey, please visit:

microsoft.com/learning/booksurvey

Acknowledgments

To Scott Schnoll, Darcy Jayne, Patricia Eddy, and the Microsoft Exchange team—you know why, and thank you!

Something wonderful and unexpected happened during the writing of this book, and I wanted to share this "happening" with readers. So here goes. When I began my research for *Microsoft Exchange Server 2010 Administrator's Pocket Consultant* back in 2008, I had no idea how challenging this project would be. To say that Exchange Server 2010 is completely different from its predecessors is a considerable understatement. Exchange Server 2010 represents a massive, top-to-bottom overhaul of Exchange Server. Every corner of Exchange Server has been tweaked, updated, or replaced entirely. In fact, I'll go so far as to say that Exchange Server 2010 seems more like an entirely different product than a new release of Exchange Server.

Exchange Server has evolved into a comprehensive messaging and collaboration platform that is completely integrated with Active Directory and fully scalable to meet the needs of the most demanding environments. What's more, just about every facet of Exchange Server 2010 is completely customizable, and many of the customizations can be performed only from the command line. With literally thousands of customizations and an extensive role-based architecture that can easily span multiple servers even in small businesses, the challenge in writing a day-to-day administrator's guide to Exchange Server 2010 lay in figuring out the best approach to organizing the material as well as in identifying essential information so that I could provide you with the critical details in one portable, precise, and concise guide.

I've been writing about Exchange Server professionally since 1999. My first Exchange Server book was published in 2000, and I've since written several others on Exchange 2003 and Exchange 2007. But I've never had the Exchange team get behind a book 100 percent, and that's what happened here. Not only did the Exchange team get behind the book, but team members Scott Schnoll, Darcy Jayne, and Patricia Eddy spent many hours providing deep technical insights and offering suggestions for improving the book. Scott and Darcy in particular were extremely helpful. Although we didn't always agree, I am certain our meeting of the minds made for a much better book. Indeed, no one anywhere knows more about Exchange Server than the team that created it. If I am in some way considered an Exchange guru, these folks are truly Exchange deities. So I want to thank the Exchange team for their helpful insights and suggestions.

With that in mind, I had to carefully review the text, making sure I organized the material appropriately, focused on the core topics, and included all the tips, tricks, and techniques you've come to expect from Pocket Consultants. The result is the book you hold in your hand, which I hope you'll agree is one of the best practical, portable guides to Exchange Server 2010.

As I've stated in other books, the team at Microsoft Press is top-notch. On this project, I worked with Carol Vu, Karen Szall, Martin DelRe, and others. Everyone was great to work with and very supportive of my unique approach to this book. Martin DelRe in particular believed in the book from the beginning and was really great to work with. Completing and publishing the book wouldn't have been possible without their help!

Unfortunately for the writer (but fortunately for readers), writing is only one part of the publishing process. Next came editing and author review. I must say, Microsoft Press has the most thorough editorial and technical review process I've seen anywhere—and I've written a lot of books for many different publishers. John Pierce was the project editor, Roger LeBlanc was the copy editor, and Todd Meister was the technical reviewer. A good experience, and thank you!

I would also like to thank Martin and everyone else at Microsoft who has helped at many points of my writing career and been there when I needed them the most. Thank you also for shepherding my many projects through the publishing process!

I hope I haven't forgotten anyone, but if I have, it was an oversight. *Honest.* ;-)

Introduction

*M*icrosoft Exchange Server 2010 Administrator's Pocket Consultant is designed to be a concise and compulsively usable resource for Exchange Server 2010 administrators. This is the readable resource guide that you'll want on your desk at all times. The book covers everything you need to perform the core administrative tasks for Exchange Server 2010, whether your servers are running on Windows Server 2008 or Windows Server 2008 R2. Because the focus of this book is on giving you maximum value in a pocket-size guide, you don't have to wade through hundreds of pages of extraneous information to find what you're looking for. Instead, you'll find exactly what you need to get the job done.

In short, this book is designed to be the one resource you turn to whenever you have questions regarding Exchange Server 2010 administration. To this end, the book zeroes in on daily administrative procedures, frequently performed tasks, documented examples, and options that are representative although not necessarily inclusive. One of the goals is to keep the content so concise that the book remains compact and easy to navigate while at the same time ensuring that the book is packed with as much information as possible—making it a valuable resource. Thus, instead of a hefty 1,000-page tome or a lightweight 100-page quick reference, you get a valuable resource guide that can help you quickly and easily perform common tasks, solve problems, and implement advanced Exchange Server 2010 technologies such as EdgeSync subscriptions, database availability groups, Outlook Anywhere, SMTP connectors, and Active Directory site links.

Who Is This Book For?

Microsoft Exchange Server 2010 Administrator's Pocket Consultant covers the Standard and Enterprise editions of Exchange Server 2010. The book is designed for the following readers:

- Current Exchange Server 2010 administrators
- Current Windows administrators who want to learn Exchange Server 2010
- Administrators upgrading to Exchange Server 2010 from Exchange 2007
- Administrators upgrading to Exchange Server 2010 from Exchange 2003
- Administrators transferring from other messaging servers
- Managers and supervisors who have been delegated authority to manage mailboxes or other aspects of Exchange Server 2010

To pack in as much information as possible, I had to assume that you have basic networking skills and a basic understanding of e-mail and messaging servers. With this in mind, I don't devote entire chapters to explaining why e-mail systems are needed or how they work. I don't devote entire chapters to installing Exchange Server 2010 either. I do, however, provide complete details on the components of

Exchange organizations and how you can use these components to build a fully redundant and highly available messaging environment. You will also find complete details on all the essential Exchange administration tasks.

I also assume that you are fairly familiar with Windows Server. If you need help learning Windows Server, I highly recommend that you buy *Windows Server 2008 Administrator's Pocket Consultant* or *Windows Server 2008 Inside Out*.

How Is This Book Organized?

Microsoft Exchange Server 2010 Administrator's Pocket Consultant is designed to be used in the daily administration of Exchange Server 2010. As such, the book is organized by job-related tasks rather than by Exchange Server 2010 features. If you are reading this book, you should be aware of the relationship between Pocket Consultants and Administrator's Companions. Both types of books are designed to be part of an administrator's library. Pocket Consultants are the down-and-dirty, in-the-trenches books, while Administrator's Companions are the comprehensive tutorials and references that cover every aspect of deploying a product or technology in the enterprise.

Speed and ease of reference are essential parts of this hands-on guide. The book has an expanded table of contents and an extensive index for finding answers to problems quickly. Many other quick reference features have been added as well. These features include quick step-by-step instructions, lists, tables with fast facts, and extensive cross-references.

The first two chapters provide an overview of Exchange servers and Exchange clients. Chapter 1 provides an overview of Exchange Server 2010 administration concepts, tools, and techniques. Chapter 2 discusses deploying Exchange Server.

Next I cover the fundamental tasks you need for Exchange Server administration. Chapter 3 details how Exchange environments are organized, how information is stored in Exchange Server, and how Exchange Server works. The chapter also explores Exchange message queues and Exchange Server service management. Chapter 4 discusses Windows PowerShell and the Exchange Management Shell, providing the essential background for using these powerful command-line environments for Exchange Server administration. Chapter 5 takes a look at creating and managing users and contacts. You'll learn all about Exchange aliases, enabling and disabling exchange mail for individual users, forwarding mail off-site, and more. Chapter 6 discusses mailbox administration, including techniques for configuring special-purpose resource mailboxes, moving mailboxes, and configuring mailbox delivery restrictions. In Chapter 7, you'll find a detailed discussion of how to use distribution groups and address lists. You'll also learn how to manage these resources. Chapter 8 covers how to implement Exchange security.

In the next several chapters, I discuss advanced tasks for managing and maintaining Exchange organizations. Chapter 9 provides the essentials for managing database availability groups and using full-text indexing. Chapter 10 examines administration of mailbox and public folder databases. The chapter also covers how to recover disconnected mailboxes and deleted messaging items. Chapter 11 looks at how you can use public folders in the enterprise.

Chapter 12 provides a comprehensive discussion of deploying and managing Hub Transport servers and Edge Transport servers. The chapter examines SMTP connectors, Active Directory sites, Active Directory links, and connecting to Exchange 2003 routing groups. The chapter also examines configuring EdgeSync subscriptions, journal rules, transport rules, and anti-spam features. Chapter 13 provides a comprehensive discussion of deploying and managing Client Access servers. The chapter examines IIS Web servers, POP3, IMAP4, and Outlook Anywhere. The chapter also examines configuring Exchange Server features for mobile devices, including Autodiscover, Direct Push, Exchange ActiveSync Mailbox Policy, Remote Device Wipe, Password Recovery, Direct File Access, Remote File Access, and WebReady Document Viewing.

In Chapter 14, you'll learn about troubleshooting essentials as well as Exchange maintenance, monitoring, and queuing. You'll learn key techniques for using message tracking, protocol logging, and connectivity logging for troubleshooting. You'll also learn techniques for automated monitoring and managing Exchange message queues—both of which can help ensure that your Exchange organization runs smoothly. Chapter 15 details how to back up and restore Exchange Server. You'll learn key techniques that can help you reliably back up and, more important, recover Exchange Server in case of failure.

Chapter 16 covers Exchange client setup and management, and Chapter 17 extends the Exchange client discussion and looks at mobile Microsoft Office Outlook users as well as Exchange Active Sync, Outlook Web App, and Outlook Anywhere. With more and more users working on the road or from home, this chapter helps ensure that you can give these mobile users the best support possible.

Conventions Used in This Book

I've used a variety of elements to help keep the text clear and easy to follow. You'll find code terms and listings in monospace type, except when I tell you to actually type a command. In that case, the command appears in **bold** type. When I introduce and define a new term, I put it in *italics*.

Other conventions include:

- **Best Practices** To examine the best technique to use when working with advanced configuration and administration concepts.
- **Cautions** To warn you of potential problems you should look out for.
- **More Info** To provide more information on the subject.
- **Notes** To provide details on a point that needs emphasis.

- **Real World** To provide real-world advice when discussing advanced topics.
- **Security Alerts** To point out important security issues.
- **Tips** To offer helpful hints or additional information.

I truly hope you find that *Microsoft Exchange Server 2010 Administrator's Pocket Consultant* provides everything you need to perform essential administrative tasks as quickly and efficiently as possible. You're welcome to send your thoughts to me at williamstanek@aol.com, or visit *http://www.williamstanek.com/*. Thank you.

Support for This Book

Every effort has been made to ensure the accuracy of this book. As corrections or changes are collected, they will be added to a Microsoft Knowledge Base article accessible via the Microsoft Help and Support site. Microsoft Press provides support for books, including instructions for finding Knowledge Base articles, at the following Web site:

http://www.microsoft.com/learning/support/books/

If you have questions regarding the book that are not answered by visiting the site above or viewing a Knowledge Base article, send them to Microsoft Press via e-mail to *mspinput@microsoft.com*.

Please note that Microsoft software product support is not offered through these addresses.

We Want to Hear from You

We welcome your feedback about this book. Please share your comments and ideas via the following short survey:

http://www.microsoft.com/learning/booksurvey

Your participation will help Microsoft Press create books that better meet your needs and your standards.

> **NOTE** We hope that you will give us detailed feedback via our survey. If you have questions about our publishing program, upcoming titles, or Microsoft Press in general, we encourage you to interact with us via Twitter at *http://twitter.com/MicrosoftPress*. For support issues, use only the e-mail address shown above.

CHAPTER 1

Exchange Server 2010 Administration Overview

I f you thought Microsoft Exchange Server 2007 was a radical departure from its predecessors, wait till you get acquainted with Microsoft Exchange Server 2010. Exchange Server 2010 completely redefines the Exchange Server messaging platform, and right up front you should know that Exchange Server 2010 does away with the concepts of storage groups, Local Continuous Replication (LCR), Single Copy Clusters (SCC), and clustered mailbox servers.

In previous releases of Exchange Server, you used storage groups to group mailbox and public folder databases into logical units of management. In Exchange Server 2010, databases are no longer associated with storage groups. For mailbox databases, database availability groups can now be used to group databases for high availability, and mailbox databases are managed at the organization level instead of at the server level. For public folder databases, database management has been moved to the organization level, but the functionality hasn't changed from how it was implemented in Exchange Server 2007.

To support these and other changes, relevant storage group functionality has been moved to the database level. Further, mailbox databases are now peers to servers in Active Directory. The Exchange store schema has been changed to remove the dependency of mailbox databases on server objects, and this reduces the Exchange store's reliance on secondary indexes maintained by the Extensible Storage Engine (ESE).

Exchange Server 2010 integrates high availability into the core architecture by enhancing aspects of Cluster Continuous Replication (CCR) and Standby Continuous Replication (SCR) and combining them into a single high-availability solution for both on-site and off-site data replication. Exchange Server 2010 also provides for automatic failover and recovery without requiring clusters when you deploy multiple mailbox servers. Because of these changes, building a high-availability mailbox server solution no longer requires cluster hardware or advanced cluster configuration. Instead, database availability groups provide the base component for high availability. Failover is automatic for mailbox databases that are part of the same database availability group.

The rules for database availability groups are simple. Each mailbox server can have multiple databases, and each database can have as many as 16 copies. A single database availability group can have up to 16 mailbox servers that provide automatic database-level recovery. Any server in a database availability group can host a copy of a mailbox database from any other server in the database availability group.

This seamless high-availability functionality is made possible because Exchange Server 2010 disconnects mailbox databases from servers and assigns the same globally unique identifier (GUID) to all copies of a mailbox database. Because storage groups no longer exist, continuous replication occurs at the database level. Transaction logs are replicated to each member of a database availability group that has a copy of a mailbox database and are replayed into the copy of the mailbox database. Failover can occur at either the database level or the server level.

Although I discuss the architectural and administrative impact of these extensive changes throughout this and other chapters of this book, you need to know this information up front because it radically changes the way you implement and manage your Exchange organization. Why? With these changes, you might not need to use Redundant Arrays Of Inexpensive Disks (RAID) for your Exchange data and you might not need to ever perform routine backups of your Exchange data. Although these are radical ideas, they are possible—especially if you implement data-retention rules as necessary for regulatory compliance and remember to rotate Exchange data to off-site storage periodically to ensure that you are protected in extreme disaster recovery scenarios.

As you get started with Exchange Server 2010, you should concentrate on the following areas:

- How Exchange Server 2010 works with your hardware
- What versions and editions of Exchange Server 2010 are available, and how they meet your needs
- How Exchange Server 2010 works with Windows–based operating systems
- How Exchange Server 2010 works with Active Directory
- What administration tools are available

Exchange Server 2010 and Your Hardware

Before you deploy Exchange Server 2010, you should carefully plan the messaging architecture. As part of your implementation planning, you need to look closely at preinstallation requirements and the hardware you will use. Exchange Server is no longer the simple messaging server that it once was. It is now a complex messaging platform with many components that work together to provide a comprehensive solution for routing, delivering, and accessing e-mail messages, voice-mail messages, faxes, contacts, and calendar information.

Successful Exchange Server administration depends on three things:

- Knowledgeable Exchange administrators
- Strong architecture
- Appropriate hardware

The first two ingredients are covered: you're the administrator, you're smart enough to buy this book to help you through the rough spots, and you've enlisted Exchange Server 2010 to provide your high-performance messaging needs. This brings us to the issue of hardware. Exchange Server 2010 should run on a system with adequate memory, processing speed, and disk space. You also need an appropriate data-protection and system-protection plan at the hardware level.

Key guidelines for choosing hardware for Exchange Server are as follows:

- **Memory** Exchange Server 2010 has been tested and developed for maximum memory configurations of 64 gigabytes (GB) for Mailbox servers and 16 GB for all other server roles except Unified Messaging. For Unified Messaging, the maximum is 8 GB. For multirole servers, the maximum is 64 GB. The minimum random access memory (RAM) is 2 GB. In most cases, you'll want to have at least twice the recommended minimum amount of memory. The primary reason for this is performance. Most of the Exchange installations I run use 4 GB of RAM as a starting point, even in small installations. In multiple Exchange server installations, the Mailbox server should have at least 2 GB of RAM plus 5 megabytes (MB) of RAM per mailbox. For all Exchange server configurations, the paging file should be at least equal to the amount of RAM in the server plus 10 MB.

- **CPU** Exchange Server 2010 runs on the x64 family of processors from AMD and Intel, including AMD64 and Intel Extended Memory 64 Technology (Intel EM64T). Exchange Server 2010 provides solid benchmark performance with Intel Xeon 3.4 GHz and higher or AMD Opteron 3.1 GHz and higher. Any of these CPUs provide good starting points for the average Exchange Server system. You can achieve significant performance improvements with a high level of processor cache. Look closely at the L1, L2, and L3 cache options available—a higher cache can yield much better performance overall. Look also at the speed of the front-side bus. The faster the bus speed, the faster the CPU can access memory.

Exchange Server 2010 runs only on 64-bit hardware. The primary advantages of 64-bit processors over 32-bit processors are related to memory limitations and data access. Because 64-bit processors can address more than 4 GB of memory at a time without physical address extension, they can store greater amounts of data in main memory, providing direct access to and faster processing of data. In addition, 64-bit processors can process data and execute instruction sets that are twice as large as 32-bit processors. Accessing 64 bits of data (versus 32 bits) offers a significant advantage when processing complex calculations that require a high level of precision.

NOTE At the time of this writing, 64-bit versions do not support Intel Itanium.

- **SMP** Exchange Server 2010 supports symmetric multiprocessors, and you'll see significant performance improvements if you use multiple CPUs. Microsoft tested and developed Exchange Server 2010 for use with dual-core and multicore CPUs as well. The minimum, recommended, and maximum number of CPUs—whether single core, dual core, or multicore—depends on a server's Exchange roles. (See the "Exchange Server Messaging Roles" section in Chapter 2, "Deploying Exchange Server 2010.") Still, if Exchange Server is supporting a small organization with a single domain, one CPU with multiple cores should be enough. If the server supports a medium or large organization or handles mail for multiple domains, you might want to consider adding processors. When it comes to processor cores, I prefer two 4-core processors to a single 8-core processor given current price and performance tradeoffs. An alternative is to distribute the workload across different servers based on where you locate resources.

- **Disk drives** The data storage capacity you need depends entirely on the number and size of the data that will pass through, be journaled on, or stored on the Exchange server. You need enough disk space to store all data and logs, plus workspace, system files, and virtual memory. Input/output (I/O) throughput is just as important as drive capacity. Rather than use one large drive, you should use several drives, which allow you to configure fault tolerance with RAID.

- **Data protection** You can add protection against unexpected drive failures by using RAID. For the boot and system disks, use RAID 1 on internal drives. However, because of the new high-availability features, you might not want to use RAID for Exchange data and logs. You also might not want to use expensive disk storage systems either. Instead, you might want to deploy multiple Exchange servers with each of your Exchange roles.

  If you decide to use RAID, remember that storage arrays typically already have an underlying RAID configuration and you might have to use a tool such as Storage Manager For SANs to help you distinguish between logical unit numbers (LUNs) and physical disks. For data, use RAID 0 or RAID 5.

For logs, use RAID 1. RAID 0 (disk striping without parity) offers good read/ write performance, but any failed drive means that Exchange Server can't continue operation on an affected database until the drive is replaced and data is restored from backup. RAID 1 (disk mirroring) creates duplicate copies of data on separate drives; you can rebuild the RAID unit to restore full operations and can continue operations if one of the drives fails. RAID 5 (disk striping with parity) offers good protection against single drive failure, but it has poor write performance. For best performance and fault tolerance, RAID 10 (also referred to as RAID 0 + 1), which consists of disk mirroring and disk striping without parity, is also an option.

- **Uninterruptible power supply**   Exchange Server 2010 is designed to maintain database integrity at all times and can recover information using transaction logs. This doesn't protect the server hardware, however, from sudden power loss or power spikes, both of which can seriously damage hardware. To prevent this, connect your server to an uninterruptible power supply (UPS). A UPS gives you time to shut down the server or servers properly in the event of a power outage. Proper shutdown is especially important on servers using write-back caching controllers. These controllers temporarily store data in cache. Without proper shutdown, this data can be lost before it is written to disk. Note that most write-back caching controllers have batteries that help ensure that changes can be written to disk after the system comes back online.

If you follow these hardware guidelines and modify them for specific messaging roles, as discussed in the next section, you'll be well on your way to success with Exchange Server 2010.

Exchange Server 2010 Editions

Several editions of Exchange Server 2010 are available, including Exchange Server 2010 Standard and Exchange Server 2010 Enterprise. The various server editions support the same core features and administration tools, which means you can use the techniques discussed throughout this book regardless of which Exchange Server 2010 edition you are using. For reference, the specific feature differences between Standard Edition and Enterprise Edition are as follows:

- **Exchange Server 2010 Standard**   Designed to provide essential messaging services for small to medium-size organizations and branch office locations. This server edition supports a limited number of databases.

- **Exchange Server 2010 Enterprise**   Designed to provide essential messaging services for organizations with increased availability, reliability, and manageability needs. This server edition supports up to 100 databases (including all active databases and copies of databases) on a particular server.

NOTE Throughout this book, I refer to Exchange Server in different ways, and each has a different meaning. Typically, I refer to the software product as *Exchange Server*. If you see this term, you can take it to mean *Microsoft Exchange Server 2010*. When necessary, I use *Exchange Server 2010* to draw attention to the fact that I am discussing a feature that's new or has changed in the most recent version of the product. Each of these terms means essentially the same thing. If I refer to a previous version of Exchange Server, I always do so specifically, such as Exchange Server 2007. Finally, I often use the term *Exchange server* (note the lowercase *S* in server) to refer to an actual server computer, as in "There are eight Exchange servers in this routing group."

REAL WORLD Microsoft provides a single binary for x64 systems, and the same binary file is used for both the Standard and Enterprise edition. The license key provided during installation is what determines which edition is established during installation. You can use a valid product key to upgrade from a trial edition to the Standard edition or the Enterprise edition of Exchange Server 2010 without having to reinstall. Using a valid product key, you can also upgrade from the Standard to the Enterprise edition. You can also relicense an Exchange server by entering a new product key for the installed edition, which is useful if you accidentally used the same product key on multiple servers and want to correct the mistake.

There are several caveats. When you change the product key on a Mailbox server, you must restart the Microsoft Exchange Information Store service to apply the change. When you change the product key on an Edge Transport server, you must resubscribe the server in the Exchange organization to apply the change. Additionally, you cannot use product keys to downgrade editions. To downgrade editions, you must uninstall Exchange Server and then reinstall Exchange Server.

You can install Exchange Server 2010 on a server running Windows Server 2008 with Service Pack 2 or later as well as on a server running Windows Server 2008 Release 2. A client accessing an Exchange server requires a Client Access License (CAL). With either Exchange Server edition, the client can use a Standard CAL, an Enterprise CAL, or both. The Standard CAL allows for the use of e-mail, shared calendaring, contacts, task management, Microsoft Outlook Web App (OWA), and Exchange ActiveSync. The Enterprise CAL allows for the use of unified messaging, advanced compliance capabilities, and antivirus/antispam protection. A client must have both a Standard CAL and an Enterprise CAL to make full use of all Exchange Server features.

Beyond the editions and CALs, Exchange Server 2010 has several variants. Microsoft offers on-premises and online implementations of Exchange Server. An on-premises Exchange Server is one that you install in your organization. An online Exchange Server is delivered as a subscription service from Microsoft. In Exchange Server 2010, you can manage both on-premises and online implementations of Exchange Server using the same management tools.

When you install Exchange Server 2010, the system partition and all disk partitions used by Exchange must be formatted using the NTFS file system. Additional preinstallation requirements are as follows:

- In the Active Directory forest where you plan to install Exchange 2010, the Schema master must be running on a server with Windows Server 2003 or a later version of Windows and Active Directory must be in at least Windows Server 2003 forest functionality mode.

- In every Active Directory site where you plan to install Exchange 2010, you must have at least one global catalog server that is running Windows Server 2003 or a later version of Windows.

- For forest-to-forest delegation and free/busy availability selection across forests, you must establish a trust between the forests that have Exchange Server installed.

- The domain should be configured to use multiple-label Domain Name System (DNS) names, such as cpandl.com or adatum.local, rather than single-label DNS names, such as cpandl or adatum. However, single label names can be used.

NOTE The full installation option of Windows Server 2008 is required for all Exchange 2010 servers. Using Active Directory with Exchange Server 2010 is covered in more detail in the "Exchange Server and Active Directory" section of this chapter and the "Integrating Exchange Server Roles with Active Directory" section of Chapter 2.

Exchange Server 2010 requires Microsoft Management Console 3.0 or later, the Microsoft .NET Framework version 3.5.1, and Windows PowerShell Version 2.0 for the Exchange Management Shell and remote management. The Windows PowerShell remoting features are supported by the WS-Management protocol and the Windows Remote Management (WinRM) service that implements WS-Management in Windows. Computers running Windows 7 and Windows Server 2008 Release 2 and later include WinRM 2.0 or later. On computers running earlier versions of Windows, you need to install Windows Management Framework, which includes Windows PowerShell 2.0 and WinRM 2.0 or later as appropriate. Other prerequisites are role-specific and discussed in Chapter 2.

If you want to manage Exchange Server 2010 from a workstation, you need to install Windows Management Framework. Because WinRM 2.0 and Windows PowerShell 2.0 are used for remote management whether you use the GUI or the command line, you need to enable remote commands on the workstation.

You can verify the availability of WinRM 2.0 and configure Windows PowerShell for remoting by following these steps:

1. Click Start, All Programs, Accessories, Windows PowerShell. Start Windows PowerShell as an administrator by right-clicking the Windows PowerShell shortcut and selecting Run As Administrator.

2. The WinRM service is configured for manual startup by default. You must change the startup type to Automatic and start the service on each computer you want to work with. At the PowerShell prompt, you can verify that the WinRM service is running by using the following command:

```
get-service winrm
```

As shown in the following example, the value of the Status property in the output should be Running:

```
Status   Name       DisplayName
------   ----       -----------
Running  WinRM      Windows Remote Management
```

If the service is stopped, enter the following command to start the service and configure it to start automatically in the future:

```
set-service -name winrm -startuptype automatic -status running
```

3. To configure Windows PowerShell for remoting, type the following command:

```
Enable-PSRemoting -force
```

You can only enable remoting when your computer is connected to a domain or private network. If your computer is connected to a public network, you need to disconnect from the public network and connect to a domain or private network and then repeat this step. If one or more of your computer's connections has the Public connection type, but you are actually connected to a domain or private network, you need to change the network connection type in Network And Sharing Center and then repeat this step.

In many cases, you will be able to work with remote computers in other domains. However, if the remote computer is not in a trusted domain, the remote computer might not be able to authenticate your credentials. To enable authentication, you need to add the remote computer to the list of trusted hosts for the local computer in WinRM. To do so, type the following:

```
winrm s winrm/config/client '@{TrustedHosts="RemoteComputer"}'
```

where *RemoteComputer* is the name of the remote computer, such as:

```
winrm s winrm/config/client '@{TrustedHosts="CorpServer56"}'
```

When you are working with computers in workgroups or homegroups, you must use HTTPS as the transport or add the remote machine to the TrustedHosts configuration settings. If you cannot connect to a remote host, verify that the service on the remote host is running and is accepting requests by running the following command on the remote host:

```
winrm quickconfig
```

This command analyzes and configures the WinRM service. If the WinRM service is set up correctly, you'll see output similar to the following:

```
WinRM already is set up to receive requests on this machine.
WinRM already is set up for remote management on this machine
```

If the WinRM service is not set up correctly, you see errors and need to respond affirmatively to several prompts that allow you to automatically configure remote management. When this process completes, WinRM should be set up correctly.

Whenever you use Windows PowerShell remoting features, you must start Windows PowerShell as an administrator by right-clicking the Windows PowerShell shortcut and selecting Run As Administrator. When starting Windows PowerShell from another program, such as the command prompt (cmd.exe), you must start that program as an administrator.

Exchange Server 2010 uses the Windows Installer (the Installer) and has a fully integrated installation process. This means you can configure Exchange Server 2010 much like you can any other application you install on the operating system. The installation can be performed remotely from a command shell as well as locally.

Chapter 2 provides detailed instructions for installing Exchange Server 2010. With an initial installation, Windows Installer first checks the system configuration to determine the status of required services and components. As part of this process, Windows Installer checks the Active Directory configuration and the availability of components, such as IIS (Internet Information Services), as well as operating system service packs, installation permissions for the default install path, memory, and hardware.

After checking the system configuration, the Installer allows you to select the roles to install. Whether you use the Standard or Enterprise edition, you have similar options. You can do any of the following:

- Install an internal messaging server by selecting the individual server roles to install and combining the Mailbox role, Client Access role, Hub Transport role, and Unified Messaging role as required for your environment. Generally, you will not want an internal Exchange server to also be configured as a domain controller with a global catalog.

  NOTE For details on how the various server roles are used, see Chapter 2, which also provides guidelines for sizing and positioning the various server roles. Before you install the Client Access role on servers with the Mailbox role, you'll want to consider whether you want to use client access arrays. A client access array is a grouping of client access servers in a load balanced array. Servers that are members of the array cannot have the Mailbox role.

- Install a Messaging server in a perimeter zone outside the organization's main network by selecting only the Edge Transport role. Edge Transport servers are not members of the internal Active Directory forest and are not configured on domain controllers. They can, however, be members of an extranet Active Directory forest, which is useful for management purposes.

- Install the management tools.
- Specify the path for the Exchange Server installation files.
- Specify the path for the Exchange Server installation.

If you want to change the configuration after installation, you can use Exchange Server 2010 maintenance mode, as discussed in the "Adding, Modifying, or Uninstalling Server Roles" section in Chapter 2.

Exchange Server 2010 includes the following antispam and antivirus capabilities:

- **Connection filtering** Allows administrators to configure IP Block lists and IP Allow lists, as well as providers who can supply these lists.

- **Content filtering** Uses intelligent message filtering to scan message content and identify spam. Spam can be automatically deleted, quarantined, or filed as junk e-mail.

TIP Using the Exchange Server management tools, administrators can manage messages sent to the quarantine mailbox and take appropriate actions, such as deleting messages, flagging them as false positives, or allowing them to be delivered as junk e-mail. Messages delivered as junk e-mail are converted to plain text to strip out any potential viruses they might contain.

- **IP reputation service** Provides Exchange Server 2010 customers with exclusive access to an IP Block list provided by Microsoft.

- **Outlook Junk E-mail Filter list aggregation** Allows the junk e-mail filter lists of individual Outlook users to be propagated to Exchange servers.

- **Recipient filtering** Allows administrators to replicate recipient data from the enterprise to the server running the Edge Transport role. This server can then perform recipient lookups on incoming messages and block messages that are for nonexistent users, which prevents certain types of attacks and malicious attempts at information discovery.

- **Sender ID verification** Verifies that incoming e-mail messages are from the Internet domain from which they claim to come. Exchange verifies the sender ID by examining the sender's IP address and comparing it to the related security record on the sender's public DNS server.

- **Sender reputation scoring** Helps to determine the relative trustworthiness of unknown senders through sender ID verification and by examining message content and sender behavior history. A sender can then be added temporarily to the Blocked Senders list.

Although these antivirus and antispam features are extensive, they are not comprehensive in scope. For comprehensive antivirus protection, you need to install Forefront Protection for Exchange Server. Forefront Protection for Exchange Server helps protect Exchange servers from viruses, worms, and other malware using multiple antivirus scan engines and file-filtering capabilities. Forefront Protection provides distributed protection for Exchange servers with the Mailbox server, Hub Transport server, and Edge Transport server roles. Although you can install Forefront Protection on Exchange servers with these roles to gain substantial antivirus protection, you do not need to install Forefront Protection on Exchange servers with only the Client Access server or Unified Messaging server role.

You can use the Forefront Protection Setup program to install the server and management components. The management components include the Forefront Server Security Administration Console and the Forefront Management Shell. When you are working with the console, you can configure the way real-time and scheduled scanning for viruses and spyware works. In the shell, you'll find Forefront-specific cmdlets for performing similar tasks.

Exchange Server and Windows

When you install Exchange Server and Forefront Protection for Exchange Server on a server operating system, Exchange Server and Forefront Protection make extensive modifications to the environment. These modifications include new system services, integrated authentication, and new security groups.

Services for Exchange Server

When you install Exchange Server and Forefront Protection for Exchange Server on Windows, multiple services are installed and configured on the server. Table 1-1 provides a summary of key services, how they are used, and which server components they are associated with.

TABLE 1-1 Summary of Key Services Used by Exchange Server 2010

SERVICE NAME	DESCRIPTION	SERVER ROLE
IIS Admin	Enables the server to administer the IIS metabase. The IIS metabase stores configuration information for Web applications used by Exchange. All roles need IIS for WinRM and remote Powershell. CAS needs IIS for OWA and Web services	Client Access
Microsoft Exchange Active Directory Topology	Provides Active Directory topology information to Exchange services. If this service is stopped, most Exchange services will not be able to start.	Hub Transport, Mailbox, Client Access, Unified Messaging
Microsoft Exchange Address Book	Manages client address book connections for Exchange Server.	Client Access

TABLE 1-1 Summary of Key Services Used by Exchange Server 2010

SERVICE NAME	DESCRIPTION	SERVER ROLE
Microsoft Exchange Anti-Spam Update	Maintains the antispam data for Fore-front Protection on an Exchange server.	Hub Transport, Edge Transport
Microsoft Exchange EdgeSync	Provides EdgeSync services between Hub and Edge servers.	Hub Transport
Microsoft Exchange File Distribution	Distributes Exchange data to other Exchange servers.	All
Microsoft Exchange Forms Based Authentication	Provides form-based authentication for Outlook Web App and the Web management interface.	Client Access
Microsoft Exchange IMAP4	Provides IMAP4 services to clients.	Client Access
Microsoft Exchange Information Store	Manages the Microsoft Exchange Information Store. This includes mailbox stores and public folder stores.	Mailbox
Microsoft Exchange Mail Submission	Submits messages from the Mailbox server to the Hub Transport servers.	Mailbox
Microsoft Exchange Mailbox Assistants	Manages assistants that are respon-sible for calendar updates and booking resources.	Mailbox
Microsoft Exchange Mailbox Replication	Enables online mailbox moves by processing mailbox move requests.	Client Access
Microsoft Exchange Monitoring	Provides support for monitoring and diagnostics.	All
Microsoft Exchange POP3	Provides Post Office Protocol version 3 (POP3) services to clients.	Client Access
Microsoft Exchange Protected Service Host	Provides secure host for Exchange Server services.	All
Microsoft Exchange Replication Service	Provides replication functionality used for continuous replication.	Mailbox
Microsoft Exchange RPC Client Access	Manages client remote procedure call (RPC) connections for Exchange Server.	Client Access
Microsoft Exchange Search Indexer	Controls indexing of mailboxes to improve search performance.	Mailbox

TABLE 1-1 Summary of Key Services Used by Exchange Server 2010

SERVICE NAME	DESCRIPTION	SERVER ROLE
Microsoft Exchange Server Extension for Windows Server Backup	Provides extensions for Windows Server Backup that allow you to backup and recover Exchange application data using Windows Server Backup.	All
Microsoft Exchange Service Host	Provides a host for essential Exchange services.	All
Microsoft Exchange Speech Engine	Provides speech processing services for Microsoft Exchange. If this service is stopped, speech recognition services will not be available to unified messaging clients.	Unified Messaging
Microsoft Exchange System Attendant	Provides monitoring, maintenance, and Active Directory lookup services.	Mailbox
Microsoft Exchange Throttling	Provides throttling functions to limit the rate of user operations.	Mailbox
Microsoft Exchange Transport	Provides mail transport for Exchange Server.	Hub Transport, Edge Transport
Microsoft Exchange Transport Log Search	Provides search capability for Exchange transport log files.	Hub Transport, Mailbox
Microsoft Exchange Unified Messaging	Enables voice and fax messages to be stored in Exchange and gives users telephone access to e-mail, voice mail, the calendar, contacts, or an automated attendant.	Unified Messaging
Microsoft Forefront Server Protection ADO/EWS Navigator	Navigates the objects in Active Directory for Forefront Protection by connecting with Exchange Web Services (EWS) or Exchange ActiveX Data Objects (ADO) to retrieve objects.	Forefront Protection
Microsoft Forefront Server Protection Controller	Controls the interaction between Forefront Protection and the Microsoft Exchange Information Store. Ensures that Forefront Protection initializes properly with the information store. The Microsoft Forefront Server Security Controller starts and stops scan jobs and applies engine updates.	Forefront Protection

TABLE 1-1 Summary of Key Services Used by Exchange Server 2010

SERVICE NAME	DESCRIPTION	SERVER ROLE
Microsoft Forefront Server Security Eventing Service	Processes incidents, and manages quarantine logging, performance logging, and notifications.	Forefront Protection
Microsoft Forefront Server Security for Exchange Registration Service	Ensures the Forefront Transport Agent is registered with Exchange Server.	Forefront Protection
Microsoft Forefront Server Security Mail Pickup	Provides mail pickup services for Forefront Protection.	Forefront Protection
Microsoft Forefront Server Security Monitor	Monitors the information store, SMTP/IMS, and Forefront Protection processes to ensure that Forefront Protection provides continuous protection.	Forefront Protection
Microsoft Search (Exchange)	Provides search services for mailboxes, address lists, and so on.	Hub Transport, Mailbox
Secure Socket Tunneling Protocol Service	Provides support for Secure Socket Tunneling Protocol (SSTP) for securely connecting to remote computers.	Client Access
Web Management Service	Enables remote and delegated management for the Web server, sites, and applications.	Client Access
Windows Remote Management Service	Implements the WS-Management protocol. Required for remote management using the Exchange console and Windows PowerShell.	All
World Wide Web Publishing Services	Provides Web connectivity and administration features for IIS.	Client Access

Exchange Server Authentication and Security

In Exchange Server 2010, e-mail addresses, distribution groups, and other directory resources are stored in the directory database provided by Active Directory. Active Directory is a directory service running on Windows domain controllers. When there are multiple domain controllers, the controllers automatically replicate directory data with each other using a multimaster replication model. This model allows any domain controller to process directory changes and then replicate those changes to other domain controllers.

The first time you install Exchange Server 2010 in a Windows domain, the installation process updates and extends Active Directory to include objects and attributes used by Exchange Server 2010. Unlike Exchange Server 2003 and earlier releases of Exchange, this process does not include updates for the Active Directory Users And Computers Snap-In for Microsoft Management Console (MMC), and you do not use Active Directory Users And Computers to manage mailboxes, messaging features, messaging options, or e-mail addresses associated with user accounts. You perform these tasks using the Exchange Management tools.

Exchange Server 2010 fully supports the Windows Server security model and relies on this security mechanism to control access to directory resources. This means you can control access to mailboxes and membership in distribution groups and you can perform other Exchange security administration tasks through the standard Windows Server permission set. For example, to add a user to a distribution group, you simply make the user a member of the distribution group in Active Directory Users And Computers.

Because Exchange Server uses Windows Server security, you can't create a mailbox without first creating a user account that will use the mailbox. Every Exchange mailbox must be associated with a domain account—even those used by Exchange for general messaging tasks. For example, the SMTP and System Attendant mailboxes that Exchange Server uses are associated by default with the built-in System user. In the Exchange Management Console, you can create a new user account as part of the process of creating a new mailbox.

NOTE To support coexistence with Exchange Server 2003, all Exchange Server 2010 servers are automatically added to a single administrative group when you install Exchange Server 2010. This administrative group is recognized in the Exchange System Manager in Exchange Server 2003 as "Exchange Administrative Group." Although Exchange Server 2003 uses administrative groups to gather Exchange objects for the purposes of delegating permission to manage those objects, Exchange Server 2007 and Exchange Server 2010 do not use administrative groups. Instead, you manage Exchange servers according to their roles and the type of information you want to manage using the Exchange Management Console. You'll learn more about this in Chapter 3, "Exchange Server 2010 Administration Essentials."

Exchange Server Security Groups

Like Exchange Server 2007, Exchange Server 2010 uses predefined universal security groups to separate administration of Exchange permissions from administration of other permissions. When you add an administrator to one of these security groups, the administrator inherits the permissions permitted by that role.

The predefined security groups have permissions to manage the following types of Exchange data in Active Directory:

- **Organization Configuration node**   This type of data is not associated with a specific server and is used to manage databases, policies, address lists, and other types of organizational configuration details.
- **Server Configuration node**   This type of data is associated with a specific server and is used to manage the server's messaging configuration.
- **Recipient Configuration node**   This type of data is associated with mailboxes, mail-enabled contacts, and distribution groups.

NOTE In Exchange Server 2010, databases have been moved from the Server Configuration node to the Organization Configuration node. This change was necessary because the Exchange schema was flattened and storage groups were removed. As a result of these changes, all storage group functionality has been moved to the database level.

The predefined groups are as follows:

- **Delegated Setup**   Members of this group have permission to install and uninstall Exchange on provisioned servers.
- **Discovery Management**   Members of this group can perform mailbox searches for data that meets specific criteria.
- **Exchange All Hosted Organizations**   Members of this group include hosted organization mailbox groups. This group is used to apply Password Setting objects to all hosted mailboxes.
- **Exchange Servers**   Members of this group are Exchange servers in the organization. This group allows Exchange servers to work together.
- **Exchange Trusted Subsystem**   Members of this group are Exchange servers that run Exchange cmdlets using WinRM. Members of this group have permission to read and modify all Exchange configuration settings as well as user accounts and groups.
- **Exchange Windows Permissions**   Members of this group are Exchange servers that run Exchange cmdlets using WinRM. Members of this group have permission to read and modify user accounts and groups.
- **ExchangeLegacyInterop**   Members of this group are granted send-to and receive-from permissions, which are necessary for routing group connections between Exchange Server 2010 and Exchange Server 2003. Exchange Server 2003 bridgehead servers must be made members of this group to allow proper mail flow in the organization. For more information on interoperability, see Chapter 2.
- **Help Desk**   Members of this group can view any property or object within the Exchange organization and have limited management permissions, including the right to change and reset passwords.
- **Hygiene Management**   Members of this group can manage the antispam and antivirus features of Exchange.

- **Organization Management**   Members of this group have full access to all Exchange properties and objects in the Exchange organization.
- **Public Folder Management**   Members of this group can manage public folders and perform most public folder management operations.
- **Recipient Management**   Members of this group have permissions to modify Exchange user attributes in Active Directory and perform most mailbox operations.
- **Records Management**   Members of this group can manage compliance features, including retention policies, message classifications, and transport rules.
- **Server Management**   Members of this group can manage all Exchange servers in the organization but do not have permission to perform global operations.
- **UM Management**   Members of this group can manage all aspects of unified messaging, including unified messaging server configuration and unified messaging recipient configuration.
- **View-Only Organization Management**   Members of this group have read-only access to the entire Exchange organization tree in the Active Directory configuration container and read-only access to all the Windows domain containers that have Exchange recipients.

Exchange Server and Active Directory

Like Exchange Server 2007, Exchange Server 2010 is tightly integrated with Active Directory. Not only does Exchange Server 2010 store information in Active Directory, but it also uses the Active Directory routing topology to determine how to route messages within the organization. Routing to and from the organization is handled using transport servers.

Understanding How Exchange Stores Information

Exchange stores four types of data in Active Directory: schema data (stored in the Schema partition), configuration data (stored in the Configuration partition), domain data (stored in the Domain partition), and application data (stored in application-specific partitions). In Active Directory, schema rules determine what types of objects are available and what attributes those objects have. When you install the first Exchange server in the forest, the Active Directory preparation process adds many Exchange-specific object classes and attributes to the schema partition in Active Directory. This allows Exchange-specific objects, such as agents and connectors, to be created. It also allows you to extend existing objects, such as users and groups, with new attributes, such as attributes that allow user objects to be used for sending and receiving e-mail. Every domain controller and global catalog server in the organization has a complete copy of the Schema partition.

During the installation of the first Exchange server in the forest, Exchange configuration information is generated and stored in Active Directory. Exchange configuration information, like other configuration information, is also stored in the Configuration partition. For Active Directory, the configuration information describes the structure of the directory, and the Configuration container includes all of the domains, trees, and forests, as well as the locations of domain controllers and global catalogs. For Exchange, the configuration information is used to describe the structure of the Exchange organization. The Configuration container includes lists of templates, policies, and other global organization-level details. Every domain controller and global catalog server in the organization has a complete copy of the Configuration partition.

In Active Directory, the Domain partition stores domain-specific objects, such as users and groups, and the stored values of attributes associated with those objects. As you create, modify, or delete objects, Exchange stores the details about those objects in the Domain partition. During the installation of the first Exchange server in the forest, Exchange objects are created in the current domain. Whenever you create new recipients or modify Exchange details, the related changes are reflected in the Domain partition as well. Every domain controller has a complete copy of the Domain partition for the domain for which it is authoritative. Every global catalog server in the forest maintains information about a subset of every Domain partition in the forest.

Understanding How Exchange Routes Messages

Within the organization, Hub Transport servers use the information about sites stored in Active Directory to determine how to route messages, and they can also route messages across site links. The Hub Transport server does this by querying Active Directory about its site membership and the site membership of other servers, and then it uses the information it discovers to route messages appropriately. Because of this, when you are deploying an Exchange Server 2010 organization, no additional configuration is required to establish routing in the Active Directory forest.

For mail delivery within the organization, additional routing configuration is necessary only in these specific scenarios:

- If you deploy Exchange Server 2010 in an existing Exchange Server 2003 organization, you must configure a two-way routing group connector from the Exchange routing group to each Exchange Server 2003 routing group that communicates with Exchange Server 2010. You must also suppress link state updates for the same.

- If you deploy an Exchange Server 2010 organization with multiple forests, you must install Exchange Server 2010 in each forest and then connect the forests using appropriate cross-forest trusts. The trust allows users to see address and availability data across the forests.

- In an Exchange Server 2010 organization, if you want direct mail flow between Exchange servers in different forests, you must configure SMTP send connectors and SMTP receive connectors on the Hub Transport servers that should communicate directly with each other.

The organization's Mail Transport servers handle mail delivery outside the organization and receipt of mail from outside servers. You can use two types of Mail Transport servers: Hub Transport servers and Edge Transport servers. You deploy Hub Transport servers within the organization. You can optionally deploy Edge Transport servers in the organization's perimeter network for added security. Typically a perimeter network is a secure network set up outside the organization's private network.

With Hub Transport servers, no other special configuration is needed for message routing to external destinations. You must configure only the standard mail setup, which includes identifying DNS servers to use for lookups. With Edge Transport servers, you can optimize mail routing and delivery by configuring one-way synchronization from the internal Hub Transport servers to the perimeter network's Edge Transport servers. Beyond this, no other special configuration is required for mail routing and delivery.

Using the Graphical Administration Tools

Exchange Server 2010 provides several types of tools for administration. The graphical tools are the ones you'll use most frequently. Exchange Server and Forefront Protection for Exchange Server have separate management consoles. If you follow the instructions for installing Exchange Server in Chapter 2, you'll be able to access the Exchange tools by selecting Start, choosing All Programs, and then using the Microsoft Exchange Server 2010 menu. To access the Forefront Protection tools, select Start, choose All Programs, and then use the Microsoft Forefront Server Security menu.

Exchange Server 2010 has several graphical tools that replace or combine features of the graphical tools in Exchange Server 2003 and earlier editions. The Exchange Management Console, shown in Figure 1-1, replaces Exchange System Manager.

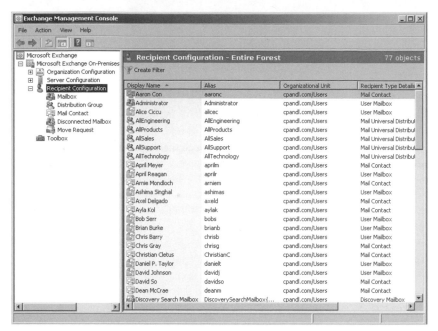

FIGURE 1-1 The Exchange Management Console.

As discussed further in Chapter 14, "Exchange Server 2010 Maintenance, Monitoring, and Queuing," and Chapter 15, "Backing Up and Restoring Exchange Server 2010," the Toolbox node in the Exchange Management Console provides access to a suite of related tools, including the following:

- **Best Practices Analyzer** Checks the configuration and health of your Exchange organization to ensure that it complies with current best practices recommended by Microsoft. Because best practices are periodically updated, the tool includes an update facility to ensure that the most current best practices are in place.

- **Details Templates Editor** Helps administrators customize client-side GUI presentation of object properties accessed through address lists. You can use this tool to customize the presentation of contacts, users, groups, public folders, and more in the client interface.

- **Mail Flow Troubleshooter** Helps troubleshoot problems related to mail flow and transport configuration by providing suggested resolutions for symptoms observed by administrators.

- **Message Tracking** Allows administrators to track messages as they are routed through the Exchange organization.

- **Performance Monitor** Allows administrators to graph system performance. Also allows administrators to create performance logs and alerts.

Wide arrays of Exchange performance objects are available for tracking performance.

- **Performance Troubleshooter** Helps troubleshoot problems related to performance by identifying possible bottlenecks and providing suggested solutions.
- **Public Folder Management Console** Allows administrators to manage public folders using a graphical interface rather than the command line.
- **Queue Viewer** Allows administrators to track message queues and mail flow. Also allows administrators to manage message queuing and remove messages.
- **Remote Connectivity Analyzer** Allows administrators to perform connectivity tests for inbound e-mail, ActiveSync, Exchange Web Services, Outlook Anywhere, and Outlook 2003 RPC over HTTP.
- **Role-Based Access Control (RBAC) User Editor** Allows administrators to assign users to RBAC groups and roles.
- **Routing Log Viewer** Helps administrators troubleshoot routing problems on transport servers by providing information about routing topology.
- **Tracking Log Explorer** Provides access to the message tracking logs for troubleshooting.

Other administration tools that you might want to use with Exchange Server are summarized in Table 1-2.

TABLE 1-2 Quick Reference Administration Tools to Use with Exchange Server 2010

ADMINISTRATIVE TOOL	PURPOSE
Computer Management	Starts and stops services, manages disks, and accesses other system management tools
DNS	Manages the DNS service.
Event Viewer	Manages events and logs.
IIS Manager	Manages Web servers used by Exchange as well as the management service configuration.
Microsoft Network Monitor	Monitors network traffic, and troubleshoots networking problems.
Server Manager	Adds, removes, and configures roles, role services, and features.

You access most of the tools listed in Table 1-2 from the Administrative Tools program group. Click Start, point to All Programs, and then point to Administrative Tools.

Using the Command-Line Administration Tools

The graphical tools provide just about everything you need to work with Exchange Server. Still, there are many times when you might want to work from the command line, especially if you want to automate installation, administration, or maintenance with scripts. To help with all your command-line needs, Exchange Server includes the Exchange Management Shell.

The Exchange Management Shell is an extension shell for Windows PowerShell that includes a wide array of built-in commands for working with Exchange Server. Windows PowerShell commands are referred to as cmdlets (pronounced *commandlets*) to differentiate these commands from less powerful commands built into the command prompt and from more full-featured utility programs that can be invoked at the command prompt.

> **NOTE** For ease of reading and reference, I'll usually refer to command prompt commands, command shell cmdlets, and command-line invoked utilities simply as commands.

The Exchange Management Shell, shown in Figure 1-2, is accessible by selecting Start, choosing All Programs, choosing Microsoft Exchange Server 2010, and then choosing Exchange Management Shell.

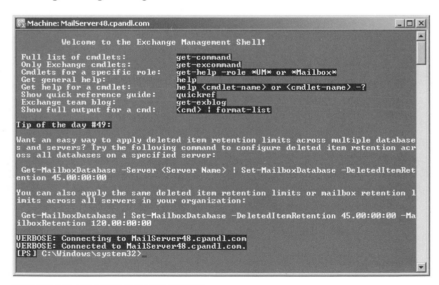

FIGURE 1-2 The Exchange Management Shell.

The basics of working with the Exchange Management Shell are straightforward:

- Type **get-command** to get a full list of all available cmdlets on the server.
- Type **get-excommand** to get a full list of all Exchange-specific cmdlets available.

- Type **help** *cmdletName* to get help information, where *cmdletName* is the name of the command you are looking up.

You'll find a comprehensive discussion of the Exchange Management Shell and Windows PowerShell in Chapter 4, "Using the Exchange Management Shell," as well as examples of using cmdlets for Exchange Server management throughout the book.

Like Exchange Server, Forefront Protection for Exchange Server has a management console and a management shell. You use the Forefront Server Security Administration console to manage Forefront Protection using a graphical interface. You use the Forefront Management Shell to manage Forefront Protection from the command line. This shell is accessible by selecting Start, choosing All Programs, choosing Microsoft Forefront Server Security, and then choosing Forefront Management Shell.

Forefront Management Shell loads extensions that allow you to manage the configuration of Forefront Protection for Exchange Server. The basics of working with the Forefront Management Shell are straightforward:

- Type **get-command** to get a full list of all available cmdlets on the server.
- Type **get-command** *fse* to get a full list of all Forefront Protection–specific cmdlets available.
- Type **help** *cmdletName* to get help information, where *cmdletName* is the name of the command you are looking up.

Because Forefront Management Shell does not load the Exchange Server cmdlets, you cannot access the Exchange-specific cmdlets from this shell by default. Because the Exchange Management Shell does not load the Forefront Protection–specific cmdlets either, you cannot access the Forefront Protection–specific cmdlets from the Exchange Management Shell by default.

Deploying Exchange Server 2010

B efore you deploy Microsoft Exchange Server 2010, you should carefully plan the messaging architecture. Every Exchange implementation has three layers in its architecture:

- **Network layer** The network layer provides the foundation for computer-to-computer communications and essential name resolution features. The network layer has both physical and logical components. The physical components include the IP addresses, the IP subnets, local area network (LAN) or wide area network (WAN) links used by messaging systems as well as the routers that connect these links, and firewalls that protect the infrastructure. The logical components are the Domain Name System (DNS) zones that define the naming boundaries and contain the essential resource records required for name resolution.

- **Directory layer** The directory layer provides the foundation necessary for authentication, authorization, and replication. The directory layer is built on the Active Directory directory service and has both physical and logical components. The physical components include the domain controllers, Global Catalog servers, and site links used for authentication, authorization, and replication. The logical components include the Active Directory forests, sites, domains, and organizational units that are used to group objects for resource sharing, centralized management, and replication control. The logical components also include the users and groups that are part of the Active Directory infrastructure.

- **Messaging layer** The messaging layer provides the foundation for messaging and collaboration. The messaging layer has both physical and logical components. The physical components include individual Exchange servers that determine how messages are delivered and mail connectors that determine how messages are routed outside an Exchange server's routing boundaries. The logical components specify the organizational boundaries for messaging, mailboxes used for storing messages, public folders used for storing data, and distribution lists used for distributing messages to multiple recipients.

Whether you are deploying Exchange Server for the first time in your organization or upgrading to Exchange Server 2010 from an earlier release of Exchange Server, you need to closely review each layer of this architecture and plan for required changes. As part of your implementation planning, you also need to look closely at the roles your Exchange servers will perform and modify the hardware accordingly to meet the requirements of these roles on a per-server basis. Exchange Server is no longer the simple messaging server that it once was. It is now a complex messaging platform with many components that work together to provide a comprehensive solution for routing, delivering, and accessing e-mail messages, voice-mail messages, faxes, contacts, and calendar information.

Exchange Server Messaging Roles

With Exchange Server Setup, you can deploy servers with specific roles throughout the enterprise. Prior to setup and configuration, you need to decide how you will use Exchange Server 2010, what roles you will deploy, and where you will locate those roles. Afterward, you can plan for your deployment and then roll out Exchange Server.

Understanding Exchange Server Messaging Roles

Exchange Server 2010 implementations have three layers in their architecture: a network layer, directory layer, and messaging layer. The messaging layer is where you define and deploy the Exchange Server roles. The Exchange servers at the core of the messaging layer can operate in the following roles:

- **Mailbox Server** A back-end server that hosts mailboxes, public folders, and related messaging data, such as address lists, resource scheduling, and meeting items. For high availability of mailbox databases, you can use database availability groups as discussed in Chapter 9, "Managing Data and Database Availability Groups."

- **Client Access Server** A middle-tier server that accepts connections to Exchange Server from a variety of clients. This server hosts the protocols used by all clients when checking messages. On the local network, Outlook MAPI clients are connected directly to the Client Access server to check mail. Remote users can check their mail over the Internet by using Outlook

Anywhere, Outlook Web App, Exchange ActiveSync, POP3, or IMAP4, as discussed in Chapter 17, "Managing Mobile Messaging Users"—remote users can connect to the Client Access server and check their messages.

- **Unified Messaging Server** A middle-tier server that integrates a private branch exchange (PBX) system with Exchange Server 2010, allowing voice messages and faxes to be stored with e-mail in a user's mailbox. Unified messaging supports call answering with automated greetings and message recording, fax receiving, and dial-in access. With dial-in access, users can use Outlook Voice Access to check voice mail, e-mail, and calendar information; to review or dial contacts; and to configure preferences and personal options. To receive faxes, you need an integrated solution from a Microsoft partner.

- **Hub Transport Server** A mail routing server that handles mail flow, routing, and delivery within the Exchange organization. This server processes all mail that is sent inside the organization before it is delivered to a mailbox in the organization or routed to users outside the organization. Processing ensures that senders and recipients are resolved and filtered as appropriate, content is filtered and has its format converted if necessary, and attachments are screened. To meet any regulatory or organizational compliance requirements, the Hub Transport server can also record, or journal, messages and add disclaimers to them.

- **Edge Transport Server** An additional mail routing server that routes mail into and out of the Exchange organization. This server is designed to be deployed in an organization's perimeter network and is used to establish a secure boundary between the organization and the Internet. This server accepts mail coming into the organization from the Internet and from trusted servers in external organizations, processes the mail to protect against some types of spam messages and viruses, and routes all accepted messages to a Hub Transport server inside the organization.

These five roles are the building blocks of Exchange organizations. Table 2-1 provides an overview of the supported processor core configurations for these roles. Processors can be single core, dual core, or multiple core. Following the configurations shown in the table, a dedicated Mailbox server has a recommended maximum number of processor cores of 12, but a server with the Mailbox and other roles combined has a recommended maximum of 16. Note that although Exchange Server 2010 can support this number of processor cores, it might make more sense to scale out to multiple servers rather than to scale up the processor cores on a single server.

TABLE 2-1 Processor Core Configurations for Exchange Server 2010 Roles

SERVER ROLE	MINIMUM	RECOMMENDED	MAXIMUM RECOMMENDED
Edge Transport	1	4	12
Hub Transport	1	4	12

TABLE 2-1 Processor Core Configurations for Exchange Server 2010 Roles

SERVER ROLE	MINIMUM	RECOMMENDED	MAXIMUM RECOMMENDED
Client Access	2	8	12
Unified Messaging	2	4	12
Mailbox	2	8	12
Multiple server roles	2	8	16

Because you can combine all of the roles except the Edge Transport server role on a single server, one of the most basic Exchange organizations you can create is one that includes a single Exchange server that provides the Mailbox server, Client Access server, and Hub Transport server roles. These three roles are the minimum required for routing and delivering messages to both local and remote messaging clients. For added security and protection, you can deploy the Edge Transport server role in a perimeter network on one or more separate servers.

Although a basic implementation of Exchange Server might include only one server, you'll likely find investing in multiple servers is more effective in terms of time, money, and resources. Why? High availability is integrated into the core architecture of Exchange Server 2010.

With the Mailbox server role, you can configure automatic failover by making the Mailbox servers members of the same database availability group. Each Mailbox server in the group can then have a copy of the mailbox databases from the other Mailbox servers in the group. Each mailbox database can have up to 16 copies, and this means you can have up to 16 Mailbox servers in a group as well.

With the Client Access role, you can enable load balancing and failover support by making Client Access servers members of the same Client Access array. Each Client Access server in the array will then be able to support all client access features, including Outlook MAPI, POP3, IMAP4, Outlook Anywhere, Outlook Web App, and Exchange ActiveSync. You can use Client Access arrays to build groups of up to 32 load-balanced servers, starting with as few a two servers and incrementally scaling as demand increases. Servers that are members of an array cannot also have the Mailbox role. If you are using the Network Load Balancing service, Microsoft recommends no more than eight load-balanced servers.

Because of the built-in, high-availability features, the hardware you use with Exchange Server 2010 might be very different from the hardware you use with earlier releases of Exchange Server. Consider the following scenario:

City Power & Light is running Exchange Server 2007 throughout its organization. The company has clustered Mailbox servers running on two nodes; it's using separate servers for client access, hub transport, and unified messaging; and it has two Edge Transport servers. Clustered Mailbox servers are connected to a storage area network (SAN). Half the disks in the SAN are configured for primary data, and the other half of the disks are configured for backups. The SAN uses RAID 0+1 and RAID 5. Other Exchange servers in the organization use internal drives—RAID 1 for their boot and system volumes, and RAID 5 for their Exchange-related volumes. Backups are rotated regularly to off-site storage.

When planning its Exchange Server 2010 environment, the company decided it no longer needed clustering hardware. It also decided that it no longer needed to dedicate half the storage space on its SAN to backups or use RAID. Instead of using clustering, the company plans on configuring three Mailbox servers as part of the same database availability group. The mailbox database copies available to each server will act as the company's on-site data backup. As a safeguard against logical corruption that replicates across the databases in the DAG, the company decided that one database copy would be lagged behind the others by 72 hours. Because the company isn't using RAID on many SAN disks, there are many more data disks available for storage. Mailbox database failover is automatic for members of the database availability group.

Because the company no longer needs to have dedicated Mailbox servers and is able to combine any roles (except Edge Transport), it decided to run the Hub Transport and Unified Messaging roles on its Mailbox servers as well. To take advantage of load balancing for client access, the company decided to set up three Client Access servers in a load-balanced array. The company will retain both Edge Transport servers as well.

This highly available configuration makes the IT team members confident that they can achieve 99.5 percent or higher uptime for Exchange services, a marked improvement over previous service-level commitments. Higher availability also allows the IT team to streamline many of its processes, especially when it comes to recovery, server backup, and data backup. Still, the team has decided that it will continue to regularly rotate backups to off-site storage.

Deploying Mailbox Servers: The Essentials

The underlying functionality of a Mailbox server is similar to that of a database server. Every mailbox-enabled recipient defined in the organization has a mailbox that is used to store messaging data. Groups of related mailboxes are organized using databases, and each database can have one or more database copies associated with it.

With Exchange Server 2007, you needed dedicated hardware for clustered Mailbox servers, those servers could not run other roles, and failover occurred at the server level. Microsoft re-engineered Exchange Server 2010 to provide continuous availability while eliminating these restrictions. This means:

- You do not need dedicated clustering hardware for highly available Mailbox servers. Key components of Windows clustering are managed automatically by Exchange Server.

- You do not need to use Local Continuous Replication (LCR), Cluster Continuous Replication (CCR), or Standby Continuous Replication (SCR). LCR has been discontinued. Key features of CCR and SCR have been combined, enhanced, and made available through database availability groups.
- You can combine multiple Exchange roles on highly available Mailbox servers. This means you can create a fully redundant Exchange organization using only two Exchange servers. In this case, each server would have the Mailbox, Client Access, and Hub Transport roles. You would also need a witness server for the DAG, which doesn't have to be an Exchange server.

The underlying technology built into database availability groups is the key ingredient that makes high availability possible. The related framework ensures failover clustering occurs in the background and doesn't normally require administrator intervention. As a result, Exchange Server 2010 doesn't need or use a cluster resource dynamic-link library (DLL) and uses only a small portion of the Windows clustering components, including heartbeat capabilities and the cluster database.

Database availability groups use continuous replication to achieve high availability. With continuous replication, Exchange Server 2010 uses its built-in asynchronous replication technology to create copies of mailbox databases and then keep the copies up to date using transaction log shipping and replay. Any server in a group can host a copy of a mailbox database from any other server in the group. When a server is added to a group, the server works with other servers in the group to provide automatic recovery from failures that affect mailbox databases, including server failure, database corruption, disk failure, and network connectivity failure.

When you create a database availability group, Exchange adds an object to Active Directory representing the group. This object stores information about the group, including details about servers that are members of the group. When you add the first server to the group, a failover cluster is created automatically and the heartbeat is initiated. As you add member servers to the group, the heartbeat components and the cluster database are used to track and manage information about the group and its member servers, including server status, database mount status, replication status, and mount location.

Because Exchange Server 2010 databases are represented at the organization level, they are effectively disconnected from the servers on which they are stored, which makes it easier to move databases from one server to another. However, it also means you can work with databases in new ways and that there are also new requirements when working with databases. Keep the following in mind when working with databases in Exchange Server 2010:

- Storage group functionality has been moved to the database level. This means you'll work with databases in new ways.
- Database names must be unique throughout your Exchange organization. This means you cannot name two databases identically even if they are on two different Mailbox servers.

- Every mailbox database, except copies, have a different globally unique identifier (GUID). Copies of a database have the same GUID.

- Mailbox servers that are part of the same database availability group do not need to and cannot use shared storage. However, the full paths for all database copies must be identical on host Mailbox servers.

- Although a Mailbox server in a DAG can have a public folder database, public folder databases cannot be part of database availability groups, and you cannot create copies of public folder databases. For redundancy and high availability of public folder databases, you should use public folder replication as discussed in Chapter 10, "Mailbox and Public Folder Store Administration."

For a successful deployment of a Mailbox server, the storage subsystem must meet the storage capacity requirements and must be able to perform the expected number of input/output (I/O) operations per second. Storage capacity requirements are determined by the number of mailboxes hosted on a server and the total storage size allowed per mailbox. For example, if a server hosts 2,500 mailboxes that you allow to store up to 2 gigabytes (GB) each, you need to ensure there are at least 5 terabytes (TB) of storage capacity above and beyond the storage needs of the operating system and Exchange itself.

I/O performance of the storage subsystem is measured in relation to the latency (delay) for each read/write operation to be performed. The more mailboxes you store on a specific drive or drive array, the more read/write operations there are performed and the greater the potential delay. To improve performance, you can use multiple mailbox databases. You might also want to store databases with their transaction log files on separate disk drives, such that database A and related logs are on disk 1, database B and related logs are on disk 2, and so on. In some scenarios, you might want the databases and logs to be on separate disks.

I/O performance in Exchange Server 2010 running on 64-bit architecture is improved substantially over 32-bit architecture. On Mailbox servers, a 64-bit architecture enables a database cache size of up to approximately 90 percent of total random access memory (RAM). A larger cache increases the probability that data requested by a client will be serviced out of memory instead of by the storage subsystem.

REAL WORLD Because of 64-bit architecture and cache optimizations for the Extensible Storage Engine (ESE), Exchange Server 2010 performs significantly better than Exchange Server 2003. Exchange Server 2010 can perform read and write operations with up to 1,024 kilobytes (KB) of data vs. 64 KB of data with Exchange Server 2003. This increases the ability to read and write larger I/O and means fewer I/O operations are necessary to service requests for data.

The streaming database file and installable file system have been removed and the database page size has been increased to 32 KB. Removing the streaming database file and installable file system reduces the overhead associated with maintaining a database. The page size is the minimum size for reading and writing to the database and is also the unit size for database caching. By using 32-KB database pages and caching these larger pages in memory, Exchange Server 2010 reduces the frequency of reads and writes. Exchange Server 2010 also makes data in the database more sequential, which increases the likelihood that related data will be grouped together. Further, each database has its own transaction log, making the database file and its associated transaction log the basic unit of backup and restore operations. See Chapter 3, "Exchange Server 2010 Administration Essentials," for more information on data storage.

Exchange Server 2010 performs substantially better than Exchange Server 2007. The store schema has been flattened to remove the dependency of mailbox databases to the server object. The schema also has been optimized by refactoring the tables used to store information and reducing the store's reliance on the secondary indices. As a result, the secondary indices no longer cause performance issues during peak usage or index maintenance periods.

Before you install the Mailbox role on a server running the Windows Server 2008 operating system, you must do the following:

1. Install the Active Directory remote management tools. One way to do this is to type the following command at an elevated, administrator PowerShell prompt:

```
Add-WindowsFeature -name RSAT-ADDS -restart
```

> **NOTE** After installing the Active Directory remote management tools, you'll likely need to restart the server. Because of this, I have added the -Restart parameter so that the server restarts automatically if required.

> **TIP** The ServerManager module provides cmdlets for listing, adding, and removing Windows features. Generally, this module is not imported into PowerShell by default, so you need to import the module before you can use the cmdlets it provides. You import the Server Manager module by entering **Import-Module ServerManager** at the PowerShell prompt. Once the module is imported, you can use it with the currently running instance of PowerShell. The next time you start PowerShell, you need to import the module again if you want to use its features.

2. If your server is running Windows Server 2008 Release 2, use the Add Feature wizard in Server Manager to install Microsoft .NET Framework version 3.5.1, if this version is not already installed. If your server is running Windows Server 2008, determine whether Microsoft .NET Framework version 3.5.1, Windows PowerShell version 2, and WinRM 2.0 are installed. If they aren't, you must install them. The main page in Exchange Setup provides links.

3. Install the 2007 Office System Converter: Microsoft Filter Pack. The filters are used by Microsoft Search components to index the contents of Office documents. Get the filters by going to *http://go.microsoft.com/fwlink/?LinkId=123380*. Make sure you download and install the 64-bit filters for your 64-bit servers.

4. If your server is running Windows Server 2008, you need to install additional components. The Internet Information Services (IIS) components include

Web Server, Basic Authentication, Windows Authentication, IIS 6 Metabase Compatibility, and IIS 6 Management Console. One way to install these components is to type the following commands at an elevated, administrator PowerShell prompt:

```
Add-WindowsFeature -name Web-Server
Add-WindowsFeature -name Web-Metabase
Add-WindowsFeature -name Web-Lgcy-Mgmt-Console
Add-WindowsFeature -name Web-Basic-Auth
Add-WindowsFeature -name Web-Windows-Auth
Add-WindowsFeature -name Web-Net-Ext
```

Deploying Client Access Servers: The Essentials

Client Access servers handle all of the client-related messaging tasks in an Exchange implementation, and the underlying functionality is similar to that of an application server that makes extensive use of Web services. Because all local and remote clients now connect to Client Access servers to check mail, Client Access servers now perform many more I/O operations than on Exchange Server 2007. This means that in addition to processors, memory, network, and disk I/O are all potential sources of bottlenecks. It also means I/O operations on Client Access servers are no longer primarily limited to protocol logging, content conversion, and paging operations. Because content conversion is performed in the TMP folder, you can improve performance by ensuring that this folder is not on the same physical disk as the paging file and operating system.

Client Access servers provide access through the Outlook MAPI, Internet Message Access Protocol version 4 revision 1 (IMAP4), Post Office Protocol version 3 (POP3), and Hypertext Transfer Protocol (HTTP) Internet protocols. Exchange Server 2010 allows local access using Outlook MAPI and remote access using Outlook Anywhere, Outlook Web App, and Exchange ActiveSync. IMAP4 and POP3 are available as alternatives to standard protocols. Client Access servers provide access to free/busy data by using the Availability service, and they enable clients to download automatic configuration settings from the Autodiscover service.

REAL WORLD In Exchange 2010, RPC connections are made directly to the MAPI RPC connection point on the Client Access server and the NSPI endpoint on the Client Access server. HTTP connections are still made to the RPC Proxy component on the Client Access server. The Client Access server then communicates with the appropriate Mailbox server. For directory information, Outlook communicates with a Name Service Provider Interface (NSPI) endpoint located on the Client Access server. NSPI replaces the DSProxy and communicates with the Active Directory driver, which then communicates with Active Directory.

If one Client Access server in a Client Access server array fails, the client immediately reconnects to another Client Access server in the array. If a mailbox server fails, the client is disconnected for about 30 seconds. Each mailbox server can handle up to 250,000 RPC connections.

Client Access servers accept connections to your Exchange 2010 server over the local network and over the Internet. Some clients, such as Windows Live Mail, use POP3 or IMAP4 connections to communicate with the Exchange server. Other clients, such as e-mail software on mobile phones, use ActiveSync, POP3, or IMAP4 to communicate with the Exchange server. You must install the Client Access server role in every Exchange organization.

Client Access arrays provide load balancing and failover support for all client access features. Servers in an array cannot also have the Mailbox role and must be members of the same Active Directory site. Each array you establish has an external domain name, and client requests are directed to this external domain name, allowing for transparent load balancing as well as failover and failback. When a load-balanced resource fails on one server, the remaining servers in the array take over the workload of the failed server. When the failed server comes back online, the server can automatically rejoin the array, and the load-balancing feature starts to distribute the load to the server automatically. Failover takes only a few seconds in most cases.

When you use Client Access arrays, the external URLs for CAS-related services should point to the array rather than to individual servers, and the internal URLs should point to individual servers. Because of this, you should set the external URLs for Exchange ActiveSync, Outlook Web applications, Exchange Control Panel, and the Offline Address Book relative to the external domain name for the array. For example, Exchange ActiveSync runs as a Web application named Microsoft-Server-ActiveSync. When setting up Exchange ActiveSync URLs on each individual mailbox server, you should configure the internal URL to point to a specific CAS server, such as *https://casserver48.cpandl.com/Microsoft-Server-ActiveSync*, and the external URL to point to a location relative to the array, such as *https://array1.cpandl.com/Microsoft-Server-ActiveSync*.

During setup of Exchange Server for a Client Access server, you have the opportunity to specify whether the Client Access server will be accessible to clients outside the organization. If you select the related check box and specify the external domain name for your CAS array, the external URLs for CAS-related services will be configured to point to locations relative to the array automatically. Otherwise, you'll need to manually configure the external URLs for each CAS-related service.

The Exchange Management Shell has several cmdlets you can use to register arrays in Active Directory and in this way tell Exchange about load-balanced arrays you've set up for Client Access servers. These cmdlets include the following:

- **Get-ClientAccessArray** Lists information about available or specified Client Access arrays.

```
Get-ClientAccessArray [-Identity ArrayIdentity]
[-DomainController FullyQualifiedName] [-Site SiteId]
```

- **New-ClientAccessArray** Creates an object in Active Directory that represents a load-balanced array of CAS servers in a specific Active Directory site

```
New-ClientAccessArray -Name ArrayName -Fqdn ExternalArrayName
-Site SiteId [-DomainController FullyQualifiedName]
```

- **Set-ClientAccessArray**   Specifies information about a named Client Access
  array.

  ```
  Set-ClientAccessArray -Identity ArrayIdentity [-Name Name]
  [-Fqdn ExternalArrayName] [-Site SiteId] [-DomainController
  FullyQualifiedName]
  ```

- **Remove-ClientAccessArray**   Removes a Client Access array from Active
  Directory.

  ```
  Remove-ClientAccessArray -Identity ArrayIdentity
  [-DomainController FullyQualifiedName]
  ```

Load balancing can be implemented using hardware or software. Windows Server includes the Network Load Balancing service. Network Load Balancing doesn't use shared resources or clustered storage devices. Instead, each server has a copy of the Client Access services and features that are being load balanced and local storage typically is used. Generally, users usually don't know that they're accessing a group of servers rather than a single server. The reason for this is that the array appears to be a single server. Clients connect to the array using the array's external domain name, and this virtual address is mapped automatically to a specific server based on availability. It is important to note that you cannot use NLB for establishing a Client Access array if the Client Access servers are co-located on a Mailbox server in a database availability group.

Before you install the Client Access role on a server running the Windows Server 2008 operating system, you must complete the following steps:

1. Install the Active Directory remote management tools. One way to do this is to type the following command at an elevated, administrator PowerShell prompt:

   ```
   Add-WindowsFeature -name RSAT-ADDS -restart
   ```

2. If your server is running Windows Server 2008 Release 2, use the Add Feature wizard in Server Manager to install Microsoft .NET Framework version 3.5.1, if this version is not already installed. If your server is running Windows Server 2008, determine whether Microsoft .NET Framework version 3.5.1, Windows PowerShell version 2, and WinRM 2.0 are installed. If they aren't, you must install them. The main page in Exchange Setup provides links.

3. If your server is running Windows Server 2008, you need to install additional components. The IIS components include Web Server, ISAPI Extensions, Basic Authentication, Digest Authentication, Windows Authentication, Dynamic

Content Compression, IIS 6 Metabase Compatibility, and IIS 6 Management Console. You also need to install the HTTP Activation component for the .NET Framework 3.5.1 and the RPC Over HTTP proxy. One way to install these components is to type the following commands at an elevated, administrator PowerShell prompt:

```
Add-WindowsFeature -name Web-Server
Add-WindowsFeature -name Web-ISAPI-Ext
Add-WindowsFeature -name Web-Metabase
Add-WindowsFeature -name Web-Lgcy-Mgmt-Console
Add-WindowsFeature -name Web-Basic-Auth
Add-WindowsFeature -name Web-Digest-Auth
Add-WindowsFeature -name Web-Windows-Auth
Add-WindowsFeature -name Web-Net-Ext
Add-WindowsFeature -name Web-Dyn-Compression
Add-WindowsFeature -name NET-HTTP-Activation
Add-WindowsFeature -name RPC-over-HTTP-proxy
```

Deploying Unified Messaging Servers: The Essentials

Unified messaging allows you to integrate voice mail, fax, and e-mail functionality so that the related data can be stored in a user's Exchange mailbox. To implement unified messaging, your organization must have a PBX that is connected to the LAN, and you must deploy a Unified Messaging server running Exchange Server 2010. After it is deployed, the Unified Messaging server has the job of providing call answering, fax receiving, subscriber access, and auto-attendant features that allow access to content over the telephone and storage of content received from the PBX.

Although some current PBXs, referred to as *IP-PBXs*, are Internet Protocol–capable, all other PBXs require a separate Internet Protocol/Voice over Internet Protocol (IP/VoIP) gateway to connect to the LAN. After you connect a PBX to the LAN, you can link it to Exchange by deploying and appropriately configuring the Unified Messaging server role. Prior to installing the Unified Messaging server role, you must install the Microsoft Speech service, Microsoft Windows Media Encoder, and Microsoft Windows Media Audio Voice Code as part of the Desktop Experience feature.

Similar to Client Access servers, Unified Messaging servers don't perform a great deal of I/O operations, and the primary potential bottlenecks for these servers are the processors, memory, and network. I/O operations on Unified Messaging servers are primarily limited to accessing routing details and dial plans, which include auto-attendant and mail policy settings.

Before you install the Unified Messaging role on a server running the Windows Server 2008 operating system, you must complete the following steps:

1. If your server is running Windows Server 2008 Release 2, use the Add Feature wizard in Server Manager to install Microsoft .NET Framework version 3.5.1, if this feature is not already installed. If your server is running Windows Server

2008, determine whether Microsoft .NET Framework version 3.5.1, Windows PowerShell version 2, and WinRM 2.0 are installed. If they aren't, you must install them. The main page in Exchange Setup provides links.

2. If your server is running Windows Server 2008, you need to install additional components. The IIS components include Web Server, Basic Authentication, Windows Authentication, IIS 6 Metabase Compatibility, and IIS 6 Management Console. One way to install these components is to type the following commands at an elevated, administrator PowerShell prompt:

```
Add-WindowsFeature -name Web-Server
Add-WindowsFeature -name Web-Metabase
Add-WindowsFeature -name Web-Lgcy-Mgmt-Console
Add-WindowsFeature -name Web-Basic-Auth
Add-WindowsFeature -name Web-Windows-Auth
Add-WindowsFeature -name Web-Net-Ext
```

3. Install the Windows Media Player audio/video codecs, which are included in the Desktop Experience feature. Because you need to restart the server to complete the installation process, I've added the –Restart parameter. One way to install this component is to type the following command at an elevated, administrator PowerShell prompt:

```
Add-WindowsFeature -name Desktop-Experience -restart
```

Deploying Transport Servers: The Essentials

The Hub Transport and Edge Transport roles are similar. You use both for messaging routing, and both have a similar set of filters to protect an organization from spam and viruses. The key difference is in where you place servers with these roles. You place a server with the Hub Transport role in the internal network and configure it as a member of the organizational domain. If you use a server with the Edge Transport role, you place it in the organization's perimeter network and you do not configure it as a member of the organizational domain.

For computers with the Hub Transport or Edge Transport role, the server cannot have the Simple Mail Transfer Protocol (SMTP) or Network News Transfer Protocol (NNTP) service installed. Although you install Edge Transport servers outside the Active Directory forest, you must have a DNS suffix configured and you must be able to perform name resolution from the Edge Transport server to any Hub Transport servers.

> **TIP** Transport servers store all incoming mail in a database file called mail.que until the transport server verifies that all of the next hops for that message have been completed. This database has an associated transaction log in which changes are first committed. If you are using an Exchange Server's internal drives for storage in a high-volume environment in which one million or more messages are persisted, you

should consider placing the database and the transaction log on separate disks for optimal performance. With SANs, it might not be immediately apparent whether disks are physically separate. This is because the volumes you see are logical references to a portion of the storage subsystem. In this case, you might be able to use the Storage Manager For SANs console or a similar tool to help you select logical unit numbers (LUNs) that are on physically separate disks.

MORE INFO Transport servers have many different queues for messages. These queues are all stored in a single ESE database called mail.que. By default, this database is located in %ExchangeInstallPath%\TransportRoles\data\Queue. Thanks to shadow redundancy, the deletion of a message in the database is delayed until the transport server verifies that all of the next hops for that message have completed delivery. If any of the next hops fail before reporting back successful delivery, the message is resubmitted for delivery to that next hop.

Both Hub and Edge Transport servers perform protocol logging and message tracking. Only Hub transports perform content conversion. Protocol logging allows you to verify whether a protocol is performing as expected and whether any issues need attention. Message tracking creates logs that track messages sent and received. Incoming mail from the Internet is converted to Summary Transport Neutral Encoding Format (STNEF) prior to being delivered. STNEF messages are always MIME-encoded and always have a Content-Transfer-Encoding value of Binary. Because content conversion is performed in the temp folder, you can improve performance by ensuring that the temp folder is not on the same physical disk as the paging file and operating system.

Before you install the Hub Transport role on a server running the Windows Server 2008 operating system, you must complete the following steps:

1. Install the Active Directory remote management tools. One way to do this is to type the following command at an elevated, administrator PowerShell prompt:

```
Add-WindowsFeature -name RSAT-ADDS -restart
```

2. If your server is running Windows Server 2008 Release 2, use the Add Feature wizard in Server Manager to install Microsoft .NET Framework version 3.5.1, if this feature is not already installed. If your server is running Windows Server 2008, determine whether Microsoft .NET Framework version 3.5.1, Windows PowerShell version 2, and WinRM 2.0 are installed. If they aren't, you must install them. If they aren't, you must install them. The main page in Exchange Setup provides links.

3. If your server is running Windows Server 2008, you need to install additional components. The IIS components include Web Server, Basic Authentication, Windows Authentication, IIS 6 Metabase Compatibility, and IIS 6

Management Console. One way to install these components is to type the following commands at an elevated, administrator PowerShell prompt:

```
Add-WindowsFeature -name Web-Server
Add-WindowsFeature -name Web-Metabase
Add-WindowsFeature -name Web-Lgcy-Mgmt-Console
Add-WindowsFeature -name Web-Basic-Auth
Add-WindowsFeature -name Web-Windows-Auth
Add-WindowsFeature -name Web-Net-Ext
```

Before you install the Edge Transport role on a server running the Windows Server 2008 operating system, you must complete these steps:

1. Install Active Directory Lightweight Directory Services (AD LDS). One way to do this is to type the following command at an elevated, administrator PowerShell prompt:

   ```
   Add-WindowsFeature -name ADLDS
   ```

2. If your server is running Windows Server 2008 Release 2, use the Add Feature wizard in Server Manager to install Microsoft .NET Framework version 3.5.1, if this feature is not already installed. If your server is running Windows Server 2008, determine whether Microsoft .NET Framework version 3.5.1, Windows PowerShell version 2, and WinRM 2.0 are installed. If they aren't, you must install them. The main page in Exchange Setup provides links. The Edge Transport role does not require IIS.

Integrating Exchange Server Roles with Active Directory

Exchange Server 2010 makes extensive use of Active Directory. Each Exchange Server 2010 role must access Active Directory to retrieve information about recipients and other Exchange server roles. Each Exchange server role uses Active Directory in other ways as well, as discussed in the sections that follow.

NOTE As discussed in Chapter 1 of *Windows Server 2008 Administrator's Pocket Consultant*, Second Edition (Microsoft Press, 2010), you can configure Windows Server 2008 domain controllers as read-only or read-writeable. As long as writeable domain controllers and writeable Global Catalog servers are available, Exchange Server 2010 can work in an environment where you've deployed read-only domain controllers and read-only Global Catalog servers. However, Exchange Server 2010 does not make use of read-only domain controllers or read-only Global Catalog servers.

Using Hub Transport Servers with Active Directory

Hub Transport servers contact Active Directory when they perform message categorization. The Categorizer queries Active Directory to perform recipient lookup, retrieves the information needed to locate a recipient's mailbox (according to the mailbox store in which it is created), and determines any restrictions or permissions that might apply to the recipient. The Categorizer also queries Active Directory to expand the membership of distribution lists and to perform the Lightweight Directory Access Protocol (LDAP) query processing when mail is sent to a dynamic distribution list.

After the Categorizer determines the location of a mailbox, the Hub Transport server uses Active Directory site configuration information to determine the routing topology and locate the site in which the mailbox is located. If the mailbox is in the same Active Directory site as the Hub Transport server, the Hub Transport server delivers the message directly to the user's mailbox. If the mailbox is in a different Active Directory site from the Hub Transport server, the Hub Transport server delivers the message to a Hub Transport server in the remote Active Directory site.

Hub Transport servers store all configuration information in Active Directory. This configuration information includes the details of any transport or journaling rules and connectors. When this information is needed, a Hub Transport server accesses it in Active Directory.

Using Client Access Servers with Active Directory

Client Access servers receive connections from local and remote clients. At a high level, when a user connection is received, the Client Access server contacts Active Directory to authenticate the user and to determine the location of the user's mailbox. If the user's mailbox is in the same Active Directory site as the Client Access server, the user is connected to his mailbox. If the user's mailbox is in an Active Directory site other than the one the Client Access server is located in, the connection is redirected to a Client Access server in the same Active Directory site as the user's mailbox.

When you use load balancing on your Client Access servers, you register CAS arrays in Active Directory to create related objects and associate each array with a specific Active Directory site. Each CAS array can be associated with only one Active Directory site. As with stand-alone CAS servers, the site information determines how connections are directed. If the user's mailbox is in the same Active Directory site as the array, the user is connected to a CAS server and via the CAS server to his mailbox. If the user's mailbox is in an Active Directory site other than the one in which the Client Access array is located, the connection is redirected.

Client Access servers communicate with Mailbox servers using RPC. You must have one Client Access server in each Active Directory site that contains a Mailbox server. At least one of your Client Access servers must be designated as Internet-facing. The Internet-facing CAS server proxies requests from Outlook Web App, Exchange ActiveSync, and Exchange Web Services to the Client Access server closest to the user's mailbox. Proxying is not used for POP3 or IMAP4. A client that is using POP3 or IMAP4 must connect to a Client Access server in the same Active Directory site as its Mailbox server.

Using Unified Messaging Servers with Active Directory

Unified Messaging servers access Active Directory to retrieve global configuration information, such as dial plans and IP gateway details. When a message is received by the Unified Messaging server, the server searches for Active Directory recipients to match the telephone number to a recipient address. When the server has resolved this information, it can determine the location of the recipient's mailbox and then submit the message to the appropriate Hub Transport server for submission to the mailbox.

Using Mailbox Servers with Active Directory

Mailbox servers are service locations for e-mail messages, voice-mail messages, and faxes. For outgoing mail, Mailbox servers can access Active Directory to retrieve information about the location of Hub Transport servers in their site. Then they can use this information to forward messages for routing. Mailbox servers also store configuration information about mailbox users, mailbox stores, agents, address lists, and policies in Active Directory. Mailbox servers retrieve this information to enforce recipient policies, mailbox policies, system policies, and global settings.

Using Edge Transport Servers with Active Directory

You deploy Edge Transport servers in perimeter networks, and they are not members of the internal domain. Because of this, Edge Transport servers do not have direct access to the organization's internal Active Directory servers for the purposes of recipient lookup or categorization. Thus, unlike Hub Transport servers, Edge Transport servers cannot contact an Active Directory server to help route messages.

To route messages into the organization, an administrator can configure a subscription from the Edge Transport server to the Active Directory site that allows it to store recipient and configuration information about the Exchange organization in its AD LDS data store. After an Edge Transport server is subscribed to an Active Directory site, it is associated with the Hub Transport servers in that site for the purpose of message routing. Thereafter, Hub Transport servers in the organization route messages being delivered to the Internet to the site associated with the Edge Transport server, and Hub Transport servers in this site relay the messages to the Edge Transport server. The Edge Transport server, in turn, routes the messages to the Internet.

The EdgeSync service running on Hub Transport servers is a one-way synchronization process that pushes information from Active Directory to the Edge Transport server. Periodically, the EdgeSync service synchronizes the data to keep the Edge Transport server's data store up to date. The EdgeSync service also establishes the connectors needed to send and receive information that is being moved between the organization and the Edge Transport server and between the Edge Transport server and the Internet. The key data pushed to the Edge Transport server includes:

- Accepted and remote domains
- Valid recipients

- Safe senders
- Send connectors
- Available Hub Transport servers
- Available SMTP servers
- Message classifications
- TLS Send and Receive Domain Secure lists

After the initial replication is performed, the EdgeSync service synchronizes the data periodically. Configuration information is synced once every hour, and it can take up to 1 hour for configuration changes to be replicated. Recipient information is synced once every 4 hours, and it can take up to 4 hours for changes to be replicated. If necessary, administrators can initiate an immediate synchronization using the Start-EdgeSynchronization cmdlet in the Exchange Management Shell.

NOTE During synchronization, objects can be added to, deleted from, or modified in the Edge Transport server's AD LDS data store. To protect the integrity and security of the organization, no information is ever pushed from the Edge Transport server's AD LDS data store to Active Directory.

Integrating Exchange Server 2010 into Existing Exchange Organizations

Existing Exchange Server 2003 and Exchange Server 2007 installations can coexist with Exchange Server 2010 installations. Generally, you do this by integrating Exchange Server 2010 into your existing Exchange Server 2003 or Exchange Server 2007 organization. Integration requires the following:

- Preparing Active Directory and the domain for the extensive Active Directory changes that will occur when you install Exchange Server 2010.
- Configuring Exchange Server 2010 so that it can communicate with servers running Exchange Server 2003 and Exchange Server 2007.

If you need a legacy server, you need to keep or add it to the Exchange organization before adding the new Exchange 2010 servers. Then, you have a coexistence implementation. You cannot upgrade existing Exchange Server 2003 or Exchange Server 2007 servers to Exchange Server 2010. You must install Exchange Server 2010 on new hardware, and then move the mailboxes from your existing installations to the new installation. See the "Transitioning to Exchange Server 2010" section later in this chapter for more details.

As an alternative to coexistence, you can deploy a new Exchange 2010 organization. After you deploy a new Exchange 2010 organization, you can't add servers that are running earlier versions of Exchange to the organization. Adding earlier versions of Exchange to an Exchange 2010 organization is not supported.

NOTE You can deploy Exchange 2010 only in an Exchange 2003 organization that operates in native mode. To use Exchange System Manager to change the Exchange organization to native mode on an Exchange 2003 server, click Start, point to Programs, point to Microsoft Exchange, and then click System Manager. Next, right-click the organization, and then click Properties. On the General tab, under Change Operations Mode, click Change Mode. Click Yes if you are sure that you want to permanently switch the organization's mode to native mode.

Preparing Active Directory for Exchange Server 2010

Exchange Server 2010 can be integrated into Exchange Server 2003 and Exchange Server 2007 organizations. If you have any servers running Exchange Server 2003, Exchange Server 2007, or both, you might want to prepare Active Directory and the domain for the extensive Active Directory changes that will occur when you install Exchange Server 2010. If so, complete the procedure in this section. Alternatively, if you run the Exchange 2010 Setup Wizard with an account that has the permissions required to prepare Active Directory and the domain, the wizard automatically prepares Active Directory and the domain and you do not need to perform the procedure in this section. However, in a large enterprise, these updates could take a long time to complete.

You can prepare Active Directory by running Exchange Server 2010 setup at an elevated, administrator command prompt with various options. The steps to complete are as follows:

1. To prepare legacy Exchange permissions in every domain in the forest that contains Exchange Enterprise Servers and Exchange Domain Servers groups, run Setup with the /PrepareLegacyExchangePermissions option on any server running Windows Server 2003 Service Pack 1 or later. Note the following:

   • To successfully run this command, you must be a member of the Enterprise Admins groups and the domain in which you run this command must be able to contact all domains in the forest.

   • If the forest has only one domain, you must be delegated the Exchange Full Administrator role and you must be a member of the Domain Admins group in the domain that you will prepare.

   • If the server cannot contact a domain that must have legacy Exchange permissions prepared, it prepares the domains that it can contact and then returns an error message that it was unable to contact some domains.

2. After all permissions have replicated across your entire Exchange organization, run Setup with the /PrepareSchema option to connect to the schema master and update the schema with attributes for Exchange Server 2010. To run this command, you must be a member of the Schema Admins group and the Enterprise Admins group. You must run this command on a computer in the same Active Directory domain and same Active Directory site as the schema master. The schema master is located in the forest root domain.

TIP If you have trouble preparing the schema, try logging on with a local administrator account on a domain controller in the forest root domain and then running Exchange Server 2010 setup with the /PrepareSchema option.

3. After all schema changes have been made, run Setup with the /PrepareAD option to configure global Exchange objects in Active Directory, create Exchange Universal Security groups in the root domain, and prepare the current domain for Exchange Server 2010. You must also use the /OrganizationName option to specify the name of your Exchange organization. To run this command, you must be a member of the Enterprise Admins group. You must run this command on a computer in the same Active Directory domain and same Active Directory site as the schema master. The schema master is located in the forest root domain.

   When this step is completed, the root domain should have a new organizational unit called Microsoft Exchange Security Groups, and this organizational unit should contain the following groups: Exchange All Hosted Organizations, Exchange Organization Administrators, Exchange Public Folder Administrators, Exchange Recipient Administrators, Exchange Self-Service Administrators, Exchange Servers, Exchange Trusted Subsystem, Exchange View-Only Administrators, Exchange Windows Permissions, and ExchangeLegacyInterop.

4. Finalize security settings for Exchange Server 2010 by preparing the local domain by running Setup with the /PrepareDomain option, or by preparing all domains by running setup with the /PrepareAllDomains option. To run this command, you must be a member of the Domain Admins groups for the local domain or the Enterprise Admins group.

   If the domain that you are preparing was created after you ran Setup with the /PrepareAD option, you must be a member of the Exchange Organization Administrators group, and you must be a member of the Domain Admins group in the domain. You must run Setup with the /PrepareAD option in every domain in which you will install Exchange 2010. You must also run this command in every domain that will contain mail-enabled users, even if the domain does not have Exchange 2010 installed.

Configuring Exchange Server 2010 for Use with Existing Exchange Organizations

All the Exchange 2010 server roles are supported for coexistence with a native-mode Exchange 2003 or 2007 organization. In the Exchange System Manager for Exchange Server 2003, all Exchange servers are displayed as members of the Exchange Administrative Group. Exchange Server 2010 servers are also displayed as members of the Exchange Routing Group. These groups are created only for the purpose of coexistence with Exchange Server 2003 and are not applicable to Exchange Server 2007.

When managing Exchange servers, you should use the administrative tools for that Exchange Server version. Exchange Server 2010 doesn't use Active Directory Users And Computers for recipient management, and instead uses only the Exchange Management Console and the Exchange Management Shell for this purpose. The Exchange Management Console and the Exchange Management Shell are the primary management tools for Exchange Server 2010.

Mailboxes located on Exchange Server 2003 and Exchange Server 2007 servers are also displayed in the Exchange Management Console. You can manage the Exchange 2003 or 2007 mailbox properties using the Exchange Management Console or the Exchange Management Shell. You can use either tool to move mailbox recipients from Exchange 2003 or Exchange 2007 to Exchange 2010.

When deploying Exchange 2010 in an Exchange 2003 or Exchange 2007 organization, keep the following in mind:

- If you want to use the Exchange Server 2010 Client Access server role, you must deploy the Client Access server role in each Active Directory site that contains the Mailbox server role. Clients will see the Outlook Web App or Exchange ActiveSync version that is on their mailbox store. With Client Access arrays, the Client Access servers must all be members of the same Active Directory site and the servers cannot also have the Mailbox role.

- If you want to use the Hub Transport server role, you must configure a two-way routing group connector from the Exchange Routing Group to each Exchange Server 2003 routing group that communicates directly with Exchange Server 2010. You must also suppress link state updates for each Exchange Routing Group that communicates with Exchange Server 2010. This does not apply to Exchange 2007.

- If you want to use the Unified Messaging server role, you must deploy the Exchange Server 2010 Hub Transport server role in the same Active Directory site as the Unified Messaging server role. Keep in mind that while Exchange 2003 mailboxes cannot be enabled with unified messaging, Exchange 2007 mailboxes can be enabled with unified messaging, but they will need an Exchange 2007 Unified Messaging server.

- If you want to use the Mailbox server role, you must deploy the Exchange Server 2010 Hub Transport server role in the same Active Directory site as the Mailbox server role.

- If you want to use the Edge Transport server role, you must configure SMTP connectors to accept mail from and send mail to the Internet. With Exchange 2003, four connector configurations are needed: Internet Send Connector, Internet Receive Connector, Legacy Send Connector, and Legacy Receive Connector. The legacy connectors are not needed for Exchange 2007. Other modifications are required to mail Exchange and smart host records. Further, you can synchronize the Edge Transport server's AD LDS data with Active Directory only if the Exchange Server 2010 Active Directory preparation process has been performed.

Moving to Exchange Server 2010

Most organizations have existing Exchange installations. When moving Exchange 2003 or Exchange 2007 installations to Exchange Server 2010, you cannot perform an in-place upgrade. Instead, you must install new Exchange Server 2010 servers into the existing organization and then either migrate or transition to Exchange Server 2010. Keep the following points in mind regarding migration and transitioning:

- **Migration** from Exchange 2003 or Exchange 2007 to Exchange 2010 involves installing Exchange Server 2010 on new hardware and then moving the mailboxes and public folders from your existing installations to the new installation. In a migration, only mailbox and public folder data is moved and any Exchange configuration data is not maintained.

- **Transitioning** from Exchange Server 2003 or Exchange 2007 to Exchange Server 2010 is a multiple-phase process that allows for the retention of Exchange configuration data as well as mailbox and public folder data. During these transitioning processes, the Exchange organization is considered to be operating in a coexistence mode.

Migrating to Exchange Server 2010

Migration from Exchange Server 2003 or Exchange 2007 to Exchange 2010 moves the mailboxes from your existing installations to your new Exchange Server 2010 installations. In a migration, only mailbox and public folder data is moved and any Exchange configuration data is not maintained.

With Exchange Server 2003, your servers must have Exchange Server 2003 Service Pack 2 or later installed. In each Active Directory site, you must have at least one Global Catalog server running Windows Server 2003 Service Pack 2 or later. Active Directory must be in Windows Server 2003 functional mode or higher.

With Exchange Server 2007, your servers must have Exchange Server 2007 Service Pack 2 or later installed. In each Active Directory site, you must have at least one Global Catalog server running Windows Server 2003 Service Pack 2 or later. Active Directory must be in Windows Server 2003 functional mode or higher.

The steps you perform to migrate from Exchange 2003 or Exchange 2007 to Exchange 2010 are as follows:

1. Plan to transition all Exchange servers in a particular routing group or site to Exchange 2010 at the same time. You must start with Internet-accessible Active Directory sites and then migrate internal Active Directory sites. With Exchange 2003, an Exchange 2003 front-end server is required to support the transition. For each Exchange 2010 Client Access server, you can configure only one Outlook Web App URL for redirection.

2. Install Exchange Server 2010 on new hardware, and make it a member of the appropriate domain in the forest. You should install the Client Access server role first and then install and transition other roles in the following order: the

Hub Transport server role, the Unified Messaging server role, the Mailbox server role. You can install these roles on a single server or on multiple servers. You must deploy an Exchange 2010 Hub Transport server in each Active Directory site that has an Exchange 2010 Mailbox server.

3. If you plan to have an Edge Transport server in your Exchange 2010 organization, you must install the Edge Transport server role on a separate computer. With Exchange 2003 organizations, you can add Exchange 2010 Edge Transport servers without having to upgrade internal servers. However, when Edge Transport servers are deployed in an Exchange organization that has not yet deployed Exchange 2010, you can't create an Edge subscription, and a limited set of features are available. If you are using the Exchange Intelligent Message Filter for antispam features, the Edge Transport servers will provide an additional layer of protection until the transition is complete.

   With Exchange 2007 organizations, you should install your Exchange 2010 Hub Transport servers first because Exchange 2010 Hub Transport servers can sync with Exchange 2007 Edge Transport servers. Then you install the Exchange 2010 Edge Transport servers. Afterward, you should remove the Exchange 2007 Edge Transport servers and related subscriptions, and then subscribe your Exchange 2010 Edge Transport servers to the Exchange 2010 Hub Transport servers.

4. Move mailboxes and public folders from your existing Exchange 2003 or Exchange 2007 installations to the new Exchange Server 2010 Mailbox server or servers. If you move a mailbox that is part of an e-mail address policy, the e-mail address for the mailbox is automatically updated based on the settings in the e-mail address policy. In this case, the new e-mail address becomes the primary address, and the old e-mail address becomes the secondary address.

   During a transition, the version of a CAS feature such as Outlook Web App that a user sees depends on where the user's mailbox is located. If the user's mailbox is on an Exchange 2003 server, she sees Exchange 2003 versions of CAS features. When you move the user's mailbox to Exchange 2010, she will see Exchange 2010 versions of CAS features.

REAL WORLD You move mailboxes from Exchange 2003 SP2 to Exchange 2010 by using an offline move process. Users will not be able to access their mailboxes during the move. Perform the move from the Exchange 2010 server using move mailbox requests, either with the Exchange Management Shell or the Exchange Management Console. You can't use the Exchange System Manager on the Exchange 2003 server to move mailboxes. You can't move mailboxes from Exchange 2003 SP1 or earlier.

You can move mailboxes from Exchange 2007 SP2 to Exchange 2010 by using an online move, and this approach allows users to access their mailboxes during the move. Perform the move from the Exchange 2010 server by using move mailbox requests, either with the Exchange Management Shell or the Exchange Management Console. You can't use the Exchange Management Console on the Exchange 2007 server to move mailboxes. You can't move mailboxes from Exchange 2007 SP1 or earlier.

5. If you want to remove your Exchange 2003 servers, you must first remove Exchange Server 2003 routing groups and all connectors to these routing groups. Also, keep in mind that Exchange Server 2010 does not support the Novell GroupWise connector for Exchange Server 2003 or the use of the Inter-Organization Replication tool to share free/busy and public folder data across forests. If you require these features, you must keep at least one Exchange Server 2003 server in your organization.

6. Remove your old Exchange 2003 or Exchange 2007 server from the organization.

CAUTION Before removing the last Exchange 2007 server, you must be sure that you will never need to introduce an Exchange 2007 server again. Once you remove the last Exchange 2007 server, you can never add another one. The same goes for Exchange 2003. Once you remove the last Exchange 2003 server, you can never add another one.

Transitioning to Exchange Server 2010

The steps you perform to transition from Exchange 2003 or Exchange 2007 to Exchange 2010 depend on the forest configuration. To transition from an Exchange 2003 or Exchange 2007 single forest organization to an Exchange 2010 single forest organization or to deploy Exchange Server 2010 in an Exchange resource forest and then transition to Exchange Server 2010, follow these steps:

1. Install Exchange Server 2010 on new hardware, and make it a member of the appropriate domain in the forest. At a minimum, you should install the Client Access server role, the Hub Transport server role, and the Mailbox server role. You can install these roles on a single server or on multiple servers. If you plan to have an Edge Transport server in your Exchange 2010 organization, you must install the Edge Transport server role on a separate computer.

2. When Mailbox servers have been deployed, you can move mailboxes from Exchange 2003 or Exchange 2007 to Exchange 2010.

3. For any public folders in your existing Exchange 2003 or Exchange 2007 organization that you want to maintain, create a replica on your Exchange Server 2010 Mailbox server or servers. For Exchange 2003, you must create the replica using Exchange System Manager in the Exchange 2003 organization. Exchange then replicates the public folder data to the Exchange Server 2010 Mailbox server or servers.

NOTE You do not need to create replicas for the offline address book (OAB) or free/busy system folders. When you install the first Exchange Server 2010 server, Exchange creates these replicas.

4. If you want to remove your Exchange 2003 servers, you must first remove Exchange Server 2003 routing groups and all connectors to these routing groups. Also, keep in mind that Exchange Server 2010 does not support the Novell GroupWise connector for Exchange Server 2003 or the use of the Inter-Organization Replication tool to share free/busy and public folder data across forests. If you require these features, you must keep at least one Exchange Server 2003 server in your organization.

5. When you are absolutely certain that you don't need your old Exchange 2003 or Exchange 2007 server, you can remove it from the organization. Once you remove it, you can never add it back again.

In some cases, you might want to have one or more forests that contain accounts and a separate resource forest for your Exchange organization. Although configuring a separate resource forest provides clear separation between accounts and your Exchange organization, it requires a great deal of predeployment planning and additional work to maintain. In the Exchange forest, you must disable any user accounts with mailboxes and then associate these disabled user accounts, and all other user accounts, with the user accounts in your other forests. To do this, you must install a Microsoft identity integration solution, and then use its GAL Synchronization feature to create mail-enabled contacts that represent recipients from other forests.

To transition from a single forest organization to a resource forest organization, follow these steps:

1. Create a new Active Directory forest, and then create a one-way, outgoing forest trust from this forest to your existing forest. This ensures that the Exchange Server 2010 resource forest trusts the existing forest. You need the trust so that you can move mailboxes from servers in the existing forest to servers in the Exchange Server 2010 forest.

2. In the Exchange Server 2010 forest, install Exchange Server 2010 on new hardware, and make it a member of the appropriate domain in this forest. At a minimum, you should install the Client Access server role, the Hub Transport server role, and the Mailbox server role. You can install these roles on a single server or on multiple servers. If you plan to have an Edge Transport server in your Exchange Server 2010 organization, you must install the Edge Transport server role on a separate computer.

3. Move all mailboxes from the existing forest to the Exchange Server 2010 forest. You must move all mailboxes. If you do not move all mailboxes, you will be in an unsupported hybrid forest scenario.

4. To complete the transition, follow steps 3 through 5 from the procedure previously described in this section.

Running and Modifying Exchange Server 2010 Setup

Exchange Server 2010 Setup is the program you use to perform installation tasks for Exchange Server 2010. You use Exchange Server 2010 Setup to install Exchange Server roles and the Exchange management tools. When you want to manage the Exchange server configuration, you use Programs And Features in Control Panel. Tasks you can perform with these utilities include:

- Installing Exchange Server roles and management tools
- Adding server roles or management tools
- Maintaining existing components
- Uninstalling Exchange Server

Installing New Exchange Servers

You can install multiple Exchange Server roles on a single computer. For servers deployed within the organization, you can deploy any combination of the Mailbox, Client Access, Hub Transport, and Unified Messaging roles on a single computer. You cannot combine the Edge Transport role with other roles, however, because this role is for the organization's perimeter network and you must install it separately from other roles.

Often, small and medium-size organizations can deploy Exchange servers that host multiple roles in each Active Directory site and might not need to have an Edge Transport server in a perimeter zone. As the size and needs of the organization increase, however, it becomes more and more beneficial to host some roles on separate servers. Keep the following in mind:

- You may be able to achieve increased efficiency for message routing and delivery by combining the Mailbox and Hub Transport roles on a single server. However, keep in mind that routing rules change when you combine Hub and Mailbox roles in a database availability group.
- You can achieve increased security by isolating the Internet-facing Client Access role and deploying it on a server other than one that also hosts the Mailbox and Hub Transport roles.
- You can improve responsiveness for dial-in and voice access by isolating the Unified Messaging role and deploying it on a server other than one that also hosts the Mailbox and Hub Transport roles.
- You can achieve high availability for the Mailbox role, simply by installing two or more Mailbox servers, creating a database availability group, adding mailbox databases to this group, and then adding database copies. You'll find detailed information on database availability groups in Chapter 9.
- You can achieve high availability for the Hub Transport role simply by installing the role on multiple servers. Thanks to the new shadow redundancy feature, a message that is submitted to a Hub Transport server is stored in the

transport database until the transport server verifies that all of the next hops for that message have completed delivery. If the next hop doesn't report successful delivery, the message is resubmitted for delivery. In addition, when messages are in the transport dumpster, they aren't removed until they are replicated to all the appropriate mailbox databases.

- You can achieve high availability for the Client Access role by installing the role on multiple servers, configuring network or hardware load balancing, and creating a load-balanced array called the Client Access Server (CAS) array. Creating a CAS array requires planning. If you are going to create and use an array, you should specify the URL of the array as the external domain name for the Client Access server during setup. This will ensure that clients connect to the array.

When you use multiple Exchange servers, you should deploy the roles in the following order:

1. Client Access server
2. Hub Transport server
3. Mailbox server
4. Unified Messaging server

For client access to work correctly, install at least one Client Access server in each Active Directory site that has a Mailbox server. For Hub Transport, Mailbox, and Unified Messaging servers, install at least one of each server role for each group of Active Directory sites that are well connected on a common LAN. For example, if the organization consists of Sites A and B, which are well connected on a common LAN, and Sites C and D, which are well connected on a common LAN, with wide area network (WAN) links connecting Sites A and B to Sites C and D, a minimal implementation would be to have Hub Transport, Mailbox, and Unified Messaging servers only in Site A and Site C. However, Microsoft recommends that you have the Client Access, Hub Transport, Mailbox, and Unified Messaging serve roles in each Active Directory site.

Because you install Edge Transport servers outside the Active Directory forest, you can deploy them at any time. By configuring multiple Edge Transport servers, you can ensure that if one server fails, Edge Transport services continue. If you also configure your Edge Transport servers with round-robin DNS, you can load-balance between them.

REAL WORLD If you are installing Exchange Server on a new network, such as one for a new company or a development environment, be sure that you've properly configured Active Directory and DNS before installing Exchange Server. You need to create a domain. Typically, you do this by installing a server and establishing the server as a domain controller in a new forest. Ideally, the operating system on the domain controller should be Windows Server 2008 Service Pack 2 or later or Windows Server 2008 Release 2. Active Directory must operate in Windows Server 2003 or higher forest functional mode.

When you set up DNS, be sure you configure the appropriate reverse lookup zones. You should have one reverse lookup zone for each subnet. If you forget to set up the reverse zones and do this after installing your servers, be sure that the appropriate PTR records have been created for your domain controllers and Exchange servers. In Active Directory Sites And Services, check that the sites and subnets are configured appropriately. You need to create a subnet in Active Directory to represent each of the subnets on your network. If DNS reverse zones and Active Directory subnets are not configured properly, you will likely experience long startup times on your servers, and Exchange services will likely not start properly.

Installing Exchange Server

The Exchange Server 2010 installation process uses Windows Installer and requires the .NET Framework version 3.5.1, Windows PowerShell 2.0, and WinRM 2.0. Some Exchange server roles also require additional components, as discussed previously.

Using Windows Installer helps to streamline and stabilize the installation process, and it makes modification of installation components fairly easy. Thanks to Windows Installer, you can do the following:

- Install additional roles or components by rerunning the Installation Wizard. With Windows Server 2008, use the Programs And Features page under Control Panel, Programs.

- Maintain installed components. With Windows Server 2008, use the Programs And Features page under Control Panel, Programs.

- Resume a failed installation or modification. Do this by rerunning Exchange Setup.

For administration purposes, you can install the Exchange management tools on a workstation computer running Windows Vista with Service Pack 2 or later, or Windows 7. This workstation must also have the .NET Framework version 3.5.1, Windows PowerShell 2.0, WinRM 2.0, IIS 6 Metabase Compatibility, and the IIS 6 Management Console. For Windows Vista SP2 or later, Windows Management Framework has most of what you need. After you install PowerShell, you can add the IIS components by entering the following commands at an elevated administrator PowerShell prompt:

```
Add-WindowsFeature -name Web-Server
Add-WindowsFeature -name Web-Metabase
```

To install Exchange Server roles on a server, complete the following steps:

1. Log on to the server using an administrator account. When you install the Mailbox, Hub Transport, Client Access, and Unified Messaging roles, you must use a domain account that is a member of the Enterprise Administrators group. If you've already prepared Active Directory, this account must also be a member of the Exchange Organization Administrators group.

2. If you are using an installation disc, insert the Exchange Server 2010 DVD into the DVD-ROM drive. If Autorun is enabled, Exchange Server 2010 Setup should start automatically. Otherwise, double-click Setup.exe on the root folder of the DVD.

3. On the Start page, you need to install required components if they are not already installed by clicking the links for steps 1, 2, and 3, each in turn. For Windows Server 2008, this helps you download and install the .NET Framework version 3.5.1 and Windows PowerShell version 2.0. Note that you also need WinRM 2.0 (which you get from Windows Management Framework) and the .NET update. For R2, these should all be available, except for .NET Framework version 3.5.1, which you can install using the Add Feature wizard in Server Manager. And for a CAS, you need to set Net.TCP Port Sharing service to Automatic startup. This service does not even appear in Windows 2008 R2 until other prerequisites are installed, so you cannot configure the service ahead of time.

4. On the Start page, click Step 3: Choose Exchange Language Option, and then choose a language installation option. You can install only languages from the DVD or all languages from the language bundle. If your e-mails messages are sent and received primarily in your native language, you probably need only the languages from the DVD. However, if you operate in a multilingual environment, you might need to install all languages from the language bundle.

5. On the Start page, click Step 4: Install Microsoft Exchange. In the Exchange Server 2010 Installation Wizard, read the introductory text and then click Next.

6. On the License Agreement page, read the license agreement. Select I Accept The Terms In The License Agreement, and then click Next.

7. On the Error Reporting page, choose Yes if you'd like to send error reports automatically to Microsoft or No if you would like to turn off automatic error reporting. Click Next.

8. On the Installation Type page, click Custom Exchange Server Installation and then click Next.

9. On the Server Role Selection Page, select the server roles that you want to install on the computer. When you select one or more roles, the wizard selects the Management Tools option automatically to install the Exchange management tools. The default installation location for Exchange Server and all its components is %SystemDrive%\Program Files\Microsoft\Exchange Server\V14. If you want to change the path for the Exchange Server 2010 installation, click Browse, locate the relevant folder in the folder tree, and then click OK. Click Next.

NOTE When you are installing production versions of Exchange Server 2010, the Management Tools option installs the 64-bit management tools. You can install the management tools on your 64-bit workstation running Windows Vista SP 2 or later or Windows 7. You can't install the management tools on 32-bit computers.

To manage Exchange Server 2010 remotely from a 32-bit Windows installation, you can install the Windows Management Framework and then use remote Windows PowerShell for management.

10. If you selected Mailbox Role, Client Access Role, Hub Transport Role, or Unified Messaging Role, and if this is the first Exchange 2010 server in your organization, on the Exchange Organization page, type a name for your Exchange organization or accept the default value of First Organization. Click Next.

11. If you selected Mailbox Role, and if this is the first Exchange 2010 server in your organization, you'll next see the Client Settings page. If you have client computers that are running Outlook 2003 and earlier or Entourage, select the Yes option so that Exchange creates a public folder database on the mailbox server. If all of your client computers are running Outlook 2007 or later or are all non-MAPI clients, public folders are optional because the OAB and free/busy information are maintained separately. If you select the No option, Exchange does not create a public folder database on the mailbox server. You can add a public folder database later if desired. Click Next.

12. If you selected Client Access Role, you'll see the Configure Client Access Server External Domain page. This page allows you to specify whether the Client Access server will be Internet facing. An internet-facing server is one that clients outside the domain can connect to using Exchange ActiveSync, Outlook Web App, or Outlook Anywhere. If your Client Access server is Internet facing, select the check box provided, and then enter the external domain name for the Client Access server, such as mail.cpandl.com. Click Next.

13. Specify whether you want to join the Exchange Customer Experience Improvement Program, and then click Next.

14. On the Readiness Checks page, Setup then checks to see whether Exchange is ready to be installed with the roles you selected. Review the status to determine whether the organization and server role prerequisite checks completed successfully. You must complete any required prerequisites before continuing. After the checks are completed successfully, click Install to install Exchange Server 2010.

15. If an error occurs, note the error and take the appropriate corrective action. Otherwise, on the Completion page, click Finish. Optionally, you can verify the installation by doing the following on the server:

   • Start the Exchange Management Shell, and type **get-ExchangeServer** to display a list of all Exchange roles installed on that server.

   • Review the application logs for events from Exchange Setup. These events have event IDs 1003 and 1004, with the source as MSExchangeSetup.

   • Review the Exchange Setup logs in the %SystemRoot%\ExchangeSetupLogs folder. Because these logs contain standard text, you can perform a search using the keyword *error* to find any setup errors that occurred.

REAL WORLD With a new Exchange Server 2010 implementation, each new recipient object (such as a mailbox, contact, distribution list, mailbox agent, or mail-enabled public folder) will have a special attribute called legacyDN that corresponds to the appropriate administrative group for the Exchange Server 2010 server. Because of this legacyDN, Microsoft Outlook will request a full OAB download from the Exchange Server 2010 server for each user in this organization that logs on. In a large organization, this could mean multiple simultaneous OAB downloads, which, in turn, could cause high network utilization.

To complete the installation for an initial deployment of Exchange into an organization, you need to perform the following tasks:

- For Client Access servers:
  - If you plan to use ActiveSync for mobile messaging clients, as discussed in Chapter 13, "Managing Client Access Servers," configure direct push, authentication, and mobile devices.
  - Configure internal and external URLs for the Outlook Web applications, Exchange ActiveSync, Exchange Control Panel, and Offline Address Book.
  - Configure authentication and display options, as appropriate.
  - Enable the server for POP3 and IMAP4, as appropriate.
- For Edge Transport servers:
  - Export the Edge Transport server subscription file, and import it on Hub Transport servers, as discussed in Chapter 12, "Managing Hub Transport and Edge Transport Servers."
  - If you are using Edge Transport servers with Exchange Server 2003 organizations, you must manually configure the necessary connectors, as discussed previously.
  - Configure DNS MX resource records for each accepted domain.
  - Configure antispam, junk e-mail, and safe sender features, as appropriate.
- For Hub Transport servers:
  - Configure domains for which you will accept e-mail. You need an accepted domain entry for each SMTP domain for which you will accept e-mail, as discussed in Chapter 12.
  - Configure Send connectors as appropriate. If you are unsure about the Send connectors that are needed, create an Internet Send connector at a minimum. Use the address space of "*" to route all outbound mail to the Internet. For more information on creating Send connectors, see "Working with SMTP Connectors, Sites, and Links" in Chapter 12.
  - If you also deployed the Edge Transport server role, you need to subscribe to the Edge Transport server so that the EdgeSync service can establish one-way replication of recipient and configuration information from Active Directory to the AD LDS store on the Edge Transport server. See Chapter 12 for details.
  - Configure DNS MX resource records for each accepted domain.

- For Mailbox servers:
  - Configure OAB distribution for Outlook 2007 and later clients, as discussed in Chapter 7, "Working with Distribution Groups and Address Lists."
  - Configure OAB distribution for Outlook 2003 or earlier clients, as discussed in Chapter 7.
  - Configure database availability groups and mailbox database copies, as discussed in Chapter 9.
- For Unified Messaging servers:
  - Configure a unified messaging dial plan, and add the server to it.
  - Configure Unified Messaging hunt groups.
  - Enable users for unified messaging, as appropriate.
  - Configure your IP/VoIP gateways or IP-PBXs to work with Exchange server.
  - Configure a Unified Messaging IP gateway in Exchange server.
  - As desired, create auto-attendant and mailbox policies and configure additional dial plans, gateways, and hunt groups.

Adding, Modifying, or Uninstalling Server Roles

After you install an Exchange server with its initial role or roles, you can add new roles or remove existing roles. With Windows Server 2008, use Programs And Features and follow these steps:

1. In Control Panel, click the Uninstall A Program link under Programs. In Programs And Features, select the Microsoft Exchange Server 2010 entry to display the Change and Uninstall buttons.
2. If you want to add roles, click Change. Select the check boxes for the roles you want to add. Click Next, and then follow the prompts.
3. If you want to remove roles, click Uninstall. Clear the check boxes for roles you want to remove. Click Next, and then follow the prompts.

Before you can remove the Mailbox role from a server, you must move or delete all mailboxes hosted in mailbox databases on the server and all offline address books hosted in public folder databases on the server. If the public folder database is the last one in the Exchange organization—which might be the case if you are uninstalling Exchange on a test or development server—you need to delete the public folder database after you've emptied it.

To remove the last public folder database in the Exchange organization, type the following command at the Exchange Management Shell prompt:

```
remove-publicfolderdatabase "CORPSVR127\Public Folder Database"
-removelastallowed -confirm:$false
```

CHAPTER 3

Exchange Server 2010 Administration Essentials

- Validating the Exchange Server Licensing **57**
- Understanding Exchange Server 2010 Organizations **59**
- Understanding Data Storage in Exchange Server 2010 **74**
- Using and Managing Exchange Server Services **81**

Whether you're using Microsoft Exchange Server 2010 for the first time or honing your skills, you'll need to master many key concepts to work effectively with Exchange Server. You'll need to know the following:

- How the Exchange environment is organized
- How information is stored in Exchange Server
- Which Windows processes are used with Exchange Server
- How Exchange Server works

You'll also need to know how to use the Exchange Management Console. These topics are all covered in this chapter.

Validating the Exchange Server Licensing

With Exchange Server 2010, you do not enter a product key during initial setup. Instead, you provide the product key after installation using the Exchange Management Console. Until you enter a product key, Exchange Server 2010 runs in trial mode.

The product key you provide determines which edition is established on an Exchange server. You can use a valid product key to go from a trial edition to a Standard Edition or Enterprise Edition of Exchange Server 2010 without having to reinstall the program.

Using the Exchange Management Console, you can determine the established edition for an Exchange server and licensing by completing the following steps:

1. In the Exchange Management Console, select the Server Configuration node.
2. In the main pane, right-click the server you want to work with and then select Properties.
3. In the Properties dialog box, the established edition and license details are listed on the General tab.

REAL WORLD You can determine the licensing configuration of multiple Exchange servers without accessing the properties of each server. In the Exchange Management Console, select the Server Configuration node. On the View menu, choose Add/Remove Columns. This displays the Add/Remove Columns dialog box. In the Add/Remove Columns dialog box, under Available Columns, click Product ID, and then click Add. Next, click Licensing, and then click Add. Click OK. This adds the Product ID and Licensing columns to the displayed columns list. In the main pane of the Exchange Management Console, scroll left or right as necessary to display the Product ID and Licensing columns for your Exchange servers. If the Product ID is listed as Unlicensed, you have not yet provided a valid product key for the Exchange server. Otherwise, the Product ID is an ID generated for the Exchange server.

Using the Exchange Management Console, you can enter a product key by completing the following steps:

1. In the Exchange Management Console, select the Server Configuration node.
2. Right-click the server that requires the product key, and then select Enter Product Key. This starts the Enter Product Key Wizard.
3. When prompted, type in the product key for the Exchange Server 2010 edition you want to establish, either Standard or Enterprise, and then click Enter.

NOTE The product key is a 25-character alphanumeric string, grouped in sets of five characters separated by hyphens. You can find the product key on the Exchange Server 2010 DVD case.

4. The wizard validates the product key and displays any appropriate warnings. Read the information provided, and then click Finish. Keep the following in mind:
   - When you change the product key on a Mailbox server, you must restart the Microsoft Exchange Information Store service to apply the change.
   - When you change the product key on an Edge Transport server, you must resubscribe the server in the Exchange organization to apply the change.
   - You cannot use product keys to downgrade editions. To downgrade editions, you must uninstall Exchange Server and then reinstall Exchange Server.

Using the Exchange Management Shell, you can enter a server's product key using the Set-ExchangeServer cmdlet. Sample 3-1 shows the syntax and usage. For the identity parameter, you use the server's name, such as MailServer25.

SAMPLE 3-1 Setting the Exchange product key syntax and usage

Syntax

```
Set-ExchangeServer -Identity 'ServerName'
-ProductKey 'ProductKey'
```

Usage

```
Set-ExchangeServer -Identity 'MailServer25'
-ProductKey 'AAAAA-BBBBB-CCCCC-DDDDD-EEEEE'
```

TIP By using a valid product key, you can change from the Standard to the Enterprise edition. You also can relicense an Exchange server by entering a new product key for the installed edition, which is useful if you accidentally used the same product key on multiple servers and want to correct the mistake. The best way to do this is to enter the product key using the Set-ExchangeServer cmdlet.

Understanding Exchange Server 2010 Organizations

The root of an Exchange environment is an *organization*. It's the starting point for the Exchange hierarchy, and its boundaries define the boundaries of any Exchange environment. Exchange Server 2010 organizations are nearly identical to Exchange Server 2007 organizations.

When you install Exchange Server 2010, you install your Exchange servers within the organizational context of the domain the server is a member of. The physical site boundaries and subnets defined for Active Directory are the same as those used by Exchange Server 2010, and the site details are determined by the IP address assigned to the server. If you are installing the first Exchange server in a domain, you set the name of the Exchange organization for that domain. The next Exchange server you install in the domain joins the existing Exchange organization automatically.

Like Exchange Server 2007, Exchange Server 2010 uses Active Directory site-based routing instead of routing groups and configuration containers instead of administrative groups. The use of site-based routing and configuration containers substantially changes the way you configure and manage Exchange Server 2010.

Using Site-Based Routing Instead of Routing Groups

With Exchange Server 2010, site-based routing is possible because Exchange servers can determine their own Active Directory site membership and the Active Directory site membership of other servers by querying Active Directory. Using Active Directory for routing eliminates the need for Exchange to have its own routing infrastructure (as was required with Exchange 2003).

How Site-Based Routing Works

Mailbox and Unified Messaging servers use site membership information to determine which Hub Transport servers are located in the same site. This allows the Mailbox or Unified Messaging server to submit messages for routing and transport to a Hub Transport server that has the same site membership.

When a Client Access server receives a user connection request, it queries Active Directory to determine which Mailbox server is hosting the user's mailbox. The Client Access server then retrieves the site membership of that Mailbox server. If the Client Access server is not in the same site as the user's Mailbox server, the connection is redirected to a Client Access server in the same site as the Mailbox server.

Normally, Hub Transport servers retrieve information from Active Directory to determine how they should transport mail inside the organization. When a user sends a message, the Categorizer running on the Hub Transport server uses the header information about the message to query Active Directory for information about where the server must deliver the message. If the recipient's mailbox is located on a Mailbox server in the same site as the Hub Transport server, the server delivers the message directly to that mailbox. If the recipient's mailbox is located on a Mailbox server in a different site, the message is transferred to a Hub Transport server in that site and then that server delivers the message to the mailbox.

Exchange servers determine site membership by matching their assigned IP address to a subnet that is defined in Active Directory Sites And Services and associated with an Active Directory site. The Exchange server then uses this information to determine which domain controllers, Global Catalog servers, and other Exchange servers exist in that site, and it communicates with those directory servers for authentication, authorization, and messaging purposes. Exchange 2010 always tries to retrieve information about recipients from directory servers that are in the same site as the Exchange 2010 server.

> **TIP** In Active Directory, you can associate a site with one or more IP subnets. Each subnet that is part of a site should be connected over reliable, high-speed links. You should configure any business locations connected over slow or unreliable links as part of separate sites. Because of this, individual sites typically represent well-connected local area networks (LANs) within an organization, and wide area network (WAN) links between business locations typically mark the boundaries of these sites. Sites cannot have overlapping subnet configurations. If subnets overlap, replication and message routing will not work correctly.

How IP Site Links Are Used

As Figure 3-1 shows, Active Directory sites are connected through IP site links. An IP site link can connect two or more sites. Each site link has a specific schedule, interval, and cost. The schedule and interval determine the frequency of Active Directory replication. The cost value determines the cost of using the link relative to other links that might be available. Active Directory replication uses the link with the lowest cost when multiple paths exist to a destination. The cost of a route is determined by adding together the cost of all site links in a transmission path. Administrators assign the cost value to a link based on relative network speed, available bandwidth, and reliability compared to other available connections. By default, IP site links always allow traffic to flow into or out of a site.

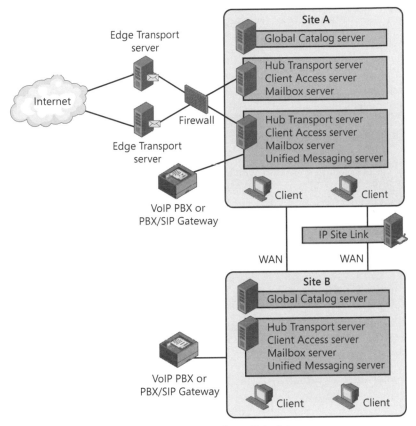

FIGURE 3-1 Message traffic between sites is routed over IP site links.

In large enterprises, message traffic might have to travel through multiple sites to get from the source site to a destination site. When transferring messages from one site to another site through other sites, a Hub Transport server always tries to connect directly to a Hub Transport server in the destination site. Because of this, messages are not relayed through each Hub Transport server in each site in the link path. Instead, they go directly from the Hub Transport server in the originating site across the link to the Hub Transport server in the destination site. If the originating server cannot connect directly to a Hub Transport server in the destination site, the originating Hub Transport server uses the link cost to determine the closest site at which to queue the message. This feature is called *queue at point of failure*.

The Hub Transport server can also use the site link information to optimize the routing of messages that users send to multiple recipients. Here, the Hub Transport server expands a distribution list and creates multiple copies of a message only when there are multiple paths in the routing topology. This feature is called *delayed fan-out*.

Understanding On-Premises, Online, and Cross-Premises Routing

Microsoft introduced Exchange Online with Exchange Server 2007. Exchange Online is what's referred to as a cloud service, meaning the service is provided via the Internet. Exchange Online allows you to outsource all or part of your Exchange services. Exchange Online differs from Exchange on-premises (the standard implementation) in several fundamental ways. With Exchange Online, the Exchange hardware resides elsewhere and users access their mailboxes over the Internet. However, administrators still retain control and management over the outsourced mailboxes.

In Exchange Server 2007, the on-premises and online Exchange configurations weren't tightly integrated. Starting with Exchange Server 2010, Microsoft corrects this deficiency by making it possible to manage both online and on-premises Exchange configurations using the same set of management tools. You can simultaneously connect to and manage both online and on-premises configurations in the Exchange Management Console.

Although Exchange Online has some advantages over an Exchange on-premises implementation, it has disadvantages as well. For users, Exchange Online provides:

- Mailbox hosting
- ActiveSync
- Microsoft Outlook Anywhere
- Microsoft Outlook Web App
- Spam filtering

For administrators, Exchange Online provides:

- Service Level Agreements
- Storage quotas
- Automatic backups
- Automatic archiving

What Exchange Online doesn't provide is immediacy of access. Users must always be connected to the Internet to get their mail. Messages typically are routed and transferred across the Internet, which can cause delays. Exchange Online also does not have Exchange voice mail, custom transport rules, and some other features.

When you configure your Exchange organization, it's important to keep in mind that Exchange Online is not an all-or-nothing implementation. You can host some mailboxes online and others on premises—and Exchange Server 2010 makes it easy to manage mailboxes regardless of where they are located. Before you transition mailboxes off-site, however, you'll probably want to perform a trial with a limited subset of users while keeping mailboxes for executives and most managers in house. In fact, you might want to plan to always keep mailboxes for executives and other high-level managers in house.

Exchange Server 2010 uses cross-premises routing to transfer messages between on-premises and hosted mailboxes. If you send a message to a user with a hosted mailbox, your organization's transport servers will route the message across the Internet to the hosted Exchange server. If you send a message to a user with an on-premises mailbox, your organization's transport servers will route the message across your organization to the appropriate Exchange server.

Exchange provides features for migrating mailboxes from online to on-premises environments and vice versa. During the migration, a mailbox might exist in both locations temporarily. When Exchange completes the migration, the mailbox exists only in the destination environment. Outlook 2007 and later include an Autodiscover feature that automatically connects messaging clients to the correct Exchange server. This feature uses the user's SMTP e-mail address during automatic discovery to determine where the mailbox is currently located.

Normally, Autodiscover works very well. However, a conflict could occur if a user has a mailbox in Exchange Online and a mailbox in Exchange on-premises or a user has the same primary SMTP e-mail address in Exchange Online and Exchange on-premises. In these scenarios, the Autodiscover feature normally does not configure Outlook for the Exchange Online environment and instead uses Exchange on-premises. This occurs because Exchange on-premises has priority over Exchange Online when there is a conflict and the user's computer is connected to the Active Directory domain. To resolve the problem, delete the original mailbox from its original location as soon as possible after a mailbox migration. If a user needs both an on-line and on-premises mailbox, do not use the same primary SMTP e-mail address for both Exchange Online and Exchange on-premises.

Using Configuration Containers Instead of Administrative Groups

Exchange Server 2010 uses configuration containers instead of administrative groups to simplify the administrative model. As you can see in Figure 3-2, you can view the logical structure of the Exchange organization in the Exchange Management Console. Start the Exchange Management Console by clicking Start, selecting All Programs, selecting Microsoft Exchange Server 2010, and selecting Exchange Management Console. When you are logged on to a computer in the Exchange forest, you can work with the local Exchange servers by using the subnodes of the Microsoft Exchange On-Premises node. Otherwise, you need to connect to the Exchange forest before you can work with Exchange servers and you need to establish one connection for each online and on-premises implementation. To do this, follow these steps:

1. In the Exchange Management Console, right-click the Microsoft Exchange node and then select Add Exchange Forest.

2. In the Add Exchange Forest dialog box, specify the friendly name for the Exchange implementation to which you want to connect. This is the name that will be displayed in the Exchange Management Console.

3. Enter the fully qualified domain name, host name, or IP address of the Exchange server you want to connect to. Normally, this is a Client Access server. However, all Exchange servers run the Remote PowerShell Web application on their instance of Internet Information Services (IIS). For an Exchange online organization, use the external name provided to you.

4. To log on with your current credentials, select Logon With Default Credential, and then click OK. Otherwise, click OK, type the name and password of a user account with Exchange administrator permissions, and then click OK again.

Regardless of whether you are connected to the Exchange forest automatically or connect to an Exchange forest manually, you are connected to an automatically selected server. You can specify an Exchange server to connect to by right-clicking the friendly name of the forest and then clicking Properties. In the Properties dialog box, the Specify A Server option is selected by default. Click Browse. Select the Exchange server you want to connect to, and then click OK. Click OK again to apply your changes.

REAL WORLD The Exchange Management Console establishes connections to a designated server in the Exchange organization via the Windows Remote Management service. The server name you enter sets the URL that the Exchange Management Console will use to connect to Exchange Server for remote management, such as https://MailServer23.cpandl.com/PowerShell/.

On a server running Exchange Server 2010, WinRM and related services are set up automatically. On your management computer, you need to install the required components and configure WinRM as discussed in the section "Exchange Server 2010 Editions" in Chapter 1, "Exchange Server 2010 Administration Overview." You can customize the WinRM configuration for your environment. In the Exchange Management Shell, the related commands are New-PowerShellVirtualDirectory, Get-PowerShellVirtual-Directory, Set-PowerShellVirtualDirectory, and Test-PowerShellConnectivity. If you enter **Get-PowerShellVirtualDirectory | Format-List,** you'll get configuration details for each Client Access server in the Exchange organization. You can use Set-PowerShellVirtualDirectory to enable or disable authentication mechanisms, including basic authentication, certificate authentication, Live ID basic authentication, Live ID NTLM negotiate authentication, and Windows authentication. You can also specify the internal and external URLs for the PowerShell virtual directory on a per-server basis. By default, servers have only internal URLs for PowerShell. For troubleshooting issues related to the PowerShell virtual directory, enter **Test-PowerShellConnectivity** followed by the URL to test, such as https://mailer1.cpandl.com/powershell.

Figure 3-2 shows the main window for the Exchange Management Console. In the Exchange Management Console, the forest-level node is the starting point for managing Exchange. When you select this node, you can use the options on the Organizational Health tab to generate and view organizational reports that include general health, licensing, and configuration statistics. Select the Click Here To Access The Latest Data link to generate or update the health statistics. Under the forest-level node, you'll find three top-level containers:

- **Organization Configuration**   Used to view and manage the global settings for all servers and recipients in an organization. Settings are organized based on the server role and applied globally throughout the organization.

- **Server Configuration**   Used to view and manage the configuration of individual servers in an organization. Servers are organized by role.

- **Recipient Configuration**   Used to view and manage recipients in an organization. Recipients are organized by type, independent of the Mailbox server on which they are stored.

NOTE   In the Exchange Management Shell, you can get organization configuration information by entering **$s=Get-OrganizationConfig; $os=$s. organizationsummary;$os | ft key,value.**

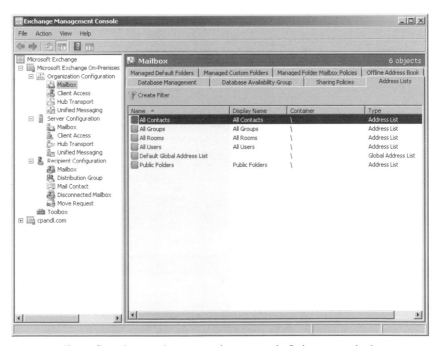

FIGURE 3-2 The configuration containers are used to manage the Exchange organization.

The sections that follow discuss these Exchange components and explain how they fit into the overall organizational structure.

Working with the Organization Configuration Node

With Exchange Server 2010, the scope of the organization is the same as the scope of your Active Directory organization. Because of this, Organization Configuration node settings apply to all Exchange servers and Exchange recipients in all domains in your Active Directory forest. When you select the Organization Configuration node, the results pane provides tabs for working with federation trusts and organizational relationships, as shown in Figure 3-3. You use these tabs as follows:

- **Federation Trusts**   Create and manage trusts between federated forests. Federated forests are Active Directory forests from different organizations or from organizations having different forest roots for which you've established trust relationships. You also can manage the identities of domains in the organization that should be federated. Every domain where users have primary e-mail services should be identified and, as appropriate, enabled for federation.

- **Organizational Relationships**   Enable and manage organizational relationships with external organizations. You use these relationships to enable secure information sharing using federation.

NOTE   After you have established federation trusts and organizational relationships, you can manage sharing policies by expanding the Organizational Configuration node, selecting the related Mailbox node, and then clicking the Sharing Policies tab. The default sharing policy allows for sharing calendar free/busy information with any external domain.

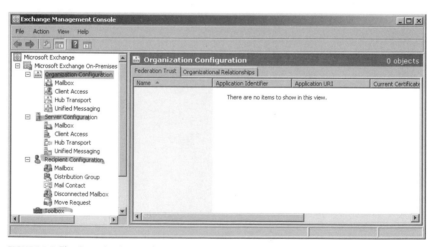

FIGURE 3-3 The Organization Configuration node extends to administrator roles as well as other organization-wide settings.

The subnodes under the Organization Configuration node provide access to the most common organization-level settings you'll work with:

- **Mailbox**   Allows you to manage Mailbox server role settings that apply to your entire Exchange 2010 organization. Mailbox server role settings that you can manage include address lists, managed folders, mailbox policies, databases, database availability groups, and offline address books. See Chapter 9, "Managing Data and Database Availability Groups," for more information, as well as Chapter 7, "Working with Distribution Groups and Address Lists."

- **Client Access** Allows you to manage Client Access server role settings that apply to your entire Exchange 2010 organization. Client Access server role settings allow you to create and manage mailbox policies for Outlook Web App and Exchange ActiveSync. See Chapter 13, "Managing Client Access Servers," for more information.

- **Hub Transport** Allows you to manage Hub Transport server role settings that apply to your entire Exchange 2010 organization. Hub Transport server role settings you can manage include antispam settings, remote and accepted domains, e-mail address policies, transport rules, journal rules, send connectors, and Edge subscriptions. See Chapter 12, "Managing Hub Transport and Edge Transport Servers," for more information.

- **Unified Messaging** Allows you to manage Unified Messaging server role settings that apply to your entire Exchange 2010 organization. Unified Messaging server role settings you can manage include dial plans, gateways, mailbox policies, and auto-attendants.

With Exchange Server organizations, most organization information is stored in Active Directory. When you start the Exchange Management Console, the console obtains the organization configuration details from the authoritative domain controller to which your computer is currently connected. In some cases, such as when you need to work with recipients and objects in a specific site or domain, you might want to connect to a specific authoritative domain controller and obtain server and Organization Configuration node details from this server.

You can specify the domain controller from which to obtain Organization Configuration node details by completing the following steps:

1. Open the Exchange Management Console.

2. Right-click the Organization Configuration node, and then select Modify Configuration Domain Controller. The Configuration Domain Controller dialog box appears, shown in Figure 3-4.

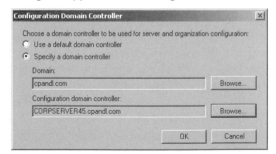

FIGURE 3-4 Specify the domain and domain controller to use.

3. Select Specify A Domain Controller. Click the Browse button to the right of the Domain text box, and then use the Select Domain dialog box to select the domain to use.

4. In the specified domain, by default you are connected to the first authoritative domain controller that responds to your request. To specify a configuration domain controller to use, click the Browse button to the right of the Configuration Domain Controller text box. Use the Select Domain Controller dialog box to select the domain controller to use according to its site membership in the previously specified domain.

5. When you click OK, the Exchange Management Console retrieves the topology information for the specified domain and site.

Working with the Server Configuration Node

All servers running Exchange Server 2010 have one or more server roles. You can deploy the Mailbox, Client Access, Hub Transport, and Unified Messaging server roles together. You can also manage these roles together using the Server Configuration node in the Exchange Management Console. When you select the Server Configuration node in the Exchange Management Console, all Exchange servers in your Exchange Server 2010 organization are listed in the results pane by name, the Exchange Server 2010 roles installed, and the Exchange Server version, as shown in Figure 3-5.

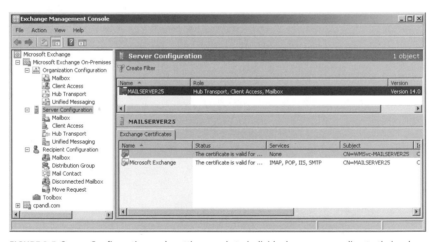

FIGURE 3-5 Server Configuration node settings apply to individual servers according to their role.

You can work with the individual server entries in several ways:

- If you right-click a server entry, you see a shortcut menu with options for managing each configured role. Selecting one of those options opens the corresponding subnode under Server Configuration, and doing this is the same as selecting the subnode and then selecting the server with which you want to work.

- If you right-click a server entry and then select Properties, you see the Properties dialog box, shown in Figure 3-6. The General tab provides summary information about the Exchange version, edition, roles, and licensing. The System Settings tab shows the domain controllers being used by Exchange and the Global Catalog servers being used by Exchange. Other server-specific configuration details are discussed elsewhere in this book.

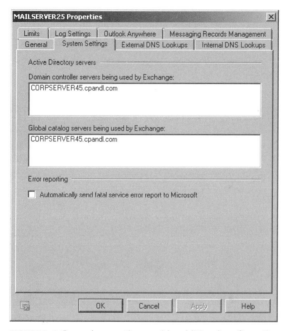

FIGURE 3-6 General properties provide additional configuration details for the selected server.

The subnodes under the Server Configuration node provide access to the most common settings you'll work with for individual servers according to their role:

- **Mailbox** Allows you to manage the mailbox configuration of a selected server. In the top pane, servers are listed by name, role, and Exchange version. If you select a server in the top pane, the related databases are listed.

- **Client Access** Allows you to manage the client access configuration of a selected server. In the top pane, servers are listed by name, role, Exchange version, and Outlook Anywhere state. If you select a server in the top pane, you can view the Web sites and Uniform Resource Locators (URLs) used with Outlook Web App, Exchange ActiveSync, POP3 And IMAP4, and Offline Address Book Distribution. See Chapter 13 for more information.

- **Hub Transport**   Allows you to manage the hub transport configuration of a selected server. In the top pane, servers are listed by name, role, Exchange version, and message-tracking state. If you select a server in the top pane, you can view the receive connectors and their status as well as the status of IP Allow and IP Block lists for antispam. See Chapter 12 for more information.

- **Unified Messaging**   Allows you to manage the unified messaging configuration of a selected server. In the top pane, servers are listed by name, role, Exchange version, unified messaging status, and associated dial plans. If you select a server in the top pane, you can view the dial plans, IP gateways, mailbox policies, and auto-attendants for that server.

As with organization-level configuration details, the configuration details for individual servers are stored in Active Directory. You can specify the domain controller from which to obtain Server Configuration node details by completing the following steps:

1. Open the Exchange Management Console.
2. Right-click the Server Configuration node, and then select Modify Configuration Domain Controller. The Configuration Domain Controller dialog box appears, shown previously in Figure 3-4.
3. Follow steps 3–5 in the procedure in the section "Working with the Organization Configuration Node."

Working with the Recipient Configuration Node

A recipient is an entity that can receive Exchange mail. Recipients include users, contacts, distribution groups, public folders, and resources. Types of resources used with Exchange include rooms and equipment used for scheduling.

You refer to recipients as either *mailbox-enabled* or *mail-enabled*. Mailbox-enabled recipients (users and resources) have mailboxes for sending and receiving e-mail messages. Mail-enabled recipients (contacts, distribution groups, and public folders) have e-mail addresses but no mailboxes. This allows users in your organization to send messages to mail-enabled recipients. Keep in mind that when you mail-enable a public folder and grant Send As permission on the folder to a user, the user can send mail on behalf of the public folder.

In addition to users, contacts, groups, resources, and public folders, Exchange Server 2010 has two unique types of recipients: linked mailboxes and dynamic distribution groups. Basically, a linked mailbox represents a mailbox that is accessed by a user in a separate, trusted forest. A dynamic distribution group is a type of distribution group that you can use to build a list of recipients whenever mail addressed to the group is received, rather than having a fixed member list.

To manage recipients in your organization, you need to know these key concepts:

- **How e-mail policies are used**   E-mail address policies define the technique Exchange uses to create e-mail addresses for users, resources, contacts, and mail-enabled groups. For example, you can set a policy for users with Exchange mailboxes that creates e-mail addresses by combining an e-mail alias with @cpandl.com. Thus, during setup of an account for William Stanek, the e-mail alias *williams* is combined with *@cpandl.com* to create the e-mail address *williams@cpandl.com*.

- **How address lists are used**   You use address lists to organize recipients and resources, making it easier to find the ones that you want to use, along with their related information. During setup, Exchange creates a number of default address lists. The most commonly used default address list is the global address list, which lists all the recipients in the organization. You can create custom address lists as well.

- **How managed folders are used**   Every recipient has a default set of managed folders that are displayed in Outlook and Outlook Web App. These folders include Inbox, Contacts, Drafts, Deleted Items, Junk E-mail, Notes, Outbox, and Sent Items. To the default folders, you can add custom managed folders. For example, if managers need to approve certain types of messages before the messages are sent, you can create a Pending Approval folder.

In the Exchange Management Console, Recipient Configuration node settings apply to individual recipients in all domains in your Active Directory forest according to their type. The subnodes under the Recipient Configuration node provide access to recipients according to their type or state:

- **Mailbox**   Allows you to view and manage user mailboxes, room mailboxes, equipment mailboxes, and linked mailboxes. See Chapter 6, "Mailbox Administration," for more details.

- **Distribution Group**   Allows you to view and manage standard and dynamic distribution groups. See Chapter 7 for more details.

- **Mail Contact**   Allows you to view and manage mail contacts. See Chapter 5, "User and Contact Administration," for more details.

- **Disconnected Mailbox**   Allows you to view and manage disconnected mailboxes. A disconnected mailbox is a mailbox that is not associated with an Active Directory user account because it has been removed and marked for deletion. By default, when you remove a mailbox, it remains as a disconnected mailbox in Exchange for 30 days. At the end of the 30-day period, the mailbox is permanently removed. See Chapter 10, "Mailbox and Public Folder Store Administration," for more information.

- **Move Request**   Allows you to view and manage mailboxes being moved from one Exchange environment to another. See Chapter 6 for more details.

When you select the Recipient Configuration node in the Exchange Management Console, or any related subnodes, Exchange recipients for your logon domain are listed in the results pane, as shown in Figure 3-7. Recipients are scoped to the logon domain by default, rather than to all domains in the Active Directory forest, because an enterprise can have many thousands of recipients, and you typically will not want to work with all recipients in all domains simultaneously.

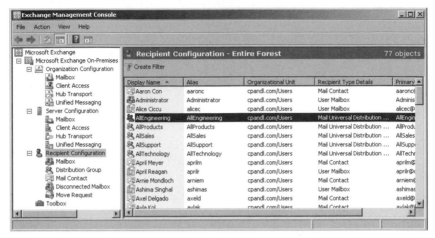

FIGURE 3-7 Recipient Configuration node settings apply to individual recipients according to their type.

You can, however, configure the recipient scope so that you can do the following:

- View all recipients in your Active Directory forest.
- View all recipients in a specific organizational unit (OU).

You can set the scope for recipient configuration by completing the following steps:

1. Open the Exchange Management Console.

2. Right-click the Recipient Configuration node, and then select Modify Recipient Scope. The Recipient Scope dialog box appears, shown in Figure 3-8.

3. If you want to view all recipients in your Active Directory forest, select View All Recipients In Forest. Information about recipients for the forest is retrieved from the global catalog. If you'd like to specify a Global Catalog server to use, select the Global Catalog check box, click Browse, and then use the Select Global Catalog dialog box to select the Global Catalog server to use according to its site membership in the forest.

4. If you want to view all recipients in a specific domain or organizational unit, select View All Recipients In Specified Organizational Unit. Information about recipients for the domain or organizational unit is retrieved from a domain controller in the domain or OU. If you'd like to specify a domain controller to use, select the Recipient Domain Controller check box, click Browse, and then

use the Select Domain Controller dialog box to select the domain controller to use according to its site membership in the related domain.

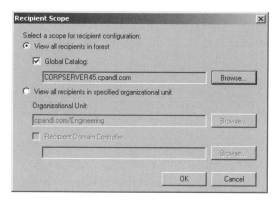

FIGURE 3-8 Specify the scope for recipient configuration.

5. When you click OK, the recipient information for the specified forest, domain, or OU is retrieved.

When you select the Recipient Configuration node in the Exchange Management Console, or any related subnodes, the maximum number of Exchange recipients you can view at any time is limited by default to 1,000. You can change the maximum number of recipients to display by completing the following steps:

1. Open the Exchange Management Console.

2. Right-click the Recipient Configuration node or the subnode you want to work with, and then click Modify The Maximum Number Of Recipients To Display. This displays the Maximum Number Of Recipients To Display dialog box, shown in Figure 3-9.

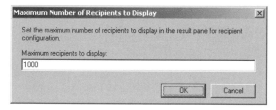

FIGURE 3-9 Specify the number of recipients to display.

3. In the text box provided, type the maximum number of recipients to display.

4. When you click OK, the recipient display is refreshed using the specified maximum number of recipients.

Understanding Data Storage in Exchange Server 2010

Depending on its role, Exchange Server stores information in several locations, including:

- Active Directory data store
- Exchange Server store
- Exchange Server queues

Working with the Active Directory Data Store

The Active Directory data store contains most directory information for Exchange Server 2010 configurations and Exchange Server 2010 recipients as well as other important directory resources. Domain controllers maintain the data store in a file called Ntds.dit. The location of this file is set when Active Directory is installed and should be on an NTFS file system drive formatted for use with Windows Server. Domain controllers save some directory data separately from the main data store.

Two key concepts to focus on when looking at Active Directory are multimaster replication and Global Catalog servers.

Using Multimaster Replication

Domain controllers replicate most changes to the data store by using multimaster replication, which allows any domain controller to process directory changes and replicate those changes to other domain controllers. Replication is handled automatically for key data types, including the following:

- **Domain data** Contains information about objects within a domain, such as users, groups, and contacts
- **Configuration data** Describes the topology of the directory, and includes a list of important domain information
- **Schema data** Describes all objects and data types that can be stored in the data store

Using Global Catalogs

Active Directory information is also made available through global catalogs. You use global catalogs for information searches and, in some cases, domain logon. A domain controller designated as a Global Catalog server stores a full replica of all objects in the data store (for its host domain).

By default, the first domain controller installed in a domain is designated as the Global Catalog server. Consequently, if there is only one domain controller in the domain, the domain controller and the global catalog are on the same server. Otherwise, the global catalog is on the domain controller configured as such.

Information searches are one of the key uses of the global catalog. Searches in the global catalog are efficient and can resolve most queries locally, thus reducing the network load and allowing for quicker responses. With Exchange, the global catalog can be used to execute Lightweight Directory Access Protocol (LDAP) queries for dynamic distribution groups. Here, the members of the distribution group are based on the results of the query sent to the Global Catalog server rather than being fixed.

Why use LDAP queries instead of a fixed member list? The idea is to reduce administrative overheard by being able to dynamically determine what the members of a distribution group should be. Query-based distribution is most efficient when the member list is relatively small (fewer than 25 members). If the member list has potentially hundreds or thousands of members, however, dynamic distribution can be inefficient and might require a great deal of processing to complete.

Here's how dynamic distribution works:

1. When e-mail is received that is addressed to the group, the Exchange Categorizer (a transport component) sends the predefined LDAP query to the Global Catalog server for the domain.

2. The Global Catalog server executes the query and returns the resulting address set.

3. The Exchange Categorizer then uses the address list to generate the recipient list and deliver the message. If the Categorizer is unable to generate the list for any reason—for instance, if the list is incomplete or an error was returned—the Categorizer might start the process over from the beginning.

NOTE To make the process more efficient, large organizations can use a dedicated expansion server. Here, LDAP queries are routed to the expansion server, which processes the query and returns the results.

Working with the Exchange Store

The Microsoft Exchange Information Store service (Store.exe) hosts the Exchange store. The Exchange store is the core storage repository for managing Exchange databases, which can include both mailbox databases and public folder databases. Mailbox databases contain the data, data definitions, indexes, flags, checksums, and other information that comprise mailboxes in your Exchange organization. Public folder databases contain the data, data definitions, indexes, flags, checksums, and other information that comprise any public folders in your Exchange organization.

Exchange Server uses transactions to control changes in databases. As with traditional databases, these transactions are recorded in a transaction log. Exchange Server then commits or rolls back changes based on the success of the transaction. The facility that manages transactions is the Microsoft Exchange Information Store service.

When working with databases, you should keep the following in mind:

- Each Mailbox server can have up to 100 databases (including both active databases and passive databases), with a maximum size per database of 64 terabytes (TB)—limited only by hardware.

- Each Mailbox server can be a member of only one database availability group and can host only one copy (either the active copy or a passive copy) of a database. Because each group can have up to 16 copies of a database, up to 16 different servers can be part of a database availability group.

To create a new mailbox or public folder database, you need about 50 megabytes (MBs) of free disk space. The files required by the database use a minimum of 23 MBs of disk space, and you'll need the extra space during creation and for read/write operations.

The Exchange store uses Extensible Storage Engine (ESE) databases for message storage. Key concepts to focus on when working with the Exchange store and databases are the following:

- Which Exchange server data files are used
- Which files are associated with databases
- How data is stored in Exchange database files

Which Exchange Server Data Files Are Used?

With Exchange Server 2010, Mailbox servers have a single database file for each mailbox or public folder database. Unlike Exchange Server 2003, Exchange Server 2010 does not use a streaming Internet content file with the .stm file extension. Although the .stm file was used to store MIME-formatted messages in Exchange Server 2003 and earlier versions, Exchange Server 2007 and 2010 store all messages and attachments in the primary data file. Exchange doesn't use an .stm file because content conversion is no longer performed on Mailbox servers but is instead performed on Client Access servers. Since Mailbox servers no longer convert the data, they no longer need to store it.

Because attachments are encapsulated and written in binary format, you don't need to convert them to Exchange format. Exchange Server uses a link table within the database to reference the storage location of attachments within it.

Two types of databases are available:

- **Mailbox databases** Contain mailboxes
- **Public Folder databases** Contain public folders

Which Files Are Associated with Databases?

As Figure 3-10 shows, each database has a primary data file and several other types of shared working files and transaction logs.

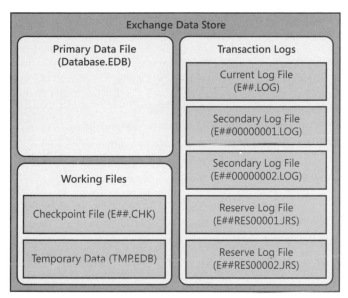

FIGURE 3-10 The Exchange data store has primary data files for each database as well as working files.

These files are used as follows:

- **Primary data file (Database.edb)**   A physical database file that holds the contents of the data store. By default, the name of the data file is the same as the name of the associated data store with the .edb file extension added. However, you can rename a database without renaming the database file.

- **Checkpoint file (E##.chk)**   A file that tracks the point up to which the transactions in the log file have been committed to databases in the storage group. Generally, the name of the checkpoint file is derived from the database prefix.

- **Temporary data (Tmp.edb)**   A temporary workspace for processing transactions.

- **Current log file (E##.log)**   A file that contains a record of all changes that have yet to be committed to the database. Generally, the name of the log file is derived from the database prefix.

- **Secondary log files (E##00000001.log, E##00000002.log, ...)**   Additional log files that are used as needed. Up to a billion unique log files can be created for each database.

- **Reserve log files (E##Res00001.jrs, E##Res00002.jrs, ...)**   Files that are used to reserve space for additional log files if the current log file becomes full.

By default, the primary data file, working files, and transaction logs are all stored in the same location. On a Mailbox server, you'll find these files in a per-database sub-folder of the %SystemRoot%\Program Files\Microsoft\Exchange Server\V14\Mailbox folder. Although these are the main files used for the data store, Exchange Server uses other files, depending on the roles for which you have configured the server.

How Is Data Stored in Exchange Database Files?

Exchange uses object-based storage. The primary data file contains several indexed tables, including a data table that contains a record for each object in the data store. Each referenced object can include object containers, such as mailboxes, and any other type of data that is stored in the data store.

Think of the data table as having rows and columns; the intersection of a row and a column is a field. The table's rows correspond to individual instances of an object. The table's columns correspond to folders. The table's fields are populated only if a folder includes stored data. The data stored in fields can be a fixed length or a variable length.

Records in the data table are stored in data pages that have a fixed size of 32 kilobytes (KBs, or 32,768 bytes). The 32-KB page file size represents a change from the 8-KB data pages used with Exchange Server 2007. This change was made to improve performance.

In an Exchange database, each data page has a page header, data rows, and free space that can contain row offsets. The page header uses the first 96 bytes of each page, leaving 32,672 bytes for data and row offsets. Row offsets indicate the logical order of rows on a page, which means that offset 0 refers to the first row in the index, offset 1 refers to the second row, and so on. If a row contains long, variable-length data, the data might not be stored with the rest of the data for that row. Instead, Exchange can store an 8-byte pointer to the actual data, which is stored in a collection of 32-KB pages that are written contiguously. In this way, an object and all its stored values can be much larger than 32 KB.

The current log file has a fixed size of 1 MB. The 1-MB log file size represents a change from the 5-MB log files used with Exchange Server 2003. This change was made so that Exchange Server 2007 could support continuous replication. When this log file fills up, Exchange closes and renames the log file (except when you are using circular logging). The secondary log files are also limited to a fixed size of 1 MB. Exchange uses the reserve log files to reserve disk space for log files that it might need to create. Because several reserve files are already created, this speeds up the transactional logging process when additional logs are needed.

Working with the Exchange Server Message Queues

Exchange Server message queues are temporary holding locations for messages that are waiting to be processed. Two general types of queues are used:

- **Persistent**   Persistent queues are always available even if no messages are waiting to be processed.

- **Nonpersistent** Nonpersistent queues are available only when messages are waiting to be processed.

With Exchange Server 2010, both Hub Transport and Edge Transport servers store messages waiting to be processed in persistent and nonpersistent queues. Table 3-1 provides an overview of the queues used. In Exchange Management Console, you can view top-level queues by selecting Toolbox in the left pane and then clicking Queue Viewer. You'll learn more about queues in Chapter 14, "Exchange Server 2010 Maintenance, Monitoring, and Queuing."

TABLE 3-1 Queues Used with Transport Servers

QUEUE NAME	SERVER ROLE	NUMBER OF QUEUES	QUEUE TYPE
Mailbox delivery	Hub Transport	One for each unique destination Mailbox server	Nonpersistent
Poison message	Hub Transport, Edge Transport	One	Persistent
Remote delivery	Hub Transport	One for each unique remote Active Directory site	Nonpersistent
Remote delivery	Edge Transport	One for each unique destination SMTP domain and smart host	Nonpersistent
Shadow redundancy	Hub Transport, Edge Transport	One for each hop to which the server delivered the primary message	Nonpersistent
Submission	Hub Transport, Edge Transport	One	Persistent
Transport dumpster	Hub Transport, Edge Transport	One for each Active Directory site	Nonpersistent
Unreachable	Hub Transport, Edge Transport	One	Persistent

The transport dumpster was introduced with Exchange Server 2007. The transport dumpster queues messages that are being delivered to recipients whose mailboxes are stored in replicated mailbox databases. When a message has been replicated to all mailbox database copies, the message is removed from the transport dumpster. This ensures that the transport dumpster stores only nonreplicated data.

In addition to the transport dumpster, Exchange Server 2010 implements shadow redundancy for queued messages. In the event of an outage or server failure, this feature works to prevent the loss of messages that are in transit by storing queued messages until the next transport server along the route reports a successful delivery of the message. If the next transport server doesn't report successful delivery, the message is resubmitted for delivery.

Shadow redundancy eliminates the reliance on the state of any specific hub or edge server and eliminates the need for storage hardware redundancy for transport servers. As long as redundant message paths exist in your routing topology, any transport server is replaceable. If a transport server fails, you can remove it and don't have to worry about emptying its queues or losing messages. If you want to upgrade or replace a hub or edge server, you can do so at any time without the risk of losing messages.

TIP Shadow redundancy uses less bandwidth than creating duplicate copies of messages on multiple servers. The only additional network traffic is the exchange of discard status between transport servers. Discard status indicates when a message is ready to be discarded from the transport database.

As Figure 3-11 shows, the various message queues are all stored in a single database. Like the Exchange store, the message queues database uses the ESE for message storage as well as for data pages.

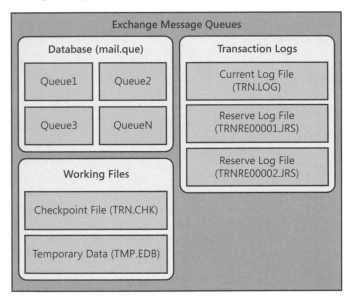

FIGURE 3-11 The Exchange message queues are all stored in a single database.

The database has a single data file associated with it and several other types of working files and transaction logs. These files are used as follows:

- **Primary data file (Mail.que)** A physical database file that holds the contents of all message queues.

- **Checkpoint file (Trn.chk)**   A file that tracks the point up to which the transactions in the log file have been committed to the database.
- **Temporary data (Tmp.edb)**   A temporary workspace for processing transactions.
- **Current log file (Trn.log)**   A log file that contains a record of all changes that have yet to be committed to the database.
- **Reserve log files (TRNRes00001.jrs, TRNRes00002.jrs, ...)**   Files that are used to reserve space for additional log files if the current log file becomes full.

The facility that manages queuing transactions is the Microsoft Exchange Transport service (MSExchangeTransport.exe). Because logs used with message queues are not continuously replicated, these log files have a fixed size of 5 MB. When the current log file for message queues fills up, Exchange closes the current log file, commits it, and continues using the same named log file. Exchange uses the reserve log files to reserve disk space for log files that might need to be created. Because several reserve files are already created, this speeds up the transactional logging process when additional logs are needed.

By default, the data file, working files, and transaction logs are all stored in the same location. On a Hub Transport or Edge Transport server, you'll find these files in the %SystemRoot%\Program Files\Microsoft\Exchange Server\V14\TransportRoles\data\Queue folder.

Using and Managing Exchange Server Services

Each Exchange server in the organization relies on a set of services for routing messages, processing transactions, replicating data, and much more. Table 1-1 in Chapter 1 lists these services.

> **TIP**   Of all the Exchange services, the one service that relies on having a network connection at startup is the Microsoft Exchange Information Store service. If you start an Exchange server and the server doesn't have a network connection, the Microsoft Exchange Information Store service might fail to start. As a result, you might have to manually start the service. Sometimes, you'll find the service has a Stopping state. In this case, you have to wait until the server completely stops the service before you restart it.

Working with Exchange Services

To manage Exchange services, you use the Services node in the Computer Management console, which you start by completing the following steps:

1. Choose Start, point to All Programs, point to Administrative Tools, and then select Computer Management. Or, in the Administrative Tools folder, select Computer Management.

2. To connect to a remote Exchange server, right-click the Computer Management entry in the console tree, and then select Connect To Another Computer from the shortcut menu. You can now choose the Exchange server for which you want to manage services.

3. Expand the Services And Applications node, and then select Services.

Figure 3-12 shows the Services view in the Computer Management console. The key fields of this window are used as follows:

- **Name** The name of the service.
- **Description** A short description of the service and its purpose.
- **Status** The status of the service as started, paused, or stopped. (Stopped is indicated by a blank entry.)
- **Startup Type** The startup setting for the service.

  NOTE Automatic services are started when the computer is started. Manual services are started by users or other services. Disabled services are turned off and can't be started. To start a disabled service, you must first enable it and then start it.

- **Log On As** The account the service logs on as. The default, in most cases, is the local system account.

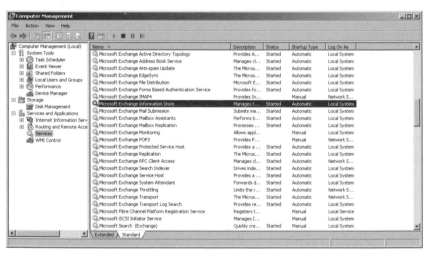

FIGURE 3-12 Use the Services node of the Computer Management console to manage Exchange Server services.

NOTE On a new Exchange Server 2010 installation, some services are configured for a manual start for security reasons. Specifically, you'll find that the Microsoft Exchange Post Office Protocol version 3 (POP3), Microsoft Exchange Internet Messaging Access Protocol 4 (IMAP4), and Microsoft Search (Exchange) services are configured to start manually. If you use these services with Exchange, you need to configure them for automatic startup and then start them using the techniques discussed in this section.

Checking Required Services

You can use Test-ServiceHealth to determine whether all Windows services that Exchange requires are running. As shown in the follow example and sample output, the command output lists required services that are running as well as required services that aren't running for each configured Exchange role:

```
test-servicehealth

Role: Mailbox Server Role
RequiredServicesRunning : True
ServicesRunning : IISAdmin, MSExchangeADTopology, MSExchangeIS,
MSExchangeMailboxAssistants, MSExchangeMailSubmission, MSExchangeRepl,
MSExchangeRPC, MSExchangeSA, MSExchangeSearch, MSExchangeServiceHost,
MSExchangeThrottling, MSExchangeTransportLogSearch, W3Svc, WinRM}
ServicesNotRunning: {}
Role : Client Access Server Role
RequiredServicesRunning : True
ServicesRunning : {IISAdmin, MSExchangeAB, MSExchangeADTopology,
MSExchangeFBA, MSExchangeFDS, MSExchangeMailboxReplication,
MSExchangeProtectedServiceHost, MSExchangeRPC, MSExchangeServiceHost,
W3Svc, WinRM}
ServicesNotRunning : {}
Role : Hub Transport Server Role
RequiredServicesRunning : True
ServicesRunning        : {IISAdmin, MSExchangeADTopology,
MSExchangeEdgeSync, MSExchangeServiceHost, MSExchangeTransport,
MSExchangeTransportLogSearch, W3Svc, WinRM}
ServicesNotRunning : {}
```

Starting, Stopping, and Pausing Exchange Server Services

As an administrator, you'll often have to start, stop, or pause Exchange services. You manage Exchange services through the Computer Management console or through the Services console.

To start, stop, or pause services in the Computer Management console, follow these steps:

1. If necessary, connect to the remote Exchange server for which you want to manage services, as discussed earlier in this section.

2. Expand the Services And Applications node, and then select Services.

3. Right-click the service you want to manipulate, and then select Start, Stop, or Pause, as appropriate. You can also choose Restart to have Windows stop and then start the service after a brief pause. Also, if you pause a service, you can use the Resume option to resume normal operation.

TIP When services that are set to start automatically fail, the status is listed as blank, and you usually receive notification in a pop-up window. Service failures can also be logged to the system's event logs. You can configure recovery actions to handle service failure automatically. For example, you can have Windows attempt to restart the service for you. See the section of this chapter titled "Configuring Service Recovery" for details.

Configuring Service Startup

Essential Exchange services are configured to start automatically and normally shouldn't be configured with another startup option. That said, if you're trouble-shooting a problem, you might want a service to start manually or you might want to temporarily disable a service.

You configure service startup by completing the following steps:

1. In the Computer Management console, connect to the Exchange server for which you want to manage services.

2. Expand the Services And Applications node, and then select Services.

3. Right-click the service you want to configure, and then select Properties.

4. On the General tab, use the Startup Type drop-down list to choose a startup option, as shown in Figure 3-13. Select Automatic to start a service when the computer starts. Select Manual to allow services to be started manually. Select Disabled to disable the service. Click OK.

NOTE The Disabled option doesn't stop the service if it's currently running. It just prevents the service from starting the next time you start the server. To stop the service, you must click Stop.

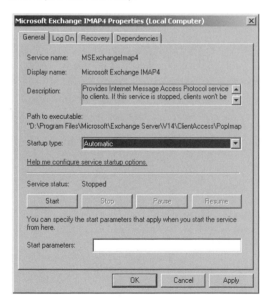

FIGURE 3-13 For troubleshooting, you might want to change the service startup option in the Properties dialog box.

Configuring Service Recovery

You can configure Windows services to take specific actions when a service fails. For example, you can attempt to restart the service or reboot the server. To configure recovery options for a service, follow these steps:

1. In the Computer Management console, connect to the computer for which you want to manage services.

2. Expand the Services And Applications node, and then select Services.

3. Right-click the service you want to configure, and then select Properties.

4. On the Recovery tab, shown in Figure 3-14, you can configure recovery options for the first, second, and subsequent recovery attempts. The available options are as follows:

   - Take No Action
   - Restart The Service
   - Run A Program
   - Restart The Computer

5. Configure other options based on your previously selected recovery options. If you elected to restart the service, you need to specify the restart delay. After stopping the service, Windows Server waits for the specified delay period before trying to start the service. In most cases, a delay of one to two minutes should be sufficient. Click OK.

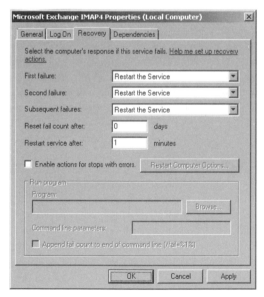

FIGURE 3-14 By using the Recovery tab in the Properties dialog box, you can configure services to automatically recover in case of failure.

When you configure recovery options for critical services, you might want to try to restart the service on the first and second attempts and then reboot the server on the third attempt. If you notice that a service keeps failing, you need to do some troubleshooting to diagnose and resolve the underlying issue causing the failure.

Customizing Remote Management Services

The Exchange management tools use the Microsoft .NET Framework version 3.5.1, Windows Remote Management (WinRM) 2.0, and Windows PowerShell version 2 for remote management. WinRM is implemented in the Windows Remote Management service, which is also referred to as the WS-Management Service or simply the Management Service. To remotely manage Exchange, your management computer must run this service and be configured to use the transports, ports, and authentication methods that your Exchange servers use. The Exchange server you want to connect to must also run this service. If this service isn't running on your management computer and on the server, remote connections will fail. For remote management, you normally connect to the PowerShell virtual directory configured in IIS on a Client Access server.

By default, the Management Service connects to and listens on TCP port 80 for HTTP connections and on TCP port 443 for Secure HTTP connections. Because firewalls and proxy servers might affect your ability to connect to remote locations over these ports, talk with your company's network or security administrator to determine what steps need to be taken to allow administration over these ports. Typically, the network/security administrator will have to open these TCP ports to allow remote communication between your computer or network and the remote server or network.

The Management Service is preconfigured to share ports with IIS when it runs on the same computer, but it does not depend on IIS. To support remote management, you need to install basic authentication and Windows authentication for IIS on your Exchange servers. These authentication techniques are used when you work remotely.

When you are working with an elevated, administrator command prompt, you can use the WinRM command-line utility to view and manage the remote management configuration. Type **winrm get winrm/config** to display detailed information about the remote management configuration. As Listing 3-1 shows, this lists the configuration details for every aspect of WinRM.

LISTING 3-1 Sample Configuration for WinRM

```
Config
    MaxEnvelopeSizekb = 150
    MaxTimeoutms = 60000
    MaxBatchItems = 32000
    MaxProviderRequests = 4294967295
    Client
        NetworkDelayms = 5000
        URLPrefix = wsman
```

```
            AllowUnencrypted = false
            Auth
                Basic = true
                Digest = true
                Kerberos = true
                Negotiate = true
                Certificate = true
                CredSSP = false
            DefaultPorts
                HTTP = 80
                HTTPS = 443
            TrustedHosts = CorpServer65
    Service
            RootSDDL = O:NSG:BAD:P(A;;GA;;;BA)S:P(AU;FA;GA;;;WD)(AU;SA;GWGX)
            MaxConcurrentOperations = 4294967295
            EnumerationTimeoutms = 60000
            MaxConnections = 25
            MaxPacketRetrievalTimeSeconds = 120
            AllowUnencrypted = false
            Auth
                Basic = false
                Kerberos = true
                Negotiate = true
                Certificate = false
                CredSSP = false
                CbtHardeningLevel = Relaxed
            DefaultPorts
                HTTP = 80
                HTTPS = 443
            IPv4Filter = *
            IPv6Filter = *
            CertificateThumbprint
    Winrs
            AllowRemoteShellAccess = true
            IdleTimeout = 180000
            MaxConcurrentUsers = 5
            MaxShellRunTime = 2147483647
            MaxProcessesPerShell = 15
            MaxMemoryPerShellMB = 150
            MaxShellsPerUser = 5
```

If you examine the listing, you'll notice there is a hierarchy of information. The base of this hierarchy, the Config level, is referenced with the path winrm/config. Then there are sublevels for client, service, and WinRS, referenced as winrm/config/client, winrm/config/service, and winrm/config/winrs, respectively. You can change the value of most configuration parameters by using the following command:

```
winrm set ConfigPath @{ParameterName="Value"}
```

where *ConfigPath* is the configuration path, *ParameterName* is the name of the parameter you want to work with, and *Value* sets the value for the parameter, such as

```
winrm set winrm/config/winrs @{MaxShellsPerUser="4"}
```

Here, you set the MaxShellsPerUser parameter under WinRM/Config/WinRS. Keep in mind that some parameters are read-only and cannot be set in this way.

WinRM requires at least one listener to indicate the transports and IP addresses on which management requests can be accepted. The transport must be HTTP, HTTPS, or both. With HTTP, messages can be encrypted only using NTLM or Kerberos encryption. With HTTPS, Secure Sockets Layer (SSL) is used for encryption. You can examine the configured listeners by typing **winrm enumerate winrm/config/ listener**. As Listing 3-2 shows, this lists the configuration details for configured listeners.

LISTING 3-2 Sample Configuration for Listeners

```
Listener
    Address = *
    Transport = HTTP
    Port = 80
    Hostname
    Enabled = true
    URLPrefix = wsman
    CertificateThumbprint
    ListeningOn = 127.0.0.1, 192.168.1.225
```

By default, your computer is likely to be configured to listen on any IP address. If so, you won't see any output. To limit WinRM to specific IP addresses, the computer's local loopback address (127.0.01) and assigned IPv4 and IPv6 addresses can be explicitly configured for listening. You can configure a computer to listen for requests on HTTP on all configured IP addresses by typing

```
winrm create winrm/config/listener?Address=*+Transport=HTTP
```

You can listen for requests on HTTPS on all IP addresses configured on the computer by typing

```
winrm create winrm/config/listener?Address=*+Transport=HTTPS
```

Here, the * indicates all configured IP addresses. Note that the Certificate-Thumbprint property must be empty for the SSL configuration to be shared with another service.

You can enable or disable a listener for a specific IP address by typing

```
winrm set winrm/config/listener?Address=IP:192.168.1.225+Transport=HTTP @
{Enabled="true"}
```

or

```
winrm set winrm/config/listener?Address=IP:192.168.1.225+Transport=HTTP @
{Enabled="false"}
```

You can enable or disable basic authentication on the client by typing

```
winrm set winrm/config/client/auth @{Basic="true"}
```

or

```
winrm set winrm/config/client/auth @{Basic="false"}
```

You can enable or disable Windows authentication using either NTLM or Kerberos (as appropriate) by typing

```
winrm set winrm/config/client @{TrustedHosts="<local>"}
```

or

```
winrm set winrm/config/client @{TrustedHosts=""}
```

In addition to managing WinRM at the command line, you can manage the service by using Group Policy. Keep in mind that Group Policy settings might override any settings you enter.

CHAPTER 4

Using the Exchange Management Shell

M icrosoft Exchange Server 2010 includes the Exchange Management Shell to complement the expanding role of Exchange Server administrators and developers. The Exchange Management Shell is an extensible command-line environment for Exchange Server that builds on the existing framework provided by Windows PowerShell. When you install Exchange Server 2010 on a server, or when you install the Exchange Server management tools on a workstation, you install Windows PowerShell and the Exchange Management Shell as part of the process. This chapter introduces Windows PowerShell and its features and then details the available commands and options of the Exchange Management Shell.

Using Windows PowerShell

Anyone with a UNIX background is probably familiar with the concept of a command shell. Most UNIX-based operating systems have several full-featured command shells available, including Korn Shell (KSH), C Shell (CSH), and Bourne Shell (SH). Although Microsoft Windows operating systems have always had a command-line environment, they've lacked a full-featured command shell, and this is where Windows PowerShell comes into the picture.

Introducing Windows PowerShell

Not unlike the less sophisticated Windows command prompt, the UNIX command shells operate by executing built-in commands, external commands, and command-line utilities and then returning the results in an output stream as text. The output stream can be manipulated in various ways, including redirecting the output stream so that it can be used as input for another command. This process of redirecting one command's output to another command's input is called *piping*, and it is a widely used shell-scripting technique.

C Shell is one of the more sophisticated UNIX shells. In many respects, C Shell is a marriage of some of the best features of the C programming language and a full-featured UNIX shell environment. The Windows PowerShell takes the idea of a full-featured command shell built on a programming language a step further. It does this by implementing a scripting language based on C# and an object model based on the Microsoft .NET Framework.

Basing the scripting language for Windows PowerShell on C# ensures that the scripting language can be easily understood by current C# developers and also allows new developers who work with PowerShell to advance to C#. Using an object model based on the .NET Framework allows the Windows PowerShell to pass complete objects and all their properties as output from one command to another. The ability to redirect objects is extremely powerful and allows for a much more dynamic manipulation of a result set. For example, not only can you get the name of a particular user, but you can also get the entire related user object. You can then manipulate the properties of this user object as necessary by referring to the properties you want to work with by name.

Running and Using Windows PowerShell

Windows PowerShell Version 2.0 (PowerShell V2) is built into Windows 7, Windows Server 2008 Release 2, and later releases of the Windows operating system. Windows PowerShell V2 has both a command-line environment and a graphical environment for running commands and scripts. The PowerShell console (powershell.exe) is a 32-bit or 64-bit environment for working with PowerShell at the command line. On 32-bit versions of Windows, you'll find the 32-bit executable in the %SystemRoot%\System32\WindowsPowerShell\v1.0 directory. On 64-bit versions of Windows, you'll find the 32-bit executable in the %SystemRoot%\SysWow64\WindowsPowerShell\v1.0 directory and the 64-bit executable in the %SystemRoot%\System32\WindowsPowerShell\v1.0 directory.

You can start the PowerShell console by using the Search box on the Start menu. Click Start, type **powershell** in the Search box, and then press Enter. Or you can click Start; point to All Programs; point to Accessories, Windows PowerShell; and then choose Windows PowerShell V2. On 64-bit systems, the 64-bit version of PowerShell is started by default. If you want to use the 32-bit PowerShell console on a 64-bit system, you must select the Windows PowerShell V2 (x86) option.

You can start Windows PowerShell from a Windows command shell (cmd.exe) by typing **powershell**. To exit Windows PowerShell and return to the command prompt, type **exit**.

Usually, when the shell starts, you will see a message similar to the following:

```
Windows PowerShell
Copyright (C) 2009 Microsoft Corporation. All rights reserved.
```

You can disable this message by starting the shell with the –Nologo parameter, such as:

```
powershell -nologo
```

Figure 4-1 shows a PowerShell window. Typically, the window is 120 characters wide and displays 50 lines of text by default. When additional text is to be displayed in the window or you enter commands and the PowerShell console's window is full, the current text is displayed in the window and prior text is scrolled up. If you want to pause the display temporarily when a command is writing output, press Ctrl+S. Afterward, press Ctrl+S to resume or Ctrl+C to terminate execution.

FIGURE 4-1 Working with Windows PowerShell.

When you start Windows PowerShell, the working environment is loaded automatically. Many features of the working environment come from profiles, which are a type of script that run when you start PowerShell. However, the working environment is also determined by imported modules, snap-ins, providers, command paths, file extensions, and file associations.

You can start Windows PowerShell without loading profiles using the –Noprofile parameter, such as:

```
powershell -noprofile
```

Whenever you work with scripts, you need to keep in mind the current execution policy and whether signed scripts are required. Execution policy controls whether and how you can run configuration files and scripts. Execution policy is a built-in security feature of Windows PowerShell that is set on a per-user basis in the Windows registry. Although the default configuration depends on which operating system and edition are installed, you can quickly determine the execution policy by typing **get-executionpolicy** at the PowerShell prompt.

The available execution policies, from least secure to most secure, are:

- **Bypass**   This policy bypasses warnings and prompts when scripts run. It is intended for use with programs that have their own security model or when a PowerShell script is built into a larger application.

- **Unrestricted**   This policy allows all configuration files and scripts to run whether they are from local or remote sources and regardless of whether they are signed or unsigned. However, if you run a configuration file or script from a remote resource, you are prompted with a warning that the file comes from a remote resource before the configuration file is loaded or the script runs.

- **RemoteSigned**   This policy requires all configuration files and scripts from remote sources to be signed by a trusted publisher. Configuration files and scripts on the local computer do not need to be signed. PowerShell does not prompt you with a warning before running scripts from trusted publishers.

- **AllSigned**   This policy requires all configuration files and scripts from all sources—whether local or remote—to be signed by a trusted publisher. Because of this requirement, configuration files and scripts on the local computer must be signed as configuration files, and scripts from remote computers must be signed. PowerShell prompts you with a warning before running scripts from trusted publishers.

- **Restricted**   This policy prevents PowerShell from loading configuration files and scripts. This means all configuration files and scripts, regardless of whether they are signed or unsigned. Because a profile is a type of script, profiles are not loaded either.

- **Undefined**   This policy removes the execution policy that is set for the current user scope. As a result, the execution policy set in Group Policy or for the LocalMachine scope is effective. If execution policy in all scopes is set to Undefined, the default execution policy, Restricted, is the effective policy.

You can use the Set-ExecutionPolicy cmdlet to change the preference for the execution policy. Changes to the policy are written to the registry. However, if the Turn On Script Execution setting in Group Policy is enabled for the computer or user, the user preference is written to the registry, but it is not effective, and Windows PowerShell displays a message explaining the conflict. You cannot use Set-ExecutionPolicy to override a group policy, even if the user preference is more restrictive than the policy setting.

To set the execution policy to require that all scripts have a trusted signature to execute, type the following command:

```
set-executionpolicy allsigned
```

To set the execution policy so that scripts downloaded from the Web execute only if they are signed by a trusted source, type:

```
set-executionpolicy remotesigned
```

To set the execution policy to run scripts regardless of whether they have a digital signature and work in an unrestricted environment, you can type the following command:

```
set-executionpolicy unrestricted
```

The change occurs immediately and is applied to the local console or application session. Because the change is written to the registry, the new execution policy will be used whenever you work with PowerShell.

Running and Using Cmdlets

Windows PowerShell introduces the concept of a cmdlet (pronounced *commandlet*). A cmdlet is the smallest unit of functionality in Windows PowerShell. You can think of a cmdlet as a built-in command. Rather than being highly complex, most cmdlets are quite simple and have a small set of associated properties.

You use cmdlets the same way you use any other commands and utilities. Cmdlet names are not case sensitive. This means you can use a combination of both uppercase and lowercase characters. After starting Windows PowerShell, you can type the name of the cmdlet at the prompt and it will run in much the same way as a command-line command.

For ease of reference, cmdlets are named using verb-noun pairs. As Table 4-1 shows, the verb tells you what the cmdlet does in general. The noun tells you what specifically the cmdlet works with. For example, the Get-Variable cmdlet gets a named Windows PowerShell environment variable and returns its value. If you don't specify which variable to get as a parameter, Get-Variable returns a list of all Windows PowerShell environment variables and their values.

TABLE 4-1 Common Verbs Associated with Cmdlets and Their Meanings

CMDLET VERB	USAGE
Add	Adds an instance of an item, such as a history entry or snap-in
Clear	Removes the contents of an item, such as an event log or variable value
New	Creates a new instance of an item, such as a new mailbox
Remove	Removes an instance of an item, such as a mailbox
Enable	Enables a setting or mail-enables a recipient
Disable	Disables an enabled setting or mail-disables a recipient
Set	Modifies specific settings of an object
Get	Queries a specific object or a subset of a type of object, such as a specified mailbox or all mailbox users

You can work with cmdlets in several ways:

- Executing commands directly at the shell prompt
- Running commands from scripts
- Calling them from C# or other .NET Framework languages

You can enter any command or cmdlet you can run at the Windows PowerShell command prompt into a script by copying the related command text to a file and saving the file with the .ps1 extension. You can then run the script in the same way you would any other command or cmdlet.

NOTE Windows PowerShell also includes a rich scripting language and allows the use of standard language constructs for looping, conditional execution, flow control, and variable assignment. Discussion of these features is beyond the scope of this book. A good resource is *Windows PowerShell 2.0 Administrator's Pocket Consultant* (Microsoft Press, 2009).

From the Windows command-line environment or a batch script, you can execute Windows PowerShell cmdlets with the –Command parameter. Typically, when you do this, you also want to suppress the Windows PowerShell logo and stop execution of profiles. After doing this, you can type the following command at a command prompt or insert it into a .BAT script:

```
powershell –nologo –noprofile –command get-service
```

Finally, when you are working with Windows PowerShell, the current directory is not part of the environment path in most instances. Because of this, you typically need to use "./" when you run a script in the current directory, such as:

```
./runtasks
```

Running and Using Other Commands and Utilities

Because Windows PowerShell runs within the context of the Windows command prompt, you can run all Windows command-line commands, utilities, and graphical applications from within Windows PowerShell. However, remember that the Windows PowerShell interpreter parses all commands before passing off the command to the command prompt environment. If Windows PowerShell has a like-named command or a like-named alias for a command, this command, and not the expected Windows command, is executed. (See the "Using Cmdlet Aliases" section later in this chapter for more information on aliases.)

Non–Windows PowerShell commands and programs must reside in a directory that is part of the PATH environment variable. If the item is found in the path, it is run. The PATH variable also controls where the Windows PowerShell looks for applications, utilities, and scripts. In Windows PowerShell, you can work with Windows environment variables using $env. If you want to view the current settings for the PATH environment variable, you type **$env:path**. If you want to add a directory to this variable, you can use the following syntax:

```
$env:path += ";DirectoryPathToAdd"
```

where *DirectoryPathToAdd* is the directory path you want to add to the path, such as

```
$env:path += ";C:\Scripts"
```

To have this directory added to the path every time you start Windows Power-Shell, you can add the command line as an entry in your profile. Keep in mind that cmdlets are like built-in commands rather than standalone executables. Because of this, they are not affected by the PATH environment variable.

Working with Cmdlets

Cmdlets provide the basic foundation for working with a computer from within the Windows PowerShell. Although there are many different cmdlets with many different available uses, cmdlets all have common features, which I'll examine in this section.

Using Windows PowerShell Cmdlets

At the Windows PowerShell prompt, you can get a complete list of cmdlets available by typing **get-command**. However, the output lists both cmdlets and functions by name and definition. With cmdlets, the definition provided is the syntax, but the full syntax rarely fits on the line. A better way to get information about cmdlets is to use Get-Help. If you type **get-help *-***, you get a list of all cmdlets, which includes a synopsis that summarizes the purpose of the cmdlet—which is much more useful than a list of commands. To get help documentation on a specific cmdlet, type **get-help** followed by the cmdlet name, such as:

```
get-help get-variable
```

Table 4-2 provides a list of cmdlets you'll commonly use for administration. Although many other cmdlets are available, these are the ones you're likely to use the most.

TABLE 4-2 Cmdlets Commonly Used for Administration

CMDLET NAME	DESCRIPTION
Add-Computer, Remove-Computer	Adds or removes a computer's membership in a domain or workgroup
Checkpoint-Computer, Restore-Computer	Creates a system restore checkpoint for a computer, or restores a computer from a checkpoint

TABLE 4-2 Cmdlets Commonly Used for Administration

CMDLET NAME	DESCRIPTION
Compare-Object, Group-Object, Sort-Object, Select-Object, New-Object	Cmdlets for comparing, grouping, sorting, selecting, and creating objects
ConvertFrom-SecureString, ConvertTo-SecureString	Cmdlets for creating or exporting secure strings
Get-Alias, New-Alias, Set-Alias, Export-Alias, Import-Alias	Cmdlets for getting, creating, setting, exporting, and importing aliases
Get-AuthenticodeSignature, Set-AuthenticodeSignature	Cmdlets for getting or setting the signature object associated with a file
Get-Command, Invoke-Command, Measure-Command, Trace-Command	Cmdlets for getting information about cmdlets, invoking commands, measuring the run time of commands, and tracing commands
Get-Counter	Gets performance counter data
Get-Credential	Gets a credential object based on a password
Get-Date, Set-Date	Gets or sets the current date and time
Get-EventLog, Write-EventLog, Clear-EventLog	Gets events, writes events, or clears events in an event log
Get-ExecutionPolicy, Set-ExecutionPolicy	Gets or sets the effective execution policy for the current shell
Get-Host	Gets information about the PowerShell host application
Get-HotFix	Gets the Quick Fix Engineering (QFE) updates that have been applied to a computer
Get-Location, Set-Location	Displays or sets the current working location
Get-Process, Start-Process, Stop-Process	Gets, starts, or stops processes on a computer
Get-PSDrive, New-PSDrive, Remove-PSDrive	Gets, creates, or removes a specified PowerShell drive
Get-Service, New-Service, Set-Service	Gets, creates, or sets system services

TABLE 4-2 Cmdlets Commonly Used for Administration

CMDLET NAME	DESCRIPTION
Get-Variable, New-Variable, Set-Variable, Remove-Variable, Clear-Variable	Cmdlets for getting, creating, setting, and removing variables as well as for clearing variable values
Import-Counter, Export-Counter	Imports or exports performance counter log files
Limit-EventLog	Sets the size and age limits for an event log
New-EventLog, Remove-EventLog	Creates or removes a custom event log and event source
Read-Host, Write-Host, Clear-Host	Reads input from, writes output to or clears the host window
Add-Computer, Remove-Computer, Stop-Computer, Restart-Computer	Adds or removes domain membership or stops or restarts a computer
Reset-ComputerMachinePassword	Changes and resets the machine account password that the computer uses to authenticate in a domain
Show-EventLog	Displays a computer's event logs in Event Viewer
Show-Service	Displays a computer's services in the Services utility
Start-Sleep	Suspends shell or script activity for the specified period
Stop-Service, Start-Service, Suspend-Service, Resume-Service, Restart-Service	Cmdlets for stopping, starting, suspending, resuming, and restarting system services
Wait-Process	Waits for a process to be stopped before accepting input
Write-Output	Writes an object to the pipeline
Write-Warning	Displays a warning message

Using Cmdlet Parameters

All cmdlet parameters are designated with an initial dash (–). To reduce the amount of typing required, some parameters are position-sensitive, so you can sometimes pass parameters in a specific order without having to specify the parameter name. For example, with Get-Service, you don't have to specify the –Name parameter, you can simply type:

```
get-service ServiceName
```

where *ServiceName* is the name of the service you want to examine, such as

```
get-service MSExchangeIS
```

This command line returns the status of the Microsoft Exchange Information Store service. Because you can use wildcards, such as *, with name values, you can also type **get-service mse*** to return the status of all Microsoft Exchange–related services. Type **get-service fs*** to return the status of all Forefront Security–related services.

All cmdlets support the common set of parameters listed in Table 4-3. However, to use these parameters, you must run the cmdlet in such a way that these parameters are returned as part of the result set.

TABLE 4-3 Common Cmdlet Parameters

PARAMETER NAME	DESCRIPTION
Confirm	Pauses processes, and requires the user to acknowledge the action before continuing. Cmdlets beginning with *Remove* and *Disable* have this parameter.
Debug	Provides programming-level debugging information about the operation.
ErrorAction	Controls the command behavior when an error occurs.
ErrorVariable	Sets the name of the variable (in addition to the standard error) in which to place objects for which an error has occurred.
OutBuffer	Sets the output buffer for the cmdlet.
OutVariable	Sets the name of the variable in which to place output objects.
Verbose	Provides detailed information about the operation.

TABLE 4-3 Common Cmdlet Parameters

PARAMETER NAME	DESCRIPTION
WarningAction	Determines how a cmdlet responds to a warning message. Valid values are SilentlyContinue (suppress the warning and continue), Continue (display the warning and continue), Inquire (display the warning and prompt to confirm before continuing), and Stop (display the warning and halt execution). The default value is Continue.
WarningVariable	Sets the name of the variable (in addition to the standard error) in which to store warnings that have occurred.
WhatIf	Allows the user to view what would happen if a cmdlet were run with a specific set of parameters. Cmdlets beginning with Remove and Disable have this parameter.

Understanding Cmdlet Errors

When you work with cmdlets, you'll encounter two standard types of errors:

- **Terminating errors**   Errors that halt execution
- **Nonterminating errors**   Errors that cause error output to be returned but do not halt execution

With both types of errors, you'll typically see error text that can help you resolve the problem that caused it. For example, an expected file might be missing or you might not have sufficient permissions to perform a specified task.

Using Cmdlet Aliases

For ease of use, Windows PowerShell lets you create aliases for cmdlets. An alias is an abbreviation for a cmdlet that acts as a shortcut for executing the cmdlet. For example, you can use the alias *gsv* instead of the cmdlet name Get-Service.

Table 4-4 provides a list of commonly used default aliases. Although there are many other aliases, these are the ones you'll use most frequently.

TABLE 4-4 Commonly Used Cmdlet Aliases

ALIAS	CMDLET
clear, cls	Clear-Host
Diff	Compare-Object
cp, copy	Copy-Item

TABLE 4-4 Commonly Used Cmdlet Aliases

ALIAS	CMDLET
Epal	Export-Alias
Epcsv	Export-Csv
Foreach	ForEach-Object
Fl	Format-List
Ft	Format-Table
Fw	Format-Wide
Gal	Get-Alias
ls, dir	Get-ChildItem
Gcm	Get-Command
cat, type	Get-Content
h, history	Get-History
gl, pwd	Get-Location
gps, ps	Get-Process
Gsv	Get-Service
Gv	Get-Variable
Group	Group-Object
Ipal	Import-Alias
Ipcsv	Import-Csv
R	Invoke-History
Ni	New-Item
Mount	New-PSDrive
Nv	New-Variable
rd, rm, rmdir, del, erase	Remove-Item
Rv	Remove-Variable
Sal	Set-Alias
sl, cd, chdir	Set-Location
sv, set	Set-Variable
Sort	Sort-Object

TABLE 4-4 Commonly Used Cmdlet Aliases

ALIAS	CMDLET
Sasv	Start-Service
Sleep	Start-Sleep
spps, kill	Stop-Process
Spsv	Stop-Service
write, echo	Write-Output

You can define additional aliases using the Set-Alias cmdlet. The syntax is

```
set-alias aliasName cmdletName
```

where *aliasName* is the alias you want to use and *cmdletName* is the cmdlet for which you are creating an alias. The following example creates a "go" alias for the Get-Process cmdlet:

```
set-alias go get-process
```

To use your custom aliases whenever you work with Windows PowerShell, enter the related command line in your profile.

Using the Exchange Management Shell

The Exchange Management Shell is a command-line management interface built on Windows PowerShell. You use the Exchange Management Shell to manage any aspect of an Exchange Server 2010 configuration that you can manage in the Exchange Management Console. This means that you can typically use either tool to configure Exchange Server 2010. However, only the Exchange Management Shell has the full complement of available commands, and this means that some tasks can be performed only at the shell prompt.

Logging Exchange Management Console Commands

When you are working with the Exchange Management Console, every action you perform is handled by the Exchange Management Shell. To view the actual commands being processed, you can turn on command logging. To do this, open the Exchange Management Console, click View, and then select View Exchange Management Shell Command Log. In the Log window, click Action, and then click Start Command Logging.

By default, the command log tracks up to 2,048 commands and then begins to overwrite itself. You can configure the maximum number of commands that are logged. In the Log window, click Action, and then click the Modify option. In the dialog box provided, enter the maximum number of commands to log, and then click OK. The valid range is 1 to 32,767.

When you are working with the Log window, you can copy selected commands by right-clicking and then selecting Copy Command(s).

Running and Using the Exchange Management Shell

After you've installed the Exchange management tools on a computer, you can start to use the Exchange Management Shell by clicking Start, pointing to All Programs, clicking Microsoft Exchange Server 2010, and then clicking Exchange Management Shell.

> **TIP** Selecting the shell in this way starts the Exchange Management Shell using your user credentials. This enables you to perform any administrative tasks allowed for your user account. As a result, you don't need to run the Exchange Management Shell in elevated, administrator mode, but you can. To do so, right-click Exchange Management Shell, and then click Run As Administrator.

This starts PowerShell and loads the Exshell.psc1 console file and the Remote-Exchange.ps1 profile file. These files are used to initialize the working environment for Exchange Server. The console file loads the Microsoft.Exchange.Management. PowerShell.E2010 snap-in. The profile file sets aliases, initializes Exchange global variables, and loads .NET assemblies for Exchange. It also modifies the standard PowerShell prompt so that it is scoped to the entire Active Directory forest and defines the following Exchange-specific functions:

- **Functions**   Allows you to list all available functions by typing **functions**.
- **Get-Exbanner**   Displays the Exchange Management Shell startup banner whenever you type **get-exbanner**.
- **Get-Exblog**   Opens Internet Explorer and accesses the Exchange blog at Microsoft whenever you type **get-exblog**.
- **Get-Excommand**   Allows you to list available Exchange commands by typing **get-excommand**.
- **Get-Pscommand**   Allows you to list available PowerShell commands by typing **get-pscommand**.
- **Get-Tip**   Displays the tip of the day whenever you type **get-tip**.
- **Quickref**   Opens Internet Explorer and allows you to download the Exchange Management Shell quick start guide whenever you type **quickref**.

The RemoteExchange.ps1 profile loads the ConnectFunctions.ps1 script, which defines a number of functions that enable AutoDiscover and Connect features. The functions include the following:

- Connect-ExchangeServer
- Discover-ExchangeServer
- _AutoDiscoverAndConnect

- _CheckServicesStarted
- _ConnectToAnyServer
- _GetCASServers
- _GetExchangeServerInSite
- _GetHostFqdn
- _GetHubMailboxUMServers
- _GetMetabases
- _GetServerFqdnFromNetworkAddress
- _GetSiteAndForest
- _GetURL
- _OpenExchangeRunSpace
- _PrintUsageAndQuit

These functions are available for you to use at this point as well as whenever you work with the Exchange Management Shell or have loaded the ConnectFunctions. ps1 script. However, only Connect-ExchangeServer and Discover-ExchangeServer are meant to be called directly. The other functions are helper functions. When you are working with the Exchange Management Shell or have run ConnectFunctions.ps1, you can view the source for a function by typing **functions** followed by the name of the function, such as **functions connect-exchangeserver**.

If you want to access Exchange features from a standard PowerShell prompt or within scripts, you need to load the Excshell.psc1 console file and the Remote-Exchange.ps1 profile file. You can find an example of the command required to do this by right-clicking the menu shortcut for the Exchange Management Shell and then selecting Properties. In the Properties dialog box, the Target text is selected by default. Press Ctrl+C to copy this text so that you can use it. For example, if you copy the Target text and paste it into an elevated command prompt (cmd.exe), you can access the Exchange Management Shell and work with Exchange Server. If you copy the Target text and paste it into a script, you can be sure that the Exchange environment is loaded when you run the script.

An extra command is added to the Target text of the menu item. This additional command is Connect-ExchangeServer –Auto, a command enabled when the ConnectFunctions.ps1 script runs.

When you use Connect-ExchangeServer with the –Auto parameter, PowerShell attempts to discover the best Exchange server to connect to automatically and then tries to create a new remote PowerShell session with this Exchange server. Power-Shell first attempts to connect to a local server and then to Client Access servers in the local site. After that, PowerShell tries to connect to Hub, Mailbox, and Unified Messaging servers. You also can automatically connect to and create a remote session by typing **connect-exchangeserver –auto**. A remote session is a runspace that establishes a common working environment for executing commands on remote computers.

To customize the initialization of remote sessions, other parameters are available:

- **–ClearCache**   A troubleshooting option that allows you to clear registry entries and exported modules and then re-create the registry settings and import modules again. After you clear the cache, you can try to connect again using options you need.

```
connect-exchangeserver -clearcache
```

- **–Forest**   Allows you to specify a single part name or the fully qualified domain name (FQDN) of the Active Directory forest in which to perform discovery. You must be able to authenticate in the forest. User credentials you provide for the –Username parameter are not used for discovery. Use with –Auto.

```
connect-exchangeserver -auto -forest ForestName
```

- **–Prompt**   Prompts you for the FQDN of the Exchange server to connect to. If you use –Prompt with –Auto, you are prompted only if PowerShell cannot connect automatically. If you use –Prompt with –ServerFqdn, you are prompted only if PowerShell cannot connect to the specified server.

```
connect-exchangeserver -auto -prompt
```

- **–ServerFqdn**   Allows you to specify the FQDN of the Exchange server to connect to.

```
connect-exchangeserver -serverfqdn ExServerFQDN
```

- **–Username**   Allows you to specify the user name to use for authentication. You will be prompted for the user's password. You can also pass in a Credential object. Use with –ServerFqdn or –Auto.

```
connect-exchangeserver -serverfqdn ExServerFQDN
-username UserName
```

REAL WORLD   When you are working with some cmdlets and objects in PowerShell, you might need to specify a credential for authentication. To do this, use Get-Credential to obtain a Credential object and save the result in a variable for later use. Consider the following example:

```
$cred = get-credential
```

When PowerShell reads this command, PowerShell prompts you for a user name and password and then stores the credentials provided in the $cred variable. You also can specify that you want the credentials for a specific user in a specific

domain. In the following example, you request the credentials for the ExAdmin
account in the Adatum domain:

```
$cred = get-credential -credential adatum\exadmin
```

A Credential object has UserName and Password properties that you can work
with. Although the user name is stored as a regular string, the password is stored as
a secure, encrypted string. Simply pass in the credential instead of the user name
as shown in this example:

```
$cred = get-credential -credential adatum\exadmin
get-hotfix -credential $cred -computername mailserver18
```

When you call Connect-ExchangeServer, one of the final things the function does
is call _OpenExchangeRunSpace to establish a remote session with an Exchange
server. In turn, _OpenExchangeRunSpace does one of two things: it opens a
remote session using implicit credentials (the credentials of the user who is running
Exchange Management Shell) or by using specified credentials (credentials you've
explicitly provided). In the script, the code for using implicit credentials is similar to
the following:

```
$global:remoteSession = new-pssession -connectionURI
https://$fqdn/powershell?serializationLevel=Full
-ConfigurationName Microsoft.Exchange -SessionOption $sessionOption
```

The code for explicit credentials is similar to the following:

```
$global:remoteSession = new-pssession -connectionURI
https://$fqdn/powershell?serializationLevel=Full
-ConfigurationName Microsoft.Exchange -Authentication Kerberos
-Credential $credential -SessionOption $sessionOption
```

These examples create a global variable named $remoteSession to hold the
remote session. A global variable is used to ensure that the session remains active
and available when the script exits. The session is established using New-PSSession
with a connection URI for a particular Exchange server. For example, if the Exchange
server's FQDN is MailServer15.Cpandl.com, the connection URI is https://
mailserver15.cpandl.com/powershell. The –ConfigurationName parameter sets the
configuration namespace as Microsoft.Exchange (in place of the default Microsoft.
PowerShell). The –Authentication parameter is set to use Kerberos authentication with explicit credentials. The –SessionOption parameter sets session options
that were defined previously using the New-PSSessionOption cmdlet. The session
options include the operation timeout value, the idle timeout value, and the open
session timeout value. By default, all three are set to 180,000 milliseconds (180 seconds) via the $sessionOptionsTimeout variable defined in the first section of the
ConnectFunctions.ps1 script.

You can use the MsExchEmsTimeout environment variable to set the default timeout values. If you set this environment variable to a value of 900,000 milliseconds or less (15 minutes or less), the timeouts are set accordingly. If you set this environment variable to a value greater than 900,000 milliseconds, the timeout values revert to the 3 minute default value.

Managing the PowerShell Application

Microsoft Internet Information Services (IIS) handles every incoming request to a Web site within the context of a Web application. A Web application is a software program that delivers Web content to users over HTTP or HTTPS. Each Web site has a default Web application and one or more additional Web applications associated with it. The default Web application handles incoming requests that aren't assigned to other Web applications. Additional Web applications handle incoming requests that specifically reference a particular application.

When you connect to a server using a URL, such as https://mailserver15.cpandl.com/powershell, you are performing remote operations via the PowerShell application running on the Web server providing Exchange services. Like all Web applications, the PowerShell application has a virtual directory associated with it. The virtual directory sets the application name and maps the application to the physical directory that contains the application's content.

You can manage the PowerShell application using IIS Manager and the Exchange Management Shell. The related commands for the Exchange Management Shell are:

- **Get-PowerShellVirtualDirectory** Displays information about the PowerShell application running on the Web server providing services for Exchange.

  ```
  Get-PowerShellVirtualDirectory [-Identity 'AppName']
  [-DomainController 'DomainControllerName']


  Get-PowerShellVirtualDirectory -Server 'ExchangeServerName'
  [-DomainController 'DomainControllerName']
  ```

- **New-PowerShellVirtualDirectory** Creates a new PowerShell application running on the Web server providing services for Exchange.

  ```
  New-PowerShellVirtualDirectory -Name 'AppName'
  [-AppPoolId 'AppPoolName'] [-BasicAuthentication <$true | $false>]
  [-CertificateAuthentication <$true | $false>] [-DomainController
  'DomainControllerName'] [-ExternalUrl 'URL'] [-InternalUrl 'URL']
  [-Path 'PhysicalDirectoryPath']
  [-WindowsAuthentication <$true | $false>]
  ```

- **Remove-PowerShellVirtualDirectory**   Removes a specified PowerShell application running on the Web server providing services for Exchange.

```
Remove-PowerShellVirtualDirectory -Identity 'AppName'
[-DomainController 'DomainControllerName']
```

- **Set-PowerShellVirtualDirectory**   Modifies the configuration settings for a specified PowerShell application running on the Web server providing services for Exchange.

```
Set-PowerShellVirtualDirectory -Identity 'AppName'
[-BasicAuthentication <$true | $false>] [-CertificateAuthentication
<$true | $false>] [-DomainController 'DomainControllerName']
[-ExternalUrl 'URL'] [-InternalUrl 'URL']
[-LiveIdBasicAuthentication <$true | $false>]
[-WindowsAuthentication <$true | $false>]
```

At the Exchange Management Shell prompt, you can confirm the location of the PowerShell application by typing **get-powershellvirtualdirectory**.

Get-PowerShellVirtualDirectory lists the name of the application, the associated directory and Web site, and the server on which the application is running, as shown in the following example:

```
Name                              Server
-------                           -------
PowerShell (Default Web Site)     CorpServer45
```

In this example, a standard configuration is being used where the application named *PowerShell* is running on Default Web Site on CorpServer45. You can use Set-PowerShellVirtualDirectory to specify the internal and external URL to use as well as the permitted authentication types. Authentication types you can enable or disable include basic authentication, Windows authentication, certificate authentication, and Live ID basic authentication. You can use New-PowerShellVirtualDirectory to create a new PowerShell application on the Web server providing services for Exchange and Remove-PowerShellVirtualDirectory to remove a PowerShell application.

REAL WORLD   Any change you make to the PowerShell virtual directory configuration requires careful pre-planning. For every potential change, you'll need to determine whether you need to modify the Windows RM configuration and the PowerShell path in ConnectFunctions.ps1 scripts on management computers and Exchange servers as well as the specific changes you'll need to make with regard to IIS on your Client Access servers.

Microsoft cautions against modifying the default configuration for the PowerShell virtual directory as any mistakes you make could prevent you from managing Exchange Server. Because Exchange configuration data is stored in Active Directory and the affected IIS metabase, you would need to be able to restore Exchange data in Active Directory and the affected IIS metabase to a previous state to recover.

Customizing Exchange Management

Now that you know how the Exchange Management Shell environment works, you can more easily customize the shell to work the way you want it to. One way to do this is to modify the menu shortcut that starts the Exchange Management Shell or create copies of this menu shortcut to change the way the Exchange Management Shell starts. For example, if you want to connect to a named Exchange server rather than any available Exchange server, you can do the following:

1. Right-click the menu shortcut for the Exchange Management Shell and then select Properties.

2. In the Properties dialog box, the Target text is selected by default. Press the right arrow key to move to the end of the command text.

3. Delete **–Auto"** and type **–ServerFqdn** followed by the FQDN of the Exchange server, such as **–ServerFQDN MailServer12.Cpandl.com**, and then type **"**. Click OK.

That said, this entire sequence of tasks is meant to simplify the task of establishing an interactive remote session with a single Exchange server. As implemented in the default configuration, you have a one-to-one, interactive approach for remote management, meaning you establish a session with a specific remote server and work with that specific server simply by executing commands.

When you are working with PowerShell outside of Exchange Management Shell, you might want to use the Enter-PSSession cmdlet to start an interactive session with an Exchange server or any other remote computer. The basic syntax is **Enter-PSSession** *ComputerName*, where *ComputerName* is the name of the remote computer, such as the following:

```
enter-pssession mailserver15
```

After you enter this command, the command prompt changes to show that you are connected to the remote computer, as shown in the following example:

```
[Server49]: PS C:\Users\wrstanek.cpandl\Documents>
```

Now, the commands that you type run on the remote computer just as if you had typed them directly on the remote computer. In most cases, you need to ensure you are running an elevated, administrator shell and that you pass credentials along in the session. When you connect to a server in this way, you use the standard PowerShell remoting configuration and do not go through the PowerShell application running on a Web server. You can end the interactive session by using the command Exit-PSSession or typing **exit**.

To access an Exchange server in the same way as the ConnectFunctions.ps1 script, you need to use the –ConnectionURI parameter to specify the connection URI, the –ConfigurationName parameter to specify the configuration namespace, the –Authentication parameter to set the authentication type to use, and optionally, the –SessionOption parameter to set session options. Consider the following example:

```
enter-pssession -connectionURI http://mailserver12.cpandl.com/powershell
-ConfigurationName Microsoft.Exchange –Authentication Kerberos
```

Here, you set the connection URI as https://mailserver12.cpandl.com/powershell, set the configuration namespace as Microsoft.Exchange, and use Kerberos authentication with the implicit credentials of your user account. If you don't specify the authentication method, the default authentication method for WinRM is used. If you want to use alternate credentials, you can pass in credentials as shown in this example:

```
$cred = get-credential –credential adatum\williams

enter-pssession -connectionURI https://mailserver12.cpandl.com/powershell
-ConfigurationName Microsoft.Exchange –credential $cred
–Authentication Kerberos
```

Here, you set the connection URI as https://mailserver12.cpandl.com/powershell, set the configuration namespace as Microsoft.Exchange, and use alternate credentials. When PowerShell reads the Get-Credential command, you are prompted for the password for the specified account. Because the authentication type is not defined, the session uses the default authentication method for WinRM.

To put this all together, one way to create a script that runs on an Exchange server is to load the Microsoft.Exchange.Management.PowerShell.E2010 snap-in, run the RemoteExchange.ps1 profile file, and then run the ConnectFunctions.ps1 script to autoconnect to Exchange. The commands you insert into your script to do this are the following:

```
Add-PSSnapin Microsoft.Exchange.Management.PowerShell.E2010
$s = $env:ExchangeInstallPath + "bin\RemoteExchange.ps1"
&$s
$t = $env:ExchangeInstallPath + "bin\ConnectFunctions.ps1"
&$t
```

Here, you use the Add-PSSnapin command to load the Exchange snap-in. Next, you define variables that point to the RemoteExchange.ps1 and ConnectFunctions scripts in the Exchange installation path, and then you use the & operator to invoke the scripts. The environment variable ExchangeInstallPath stores the location of the Exchange installation. If you enter the full path to a script, you don't need to assign the path to a variable and then invoke it. However, you then have a fixed path and might need to edit the path on a particular Exchange server. Be sure to run the script at an elevated, administrator PowerShell prompt.

If you want to create a script that runs on your management computer and then executes commands remotely on an Exchange server, you'll probably want to insert commands in your script to create a new session and then invoke commands in the session using the techniques discussed in the next section.

Performing One-to-Many Remote Management

PowerShell also lets you perform one-to-many remote management. Here, you must work with an elevated, administrator shell and can either invoke remote commands on multiple computers or establish remote sessions with multiple computers. When you remotely invoke commands, PowerShell runs the commands on the remote computers, returns all output from the commands, and establishes connections to the remote computers only for as long as is required to return the output. When you establish remote sessions, you can create persistent connections to the remote computers and then execute commands within the session. Any command you enter while working in the session is executed on all computers to which you are connected, whether this is 1 computer, 10 computers, or 100 computers.

> **TIP** As discussed in Chapter 1, "Exchange Server 2010 Administration Overview," WinRM must be appropriately configured on any computer you want to remotely manage. While WinRM is configured on Exchange servers and most others computers running Windows 7 and Windows Server 2008 Release 2, WinRM listeners generally are not created by default. You can create the required listeners by running winrm quickconfig.

The following command entered as a single line invokes the Get-Service and Get-Process commands on the named servers:

```
invoke-command -computername MailServer12, MailServer21, MailServer32
-scriptblock {get-service; get-process}
```

The following command establishes a remote session with the named computers:

```
$s = new-PSSession -computername MailServer12, MailServer21, MailServer32
-Credential Cpandl\WilliamS
```

When you connect to a server in this way, you use the standard PowerShell remoting configuration and are not going through the PowerShell application running on a Web server. After you establish the session, you can then use the $s session with Invoke-Command to return commands on all remote computers you are connected to. In this example, you look for stopped Exchange services on each computer:

```
invoke-command -session $s
-scriptblock {get-service msc* | where { $_.status -eq "stopped"}}
```

In this example, you pipe the output of Get-Service to the Where-Object cmdlet and filter based on the Status property. As the $_ automatic variable operates on the current object in the pipeline, PowerShell examines the status of each service in turn and lists only those that are stopped in the output.

In addition to working with remote commands and remote sessions, some cmdlets have a –ComputerName parameter that lets you work with a remote computer without using Windows PowerShell remoting. PowerShell supports remote background jobs as well. A background job is a command that you run asynchronously in an interactive or noninteractive session. When you start a background job, the command prompt returns immediately and you can continue working while the job runs. For a complete discussion of these remoting features, see Chapter 4 "Using Sessions, Jobs, and Remoting" in *Windows PowerShell 2.0 Administrator's Pocket Consultant* (Microsoft Press, 2009).

Finally, compared to all the behind-the-scenes tasks that are performed when you work with the Exchange Management Shell, the Forefront Management Shell is very simple. When you select the related menu item, Windows runs PowerShell and loads the FSSPSnapin. Because PowerShell is run with no security context, you won't be able to perform administrative tasks. To resolve this, you need to right-click the Forefront Management Shell and then select Run As Administrator to open an elevated, administrator shell. If you want to run Forefront commands while working with the Exchange Management Shell, all you need to do is type the following command:

```
Add-PSSnapin FSSPSSnapin
```

Adding this command to your scripts allows you to work with Forefront Security in your scripts as well.

Troubleshooting Exchange Management

Note that the ConnectionFunctions.ps1 script relies on your organization having a standard Exchange Server configuration. By default, Exchange is configured for management using HTTP with the URL http://ServerName/powershell. If you've modified the Web Server configuration on your Exchange servers to use a different path, such as might be required to enhance security, you need to update the connection URIs used in the ConnectionFunctions.ps1 script.

When you invoke the PowerShell application, the Web server to which you connect runs the PowerShell plug-in (Pwrshplugin.dll) and the Exchange Authorization plug-in (Microsoft.Exchange.AuthorizationPlugin.dll). The PowerShell plug-in runs as a Microsoft.Exchange shell and has the following initialization parameters:

- PSVersion, which sets the PowerShell version as 2.0
- ApplicationBase, which sets the base path for the Exchange server as %ExchangeInstallPath%Bin
- AssemblyName, which sets the name of the .NET assembly to load as Microsoft.Exchange.Configuration.ObjectModel.dll

The Authorization plug-in handles Exchange authorization and authentication. Together, these plug-ins create an authorized shell environment for the remote session.

The physical directory for the PowerShell application is %ExchangeInstallPath%\ClientAccess\PowerShell. This application runs in the context of an application pool named MSExchangePowerShellAppPool. In a large organization, you might want to optimize settings for this and other application pools, as discussed in Chapter 9, "Managing Applications, Application Pools, and Worker Processes," in the *Internet Information Services (IIS) 7.0 Administrator's Pocket Consultant* (Microsoft, 2007).

In the %ExchangeInstallPath%\ClientAccess\PowerShell directory on your server, you'll find a web.config file that defines the settings for the PowerShell application. This file contains a role-based access control (RBAC) configuration section that loads the assemblies and Web controls for the application.

TIP Microsoft recommends against changing the PowerShell application configuration. However, there's nothing magical or mystical about the PowerShell application or MSExchangePowerShellAppPool. You can re-create these features to enable remote management in alternate configurations, such as on nondefault Web sites or Web sites with alternate names. However, be sure to copy the PowerShell application's web.config file to the physical directory for your base application. Before you make any changes to a live production environment, you should plan and test your changes in a nonproduction test environment.

The Web Server to which you connect processes your remote actions via the Exchange Control Panel (ECP) application running on the default Web site. The physical directory for this application is %ExchangeInstallPath%\ClientAccess\Ecp. This application runs in the context of an application pool named MSExchangeECPAppPool.

In the %ExchangeInstallPath%\ClientAccess\ECP directory on your server, you'll find a web.config file that defines the settings for the ECP application. This file contains an RBAC configuration section that loads the assemblies and Web controls for the application.

Because of the interdependencies created by accessing Exchange via Web applications, you'll want to examine related features as part of troubleshooting any issues you experience with remote sessions. Generally, your troubleshooting should follow these steps:

1. Examine the status and configuration of the WinRM on your local computer and the target Exchange server. The service must be started and responding.

2. Check the settings of any firewall running on your local computer, the target Exchange server, or any device in between the two, such as a router with a firewall.

3. Check the status of the World Wide Web Publishing Service on the Exchange server. The service must be started and responding.

4. Check the configuration settings of the PowerShell and ECP applications on the Web server. By default, the applications don't have access restrictions, but another administrator could have set restrictions.

5. Check the status of MSExchangePowerShellAppPool and MSExchange-ECPAppPool. You might want to recycle the application pools to stop and then start them.

6. Check the configuration settings of MSExchangePowerShellAppPool and MSExchangeECPAppPool. By default, the application pools are configured to use only one worker process to service requests.

7. Check to ensure the PowerShell application's web.config file is present in the physical directory for the application, and also that the file has the appropriate settings.

8. Check to ensure the ECP application's web.config file is present in the physical directory for the application and also that the file has the appropriate settings.

Working with Exchange Cmdlets

When you are working with the Exchange Management Shell, additional Exchange-specific cmdlets are available. As with Windows PowerShell cmdlets, you can get help information on Exchange cmdlets:

-   To view a list of all Exchange cmdlets, type **get-excommand** at the shell prompt.

-   To view Exchange cmdlets related to a specific server role, type **get-help** **–role *RoleName***, where *RoleName* is the name of the server role you want to examine. You can use the following role names:

    -   *UM* for cmdlets related to the Unified Messaging server role

    -   *Mailbox* for cmdlets related to the Mailbox server role

    -   *ClientAccess* for cmdlets related to the Client Access server role

When you work with the Exchange Management Shell, you'll often work with Get, Set, Enable, Disable, New, and Remove cmdlets (the groups of cmdlets that begin with these verbs). These cmdlets all accept the –Identity parameter, which identifies the unique object with which you are working.

Typically, a cmdlet that accepts the –Identity parameter has this parameter as its first parameter, allowing you to specify the identity, with or without the parameter name. When identities have names as well as aliases, you can specify either value as the identity. For example, you can use any of the following techniques to retrieve the mailbox object for the user William Stanek with the mail alias Williams:

```
get-mailbox -identity williams
get-mailbox -identity 'William Stanek'
get-mailbox Williams
get-mailbox "William Stanek"
```

With Get cmdlets, you typically can return an object set containing all related items simply by omitting the identity. For example, if you type **get-mailbox** at the shell prompt without specifying an identity, you get a list of all mailboxes in the enterprise (up to the maximum permitted to return in a single object set).

By default, all cmdlets return data in table format. Because there are often many more columns of data than you can fit across the screen, you might need to switch to Format-List output to see all of the data. To change to the Format-List output, redirect the output using the pipe symbol (|) to the Format-List cmdlet, as shown in this example:

```
get-mailbox -identity williams | format-list
```

You can abbreviate Format-List as *fl*, as in this example:

```
get-mailbox -identity williams | fl
```

Either technique typically ensures that you see much more information about the object or the result set than if you were retrieving table-formatted data.

Working with Object Sets and Redirecting Output

When you are working with the Exchange Management Shell, you'll often need to redirect the output of one cmdlet and pass it as input to another cmdlet. You can do this using the pipe symbol. For example, if you want to view mailboxes for a specific mailbox database rather than all mailboxes in the enterprise, you can pipe the output of Get-MailboxDatabase to Get-Mailbox, as shown in this example:

```
get-mailboxdatabase -Identity "Engineering" | get-mailbox
```

Here, you use Get-MailboxDatabase to get the mailbox database object for the Engineering database. You then send this object to the Get-Mailbox cmdlet as input, and Get-Mailbox iterates through all the mailboxes in this database. If you don't perform any other manipulation, the mailboxes for this database are listed as output, as shown here:

```
Name            Alias           Server      ProhibitSendQuota
Administrator   Administrator   corpsvr127  unlimited
William S       williams        corpsvr127  unlimited
Tom G           tomg            corpsvr127  unlimited
David W         davidw          corpsvr127  unlimited
Kari F          karif           corpsvr127  unlimited
Connie V        conniev         corpsvr127  unlimited
Mike D          miked           corpsvr127  unlimited
```

You can also pipe this output to another cmdlet to perform an action on each individual mailbox in this database. If you don't know the name of the mailbox database you want to work with, enter **get-mailboxdatabase** without any parameters to list all available mailbox databases.

CHAPTER 5

User and Contact Administration

- Understanding Users and Contacts   **117**
- Understanding the Basics of E-Mail Routing   **119**
- Managing User Accounts and Mail Features   **120**
- Managing Contacts   **149**

Often, one of your primary tasks as a Microsoft Exchange administrator is to manage user accounts and contacts. User accounts enable individual users to log on to the network and access network resources. In Active Directory, users are represented by User and InetOrgPerson objects. User objects represent standard user accounts; InetOrgPerson objects represent user accounts imported from non-Microsoft Lightweight Directory Access Protocol (LDAP) or X.500 directory services. User and InetOrgPerson are the only Active Directory objects that can have Exchange mailboxes associated with them. Contacts, on the other hand, are people who you or others in your organization want to get in touch with. Contacts can have street addresses, phone numbers, fax numbers, and e-mail addresses associated with them. Unlike user accounts, contacts don't have network logon privileges.

Understanding Users and Contacts

In Active Directory, users are represented as objects that can be mailbox-enabled or mail-enabled. A *mailbox-enabled* user account has an Exchange mailbox associated with it. Mailboxes are private storage areas for sending and receiving mail. A user's display name is the name Exchange presents in the global address list and in the From text box of e-mail messages.

Another important identifier for mailbox-enabled user accounts is the Exchange alias. The alias is the name that Exchange associates with the account for mail addressing. When your mail client is configured to use Microsoft

Exchange Server, you can type the alias or display name in the To, Cc, or Bcc text boxes of an e-mail message and have Exchange Server resolve the alias or name to the actual e-mail address.

Although you'll likely configure most Windows user accounts as mailbox-enabled, user accounts don't have to have mailboxes associated with them. You can create user accounts without assigning a mailbox. You can also create user accounts that are *mail-enabled* rather than mailbox-enabled, which means that the account has an off-site e-mail address associated with it but doesn't have an actual mailbox. Mail-enabled users have Exchange aliases and display names that Exchange Server can resolve to actual e-mail addresses. Internal users can send a message to the mail-enabled user account using the Exchange display name or alias, and the message will be directed to the external address. Users outside the organization can use the Exchange alias to send mail to the user.

It's not always easy to decide when to create a mailbox for a user. To better understand the decision-making process, consider the following scenario:

1. You've been notified that two new users, Elizabeth and Joe, will need access to the domain.

2. Elizabeth is a full-time employee who starts on Tuesday. She'll work on-site and needs to be able to send and receive mail. People in the company need to be able to send mail directly to her.

3. Joe, on the other hand, is a consultant who is coming in to help out temporarily. His agency maintains his mailbox, and he doesn't want to have to check mail in two places. However, people in the company need to be able to contact him, and he wants to be sure that his external address is available.

4. You create a mailbox-enabled user account for Elizabeth. Afterward, you create a mail-enabled user account for Joe, ensuring that his Exchange information refers to his external e-mail address.

Mail-enabled users are one of several types of custom recipients that you can create in Exchange Server. Another type of custom recipient is a *mail-enabled* contact. You create a mail-enable contact by specifying the external e-mail address that users can use to send e-mail to that contact.

The Exchange Management Shell provides many commands for working with mailbox-enabled users, mail-enabled users, and contacts. The main commands you'll use are shown in the following list:

MAILBOX-ENABLED USER	MAIL-ENABLED USERS	CONTACTS
Connect-Mailbox	Disable-MailUser	Disable-MailContact
Disable-Mailbox	Enable-MailUser	Enable-MailContact
Enable-Mailbox	Get-MailUser	Get-MailContact
Export-Mailbox	New-MailUser	New-MailContact
Get-Mailbox	Remove-MailUser	Remove-MailContact

MAILBOX-ENABLED USER	MAIL-ENABLED USERS	CONTACTS
Import-Mailbox	Set-MailUser	Set-MailContact
Move-Mailbox		
New-Mailbox		
Remove-Mailbox		
Restore-Mailbox		
Search-Mailbox		
Set-Mailbox		

Understanding the Basics of E-Mail Routing

Exchange uses e-mail addresses to route messages to mail servers inside and outside the organization. When routing messages internally, Hub Transport servers use mail connectors to route messages to other Exchange servers, as well as to other types of mail servers that your company might use. Two standard types of connectors are used:

- Send connectors
- Receive connectors

Send and Receive connectors use Simple Mail Transfer Protocol (SMTP) as the default transport and provide a direct connection among Hub Transport servers in an organization. Hub Transport and Edge Transport servers can also receive mail from and send mail to other types of mail servers.

You can use these connectors to connect Hub Transport servers in an organization. When routing messages outside the company, Hub Transport and Edge Transport servers use mail gateways to transfer messages. The default gateway is SMTP.

Exchange Server 2010 uses directory-based recipient resolution for all messages that are sent from and received by users throughout the organization. The Exchange component responsible for recipient resolution is the Categorizer. The Categorizer must be able to associate every recipient in every message with a corresponding recipient object in Active Directory.

All senders and recipients must have a primary SMTP address. If the Categorizer discovers a recipient that does not have a primary SMTP address, it will determine what the primary SMTP address should be or replace the non-SMTP address. Replacing a non-SMTP address involves encapsulating the address in a primary SMTP address that will be used while transporting the message.

NOTE Non-SMTP e-mail address formats include fax, X.400, and messages originating from Lotus Notes. The Categorizer encapsulates e-mail addresses using non-SMTP formats in the Internet Mail Connector Encapsulated Addressing (IMCEA) format. For example, the Categorizer encapsulates the fax address, FAX:888-555-1212, as

IMCEA-FAX-888-555-1212@yourdomain.com. Any e-mail address that is longer than what SMTP allows is transmitted as an extended property in the XExch50 field.

In addition to primary SMTP e-mail addresses, you can configure alternative recipients and forwarding addresses for users and public folders. If there is an alternative recipient or forwarding address, redirection is required during categorization. You specify the addresses to which messages will be redirected in Active Directory, and redirection history is maintained with each message.

Managing User Accounts and Mail Features

With Exchange Server 2010, the Exchange Management Console and the Exchange Management Shell are the primary administration tools you use to manage mailboxes, distribution groups, and mail contacts. You can use these tools to create and manage mail-enabled user accounts, mailbox-enabled user accounts, and mail-enabled contacts as well as any other configurable aspect of Exchange Server.

Exchange Server 2010 also includes the Exchange Control Panel. The Exchange Control Panel provides browser-based management of mailbox-enabled user accounts, mail-enabled contacts, and distribution groups as well as transport rules and delivery reports. To perform remote management with the Exchange Control Panel, a user must have appropriate permissions in the Exchange organization.

The sections that follow examine techniques that you can employ to manage user accounts and the Exchange features of those accounts.

NOTE Domain administrators can create user accounts and contacts using Active Directory Users And Computers. If any existing user accounts need to be mail-enabled or mailbox-enabled, you perform these tasks using the Exchange management tools. If existing contacts need to be mail-enabled, you also perform this task using the Exchange management tools.

Configuring the Exchange Control Panel

The Exchange Control Panel (ECP) is a Web application running on a Client Access server providing services for the Exchange organization. This application is installed automatically when you install a Client Access server. To perform Exchange management from just about anywhere, you simply need to enter the Uniform Resource Locator (URL) path for the application in your browser's Address field. You can then access the Exchange Control Panel. By default, the Exchange Control Panel URL is *https://yourserver.yourdomain.com/ecp*.

The Client Access server to which you connect processes your remote actions via the ECP application running on the default Web site. The physical directory for this application is %ExchangeInstallPath%\ClientAccess\Ecp. This application runs in the context of an application pool named MSExchangeECPAppPool. In the

%ExchangeInstallPath%\ClientAccess\Ecp directory on your server, you'll find a web.config file that defines the settings for the ECP application.

When you install an Exchange server, the setup process creates a self-signed security certificate. Because this default certificate is not issued by a trusted authority, you see a related error message whenever you use HTTPS to access services hosted by your Client Access servers, including the Exchange Control Panel, the PowerShell application, and Microsoft Outlook Web App.

The best way to eliminate this error message is to install a certificate from a trusted authority on your Client Access servers. If you organization has a certification authority (CA), have your security administrator issue a certificate. Otherwise, you can purchase a certificate from a trusted third-party authority. Web browsers should already be configured to trust certificates issued by your organization's CA or by a trusted third-party authority. Typically, browsers need additional configuration only when you use your own CA with non-domain-joined machines. For more information on creating certificates or configuring CAs, see Chapter 11, "Managing Active Directory Certificate Services and SSL," in *Internet Information Services (IIS) 7.0 Administrator's Pocket Consultant* (Microsoft, 2008).

In Exchange Management Console, you can view, install, and manage certificates by selecting the Server Configuration node in the left pane and then clicking the server you want to work with in the main pane. Certificates available on the server are listed in the lower pane. If you right-click in the lower pane, you can choose New Exchange Certificate to create a new certificate request, or choose Import Exchange Certificate to import a certificate issued by a CA from a file. After you import or create a certificate, right-click the certificate, and then select Assign Services To Certificate to permit the certificate to be used with designated Exchange services.

The services a certificate can be used with include Internet Message Access Protocol (IMAP), Post Office Protocol (POP), SMTP, Internet Information Services (IIS), and Unified Messaging (UM). The default self-signed certificate is assigned services automatically during setup based on the roles installed on the Exchange server.

Accessing and Using the Exchange Control Panel

You access the Exchange Control Panel by following these steps:

1. Open your Web browser, and then enter the secure URL for the Exchange Control Panel, such as *https://mailserver48.cpandl.com/ecp*.

2. If your browser displays a security alert stating there's a problem with the site's security certificate, click the Continue To This Web Site link.

3. You'll see the logon page for Outlook Web App. After you specify whether you are using a public or a private computer, enter your user name and password, and then click Sign In.

4. The first time you sign in to OWA, you need to specify the language you want to use and your time zone. You also can specify that you want to use the blind or low-vision experience. Click OK to continue to your mailbox.

In your browser, you use the Select What To Manage list to choose whether you want to manage the Exchange organization on your mailbox or another user's mailbox. If you choose your mailbox, you are redirected to the virtual directory for Outlook Web App. When you are managing your organization, you have several management categories available, including Users & Groups and Reporting. When you are managing your organization, you can switch between these management categories by clicking the links provided in the left pane.

When Users & Groups is selected in the left pane, the Mailboxes view is displayed by default. As shown in Figure 5-1, the Mailboxes view lists mail-enabled user accounts according to their display name and e-mail address. While working with this view, you can do the following:

- Double-click an entry in the Mailboxes list to view and manage mailbox settings. The information you can view and manage is a subset of the information available in the related Properties dialog box in the Exchange Management Console.

- Click Refresh to update the Mailboxes list.

- Enter a search value, and click the Search button to search the mailboxes by display name or e-mail address.

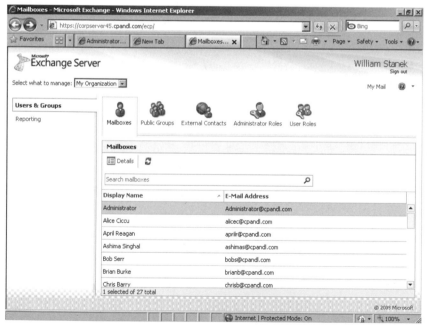

FIGURE 5-1 Access mailbox-enabled users in the Exchange Control Panel.

By clicking Users & Groups and then clicking External Contacts, you can display mail-enabled contacts in the organization, as shown in Figure 5-2. The External Contacts view lists mail-enabled contacts according to their display name and e-mail address. While working with this view, you can do the following:

- Click New to create a new mail-enabled contact. The information you need to provide to create a contact is the same as the information you must enter on the Contact Information page in the New Mail Contact Wizard when you are working with the Exchange Management Console.

- Double-click an entry in the External Contacts list to view and manage contact settings. The information you can view and manage is a subset of the information available in the related Properties dialog box in the Exchange Management Console.

- Select an entry in the External Contacts list, and then click Delete to remove the contact.

- Click Refresh to update the External Contacts list.

- Enter a search value, and then click the Search button to search the contacts by display name or e-mail address.

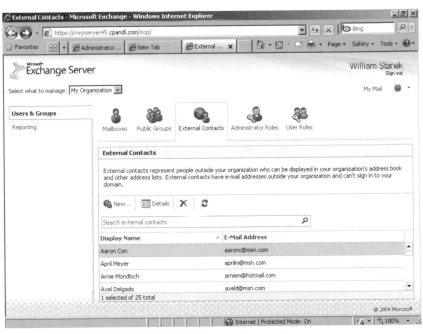

FIGURE 5-2 Access mail-enabled contacts in the Exchange Control Panel.

By clicking Users & Groups and then clicking Groups, you can display distribution groups in the organization, as shown in Figure 5-3. The Groups view lists distribution groups according to their display name and e-mail address. While working with this view, you can do the following:

- Click New to create a distribution group. The information you need to provide to create a distribution group is the same as the information you must enter on the Group Information page in the New Distribution Group Wizard when you are working with the Exchange Management Console. However, you can also configure settings for ownership, membership, and membership approval. With the New Distribution Group Wizard, you need to create the group and then edit the properties to manage these additional settings.

- Double-click an entry in the Groups list to view and manage group settings. The information you can view and manage is a subset of the information available in the related Properties dialog box in the Exchange Management Console.

- Select an entry in the Groups list and then click Delete to remove a group.

- Click Refresh to update the Groups list.

- Enter a search value, and then click the Search button to search distribution groups by display name or e-mail address.

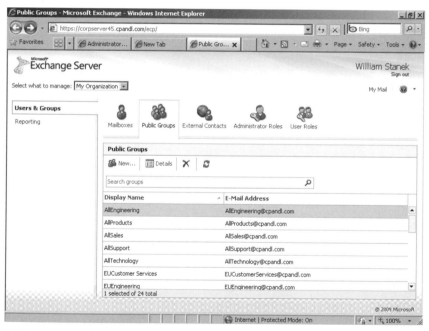

FIGURE 5-3 Access distribution groups in the Exchange Control Panel.

You can configure the Exchange Control Panel for single-server and multiserver environments. In a single-server environment, you use one Client Access server for all your remote management needs. In a multiple-server environment, you can instruct administrators to use different URLs to access different Client Access servers, or you can use Client Access arrays with multiple, load-balanced servers and give all administrators the same access URL.

REAL WORLD If you have multiple Client Access servers in the same Active Directory site, you put them all in the same single CAS array, and then you point to the CAS array. Note that the load balancing performed by the array automatically is for RPC Client Access only. You need to use some other means to load balance the HTTPS requests against the array.

NOTE You can use the Exchange Control Panel with firewalls. You configure your network to use a perimeter network with firewalls in front of the designated Client Access servers and then open port 443 to the IP addresses of your Client Access servers. If Secure Sockets Layer (SSL) is enabled and you want to use SSL exclusively, you only need port 443, and you don't need to open port 80.

You can manage the Exchange Control Panel application using Internet Information Services (IIS) Manager or the Exchange Management Shell. The related commands for the Exchange Management Shell are as follows:

- **Get-ECPVirtualDirectory** Displays information about the ECP application running on the Web server providing services for Exchange.

```
Get-ECPVirtualDirectory [-Identity AppName]
[-DomainController DomainControllerName]


Get-ECPVirtualDirectory -Server ExchangeServerName
[-DomainController DomainControllerName]
```

- **New-ECPVirtualDirectory** Creates a new ECP application running on the Web server providing services for Exchange. You should use this command only for troubleshooting scenarios where you are required to remove and re-create the ECP virtual directory.

```
New-ECPVirtualDirectory [-AppPoolId AppPoolName]
[-DomainController DomainControllerName] [-ExternalUrl URL]
[-InternalUrl URL] [-WebSiteName SiteName]
```

- **Remove-ECPVirtualDirectory** Use the Remove-ECPVirtualDirectory cmdlet to remove a specified ECP application running on the CAS server providing services for Exchange.

```
Remove-ECPVirtualDirectory -Identity AppName
[-DomainController DomainControllerName]
```

- **Set-ECPVirtualDirectory** Modifies the configuration settings for a specified ECP application running on the CAS server providing services for Exchange.

```
Set-ECPVirtualDirectory -Identity AppName
[-BasicAuthentication <$true | $false>] [-DomainController
DomainControllerName] [-ExternalAuthenticationMethods Methods]
[-FormsAuthentication <$true | $false>]
[-ExternalUrl URL] [-GzipLevel <Off | Low | High | Error>]
[-InternalUrl URL] [-LiveIdAuthentication <$true | $false>]
[-WindowsAuthentication <$true | $false>]
```

At the Exchange Management Shell prompt, you can confirm the location of the Exchange Control Panel application by typing **get-ecpvirtualdirectory**.

Get-ECPVirtualDirectory lists the name of the application, the associated Web site, and the server on which the application is running, as shown in the following example:

```
Name                            Server
-------                         -------
ecp (Default Web Site)          CorpServer45
```

In this example, a standard configuration is being used on which the application named ECP is running on the Default Web Site on CorpServer45. You can use Set-ECPVirtualDirectory to specify the internal and external URL to use as well as the permitted authentication types. Authentication types you can enable or disable include basic authentication, Windows authentication, and Live ID basic authentication. You can use New-ECPVirtualDirectory to create an ECP application on the Web server providing services for Exchange and Remove-ECPVirtualDirectory to remove an ECP application.

Finding Existing Mailboxes, Contacts, and Groups

In the Exchange Management Console, you can view current mailboxes, mail-enabled users, contacts, and groups by following these steps:

1. As shown in Figure 5-4, expand the Recipient Configuration node by double-clicking it.

2. Select the related Mailbox, Distribution Group, or Mail Contact node, as appropriate for the type of recipient you want to work with.

3. By default, the Exchange Management Console displays only the recipients in the current domain or organizational unit. To view recipients in other domains or organizational units, right-click the Recipient Configuration node, and then select Modify Recipient Scope. Use the options provided to configure the scope to use, and then click OK.

4. By default, the maximum number of Exchange recipients you can view at any time is limited to 1,000. You can change the maximum number of recipients to display by right-clicking the Recipient Configuration node or the subnode you want to work with and then selecting Modify The Maximum Number Of Recipients To Display. Type the number of recipients to display, and then click OK.

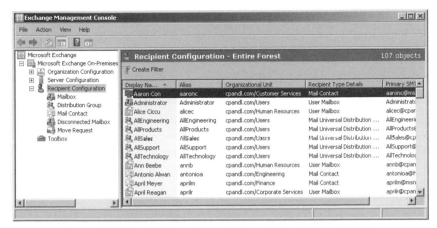

FIGURE 5-4 Access the Recipient Configuration node to work with mailboxes, distribution groups, and mail contacts.

In the Exchange Management Shell, you can find mailboxes, contacts, and groups by using the following commands:

- **Get-User** Use the Get-User cmdlet to retrieve all users in the forest that match the specified conditions.

```
Get-User [-Identity UserId -Anr Identifier] [ Arbitration <$true | $false>]
[-Credential Credential] [-DomainController DomainControllerName]
[-Filter FilterString] [-IgnoreDefaultScope <$true | $false>]
[-Organization OrgName] [-OrganizationalUnit OUName]
[-ReadFromDomainController <$true | $false>]
[-RecipientTypeDetails Details] [-ResultSize Size]
[-SortBy String]
```

- **Get-Contact** Use the Get-Contact cmdlet to retrieve information about a specified contact or contacts.

```
Get-Contact [-Identity ContactId | -Anr ContactID]
[-Credential Credential] [-DomainController DomainControllerName]
[-Filter FilterString] [-IgnoreDefaultScope <$true | $false>]
[-Organization OrgName] [-OrganizationalUnit OUName]
[-ReadFromDomainController <$true | $false>]
[-RecipientTypeDetails Details] [-ResultSize Size] [-SortBy Value]
```

- **Get-Group** Use the Get-Group cmdlet to query for existing groups.

```
Get-Group [-Identity GroupId | -Anr GroupID]
[-Credential Credential] [-DomainController FullyQualifiedName]
[-Filter FilterString] [-IgnoreDefaultScope <$true | $false>]
[-Organization OrgName] [-OrganizationalUnit OUName]
[-ReadFromDomainController <$true | $false>]
```

```
[-RecipientTypeDetails {"Contact" | "MailContact" | "MailUser" |
"RoleGroup" | "User" | "UserMailbox" | ... }]
[-ResultSize Size] [-SortBy Value]
```

Creating Mailbox-Enabled and Mail-Enabled User Accounts

Generally speaking, you need to create a user account for each user who wants to use network resources. The following sections explain how to create domain user accounts that are either mailbox-enabled or mail-enabled, and how to add a mailbox to an existing user account. If a user needs to send and receive e-mail, you need to create a new mailbox-enabled account for the user or add a mailbox to the user's existing account. Otherwise, you can create a mail-enabled account.

Understanding Logon Names and Passwords

Before you create a domain user account, you should think for a moment about the new account's logon name and password. You identify all domain user accounts with a logon name. This logon name can be (but doesn't have to be) the same as the user's e-mail address. In Windows domains, logon names have two parts:

- **User name**   The account's text label
- **User domain**   The domain where the user account exists

For the user Williams whose account is created in adatum.com, the full logon name for Windows is williams@adatum.com.

User accounts can also have passwords and public certificates associated with them. *Passwords* are authentication strings for an account. *Public certificates* combine a public and private key to identify a user. You log on with a password by typing the password. You log on with a public certificate by using a smart card and a smart card reader.

Although Windows displays user names to describe privileges and permissions, the key identifiers for accounts are security identifiers (SIDs). SIDs are unique identifiers that Windows generates when you create accounts. SIDs consist of the domain's security ID prefix and a unique relative ID. Windows uses these identifiers to track accounts independently from user names. SIDs serve many purposes; the two most important are to allow you to easily change user names and to allow you to delete accounts without worrying that someone could gain access to resources simply by re-creating an account with the same user name.

When you change a user name, you tell Windows to map a particular SID to a new name. When you delete an account, you tell Windows that a particular SID is no longer valid. Afterward, even if you create an account with the same user name, the new account won't have the same privileges and permissions as the previous one because the new account will have a new SID.

Creating Mail-Enabled User Accounts

Mail-enabled users are defined as custom recipients in Exchange Server. They have an Exchange alias and an external e-mail address, but they do not have an Exchange mailbox. All e-mail messages sent to a mail-enabled user are forwarded to the remote e-mail address associated with the account.

In the Exchange Management Console, mail-enabled users are listed as such in the Recipient Configuration node and in the Mail Contact node. You can manage mail-enabled users through the Exchange Management Console and the Exchange Management Shell.

In the Exchange Management Console, you can create a new mail-enabled user by completing the following steps:

1. In the Exchange Management Console, expand and then select the Recipient Configuration node.

    NOTE If you want to create the user account in a domain other than the current one, you first need to set the scope for the Recipient Configuration node, as discussed previously in "Finding Existing Mailboxes, Contacts, and Groups."

2. Right-click the Recipient Configuration node, and then select New Mail User. This starts the New Mail User Wizard.

3. Click Next to accept the default selections on the Introduction page (to create a mail user).

4. On the User Information page, shown in Figure 5-5, the Organizational Unit text box shows where in Active Directory the user account will be created. By default, this is the Users container in the current domain. Because you'll usually need to create new user accounts in a specific organizational unit rather than in the Users container, select the Specify The Organizational Unit check box, and then click Browse. In the Select Organizational Unit dialog box, choose the location in which to store the account and then click OK.

5. Type the user's first name, middle initial, and last name in the text boxes provided. These values are used to create the Name entry, which is the user's display name.

6. As necessary, make changes to the Name text box. For example, you might want to type the name in LastName FirstName MiddleInitial format or in FirstName MiddleInitial LastName format. The name must be no more than 64 characters in length.

7. In the User Logon Name text box, type the user's logon name. Use the drop-down list to select the domain with which you want to associate the account. This sets the fully qualified logon name.

8. The first 20 characters of the logon name are used to set the pre–Windows 2000 logon name, which must be unique in the domain. If necessary, change the pre–Windows 2000 logon name.

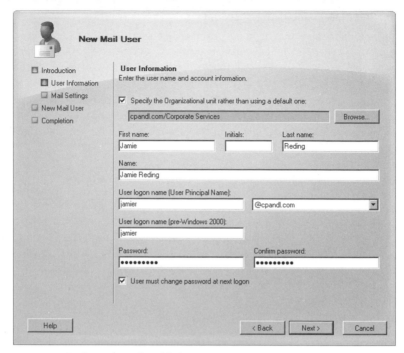

FIGURE 5-5 Configure the mail-enabled user's settings.

9. Type and then confirm the password for the account. This password must follow the conventions of your organization's password policy. Typically, this means that the password must be at least six characters in length and must use three of the four available character types: lowercase letters, uppercase letters, numbers, and symbols.

10. If you want to ensure that the user changes the password at next logon, select the User Must Change Password At Next Logon check box. Click Next.

    As shown in Figure 5-6, the Exchange alias is set to the user's logon name by default. You can change this value by entering a new alias. The Exchange Management Console uses the alias to set the user's e-mail address.

11. To the right of the External E-Mail Address text box is an Edit button. Click the down arrow next to the Edit button to display two options:

    ■ **SMTP Address**   Select SMTP Address to associate a standard SMTP e-mail address with the user. Enter the e-mail address, and then click OK.

    ■ **Custom Address**   Click Custom Address to associate a custom e-mail address with the user. Enter the e-mail address, and then enter the e-mail address type. Click OK.

12. Click Next, and then click New. The Exchange Management Console creates the new user and mail-enables it. If an error occurs, the user will not be

created. You will need to correct the problem and repeat this procedure. Click Finish.

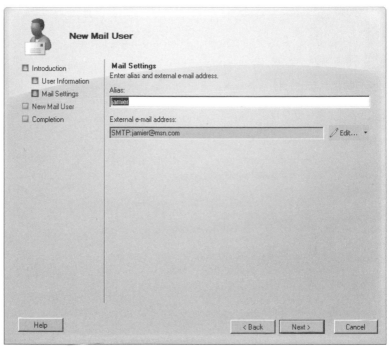

FIGURE 5-6 Configure the user's mail settings.

You can list all mail-enabled users by typing **get-mailuser** at the Exchange Management Shell prompt. Sample 5-1 provides the full syntax and usage for Get-MailUser.

SAMPLE 5-1 Get-MailUser cmdlet syntax and usage

Syntax
```
Get-MailUser [-Identity Identifier | -Anr Name] [-Credential Credential]
[-DomainController FullyQualifiedName] [-Filter FilterString]
[-IgnoreDefaultScope {$true | $false}] [-Organization OrgName]
[-OrganizationalUnit OUName] [-ReadFromDomainController {$true | $false}]
[-ResultSize Size] [-SortBy Value]
```

Usage
```
Get-MailUser -Identity "aaron1" | fl

Get-MailUser -OrganizationalUnit "marketing" | fl
```

NOTE By default, Get-MailUser lists the name and recipient type for matches. In the example, fl is an alias for Format-List and is used to get detailed information about matching entries.

You can create a new mail-enabled user account using the New-MailUser cmdlet. Sample 5-2 shows the syntax and usage. When prompted, provide a secure password for the user account.

NOTE The syntax and usage are entered on multiple lines for ease of reference. You must enter the command-line values for a cmdlet on a single line.

SAMPLE 5-2 New-MailUser cmdlet syntax and usage

```
Syntax
New-MailUser -Name DisplayName -ExternalEmailAddress EmailAddress
{AddtlParams1}

New-MailUser -Name DisplayName -ExternalEmailAddress EmailAddress
-Password Password -UserPrincipalName UserNameAndSuffix {AddtlParams1}

New-MailUser -Name DisplayName -FederatedIdentity FederatedId
-WindowsLiveID WindowsLiveId {AddtlParams2}

New-MailUser -Name DisplayName -Password Password -WindowsLiveID
WindowsLiveId [-EvictLiveId {$true | $false}] {AddtlParams2}

New-MailUser -Name DisplayName -WindowsLiveID WindowsLiveId
-UseExistingLiveId {$true | $false} {AddtlParams2}

{AddtlParams1}
[-Alias ExchangeAlias] [-ArbitrationMailbox ModeratorMailbox]
[-DisplayName Name] [-DomainController FullyQualifiedName] [-FirstName
FirstName] [-Initials Initials] [-LastName LastName]
[-MacAttachmentFormat <BinHex | UuEncode | AppleSingle | AppleDouble>]
[-MessageBodyFormat <Text | Html | TextAndHtml>] [-MessageFormat <Text |
Mime>] [-ModeratedBy Moderators] [-ModerationEnabled <$true | $false>]
[-Organization OrgName] [-OrganizationalUnit OUName] [-PrimarySmtpAddress
}SmtpAddress] [-ResetPasswordOnNextLogon <$true | $false>]
}[-SamAccountName PreWin2000Name] [-SendModerationNotifications <Never |
Internal | Always>] [-UsePreferMessageFormat <$true | $false>]

{AddtlParams2}
[-Alias ExchangeAlias] [-ArbitrationMailbox ModeratorMailbox]
[-DisplayName Name] [-DomainController FullyQualifiedName] [-FirstName
FirstName] [-Initials Initials] [-LastName LastName] [-ModeratedBy
Moderators] [-ModerationEnabled <$true | $false>] [-Organization OrgName]
[-OrganizationalUnit OUName] [-PrimarySmtpAddress SmtpAddress]
[-RemotePowerShellEnabled <$true:$false>] [-ResetPasswordOnNextLogon
<$true | $false>] [-SamAccountName PreWin2000Name]
[-SendModerationNotifications <Never | Internal | Always>]
```

Usage
```
New-MailUser -Name "Frank Miller" -Alias "Frankm"
-OrganizationalUnit "cpandl.com/Technology"
-UserPrincipalName "Frankm@cpandl.com" -SamAccountName "Frankm"
-FirstName "Frank" -Initials "" -LastName "Miller"
-ResetPasswordOnNextLogon $false
-ExternalEmailAddress "SMTP:Frankm@hotmail.com"
```

Mail-Enabling Existing User Accounts

When a user already has an account in Active Directory, you can mail-enable the account using the Exchange Management Console and the Exchange Management Shell. In the Exchange Management Console, you can mail-enable an existing user account by completing the following steps:

1. In the Exchange Management Console, expand and then select the Recipient Configuration node.

   NOTE If you want to create the user account in a domain other than the current one, you first need to set the scope for the Recipient Configuration node, as discussed previously in "Finding Existing Mailboxes, Contacts, and Groups."

2. Right-click the Recipient Configuration node, and then select New Mail User. This starts the New Mail User Wizard.

3. On the Introduction page, select Existing User and then click Browse. This displays the Select User dialog box.

4. In the Select User dialog box, select the user account you want to mail-enable and then click OK. User accounts for the current domain are listed by name and organizational unit.

   NOTE Accounts listed don't yet have an Exchange mailbox or e-mail association. If you don't see the user you want to use, you may need to change the scope by selecting Modify Recipient Picker Scope on the Scope menu, selecting the appropriate scope using the options provided, and then clicking OK.

5. Click Next. On the Mail Settings page, enter an Exchange alias for the user. The Exchange Management Console uses the alias to set the user's e-mail address.

6. To the right of the External E-Mail Address text box is an Edit button. Click the down arrow next to the Edit button to display two options:

   - **SMTP Address** Select SMTP Address to associate a standard SMTP e-mail address with the user. Enter the e-mail address, and then click OK.

   - **Custom Address** Click Custom Address to associate a custom e-mail address with the user. Enter the e-mail address, and then enter the e-mail address type. Click OK.

7. Click Next, and then click New. Exchange Management Console mail-enables the user account you previously selected. If an error occurs, the user account will not be mail-enabled. You will need to correct the problem and repeat this procedure. Click Finish.

You can mail-enable an existing user account using the Enable-MailUser cmdlet. Sample 5-3 shows the syntax and usage. For the identity parameter, you can use the user's display name, logon name, or user principal name.

SAMPLE 5-3 Enable-MailUser cmdlet syntax and usage

Syntax
```
Enable-MailUser -Identity Identity -ExternalEmailAddress EmailAddress
[-Alias ExchangeAlias] [-DisplayName Name] [-DomainController
FullyQualifiedName] [-MacAttachmentFormat <BinHex | UuEncode |
AppleSingle | AppleDouble>] [-MessageBodyFormat <Text | Html |
TextAndHtml>] [-MessageFormat <Text | Mime>] [-PrimarySmtpAddress
SmtpAddress] [-UsePreferMessageFormat <$true | $false>]
```

Usage
```
Enable-MailUser -Identity "cpandl.com/Marketing/Frank Miller"
-Alias "Frankm" -ExternalEmailAddress "SMTP:Frankm@hotmail.com"
```

Managing Mail-Enabled User Accounts

You can manage mail-enabled users in several ways. If a user account should no longer be mail-enabled, you can disable mail forwarding. To disable mail forwarding in the Exchange Management Console, right-click Mail User and then select Disable. When prompted to confirm, click Yes. At the Exchange Management Shell prompt, you can disable mail forwarding using the Disable-MailUser cmdlet, as shown in Sample 5-4.

SAMPLE 5-4 Disable-MailUser cmdlet syntax and usage

Syntax
```
Disable-MailUser -Identity Identity [-DomainController
FullyQualifiedName] [-IgnoreDefaultScope {$true | $false}]
```

Usage
```
Disable-MailUser -Identity "Frank Miller"
```

If you no longer need a mail-enabled user account, you can permanently remove it from Active Directory. To remove a mail-enabled user account in the Exchange Management Console, right-click the Mail User and then select Remove. When prompted to confirm, click Yes. At the Exchange Management Shell prompt, you can remove a mail-enabled user account by using the Remove-MailUser cmdlet, as shown in Sample 5-5.

Syntax
```
Remove-MailUser -Identity "Identity" [-DomainController DCName]
[-IgnoreDefaultScope {$true | $false}]
[-KeepWindowsLiveID {$true | $false}]
```

Usage
```
Remove-MailUser -Identity "Frank Miller"
```

Creating Domain User Accounts with Mailboxes

In the Exchange Management Console, you can create a new user account with a mailbox by completing the following steps:

1. In the Exchange Management Console, expand and then select the Recipient Configuration node.

   NOTE If you want to create the user account in a domain other than the current one, you first need to set the scope for the Recipient Configuration node, as discussed previously in "Finding Existing Mailboxes, Contacts, and Groups."

2. Right-click the Recipient Configuration node, and then select New Mailbox. This starts the New Mailbox Wizard.

3. Click Next twice to accept the default selections on the Introduction page (to create a user mailbox) and the User Type page (to create a new user account with a mailbox).

4. On the New Mailbox User Information page, shown in Figure 5-7, the Organizational Unit text box shows where in Active Directory the user account will be created. By default, this is the Users container in the current domain. Because you'll usually need to create new user accounts in a specific organizational unit rather than in the Users container, select the Specify The Organizational Unit check box and then click Browse. Use the Select Organizational Unit dialog box to choose the location in which to store the account, and then click OK.

5. Type the user's first name, middle initial, and last name in the text boxes provided. These values are used to create the Name entry, which is the user's display name.

6. As necessary, make changes to the Name text box. For example, you might want to type the name in LastName FirstName MiddleInitial format or in FirstName MiddleInitial LastName format. The full name must be no more than 64 characters in length.

7. In the User Logon Name text box, type the user's logon name. Use the drop-down list to select the domain with which you want to associate the account. This sets the fully qualified logon name.

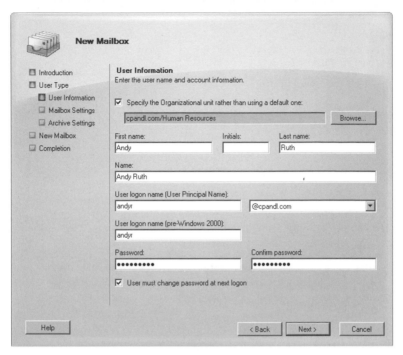

FIGURE 5-7 Configure the user's domain settings.

8. The first 20 characters of the logon name are used to set the pre–Windows 2000 logon name, which must be unique in the domain. If necessary, change the pre–Windows 2000 logon name.

9. Type and then confirm the password for the account. This password must follow the conventions of your organization's password policy. Typically, this means that the password must be at least six characters in length and must use three of the four available character types: lowercase letters, uppercase letters, numbers, and symbols.

10. If you want to ensure that the user changes the password at next logon, select the User Must Change Password At Next Logon check box. Click Next.

11. As shown in Figure 5-8, enter an Exchange alias for the user. The Exchange Management Console uses the alias to set the user's e-mail address.

12. If you want to specify a mailbox database rather than use one that is selected automatically, select the Specify Mailbox Database check box, and then click the Browse button to the right of the Mailbox Database text box. In the Se-lect Mailbox Database dialog box, choose the mailbox database in which the mailbox should be stored. Mailbox databases are listed by name as well as by associated server.

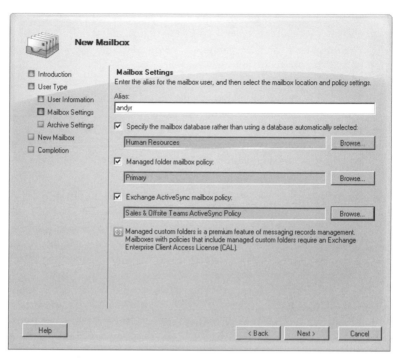

FIGURE 5-8 Configure the user's Exchange mailbox.

Exchange uses the mailbox provisioning load balancer to select a database to use when you create a mailbox and do not specify the mailbox database to use. For more information, see "Working with Active Mailbox Databases" and "Creating Mailbox Databases" in Chapter 10, "Mailbox and Public Folder Database Administration."

13. If you want to apply a managed folder mailbox policy to the mailbox, select the Managed Folder Mailbox Policy check box, and then click the related Browse button. In the Select Managed Folder Mailbox Policy dialog box, choose the policy to apply and then click OK.

Exchange Server 2010 uses managed folder mailbox policies in the same way as Exchange Server 2007. These policies are part of the Messaging Records Management feature. However, managed folder mailbox policies are being phased out in favor of retention policies and retention tagging. Because no default policy is applied to a new mailbox, you must explicitly assign a policy, either when you create the mailbox or later by editing the mailbox's properties.

TIP In a mailbox's Properties dialog box, you can specify the managed mailbox folder policy to use by double-clicking the Messaging Records Management option on the Mailbox Settings tab, selecting the Managed Folder Mailbox Policy check box, and clicking the related Browse button. In the dialog box provided, select the policy to use and then click OK.

14. If you want to apply an Exchange ActiveSync policy to the mailbox, select the Exchange ActiveSync Mailbox Policy check box, and then click the related Browse button. In the Exchange ActiveSync Mailbox Policy dialog box, choose the policy to apply and then click OK.

    When you install Exchange Server, a default Exchange ActiveSync mailbox policy is created, as discussed in "Understanding and Using Exchange Active-Sync Mailbox Policy" in Chapter 13, "Managing Client Access Servers." This policy is applied automatically to all new mailboxes you create unless you specify a different policy to use. To view the settings for the default policy, enter **get-activesyncmailboxpolicy –identity "Default"** in the Exchange Management Shell.

15. Click Next. If you want to create an archive mailbox for the user, select the related check box. Items in the user's mailbox will be moved automatically to the archive mailbox based on the default retention policy.

    When you install Exchange Server, a default retention policy is created for all archive mailboxes, as discussed in "Understanding and Using Retention Policy" in Chapter 6, "Mailbox Administration." This policy is applied automatically to all new mailboxes you create unless you specify a different policy to use. To view the settings for the default policy, enter **get-retentionpolicy –identity "Default Archive Policy"** in the Exchange Management Shell.

16. Click Next, and then click New to create the account and the related mailbox. If an error occurs during account or mailbox creation, the Exchange Management Console will create neither the account nor the related mailbox. You need to correct the problem and repeat this procedure.

17. Click Finish. For all mailbox-enabled accounts, an SMTP e-mail address is configured automatically. You can also add more addresses of the same type. For example, if Brian Johnson is the company's human resources administrator, he might have the primary SMTP address of brianj@adatum.com and an alternate SMTP address of resumes@adatum.com.

18. Creating the user account and mailbox isn't the final step. You might also want to do the following:

    - Add detailed contact information for the user, such as a business phone number and title.
    - Add the user to security and distribution groups.
    - Associate additional e-mail addresses with the account.
    - Enable or disable Exchange features for the account.
    - Modify the user's default delivery options, storage limits, and restrictions on the account.
    - Apply a retention policy other than the default to the mailbox.

In the Exchange Management Shell, you can create a user account with a mailbox by using the New-Mailbox cmdlet. Sample 5-6 provides the syntax and usage. When you are prompted, enter a secure password for the new user account.

SAMPLE 5-6 New-Mailbox cmdlet syntax and usage

```
Syntax
New-Mailbox -Name Name -Password Password
-UserPrincipalName UserNameAndSuffix
[-MailboxPlan <MailboxPlanIdParameter>] {AddtlParams} {ModParams}


New-Mailbox -Name Name -Password Password -WindowsLiveID WindowsLiveId
[-EvictLiveId {$true | $false}] [-MailboxPlan MailboxPlanId]
{AddtlParams} {ModParams}


New-Mailbox -Name Name -UserPrincipalName UserNameAndSuffix
[-MailboxPlan MailboxPlanId] {AddtlParams} {ModParams}


New-Mailbox -Name Name -UseExistingLiveId {$true | $false} -WindowsLiveID
WindowsLiveId [-MailboxPlan MailboxPlanId] {AddtlParams} {ModParams}


New-Mailbox -Name Name -Shared {$true | $false} -UserPrincipalName
UserNameAndSuffix [-Password Password] {AddtlParams} {ModParams}


New-Mailbox -Name Name -Room {$true | $false} -UserPrincipalName
UserNameAndSuffix [-Password Password] {AddtlParams} {ModParams}


New-Mailbox -Name Name -Equipment {$true | $false} -UserPrincipalName
UserNameAndSuffix [-Password Password] {AddtlParams} {ModParams}


New-Mailbox -Name Name -LinkedDomainController DCName
-LinkedMasterAccount Identity -UserPrincipalName UserNameAndSuffix
[-LinkedCredential Credential] [-Password Password]
{AddtlParams} {ModParams}


New-Mailbox -Name Name -ImportLiveId {$true | $false} -WindowsLiveID
WindowsLiveId {AddtlParams} {ModParams}


New-Mailbox -Name Name -Arbitration {$true | $false} -UserPrincipalName
UserNameAndSuffix [-Password Password] {AddtlParams}


New-Mailbox -Name Name -FederatedIdentity FederatedId -WindowsLiveID
WindowsLiveId {AddtlParams}


{ModParams}
[-ArbitrationMailbox ModeratorMailbox] [-ModeratedBy Moderators]
[-ModerationEnabled <$true | $false>] [-SendModerationNotifications
<Never | Internal | Always>]
```

```
{AddtlParams}
[-ActiveSyncMailboxPolicy MailboxPolicyId] [-Alias ExchangeAlias]
[-Archive {$true | $false}] [-Database DatabaseId] [-DisplayName Name]
[-DomainController FullyQualifiedName] [-FirstName FirstName]
[-Initials Initials] [-LastName LastName] [-ManagedFolderMailboxPolicy
MailboxPolicyId] [-ManagedFolderMailboxPolicyAllowed {$true | $false}]
[-Organization OrgName] [-OrganizationalUnit OUName] [-PrimarySmtpAddress
SmtpAddress] [-QueryBaseDNRestrictionEnabled <$true | $false>]
[-RemoteAccountPolicy RemoteAccountPolicyId] [-ResetPasswordOnNextLogon
<$true | $false>] [-SamAccountName PreWin2000Name] [-SharingPolicy
SharingPolicyId] [-ThrottlingPolicy ThrottlingPolicyId]


Usage
New-Mailbox -Name "Shane S. Kim" -Alias "shanek"
-OrganizationalUnit "cpandl.com/Engineering"
-Database "Engineering Primary"
-UserPrincipalName "shanek@cpandl.com" -SamAccountName "shanek"
-FirstName "Shane" -Initials "S" -LastName "Kim"
-ResetPasswordOnNextLogon $true -Archive $true
```

Adding Mailboxes to Existing Domain User Accounts

You don't have to create an Exchange mailbox when you create a user account.
You can create a mailbox for a user account any time you determine the mailbox is
needed. Using the Exchange Management Console, you can create mailboxes for
multiple user accounts at the same time by using bulk creation mode, or you can
create a single mailbox for a specific user by completing the following steps:

1. In the Exchange Management Console, expand and then select the Recipient
   Configuration node.

   NOTE If you want to create the user account in a domain other than the current
   one, you first need to set the scope for the Recipient Configuration node, as discussed previously in "Finding Existing Mailboxes, Contacts, and Groups."

2. Right-click the Recipient Configuration node, and then select New Mailbox.
   This starts the New Mailbox Wizard. Click Next on the New Mailbox page to
   accept the default action to create a user mailbox.

3. On the User Type page, select Existing Users and then click Add. This displays
   the Select User dialog box. In the Select User dialog box, shown in Figure 5-9,
   select the user account or accounts you want to mailbox-enable and then
   click OK. User accounts that are not yet mail-enabled or mailbox-enabled for
   the current domain are listed by name and organizational unit.

NOTE You can select multiple accounts individually by holding down the Ctrl key and then clicking the left mouse button on each object you want to select. You can select a series of accounts at once by holding down the Shift key, selecting the first object, and then clicking the last object.

4. Click Next. On the Mailbox Settings page, enter an Exchange alias for the user. The Exchange alias is used to set the user's e-mail address. When you are creating mailboxes for multiple accounts, the Exchange alias is set to the logon name by default, and you cannot change the default value.

5. Follow steps 12 to 17 in the previous section, "Creating Domain User Accounts with Mailboxes." A key exception is that you can't create an archive mailbox. If you want to create an archive mailbox for the user or users, do so after creating the mailbox. Select the Mailbox node in the Exchange Management Console, then select and right-click the mailboxes, and then select Enable Archive. When prompted to confirm, click Yes.

NOTE A mailbox can use either managed mailbox folder policy or retention policy, not both. If managed mailbox folder policy is enabled on a mailbox, you can't create an archive mailbox and enable retention policy.

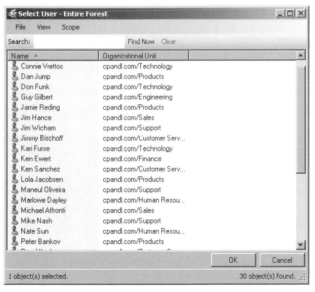

FIGURE 5-9 Find the user account you want to mailbox-enable.

In the Exchange Management Shell, you can add a mailbox to individual user accounts using the Enable-Mailbox cmdlet. Sample 5-7 provides the syntax and usage. If you want to create mailboxes for multiple accounts, you need to enter a separate command for each account.

Syntax
```
Enable-Mailbox -Identity Identity [-MailboxPlan MailboxPlanId]
{AddtlParams}


Enable-Mailbox -Identity Identity -Arbitration {$true | $false}
{AddtlParams}


Enable-Mailbox -Identity Identity -Room {$true | $false} {AddtlParams}


Enable-Mailbox -Identity Identity -Equipment {$true | $false}
{AddtlParams}


Enable-Mailbox -Identity Identity -Shared {$true | $false} {AddtlParams}


Enable-Mailbox -Identity Identity -LinkedDomainController DCName
-LinkedMasterAccount Identity [-LinkedCredential Credential]
{AddtlParams}


{AddtlParams}
[-ActiveSyncMailboxPolicy MailboxPolicyId] [-Alias ExchangeAlias]
[-Database DatabaseId] [-DisplayName Name] [-DomainController
FullyQualifiedName] [-MailboxPlan MailboxPlanId]
[-ManagedFolderMailboxPolicy MailboxPolicyId]
[-ManagedFolderMailboxPolicyAllowed {$true | $false}]
[-PrimarySmtpAddress SmtpAddress]
```

Usage
```
Enable-Mailbox -Identity "cpandl.com/Engineering/Oliver Lee"
-Alias "Oliver1" -Database "Engineering Primary"
```

Setting or Changing the Display Name and Logon Name for User Accounts

All user accounts have a display name, logon name, and pre–Windows 2000 logon name. These names can be different from the mailbox name and mailbox alias used by Exchange Server.

You can set contact information for a user account by completing the following steps:

1. In the Exchange Management Console, expand the Recipient Configuration node and then select the related Mailbox node.

2. Double-click the mailbox entry for the user with which you want to work.

3. On the User Information tab, use the following text boxes to set the user's display name and logon name:

   - **First Name, Initials, Last Name** Sets the user's full name
   - **Name** Sets the user's display name as seen in logon sessions and in Active Directory

NOTE The Simple Display Name field sets the display name used by systems that cannot interpret all the characters in the regular display name. Because the Simple Display Name field accepts only ASCII characters, the name is displayed correctly in all versions of the Exchange management interfaces.

4. Click OK to save your changes.

Setting or Changing Contact Information for User Accounts

You can set contact information for a user account by completing the following steps:

1. In the Exchange Management Console, expand the Recipient Configuration node and then select the related Mailbox node.
2. Double-click the mailbox entry for the user with which you want to work.
3. On the User Information tab, use the Web Page text box to set the URL of the user's home page, which can be on the Internet or the company intranet.
4. Click the Address And Phone tab. Use the text boxes provided to set the user's business address or home address. Normally, you'll want to enter the user's business address. This way, you can track the business locations and mailing addresses of users at various offices.
5. Use the Phone Numbers text boxes to set the user's primary business telephone, pager, fax, home telephone, and mobile telephone numbers.

NOTE You need to consider privacy issues before entering private information, such as home addresses and home phone numbers, for users. Discuss the matter with the appropriate groups in your organization, such as the human resources and legal departments. You might also want to get user consent before releasing home addresses.

6. Click the Organization tab. As appropriate, type the user's title, company, department, and office.
7. To specify the user's manager, select the Manager check box and then click Browse. In the Select Recipient User Or Contact dialog box, select the user's manager and then click OK. When you specify a manager, the user shows up as a direct report in the manager's account. Click Apply or OK to apply the changes.

Changing a User's Exchange Server Alias and Display Name

Each mailbox has an Exchange alias and display name associated with it. The Exchange alias is used with address lists as an alternative way of specifying the user in the To, Cc, or Bcc text boxes of an e-mail message. The alias also sets the primary SMTP address associated with the account.

TIP Whenever you change the Exchange alias, a new e-mail address can be generated and set as the default address for SMTP. The previous e-mail addresses for the account aren't deleted. Instead, these remain as alternatives to the defaults. To learn how to change or delete these additional e-mail addresses, see "Adding, Changing, and Removing E-Mail Addresses" later in this chapter.

To change the Exchange alias and mailbox name on a user account, complete the following steps:

1. In the Exchange Management Console, expand the Recipient Configuration node and then select the related Mailbox node.

2. Double-click the mailbox entry for the user with which you want to work.

3. On the General tab, the first text box sets the mailbox name. Change this text box if you'd like the mailbox to have a different display name.

4. The Alias text box sets the Exchange alias. If you'd like to assign a new alias, enter the new Exchange alias in this text box. Click OK.

Adding, Changing, and Removing E-Mail Addresses

When you create a mailbox-enabled user account, default e-mail addresses are created. Any time you update the user's Exchange alias, a new default e-mail address can be created. However, the old addresses aren't deleted. They remain as alternative e-mail addresses for the account.

To add, change, or remove an e-mail address, follow these steps:

1. In the Exchange Management Console, expand the Recipient Configuration node and then select the related Mailbox node.

2. Double-click the mailbox entry for the user with which you want to work.

3. On the E-Mail Addresses tab, shown in Figure 5-10, you can use the following techniques to manage the user's e-mail addresses:

   - **Create a new SMTP address** Click Add. Enter the SMTP e-mail address, and then click OK.

   - **Create a custom address** Click the small arrow to the right of the Add button, and then select Custom Address. Enter the e-mail address, and then enter the e-mail address type. Click OK.

   TIP Use SMTP as the address type for standard Internet e-mail addresses. For custom address types, such as X.400, you must manually enter the address in the proper format.

   - **Edit an existing address** Double-click the address entry, or click Edit on the toolbar. Modify the settings in the Address dialog box, and then click OK.

   - **Delete an existing address** Select the address, and then click the Remove button.

NOTE You can't delete the primary SMTP address without first promoting another e-mail address to the primary position. Exchange Server uses the primary SMTP address to send and receive messages.

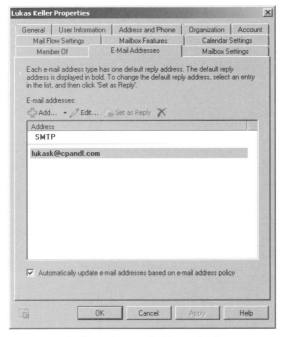

FIGURE 5-10 Configure the e-mail addresses for the user account.

Setting a Default Reply-To Address for a User Account

Each e-mail address type has one default reply address. This e-mail address sets the value of the Reply To text box. To change the default reply address, follow these steps:

1. In the Exchange Management Console, expand the Recipient Configuration node and then select the related Mailbox node.

2. Double-click the mailbox entry for the user with which you want to work.

3. Click the E-Mail Addresses tab. Current default e-mail addresses are highlighted with bold text. E-mail addresses that aren't highlighted are used only as alternative addresses for delivering messages to the current mailbox.

4. To change the current default settings, select an e-mail address that isn't highlighted and then click Set As Reply.

Changing a User's Web, Wireless Service, and Protocol Options

When you create user accounts with mailboxes, global settings determine the Web, wireless services, and protocols that are available. You can change these settings for individual users at any time by completing the following steps:

1. In the Exchange Management Console, expand the Recipient Configuration node and then select the related Mailbox node.

2. Double-click the mailbox entry for the user with which you want to work.

3. Click the Mailbox Features tab. As shown in Figure 5-11, configure the following Web, wireless services, and protocols for the user:

   - **Outlook Web App**   Permits the user to access the mailbox with a Web browser. Properties allow you to specify an Outlook Web App mailbox policy.

   - **Exchange ActiveSync**   Allows the user to synchronize the mailbox and to browse wireless devices. Properties allow you to specify an Exchange ActiveSync policy.

   - **Unified Messaging**   Allows the user to access unified messaging features, such as the voice browser. To enable or disable unified messaging, right-click the mailbox entry in the Exchange Management Console, click Enable Unified Messaging or Disable Unified Messaging as appropriate, and then follow the prompts.

   - **MAPI**   Permits the user to access the mailbox with a Messaging Application Programming Interface (MAPI) e-mail client

   - **POP3**   Permits the user to access the mailbox with a Post Office Protocol version 3 (POP3) e-mail client. Properties allow you to specify the MIME format of messages that are retrieved from the server.

   - **Internet Message Access Protocol version 4 (IMAP4)**   Permits the user to access the mailbox with an IMAP4 e-mail client Properties allow you to specify the MIME format of messages that are retrieved from the server.

   - **Archive**   Indicates whether an archive mailbox has been created for the user. Properties allow you to specify the name of the archive mailbox. To enable or disable an archive mailbox, right-click the mailbox entry in the Exchange Management Console, click Enable Archive or Disable Archive as appropriate, and then follow the prompts.

4. Select an option and then click Enable or Disable, as appropriate, to change the status. If an option has configurable properties and you want to change the properties, select the option and then click Properties. Make your changes, and then click OK. Click OK again to close the Properties dialog box.

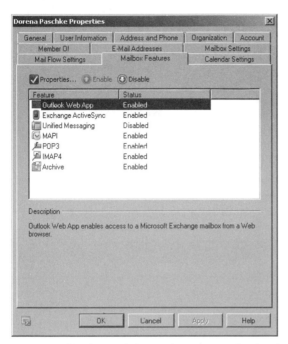

FIGURE 5-11 You change wireless service and protocol options for users in the Properties dialog box for each user.

Requiring User Accounts to Change Passwords

Group Policy settings typically require users to periodically change their passwords. Sometimes, you might have to ensure that a user changes her password the next time she logs on. For example, if you have to reset a user's password and you give her the password over the phone, you might want the user to change the password the next time she logs on.

You can set a user account to require the password to be changed on next logon by completing the following steps:

1. In the Exchange Management Console, expand the Recipient Configuration node and then select the related Mailbox node.

2. Double-click the mailbox entry for the user with which you want to work.

3. On the Account tab, select the User Must Change Password At Next Logon check box. Click OK.

You can use the Set-User cmdlet to perform the same task, following the syntax shown in Sample 5-8.

SAMPLE 5-8 Requiring a user password change

Syntax
```
Set-User -Identity UserIdentity
-ResetPasswordOnNextLogon <$false|$true>
```

Usage
```
Set-User -Identity "Oliver Lee" -ResetPasswordOnNextLogon $true
```

Deleting Mailboxes from User Accounts

When you disable a mailbox for a user account using the Exchange management tools, you permanently remove all Exchange attributes from the user object in Active Directory and mark the primary mailbox for deletion. Exchange Server then deletes the mailbox according to the retention period you set on the account or on the mailbox database. Because you only removed the user account's Exchange attributes, the user account still exists in Active Directory.

In the Exchange Management Console, you can delete a mailbox from a user account and all related Exchange attributes by right-clicking the mailbox and selecting Disable. When prompted to confirm this action, click Yes.

You can use the Disable-Mailbox cmdlet to delete mailboxes while retaining the user accounts as well. Sample 5-9 shows the syntax and usage.

SAMPLE 5-9 Disable-Mailbox cmdlet syntax and usage

Syntax
```
Disable-Mailbox -Identity Identifier [-DomainController DCName]
```

Usage
```
Disable-Mailbox -Identity "Oliver Lee"
```

Deleting User Accounts and Their Mailboxes

When you delete a user account and its mailbox using the Exchange management tools, you permanently remove the account from Active Directory and mark the primary mailbox for deletion. Exchange Server then deletes the mailbox according to the retention period you set on the account or on the mailbox database.

After you delete an account, you can't create an account with the same name and have the account automatically retain the same permissions as the original account. This is because the SID for the new account won't match the SID for the old account. However, that doesn't mean that after you delete an account, you can never again create an account with that same name. For example, a person might leave the company only to return a short while later. You can create an account using the same naming convention as before, but you'll have to redefine the permissions for that account.

Because deleting built-in accounts could have far-reaching effects on the domain, Windows doesn't let you delete built-in user accounts. In the Exchange Management Console, you can remove other types of accounts and the mailboxes associated with those accounts by right-clicking the mailboxes and selecting Remove. When prompted to confirm this action, click Yes.

NOTE Because Exchange security is based on domain authentication, you can't have a mailbox without an account. If you still need the mailbox for an account you want to delete, you can disable the account using Active Directory Users And Computers. Disabling the account in Active Directory prevents the user from logging on, but you can still access the mailbox if you need to. To disable an account, right-click the account in Active Directory Users And Computers and then select Disable Account. If you don't have permissions to use Active Directory Users And Computers, ask a domain administrator to disable the account for you.

You can use the Remove-Mailbox cmdlet to delete user accounts as well. Sample 5-10 shows the syntax. By default, the –Permanent flag is set to $false and mailboxes are retained in a disconnected state according to the mailbox retention policy. If you set the –Permanent flag to $true, the mailbox is removed from Exchange.

SAMPLE 5-10 Remove-Mailbox cmdlet syntax and usage

```
Syntax
Remove-Mailbox -Identity UserIdentity {AddtlParams}

Remove-Mailbox –Database DatabaseId -StoreMailboxIdentity StoreMailboxId
{AddtlParams}

{AddtlParams}
[-Arbitration <$false|$true>] [-DomainController DCName]
[-IgnoreDefaultScope {$true | $false}] [-KeepWindowsLiveID {$true |
$false}] [-Permanent <$false|$true>]
[-RemoveLastArbitrationMailboxAllowed {$true | $false}]
```

```
Usage
Remove-Mailbox -Identity "Oliver Lee"

Remove-Mailbox -Identity "Oliver Lee" –Permanent $true
```

Managing Contacts

Contacts represent people with whom you or others in your organization want to get in touch. Contacts can have directory information associated with them, but they don't have network logon privileges.

The only difference between a standard contact and a mail-enabled contact is the presence of e-mail addresses. A mail-enabled contact has one or more e-mail addresses associated with it; a standard contact doesn't. When a contact has an e-mail address, you can list the contact in the global address list or other address lists. This allows users to send messages to the contact.

In the Exchange Management Console, mail-enabled contacts and mail-enabled users are both listed in the Mail Contact node. Mail-enabled contacts are listed with the recipient type Mail Contact, and mail-enabled users are listed with the recipient type Mail User.

Creating Mail-Enabled Contacts

You can create and mail-enable a new contact by completing the following steps:

1. In the Exchange Management Console, expand the Recipient Configuration node and then select the related Mail Contact node.

2. Right-click the Mail Contact node, and then select New Mail Contact. This starts the New Mail Contact Wizard.

3. Click Next to accept the default selection on the Introduction page to create a new contact.

4. On the Contact Information page, shown in Figure 5-12, the Organizational Unit text box shows where in Active Directory the contact will be created. By default, this is the Users container in the current domain. Because you'll usually need to create new contacts in a specific organizational unit rather than in the Users container, select the Specify The Organizational Unit check box and then click Browse. Use the Select Organizational Unit dialog box to choose the location in which to store the contact, and then click OK.

5. Type the contact's first name, middle initial, and last name in the text boxes provided. These values are used to automatically create the following entries:

   - **Contact Name** The Contact Name is the name used in the Exchange Management Console.

   - **Display Name** The Display Name is displayed in the global address list and other address lists created for the organization. It is also used when addressing e-mail messages to the contact.

   - **Alias** The Alias is the Exchange alias for the contact. Aliases provide an alternative way of addressing users and contacts in To, Cc, and Bcc text boxes of e-mail messages.

6. To the right of the External E-Mail Address text box is an Edit button. Click the down arrow next to the Edit button to display two options:

   - **SMTP Address** Select SMTP Address to associate a standard SMTP e-mail address with the contact. Enter the e-mail address, and then click OK.

   - **Custom Address** Click Custom Address to associate a custom e-mail address with the contact. Enter the e-mail address, and then enter the e-mail address type. Click OK.

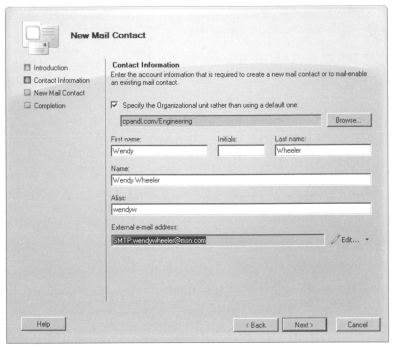

New Mail Contact

Introduction
Contact Information
New Mail Contact
Completion

Contact Information
Enter the account information that is required to create a new mail contact or to mail-enable an existing mail contact.

☑ Specify the Organizational unit rather than using a default one:

cpandl.com/Engineering   Browse...

First name: Initials: Last name:
Wendy   Wheeler

Name:
Wendy Wheeler

Alias:
wendyw

External e-mail address:
SMTP:wendywheeler@msn.com   ✎ Edit... ▾

Help   < Back   Next >   Cancel

FIGURE 5-12 Configure the contact information.

7. Click Next, and then click New. The Exchange Management Console creates the new contact and mail-enables it. If an error occurs, the contact will not be created. You will need to correct the problem and repeat this procedure.

8. Click Finish.

In the Exchange Management Shell, you can create a new mail-enabled contact using the New-MailContact cmdlet. Sample 5-11 provides the syntax and usage.

SAMPLE 5-11 New-MailContact cmdlet syntax and usage

Syntax
```
New-MailContact –Name Name –ExternalEmailAddress TYPE:EmailAddress
[-ArbitrationMailbox ModeratorMailbox] [-Alias ExchangeAlias]
[-DisplayName Name] [-DomainController DCName] [-FirstName FirstName]
[-Initials Initials] [-LastName LastName] [-MacAttachmentFormat <BinHex |
UuEncode | AppleSingle | AppleDouble>] [-MessageBodyFormat <Text | Html |
TextAndHtml>] [-MessageFormat <Text | Mime>] [-ModeratedBy Moderators]
[-ModerationEnabled <$true | $false>] [-Organization OrgName]
[-OrganizationalUnit OUName] [-PrimarySmtpAddress
SmtpAddress] [-SendModerationNotifications <Never | Internal | Always>]
[-UsePreferMessageFormat <$true | $false>]
```

```
New-MailContact -ExternalEmailAddress "SMTP:wendywheeler@msn.com"
-Name "Wendy Wheeler" -Alias "WendyWheeler"
-OrganizationalUnit "cpandl.com/Corporate Services"
-FirstName "Wendy" -Initials "" -LastName "Wheeler"
```

Mail-Enabling Existing Contacts

You can mail-enable an existing contact by completing the following steps:

1. In the Exchange Management Console, expand the Recipient Configuration node and then select the related Mail Contact node.

2. Right-click the Mail Contact node, and then choose New Contact. This starts the New Mail Contact Wizard.

3. On the Introduction page, select Existing Contact and then click Browse. This displays the Select Contact dialog box.

4. In the Select Contact dialog box, select the contact you want to mail-enable and then click OK. Contacts for the current domain are listed by name and organizational unit. You'll need to change the scope, as discussed previously, if you don't see the contact you want to use.

5. Click Next. To the right of the External E-Mail Address text box is an Edit button. Click the down arrow next to the Edit button to display two options:

   - **SMTP Address**   Click SMTP Address to associate a standard SMTP e-mail address with the contact. Enter the e-mail address, and then click OK.

   - **Custom Address**   Click Custom Address to associate a custom e-mail address with the contact. Enter the e-mail address, and then enter the e-mail address type. Click OK.

6. Click Next, and then click New. The Exchange Management Console mail-enables the selected contact. If an error occurs, the contact will not be created. You will need to correct the problem and repeat this procedure.

7. Click Finish.

In the Exchange Management Shell, you can mail-enable an existing contact using the Enable-MailContact cmdlet. Sample 5-12 provides the syntax and usage.

SAMPLE 5-12 Enable-MailContact cmdlet syntax and usage

```
Enable-MailContact -Identity ContactId -ExternalEmailAddress EmailAddress
[-Alias ExchangeAlias] [-DisplayName Name] [-DomainController
FullyQualifiedName] [-MacAttachmentFormat <BinHex | UuEncode |
AppleSingle | AppleDouble>] [-MessageBodyFormat <Text | Html |
TextAndHtml>] [-MessageFormat <Text | Mime>] [-PrimarySmtpAddress
SmtpAddress] [-UsePreferMessageFormat <$true | $false>]
```

Setting or Changing a Contact's Name and Alias

All mail-enabled contacts and users have the following name components:

- **First Name, Initials, Last Name**   The first name, initials, and last name of the contact
- **Exchange Name**   The name used in the Exchange Management Console
- **Display Name**   The name displayed in the global address list
- **Alias**   The Exchange alias for the contact

You can set or change name and alias information for a mail-enabled contact or user by completing the following steps:

1. In the Exchange Management Console, expand the Recipient Configuration node and then select the related Mail Contact node.
2. Double-click the name of the mail-enabled contact or user you want to work with. The Properties dialog box appears.
3. On the General tab, the first text box sets the name used in the Exchange Management Console. Change this text box if you'd like the mail-enabled contact or user to have a different name.
4. The Alias text box sets the Exchange alias. If you'd like to assign a new alias, enter the new Exchange alias in this text box.
5. On the Contact Information or User Information tab, use the following text boxes to set the full name and display name to use:
   - **First Name, Initials, Last Name**   Sets the contact's full name
   - **Name**   Sets the contact's display name as seen in the global address list
6. Click OK to save your changes.

Setting Additional Directory Information for Contacts

You can set additional directory information for a mail-enabled contact or user by completing the following steps:

1. In the Exchange Management Console, expand the Recipient Configuration node and then select the related Mail Contact node.
2. Double-click the name of the mail-enabled contact or user you want to work with. The Properties dialog box appears.
3. On the Contact Information or User Information tab, use the Web Page text box to set the URL of the home page for the mail-enabled contact or user, which can be on the Internet or the company intranet.

4. On the Address And Phone tab, use the text boxes provided to set the business address or home address to use. Normally, you'll want to enter the business address rather than a personal address. This way, you can track the business locations and mailing addresses of contacts at various offices.

5. Use the Phone Numbers text boxes to set the primary business telephone, pager, fax, home telephone, and mobile telephone numbers.

6. On the Organization tab, type the title, company, department, and office, as appropriate.

7. To specify the manager of a mail-enabled contact or user, select the Manager check box and then click Browse. In the Select Recipient User Or Contact dialog box, select the contact's manager. When you specify a manager, the contact shows up as a direct report in the manager's account. Click Apply or OK to apply the changes.

Changing E-Mail Addresses Associated with Contacts

Mail-enabled contacts and users have several types of e-mail addresses associated with them:

- An internal, automatically generated e-mail address used for routing within the organization

- An external e-mail address to which mail routed internally is forwarded for delivery

You can change the e-mail addresses associated with a mail-enabled contact or user by completing the following steps:

1. In the Exchange Management Console, expand the Recipient Configuration node and then select the related Mail Contact node.

2. Double-click the name of the mail-enabled contact or user you want to work with. The Properties dialog box appears.

3. On the E-Mail Addresses tab, e-mail addresses are listed by protocol and type. If an e-mail address is also specified as an external address, it is listed according to its protocol type, such as SMTP or X.400, and under the External heading. You can use the following techniques to manage a contact's e-mail addresses:

   - **Create a new SMTP address**   Click the down arrow next to the Add button, and then select SMTP Address. Enter the e-mail address, and then click OK.

   - **Create a custom address**   Click the down arrow next to the Add button, and then select Custom Address. Enter the e-mail address, enter the e-mail address type, and click OK.

   - **Edit an existing address**   Double-click the address entry, or click Edit on the toolbar. Modify the settings in the Address dialog box, and then click OK.

   - **Delete an existing address**   Select the address, and then click the Remove button.

4. To set an e-mail address as the default Reply To address, select it, and then click Set As Reply.

5. To specify that an e-mail address is an external address, select it, and then click Set As External. Click OK.

Disabling Contacts and Removing Exchange Attributes

When you disable a contact using the Exchange management tools, you permanently remove the contact from the Exchange database, but you do not remove it from Active Directory. In the Exchange Management Console, you can remove contacts by right-clicking them and selecting Disable. When prompted to confirm this action, click Yes.

You can use the Disable-MailContact cmdlet to remove Exchange attributes from contacts while retaining the contact in Active Directory. Sample 5-13 shows the syntax and usage.

SAMPLE 5-13 Disable-MailContact cmdlet syntax and usage

Syntax
```
Disable-MailContact -Identity ContactIdentity
```

Usage
```
Disable-MailContact -Identity "David So"
```

Deleting Contacts

When you delete a contact using the Exchange management tools, you permanently remove it from Active Directory and from the Exchange database. In the Exchange Management Console, you can delete contacts by right-clicking them and selecting Remove. When prompted to confirm this action, click Yes.

You can use the Remove-MailContact cmdlet to delete contacts as well. Sample 5-14 shows the syntax and usage.

SAMPLE 5-14 Remove-MailContact cmdlet syntax and usage

Syntax
```
Remove-MailContact -Identity ContactIdentity
```

Usage
```
Remove-Mailbox -Identity "Henrik Larsen"
```

Mailbox Administration

The difference between a good Microsoft Exchange administrator and a great one is the attention he or she pays to mailbox administration. Mailboxes are private storage places for messages you've sent and received, and they are created as part of private mailbox databases in Exchange. Mailboxes have many properties that control mail delivery, permissions, and storage limits. You can configure most mailbox settings on a per-mailbox basis. However, you cannot change some settings without moving mailboxes to a different mailbox database or changing the settings of the mailbox database itself. For example, you set the storage location on the file system, the default public folder database for the mailbox, and the default offline address book on a per-mailbox-database basis. Keep this in mind when performing capacity planning and when deciding which mailbox database to use for a particular mailbox.

Creating Special-Purpose Mailboxes

Exchange Server 2010 makes it easy to create several special-purpose mailbox types, including:

- **Room mailbox**   A room mailbox is a mailbox for room scheduling.
- **Equipment mailbox**   An equipment mailbox is a mailbox for equipment scheduling.
- **Linked mailbox**   A linked mailbox is a mailbox for a user from a separate, trusted forest.
- **Forwarding mailbox**   A forwarding mailbox is a mailbox that can receive mail and forward it off-site.

- **Archive mailbox**   An archive mailbox is used to store a user's messages, such as might be required for executives and needed by some managers.
- **Arbitration mailbox**   An arbitration mailbox is used to manage approval requests, such as may be required for handling moderated recipients and distribution group membership approval.
- **Discovery mailbox**   A discovery mailbox is the target for Discovery searches and can't be converted to another mailbox type once it's created.
- **Shared mailbox**   A shared mailbox is a mailbox that is shared by multiple users, such as a general mailbox for customer inquiries.

The sections that follow discuss techniques for working with these special-purpose mailboxes.

Using Room and Equipment Mailboxes

You use room and equipment mailboxes for scheduling purposes only. You'll find that

- Room mailboxes are useful when you have conference rooms, training rooms, and other rooms for which you need to coordinate the use.
- Equipment mailboxes are useful when you have projectors, media carts, or other items of equipment for which you need to coordinate the use.

Every room and equipment mailbox must have a separate user account associated with it. Although these accounts are required so that the mailboxes can be used for scheduling, the accounts are disabled by default so that they cannot be used for logon. To ensure that the resource accounts do not get enabled accidentally, you need to coordinate closely with other administrators in your organization.

NOTE The Exchange Management Console doesn't show the enabled or disabled status of user accounts. The only way to check the status is to use domain administration tools.

Because the number of scheduled rooms and amount of equipment grows as your organization grows, you'll want to carefully consider the naming conventions you use with rooms and equipment:

- With rooms, you'll typically want to use display names that clearly identify the rooms' physical locations. For example, you might have rooms named "Conference Room 28 on Fifth Floor" or "Building 83 Room 15."
- With equipment, you'll typically want to identify the type of equipment, the equipment's characteristics, and the equipment's relative location. For example, you might have equipment named "NEC HD Projector at Seattle Office" or "Fifth Floor Media Cart."

As with standard user mailboxes, room and equipment mailboxes have contact information associated with them. To make it easier to find rooms and equipment, you should provide as much information as possible. Specifically, you can make rooms easier for users to work with by using these techniques:

- If a room has a conference or call-in phone, enter this phone number as the business phone number on the Address And Phone tab of the Mailbox Properties dialog box.
- Specify the location details in the Office text box on the Organization tab of the Mailbox Properties dialog box.
- Specify the room capacity in the Resource Capacity text box on the Resource Information tab of the Mailbox Properties dialog box.

The business phone, location, and capacity are displayed in Microsoft Office Outlook.

After you've set up mailboxes for your rooms and equipment, scheduling the rooms and equipment is straightforward. In Exchange, room and equipment availability is tracked using free/busy data. In Outlook, a user who wants to reserve rooms, equipment, or both simply makes a meeting request that includes the rooms and equipment that are required for the meeting.

The steps to schedule a meeting and reserve equipment are as follows:

1. Create a meeting request:
   - In Outlook 2007, click New, and then select Meeting Request. Or press Ctrl+Shift+Q.
   - In Outlook 2010, click New Items, and then select Meeting. Or press Ctrl+Shift+Q.

2. In the To text box, invite the individuals who should attend the meeting by typing their display names, Exchange aliases, or e-mail addresses, as appropriate. (See Figure 6-1.)

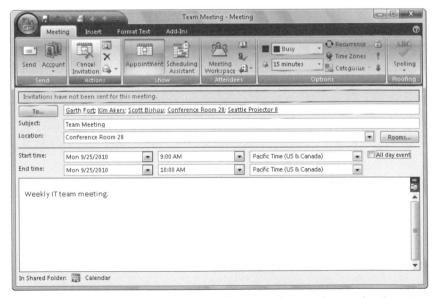

FIGURE 6-1 You can schedule a meeting that includes a reserved room and reserved equipment.

3. Type the display name, Exchange alias, or e-mail address for any equipment you need to reserve.

4. Click the Rooms button to the right of the Location text box. The Select Rooms dialog box appears, as shown in Figure 6-2. By default, the Select Rooms dialog box uses the All Rooms address book. Rooms are added to this address book automatically when you create them.

5. Double-click the room you want to use. This adds the room to the Rooms list. Click OK to close the Select Rooms dialog box.

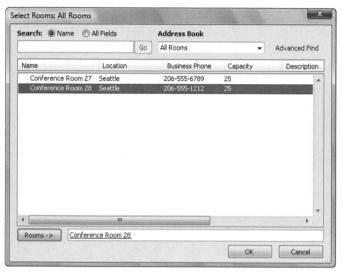

FIGURE 6-2 Select a room to use for the meeting.

6. In the Subject text box, type the meeting subject.

7. Use the Start Time and End Time options to schedule the start and end times for the meeting.

8. Click Scheduling Assistant to view the free/busy data for the invited users and the selected resources.

9. After you type a message to accompany the meeting request, click Send.

Creating Room and Equipment Mailboxes

You can create room and equipment mailboxes by completing the following steps:

1. In the Exchange Management Console, expand the Recipient Configuration node and then select the Mailbox node.

NOTE If you want to create the user account for the room or equipment mailbox in a domain other than the current one, you first need to set the scope for the Mailbox node, as discussed in the "Finding Existing Mailboxes, Contacts, and Groups" section of Chapter 5, "User and Contact Administration."

2. Right-click the Mailbox node, and then select New Mailbox. This starts the New Mailbox Wizard.

3. On the Introduction page, select either Room Mailbox or Equipment Mailbox, as appropriate, and then click Next.

4. On the User Type page, verify that New User is selected and then click Next. Each room or piece of equipment must have a separate user account. This is necessary to track the unique free/busy data for the room or piece of equipment.

5. On the User Information page, the Organizational Unit text box shows where in Active Directory the user account will be created. By default, this is the Users container in the current domain. Because you'll usually need to create room and equipment accounts in a specific organizational unit rather than in the Users container, select the Specify The Organizational Unit check box and then click Browse. Use the Select Organizational Unit dialog box to choose the location in which to store the account, and then click OK.

6. Type a descriptive display name in the Name text box.

7. In the User Logon Name text box, type the logon name. Use the drop-down list to select the domain with which the account is to be associated. This sets the fully qualified logon name.

8. The first 20 characters of the logon name are used to set the pre–Microsoft Windows 2000 logon name, which must be unique in the domain. If necessary, change the pre–Windows 2000 logon name.

9. Type and then confirm the password for the account. Even though the account is disabled by default, this password must follow the conventions of your organization's password policy.

10. Click Next. On the Mailbox Settings page, enter an Exchange alias. The Exchange alias is used to set the default e-mail address.

11. If you want to specify a mailbox database rather than use an automatically selected one, select the Specify Mailbox Database check box, and then click the Browse button to the right of the Mailbox Database text box. In the Select Mailbox Database dialog box, choose the mailbox database in which the mailbox should be stored. Mailbox databases are listed by name as well as by associated server.

12. If you want to create an archive mailbox for the resource, select the related check box. Items in the mailbox will be moved automatically to the archive mailbox based on the default retention policy.

13. Click Next, and then click New to create the account and the related mailbox. If an error occurs during account or mailbox creation, neither the account nor the related mailbox will be created. You need to correct the problem and repeat this procedure.

14. Click Finish. For all mailbox-enabled accounts, a Simple Mail Transfer Protocol (SMTP) e-mail address is configured automatically.

In the Exchange Management Shell, you can create a user account with a mailbox for rooms and equipment by using the New-Mailbox cmdlet. Sample 6-1 provides the syntax and usage. Although the account is disabled by default, you must enter a secure password for the account when prompted.

NOTE For rooms, you must use the –Room parameter. For equipment, you must use the –Equipment parameter. By default, when you use either parameter, the related value is set as $true.

SAMPLE 6-1 Creating room and equipment mailboxes

Syntax

```
New-Mailbox -Name 'DisplayName' -Alias 'ExchangeAlias'
 -OrganizationalUnit 'OrganizationalUnit'
 -UserPrincipalName 'LogonName' -SamAccountName 'prewin2000logon'
 -FirstName '' -Initials '' -LastName ''
 -Database 'Server\MailboxDatabase'
 [-Room <$false|$true> | -Equipment <$false|$true> ]
```

Usage

```
New-Mailbox -Name 'Conference Room 27' -Alias 'room27'
 -OrganizationalUnit 'cpandl.com/Sales'
 -UserPrincipalName 'room27@cpandl.com' -SamAccountName 'room27'
 -FirstName '' -Initials '' -LastName ''
 -Database 'Sales Primary'
 -Room
```

Creating Linked Mailboxes

A linked mailbox is a mailbox that is accessed by a user in a separate, trusted forest. Typically, you use linked mailboxes when your organization's mailbox servers are in a separate resource forest and you want to ensure that users can access free/busy data across these forests.

All linked mailboxes have two user account associations:

- A unique user account in the same forest as the Mailbox server. The same forest user account is disabled automatically so that it cannot be used for logon.

- A unique user account in a separate forest for which you are creating a link. The separate forest user account is enabled so that it can be used for logon.

You can create a linked mailbox by completing the following steps:

1. In the Exchange Management Console, expand the Recipient Configuration node and then select the Mailbox node.

2. Right-click the Mailbox node, and then select New Mailbox. This starts the New Mailbox Wizard.

3. On the Introduction page, select Linked Mailbox and then click Next.

4. On the User Type page, verify that New User is selected and then click Next.

5. On the User Information page, the Organizational Unit text box shows where in Active Directory the user account will be created. By default, this is the Users container in the current domain. Select the Specify The Organizational Unit check box and then click Browse to create the new user account in a different container. Use the Select Organizational Unit dialog box to choose the location in which to store the account, and then click OK.

6. Type the user's first name, middle initial, and last name in the text boxes provided. These values are used to create the Name entry, which is the user's display name.

7. In the User Logon Name text box, type the user's logon name. Use the drop-down list to select the domain with which the account is to be associated. This sets the fully qualified logon name.

8. The first 20 characters of the logon name are used to set the pre–Windows 2000 logon name, which must be unique in the domain. If necessary, change the pre–Windows 2000 logon name.

9. Type and then confirm the password for the account. Although the account will not be used for logon, this password must follow the conventions of your organization's password policy.

10. Click Next. Enter an Exchange alias for the user. Make sure the alias matches the one used in the resource forest.

11. If you want to specify a mailbox database rather than use an automatically selected on, select the Specify Mailbox Database check box, and then click the Browse button to the right of the Mailbox Database text box. In the Select Mailbox Database dialog box, choose the mailbox database in which the mailbox should be stored. Mailbox databases are listed by name as well as by associated server.

12. Click Next. On the Master Account page, click Browse to the right of the Linked Forest text box. In the Select Trusted Forest Or Domain dialog box, select the linked forest or domain in which the user's original account is located and then click OK.

13. If you need additional administrative permissions to access the linked forest, select the Use The Following Windows Account check box. Then type the user name and password for an administrator account in this forest.

14. Click the Browse button to the right of the Linked Domain Controller text box. In the Select Domain Controller dialog box, select a domain controller in the linked forest and then click OK.

15. Click the Browse button to the right of the Linked Master Account text box. Use the options in the Select User dialog box to select the original user account in the linked forest, and then click OK.

16. Click Next, and then click New to create the account and the related mailbox. If an error occurs during account or mailbox creation, neither the account nor the related mailbox will be created. You will need to correct the problem and repeat this procedure.

17. Click Finish. For all mailbox-enabled accounts, an SMTP e-mail address is configured automatically.

In the Exchange Management Shell, you can create a user account with a linked mailbox by using the New-Mailbox cmdlet. Sample 6-2 provides the syntax and usage. You'll be prompted for two sets of credentials: one for the new user account and one for an administrator account in the linked forest.

SAMPLE 6-2 Creating linked mailboxes

Syntax

```
New-Mailbox -Name 'DisplayName' -Alias 'ExchangeAlias'
 -OrganizationalUnit 'OrganizationalUnit'
 -Database 'Database'
 -UserPrincipalName 'LogonName' -SamAccountName 'prewin2000logon'
 -FirstName 'FirstName' -Initials 'Initial' -LastName 'LastName'
 -ResetPasswordOnNextLogon State
 -LinkedDomainController 'LinkedDC'
 -LinkedMasterAccount 'domain\user'
 -LinkedCredential:(Get-Credential 'domain\administrator')
```

Usage

```
New-Mailbox -Name 'Wendy Richardson' -Alias 'wendyr'
 -OrganizationalUnit 'cpandl.com/Sales'
 -Database 'Corporate Services Primary'
 -UserPrincipalName 'wendyr@cpandl.com' -SamAccountName 'wendyr'
 -FirstName 'Wendy' -Initials '' -LastName 'Richardson'
 -ResetPasswordOnNextLogon $true
 -LinkedDomainController 'CohoDC58'
 -LinkedMasterAccount 'coho\wrichardson'
 -LinkedCredential:(Get-Credential 'coho\williams')
```

Creating Forwarding Mailboxes

Custom recipients, such as mail-enabled users and contacts, don't normally receive mail from users outside the organization because a custom recipient doesn't have an e-mail address that resolves to a specific mailbox in your organization. At times, though, you might want external users, applications, or mail systems to be able to send mail to an address within your organization and then have Exchange forward this mail to an external mailbox.

> **TIP** You can send and receive text messages using Outlook Web App in Exchange 2010, or you can send text messages the old fashioned way. In my organization, I've created forwarding mailboxes for text-messaging and pager alerts. This simple solution lets managers (and monitoring systems) within the organization quickly and easily send text messages to IT personnel. Here, I've set up mail-enabled contacts for each text messaging e-mail address, such as 8085551212@adatum.com, and then created a mailbox that forwards e-mail to the custom recipient. Generally, the display name of the mail-enabled contact is in the form Alert *User Name*, such as Alert William Stanek. The display name and e-mail address for the mailbox are in the form Z *LastName* and AE-*MailAddress@myorg.com*, such as Z Stanek and AWilliamS@adatum.com, respectively. Afterward, I hide the mailbox so that it isn't displayed in the global address list or in other address lists; this way, users can see only the Alert William Stanek mailbox.

To create a user account to receive mail and forward it off-site, follow these steps:

1. Using the Exchange Management Console, create a mail-enabled contact for the user. Name the contact Alert *User Name,* such as Alert William Stanek. Be sure to establish an external e-mail address for the contact that refers to the user's Internet address.

2. Using the Exchange Management Console, create a mailbox-enabled user account in the domain. Name the account with the appropriate display name, such as Z William Stanek. Be sure to create an Exchange mailbox for the account, but don't grant any special permission to the account. You might want to restrict the account so that the user can't log on to any servers in the domain.

3. Using the Exchange Management Console, access the Properties dialog box for the user's mailbox.

4. On the Mail Flow Settings tab, select Delivery Options and then click Properties.

5. In the Delivery Options dialog box, select the Forward To check box and then click Browse.

6. In the Select Recipient dialog box, select the mail-enabled contact you created earlier and then click OK three times. You can now use the user account to forward mail to the external mailbox.

Creating Archive Mailboxes

Each user can have an alternate mailbox for archives. An archive mailbox is used to store a user's old messages, such as might be required for executives and needed by some managers. In Outlook and Outlook Web App, users can access archive mailboxes in much the same way as they access their regular mailbox.

You can create a user's archive mailbox at the same time you create the user's standard mailbox. To create an archive mailbox, right-click the standard mailbox in the Exchange Management Console, select Enable Archive, review the dialog box, and then click Yes when prompted to confirm. Using the Exchange Management Shell, you can create an archive mailbox using Enable-Mailbox. The basic syntax is as follows:

```
Enable-Mailbox [-Identity] Identity -Archive
```

such as:

```
enable-mailbox cpandl.com/engineering/tonyg -archive
```

Because each user can have only one archive mailbox, you get an error if the user already has an archive mailbox. Items in the user's mailbox will be moved automatically to the archive mailbox based on the default retention policy. When you install Exchange Server, a default retention policy is created for all archive mailboxes.

Whether you use the Exchange Management Console or the Exchange Management Shell, several other parameters are set for archive mailboxes. The default name for the archive mailbox is set as Online Archive – *UserDisplayName,* such as Online Archive – Vamsi Kuppa. The default quota and warning quota are set as unlimited.

You can change the archive name and set quotas by using Set-Mailbox. The basic syntax is as follows:

```
Set-Mailbox [-Identity] Identity -ArchiveName Name
-ArchiveQuota Quota -ArchiveWarningQuota Quota
```

When you set a quota, specify the value with MB (for megabytes), GB (for gigabytes), or TB (for terabytes), or enter 'Unlimited' to remove the quota. Here is an example:

```
set-mailbox cpandl.com/engineering/tonyg
-ArchiveQuota '2GB' -ArchiveWarningQuota '900MB'
```

In the Exchange Management Console, you can set or remove a quota warning for an archive mailbox by right-clicking the entry for the user's standard mailbox and selecting Properties. In the Properties dialog box, on the Mailbox Settings tab, double-click Archive Quota. To set a quota warning, select Issue Warning At, and then enter a quota in megabytes. To remove a quota, clear Issue Warning At.

To disable an archive mailbox, right-click the mailbox in the Exchange Management Console, select Disable Archive, and then click Yes when prompted to confirm. In the Exchange Management Shell, you can disable an archive mailbox by using Disable-Mailbox. The basic syntax is as follows:

```
Disable-Mailbox [-Identity] Identity -Archive
```

such as:

```
disable-mailbox cpandl.com/engineering/tonyg -archive
```

Creating Arbitration Mailboxes

Exchange moderated transport requires all e-mail messages sent to specific recipients to be approved by moderators. You can configure any type of recipient as a moderated recipient, and Exchange will ensure that all messages sent to those recipients go through an approval process.

Distribution groups are the only types of recipients that use moderation by default. Membership in distribution groups can be closed, owner approved or open. While any Exchange recipient can join an open distribution group, joining a closed group requires approval. Group owners receive join and remove requests and can either approve or deny those requests.

Distribution groups can also be unmoderated or moderated. With unmoderated groups, any approved sender (which is all senders by default) can send messages to the group. With moderated groups, messages are sent to moderators for approval before being distributed to members of the group. The only exception is for a message sent by a moderator. A message from a moderator is delivered immediately because a moderator has the authority to determine what is and isn't an appropriate message.

NOTE The default moderator for a distribution group is the group's owner.

Arbitration mailboxes are used to store messages that are awaiting approval. When you install Exchange Server 2010, a default arbitration mailbox is created. For the purposes of load balancing or for other reasons, you can convert other mailboxes to the Arbitration mailbox type by using the Enable-Mailbox cmdlet. The basic syntax is as follows:

```
Enable-Mailbox [-Identity] Identity -Arbitration
```

such as:

```
enable-mailbox cpandl.com/users/moderatedmail -Arbitration
```

You can create an arbitration mailbox by using New-Mailbox as shown in this example:

```
New-Mailbox ModeratedMail -Arbitration -UserPrincipalName
ModeratedMail@cpand1.com
```

Creating Discovery Mailboxes

Exchange Discovery helps organizations comply with legal discovery require-ments and can also be used as an aid in internal investigations or as part of regular monitoring of e-mail content. Exchange Discovery uses content indexes created by Exchange Search to speed up the search process.

> **NOTE** By default, Exchange administrators do not have sufficient rights to perform Discovery searches. Only users with the Discovery Management role can perform Discovery searches.

You use the Exchange Control Panel (ECP) to perform searches. After you log on, click Reporting in the left pane, and then click the Mailbox Searches tab. Discov-ery searches are performed against designated mailboxes or all mailboxes in the Exchange organization. Items in mailboxes that match the Discovery search are copied to a target mailbox. Only mailboxes specifically designated as Discovery mailboxes can be used as targets.

> **TIP** By default, Discovery search does not include items that cannot be indexed by Exchange Search. To include such items in the search results, select the Include Items That Can't Be Searched check box in Exchange Control Panel.

When you install Exchange Server 2010, a default discovery mailbox is created. You can convert other mailboxes to the Discovery mailbox type by using the Enable-Mailbox cmdlet. The basic syntax is as follows:

```
Enable-Mailbox [-Identity] Identity -Discovery
```

such as:

```
enable-mailbox cpand1.com/hr/legalsearch -discovery
```

You can create a Discovery mailbox by using New-Mailbox as shown in this example:

```
New-Mailbox LegalSearch -Discovery -UserPrincipalName
LegalSearch@cpand1.com
```

Once a Discovery mailbox is established, you can't convert it to another mailbox type. You can't use Exchange Management Console to create Discovery mailboxes.

Creating Shared Mailboxes

Shared mailboxes are mailboxes that are shared by multiple users. Although shared mailboxes must have an associated user account, this account is not used for logon in the domain and is disabled by default. Users who access the shared mailbox do so using access permissions.

You can create a shared mailbox by using New-Mailbox, as shown in this example:

```
New-Mailbox CustomerService -Shared -UserPrincipalName
customerservice@cpandl.com
```

A user account named CustomerService is created for this mailbox. This user account is disabled by default to prevent logon using this account. To share the mailbox with users who need to be able to access it, right-click the mailbox in the Exchange Management Console, select Manage Full Access Permission, and then follow the prompts.

Managing Mailboxes: The Essentials

You often need to manage mailboxes the way you do user accounts. Some of the management tasks are intuitive and others aren't. If you have questions, be sure to read the sections that follow.

You can work with multiple recipients at the same time. To select multiple resources not in sequence, hold down the Ctrl key and then click the left mouse button on each resource you want to select. To select a series of resources, select the first resource, hold down the Shift key, and then click the last resource.

The actions you can perform on multiple resources depend on the types of recipients you've selected. Generally, you'll want to work with recipients of the same type, such as either user mailboxes or room mailboxes, but not both types at the same time. The actions you can perform on multiple mailboxes include:

- Disable
- Disable Archive
- New Local Move Request
- New Remote Move Request
- Remove
- Send Mail

You also can edit the properties of multiple recipients at the same time. To do this, select the recipients you want to work with, right-click and then select Properties. Just about any property that can be set for an individual recipient can be set for multiple recipients.

TIP If the Properties option isn't available when you right-click, you've probably selected one or more recipients of different types. For example, you might have intended to select only user mailboxes but selected a room mailbox as well.

Viewing Current Mailbox Size, Message Count, and Last Logon

You can use the Exchange Management Console to view who last logged on to a mailbox, the last logon date and time, the mailbox size, and the message count by completing these steps:

1. Expand the Recipient Configuration node and then select the Mailbox node.
2. Double-click the mailbox with which you want to work.
3. On the General tab, the Last Logged On By text box shows who last logged on to the mailbox, and the Modified entry shows the date and time the mailbox was last modified. (See Figure 6-3.)
4. On the General tab, the Total Items and Size (KB) areas show the number of messages in the mailbox and the current mailbox size in kilobytes, respectively.

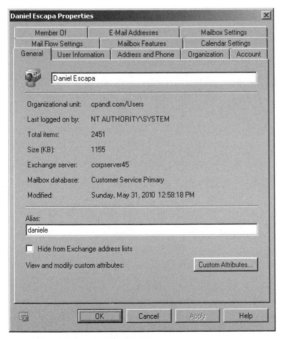

FIGURE 6-3 View mailbox statistics.

If you want to view similar information for all mailboxes on a server, the easiest way is to use the Get-MailboxStatistics cmdlet. Sample 6-3 shows examples using this cmdlet. Use the –Archive parameter to return mailbox statistics for the archive mailbox associated with a specified mailbox.

SAMPLE 6-3 Getting statistics for multiple mailboxes

Syntax

```
Get-MailboxStatistics -Identity 'Identity' [-Archive <$true|$false>]
[-DomainContoller DomainController] [-IncludeMoveHistory <$true|$false>]
[-IncludeMoveReport <$true|$false>]

Get-MailboxStatistics -Server 'Server' | -Database 'Database'
[-DomainContoller DomainController]
```

Usage

```
Get-MailboxStatistics -Server 'corpsvr127'

Get-MailboxStatistics -Database 'Engineering Primary'

Get-MailboxStatistics -Tdentity 'cpandl\williams'
```

When you are working with the Exchange Management Shell, the standard output won't necessarily provide all the information you are looking for. Often, you need to format the output as a list or table using Format-List or Format-Table, respectively, to get the additional information you are looking for. Format-List comes in handy when you are working with a small set of resources or want to view all the properties that are available. Once you know what properties are available for a particular resource, you can format the output as a table to view specific properties. For example, if you format the output of Get-MailboxStatistics as a list, you see all the properties that are available for mailboxes, as shown in this example and sample output:

```
get-mailboxstatistics -identity "cpandl\daniele" | format-list
```

```
AssociatedItemCount       : 2655
DeletedItemCount          : 121
DisconnectDate            :
DisplayName               : Daniel Escapa
ItemCount                 : 2451
LastLoggedOnUserAccount   : NT AUTHORITY\SYSTEM
LastLogoffTime            : 6/15/2010 12:58:18 PM
LastLogonTime             : 6/15/2010 12:58:14 PM
LegacyDN                  : /O=FIRST ORGANIZATION/OU=EXCHANGE
ADMINISTRATIVE GROUP/CN=RECIPIENTS/CN=DANIEL ESCAPA
MailboxGuid               : d3f6ce55-fe3d-4beb-ae65-9c9f7edaf995c
```

```
ObjectClass              : Mailbox
StorageLimitStatus       : BelowLimit
TotalDeletedItemSize     : 97 KB (97,235 bytes)
TotalItemSize            : 1155.11 KB (1,155,445 bytes)
Database                 : Customer Service Primary
ServerName               : CORPSERVER45
DatabaseName             : Customer Service Primary
MoveHistory              :
IsQuarantined            : False
IsArchiveMailbox         : False
Identity                 : d3f6ce44-fe0c-4beb-ae79-9c9f8eaf123c
MapiIdentity             : d3f6ce44-fe0c-4beb-ae79-9c9f8eaf123c
OriginatingServer        : corpserver45.cpandl.com
IsValid                  : True
```

Once you know the available properties, you can format the output as a table to get exactly the information you want to see. In this example, you get information about all the mailboxes in the Engineering Primary database and format the output as a table:

```
Get-MailboxStatistics -Database 'Engineering Primary' | format-table
DisplayName, TotalItemSize, TotalDeletedItemSize, Database, ServerName
```

Setting Alternate Mailbox Display Names for Multilanguage Environments

In some cases, the full display name for a mailbox won't be available for display. This can happen when multiple language versions of the Exchange snap-in are installed on the network or when multiple language packs are installed on a system. Here, the system cannot interpret some or all of the characters in the display name and, as a result, doesn't show the display name. To correct this problem, you can set an alternate display name using a different character set. For example, you could use Cyrillic or Kanji characters instead of standard ANSI characters.

You can set an alternate display name for a mailbox by following these steps:

1. Open the Properties dialog box for the mailbox-enabled user account by double-clicking the user name in the Exchange Management Console.

2. On the User Information tab, type the alternate display name in the Simple Display Name text box and then click OK.

Hiding Mailboxes from Address Lists

Occasionally, you might want to hide a mailbox so that it doesn't appear in the global address list or other address lists. One reason for doing this is if you have administrative mailboxes that you use only for special purposes. To hide a mailbox from the address lists, follow these steps:

1. Open the Properties dialog box for the mailbox-enabled user account by double-clicking the user name in the Exchange Management Console.
2. On the General tab, select the Hide From Exchange Address Lists check box and then click OK.

Defining Custom Mailbox Attributes for Address Lists

Address lists, such as the global address list, make it easier for users and administrators to find available Exchange resources, including users, contacts, distribution groups, and public folders. The fields available for Exchange resources are based on the type of resource. If you want to add more values that should be displayed or searchable in address lists, such as an employee identification number, you can assign these values as custom attributes.

Exchange provides 15 custom attributes—labeled Customer Attribute 1, Custom Attribute 2, and so on through Custom Attribute 15. You can assign a value to a custom attribute by completing the following steps:

1. Open the Properties dialog box for the mailbox-enabled user account by double-clicking the user name in the Exchange Management Console.
2. On the General tab, click Custom Attributes. The Custom Attributes dialog box appears.
3. Enter attribute values in the text boxes provided, and click OK twice.

Moving Mailboxes

To complete an upgrade, balance the server load, manage drive space, or relocate mailboxes when users move to a different location, you can move mailboxes from one server or database to another server or database. Exchange Server 2010 supports online mailbox moves.

Moving Mailboxes: The Essentials

In earlier releases of Exchange, moving mailboxes while they were actively being used wasn't a good idea because it caused some disruption to the affected users. For this reason, Exchange Server 2010 performs move operations as a series of steps that allow a mailbox to remain available to a user while the move operation is being completed. When the move is completed, the user begins accessing the mailbox in the new location. Because users can continue to access their e-mail account during the move, you can perform online moves at any time.

The destination database for a move can be on the same server, on a different server, in a different domain, in a different Active Directory site, or in another forest. However, some caveats apply:

- When your source and destination Mailbox servers are running Exchange Server 2010 or Exchange Server 2007 SP2 or later and are in the same or different forests, you can use the Exchange Management Console or the

New-MoveRequest cmdlet to perform an online mailbox move. This might be necessary when you are moving mailboxes between an on-premises and an online Exchange organization. You perform the move from the Exchange 2010 Mailbox server. You can't move mailboxes from Exchange 2007 SP1 or earlier.

- When your source servers are running Exchange Server 2003 SP2 or later and your destination servers are running Exchange Server 2010, you cannot perform an online mailbox move. You need to perform an offline mailbox move instead. You do this by starting the move operation on the Exchange 2010 Mailbox server with the New-MoveRequest cmdlet. You can't move mailboxes from Exchange 2003 SP1 or earlier.

Performing online moves is a multistep process that is initiated with a Move Mailbox request that is sent to the Microsoft Exchange Mailbox Replication Service (MRS) running on a Client Access server in the source forest. The MRS queues the request for processing, handling all requests on a first-in, first-out basis. When a request is at the top of the queue, the replication service begins replicating mailbox data to the destination database. When the replication service finishes its initial replication of a mailbox, it marks the mailbox as Ready To Complete and periodically performs data synchronization between the source and destination database to ensure that the contents of a mailbox are up to date. After a mailbox has been moved, you can complete the move request and finalize the move.

In the Exchange Management Console, you can track the status of move requests by expanding Recipient Configuration and then selecting the Move Request node (see Figure 6-4). If a move request fails, you can get more information about the failure by double-clicking the move request and then clicking the View button to the right of the Failed Message entry.

FIGURE 6-4 Check the status of move requests.

When you move mailboxes from one server to another, or even to a different database on the same sever, keep in mind that the Exchange policies of the new mailbox database might be different from the old one. Because of this, consider the following issues before you move mailboxes to a new server or database:

- **General policy** Changes to watch out for include those in the default public folder database, the offline address book, and message settings. The risk is that the users whose mailboxes you move could lose or gain access to public folders. They might have a different offline address book, which might have different entries. This address book will also have to be downloaded in its entirety the first time the user's mail client connects to Exchange after the move.

- **Database policy** Changes to watch out for pertain to the maintenance interval and automatic mounting. If Exchange performs maintenance when these users are accessing their mail, they might have slower response times. If the mailbox database is configured so that it isn't mounted at startup, restarting the Exchange services could result in the users not being able to access their mailboxes.

- **Limits** Changes to watch out for pertain to storage limits and deletion settings. Users might be prohibited from sending and receiving mail if their mailbox exceeds the storage limits of the new mailbox database. Users might notice that deleted items stay in their Deleted Items folder longer or are deleted sooner than expected if the Keep Deleted Items setting is different.

Performing Online Mailbox Moves

With online moves, you can move mailboxes between databases on the same server. You also can move mailboxes from a database on one server to a database on another server regardless of whether the servers are in a different Active Directory site or in another Active Directory forest.

Normally, when you perform online moves, the move process looks like this:

1. You create a new move request for the mailbox or mailboxes that you want to move using either the Exchange Management Console or Exchange Management Shell.

2. The move request is sent to the Mailbox Replication Service running on a Client Access server in the current Active Directory site. This server acts as the Mailbox Replication Service proxy.

3. The Mailbox Replication Service (MRS) adds the mailboxes to the Move Request queue and assigns the status Queued For Move to each mailbox. This indicates the move has been requested but the move has not started.

4. When a move request is at the top of the queue, the MRS begins replicating the related mailbox to the destination database and assigns the Move In Progress status to mailboxes being moved. By default, the replication service can move up to 5 mailboxes on a single database at one time and up to 50 mailboxes at a time in total.

5. When the MRS finishes its initial replication of the mailbox, the service assigns the Ready To Complete status to the mailbox.

6. The mailbox remains in the Ready To Complete state until you or another administrator specifies that you either want to complete the move request or cancel the move request. If you complete the move request, the MRS assigns the Completing status while it performs a final data synchronization and then marks the move as completed.

7. When the move is completed, the mailbox or mailboxes are available in the new location. Because users can continue to access their e-mail account during a move, you can perform online moves at any time.

One way to perform online mailbox moves within the same Exchange forest is by using the Exchange Management Shell. The commands for performing online mailbox moves include the following:

- **Get-MoveRequest** View the detailed status of an ongoing mailbox move that was initiated using the New-MoveRequest cmdlet.

```
Get-MoveRequest -Identity Identity [-Credential Credential]
[-DomainController FullyQualifiedName] [-Organization
OrganizationId] [-OrganizationalUnit OrganizationalUnitId]
[-ResultSize Size] [-SortBy String]


Get-MoveRequest [-BatchName BatchRequestName] [-Credential
Credential] [-DomainController FullyQualifiedName]
[-MoveStatus Status] [-Offline <$true | $false>]
[-Organization OrganizationId] [-OrganizationalUnit
OrganizationalUnitId>] [-Protect <$true | $false>]
[-RemoteHostName FullyQualifiedName] [-ResultSize Size]
[-SortBy String] [-SourceDataBase DatabaseId]
[-Suspend <$true | $false>]
[-SuspendWhenReadyToComplete <$true | $false>]
[-TargetDatabase DatabaseId]
```

- **New-MoveRequest** Start a mailbox move. You also can verify readiness to move by using the –WhatIf parameter. Use the –Protect parameter to protect the move request for tenant administrators.

```
New-MoveRequest -Identity Identity [-TargetDatabase DatabaseId]
{AddtlParams}


New-MoveRequest -Identity Identity -Remote {$true | $false}
–RemoteHostName HostName -TargetDeliveryDomain Domain
[-RemoteCredential Credential] [-RemoteGlobalCatalog GCServer]
[-RemoteTargetDatabase DatabaseID] [-TargetDatabase DatabaseID]
{AddtlParams}


New-MoveRequest -Identity Identity -RemoteGlobalCatalog GCServer
-RemoteLegacy <$true|$false> -TargetDeliveryDomain Domain
```

```
[-RemoteCredential Credential] [-RemoteTargetDatabase DatabaseID]
[-TargetDatabase DatabaseID] {AddtlParams}


{AddtlParams}
[-BadItemLimit Limit] [-BatchName BatchRequestName]
[-DomainController FullyQualifiedName] [-IgnoreRuleLimitErrors
<$true|$false>] [-MRSServer CASServer] [-Protect
<$true|$false>] [-Suspend <$true|$false>] [-SuspendComment String]
[-SuspendWhenReadyToComplete <$true|$false>]
```

- **Resume-MoveRequest**   Resumes a move request that has been suspended or failed.

```
Resume-MoveRequest -Identity MoveRequestIdentity
[-DomainController FullyQualifiedName]
```

- **Set-MoveRequest**   Changes a move request after it has been started.

```
Set-MoveRequest -Identity MoveRequestIdentity
[-BadItemLimit Limit] [-DomainController FullyQualifiedName]
[-IgnoreRuleLimitErrors <$true|$false>] [-Protect <$true|$false>]
[-RemoteCredential Credential] [-RemoteGlobalCatalog GCServer]
[-RemoteHostName HostName] [-SuspendWhenReadyToComplete
<$true|$false>]
```

- **Suspend-MoveRequest**   Suspends a move request that has been started but has not yet been completed.

```
Suspend-MoveRequest -Identity MoveRequestIdentity
[-SuspendComment Comment]
[-DomainController FullyQualifiedName]
```

- **Remove-MoveRequest**   Cancels a mailbox move initiated using the New-MoveRequest cmdlet. You can use the Remove-MoveRequest command any time after initiating the move but only if the move request is not yet complete. If the move request was initiated with the –Protect parameter, you must use the –Protect parameter to cancel the move request.

```
Remove-MoveRequest -Identity Identity [-MRSServer CASServer]
[-DomainController FullyQualifiedName] [-Protect {$true | $false}]
```

Moving Mailboxes Within a Single Forest

You perform online mailbox moves within a single forest by using the Exchange Management Shell. To verify move readiness, use New-MoveRequest with the –WhatIf parameter for each mailbox you plan to move. The following examples show two different ways you can verify whether Garrett Vargas's mailbox can be moved:

```
New-MoveRequest -Identity 'garrettv'
-TargetDatabase "Engineering Primary" -WhatIf

'cpandl.com/users/Garrett Vargas' | New-MoveRequest -TargetDatabase
'Engineering Primary' -WhatIf
```

To initiate an online move, you use New-MoveRequest for each mailbox you want to move. The following examples show two different ways you can move Garrett Vargas's mailbox:

```
New-MoveRequest -Identity 'garrettv' -Remote -RemoteHostName
'mailserver17.cpandl.com' -mrsserver 'casserver21.cpandl.com'
-TargetDatabase "Engineering Primary"

'cpandl.com/users/Garrett Vargas' | New-MoveRequest -Remote
-RemoteHostName 'mailserver17.cpandl.com' -mrsserver
'casserver21.cpandl.com' -TargetDatabase 'Engineering Primary'
```

After you initiate a move, you can check the status of the online move using Get-MoveRequest. As shown in the following example, the key parameter to provide is the identity of the mailbox you want to check:

```
Get-MoveRequest -Identity 'garrettv'
```

By default, basic information about the move request is displayed. To get more detailed information, add the –IncludeReport parameter as shown in this example:

```
Get-MoveRequest -Identity 'garrettv' -IncludeReport
```

You can use Suspend-MoveRequest to suspend a move request that has not yet completed, and Resume-MoveRequest to resume a suspended move request. Resuming a suspended request allows it to complete.

You can cancel a move at any time prior to running the move request being completed by Exchange. To do this, run Remove-MoveRequest and specify the identity of the mailbox that shouldn't be moved. An example follows:

```
Remove-MoveRequest -Identity 'garrettv'
```

When your source and destination Mailbox servers are running Exchange Server 2010 and are in the same forest, you can move mailboxes by completing these steps:

1. In the Exchange Management Console, expand the Recipient Configuration node, and then select the related Mailbox node.

2. Right-click the mailbox, and then select New Local Move Request. This starts the New Local Move Request Wizard, as shown in Figure 6-5.

TIP You can select and move multiple mailboxes at the same time. To select multiple users individually, hold down the Ctrl key, and then click each user account that you want to select. To select a sequence of accounts, select the first user account, hold down the Shift key, and then click the last user account.

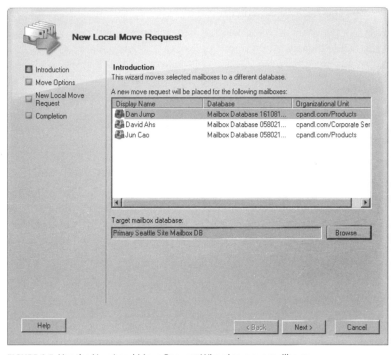

FIGURE 6-5 Use the New Local Move Request Wizard to move mailboxes.

3. Click the Browse button to the right of the Target Mailbox Database text box. In the Select Mailbox Database dialog box, choose the mailbox database to which the mailbox should be moved. Mailbox databases are listed by name as well as by associated server.

4. Click Next. If corrupted messages are found in a mailbox, specify how you would like those messages to be handled. To skip the mailbox if corrupted messages are found, select Skip The Mailbox. To skip the corrupted messages if any are found but still move the mailbox, select Skip The Corrupted Messages.

5. If you elected to skip corrupted messages, you must also specify the maximum number of corrupted messages to skip. If this value is exceeded, the mailbox will not be moved.

6. When you click Next and then click New, Exchange Server creates a new move request. Click Finish.

7. Moving mailboxes can take several hours, depending on the size of the mailboxes you are moving. You can check the status of move requests by selecting the Move Request node under Recipient Configuration. While the move request is in the Moving or Queued state, you can cancel the move request by right-clicking it and then selecting Remove Move Request.

Moving Mailboxes Between Forests

You can perform online mailbox moves between different Exchange forests using the Exchange Management Console or Exchange Management Shell. When you are moving mailboxes between forests, you'll want to verify that mailboxes are ready to be moved before you submit a move request. To verify readiness, the Microsoft Exchange Mailbox Replication service proxy in the source forest checks the status of each mailbox you are moving and also ensures you have the permissions required to move the mailboxes from the source forest to the target forest. If a user has an archive mailbox or subscriptions, you will likely need to remove the archive mailbox, the subscriptions, or both before you are able to move the mailbox.

You can verify move readiness in the Exchange Management Shell by using New-MoveRequest with the –WhatIf parameter for each mailbox you plan to move. The following examples show two different ways you can verify whether Charlie Keen's mailbox can be moved:

```
New-MoveRequest -Identity 'charliek' –Remote
-RemoteHost 'mailserver17.cpandl.com'-mrsserver 'casserver21.cpandl.com'
-TargetDatabase "Engineering Primary" -WhatIf

'cpandl.com/users/Charlie Keen' | New-MoveRequest –Remote
-RemoteHost 'mailserver17.cpandl.com' -mrsserver 'casserver21.cpandl.com'
-TargetDatabase 'Engineering Primary' -WhatIf
```

You can perform online mailbox moves between forests by following these steps:

1. In the Exchange Management Console, select the mailbox or mailboxes that you want to move. Right-click, and then select New Remote Move Request. This starts the New Remote Move Request Wizard.

   The mailboxes you selected are listed as the ones that will be moved. Click Next.

2. The source forest is the forest to which you are connected. In the Target Forest list, select the forest to which you are moving the mailboxes.

3. In the text box provided, type the fully qualified domain name of a Client Access server in the source forest that will act as the proxy server.

4. If you want to provide alternate credentials for the source forest, select the Use The Following Source Forest's Credential, type the user name, and then type the password for the account.

5. When the move request is complete, mail sent to the relocated users in the source forest will be redirected to the target forest. Enter the post-move external e-mail address for the user or users in the source forest.

6. When you click Next and then click New to initiate the move request, the Exchange Management Console calls into the shell and the shell runs New-MoveRequest for each mailbox you selected. Moving the mailboxes can take several hours, depending on the size of the mailboxes you are moving.

You can perform online moves in the Exchange Management Shell by using New-M oveRequest for each mailbox you plan to move. The following examples show two different ways you can move Bruno Denuit's mailbox:

```
New-MoveRequest -Identity 'brunod' -Remote
-RemoteHost 'mailserver17.cpandl.com'-mrsserver 'casserver21.cpandl.com'
-TargetDatabase "Engineering Primary"


'cpandl.com/users/Bruno Denuit' | New-MoveRequest -Remote
-RemoteHost 'mailserver17.cpandl.com' -mrsserver 'casserver21.cpandl.com'
-TargetDatabase 'Engineering Primary'
```

After you initiate a move, you can check the status of the online move by using Get-MoveRequest. As shown in the following example, the key parameters to provide are the identity of the mailbox you want to check and the name of the proxy server:

```
Get-MoveRequest -Identity 'brunod' -mrsserver 'casserver21.cpandl.com'
```

By default, basic information about the move request is displayed. To get more detailed information, add the –IncludeReport parameter as shown in this example:

```
Get-MoveRequest -Identity 'brunod' -mrsserver 'casserver21.cpandl.com'
-IncludeReport
```

You can use Suspend-MoveRequest to suspend a move request that is not yet complete, and Resume-MoveRequest to resume a suspended move request. Resuming a suspended request allows it to complete.

At any time prior to running the move request completing, you can cancel the move by running Remove-MoveRequest and specifying the identify of the mailbox that shouldn't be moved, such as:

```
Remove-MoveRequest -Identity 'brunod' -mrsserver 'casserver21.cpandl.com'
```

Configuring Mailbox Delivery Restrictions, Permissions, and Storage Limits

You use mailbox properties to set delivery restrictions, permissions, and storage limits. To change these configuration settings for mailboxes, follow the techniques discussed in this section.

Setting Message Size Restrictions for Contacts

You set message size restrictions for contacts in much the same way that you set size restrictions for users. Follow the steps listed in the next section.

Setting Message Size Restrictions on Delivery to and from Individual Mailboxes

Using the When The Size Of Any Attachment Is Greater Than Or Equal To Limit transport rule condition, you can set restrictions regarding the size of message attachments and specify what action to take if a message has an attachment that exceeds this limit. Sometimes, you need to set exceptions for specific users. For example, some users might need to be able to send large files as part of their job.

You set individual delivery restrictions by completing the following steps:

1. Open the Properties dialog box for the mailbox-enabled user account by double-clicking the user name in the Exchange Management Console.

2. On the Mail Flow Settings tab, double-click Message Size Restrictions. As shown in Figure 6-6, you can now set the following send and receive restrictions:

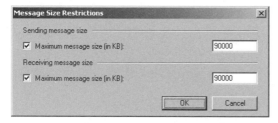

FIGURE 6-6 You can apply individual delivery restrictions on a per-user basis.

- **Sending Message Size** Sets a limit on the size of messages the user can send. The value is set in kilobytes (KBs). If an outgoing message exceeds the limit, the message isn't sent and the user receives a non-delivery report (NDR).

- **Receiving Message Size** Sets a limit on the size of messages the user can receive. The value is set in KBs. If an incoming message exceeds the limit, the message isn't delivered and the sender receives an NDR.

3. Click OK. The restrictions that you set override the global default settings.

Setting Send and Receive Restrictions for Contacts

You set message send and receive restrictions for contacts in the same way that you set these restrictions for users. Follow the steps listed in the next section.

Setting Message Send and Receive Restrictions on Individual Mailboxes

By default, user mailboxes are configured to accept messages from anyone. To override this behavior, you can do the following:

- Specify that only messages from the listed users, contacts, or groups be accepted.
- Specify that messages from specific users, contacts, or groups listed be rejected.
- Specify that only authenticated users—meaning users who have logged on to the Exchange system or the domain—be accepted.

You set message send and receive restrictions by completing the following steps:

1. Open the Properties dialog box for the mailbox-enabled user account by double-clicking the user name in the Exchange Management Console.

2. On the Mail Flow Settings tab, double-click Message Delivery Restrictions. As shown in Figure 6-7, you can now set message acceptance restrictions.

FIGURE 6-7 You can apply send and receive restrictions on messages on a per-user basis.

3. If you want to ensure that messages are accepted only from authenticated users, select the Require That All Senders Are Authenticated check box.

4. To accept messages from all e-mail addresses except those on the reject list, under Accept Messages From, select All Senders.

5. To specify that only messages from the listed users, contacts, or groups be accepted, select the Only Senders In The Following List option and then add acceptable recipients by following these steps:
   - Click Add to display the Select Recipient dialog box.
   - Select a recipient, and then click OK. Repeat as necessary.

   TIP You can select multiple recipients at the same time. To select multiple recipients individually, hold down the Ctrl key and then click each recipient that you want to select. To select a sequence of recipients, select the first recipient, hold down the Shift key, and then click the last recipient.

6. To specify that no recipients should be rejected, under Reject Messages From, select No Senders.

7. To reject messages from specific recipients, under Reject Messages From, select Senders In The Following List and then add unacceptable recipients by following these steps:
   - Click Add to display the Select Recipients dialog box.
   - Select a recipient, and then click OK. Repeat as necessary.

8. Click OK.

Permitting Others to Access a Mailbox

Occasionally, users need to access someone else's mailbox, and in certain situations, you should allow this. For example, if John is Susan's manager and Susan is going on vacation, John might need access to her mailbox while she's away. Another situation in which someone might need access to another mailbox is when you've set up special-purpose mailboxes, such as a mailbox for Webmaster@domain.com or a mailbox for Info@domain.com.

You can grant permissions for a mailbox in two ways:

- You can grant access to a mailbox and its content.
- You can grant the right to send messages as the mailbox owner.

If you want to grant access to a mailbox and its contents but not grant Send As permissions, use the Manage Full Access Permission Wizard. In the Exchange Management Console, right-click the mailbox you want to work with and then select Manage Full Access Permission. In the Manage Full Access Permission Wizard, click Add, and then use the Select User Or Group dialog box to choose the user or users who should have access to the mailbox. To revoke the authority to access the mailbox, select an existing user name in the Security Principal list box and then click Remove. Click Manage to set the desired access permissions.

If you want to grant Send As permissions, use the Manage Send As Permission Wizard. In the Exchange Management Console, right-click the mailbox you want to work with and then select Manage Send As Permission. In the Manage Send As Permission Wizard, click Add, and then use the Select Recipient dialog box to choose the user or users who should have this permission. To revoke this permission, select an existing user name in the Security Principal list box and then click Remove. Click Manage to set the desired Send As permissions.

In the Exchange Management Shell, you can use the Add-MailboxPermission and Remove-MailboxPermission cmdlets to manage full access permissions. Samples 6-4 and 6-5 show examples of using these cmdlets. In these examples, the AccessRights parameter is set to FullAccess to indicate you are setting full access permissions on the mailbox.

SAMPLE 6-4 Adding full access permissions

Syntax

```
Add-MailboxPermission -Identity UserBeingGrantedPermission
 -User UserWhoseMailboxIsBeingConfigured -AccessRights 'FullAccess'
```

Usage

```
Add-MailboxPermission -Identity
'CN=Jerry Orman,OU=Engineering,DC=cpandl,DC=com'
-User 'CPANDL\boba' -AccessRights 'FullAccess'
```

SAMPLE 6-5 Removing full access permissions

Syntax

```
Remove-MailboxPermission -Identity 'UserBeingGrantedPermission'
 -User 'UserWhoseMailboxIsBeingConfigured' -AccessRights 'FullAccess'
-InheritanceType 'All'
```

Usage

```
Remove-MailboxPermission -Identity 'CN=Jerry Orman,
OU=Engineering,DC=cpandl,DC=com'
 -User 'CPANDL\boba' -AccessRights 'FullAccess' -InheritanceType 'All'
```

If you want to allow another user to send messages as the mailbox owner, you can do this using the Manage Send As Permission Wizard. In the Exchange Management Console, right-click the mailbox you want to work with and then select Manage Send As Permission. In the Manage Send As Permission Wizard, click Add, and then use the Select User Or Group dialog box to choose the user or users who should have Send As permission on the mailbox. To revoke Send As permission, select an existing user name in the Security Principal list box and then click Remove. Click Manage to set the desired access permissions.

In the Exchange Management Shell, you can use the Add-ADPermission and Remove-ADPermission cmdlets to manage Send As permissions. Samples 6-6 and 6-7 show examples using these cmdlets. In these examples, the ExtendedRights parameter is set to Send-As to indicate you are setting Send As permissions on the mailbox.

SAMPLE 6-6 Adding Send As permissions

Syntax

```
Add-ADPermission –Identity UserBeingGrantedPermission
-User UserWhoseMailboxIsBeingConfigured –ExtendedRights 'Send-As'
```

Usage

```
Add-ADPermission –Identity 'CN=Jerry
Orman,OU=Engineering,DC=cpandl,DC=com'
-User 'CPANDL\boba' –ExtendedRights 'Send-As'
```

SAMPLE 6-7 Removing Send As permissions

Syntax

```
Remove-ADPermission –Identity UserBeingRevokedPermission
-User UserWhoseMailboxIsBeingConfigured –ExtendedRights 'Send-As'
-InheritanceType 'All' –ChildObjectTypes $null
-InheritedObjectType $null -Properties $null
```

Usage

```
Remove-ADPermission –Identity 'CN=Jerry
Orman,OU=Engineering, DC=cpandl,DC=com'
 –User 'CPANDL\boba' –ExtendedRights 'Send-As' –InheritanceType 'All'
-ChildObjectTypes $null –InheritedObjectTypes $null
-Properties $null
```

NOTE Another way to grant access permissions to mailboxes is to do so through Outlook. Using Outlook, you have more granular control over permissions. You can allow a user to log on as the mailbox owner, delegate mailbox access, and grant various levels of access. For more information on this issue, see the "Accessing Multiple Exchange Server Mailboxes" and "Granting Permission to Access Folders Without Delegating Access" sections in Chapter 16.

Forwarding E-Mail to a New Address

Except when rights management prevents it, any messages sent to a user's mailbox can be forwarded to another recipient. This recipient can be another user or a mail-enabled contact. You can also specify that messages should be delivered to both the forwarding address and the current mailbox.

To configure mail forwarding, follow these steps:

1. Open the Properties dialog box for the mailbox-enabled user account by double-clicking the user name in the Exchange Management Console.

2. On the Mail Flow Settings tab, double-click Delivery Options.

3. To remove forwarding, in the Forwarding Address panel, clear the Forward To check box.

4. To add forwarding, select the Forward To check box and then click Browse. Use the Select Recipient dialog box to choose the alternate recipient.

5. If messages should go to both the alternate recipient and the current mailbox owner, select the Deliver Messages To Both Forwarding Address And Mailbox check box. (See Figure 6-8.) Click OK.

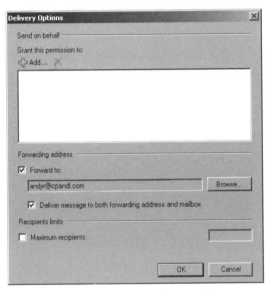

FIGURE 6-8 Using the Delivery Options dialog box, you can specify alternate recipients for mailboxes and deliver mail to the current mailbox as well.

Setting Storage Restrictions on an Individual Mailbox

You can set storage restrictions on multiple mailboxes using global settings for each mailbox database or on individual mailboxes using per-user restrictions. Global restrictions are applied when you create a mailbox and are reapplied when you define new global storage restrictions. Per-user storage restrictions are set individually for each mailbox and override the global default settings.

> **NOTE** Storage restrictions apply only to mailboxes stored on the server. They don't apply to personal folders. Personal folders are stored on the user's computer.

You'll learn how to set global storage restrictions in Chapter 10, "Mailbox and Public Folder Database Administration." See the "Setting Mailbox Database Limits and Deletion Retention" section in that chapter.

You set individual storage restrictions by completing the following steps:

1. Open the Properties dialog box for the mailbox-enabled user account by double-clicking the user name in the Exchange Management Console.

2. On the Mailbox Settings tab, double-click Storage Quotas. This displays the Storage Quotas dialog box, shown in Figure 6-9.

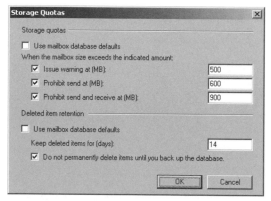

FIGURE 6-9 Using the Storage Quotas dialog box, you can specify storage limits and deleted item retention on a per-user basis when necessary.

3. To set mailbox storage limits, in the Storage Quotas panel, clear the Use Mailbox Database Defaults check box. Then set one or more of the following storage limits:

   ■ **Issue Warning At (MB)**   This limit specifies the size, in megabytes, that a mailbox can reach before a warning is issued to the user. The warning tells the user to clean out the mailbox.

   ■ **Prohibit Send At (MB)**   This limit specifies the size, in megabytes, that a mailbox can reach before the user is prohibited from sending any new mail. The restriction ends when the user clears out the mailbox and the mailbox size is under the limit.

   ■ **Prohibit Send And Receive At (MB)**   This limit specifies the size, in megabytes, that a mailbox can reach before the user is prohibited from sending and receiving mail. The restriction ends when the user clears out the mailbox and the mailbox size is under the limit.

   CAUTION   Prohibiting send and receive might cause the user to think they've lost e-mail. When someone sends a message to a user who is prohibited from receiving messages, an NDR is generated and delivered to the sender. The original recipient never sees the e-mail. Because of this, you should rarely prohibit send and receive.

4. Click OK twice.

Setting Deleted Item Retention Time on Individual Mailboxes

Normally, when a user deletes a message in Microsoft Office Outlook, the message is placed in the Deleted Items folder. The message remains in the Deleted Items folder until the user deletes it manually or allows Outlook to clear out the Deleted Items folder. With personal folders, the message is then permanently deleted and you can't restore it. With server-based mailboxes, the message isn't actually deleted from the Exchange database. Instead, the message is marked as hidden and kept for a specified period of time called the *deleted item retention period*.

NOTE The standard processes can be modified in several different ways. A user could press Shift+Delete to bypass Deleted Items. As an administrator, you can create and apply policies that prevent users from deleting items (even if they try to use Shift+Delete). You can also configure policy to retain items indefinitely.

Default retention settings are configured for each mailbox database in the organization. You can change these settings, as described in Chapter 10 in the "Setting Mailbox Database Limits and Deletion Retention" section, or override the settings on a per-user basis by completing these steps:

1. Open the Properties dialog box for the mailbox-enabled user account by double-clicking the user name in the Exchange Management Console.

2. On the Mailbox Settings tab, double-click Storage Quotas. This displays the Storage Quotas dialog box, shown previously in Figure 6-9.

3. In the Deleted Item Retention panel, clear the Use Mailbox Database Defaults check box.

4. In the Keep Deleted Items For (Days) text box, enter the number of days to retain deleted items. An average retention period is 14 days. If you set the retention period to 0 and aren't using policies that prevent deletion, messages aren't retained and can't be recovered. If you set the retention period to 0 but are using policies that prevent deletion, the messages are retained according to the established policies.

5. You can also specify that deleted messages should not be permanently removed until the mailbox database has been backed up. This option ensures that the deleted items are archived into at least one backup set. Click OK twice.

REAL WORLD Deleted item retention is convenient because it allows the administrator the chance to salvage accidentally deleted e-mail without restoring a user's mailbox from backup. I strongly recommend that you enable this setting, either in the mailbox database or for individual mailboxes, and configure the retention period accordingly.

CHAPTER 7

Working with Distribution Groups and Address Lists

D istribution groups and address lists are extremely important in Microsoft Exchange Server 2010 administration. Careful planning of your organization's groups and address lists can save you countless hours in the long run. Unfortunately, most administrators don't have a solid understanding of these subjects, and the few who do spend most of their time on other duties. To save yourself time and frustration, study the concepts discussed in this chapter and then use the step-by-step procedures to implement the groups and lists for your organization.

Using Security and Distribution Groups

You use groups to grant permissions to similar types of users, to simplify account administration, and to make it easier to contact multiple users. For example, you can send a message addressed to a group, and the message will go to all the users in that group. Thus, instead of having to enter 20 different e-mail addresses in the message header, you enter one e-mail address for all of the group members.

Group Types, Scope, and Identifiers

Windows defines several different types of groups, and each of these groups can have a unique scope. In Active Directory domains, you use three group types:

- **Security**   You use security groups to control access to network resources. You can also use user-defined security groups to distribute e-mail.

- **Standard distribution** Standard distribution groups have fixed membership, and you use them only as e-mail distribution lists. You can't use these groups to control access to network resources.

- **Dynamic distribution** Membership for dynamic distribution groups is determined based on a Lightweight Directory Access Protocol (LDAP) query; you use these groups only as e-mail distribution lists. The LDAP query is used to build the list of members whenever messages are sent to the group.

> **NOTE** Dynamic distribution groups created for Exchange Server 2007 are compatible with Exchange Server 2010. However, dynamic distribution groups created for Exchange Server 2003 or Exchange 2000 Server are not compatible with Exchange Server 2010 and aren't displayed in the Exchange Management Console. You can resolve this by forcing an upgrade. See "Modifying Dynamic Distribution Groups Using Cmdlets" later in this chapter for details.

Security groups can have different scopes—*domain local, global,* and *universal*—so that they are valid in different areas of your Active Directory forest. With Exchange Server 2003, you could also create distribution groups with different scopes as well. To simplify group management, Exchange Server 2007 and Exchange Server 2010 support only groups with universal scope. You can mail-enable security groups with universal scope, and you can create new distribution groups with universal scope.

> **REAL WORLD** If your organization has existing mail-enabled security groups or distribution groups with global scope, you will not be able to use those groups with Exchange Server 2007 and later editions of Exchange. You will either need to create a new architecture for your groups or convert those groups to universal groups. Using Active Directory Users And Computers, domain administrators can easily convert global groups to universal groups. They simply need to double-click the group entry, select Universal under Group Scope, and then click OK. However, some conversion restrictions apply. For example, you can convert a global group only if it isn't a member of another global group. In addition, pre-planning is recommended to determine the impact on Active Directory. You also can use Set-Group to convert groups.

Groups with universal scope can do the following:

- Contain users and groups from any domain in the forest
- Be put into other groups and assigned permissions in any domain in the forest

When you work with dynamic distribution groups, keep in mind that the membership can include only members of the local domain, or it can include users and groups from other domains, domain trees, or forests. Scope is determined by the default apply-filter container you associate with the group when you create it. More specifically, the default apply-filter container defines the root of the search hierarchy and the LDAP query filters to recipients in and below the specified container. For example, if the apply-filter container you associate with the group is cpandl.com, the query filter is applied to all recipients in this domain. If the apply-filter container you associate with the organizational unit is Engineering, the query filter is applied to all recipients in or below this container.

As with user accounts, Windows uses unique security identifiers (SIDs) to track groups. This means that you can't delete a group, re-create it with the same name, and then expect all the permissions and privileges to remain the same. The new group will have a new SID, and all the permissions and privileges of the old group will be lost.

When to Use Security and Standard Distribution Groups

Exchange Server 2007 and Exchange Server 2010 change the earlier rules about how you can use groups. Previously, you could use groups with different scopes, but now you can use only groups with universal scope. As a result, you might need to rethink how and when you use groups.

You must change the scope of any global group to universal before you can mail-enable it. Rather than duplicating your existing security group structure with distribution groups that have the same purpose, you might want to selectively mail-enable your universal security groups, which converts them to distribution groups. For example, if you have a universal security group called Marketing, you don't need to create a MarketingDistList distribution group. Instead, you could enable Exchange mail on the original universal security group, which would then become a distribution group.

You might also want to mail-enable universal security groups that you previously defined. Then, if existing distribution groups serve the same purpose, you can delete the distribution groups.

To reduce the time administrators spend managing groups, Exchange Server 2010 defines several additional control settings, including

- **Group ownership** Mail-enabled security groups, standard distribution groups, and dynamic distribution groups can have one or more owners. A group's owners are the users assigned as its managers, and they can control membership in the group. A group's managers are listed when users view the properties of the group in Microsoft Office Outlook. Additionally, managers can receive delivery reports for groups if you select the Send Delivery Reports To Group Manager option on the Advanced tab.

- **Membership approval** Mail-enabled security groups and standard distribution groups can have open or closed membership. There are separate settings for joining and leaving a group. For joining, the group can be open to allow users to join without requiring permission, closed to allow only group owners and administrators to add members, or require owner approval to allow users to request membership in a group. Membership requests must be approved by a group owner. For leaving, a group can either be open to allow users to leave a group without requiring owner approval or closed to allow only group owners and administrators to remove members.

Your management tool of choice will determine your options for configuring group ownership and membership approval. When you create distribution groups in the Exchange Control Panel, you can specify ownership and membership approval settings when you create the group and can edit these settings at any time by editing the group's properties. When you create distribution groups in the Exchange Management Console, you create the group first and then edit the group's properties to specify the desired ownership and membership approval settings.

When to Use Dynamic Distribution Groups

It's a fact of life that over time users will move to different departments, leave the company, or accept different responsibilities. With standard distribution groups, you'll spend a lot of time managing group membership when these types of changes occur—and that's where dynamic distribution groups come into the picture. With dynamic distribution groups, there isn't a fixed group membership and you don't have to add or remove users from groups. Instead, group membership is determined by the results of an LDAP query sent to your organization's Global Catalog (or dedicated expansion) server whenever mail is sent to the distribution group.

Dynamic distribution groups can be used with or without a dedicated expansion server. You'll get the most benefit from dynamic distribution without a dedicated expansion server when the member list returned in the results is relatively small (fewer than 25 members). In the case of potentially hundreds or thousands of members, however, dynamic distribution is inefficient and could require a great deal of processing to complete. To resolve this problem, you can shift the processing requirements from the Global Catalog server to a dedicated expansion server (a server whose only task is to expand the LDAP queries). However, it could still take several minutes to resolve and expand large distribution lists. For more information on expansion servers, see "Designating an Expansion Server" and "Modifying Dynamic Distribution Groups Using Cmdlets" later in this chapter.

One other thing to note about dynamic distribution is that you can associate only one specific query with each distribution group. For example, you could create separate groups for each department in the organization. You could have groups called QD-Accounting, QD-BizDev, QD-Engineering, QD-Marketing, QD-Operations, QD-Sales, and QD-Support. You could, in turn, create a standard distribution group or a dynamic distribution group called AllEmployees that contains these groups as members—thereby establishing a distribution group hierarchy.

When using multiple parameters with dynamic distribution, keep in mind that multiple parameters typically work as logical AND operations. For example, if you create a query with a parameter that matches all employees in the state of Washington with all employees in the Marketing department, the query results do not contain a list of all employees in Washington or all Marketing employees. Rather, the results contain a list of recipients who are in Washington and are members of the Marketing group. In this case, you get the expected results by creating a dynamic distribution group for all Washington State employees, another dynamic distribution group for all Marketing employees, and a final group that has as members the other two distribution groups.

Working with Security and Standard Distribution Groups

As you set out to work with groups, you'll find that some tasks are specific to each type of group and some tasks can be performed with any type of group. Because of this, I've divided the group management discussion into three sections. In this section, you'll learn about the typical tasks you perform with security and standard distribution groups. The next section discusses tasks you'll perform only with dynamic distribution groups. The third section discusses general management tasks.

You can use the Exchange Management Console or the Exchange Management Shell to work with groups.

Creating Security and Standard Distribution Groups

You use groups to manage permissions and to distribute e-mail. As you set out to create groups, remember that you create groups for similar types of users. Consequently, the types of groups you might want to create include the following:

- **Groups for departments within the organization** Generally, users who work in the same department need access to similar resources and should be a part of the same e-mail distribution lists.

- **Groups for roles within the organization** You can also organize groups according to the users' roles within the organization. For example, you could use a group called Executives to send e-mail to all the members of the executive team and a group called Managers to send e-mail to all managers and executives in the organization.

- **Groups for users of specific projects** Often, users working on a major project need a way to send e-mail to all the members of the team. To solve this problem, you can create a group specifically for the project.

You can create groups two ways. You can mail-enable an existing universal security group, or you can create an entirely new distribution group.

Mail-Enabling an Existing Universal Security Group

To mail-enable an existing universal security group, complete the following steps:

1. In the Exchange Management Console, expand the Recipient Configuration node and then select the Distribution Group node.

    NOTE Only recipients in the current domain or organizational unit are displayed. To view recipients in other domains or organizational units, right-click the Recipient Configuration node and then select Modify Recipient Scope. Use the options provided to configure the scope to use and then click OK.

2. Right-click the Distribution Group node, and then select New Distribution Group. This starts the New Distribution Group Wizard.

3. On the Introduction page, select Existing Group and then click Browse.

4. In the Select Group dialog box, shown in Figure 7-1, select the universal security group you want to mail-enable and then click OK. Universal security groups for the current domain are listed by name and group type.

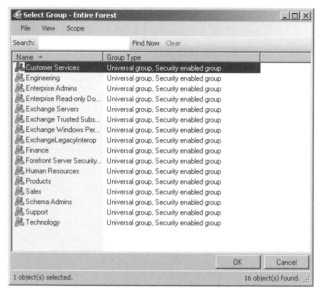

FIGURE 7-1 Use the Select Group dialog box to select the existing universal security group to mail-enable.

5. Click Next. On the Group Information page, the name details for the group are filled in automatically based on the details for the group you selected. You cannot change the group name or the pre–Windows 2000 group name.

6. Like users, groups have an Exchange alias. Enter an alias. The Exchange alias is used to set the group's e-mail address. If necessary, change the default alias.

7. Click Next, and then click New to create the group. An e-mail address is configured automatically for Simple Mail Transfer Protocol (SMTP). Exchange Server uses the SMTP address for receiving messages. After Exchange creates the group, click Finish.

8. Mail-enabling the group isn't the final step. Afterward, you might want to do the following:

- Add members to the group.
- Make the group a member of other groups.
- Assign a manager as a point of contact and control for the group.

- Configure membership approval settings for joining and leaving the group.
- Set message size restrictions for messages mailed to the group.
- Limit users who can send to the group.
- Change or remove default e-mail addresses.
- Add more e-mail addresses.

NOTE By default, the mail-enabled group will have closed membership. This means members won't be able to join or leave the group.

In the Exchange Management Shell, you can mail-enable a universal security group using the Enable-DistributionGroup cmdlet. Sample 7-1 provides the syntax and usage.

SAMPLE 7-1 Enable-DistributionGroup cmdlet syntax and usage

Syntax

```
Enable-DistributionGroup -Identity GroupIdentity [-Alias ExchangeAlias]
[-DisplayName DisplayName] [-DomainController FullyQualifiedName]
[-PrimarySmtpAddress SmtpAddress]
```

Usage

```
Enable -DistributionGroup -Identity 'cpandl.com/Users/AllSales'
-DisplayName 'All Sales'
-Alias 'AllSales'
```

You can manage mail-enabled security groups in several ways. You can add or remove group members as discussed in the "Assigning and Removing Membership for Individual Users, Groups, and Contacts" section of this chapter. If a group should no longer be mail-enabled, you can right-click it in the Exchange Management Console and select Disable to remove the Exchange settings from the group. If you no longer need a mail-enabled security group and it is not a built-in group, you can permanently remove it from Active Directory by right-clicking it in the Exchange Management Console and selecting Remove.

Using the Exchange Management Shell, you can disable a group's Exchange features using the Disable-DistributionGroup cmdlet, as shown in Sample 7-2.

SAMPLE 7-2 Disable-DistributionGroup cmdlet syntax and usage

Syntax

```
Disable-DistributionGroup -Identity GroupIdentity
[-DomainController FullyQualifiedName]
[-IgnoreDefaultScope {$true | $false}]
```

Usage

```
Disable-DistributionGroup -Identity 'cpandl.com/Users/AllSales'
```

Creating a New Distribution Group

You can create a new distribution group by completing the following steps:

1. In the Exchange Management Console, expand the Recipient Configuration node and then select the Distribution Group node.

    NOTE Only recipients in the current domain or organizational unit are displayed. To view recipients in other domains or organizational units, right-click the Recipient Configuration node and then select Modify Recipient Scope. Use the options provided to configure the scope to use and then click OK.

2. Right-click the Distribution Group node, and then select New Distribution Group. This starts the New Distribution Group Wizard.

3. On the Introduction page, accept the default selection to create a new group and click Next.

4. On the Group Information page, shown in Figure 7-2, the Organizational Unit field shows where in Active Directory the group will be created. By default, this is the Users container in the current domain. Because you'll usually need to create new groups in a specific organizational unit rather than in the Users container, select the Specify an Organizational Unit check box and then click Browse. Use the Select Organizational Unit dialog box to choose the location in which to store the account, and then click OK.

5. Select a group type—either Security or Distribution. Generally, you'll want to create a mail-enabled security group if you also want to use the group to manage access permissions. Otherwise, you'll want to create a distribution group to use the group only for mail distribution.

6. Type a name for the group. Group names aren't case-sensitive and can be up to 64 characters long.

7. The first 20 characters of the group name are used to set the pre–Windows 2000 group name. This group name must be unique in the domain. If necessary, change the pre–Windows 2000 group name.

8. Like users, groups have an Exchange alias. Enter an alias. The Exchange alias is used to set the group's e-mail address.

9. Click Next, and then click New to create the group. An e-mail address is configured automatically for SMTP. Exchange Server uses the SMTP address for receiving messages. Click Finish after creation of the group is complete.

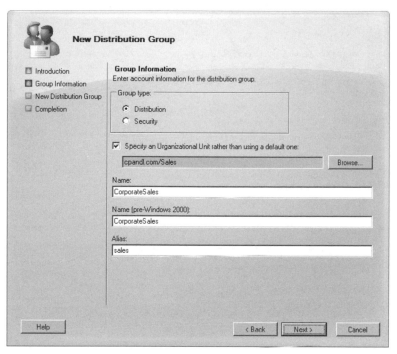

New Distribution Group

Introduction
Group Information
New Distribution Group
Completion

Group Information
Enter account information for the distribution group.

Group type:

- Distribution
- Security

☑ Specify an Organizational Unit rather than using a default one:

cpandl.com/Sales [Browse...]

Name:
CorporateSales

Name (pre-Windows 2000):
CorporateSales

Alias:
sales

[Help] [< Back] [Next >] [Cancel]

FIGURE 7-2 Configure the group's domain settings.

10. Creating the group isn't the final step. Afterward, you might want to do the following:

   - Add members to the group.
   - Make the group a member of other groups.
   - Assign a manager as a point of contact and control for the group.
   - Configure membership approval settings for joining and leaving the group.
   - Set message size restrictions for messages mailed to the group.
   - Limit users who can send to the group.
   - Change or remove default e-mail addresses.
   - Add more e-mail addresses.

   NOTE By default, the new distribution group will be closed for joining but open for leaving.

In the Exchange Management Shell, you can create a new distribution group using the New-DistributionGroup cmdlet. Sample 7-3 provides the syntax and usage. You can set the Type parameter to Distribution for a distribution group or to Security for a mail-enabled security group.

Syntax

```
New-DistributionGroup -Name ExchangeName [-Alias ExchangeAlias]
[-DisplayName DisplayName] [-OrganizationalUnit OUName]
[-PrimarySmtpAddress SmtpAddress] [-SamAccountName PreWin2000Name]
[-Type <Distribution | Security>] {AddtlParams}


{AddtlParams}
[-ArbitrationMailbox ModeratorMailbox] [-AutoApproveNestedDLEnabled
<$true | $false>] [-BypassNestedModerationEnabled <$true | $false>]
[-CopyOwnerToMember {$true | $false}] [-DomainController
FullyQualifiedName] [-ExternalManaged {$true | $false}] [-ManagedBy
RecipientIdentities] [-MemberDepartRestriction <Closed | Open |
ApprovalRequired>] [-MemberJoinRestriction <Closed | Open |
ApprovalRequired>] [-Members RecipientIdentities] [-ModeratedBy
Moderators] [-ModerationEnabled <$true | $false>] [-Notes String]
[-Organization OrgName] [-RoomList {$true | $false}]
[-SendModerationNotifications <Never | Internal | Always>]
```

Usage

```
New-DistributionGroup -Name 'CorporateSales' -Type 'Distribution'
 -OrganizationalUnit 'cpandl.com/Sales'
 -SamAccountName 'CorporateSales'
 -DisplayName 'Corporate Sales'
 -Alias 'CorporateSales'
```

Assigning and Removing Membership for Individual Users, Groups, and Contacts

All users, groups, and contacts can be members of other groups. To configure a group's membership, follow these steps:

1. In the Exchange Management Console, double-click the group entry. This opens the group's Properties dialog box.

2. On the Members tab, you'll see a list of current members. Click Add to add objects to the group. The Select Recipient dialog box appears. You can now choose objects that should be members of this currently selected group. Select the recipients you want to add to the group and then click OK.

3. To remove a member from a group, select an object, and then click Remove. When you're finished, click OK.

In the Exchange Management Shell, you can view group members using the Get-DistributionGroupMember cmdlet. Sample 7-4 provides the syntax and usage.

Syntax

```
Get-DistributionGroupMember -Identity GroupIdentity [-Credential
Credential] [-DomainController FullyQualifiedName]
[-IgnoreDefaultScope {$true | $false}] [-ReadFromDomainController {$true
| $false}] [-ResultSize Size]
```

Usage

```
Get-DistributionGroupMember -Identity 'cpandl.com/Users/CorpSales'
```

You add members to a group using the Add-DistributionGroupMember cmdlet. Sample 7-5 provides the syntax and usage.

SAMPLE 7-5 Add-DistributionGroupMember cmdlet syntax and usage

Syntax

```
Add-DistributionGroupMember -Identity GroupIdentity [-Member
RecipientIdentity] [-BypassSecurityGroupManagerCheck {$true | $false}]
[-DomainController FullyQualifiedName]
[-ExternalManaged {$true | $false}]
```

Usage

```
Add-DistributionGroupMember -Identity 'cpandl.com/Users/CorpSales'
 -Member 'cpandl.com/Sales/Kim Akers'
```

You remove members from a group using the Remove-DistributionGroupMember cmdlet. Sample 7-6 provides the syntax and usage.

SAMPLE 7-6 Remove-DistributionGroupMember cmdlet syntax and usage

Syntax

```
Remove-DistributionGroupMember -Identity GroupIdentity [-Member
RecipientIdentity] [-BypassSecurityGroupManagerCheck {$true | $false}]
[-DomainController FullyQualifiedName]
[-ExternalManaged {$true | $false}]
```

Usage

```
Remove-DistributionGroupMember -Identity 'cpandl.com/Users/CorpSales'
 -Member 'cpandl.com/Sales/Kim Akers'
```

Adding and Removing Managers

To configure a group's managers, follow these steps:

1. In the Exchange Management Console, double-click the group entry. This opens the group's Properties dialog box.

2. On the Group Information tab, click Add to add managers to the group. The Select Mailbox or Mail-Enabled Used dialog box appears. You can now choose mailbox-enabled or mail-enabled users that should be managers of this group. Select the recipients you want to add as managers and then click OK.

3. To remove a manager from a group, select the manager in the Managed By list and then click Remove. When you're finished, click OK.

In the Exchange Management Shell, you can add or remove group managers using the –ManagedBy parameter of the Set-DistributionGroup cmdlet. To set this parameter, you must specify the full list of managers for the group by doing the following:

- Add managers by including existing managers and specifying the additional managers when you set the parameter.

- Remove managers by specifying only those who should be managers and excluding those who should not be managers.

If you don't know the current managers of a group, you can list the managers using Get-DistributionGroup. You'll need to format the output and examine the value of the ManagedBy property.

Sample 7-7 provides syntax and usage examples for adding and removing group managers.

SAMPLE 7-7 Adding and removing group managers

Syntax

```
Get-DistributionGroup -Identity GroupIdentity | format-table
-property ManagedBy


Set-DistributionGroup -Identity GroupIdentity -ManagedBy GroupManagers
```

Usage

```
Get-DistributionGroup -Identity 'cpandl.com/Users/CorpSales' |
format-table -property ManagedBy


Set-DistributionGroup -Identity 'cpandl.com/Users/CorpSales'
-ManagedBy 'cpandl.com/Sales/Daniel Escapa',
'cpandl.com/Users/Charlie Keen'
```

```
$g = Get-DistributionGroup -Identity 'cpandl.com/Users/CorpSales'
$h = $g.managedby + 'cpandl.com/Users/William Stanek'

Set-DistributionGroup -Identity 'cpandl.com/Users/CorpSales'
-ManagedBy $h
```

Configuring Member Restrictions and Moderation

Membership in distribution groups can be restricted in several ways. Groups can be open or closed for joining or require group owner approval for joining. Groups can be open or closed for leaving. Groups also can be moderated. With moderated groups, messages are sent to designated moderators for approval before being distributed to members of the group. The only exception is for a message sent by a designated moderator. A message from a moderator is delivered immediately because a moderator has the authority to determine what is and isn't an appropriate message.

To configure member restrictions and moderation, follow these steps:

1. In the Exchange Management Console, double-click the group entry. This opens the group's Properties dialog box.

2. On the Membership Approval tab, choose settings for joining the group. The options are:

   - **Open**   Anyone can join this group without being approved by the group owners.

   - **Closed**   Members can be added only by the group owners. All requests to join will be rejected automatically.

   - **Owner Approval**   Approval by the group owners is required.

3. Choose settings for leaving the group. The options are:

   - **Open**   Anyone can leave this group without being approved by the group owners.

   - **Closed**   Members can be removed only by the group owners. All requests to leave will be rejected automatically.

   When you're finished, click OK.

4. On the Mail Flow Settings tab, double-click Message Moderation. This opens the Message Moderation dialog box. To disable moderation, click the Messages Sent To This Group Have To Be Approved By A Moderator check box. To enable moderation, select the Messages Sent To This Group Have To Be Approved By A Moderator check box, and then use the options provided to specify group moderators, specify senders who don't require message approval, and configure moderation notifications. Click OK to save your changes.

In the Exchange Management Shell, you manage distribution group settings using Set-DistributionGroup. You configure member restrictions for joining a group using the MemberJoinRestriction parameter and configure member restrictions for leaving a group using the MemberDepartRestriction parameter. If you want to check the current restrictions, you can do this using Get-DistributionGroup. You'll need to format the output and examine the values of the MemberJoinRestriction property, the MemberDepartRestriction property, or both.

Sample 7-8 provides syntax and usage examples for configuring member restrictions.

SAMPLE 7-8 Configuring member restrictions for groups

Syntax

```
Get-DistributionGroup -Identity GroupIdentity | format-table -property
Name, MemberJoinRestriction, MemberDepartRestriction

Set-DistributionGroup -Identity GroupIdentity
[-MemberJoinRestriction <Closed | Open | ApprovalRequired>]
[-MemberDepartRestriction <Closed | Open | ApprovalRequired>]
```

Usage

```
Get-DistributionGroup -Identity 'cpandl.com/Users/AllMarketing' |
format-table -property Name, MemberJoinRestriction,
MemberDepartRestriction

Set-DistributionGroup -Identity 'cpandl.com/Users/AllMarketing'
-MemberJoinRestriction 'Closed' -MemberDepartRestriction 'Closed'
```

Set-DistributionGroup parameters for configuring moderation include ModerationEnabled, ModeratedBy, BypassModerationFromSendersOrMembers, and SendModerationNotifications. You enable or disable moderation by using ModerationEnabled. If moderation is enabled, you can do the following:

- Designate moderators using ModeratedBy.
- Specify senders who don't require message approval by using Bypass-ModerationFromSendersOrMembers.
- Configure moderation notifications using SendModerationNotifications.

Sample 7-9 provides syntax and usage examples for configuring moderation.

SAMPLE 7-9 Configuring moderation for groups

Syntax

```
Get-DistributionGroup -Identity GroupIdentity | format-table -property
Name, ModeratedBy, BypassModerationFromSendersOrMembers,
SendModerationNotifications
```

```
Set-DistributionGroup -Identity GroupIdentity
[-ModeratedBy Moderators] [-ModerationEnabled <$true | $false>]
[-BypassModerationFromSendersOrMembers Recipients]
[-SendModerationNotifications <Never | Internal | Always>]
```

Usage

```
Get-DistributionGroup -Identity 'cpandl.com/Users/AllMarketing' |
format-table -property Name, ModeratedBy,
BypassModerationFromSendersOrMembers, SendModerationNotifications


Set-DistributionGroup -Identity 'cpandl.com/Users/AllMarketing'
-ModerationEnabled $true -Moderators 'cpandl.com/Users/AprilC'
-SendModerationNotifications 'Internal'
```

Working with Dynamic Distribution Groups

Just as there are tasks that apply only to security and standard distribution groups, there are also tasks that apply only to dynamic distribution groups. These tasks are discussed in this section.

Creating Dynamic Distribution Groups

With dynamic distribution groups, group membership is determined by the results of an LDAP query. You can create a dynamic distribution group and define the query parameters by completing the following steps:

1. In the Exchange Management Console, expand the Recipient Configuration node and then select the related Distribution Group node.

2. Right-click the Distribution Group node, and then select New Dynamic Distribution Group. This starts the New Dynamic Distribution Group Wizard.

3. On the Group Information page, the Organizational Unit field shows where in Active Directory the group will be created. By default, this is the Users container in the current domain. Because you'll usually need to create new groups in a specific organizational unit rather than the Users container, select the Specify the Organizational Unit check box, and then click Browse. Use the Select Organizational Unit dialog box to choose the location in which to store the account, and then click OK.

4. Type a name for the group. Group names aren't case-sensitive and can be up to 64 characters long.

5. The group name is used to set the display name. The display name is the name displayed in Microsoft Office Outlook address lists. If necessary, change the default display name.

6. Like users, groups have an Exchange alias. Enter an alias. The Exchange alias is used to set the group's e-mail address.

7. Click Next to display the Filter Settings page, shown in Figure 7-3. The container in which you apply the query filter defines the scope of the query, which is the LDAP query you define for the group filters to recipients in and below the specified container. The default apply-filter container is the one in which you are creating the group. To specify a different container for limiting the query scope, click Browse and then use the Select Organizational Unit dialog box to select a container. In most cases, you'll want to select the domain container.

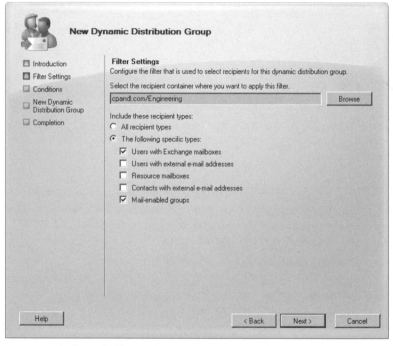

FIGURE 7-3 Configure the filter settings.

8. Use the Include These Recipient Types options to specify the types of recipients to include in the query. Select All Recipient Types or select The Following Specific Types, and then select the types of recipients you want to include in the dynamic distribution group.

9. Click Next. On the Conditions page, shown in Figure 7-4, you can now set the filter conditions. The following types of conditions are available as well as conditions for custom attributes:

   - **Recipient Is In A State Or Province** Filters recipients based on the value of the State/Province text box on the Address And Phone tab in the related Properties dialog box. Click the related In The Specified State Or Province(s) link. In the Specify State Or Province dialog box, type a state or province to use as a filter condition and then press Enter or click Add. Repeat as necessary, and then click OK.

- **Recipient Is In A Department**   Filters recipients based on the value of the Department text box on the Organization tab in the related Properties dialog box. Click the related In The Specified Department(s) link. In the Specify Department dialog box, type a department to use as a filter condition and then press Enter or click Add. Repeat as necessary, and then click OK.

- **Recipient Is In A Company**   Filters recipients based on the value of the Company text box on the Organization tab in the related Properties dialog box. Click the related In The Specified Company(s) link. In the Specify Company dialog box, type a company name to use as a filter condition and then press Enter or click Add. Repeat as necessary, and then click OK.

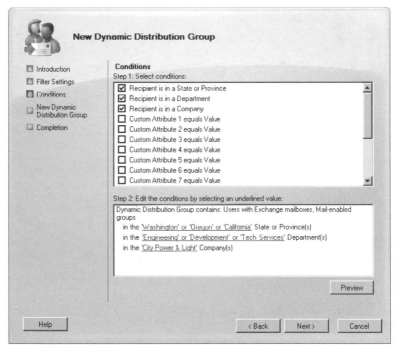

FIGURE 7-4 Set the filter conditions.

10. Click Preview to run the query and display a list of matching recipients by display name, alias, and organizational unit. Click OK.

11. Click Next and then click New to create the group. An e-mail address is configured automatically for SMTP. Exchange Server uses the SMTP address for receiving messages. Click Finish.

12. Creating the group isn't the final step. Afterward, you might want to do the following:

- Assign a manager as a point of contact for the group.
- Set message size restrictions for messages mailed to the group.
- Limit users who can send to the group.
- Change or remove default e-mail addresses.
- Add more e-mail addresses.

In the Exchange Management Shell, you can create a dynamic distribution group using the New-DynamicDistributionGroup cmdlet. Sample 7-10 provides the syntax and usage.

SAMPLE 7-10 New-DynamicDistributionGroup cmdlet syntax and usage

Syntax

```
New-DynamicDistributionGroup -Name ExchangeName
-IncludedRecipients <None, UserMail, MailContacts, MailGroups, Resources,
AllRecipients> [-Alias ExchangeAlias]
[-DisplayName DisplayName] [-OrganizationalUnit OUName]
[-ConditionalCompany CompanyNameFilter1, CompanyNameFilter2,...]
[-ConditionalCustomAttributeX Value1, Value2,...]
[-ConditionalDepartment DeptNameFilter1, DeptNameFilter2, ... ]
[-ConditionalStateOrProvince StateNameFilter1, StateNameFilter2, ...]
[-RecipientContainer ApplyFilterContainer] {AddtlParams}

New-DynamicDistributionGroup -Name ExchangeName -RecipientFilter Filter
[-Alias ExchangeAlias] [-DisplayName DisplayName] [-OrganizationalUnit
OUName] [-RecipientContainer ApplyFilterContainer] {AddtlParams}

{AddtlParams}
[-ArbitrationMailbox ModeratorMailbox] [-DomainController
FullyQualifiedName] [-ModeratedBy Moderators] [-ModerationEnabled <$true
| $false>] [-Organization OrgName] [-PrimarySmtpAddress SmtpAddress]
[-SendModerationNotifications <Never | Internal | Always>]
```

Usage

```
New-DynamicDistributionGroup -Name 'CrossSales'
 -OrganizationalUnit 'cpandl.com/Users' -DisplayName 'CrossSales'
 -Alias 'CrossSales'
 -IncludedRecipients 'UserMail, MailContacts, MailGroups'
 -ConditionalCompany 'City Power & Light'
 -ConditionalDepartment 'Sales','Marketing'
 -ConditionalStateOrProvince 'Washington','Oregon','California'
 -RecipientContainer 'cpandl.com'
```

Changing Query Filters

With dynamic distribution groups, the container in which you apply a query filter determines the scope of the query, which is the LDAP query you define for the group filters to recipients in and below the specified container. You can change the apply-filter container or modify the types of recipients to search for by completing the following steps:

1. In the Exchange Management Console, double-click the dynamic distribution group entry. This opens the group's Properties dialog box.

2. On the Filter tab, the current apply-filter container is listed. To specify a different container for limiting the query scope, click Browse, and then use the Select Organizational Unit dialog box to select a container.

3. Use the Include These Recipient Types options to specify the type of recipients to include in the query. Select either All Recipient Types or select The Following Specific Types, and then select the types of recipients. Click OK.

Changing Filter Conditions

With dynamic distribution groups, the filter conditions determine the exact criteria that must be met for a recipient to be included in the dynamic distribution group. You can modify the filter conditions by completing the following steps:

1. In the Exchange Management Console, double-click the dynamic distribution group entry. This opens the group's Properties dialog box.

2. On the Conditions tab, the current conditions are listed. The following types of conditions are available as well as conditions for custom attributes:

   - **Recipient Is In A State Or Province** Filters recipients based on the value of the State/Province field on the Address And Phone tab in the related Properties dialog box. Click the related In The Specified State Or Province(s) link. In the Specify State Or Province dialog box, add or remove states or provinces as necessary and then click OK.

   - **Recipient Is In A Department** Filters recipients based on the value of the Department field on the Organization tab in the related Properties dialog box. Click the related In The Specified Department(s) link. In the Specify Department dialog box, add or remove departments as necessary and then click OK.

   - **Recipient Is In A Company** Filters recipients based on the value of the Company field on the Organization tab in the related Properties dialog box. Click the related In The Specified Company(s) link. In the Specify Company dialog box, add or remove company names and then click OK.

3. Click OK.

Designating an Expansion Server

When there are potentially hundreds or thousands of members, dynamic distribution groups are inefficient and can require a great deal of processing to complete. This is why the expansion process normally is handled by your organization's Global Catalog servers. However, in some cases, you might want a dedicated expansion server to handle expansion processing. The dedicated expansion server can be any Hub Transport server in your organization, and you'll usually want to configure at least one dedicated expansion server per Active Directory site.

You can specify a dedicated expansion server for a dynamic distribution group by completing these steps:

1. In the Exchange Management Console, double-click the dynamic distribution group entry. This opens the group's Properties dialog box.

2. On the Advanced tab, select the Set Expansion Server check box, and then click Browse to select the expansion server you want to use. Click OK.

Modifying Dynamic Distribution Groups Using Cmdlets

In the Exchange Management Shell, you can get information about dynamic distribution groups using the Get-DynamicDistributionGroup cmdlet and modify the filters and conditions associated with a dynamic distribution group using the Set-DynamicDistributionGroup cmdlet. The Set-DynamicDistributionGroup cmdlet has several other uses as well. You can use it to do the following:

- Specify a dedicated expansion server to enhance query processing. Set the –ExpansionServer parameter to the identity of the Global Catalog server to use.

- Upgrade dynamic distribution groups created for Exchange 2003 and Exchange 2000 to allow incompatible dynamic distribution groups to be re-written to work with Exchange Server 2010. Set –ForceUpgrade $true, and then modify any incompatible included recipients or recipient filters as necessary.

Sample 7-11 provides the syntax and usage for the Get-DynamicDistribution-Group cmdlet.

SAMPLE 7-11 Get-DynamicDistributionGroup cmdlet syntax and usage

Syntax

```
Get-DynamicDistributionGroup [-Identity GroupIdentity | -Anr Name]
[-Credential Credential]
[-DomainController FullyQualifiedName]
[-Filter FilterString]
[-IgnoreDefaultScope {$true | $false}]
[-ManagedBy Managers]
[-Organization OrgName]
[-OrganizationalUnit OUName]
[-ReadFromDomainController {$true | $false}]
[-ResultSize Size]
[-SortBy Value]
```

```
Get-DynamicDistributionGroup -Identity 'cpandl.com/Users/CrossSales'
```

Sample 7-12 provides the syntax and usage for the Set-DynamicDistribution-Group cmdlet.

SAMPLE 7-12 Set-DynamicDistributionGroup cmdlet syntax and usage

Syntax

```
Set-DynamicDistributionGroup -Identity GroupIdentity
[-Alias NewAlias] [-AcceptMessagesOnlyFrom Recipients]
[-AcceptMessagesOnlyFromDLMembers Recipients]
[-AcceptMessagesOnlyFromSendersOrMembers Recipients]
[-ArbitrationMailbox ModeratorMailbox]
[-BypassModerationFromSendersOrMembers Recipients]
[-ConditionalCompany Values] [-ConditionalDepartment Values]
[-ConditionalCustomAttributeX Values]
[-ConditionalStateOrProvince Values] [-CreateDTMFMap <$true | $false>]
[-DisplayName Name] [-DomainController DCName]
[-EmailAddresses ProxyAddress]
[-EmailAddressPolicyEnabled <$false|$true>]
[-ExpansionServer Server] [-ForceUpgrade <$false|$true>]
[-GrantSendOnBehalfTo Mailbox]
[-HiddenFromAddressListsEnabled <$false|$true>]
[-IgnoreDefaultScope {$true | $false}]
[-IncludedRecipients <None, UserMail, MailContacts, MailGroups,
Resources, AllRecipients>] [-MailTip String]
[-MailTipTranslations Locale:TipString, Locale:TipString, ...]
[-ManagedBy Managers] [-MaxReceiveSize Size] [-MaxSendSize Size]
[-ModeratedBy Moderators] [-ModerationEnabled <$true | $false>]
[-Name Name] [-Notes Value] [-PhoneticDisplayName PhName]
[-PrimarySmtpAddress SmtpAddress]
[-RecipientContainer OUName] [-RecipientFilter String]
[-RejectMessagesFrom Recipients]
[-RejectMessagesFromDLMembers Recipients]
[-RejectMessagesFromSendersOrMembers Recipients]
[-ReportToManagerEnabled <$false|$true>]
[-ReportToOriginatorEnabled <$false|$true>]
[-RequireSenderAuthenticationEnabled <$false|$true>]
[-SendModerationNotifications <Never | Internal | Always>]
[-SendOofMessageToOriginatorEnabled <$false|$true>]
[-SimpleDisplayName Name] [-UMDtmfMap Values]
[-WindowsEmailAddress SmtpAddress]
```

Usage

```
Set-DynamicDistributionGroup -Identity 'cpandl.com/Users/CrossSales'
-IncludedRecipients 'AllRecipients'
```

```
-ConditionalCompany 'City Power & Light'
-ConditionalDepartment 'Sales','Accounting'
-ConditionalStateOrProvince 'Washington','Idaho','Oregon'
-RecipientContainer 'cpandl.com'
```

Usage

```
Set-DynamicDistributionGroup -Identity 'cpandl.com/Users/CrossSales'
 -ForceUpgrade $true
```

Usage

```
Set-DynamicDistributionGroup -Identity 'cpandl.com/Users/CrossSales'
 -ExpansionServer 'CorpSvr127'
```

Previewing Dynamic Distribution Group Membership

You can preview a dynamic distribution group to confirm its membership and
determine how long it takes to return the query results. The specific actions you
take depend on the following factors:

- In some cases, you might find that the membership isn't what you expected.
  If this happens, you need to change the query filters, as discussed earlier.

- In other cases, you might find that it takes too long to execute the query
  and return the results. If this happens, you might want to rethink the query
  parameters. You might want to create several query groups.

To preview dynamic distribution group membership, follow these steps:

1. In the Exchange Management Console, double-click the dynamic distribution
   group entry. This opens the group's Properties dialog box.

2. On the Conditions tab, click Preview.

3. When you are finished reviewing the results of the query, click OK twice.

Other Essential Tasks for Managing Groups

Previous sections covered tasks that were specific to a type of group. As an
Exchange administrator, you'll find that you need to perform many additional group
management tasks. These essential tasks are discussed in this section.

Changing a Group's Name Information

Each mail-enabled group has a display name, an Exchange alias, and one or more
e-mail addresses associated with it. The display name is the name that appears in
address lists. The Exchange alias is used to set the e-mail addresses associated with
the group.

Whenever you change a group's naming information, new e-mail addresses can be generated and set as the default addresses for SMTP. These e-mail addresses are used as alternatives to e-mail addresses previously assigned to the group. To learn how to change or delete these additional e-mail addresses, see the "Changing, Adding, or Deleting a Group's E-Mail Addresses" section later in this chapter.

To change the group's Exchange name details, complete the following steps:

1. In the Exchange Management Console, double-click the group entry. This opens the group's Properties dialog box.

2. On the General tab, the first text box shows the display name of the group. If necessary, type a new display name.

3. The Alias text box shows the Exchange alias. If necessary, type a new alias. Click OK.

NOTE When you change a group's display name, you give the group a new label. Changing the display name doesn't affect the SID, which is used to identify, track, and handle permissions independently from group names.

Changing, Adding, or Deleting a Group's E-Mail Addresses

When you create a mail-enabled group, default e-mail addresses are created for SMTP. Any time you update the group's Exchange alias, new default e-mail addresses can be created. The old addresses aren't deleted, however; they remain as alternative e-mail addresses for the group.

To change, add, or delete a group's e-mail addresses, follow these steps:

1. In the Exchange Management Console, double-click the group entry. This opens the group's Properties dialog box.

2. On the E-Mail Addresses tab, you can use the following techniques to manage the group's e-mail addresses:

   - **Create a new SMTP address** Click the arrow to the right of Add, and then select SMTP Address. Enter the e-mail address, and then click OK.

   - **Create a custom address** Click the arrow to the right of Add, and then select Custom Address. Enter the e-mail address, and then enter the e-mail address type. Click OK.

     TIP Use SMTP as the address type for standard Internet e-mail addresses. For custom address types, such as X.400, you must manually enter the address in the proper format.

   - **Set a new Reply To address** Select the address you want to be the new default, and then click Set As Reply.

   - **Edit an existing address** Double-click the address entry. Modify the settings in the Address dialog box, and then click OK.

   - **Delete an existing address** Select the address, and then click the Remove button.

Hiding Groups from Exchange Address Lists

By default, any mail-enabled security group or other distribution group that you create is shown in Exchange address lists, such as the global address list. If you want to hide a group from the address lists, follow these steps:

1. In the Exchange Management Console, double-click the group entry. This opens the group's Properties dialog box.

2. On the Advanced tab, select the Hide Group From Exchange Address Lists check box. Click OK.

NOTE When you hide a group, it isn't listed in Exchange address lists. However, if a user knows the name of a group, he or she can still use it in the mail client. To prevent users from sending to a group, you must set message restrictions, as discussed in the next section, "Setting Usage Restrictions on Groups."

TIP Hiding group membership is different from hiding the group itself. In Outlook, users can view the membership of groups. In Exchange Server 2010, you cannot prevent viewing the group membership. In addition, membership of dynamic distribution groups is not displayed in global address lists because it is generated only when mail is sent to the group.

Setting Usage Restrictions on Groups

Groups are great resources for users in an organization. They let users send mail quickly and easily to other users in their department, business unit, or office. However, if you aren't careful, people outside the organization can use groups as well. Would your boss like it if spammers sent unsolicited e-mail messages to company employees through your distribution lists? Probably not—and you'd probably be sitting in the hot seat, which would be uncomfortable, to say the least.

To prevent unauthorized use of mail-enabled groups, you can specify that only certain users or members of a particular group can send messages to the group. For example, if you create a group called AllEmployees, of which all company employees were members, you can specify that only the members of AllEmployees can send messages to the group. You do this by specifying that only messages from members of AllEmployees are acceptable.

To prevent mass spamming of other groups, you can set the same restriction. For example, if you have a group called Technology, you can specify that only members of AllEmployees can send messages to that group.

REAL WORLD If you have users who telecommute or send e-mail from home using a personal account, you might be wondering how these users can send mail after you put a restriction in place. What I've done in the past is create a group called OffsiteE-mailUsers and then added this as a group that can send mail to my mail-enabled groups. The OffsiteEmailUsers group contains separate mail-enabled contacts for each authorized off-site e-mail address. Alternatively, users could simply log on to Outlook

Anywhere, Outlook Web App, or Exchange ActiveSync and send mail to the group; this is an approach that doesn't require any special groups with permissions to be created or maintained.

Another way to prevent unauthorized use of mail-enabled groups is to specify that only mail from authenticated users is accepted. An authenticated user is any user accessing the system through a logon process. It does not include anonymous users or guests, and it is not used to assign permissions. If you use this option, keep in mind that off-site users will need to log on to Exchange before they can send mail to restricted groups, which might present a problem for users who are at home or on the road.

You can set or remove usage restrictions by completing the following steps:

1. In the Exchange Management Console, double-click the group entry. This opens the group's Properties dialog box.

2. On the Mail Flow Settings tab, double-click Message Delivery Restrictions.

3. If you want to ensure that messages are accepted only from authenticated users, select the Require That All Senders Are Authenticated check box.

4. To accept messages from all e-mail addresses except those on the reject list, under Accept Messages From, select All Senders.

5. To specify that only messages from the listed users, contacts, or groups be accepted, under Accept Messages From, select the Only Senders In The Following List option, and then add acceptable recipients:

    • Click Add to display the Select Recipient dialog box.

    • Select a recipient, and then click OK. Repeat as necessary.

    TIP You can select multiple recipients at the same time. To select multiple recipients individually, hold down the Ctrl key and then click each recipient that you want to select. To select a sequence of recipients, select the first recipient, hold down the Shift key, and then click the last recipient.

6. To specify that no recipients should be rejected, under Reject Messages From, select No Senders.

7. To reject messages from specific recipients, under Reject Messages From, select Senders In The Following List, and then add unacceptable recipients:

    • Click Add to display the Select Recipient dialog box.

    • Select a recipient, and then click OK. Repeat as necessary.

8. Click OK.

Setting Message Size Restrictions for Delivery to Groups

By default, messages of any size can be sent to distribution groups. You can change this behavior by limiting the size of messages that users can send to distribution groups. To do this, complete the following steps:

1. Open the Properties dialog box for the group by double-clicking the group name in the Exchange Management Console.
2. On the Mail Flow Settings tab, double-click Message Size Restrictions.
3. Select the Maximum Message Size (In KB) check box.
4. In the text box provided, enter the maximum message size in kilobytes (KB). Be sure to set a size that allows the sending of suitably sized attachments. Click OK twice.

If a message addressed to the group exceeds the limit, the message isn't distributed to members of the group, and the user receives a nondelivery report (NDR).

Setting Out-of-Office and Delivery Report Options for Groups

By default, distribution groups are configured so that delivery reports are sent to the person who sent the mail message. You can change this so that delivery reports are sent to the group owner or not sent at all. You can also specify out-of-office messages that are returned in response to messages from the sender. To set these options, complete the following steps:

1. Open the Properties dialog box for the group by double-clicking the group name in the Exchange Management Console.
2. On the Advanced tab, if you want out-of-office messages to be delivered to the sender, select the Send Out-Of-Office Message To Originator check box.
3. If you want to stop sending delivery reports, select Do Not Send Delivery Reports. Alternately, you can send delivery reports to the group manager or the message originator. Click OK.

Deleting Groups

Deleting a group removes it permanently. After you delete a group, you can't create a group with the same name and automatically restore the permissions that the original group was assigned because the SID for the new group won't match the SID for the old group. You can reuse group names, but remember that you'll have to re-create all permissions settings.

Windows doesn't let you delete built-in groups. In the Exchange Management Console, you can remove other types of groups by right-clicking them and selecting Remove. When prompted, click Yes to delete the group. If you click No, the Exchange Management Console will not delete the group.

In the Exchange Management Shell, only a group's manager or other authorized user can remove a group. You can use the Remove-DistributionGroup cmdlet to remove distribution groups, as shown in Sample 7-13.

Syntax

```
Remove-DistributionGroup -Identity GroupIdentity
[-BypassSecurityGroupManagerCheck {$true | $false}]
[-DomainController FullyQualifiedName]
[-ExternalManaged {$true | $false}]
[-IgnoreDefaultScope {$true | $false}]
```

Usage

```
Remove-DistributionGroup -Identity 'cpandl.com/Users/AllSales'
```

To remove dynamic distribution groups, you can use the Remove-Dynamic-DistributionGroup cmdlet. Sample 7-14 shows the syntax and usage.

SAMPLE 7-14 Remove-DynamicDistributionGroup cmdlet syntax and usage

Syntax

```
Remove-DynamicDistributionGroup -Identity GroupIdentity
[-DomainController FullyQualifiedName]
[-IgnoreDefaultScope {$true | $false}]
```

Usage

```
Remove-DynamicDistributionGroup -Identity 'cpandl.com/Users/CrossSales'
```

Managing Online Address Lists

Address lists help administrators organize and manage Exchange recipients. You can use address lists to organize recipients by department, business unit, location, type, and other criteria. The default address lists that Exchange Server creates, as well as any new address lists that you create, are available to the user community. Users can navigate these address lists to find recipients to whom they want to send messages.

Using Default Address Lists

During setup, Exchange Server creates a number of default address lists, including the following:

- **Default Global Address List** Lists all mail-enabled users, contacts, and groups in the organization.
- **Default Offline Address Book** Provides an address list for viewing offline that contains information on all mail-enabled users, contacts, and groups in the organization.
- **All Contacts** Lists all mail-enabled contacts in the organization.

- **All Groups** Lists all mail-enabled groups in the organization.
- **All Rooms** Lists all resource mailboxes for rooms.
- **Public Folders** Lists all public folders in the organization.
- **All Users** Lists all mail-enabled users in the organization.

The most commonly used address lists are the global address list and the offline address book.

In the Exchange Management Console, you access online address lists and offline address books by expanding the Organization Configuration node and then selecting the Mailbox node. As Figure 7-5 shows, the details pane then provides a group of tabs for managing organizational-level settings for mailbox servers. You use the Address Lists tab to manage online address lists and the Offline Address Book tab to manage offline address books.

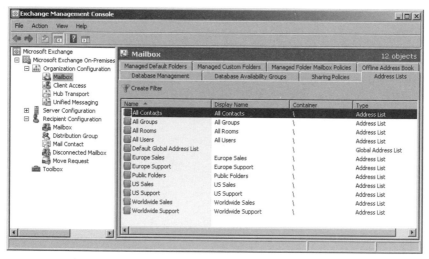

FIGURE 7-5 Access online address lists and offline address books under the Organization Configuration node.

Creating and Applying New Address Lists

You can create new address lists to accommodate your organization's special needs. For example, if your organization has offices in Seattle, Portland, and San Francisco, you might want to create separate address lists for each office.

To create an address list that users can select in their Outlook mail clients, follow these steps:

1. In the Exchange Management Console, expand the Organization Configuration node and then select the related Mailbox node.

2. Right-click the Mailbox node in the console tree, and then select New Address List. This starts the New Address List Wizard.

3. Type an internal Exchange name and a display name for the address list, as shown in Figure 7-6. The display name should describe the types of recipients that are viewed through the list. For example, if you're creating a list for recipients in the Boston office, you can call the list Boston E-Mail Addresses.

4. The container on which you base the address list sets the scope of the list. The list will include recipients in address lists in and below the specified container. The default (root) container, \, specifies that all address lists are included by default. To specify a different container for limiting the list scope, click Browse, and then use the Select Address List dialog box to select a container. In most cases, you'll want to select the default (root) container.

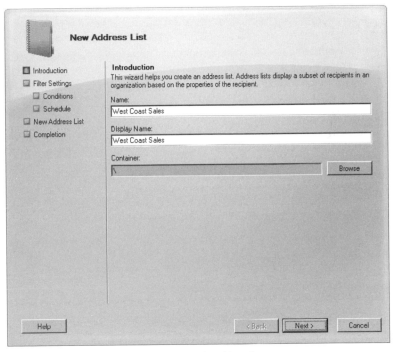

FIGURE 7-6 Determine a name and configure the address list.

5. Click Next. Use the Include These Recipient Types options to specify the types of recipients to include in the query. Select All Recipient Types or select The Following Specific Types, and then select the types of recipients. You can include mailbox users, mail-enabled contacts, mail-enabled groups, mail-enabled users, and resource mailboxes.

6. Click Next. On the Conditions page, you can now set the filter conditions. The following types of conditions are available as well as conditions for custom attributes:

   - **Recipient Is In A State Or Province** Filters recipients to be included in the address list based on the value of the State/Province field on the

Address And Phone tab in the related Properties dialog box. Click the related In The Specified State Or Province(s) link. In the Specify State Or Province dialog box, type a state or province to use as a filter condition and then press Enter or click Add. Repeat as necessary, and then click OK.

- **Recipient Is In A Department** Filters recipients to be included in the address list based on the value of the Department field on the Organization tab in the related Properties dialog box. Click the related In The Specified Department(s) link. In the Specify Department dialog box, type a department to use as a filter condition and then press Enter or click Add. Repeat as necessary, and then click OK.

- **Recipient Is In A Company** Filters recipients to be included in the address list based on the value of the Company field on the Organization tab in the related Properties dialog box. Click the related In The Specified Company(s) link. In the Specify Company dialog box, type a company name to use as a filter condition and then press Enter or click Add. Repeat as necessary, and then click OK.

7. Click Next. If you want to create and apply the address list immediately, select Immediately. To schedule the address list creation and application, select At The Following Time, and then set the date and time to create and apply the list.

   TIP Creating address lists can be resource intensive. If you want to create the list later, select Do Not Apply. Later, when you are ready to create the list, right-click the list in the Exchange Management console, and then click Apply. Exchange will create the list for you eventually (as part of routine maintenance).

8. To specify the maximum length of time that the server can spend creating and applying the address list, select the Cancel Tasks That Are Still Running After (Hours) check box, and then set the maximum number of hours the address list task can run.

   NOTE Canceling after a maximum number of hours is designed to ensure that address list tasks that are blocked or not proceeding as expected are canceled. Most address list tasks should be completed in two hours or less, but the exact duration depends on the number of recipients involved and the complexity of the filters.

9. Click Next, and then click New to create and schedule the address list to be created. After the address list is created, users will be able to use the new address list the next time they start Outlook. Click Finish.

In the Exchange Management Shell, creating and applying address lists are two separate tasks. You can create address lists using the New-AddressList cmdlet. You apply address lists using the Update-AddressList cmdlet. Sample 7-15 provides the syntax and usage for the New-AddressList cmdlet. Sample 7-16 provides the syntax and usage for the Update-AddressList cmdlet. For IncludedRecipients, you can include mailbox users, mail-enabled contacts, mail-enabled groups, mail-enabled users, and resource mailboxes.

TIP Exchange Server 2010 does not support Recipient Update Service (RUS). To replace the functionality of RUS, you can schedule the Update-AddressList and Update-EmailAddressPolicy cmdlets to run periodically using Task Scheduler. Alternatively, you can run the cmdlets manually when you modify addresses.

SAMPLE 7-15 New-AddressList cmdlet syntax and usage

Syntax

```
New-AddressList -Name ListName [-Container BaseAddressList]
[-DisplayName DisplayName] [-IncludedRecipients <None, UserMail,
MailContacts, MailGroups, Resources, AllRecipients>]
[-ConditionalCompany CompanyNameFilter1, CompanyNameFilter2,... ]
[-ConditionalCustomAttributeX Value1, Value2, ...]
[-ConditionalDepartment DeptNameFilter1, DeptNameFilter2, ... ]
[-ConditionalStateOrProvince StateFilter1, StateFilter2, ... ]
[-DomainController FullyQualifiedName] [-Organization OrgName]
[-RecipientContainer ApplyFilterContainer]

New-AddressList -Name ListName [-Container BaseAddressList]
[-DisplayName DisplayName] [-DomainController FullyQualifiedName]
[-Organization OrgName] [-RecipientContainer ApplyFilterContainer]
[-RecipientFilter Filter]
```

Usage

```
New-AddressList -Name 'West Coast Sales' -Container '\'
-DisplayName 'West Coast Sales' -IncludedRecipients 'UserMail,
MailContacts, MailGroups, Resources'
-ConditionalCompany 'City Power & Light'
-ConditionalDepartment 'Sales','Marketing'
-ConditionalStateOrProvince 'Washington','Idaho','Oregon'
```

SAMPLE 7-16 Update-AddressList cmdlet syntax and usage

Syntax

```
Update-AddressList -identity ListIdentity
[-DomainController FullyQualifiedName]
```

Usage

```
Update-AddressList -Identity '\West Coast Sales'
```

Configuring Clients to Use Address Lists

Address books are available to clients that are configured for corporate or work-group use. To set the address lists used by the client, complete these steps:

1. In Office Outlook 2007, from the Tools menu, select Address Book.

2. In the Address Book dialog box, from the Tools menu, select Options, and then set the following options to configure how address lists are used:

   - **Show This Address List First**   Sets the address book that the user sees first whenever he or she works with the address book.

   - **Keep Personal Addresses In**   Specifies the default address book for storing new addresses.

   - **When Sending Mail, Check Names Using These Address Lists In The Following Order**   Sets the order in which Outlook searches address books when you send a message or click Check Names. Use the up and down arrows to change the list order.

3. Click OK.

TIP   When checking names, you'll usually want the global address list (GAL) to be listed before the user's own contacts or other types of address lists. This is important because users often put internal mailboxes in their personal address lists. The danger of doing this without first resolving names against the GAL is that although the display name might be identical, the properties of a mailbox might change. When changes occur, the entry in the user's address book is no longer valid and any mail sent bounces back to the sender with a nondelivery report (NDR). To correct this, the user should either remove that mailbox from his or her personal address list and add it based on the current entry in the GAL, or change the check names resolution order to use the GAL before any personal lists.

Updating Address List Configuration and Membership Throughout the Domain

Exchange Server doesn't immediately replicate changes to address lists through-out the domain. Instead, changes are replicated during the normal replication cycle, which means that some servers might temporarily have outdated address list information. Rather than waiting for replication, you can manually update address list configuration, availability, and membership throughout the domain. To do this, follow these steps:

1. In the Exchange Management Console, expand the Organization Configura-tion node by double-clicking it, and then select the related Mailbox node.

2. On the Address Lists tab, right-click the address list you want to update and then select Apply.

3. If you want to update the address list immediately, select Immediately. To schedule the address list creation and application, select At The Following Time, and then set the date and time to create and apply the list.

4. To specify the maximum length of time that the server can spend creating and applying the address list, select the Cancel Tasks That Are Still Running After (Hours) check box and then set the maximum number of hours the address list task can run.

5. Click Next and then click Apply. Click Finish.

Sample 7-16, shown earlier, illustrates how to update and apply address lists.

Editing Address Lists

Although you can't change the properties of default address lists, you can change the properties of address lists that you create. To do this, complete the following steps:

1. In the Exchange Management Console, expand the Organization Configuration node and then select the related Mailbox node.

2. On the Address Lists tab, right-click the address list you want to edit and then select Edit. This starts the Edit Address List Wizard.

3. Modify the name as necessary, and then click Next. Use the Include These Recipient Types options to specify the types of recipients to include in the query. Select All Recipient Types or select The Following Specific Types, and then select the types of recipients.

4. Click Next. On the Conditions page, you can manage the filter conditions.

5. Click Next. If you want to modify the address list but apply the changes as part of Exchange's regular housekeeping, select Do Not Apply. To apply the address list changes now, select Immediately. To schedule the address list creation and application, select At The Following Time, and then set the date and time to create and apply the list.

6. To specify the maximum length of time that the server can spend creating and applying the address list, select the Cancel Tasks That Are Still Running After (Hours) check box and then set the maximum number of hours the address list task can run.

7. Click Next, and then click Edit to apply the changes.

8. Click Finish.

In the Exchange Management Shell, you can modify an address list using the Set-AddressList cmdlet. Sample 7-17 provides the syntax and usage. Address lists created for Exchange Server 2003 are compatible with Exchange Server 2010. You can upgrade address lists created for Exchange Server 2003 so that they work with Exchange Server 2010 by using –ForceUpgrade $true and then modifying any incompatible included recipients or recipient filters as necessary. After you update an address list, you can make the changes visible by using the Update-AddressList cmdlet, as shown previously in Sample 7-16. You don't need to upgrade address lists created for Exchange Server 2007.

SAMPLE 7-17 Set-AddressList cmdlet syntax and usage

Syntax

```
Set-AddressList -Identity ListName
[-DisplayName DisplayName] [-IncludedRecipients <None, UserMail,
MailContacts, MailGroups, Resources, AllRecipients>]
[-ConditionalCompany CompanyNameFilter1, CompanyNameFilter2,... ]
[-ConditionalDepartment DeptNameFilter1, DeptNameFilter2, ... ]
[-ConditionalStateOrProvince StateFilter1, StateFilter2, ... ]
[-DomainController FullyQualifiedName] [-ForceUpgrade <$false|$true>]
[-RecipientContainer ApplyFilterContainer] [-RecipientFilter Filter]
```

Usage

```
Set-AddressList -Identity '\West Coast Sales' -Name 'Sales Team-West'
-IncludedRecipients 'UserMail, MailContacts, MailGroups'
 -Company 'City Power & Light'
 -Department 'Sales','Marketing'
 -StateOrProvince 'Washington','Idaho','Oregon'
```

Usage

```
Set-AddressList -Identity '\West Coast Sales' -Name 'Sales Team-West'
 -IncludedRecipients 'UserMail, MailContacts, MailGroups'
 -ForceUpgrade $true
```

Renaming and Deleting Address Lists

Although the Exchange Management Console will let you rename and delete default address lists, you really shouldn't do this. Instead, you should rename or delete
only user-defined address lists.

- **Renaming address lists**   To rename an address list, in the Exchange Management Console, right-click its entry and then select Edit. Type a new name
  in the Name text box. Click Next four times. Click Edit, and then click Finish.

- **Deleting address lists**   To delete an address list, in the Exchange Management Console, right-click its entry and then select Remove. When prompted
  to confirm the action, click Yes.

In the Exchange Management Shell, you can remove address lists using the
Remove-AddressList cmdlet. Sample 7-18 provides the syntax and usage. If you also
want to remove address lists that reference the address list you are removing and
match a portion of it (child address lists), you can set the Recursive parameter to
$true. By default, the cmdlet does not remove child address lists of the specified list.

Syntax

```
Remove-AddressList -Identity ListIdentity
[-DomainController FullyQualifiedName] [-Recursive {$true | $false}]
```

Usage

```
Remove-AddressList -Identity '\West Coast Sales'
```

Managing Offline Address Books

You configure offline address books differently than online address lists. To use an offline address book, the client must be configured to have a local copy of the server mailbox, or you can use personal folders. Clients using Outlook 2003 or earlier versions of Outlook retrieve the offline address books from Exchange using the Messaging Application Programming Interface (MAPI) protocol. Clients using Office Outlook 2007 or later versions of Outlook retrieve the offline address book from the designated offline address book (OAB) distribution point.

> **NOTE** An OAB distribution point is a virtual directory to which Office Outlook 2007 and later clients can connect to download the OAB. OAB distribution points are hosted by servers running Internet Information Services (IIS) as virtual directories. Each distribution point can have two URLs associated with it: one URL for internal (on-site) access and another for external (off-site) access. See Chapter 13, "Managing Client Access Servers," for details on configuring OAB distribution points.

Creating Offline Address Books

By default, the default offline address book includes all the addresses in the global address list. It does this by including the default global address list. All other offline address books are created by including the default global address list or a specific online address list as well.

You can create other custom offline address books by completing the following steps:

1. In the Exchange Management Console, expand the Organization Configuration node by double-clicking it, and then select the related Mailbox node.

2. Right-click the Mailbox node in the console tree, and then select New Offline Address Book. This starts the New Offline Address Book Wizard.

3. Type a name for the address book, as shown in Figure 7-7. The name should describe the types of recipients that are viewed through the offline address book.

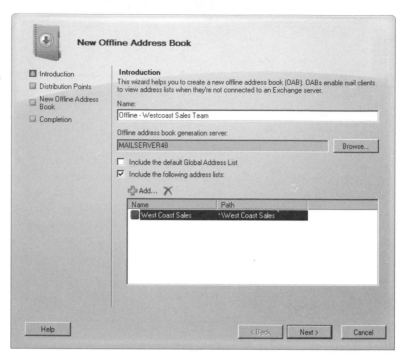

New Offline Address Book

☑ Introduction
☐ Distribution Points
☐ New Offline Address Book
☐ Completion

Introduction

This wizard helps you to create a new offline address book (OAB). OABs enable mail clients to view address lists when they're not connected to an Exchange server.

Name:

Offline - Westcoast Sales Team

Offline address book generation server:

MAILSERVER48   Browse...

☐ Include the default Global Address List
☑ Include the following address lists:

➕ Add... ✖

Name	Path
West Coast Sales	\West Coast Sales

Help   < Back   Next >   Cancel

FIGURE 7-7 Set the name and configure the offline address book.

4. Offline address books are generated on designated mailbox servers. To specify the server to use to generate the address book, click Browse. In the Select Mailbox Server dialog box, select the mailbox server to use and then click OK.

5. The default global address list is included by default. Clear the Include The Default Global Address List check box if you do not want to include it.

6. To include other address lists, select the Include The Following Address Lists check box. Click Add. In the Select Address List dialog box, click the address list to use and then click OK. Repeat this step as necessary to include other address lists. Click Next.

7. On the Distribution Points page, shown in Figure 7-8, select the distribution points to use. The default settings depend on the way Exchange Server was installed.

8. To support Outlook 2007 and later clients, you must enable Web-based distribution. Select the Enable Web-Based Distribution check box, and then click Add. In the Select OAB Virtual Directory dialog box, select the OAB virtual directory to use and then click OK. Repeat as necessary.

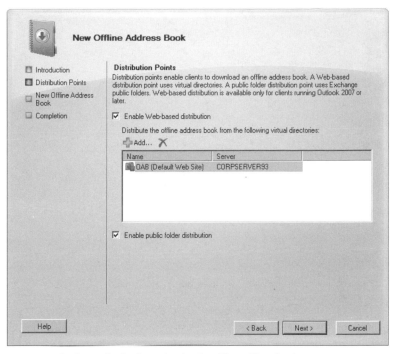

FIGURE 7-8 Configure distribution points for the offline address book.

9. To support Outlook 2003, you must enable public folder distribution. Select the Enable Public Folder Distribution check box.

10. Click Next, and then click New to create the offline address book. Click Finish.

REAL WORLD Exchange uses public folders to distribute offline address books to client computers that are running Outlook 2003 or Entourage. If you haven't already created a public folder database for your organization, you'll need to do this before you can enable public folder distribution. Note that if all of your client computers are running Outlook 2007 or later, the OAB and free/busy information are maintained separately from public folder infrastructure and you don't need to create public folder databases or public folders for this explicit purpose.

In the Exchange Management Shell, you can create offline address books using the New-OfflineAddressBook cmdlet. You apply offline address books using the Update-OfflineAddressBook cmdlet. Sample 7-19 provides the syntax and usage for the New-OfflineAddressBook cmdlet. Sample 7-20 provides the syntax and usage for the Update-OfflineAddressBook cmdlet.

SAMPLE 7-19 New-OfflineAddressBook cmdlet syntax and usage

Syntax

```
New-OfflineAddressBook -Name ListName  -Server GenerationServer
 -AddressLists AddressList1, AddressList2, ...
[-PublicFolderDistributionEnabled <$false|$true> ]
[-VirtualDirectories  VirtualDir1, VirtualDir2, ...] {AddtlParams}

{AddtlParams}
[-DiffRetentionPeriod RetentionPeriod]
[-DomainController FullyQualifiedName]
[-GlobalWebDistributionEnabled <$true | $false>]
[-IsDefault <$true | $false>] [-Organization OrgName]
[-PublicFolderDatabase DatabaseIdentity]
[-Schedule Schedule] [-Server ServerName]
[-SkipPublicFolderInitialization {$true | $false}]
[-Versions Versions]
```

Usage

```
New-OfflineAddressBook -Name 'Offline - West Coast Sales'
 -Server 'CorpSvr127'
 -AddressLists '\West Coast Sales'
 -PublicFolderDistributionEnabled $true
 -VirtualDirectories 'CORPSVR127\OAB (Default Web Site)'
```

SAMPLE 7-20 Update-OfflineAddressBook cmdlet syntax and usage

Syntax

```
Update-OfflineAddressBook -Identity OABName
[-DomainController FullyQualifiedName]
```

Usage

```
Update-OfflineAddressBook -Identity '\Offline - West Coast Sales'
```

Configuring Clients to Use an Offline Address Book

Offline address lists are available only when users are working offline. You can configure how clients use offline address books by completing the following steps:

1. Do one of the following:
   - In Office Outlook 2007, click Tools, select Send/Receive, and then select Download Address Book. The Offline Address Book dialog box appears.
   - In Office Outlook 2010, click the Office button. On the Info pane, select Download Address Book. The Offline Address Book dialog box appears.

2. Select the Download Changes Since Last Send/Receive check box to download only items that have changed since the last time you synchronized the address list. Clear this check box to download the entire contents of your address book.

3. Specify the information to download as either of the following two options:

   - **Full Details** Select this option to download the address book with all address information details. Full details are necessary if the user needs to encrypt messages when using remote mail.

   - **No Details** Select this option to download the address book without address information details. This reduces the download time for the address book.

4. If multiple address books are available, use the Choose Address Book drop-down list to specify which address book to download. Click OK.

Assigning a Time to Rebuild an Offline Address Book

The default offline address book is rebuilt daily at 1:00 A.M. Other offline address books are rebuilt daily at 5:00 A.M. You can change the time when the rebuild occurs by completing these steps:

1. In the Exchange Management Console, expand the Organization Configuration node by double-clicking it, and then select the related Mailbox node.

2. On the Offline Address Book tab, right-click the offline address book you want to configure, and then select Properties.

3. Use the Update Schedule drop-down list to set the rebuild time. The available options are as follows:

   - Run Daily At 1:00 A.M.
   - Run Daily At 2:00 A.M.
   - Run Daily At 3:00 A.M.
   - Run Daily At 4:00 A.M.
   - Run Daily At 5:00 A.M.
   - Never Run
   - Use Custom Schedule

   TIP If you select Use Custom Schedule, click Customize to define your own rebuild schedule.

4. Click OK.

Rebuilding Offline Address Books Manually

Normally, offline address books are rebuilt at a specified time each day. You can also rebuild offline address books manually. To do this, complete the following steps:

1. In the Exchange Management Console, expand the Organization Configuration node by double-clicking it, and then select the related Mailbox node.

2. On the Offline Address Book tab, right-click the offline address book you want to rebuild, and then select Update.

3. When prompted to confirm the action, click Yes. Rebuilding address lists can take a long time. Be patient. Users will see the updates the next time they start Outlook.

Setting the Default Offline Address Book

Although you can create many offline address books, clients download only one. This address list is called the default offline address book, and you can set it by completing these steps:

1. In the Exchange Management Console, expand the Organization Configuration node by double-clicking it, and then select the related Mailbox node.

2. On the Offline Address Book tab, right-click the offline address book you want to configure, and then select Set As Default. Users will use the new default offline address book the next time they start Outlook.

Changing Offline Address Book Properties

The offline address book is based on other address lists that you've created in the organization. You can modify the lists that are used to create the offline address book by completing the following steps:

1. In the Exchange Management Console, expand the Organization Configuration node by double-clicking it, and then select the related Mailbox node.

2. On the Offline Address Book tab, right-click the offline address book you want to configure, and then select Properties.

3. On the Address Lists tab, you can make additional address lists a part of the master offline address book by clicking Add, selecting the list you want to use, and then clicking OK. If you no longer want an address list to be a part of the offline address book, select the address list, and then click the Remove button.

4. On the Distribution tab, to change the clients supported, select or clear the client-related check boxes as appropriate.

5. To enable or disable distribution points for Outlook 2007 and later clients, select or clear the Enable Web-Based Distribution check box, as appropriate. You can configure additional distribution points by clicking Add, selecting the distribution point you want to use, and then clicking OK. If you no longer want to use a distribution point, select the distribution point, and then click the Remove button.

6. To enable or disable distribution points for Outlook 2003 and other MAPI clients, select or clear the Enable Public Folder Distribution check box, as appropriate. Click OK.

In the Exchange Management Shell, you can modify offline address books using the Set-OfflineAddressBook cmdlet. Sample 7-21 provides the syntax and usage.

SAMPLE 7-21 Set-OfflineAddressBook cmdlet syntax and usage

Syntax

```
Set-OfflineAddressBook -Identity OABName
[-AddressLists AddressList1, AddressList2, ... ]
[-ApplyMandatoryProperties {$true | $false}]
[-ConfiguredAttributes Attributes]
[-DiffRetentionPeriod RetentionPeriod]
[-DomainController FullyQualifiedName]
[-GlobalWebDistributionEnabled <$true | $false>]
[-IsDefault <$true | $false>] [-MaxBinaryPropertySize Size]
[-MaxMultivaluedBinaryPropertySize Size]
[-MaxMultivaluedStringPropertySize Size] [-MaxStringPropertySize Size]
[-Name Name] [-PublicFolderDistributionEnabled <$false|$true> ]
[-Schedule Schedule] [-UseDefaultAttributes {$true | $false}]
[-Versions Versions] [-VirtualDirectories VirtualDir1, VirtualDir2, ...]
```

Usage

```
Set-OfflineAddressBook -Identity '\Offline – West Coast Sales'
 -Name 'West Coast Sales - Offline'
 -AddressLists '\West Coast Sales'
 -PublicFolderDistributionEnabled $true
 -VirtualDirectories 'CORPSVR127\OAB (Default Web Site)'
```

Changing the Offline Address Book Server

In a large organization in which lots of users are configured to use offline folders, managing and maintaining offline address books can put a heavy burden on Exchange Server. To balance the load, you might want to designate a server other than your primary Exchange servers to manage and propagate offline address books.

You can change the offline address book server by completing these steps:

1. In the Exchange Management Console, expand the Organization Configuration node by double-clicking it, and then select the Mailbox node.

2. On the Offline Address Book tab, right-click the offline address book you want to configure, and then select Move. This starts the Move Offline Address Book Wizard.

3. The current offline address book server is listed in the Offline Address Book Generation Server field. To use a different server, click Browse, and then, in the Select Mailbox Server dialog box, choose a different server. Click OK.

4. Click Move, and then click Finish.

In the Exchange Management Shell, you can change the offline address book server using the Move-OfflineAddressBook cmdlet. Sample 7-22 provides the syntax and usage.

SAMPLE 7-22 Move-OfflineAddressBook cmdlet syntax and usage

Syntax

```
Move-OfflineAddressBook -Identity 'OfflineAddressBookIdentity'
[-Server 'Server'] [-DomainController FullyQualifiedName]
```

Usage

```
Move-OfflineAddressBook -Identity '\Offline - West Coast Sales'
-Server 'CorpSvr127'
```

Deleting Offline Address Books

If an offline address book is no longer needed, you can delete it as long as it isn't the default offline address book. Before you can delete the default offline address book, however, you must set another address book as the default.

You can delete an offline address book by completing the following steps:

1. In the Exchange Management Console, expand the Organization Configuration node by double-clicking it, and then select the Mailbox node.

2. On the Offline Address Book tab, right-click the offline address book you want to configure, and then select Remove.

3. When prompted to confirm, click Yes.

In the Exchange Management Shell, you can delete an offline address book using the Remove-OfflineAddressBook cmdlet. Sample 7-23 provides the syntax and usage. Set the Force parameter to $true to force the immediate removal of an offline address book.

SAMPLE 7-23 Remove-OfflineAddressBook cmdlet syntax and usage

Syntax

```
Remove-OfflineAddressBook -Identity 'OfflineAddressBookIdentity'
[-Force <$false|$true>] [-DomainController FullyQualifiedName]
```

Usage

```
Remove-OfflineAddressBook -Identity '\Offline - West Coast Sales'
```

CHAPTER 8

Implementing Exchange
Server 2010 Security

In this chapter, you'll learn how to implement Microsoft Exchange Server 2010 security and auditing. In Active Directory, you manage security using permissions. Users, contacts, and security groups all have permissions assigned to them. These permissions control the resources that users, contacts, and groups can access and the actions they can perform. You use auditing to track the use of these permissions, as well as logons and logoffs. You manage Exchange permissions using either the Active Directory tools or the Exchange management tools.

Exchange 2010 includes a new permissions model called *role-based access control* (RBAC). This model is implemented in tandem with the standard permissions model. Because you can use both models to control access to an Exchange organization, I will examine the standard model first and then discuss the new model. Note that when you integrate Exchange 2010 into an Exchange 2003 or Exchange 2007 organization, the permission models used with these older Exchange implementations will coexist with the standard and new permissions models used by Exchange 2010. You'll need to transition permissions from the old model to the permissions models used by Exchange 2010.

Configuring Standard Permissions for Exchange Server

Most Exchange information is stored in Active Directory. You can use the features of Active Directory to manage these standard permissions across the Exchange organization.

Assigning Exchange Server Permissions to Users, Contacts, and Groups

Users, contacts, and groups are represented in Active Directory as objects. These objects have many attributes that determine how they are used. The most important attributes are the permissions assigned to the object. Permissions grant or deny access to objects and resources. For example, you can grant a user the right to create public folders but deny that same user the right to view the status of the information store.

Permissions assigned to an object can be applied directly to the object, or they can be inherited from another object. Generally, objects inherit permissions from *parent objects*. A parent object is an object that is above another object in the object hierarchy. However, you can override inheritance. One way to do this is to assign permissions directly to an object. Another way is to specify that an object shouldn't inherit permissions.

In Exchange Server 2010, permissions are inherited through the organizational hierarchy. The root of the hierarchy is the *Organization node*. All other nodes in the tree inherit the Exchange permissions of this node. For example, the permissions on the Recipient Configuration node are inherited from the Organization node.

For the management of Exchange information and servers, Exchange Server 2010 uses several predefined groups. These predefined security groups have permissions to manage Exchange organization, Exchange server, and Exchange recipient data in Active Directory. In Active Directory Users And Computers, you can view and work with the Exchange-related groups using the Microsoft Exchange Security Groups node. (See Figure 8-1.)

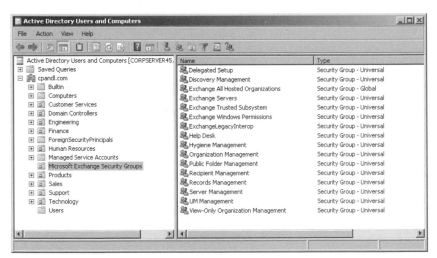

FIGURE 8-1 You can use Active Directory Users And Computers to work with Exchange management groups.

TIP In Active Directory Users And Computers, there's a hidden container of Exchange objects called Microsoft Exchange System Objects. You can display this container by selecting Advanced Features on the View menu.

Understanding the Exchange Management Groups

Table 8-1 lists predefined groups created in Active Directory for Exchange Server 2010. As the table shows, each group has a slightly different usage and purpose. Several of the groups are used by Exchange servers. These groups are Exchange Servers, Exchange Trusted Subsystem, Exchange Windows Permissions, and ExchangeLegacyInterop. As indicated in the table, you use the other groups for role-based access control and assigning management permissions.

NOTE Exchange 2003 and Exchange 2007 use a different set of security groups for managing Exchange permissions. If you want a user or group that had permissions in Exchange 2003 or Exchange 2007 to have permission in Exchange 2010, you need to configure the appropriate Exchange 2010 permissions for that user or group.

TABLE 8-1 Security Groups Created for Exchange

GROUP	GROUP TYPE	DESCRIPTION	ROLE GROUP
Delegated Setup	Universal Security Group	Members of this group have permission to install and uninstall Exchange on provisioned servers.	Yes
Discovery Management	Universal Security Group	Members of this group can perform mailbox searches for data that meets specific criteria.	Yes
Exchange All Hosted Organizations	Global Security Group	Members of this group include hosted organization mailbox groups. This group is used to apply Password Setting objects to all hosted mailboxes.	No
Exchange Install Domain Servers	Global Security Group	Members of this group include domain controllers on which Exchange Server is installed. You can see this group only when you select View and then click Advanced Features in Active Directory Users And Computers.	No

TABLE 8-1 Security Groups Created for Exchange

GROUP	GROUP TYPE	DESCRIPTION	ROLE GROUP
Exchange Servers	Universal Security Group	Members of this group are Exchange servers in the organization. This group allows Exchange servers to work together. By default, all computers running Exchange Server 2010 are members of this group; you should not change this setup.	No
Exchange Trusted Subsystem	Universal Security Group	Members of this group are Exchange servers that run Exchange cmdlets using Windows Remote Management (WinRM). Members of this group have permission to read and modify all Exchange configuration settings as well as user accounts and groups.	No
Exchange Windows Permissions	Universal Security Group	Members of this group are Exchange servers that run Exchange cmdlets using WinRM. Members of this group have permission to read and modify user accounts and groups.	No
ExchangeLegacyInterop	Universal Security Group	Members of this group are granted send-to and receive-from permissions, which are necessary for routing group connections between Exchange Server 2010 and Exchange Server 2003. Exchange Server 2003 bridgehead servers must be made members of this group to allow proper mail flow in the organization. For more information on interoperability, see Chapter 2, "Deploying Exchange Server 2010."	No

TABLE 8-1 Security Groups Created for Exchange

GROUP	GROUP TYPE	DESCRIPTION	ROLE GROUP
Help Desk	Universal Security Group	Members of this group can view any property or object within the Exchange organization and have limited management permissions.	Yes
Hygiene Management	Universal Security Group	Members of this group can manage the antispam and antivirus features of Exchange.	Yes
Organization Management	Universal Security Group	Members of this group have full access to all Exchange properties and objects in the Exchange organization.	Yes
Public Folder Management	Universal Security Group	Members of this group can manage public folders and perform most public folder management operations.	Yes
Recipient Management	Universal Security Group	Members of this group have permissions to modify Exchange user attributes in Active Directory and perform most mailbox operations.	Yes
Records Management	Universal Security Group	Members of this group can manage compliance features, including retention policies, message classifications, and transport rules.	Yes
Server Management	Universal Security Group	Members of this group can manage all Exchange servers in the organization but do not have permission to perform global operations.	Yes
UM Management	Universal Security Group	Members of this group can manage all aspects of unified messaging (UM), including Unified Messaging server configuration and UM recipient configuration.	Yes

TABLE 8-1 Security Groups Created for Exchange

GROUP	GROUP TYPE	DESCRIPTION	ROLE GROUP
View-Only Organization Management	Universal Security Group	Members of this group have read-only access to the entire Exchange organization tree in the Active Directory configuration container and read-only access to all the Windows domain containers that have Exchange recipients.	Yes

When working with Exchange-related groups, be sure to keep in mind that Organization Management grants the widest set of Exchange management permissions possible. Members of this group can perform any Exchange management task, including organization, server, and recipient management. Members of the Recipient Management group, on the other hand, can manage only recipient information, and Public Folder Management can manage only public folder information. View-Only Organization Management can view Exchange organization, server, and recipient information, but this group cannot manage any aspects of Exchange.

Table 8-2 provides an overview of the default group membership for the Exchange groups. Membership in a particular group grants the member the permissions of the group. Exchange groups that aren't listed don't have any default members or membership.

TABLE 8-2 Default Membership for Exchange Security Groups

GROUP	MEMBERS	MEMBER OF
Exchange Install Domain Servers	Individual Exchange servers	Exchange Servers
Exchange Servers	Exchange Install Domain Servers, individual Exchange servers	Windows Authorization Access Group
Exchange Trusted Subsystem	Individual Exchange servers	Exchange Windows Permissions
Exchange Windows Permissions	Exchange Trusted Subsystem	n/a

Assigning Standard Exchange Management Permissions

To grant Exchange management permissions to a user or group of users, all you need to do is make the user or group a member of the appropriate Exchange management group. The tool of choice for managing users in a domain is Active Directory Users And Computers. You can make users, contacts, computers, or other groups members of an Exchange management group by completing the following steps:

1. Click Start, point to All Programs, select Administrative Tools, and select Active Directory Users And Computers.

2. In Active Directory Users And Computers, double-click the Exchange management group you want to work with. This opens the group's Properties dialog box.

3. Click the Members tab, as shown in Figure 8-2.

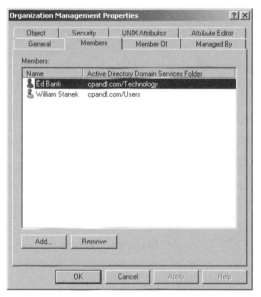

FIGURE 8-2 Use the Members tab to view and manage membership in a group.

4. To make a user or group a member of the selected group, click Add. The Select Users, Contacts, Computers, Service Accounts, Or Groups dialog box appears, as shown in Figure 8-3.

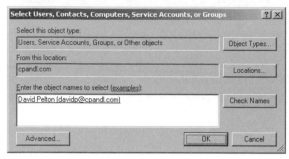

FIGURE 8-3 Specify the name of the user, contact, computer, service account, or group to add.

5. Type the name of the account to which you want to grant permissions, and then click Check Names. If matches are found, select the account you want to use and then click OK. If no matches are found, update the name you entered, and try searching again. Repeat this step as necessary. Click OK.

You can remove a user, contact, computer, service account, or other group from an Exchange management group by completing the following steps:

1. Open Active Directory Users And Computers.

2. In Active Directory Users And Computers, double-click the Exchange management group with which you want to work. This opens the group's Properties dialog box.

3. On the Members tab, click the user or group you want to remove and then click Remove. When prompted to confirm, click Yes, and then click OK.

You can use the Exchange Control Panel (ECP) to manage membership in role groups. By default, the Exchange Control Panel URL is *https://yourserver .yourdomain.com/ecp*. When you are managing the organization and Users & Groups is selected in the left pane, you can select the Administrator Roles tab to work with Exchange role groups. When you select a role, the right-most pane provides a description of the role, lists the assigned roles, and also shows the current members. While working with this view, you can double-click a group entry to view and manage its membership.

Understanding Advanced Exchange Server Permissions

Active Directory objects are assigned a set of permissions. These permissions are standard Microsoft Windows permissions, object-specific permissions, and extended permissions.

Table 8-3 summarizes the most common object permissions. Keep in mind that some permissions are generalized. For example, with Read Value(s) and Write Value(s), Value(s) is a placeholder for the actual type of value or values.

TABLE 8-3 Common Permissions for Active Directory Objects

PERMISSION	DESCRIPTION
Full Control	Permits reading, writing, modifying, and deleting
List Contents	Permits viewing object contents
Read All Properties	Permits reading all properties of an object
Write All Properties	Permits writing to all properties of an object
Read Value(s)	Permits reading the specified value(s) of an object, such as general information or group membership
Write Value(s)	Permits writing the specified value(s) of an object, such as general information or group membership
Read Permissions	Permits reading object permissions
Modify Permissions	Permits modifying object permissions
Delete	Permits deleting an object
Delete Subtree	Permits deleting the object and its child objects
Modify Owner	Permits changing the ownership of the object
All Validated Writes	Permits all types of validated writes
All Extended Writes	Permits all extended writes
Create All Child Objects	Permits creating all child objects
Delete All Child Objects	Permits deleting all child objects
Add/Remove Self As Member	Permits adding and removing the object as a member
Send To	Permits sending to the object
Send As	Permits sending as the object
Change Password	Permits changing the password for the object
Receive As	Permits receiving as the object

Table 8-4 summarizes Exchange-specific permissions for objects. If you want to learn more about other types of permissions, I recommend that you read *Windows Server 2008 Administrator's Pocket Consultant,* Second Edition (Microsoft Press, 2010) or *Windows 7 Administrator's Pocket Consultant* (Microsoft Press, 2009).

TABLE 8-4 Extended Permissions for Exchange Server

PERMISSION	DESCRIPTION
Read Exchange Information	Permits reading general Exchange properties of the object
Write Exchange Information	Permits writing general Exchange properties of the object
Read Exchange Personal Information	Permits reading personal identification and contact information for an object
Write Exchange Personal Information	Permits writing personal identification and contact information for an object
Read Phone and Mail Options	Permits reading phone and mail options of an object
Write Phone and Mail Options	Permits writing phone and mail options of an object

Although you can use standard Windows permissions, object-specific permissions, and extended permissions to control Exchange management and use, Microsoft recommends that you use the new role-based access controls instead. My recommendation is to use the role-based access controls whenever possible in place of specific permissions. However, you might want to duplicate the old style permissions during your transition from Exchange 2003 or Exchange 2007 to Exchange 2010. This can simplify the transition by allowing you to configure new Exchange groups, such as Organization Management or Recipient Management, exactly as they are configured in the Exchange 2003 or Exchange 2007 organization. In this case, after you've ensured permissions are configured as required for proper operations and support of any applications that work with Exchange data, you can start implementing a role-based model for your organization.

Assigning Advanced Exchange Server Permissions

In Active Directory, different types of objects can have different sets of permissions. Different objects can also have general permissions that are specific to the container in which they're defined. For troubleshooting or fine-tuning your environment, you might occasionally need to modify advanced permissions. You can set advanced permissions for Active Directory objects by following these steps:

1. Open Active Directory Users And Computers. If advanced features aren't currently being displayed, select Advanced Features on the View menu.

2. Right-click the user, group, service account, or computer account with which you want to work.

CAUTION Only administrators with a solid understanding of Active Directory and Active Directory permissions should manipulate advanced object permissions. Incorrectly setting advanced object permissions can cause problems that are difficult to track down and may also cause irreparable harm to the Exchange organization.

3. Select Properties from the shortcut menu, and then click the Security tab in the Properties dialog box, as shown in Figure 8-4.

4. Users or groups with access permissions are listed in the Group Or User Names list box. You can change permissions for these users and groups by doing the following:

   • Select the user or group you want to change.

   • Use the Permissions list box to grant or deny access permissions.

   • When inherited permissions are dimmed, override inherited permissions by selecting the opposite permissions.

5. To set access permissions for additional users, computers, or groups, click Add. Then use the Select Users, Computers, Security Accounts, Or Groups dialog box to add users, computers, security accounts, or groups.

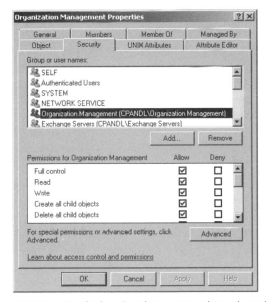

FIGURE 8-4 Use the Security tab to manage advanced permissions.

6. Select the user, computer, service account, or group you want to configure in the Group Or User Names list box, click Add, and then click OK. Then use the fields in the Permissions area to allow or deny permissions. Repeat this step for other users, computers, service accounts, or groups. Click OK when you're finished.

Configuring Role-Based Permissions for Exchange Server

Exchange Server 2010 implements role-based access controls that allow you to easily customize permissions for users in the organization. You use role-based access controls to do the following:

- Assign permissions to groups of users.
- Define policies that assign permissions.
- Assign permissions directly to users.

Before I discuss each of these tasks, I'll discuss essential concepts related to role-based permissions. Because the permissions model is fairly complex, I recommend reading this entire section to understand your implementation options before starting to assign permissions.

Understanding Role-Based Permissions

Role-based access control is a permissions model that uses role assignment to define the management tasks a user or group of users can perform in the Exchange organization. Exchange defines many built-in management roles that you can use to manage your Exchange organization. Each built-in role acts as a logical grouping of permissions that specify the management actions that those assigned the role can perform. You also can create your own custom roles.

You can assign roles to role groups or directly to users. You also can assign roles through role policies that are then applied to role groups, users, or both. By assigning roles, you grant permission to perform management tasks.

At the top of the permission model is the role group, which is a special type of security group that has been assigned one or more roles. Keep the following in mind when working with role-based permissions:

- You can assign role-based permissions to any mailbox-enabled user account. Assigning a role to a user grants the user the ability to perform a specific management action.
- You can assign role-based permissions to any universal security group. Assigning a role to a group grants members of the group the ability to perform a specific management action.
- You cannot assign role-based permissions to security groups with the domain local or global scope.
- You cannot assign role-based permissions to distribution groups regardless of scope.

As Table 8-1 showed previously, Exchange Server 2010 includes a number of predefined role groups. These role groups are assigned fixed management roles by default. As a result, you do not need to explicitly add roles to these groups to enable management, nor can you add or remove roles associated with the built-in groups.

You can, however, manage the members of the predefined role groups using the procedures discussed previously. You can also create your own role groups and manage the membership of those groups.

When you assign a role to a group, the management scope determines where in the Active Directory hierarchy that objects can be managed by users assigned a management role. The scope is either implicitly or explicitly assigned. Implicit scopes are the default scopes that apply based on a particular type of management role.

Table 8-5 lists the management roles with an organization scope. A role with an organization scope applies across the whole Exchange organization. Table 8-6 lists the management roles with a server scope. A role with a server scope applies to an individual server. Table 8-7 lists the management roles with a user scope. A role with a user scope applies to an individual user. When you create a role group, you also can set an explicit scope, such as for objects in the Customer Service organization unit or objects in the Technology organizational unit.

TABLE 8-5 Management Roles with an Organization Scope

MANAGEMENT ROLE	ENABLES MANAGERS TO...
Active Directory Permissions	Configure Active Directory permissions in an organization. Keep in mind that permissions set directly on Active Directory objects cannot be enforced through RBAC.
Address Lists	Manage address lists, the global address list, and offline address lists in an organization.
Audit Logs	Manage audit logs in an organization.
Cmdlet Extension Agents	Manage cmdlet extension agents in an organization.
Database Availability Groups	Manage database availability groups in an organization.
Disaster Recovery	Restore mailboxes and database availability groups in an organization.
Distribution Groups	Create and manage distribution groups and distribution group members in an organization.
Edge Subscriptions	Manage edge synchronization and subscription configuration between Edge Transport servers and Hub Transport servers in an organization.
E-Mail Address Policies	Manage e-mail address policies in an organization.
Exchange Connectors	Manage routing group connectors, delivery agent connectors, and other connectors used for transport. This role doesn't enable administrators to manage Send and Receive connectors.

TABLE 8-5 Management Roles with an Organization Scope

MANAGEMENT ROLE	ENABLES MANAGERS TO...
Federated Sharing	Manage cross-forest and cross-organization sharing in an organization.
Information Rights Management	Manage the Information Rights Management (IRM) features of Exchange in an organization.
Journaling	Manage journaling configuration in an organization.
Legal Hold	Configure whether data within a mailbox should be retained for litigation purposes in an organization.
Mail Enabled Public Folders	Configure whether individual public folders are mail-enabled or mail-disabled in an organization.
Mail Recipient Creation	Create mailboxes, mail users, mail contacts, distribution groups, and dynamic distribution groups in an organization.
Mail Recipients	Manage existing mailboxes, mail users, mail contacts, distribution groups, and dynamic distribution groups in an organization. This does not enable administrators to create these recipients.
Mail Tips	Manage mail tips in an organization.
Mailbox Import Export	Import or example mailbox content as well as to purge unwanted content.
Mailbox Search	Search the content of one or more mailboxes in an organization.
Message Tracking	Track messages in an organization.
Monitoring	Monitor the Microsoft Exchange services and component availability in an organization.
Move Mailboxes	Move mailboxes between servers in an organization and between servers in the local organization and another organization.
Organization Client Access	Manage Client Access server settings in an organization.
Organization Configuration	Manage basic organization-wide settings. This role type doesn't include the permissions included in the Organization Client Access or Organization Transport Settings role types.

TABLE 8-5 Management Roles with an Organization Scope

MANAGEMENT ROLE	ENABLES MANAGERS TO...
Organization Transport Settings	Manage organization-wide transport settings, including system messages, site configuration, and so forth. This role doesn't enable administrators to create or manage transport Receive or Send connectors, queues, hygiene, agents, remote and accepted domains, or rules.
Public Folder Replication	Start and stop public folder replication in an organization.
Public Folders	Manage public folders in an organization. This role type doesn't enable you to manage whether public folders are mail-enabled or to manage public folder replication.
Recipient Policies	Manage recipient policies, such as provisioning policies, in an organization.
Retention Management	Manage retention policies in an organization.
Role Management	Manage management role groups, role assignment policies, management roles, role entries, assignments, and scopes in an organization. Users assigned roles associated with this role type can override the Managed By property for role groups, configure any role group, and add or remove members to or from any role group.
Security Group Creation and Membership	Create and manage security groups and their memberships in an organization.
Send Connectors	Manage transport Send connectors in an organization.
Support Diagnostics	Perform advanced diagnostics under the direction of Microsoft support services.
Transport Agents	Manage transport agents in an organization.
Transport Hygiene	Manage antivirus and antispam features in an organization.
Transport Rules	Manage transport rules.
UM Mailboxes	Manage the unified messaging (UM) configuration of mailboxes and other recipients.
UM Prompts	Create and manage custom UM voice prompts.

TABLE 8-5 Management Roles with an Organization Scope

MANAGEMENT ROLE	ENABLES MANAGERS TO...
Unified Messaging	Manage Unified Messaging servers. This role doesn't enable administrators to manage UM-specific mailbox configuration or UM prompts.
Unscoped Role Management	Create and manage unscoped top-level management roles.
User Options	View the Microsoft Outlook Web Access options for users.
View-Only Configuration	View all of the nonrecipient Exchange configuration settings.
View-Only Recipients	View the configuration of recipients, including mailboxes, mail users, mail contacts, distribution groups, and dynamic distribution groups.

TABLE 8-6 Management Roles with a Server Scope

MANAGEMENT ROLE	ENABLES MANAGERS TO...
Database Copies	Manage mailbox database copies on individual servers.
Databases	Create, manage, mount, and dismount mailbox and public folder databases on individual servers.
Exchange Server Certificates	Create, import, export, and manage Exchange server certificates on individual servers.
Exchange Servers	Manage Exchange server configuration on individual servers.
Exchange Virtual Directories	Manage Autodiscover, Outlook Web App, Exchange ActiveSync, offline address book (OAB), Windows PowerShell, and Web administration interface virtual directories on individual servers.
Migration	Migrate mailboxes and mailbox content into or out of a server.
POP3 and IMAP4 Protocols	Manage Post Office Protocol version 3 (POP3) and Internet Message Access Protocol version 4 (IMAP4) configuration, such as authentication and connection settings, on individual servers.
Receive Connectors	Manage transport Receive connector configuration, such as size limits on an individual server.
Transport Queues	Manage transport queues on an individual server.

TABLE 8-7 Management Roles with a User Scope

MANAGEMENT ROLE	ENABLES INDIVIDUAL USERS TO...
MyBaseOptions	View and modify the basic configuration of their own mailbox and associated settings.
MyContactInformation	Modify their contact information. This information includes their address and phone numbers.
MyDistributionGroupMembership	View and modify their membership in distribution groups in an organization, provided that those distribution groups allow manipulation of group membership.
MyDistributionGroups	Create, modify, and view distribution groups and modify, view, remove, and add members to distribution groups they own.
MyProfileInformation	Modify their name.
MyRetentionPolicies	View their retention tags, and view and modify their retention tag settings and defaults.
MyVoiceMail	View and modify their voice mail settings.

Role assignment policies grant users permissions to configure their Outlook Web App options and perform limited management tasks. When you install Exchange server, the setup process creates the Default Role Assignment Policy and sets this as the default for all new mailboxes. This policy grants users the MyBaseOptions, MyContactInformation, MyDistributionGroupMembership, and MyVoiceMail roles, but it does not grant users the MyDistributionGroups and MyProfileInformation roles.

As discussed later in this chapter, you can create other role assignment policies as well. One way to manage existing policies is to use the Exchange Control Panel. When you are managing the organization and Users & Groups is selected in the left pane, you can select the User Roles tab to work with existing role assignment policies. Double-click the related entry to configure role assignment. To grant a role to users, select the related check box. To not grant a role to users, clear the related check box. Click Save to save your changes.

Creating and Managing Role Groups

By default, members of the Organization Management group can manage any role group in the Exchange organization. Anyone designated as a manager of a role group can manage the role group. You assign a user as a manager of a role group using the –ManagedBy parameter, which can be set when you create or modify a role group.

In the Exchange Management Shell, commands you use to work with role groups include the following:

- **Get-RoleGroup**   Displays a complete or filtered list of role groups. When specifying filters, use parentheses to define the filter, such as **–Filter { RolegroupType –Eq "Linked" }**.

```
Get-RoleGroup [-Identity RoleGroupName] {AddtlParams}


{AddtlParams}
[-DomainController FullyQualifiedName] [-Filter {LinkedGroup |
ManagedBy | Members | Name | RoleGroupType | DisplayName}]
[-Organization OrganizationID] [-ReadFromDomainController
{$True|$False}] [-ResultSize Size] [-SortBy {LinkedGroup |
ManagedBy | Members | Name | RoleGroupType | DisplayName}]
```

- **New-RoleGroup**   Creates a new role group. When specifying roles, you must use the full role name, including spaces. Enclose the role names in quotation marks and separate each role with a comma, such as "**Mail Recipient Creation**", "**Mail Recipients**", "**Recipient Policies**".

```
New-RoleGroup –Name RoleGroupName [-Roles Roles]
[-ManagedBy ManagerIds] [-Members MemberIds] {AddtlParams}


{AddtlParams}
[-CustomConfigWriteScope Scope] [-CustomRecipientWriteScope Scope]
[-Description Description] [-DisplayName DisplayName]
[-DomainController FullyQualifiedName] [-Organization
OrganizationID] [-RecipientOrganizationalUnitScope Scope]
[-SamAccountName PreWin2000Name]


[-LinkedCredential Credential] [-LinkedDomainController LinkedDC]
[-LinkedForeignGroup LinkedGroup]
```

- **Remove-RoleGroup**   Removes a role group. If a role group has designated managers, you must be listed as a manager to remove the role group or use the –BypassSecurityGroupManagerCheck parameter and be an organization manager.

```
Remove-RoleGroup –Identity RoleGroupName {AddtlParams}


{AddtlParams}
[-BypassSecurityGroupManagerCheck {$True|$False}]
[-DomainController FullyQualifiedName]
```

- **Set-RoleGroup**   Configures role group properties. If you specify managers, you must provide the complete list of managers because the list you provide overwrites the existing list of managers. To manage role assignment, see the "Assigning Roles Directly or via Policy" section later in the chapter.

```
Set-RoleGroup -Identity RoleGroupName [-ManagedBy ManagerIds]
[-Name NewName] {AddtlParams}

{AddtlParams}
[-BypassSecurityGroupManagerCheck {$True|$False}]
[-Description Description] [-DomainController FullyQualifiedName]

[-LinkedCredential Credential] [-LinkedDomainController LinkedDC]
[-LinkedForeignGroup LinkedGroup]
```

You use New-RoleGroup to create role groups. When you create a role group, you must specify the group name and the roles assigned to the group. You should also specify the managers and members of the group. The managers and members can be individual users or groups identified by their display name, alias, or distinguished name. If you want to specify more than one manager or member, separate each entry with a comma. In the following example, you create the Special Recipient Management role group to allow members of the group to manage (but not create) recipients:

```
New-RoleGroup -Name "Special Recipient Management"
-Roles "mail recipients", "recipient policies"
-ManagedBy "juliec", "tylerk", "ulij"
-Member "mikeg", "lylep", "rubyc", "yus"
```

By default, the scope of the role group is the organization. You can also set a specific scope for an organizational unit. In the following example, you create a role group named LA Recipient Management and set the scope to the LA Office organizational unit to allow members of the group to manage recipients in the LA Office organizational unit:

```
New-RoleGroup -Name "LA Recipient Management"
-Roles "mail recipient creation", "mail recipients", "recipient policies"
-ManagedBy "LA Managers" -Member "LA Help Desk"
-RecipientOrganizationalUnitScope "LA Office"
```

A linked role group links the role group to a universal security group in another forest. Creating a linked role group is useful if your Exchange servers reside in a resource forest and your users and managers reside in a separate user forest. If you create a linked role group, you can't add members directly to it. You must add the members to the universal security group in the foreign forest.

When you are creating linked role groups, you use the –LinkedDomainController parameter to specify the fully qualified domain name or IP address of a domain controller in the foreign forest. This domain controller is used to get security information for the foreign universal security group, which is specified by the –Linked-ForeignGroup parameter. If you use the –LinkedDomainController parameter, you must specify a foreign universal security group with the –LinkedForeignGroup parameter, and you can't use the –Members parameter. Optionally, you can use the –LinkedCredential parameter to specify credentials to use to access the foreign forest. To pass in the credentials, you'll want to use a Credential object.

In the following example, you create a linked role group that enables the members of the Chicago Managers universal security group to manage recipients located in the Chicago office:

```
$cred = Get-Credentials

New-RoleGroup -Name "Chicago Recipient Managers"
-LinkedDomainController corpserver26.cpusers.cpand1.com
-LinkedCredential $cred -LinkedForeignGroup "Chicago Managers"
-CustomRecipientWriteScope "Chicago Recipients" -Roles "mail recipients"
```

In this example, Chicago Managers is a group created in the user forest and you are logged on to the resource forest. When PowerShell reads the Get-Credentials command, you are prompted for the user name and password for the user forest.

Role groups are created as universal security groups in the Active Directory database. In Active Directory Users And Computers, you'll find role groups in the Microsoft Exchange Security Groups container. After you create a role group, you can manage it using Active Directory Users And Computers or the Exchange Management Shell. The management tasks you can perform depend on which tool you are using. In Active Directory Users And Computers, you can manage group membership, rename the group, or delete the group. Additional tasks you can perform when you use the Exchange Management Shell include setting managers and modifying role assignments.

NOTE Although you can edit a group's managers or other attributes in Active Directory Users And Computers, you shouldn't do this because some values are linked and set differently than you'd expect. For example, you set the ManagedBy property to the distinguished name of the first manager and define additional managers using the msExchCoManagedByLink property.

You can list available role groups using Get-RoleGroup. If you type Get-Role-Group at the Exchange Management Shell prompt, you see a list of all role groups defined in the Exchange organization to which you are connected. You can filter the output in a variety of ways using standard PowerShell filtering techniques. Get-Role-Group also has a –Filter parameter that you can use to filter the output according to specific criteria you set. The following example looks for a role group named CS Recipient Management and lists all its properties:

```
get-rolegroup -filter {Name -eq "CS Recipient Management"} |
format-list
```

You can use Set-RoleGroup to change the name of a role group or to define a new list of managers. To delete a role group, use Remove-RoleGroup.

Viewing, Adding or Removing Role Group Members

By default, members of the Organization Management group can manage the membership of any role group in the Exchange organization. Anyone designated as a manager of a role group can manage the membership of that role group as well.

In the Exchange Management Shell, commands you use to configure role group membership include the following:

- **Add-RoleGroupMember** Adds a user or universal security group as a member of a role group. If a role group has designated managers, you must be listed as a manager to add role group members or use the –BypassSecurityGroupManagerCheck parameter and be an organization manager.

  ```
  Add-RoleGroupMember -Identity RoleGroupName -Member MemberIds
  [-BypassSecurityGroupManagerCheck {$True|$False}]
  [-DomainController FullyQualifiedName]
  ```

- **Get-RoleGroupMember** Lists the members of a role group.

  ```
  Get-RoleGroupMember -Identity RoleGroupName
  [-DomainController FullyQualifiedName]
  [-ReadFromDomainController {$True|$False}]
  [-ResultSize Size]
  ```

- **Remove-RoleGroupMember** Removes a user or universal security group from a role group. If a role group has designated managers, you must be listed as a manager to remove role group members or use the –BypassSecurityGroupManagerCheck parameter and be an organization manager.

  ```
  Remove-RoleGroupMember -Identity RoleGroupName -Member MemberIds
  [-BypassSecurityGroupManagerCheck {$True|$False}]
  [-DomainController FullyQualifiedName]
  ```

- **Update-RoleGroupMember** Replaces the current group membership with the list of members you provide.

  ```
  Update-RoleGroupMember -Identity RoleGroupName -Members NewMemberIds
  [-BypassSecurityGroupManagerCheck {$True|$False}]
  [-DomainController FullyQualifiedName]
  ```

You add members to a role group using Add-RoleGroupMember. When you add a member to a role group, the member is given the effective permissions provided by the management roles assigned to the role group. If the role group has designated managers, you must be a role group manager or use the –BypassSecurityGroup-ManagerCheck parameter to override the security group management check.

In the following example, you add a user to the LA Recipient Management role group:

```
Add-RoleGroupMember –Identity "LA Recipient Management"
-Member "joym"
```

When you are working with the Exchange Management Shell, don't forget that all the features of PowerShell are at your disposal. In the following example, you get a list of all users with mailboxes in the Technology department and add them to the Technology Management role group:

```
Get-User –Filter { Department -Eq "Technology" -And –RecipientType
-Eq "UserMailbox" } | Get-Mailbox | Add-RoleGroupMember
"Technology Management"
```

You can list members of a particular role group using Get-RoleGroupMember. Members are listed by name and recipient type as shown in the following example and sample output:

```
Get-RoleGroupMember –Identity "CS Recipient Management"


Name                          RecipientType
----                          -------------
Jae Pak                       UserMailbox
Raman Iyer                    UserMailbox
```

You can delete role group members using Remove-RoleGroupMember. When you remove a member from a role group, the user or group of users can no longer perform the management tasks made available by that role group. However, keep in mind that the user or group of users might be a member of another role group that grants management permissions. If so, the user or group of users will still be able to perform management tasks.

NOTE For linked role groups, you can't use Remove-RoleGroupMember to remove members from the role group. Instead, you need to remove members from the foreign universal security group (USG) that's linked to the linked role group. Use Get-RoleGroup to identify the foreign group.

Assigning Roles Directly or via Policy

You can assign built-in or custom roles to users, role groups, and universal security groups in one of two ways:

- Directly using role assignment
- Via assignment policy

Directly assigning roles is accomplished using role assignment commands. By adding, removing, or modifying role assignments, you can control the management tasks that users can perform. Although you can assign roles directly to users or universal security groups, this approach increases the complexity of the permissions model in your Exchange organization. A more flexible solution is to assign roles via assignment policy. Assigning roles via assignment policy requires you to do the following:

1. Create assignment policies.
2. Assign roles to these policies.
3. Assign policies to users or groups as appropriate.

Management roles define the specific tasks that can be performed by the members of a role group assigned the role. A role assignment links a management role and a role group. Assigning a management role to a role group grants members of the role group the ability to perform the management tasks defined in the management role. Role assignments can use management scopes to control where the assignment can be used.

In the Exchange Management Shell, commands you use to work with role assignment include the following:

- **Get-ManagementRoleAssignment** Displays a complete or filtered list of role assignments for a role group. You can examine role assignments by name, assignment type, or scope type as well as whether the assignment is enabled or disabled.

```
Get-ManagementRoleAssignment [-Identity RoleAssignmentToRetrieve]
{AddtlParams}


Get-ManagementRoleAssignment [-RoleAssignee IdentityToCheck]
[-AssignmentMethod {Direct | SecurityGroup |
RoleAssignmentPolicy}] {AddtlParams}


{AddtlParams}
[-ConfigWriteScope <None | NotApplicable | OrganizationConfig |
CustomConfigScope | PartnerDelegatedTenantScope |
ExclusiveConfigScope>] [-CustomConfigWriteScope ManagementScopeId]
[-CustomRecipientWriteScope ManagementScopeId] [-Delegating <$true
| $false>] [-DomainController FullyQualifiedName] [-Enabled <$true
| $false>] [-Exclusive <$true | $false>]
[-ExclusiveConfigWriteScope ManagementScopeId]
[-ExclusiveRecipientWriteScope ManagementScopeId]
[-GetEffectiveUsers <$true | $false>] [-Organization
OrganizationId] [-RecipientOrganizationalUnitScope
OrganizationalUnitId] [-RecipientWriteScope <None | NotApplicable
| Organization | MyGAL | Self | MyDirectReports | OU |
CustomRecipientScope | MyDistributionGroups | MyExecutive |
ExclusiveRecipientScope>] [-Role RoleId] [-RoleAssigneeType <User |
SecurityGroup | RoleAssignmentPolicy | MailboxPlan |
ForeignSecurityPrincipal | RoleGroup | LinkedRoleGroup>]
[-WritableRecipient GeneralRecipientId] [-WritableServer ServerId]
```

- **New-ManagementRoleAssignment** Creates a new role assignment, and
  assigns it directly to a user or group or assigns it via an assignment policy.

```
New-ManagementRoleAssignment –Name RoleAssignmentName
-Policy Policy –Role Roles {AddtlParams}

New-ManagementRoleAssignment –Name RoleAssignmentName
-SecurityGroup Group –Role Roles {AddtlParams}

New-ManagementRoleAssignment –Name RoleAssignmentName
-User User –Role Roles {AddtlParams}

{AddtlParams}
[-CustomConfigWriteScope Scope][-CustomRecipientWriteScope Scope]
[-Delegating {$True|$False}] [-DomainController FullyQualifiedName]
[-ExclusiveConfigWriteScope Scope] [-ExclusiveRecipientWriteScope
Scope] [-Organization OrganizationId]
[-RecipientOrganizationalUnitScope Scope]
[-RecipientRelativeWriteScope <None | NotApplicable | Organization
| MyGAL | Self | MyDirectReports | OU |CustomRecipientScope |
MyDistributionGroups | MyExecutive | ExclusiveRecipientScope>]
[-UnscopedTopLevel {$True|$False}]
```

- **Remove-ManagementRoleAssignment** Removes a role assignment.

```
Remove-ManagementRoleAssignment –Identity RoleAssignmentName
[-DomainController FullyQualifiedName]
```

- **Set-ManagementRoleAssignment** Configures role assignment properties.

```
Set-ManagementRoleAssignment –Identity RoleAssignmentName
[-DomainController FullyQualifiedName] [-Enabled {$True|$False}]
{AddtlParams1 | AddtlParams2 | AddtlParams3 | AddtlParams4}

{AddtlParams1}
[-CustomConfigWriteScope Scope] [-RecipientOrganizationalUnitScope
OUId] [-RecipientRelativeWriteScope <None | NotApplicable |
Organization | MyGAL | Self | MyDirectReports | OU |
CustomRecipientScope | MyDistributionGroups | MyExecutive |
ExclusiveRecipientScope>]

{AddtlParams2}
[-CustomConfigWriteScope Scope]
[-CustomRecipientWriteScope Scope]

{AddtlParams3}
 [-CustomConfigWriteScope Scope]
[-DomainController FullyQualifiedName]

{AddtlParams4}
[-ExclusiveConfigWriteScope Scope]
[-ExclusiveRecipientWriteScope Scope]
```

You can list role assignments using Get-ManagementRoleAssignment. You use New-ManagementRoleAssignment to assign roles. In the following example, you assign the Retention Management role to the Central Help Desk group:

```
New-ManagementRoleAssignment -Name "Central Help Desk_Retention"
-Role "Retention Management" -SecurityGroup "Central Help Desk"
```

In the following example, you assign the Mail Recipients role to members of the Marketing Help Desk group and restrict the write scope to the Marketing organizational unit:

```
New-ManagementRoleAssignment -Name "Marketing_Options"
-Role "Mail Recipients" -SecurityGroup "Marketing Help Desk"
-RecipientOrganizationalUnitScope "cpandl.com/Marketing"
```

This allows users who are members of the Marketing Help Desk to manage existing mailboxes, mail users, mail contacts, distribution groups, and dynamic distribution groups in the Marketing organizational unit. This does not enable these users to create recipients in this organizational unit. To create recipients, the users need to be assigned the Mail Recipient Creation role.

You can modify role assignment using Set-ManagementRoleAssignment. In the following example, you disable the Central Help Desk_Retention role assignment:

```
Set-ManagementRoleAssignment -Identity "Central Help Desk_Retention"
-Enabled $False
```

When you disable a role assignment, the users assigned the role can no longer perform the management tasks granted by the role. However, keep in mind that a user might have been granted the permission in another way. By disabling a role assignment rather than removing it, you can easily enable the role assignment again as shown in the following example:

```
Set-ManagementRoleAssignment -Identity "Central Help Desk_Retention"
-Enabled $True
```

However, if you are sure you no longer want to use a particular role assignment, you can remove it using Remove-ManagementRoleAssignment as shown in the following example:

```
Remove-ManagementRoleAssignment -Identity "Central Help Desk_Retention"
```

When you create a new assignment policy, you can assign it to users using the New-Mailbox, Set-Mailbox, or Enable-Mailbox cmdlet. If you make the new assignment policy the default assignment policy, it's assigned to all new mailboxes that don't have an explicitly designated assignment policy. After you create an assignment policy, you must assign at least one management role to it for it to apply permissions to a mailbox. Without any roles assigned to it, users assigned the policy won't be able to manage any of their mailbox configurations. To assign a management role, use New-ManagementRoleAssignment.

In the Exchange Management Shell, commands you use to work with role assignment policy include the following:

- **Get-RoleAssignmentPolicy**   Lists all policies or a specified role assignment policy.

```
Get-RoleAssignmentPolicy [-Identity AssignmentPolicyName]
[-DomainController FullyQualifiedName] [-Organization
OrganizationId]
```

- **New-RoleAssignmentPolicy**   Creates a new role assignment policy.

```
New-RoleAssignmentPolicy -Name AssignmentPolicyName
[-Description Description] [-DomainController FullyQualifiedName]
[-IsDefault {$True|$False}] [-Organization OrganizationId]
```

- **Remove-RoleAssignmentPolicy**   Removes a role assignment policy.

```
Remove-RoleAssignmentPolicy -Identity AssignmentPolicyName
[-DomainController FullyQualifiedName]
```

- **Set-RoleAssignmentPolicy**   Changes the name of a role assignment policy, or sets a role assignment policy as the default.

```
Set-RoleAssignmentPolicy -Identity AssignmentPolicyName
[-Description Description] [-DomainController FullyQualifiedName]
[-IsDefault {$True|$False}] [-Name NewName]
```

You can list role assignment policies using Get-RoleAssignmentPolicy. Rather than view all available assignment policies, you can easily filter the output to look for default assignment policies. Here is an example:

```
Get-RoleAssignmentPolicy | Where { $_.IsDefault -eq $True }
```

You use New-RoleAssignmentPolicy to create role assignment policies. In the following example, you create the Standard User Policy and assign it as the default:

```
New-RoleAssignmentPolicy -Name "Standard User Policy"
```

When you create a new assignment policy, you can assign it to users using New-Mailbox, Set-Mailbox, or Enable-Mailbox as shown in the following example:

```
Set-Mailbox -Identity "tommyj" -RoleAssignmentPolicy "Standard User
Policy"
```

If you make the new assignment policy the default assignment policy, it's assigned to all new mailboxes that don't have an explicitly designated assignment policy. You can specify that a policy is the default when you create it using –IsDefault. You can also designate a policy as the default using Set-RoleAssignment-Policy as shown in this example:

```
Set-RoleAssignmentPolicy –Identity "Standard User Policy" -IsDefault
```

After you create an assignment policy, you must assign at least one management role to it for it to apply permissions to a mailbox. Without any roles assigned to it, users assigned the policy won't be able to manage any of their mailbox configuration. To assign a management role, use New-ManagementRoleAssignment.

You can remove policies using Remove-RoleAssignmentPolicy. The assignment policy you want to remove can't be assigned to any mailboxes or management roles. Also, if you want to remove the default assignment policy, it must be the last assignment policy. Because of this, you need to use Set-Mailbox to change the assignment policy for any mailbox that's assigned the assignment policy before you can remove it. If the assignment policy is the default assignment policy, use Set-RoleAssignmentPolicy to select a new default assignment policy before you remove the old default policy. You don't need to do this if you're removing the last assignment policy. Additionally, keep in mind that you can use Remove-Management-RoleAssignment to remove any management role assignments assigned to a policy.

With this in mind, a series of examples follow that show how you can modify and remove assignment policy. The following example removes the assignment policy called "Standard User Policy" by finding all of the mailboxes assigned the policy and then assigning a different policy:

```
Get-Mailbox | Where {$_.RoleAssignmentPolicy -Eq "Standard User Policy"}
| Set-Mailbox -RoleAssignmentPolicy "New User Policy"
```

Next, you can remove all the role assignments assigned to an assignment policy:

```
Get-ManagementRoleAssignment -RoleAssignee "Standard User Policy" |
Remove-ManagementRoleAssignment
```

Afterward, you can remove the assignment policy by entering the following:

```
Remove-RoleAssignmentPolicy "Standard User Policy"
```

Performing Advanced Permissions Management

Advanced permissions areas you can work with are related to custom management roles, management scopes, and role entries. Management roles define the management tasks users can perform. Management scopes identify the objects that are allowed to be managed. Role entries are the individual permission entries on a management role that allow users to perform management tasks.

Creating Custom Roles

The built-in roles were listed previously in Tables 8-5 to 8-7. The built-in roles are fixed, and you cannot create role entries to define additional management tasks for built-in roles. You can, however, create your own custom roles based on built-in roles and then extend the custom roles as necessary to meet the needs of your organization. In this way, custom management roles allow you to do things you can't do with the built-in roles.

Commands you use to create your own custom roles and to view any existing roles include the following:

- **Get-ManagementRole**   Displays a complete or filtered list of management roles defined in the organization. Role types are the same as those listed previously without spaces in their names.

```
Get-ManagementRole [-Identity RoleName] [-DomainController
FullyQualifiedName] [-Organization OrganizationId] [-RoleType
RoleType] {AddtlParams}

{AddtlParams}
{ [-Cmdlet Cmdlet] [-CmdletParameters Parameters] |
[-GetChildren {$True|$False}] |
[-Script Script] [-ScriptParameters Parameters] |
[-Recurse {$True|$False}] }
```

- **New-ManagementRole**   Creates a new management role.

```
New-ManagementRole –Name RoleName
[-Parent ParentRoleToCopy | -UnScopedTopLevel {$True|$False}]
[-Description Description] [-DomainController FullyQualifiedName]
[-Organization OrganizationId]
```

- **Remove-ManagementRole**   Removes a management role.

```
Remove-ManagementRole [-Identity RoleName]
[-DomainController FullyQualifiedName] [-Recurse {$True|$False}]
[-UnScopedTopLevel {$True|$False}]
```

To view management roles, you use Get-ManagementRole. Entering Get-ManagementRole by itself without parameters lists all the roles in your organization. Additional options include using

- **–Identity**, to view information about a specific role
- **–Cmdlet**, to list all roles that include a specified cmdlet
- **–CmdletParameters**, to list all roles that include the specified cmdlet parameter or parameters

- **–GetChildren**, to list only the child roles of a specified parent role
- **–Recurse**, to list the role specified in the –Identity parameter, its child roles, and their children
- **–RoleType**, to list all roles of a particular type
- **–Script**, to list all roles that include a specified script
- **–ScriptParameters**, to list all roles that include the specified script parameter or parameters

In the following example, you list all the roles associated with the Mail Recipient Creation role:

```
Get-ManagementRole "Mail Recipient Creation" -Recurse
```

You can create your own custom roles using New-ManagementRole. New roles can either be empty top-level roles or based on an existing parent role. In this example, you create an empty role:

```
New-ManagementRole -Name "Change Management"
-UnscopedTopLevel
```

In the following example, you create a new role based on the Organization Client Access role:

```
New-ManagementRole -Name "Organization Client Access View-Only"
-Parent "Organization Client Access"
```

After you create a role based on another role, you might need to remove role entries that are not required. In the following example, you ensure the Organization Client Access View-Only role grants only permission to view Client Access information by removing any entries for commands that don't begin with Get:

```
Get-ManagementRoleEntry "Organization Client Access View-Only\*" |
Where { $_.Name -NotLike "Get*" } | Remove-ManagementRoleEntry
```

To remove a custom role, you use Remove-ManagementRole. You can remove a role by name as shown in the following example:

```
Remove-ManagementRole "Organization Client Access View-Only"
```

Using the –Recurse parameter, you can remove all child roles of a role. Using the –UnscopedTopLevel parameter, you can remove an unscoped top-level role. You also can use Get-ManagementRole to obtain a list of roles to remove as shown in this example:

```
Get-ManagementRole *MyTestRole* | Remove-ManagementRole
```

TIP To avoid accidentally removing a number of important roles, you should run Get-ManagementRole by itself first or add the –WhatIf parameter to Remove-ManagementRole. Either technique will ensure you know exactly which roles you are working with.

Creating Custom Role Scopes

Every management role has a management scope that determines where in Active Directory objects can be viewed or modified by users assigned the management role. Management scopes can be defined as either regular or exclusive. Regular scopes can be either implicitly or explicitly created. They are simply the standard type of scope, and they define the set of recipients that can be managed. Exclusive scopes on the other hand must always be explicitly created, and they allow you to deny users access to objects contained within the exclusive scope if those users aren't assigned a role associated with the exclusive scope.

Scopes can be

- Inherited from the management role
- Specified as a predefined relative scope on a management role assignment
- Created using custom filters, and added to a management role assignment.

Scopes inherited from management roles are called *implicit scopes,* while predefined and custom scopes are called *explicit scopes.* Implicit scopes include

- **Recipient read scope** Determines which recipient objects the user assigned the management role is allowed to read from Active Directory.
- **Recipient write scope** Determines which recipient objects the user assigned the management role is allowed to modify in Active Directory.
- **Configuration read scope** Determines which configuration objects the user assigned the management role is allowed to read from Active Directory.
- **Configuration write scope** Determines which organizational and server objects the user assigned the management role is allowed to modify in Active Directory.

Commands you use to work with scopes include the following:

- **Get-ManagementScope** Displays a complete or filtered list of management scopes defined in the organization.

```
Get-ManagementScope [-Identity ScopeName]
[-Exclusive {$True|$False}] [-DomainController FullyQualifiedName]
[-Organization OrganizationId] [-Orphan {$True|$False}]
```

- **New-ManagementScope** Creates a new management scope.

```
New-ManagementScope -Name ScopeName -RecipientRestrictionFilter
Filter [-RecipientRoot Root] {AddtlParams}
```

```
New-ManagementScope -Name ScopeName
-ServerList Servers | -ServerRestrictionFilter Filter {AddtlParams}

{AddtlParams}
[-DomainController FullyQualifiedName] [-Organization
OrganizationId] [-Exclusive {$True|$False}] [-Force {$True|$False}]
```

- **Remove-ManagementScope**   Removes a management scope.

```
Remove-ManagementScope [-Identity Scope]
[-DomainController FullyQualifiedName]
```

- **Set-ManagementScope**   Modifies the settings of a management scope.

```
Set-ManagementScope -Identity ScopeName -ServerRestrictionFilter
Filter [-DomainController FullyQualifiedName] [-Name Name]

Set-ManagementScope -Identity ScopeName -RecipientRestrictionFilter
Filter [-RecipientRoot Root] [-DomainController FullyQualifiedName]
[-Name Name]
```

You use Get-ManagementScope to retrieve a list of existing management scopes. If you want to list only exclusive scopes, use the –Exclusive parameter. If you want to list only management scopes that aren't associated with role assignments, use the –Orphan parameter, as shown here:

```
Get-ManagementScope -Orphan
```

You can create custom management scopes using New-ManagementScope. After you create a regular or exclusive scope, you need to associate the scope with a management role assignment. One way to do this is to use New-ManagementRole Assignment.

You define scopes using recipient restriction filters, explicit server lists, or server restriction filters. In the following example, you create the Sales Team scope that applies only to mailboxes located in the Sales organizational unit:

```
New-ManagementScope -Name "Sales Team Scope" -RecipientRoot
"cpandl.com/Sales" -RecipientRestrictionFilter {RecipientType -eq
"UserMailbox"}
```

In the following example, you create a scope that applies only to MailServer14 and MailServer18:

```
New-ManagementScope -Name "Main Server Scope" -ServerList
"MailServer14", "MailServer18"
```

In the following example, you create a scope that applies only to servers in the Active Directory site called Seattle-First-Site:

```
New-ManagementScope -Name "Seattle Site Scope" -ServerRestrictionFilter
{ServerSite -eq "Seattle-First-Site"}
```

Exclusive scopes work a bit differently. When an exclusive scope is created, all users are immediately blocked from modifying the recipients that match the exclusive scope until the scope is associated with a management role assignment. If other role assignments are associated with other exclusive scopes that match the same recipients, those assignments can still modify the recipients. In the following example, you create a Protected Managers exclusive scope for users that contain the string "Manager" in their job title:

```
New-ManagementScope -Name "Protected Managers"
-RecipientRestrictionFilter { Title -Like "*Manager*" } -Exclusive
```

You then need to associate the exclusive scope with a management role assignment that assigns the appropriate management roles to the appropriate role group or groups. In the following example, members of the Level 5 Administrators security group are granted permission to work with Protected Manager mailboxes:

```
New-ManagementRoleAssignment -Name "Level 5 Administrators_Mail
Recipients" -SecurityGroup "Level 5 Administrators" -Role "Mail
Recipients" -CustomRecipientWriteScope "Protected Managers"
```

You use Set-ManagementScope to modify the settings of a management scope. If you change a scope that has been associated with management role assignments, the updated scope applies to all of the associated role assignments. To remove a management scope, you can use Remove-ManagementScope. However, you can't remove a management scope if it's associated with a role assignment.

Creating Custom Role Entries

Role entries determine the management actions that members of a role group can perform. You create a role entry by specifying the permitted management command and any permitted command parameters.

When you assign a management role to a role group, this is essentially similar to creating the related role entries that allow a user or group to perform related management tasks. Another way to grant permission to perform a management action is to create a management role entry and add it to a management role. However, keep in mind that you can't add role entries to built-in roles.

Commands you use to work with role entries include

- **Add-ManagementRoleEntry** Adds role entries to a custom management role. You can't add role entries to built-in roles. The –UnScopedTopLevel parameter allows you to specify that you're adding a custom script or non-Exchange cmdlet to an unscoped top-level management role.

```
Add-ManagementRoleEntry -Identity RoleEntryToAdd
[-DomainController FullyQualifiedName] [-Overwrite {$True|$False}]
[-Parameters CmdletParametersToUse]
[-PSSnapinName SnapinThatContainsCmdlet]
[-Type <Cmdlet | Script | ApplicationPermission | All>]
[-UnScopedTopLevel {$True|$False}]

Add-ManagementRoleEntry -ParentRoleEntry ParentRoleEntry
-Role Role [-DomainController FullyQualifiedName]
[-Overwrite {$True|$False}]
```

- **Get-ManagementRoleEntry**   Lists the role entries configured on a particular role. You can list role entries that match specific criteria such as role name, cmdlet name, parameter name, role entry type, or associated PowerShell snap-in.

```
Get-ManagementRoleEntry -Identity RoleEntry
[-DomainController FullyQualifiedName]
[-Parameters CmdletParameters] [-PSSnapinName Snapin]
[-Type <Cmdlet | Script | ApplicationPermission | All>]
```

- **Remove-ManagementRoleEntry**   Removes a management role entry.

```
Remove-ManagementRoleEntry -Identity RoleEntry
[-DomainController FullyQualifiedName]
```

- **Set-ManagementRoleEntry**   Modifies a management role entry.

```
Set-ManagementRoleEntry -Identity RoleEntry
[-AddParameter {$True|$False} | -RemoveParameter {$True|$False}]
[-Parameters ParametersToAddOrRemove]

[-DomainController FullyQualifiedName]
[-UnScopedTopLevel {$True|$False}]
```

Every management role must have at least one management role entry. A role entry consists of a single cmdlet and its parameters, a script, or a special permission that you want to make available. If a cmdlet or script doesn't appear as an entry on a management role, that cmdlet or script isn't accessible via that role. Similarly, if a parameter isn't specified in a role entry, the parameter on that cmdlet or script isn't accessible via that role.

The way you create and work with role entries depends on whether they are based on the built-in roles or unscoped roles. Roles based on built-in roles can contain only role entries that are Exchange 2010 cmdlets. To use custom scripts or non-Exchange cmdlets, you need to add them as unscoped role entries to an unscoped top-level role.

You can't add management role entries to child roles if the entries don't appear in parent roles. For example, if the parent role doesn't have an entry for New-Mailbox, the child role can't be assigned that cmdlet. Additionally, if Set-Mailbox is on the parent role but the –Database parameter has been removed from the entry, the –Database parameter on the Set-Mailbox cmdlet can't be added to the entry on the child role. With this in mind, you need to carefully choose the parent role to copy when you want to create a new customized role.

Role entry names are a combination of the management role that they're associated with and the name of the cmdlet or script that you want to make available. The role name and the cmdlet or script are separated by a backslash character (\). For example, the role entry name for the New-Mailbox cmdlet on the Mail Recipient Creation role is Mail Recipient Creation\New-Mailbox.

You can use the wildcard character (*) in the role entry name to return all of the role entries that match the input you provide. The wildcard character can be used with role names as well as with cmdlet or script names. For example, you can use ** to return a list of all role entries for all roles, *\New-Mailbox to return a list of all role entries that contain the New-Mailbox cmdlet, or Mail Recipient Creation* to return a list of all role entries on the Mail Recipient Creation role.

When you create a role entry, you need to specify all of the parameters that can be used. Exchange will try to verify the parameters that you provide when you add the role entry. Only the parameters that you include are available to the users assigned to the role. You need to update role entries manually if parameters available for cmdlets or scripts change.

To avoid errors, keep the following in mind:

- Scripts that you add to an unscoped role entry must reside in the Exchange 2010 scripts directory on every server where administrators and users connect using the Exchange Management Shell. The default scripts directory is C:\Program Files\Microsoft\Exchange Server\V14\Scripts.

- Non-Exchange cmdlets that you add to an unscoped role entry must be installed on every Exchange 2010 server where administrators and users connect using the Exchange Management Shell. When you add a non-Exchange cmdlet, you must specify the Windows PowerShell snap-in name that contains the non-Exchange cmdlet.

You use Get-ManagementRoleEntry to list role entries that have been configured on roles. In the following example, you list all the role entries that exist on the Mail Recipient Creation role:

```
Get-ManagementRoleEntry "Mail Recipient Creation\*"
```

You also can list all the role entries that contain a particular command, as shown here:

```
Get-ManagementRoleEntry *\Get-Recipient
```

You can list role entries that match specific criteria such as role name or cmdlet name. Using Add-ManagementRoleEntry, you can specify role entries to add to a role. You specify the role entry to add using the –Identity parameter and the basic syntax for the identity as RoleName\CmdletName. Role entries are either based on a parent role entry or are unscoped (the default), specified using the –ParentRoleEntry or –UnScopedTopLevel parameter, respectively. The –Role parameter specifies the role to which the new role entry is added.

In the following example, you add a role entry for the Get-Mailbox cmdlet to the LA Recipient Managers role:

```
Add-ManagementRoleEntry -Identity "LA Recipient Managers\Get-Mailbox"
```

This entry assigns permission for the Get-Mailbox cmdlet to members of the LA Recipient Managers role. You can specify the exact parameters that are permitted as shown in the following example:

```
Add-ManagementRoleEntry -Identity "LA Recipient Managers\Get-Mailbox"
-Parameters Archive, Identity, Filter, OrganizationalUnit, SortBy
```

You can also assign permission for multiple commands. Consider the following example:

```
Get-ManagementRoleEntry "Mail Recipients\Get-Mailbox*" |
Add-ManagementRoleEntry -Role "Central Help Desk"
```

Here, you use Get-ManagementRoleEntry to retrieve a list of all the role entries for the Mail Recipients role that begin with the string "Get-Mailbox" in the cmdlet name, and then add them to the Central Help Desk role using the Add-ManagementRoleEntry cmdlet. The role entries are added to the child role exactly as they're configured on the parent role, Mail Recipients.

You use Set-ManagementRoleEntry to change the available parameters on an existing management role entry. With the –AddParameter parameter, the parameters you specify are added to the role entry. With the –RemoveParameter parameter, the parameters you specify are removed from the role entry. Otherwise, only the parameters you specify are included in the role entry. For example, with Get-Mailbox you might want users to be able to specify a server and limit the result set size, and you can do this by adding the –Server and –ResultSize parameters as shown in this example:

```
Set-ManagementRoleEntry -Identity "LA Recipient Managers\Get-Mailbox"
-AddParameter Server, ResultSize
```

To remove all parameters, set –Parameters to $Null and don't use either –AddParameter or –RemoveParameter as shown in this example:

```
Set-ManagementRoleEntry -Identity "LA Recipient Managers\Get-Mailbox"
-Parameters $Null
```

You use Remove-ManagementRoleEntry to remove role entries. However, you can't remove role entries from built-in management roles.

Auditing Exchange Server Usage

Auditing lets you track what's happening with Exchange Server. You can use auditing to collect information related to information logons and logoffs, permission use, and much more. Any time an action that you've configured for auditing occurs, this action is written to the system's security log, where it's stored for your review. You can access the security log from Event Viewer.

Using Auditing

You enable auditing in the domain through Group Policy. You can think of group policies as sets of rules that help you manage resources. You can apply group policies to domains, organizational units within domains, and individual systems. Policies that apply to individual systems are referred to as *local group policies* and are stored only on the local system. Other group policies are linked as objects in Active Directory.

You can audit Exchange activity by enabling auditing in a Group Policy object applied to your Exchange servers. This policy object can be a local Group Policy object or an Active Directory Group Policy object. You manage a server's local Group Policy object using the Local Security Policy tool. You manage Active Directory Group Policy using the Group Policy Management Console (GPMC). GPMC is included as a Windows feature with Windows Vista and later versions of the Windows operating system. After you add GPMC as a feature, you can access it on the Administrative Tools menu.

Configuring Auditing

You can enable Exchange auditing by completing the following steps:

1. Start the Group Policy Management Console by clicking Start, All Programs, Administrative Tools, Group Policy Management. You can now navigate through the forest and domains in the organization to view individual Group Policy objects.

2. To specifically audit users' actions on Exchange Server, you should consider creating an organizational unit (OU) for Exchange servers and then define auditing policy for a Group Policy object applied to the OU. After you've created the OU or if you have an existing OU for Exchange servers, right-click

the related policy object, and then select Edit to open the policy object for editing in Group Policy Management Editor.

3. As shown in Figure 8-5, you access the Audit Policy node by working your way down through the console tree. Expand Computer Configuration, Policies, Windows Settings, Security Settings, and Local Policies. Then select Audit Policy.

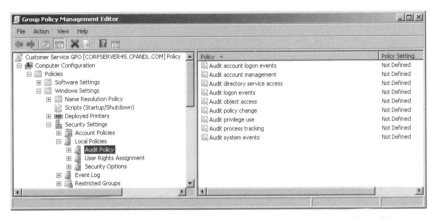

FIGURE 8-5 Use the Audit Policy node in Group Policy Management Editor to enable auditing.

4. You should now see the following auditing options:

- **Audit Account Logon Events** Tracks user account authentication during logon. Account logon events are generated on the authenticating computer when a user is authenticated.

- **Audit Account Management** Tracks account management by means of Active Directory Users And Computers. Events are generated any time user, computer, or group accounts are created, modified, or deleted.

- **Audit Directory Service Access** Tracks access to Active Directory. Events are generated any time users or computers access the directory.

- **Audit Logon Events** Tracks local logon events for a server or workstation.

- **Audit Object Access** Tracks system resource usage for mailboxes, information stores, and other types of objects.

- **Audit Policy Change** Tracks changes to user rights, auditing, and trust relationships.

- **Audit Privilege Use** Tracks the use of user rights and privileges, such as the right to create mailboxes.

- **Audit Process Tracking** Tracks system processes and the resources they use.

- **Audit System Events** Tracks system startup, shutdown, and restart, as well as actions that affect system security or the security log.

5. To configure an auditing policy, double-click or right-click its entry, and then select Properties. This opens a Properties dialog box for the policy.

6. Select the Define These Policy Settings check box, and then select the Success check box, the Failure check box, or both. Success logs successful events, such as successful logon attempts. Failure logs failed events, such as failed logon attempts.

7. Repeat steps 5 and 6 to enable other auditing policies. The policy changes won't be applied until the next time you start the Exchange server.

Configuring Compliance and Messaging Retention

To enhance your ability to comply with regulations related to messaging retention, protect personal information, and fulfill legal discovery requests for messaging records, Exchange supports the following:

- **Messaging Records Management**   Allows your organization to implement message retention policies. Messaging retention policies combine retention tags, retention policies, and autotagging. Mailbox folders and individual mail items use retention tags to apply retention settings. Users can use tags to mark folders or items for retention. A default tag associated with a retention policy applies to items not tagged manually by a user or to items in folders that do not have tags applied. Although users can use rules and default tags to automatically assign tags to incoming e-mail, autotagging allows Exchange to learn from users' tagging preferences and assign tags to incoming messages automatically. Users can manually override any automatically assigned tags.

- **Discovery Management**   Allows a user who is assigned the Discovery Management role to search mailbox content in selected mailboxes across an Exchange organization. The scope of the role assignment determines which mailboxes a user can search. Messages returned by the search are copied to a folder in the designated Discovery mailbox, which ensures compliance with legal discovery requirements and also allows authorized personal to search message content for purposes such as internal investigations and messaging-policy compliance.

- **Transport Protection Rules**   Allows you to secure messaging content against unauthorized access and reviews by protecting e-mail messages and attachments. Transport Protection Rules apply rights management settings to messages in transport, determining which recipients can access a message and what actions recipients can perform. For example, a recipient might be permitted to view a message and attachments but not be permitted to print a message and attachments.

Other compliance features include the following:

- Archive mailboxes
- Journaling

- Message classifications
- Hold policy

I've discussed most of these features in previous chapters, so I'll focus on messaging records management here. Exchange Server 2010 implements messaging records management to help retain messaging content that your organization might need for business or legal reasons and to delete messages that are no longer needed. You specify the retention period and the types of messaging content that management settings should apply to. Messaging records management is configured globally for your Exchange organization and implemented on a per-server basis by enabling records management enforcement.

Understanding Message Retention Policies and Tags

Message retention policies replace managed folders as the preferred method for implementing messaging records management. For backward compatibility with existing records management implementations, you can use managed folders. A managed folder is simply a Microsoft Office Outlook folder to which you can apply retention policies. Exchange uses two types of managed folders: managed default folders and managed custom folders. Managed default folders include the standard folders available in Outlook. Managed custom folders are additional folders that you can create and deploy.

You work with managed folders in several ways. If you want to control the contents of managed folders, you can apply managed content settings. For example, you can apply managed content settings to the Inbox folder, specifying that Exchange Server should automatically delete or move the folder's contents to another folder after 90 days. Although managed default folders appear in Outlook automatically, managed custom folders do not. To add a managed custom folder to a mailbox, you must create a Managed Folder Mailbox policy that deploys the folder. You can use a single Managed Folder Mailbox policy to deploy multiple managed custom folders.

By automating records management, Exchange Server 2010 helps your organization comply with legal requirements while minimizing the impact on administrators. The process relies on users to classify their own messaging content and on automatic tagging. Users can file items by placing them in the managed folder that is appropriate for that type of content, or messaging content can be sorted into the appropriate folder by using rules and tagging. This ensures that messaging content is classified according to users' wants and helps eliminate the mishandling of messaging content that can occur with completely automated messaging management solutions.

Managed folders are similar to the other folders in users' mailboxes except that users cannot remove, rename, or delete the folders after Exchange Server has deployed them. Exchange Server uses the retention policies you define to periodically process messaging content that users put in managed folders. You can configure retention policies by content age and by message type, and you can apply them to any of the folders in users' mailboxes. When messages reach a retention limit, Exchange Server can retain required messaging content and delete unneeded messaging content without requiring administrator intervention.

You can retain any messaging content that you want to keep by applying managed content settings that create journal copies of the content in another location. This can be any location with a Simple Mail Transfer Protocol (SMTP) e-mail address, including another Exchange mailbox.

You can configure Exchange Server to delete any messaging content that is no longer needed by specifying a deletion action. You can delete content permanently or delete it so that users can still recover it. You can also move content to a managed folder that is set up for user review prior to deletion, and you can mark content as expired in a user's mailbox in Outlook. This ensures that the user is prompted to take any required action.

When you apply managed content settings, you can also specify that messaging content should be journaled. A journal is an automatically forwarded copy of an item saved in an alternate location. Typically, you'll create journal copies of items in a mailbox specifically set up for this purpose. You can use journaling to help your organization meet additional compliance or regulatory requirements.

REAL WORLD Mailboxes can use either managed folders or retention tags, not both. If you no longer want to use managed folders for messaging records management, you can remove all records management settings from a Mailbox server by deleting managed custom folders and managed mailbox polices. When you remove all managed custom folders and all managed mailbox policies, the Managed Folder Assistant performs the following tasks the next time it runs for all mailboxes with records management enabled: removes mailbox policy settings from managed folders, removes empty managed custom folders, converts managed custom folders with items to standard folders. When you are sure the Managed Folder Assistant has run and completed the cleanup, you'll know managed folders are no longer being used.

Hold policy can help you recover accidentally deleted items and can also be used as part of retention. Previously, if a user wanted items that were written to backups, you had to find the backup media that contains the data, find the items, and return them to the user. Exchange 2010 includes the Recoverable Items folder to make this process easier.

The Recoverable Items folder is the storage location in which items deleted from the Deleted Items folder are located until they're purged from the Mailbox database. With this folder and the hold policy that can be applied to it, Exchange can retain all deleted and modified data for a specified period of time, and you can recover items directly from it, streamlining an otherwise lengthy process.

When you are using the Search-Mailbox cmdlet, you can set the –SearchDumpster parameter to $true to search the Recoverable Items folder. With Set-Mailbox, you can set the –LitigationHoldEnabled parameter to $true to specify that a mailbox is under litigation hold and that its messages can't be deleted. After a mailbox is placed on litigation hold, deleted items and all versions of changed items are retained in the Recoverable Items folder. Items that are purged from the dumpster are also retained, and the items are held indefinitely.

Creating and Applying Retention Tags

You deploy retention tags by creating retention policy tags for default folders and then creating and applying retention policies to mailboxes. You work with retention tags and policies in the Exchange Management Shell. Keep the following in mind:

- Commands for creating and working with retention policy tags include Get-RetentionPolicyTag, New-RetentionPolicyTag, Set-RetentionPolicyTag, and Remove-RetentionPolicyTag.

- Commands for creating and working with retention policies include Get-RetentionPolicy, New-RetentionPolicy, Set-RetentionPolicy, and Remove-RetentionPolicy.

To create a retention policy tag, you use the Type parameter to specify a default folder that the retention policy tag applies to, as shown in this example:

```
New-RetentionPolicyTag "Managers-DeletedItems" -Type "DeletedItems"
-MessageClass "AllMailboxContent" -RetentionEnabled $true
-AgeLimitForRetention 30 -RetentionAction PermanentlyDelete
```

Here, you configure retention for the DeletedItems folder. You also could have configured retention for Calendar, Contacts, Drafts, Inbox, JunkMail, Journal, Notes, Outbox, SentItems, Tasks, or All. The –MessageClass specifies the type of item to retain, such as CallItems, Contacts, Documents, E-Mail, Faxes, Journal, MeetingRequest, MissedCall, Notes, Posts, Tasks, and Voicemail. Once the age limit has expired, the retention action is performed. Retention actions include MoveToDeletedItems, MoveToFolder, DeleteAndAllowRecovery, PermanentlyDelete, MarkAsRetentionLimit, and MoveToArchive.

NOTE PermanentlyDelete permanently deletes a message. A message that has been permanently deleted can't be recovered using the Recoverable Items folder. Permanently deleted messages are not returned in a Discovery search unless a litigation hold is enabled for the mailbox.

Retention policies contain retention tags with managed content settings and are applied to mailboxes to control retention. After you create your retention tags, you can specify the list of tags to associate with a retention policy, as shown in this example:

```
Set-RetentionPolicy -Identity ManagersRP
-RetentionPolicyTagLinks "Managers-Default", "Managers-Inbox",
"Managers-DeletedItems"
```

Because the list of tags you provide replaces any previous list of associated tags, you'll want to get any existing tags associated with the policy and append new tags as shown in this example:

```
$tags = (Get-RetentionPolicy ManagersRP).RetentionPolicyTagLinks
$newtag1 = Get-RetentionPolicyTag Managers-Default
$newtag2 = Get-RetentionPolicyTag Managers-Inbox
$newtag3 = Get-RetentionPolicyTag Managers-DeletedItems
$tags += $newtag1 + $newtag2 + $newtag3
Set-RetentionPolicy ManagersRP -RetentionPolicyTagLinks $tags
```

After you associate retention tags with retention policies, you'll want to apply retention policies to mailboxes using Set-Mailbox with the –RetentionPolicy parameter, as shown in this example:

```
Set-Mailbox "timj" –RetentionPolicy ManagersRP
```

You can also apply a retention policy to the current members of a specific distribution group, as shown in this example:

```
Get-DistributionGroupMember -Identity "Managers" | Set-Mailbox
-RetentionPolicy ManagersRP
```

Autotagging automatically assigns retention tags to items in mailboxes based on a user's past tagging behavior. To use autotagging, a retention policy must be assigned to a mailbox. You can enable autotagging for a mailbox as shown in this example:

```
Set-MailboxComplianceConfiguration -Identity "timj"
-RetentionAutoTaggingEnabled $true
```

You can also apply autotagging to the current members of a specific distribution group, as shown in this example:

```
Get-DistributionGroupMember -Identity "Managers" |
Set-MailboxComplianceConfiguration -RetentionAutoTaggingEnabled $true
```

If you want to temporarily suspend processing of retention policies for a mailbox, such as when a user is on vacation or maternity leave, you can place the mailbox on retention hold. To do this in the Exchange Management Console, double-click the user's mailbox to open the related Properties dialog box. On the Mailbox Settings tab, double-click Messaging Records Management. Select Enable Retention Hold For Items In This Mailbox. Optionally, set a start date and an end date for the retention hold. Click OK to save your settings.

Applying Records Management to a Mailbox Server

After you've configured records management for your organization and applied policies to user mailboxes, you can begin managing records on the individual Mailbox servers in your organization. In Exchange Server 2010, the Managed Folder Assistant is responsible for applying records management settings. The Assistant does the following:

- Creates the necessary managed custom folders in user mailboxes
- Moves or removes items according to their retention settings
- Creates journal items in mailboxes in other locations

Each Mailbox server in your organization has a Managed Folder Assistant that runs according to a schedule you specify. It attempts to process all the mailboxes on a server in the specified amount of time. If it does not finish during the allotted time, it resumes processing where it left off the next time it runs.

In the Exchange Management Console, you can enable records management and schedule the Managed Mailbox Assistant to run by completing the following steps:

1. In the Exchange Management Console, expand the Server Configuration node, and then select the related Mailbox node.
2. Right-click the Mailbox server you want to configure, and then select Properties. In the Properties dialog box, click the Messaging Records Management tab.
3. Select Use Custom Schedule from the list, and then click Customize.
4. In the Schedule dialog box, select the times and days during which you want the Managed Folder Assistant to run. Click OK to close the Schedule dialog box, and then click OK to close the server's Properties dialog box.

In the Exchange Management Console, you can disable records management by completing the following steps:

1. In the Exchange Management Console, expand the Server Configuration node, and then select the related Mailbox node.
2. Right-click the Mailbox server you want to configure, and then select Properties.
3. In the Properties dialog box, click the Messaging Records Management tab.
4. In the Start Messaging Records Management Enforcement Process list, select Never. Click OK.

In the Exchange Management Shell, you can enable and disable records management by using the -ManagedFolderAssistantSchedule parameter of the set-MailboxServer cmdlet. Sample 8-1 provides the syntax and usage. Note that it is easiest to schedule run times using a 24-hour clock.

SAMPLE 8-1 Enabling and disabling records management

Syntax

```
Set-MailboxServer -Identity 'ServerIdentity'
-ManagedFolderAssistantSchedule 'Schedule'
```

Usage for enabling records management

```
set-MailboxServer -Identity 'CorpSvr127'
-ManagedFolderAssistantSchedule 'Sun.01:00-Sun.05:00',
'Wed.01:00-Wed.05:00'
```

Usage for disabling records management

```
Set-MailboxServer -Identity 'CorpSvr127'
 -ManagedFolderAssistantSchedule $null
```

In the Exchange Management Shell, you can manually start and stop records management by using the Start-ManagedFolderAssistant and Stop-ManagedFolder-Assistant cmdlets, respectively. When you start the assistant manually, any current processing of mailboxes stops, and the assistant reprocesses all mailboxes on the server. Sample 8-2 provides the syntax and usage.

SAMPLE 8-2 Starting and stopping records management manually

Syntax

```
Start-ManagedFolderAssistant -Identity 'ServerIdentity'

Stop-ManagedFolderAssistant -Identity 'ServerIdentity'
```

Usage

```
Start-ManagedFolderAssistant -Identity 'CorpSvr127'
```

CHAPTER 9

Managing Data and Database Availability Groups

One of your most important tasks as a Microsoft Exchange Server 2010 administrator is managing the information store. Each mailbox server deployed in an organization has an information store, which can contain databases and information about database availability groups (DAGs). This chapter introduces databases and focuses on the management of database availability groups. You'll learn the following:

■ How to enable, create, and use database availability groups

■ How to manage databases and their related transaction logs

■ How to improve mailbox server availability

■ How to manage full-text indexing of Exchange databases

To learn how to manage databases, see Chapter 10, "Mailbox and Public Folder Database Administration."

Navigating the Information Store

Exchange 2010 integrates high availability and messaging resilience into the core architecture, providing a simple unified framework for both high availability and disaster recovery. This approach allows Exchange 2010 to improve continuous replication and replace the clustering features in Exchange 2007 with a more robust solution that doesn't require expensive hardware and also requires less maintenance.

Using Databases

Mailbox databases continue to be the primary type of database used with Exchange Server. Exchange Server 2010 also supports public folder databases. However, Exchange Server 2010 does not make public folders mandatory because Microsoft Office Outlook 2007 and later releases do not use public folders for accessing free/busy data or the offline address book (OAB). Instead, Outlook 2007 and later access this information from the organization's Client Access servers. How does this work? Client Access servers provide Web services, which in turn allow clients to access mail, free/busy data, OAB data, and other Exchange data using Hypertext Transfer Protocol (HTTP).

Outlook 2003 clients and earlier clients require a public folder database to connect to Exchange Server. These clients use public folders to access free/busy information and the OAB. If you have Outlook 2003 or earlier clients, as well as other Messaging Application Programming Interface (MAPI) clients, these clients can continue to access public folders on mailbox servers running Exchange Server 2010. You manage public folder configuration using the Public Folder Management Console and the Exchange Management Shell.

NOTE Exchange Server 2010 does not support public folder access using Network News Transfer Protocol (NNTP) or public folder access using Internet Message Access Protocol version 4 (IMAP4). Exchange Server 2010 also does not support non-MAPI top-level folders in your public folder databases. The only way to maintain this functionality in an Exchange 2010 organization is to maintain a server running Exchange Server 2003.

When you install the first mailbox server in the organization, this server's information store typically has a single, default mailbox database and a single, default public folder database. However, the specific configuration depends on your responses during setup. When you are installing the first mailbox server, Setup prompts you to:

- Specify whether you want to create the default mailbox database. If you decide to create one, you can also specify its name and location.

- Specify whether any client computers run Outlook 2003 or earlier or Entourage. If you answer yes, a default public folder database is created. If you answer no, a default public folder database is not created.

NOTE In an Exchange organization with existing Exchange 2003 servers, you are not prompted about clients running Outlook 2003 or earlier or Entourage. In a mixed organization like this, Setup creates a public folder database automatically to ensure backward compatibility.

When you install additional mailbox servers in the organization, these servers have only one database initially—the default mailbox database, if you choose to create it. The reason for this default configuration is that the decision whether a public folder database is needed in the organization is determined only when you install the first mailbox server. When you install additional mailbox servers, you are not prompted about clients running Outlook 2003 and earlier or Entourage. A key reason for this is that only one public folder database is required in an Exchange organization and any other public folder databases are optional. Keep in mind that regardless of your selections during setup, you can create a default public folder database as well as additional public folder databases at any time using the Exchange Management tools.

Understanding Database Structures

Unlike earlier releases of Exchange, Exchange Server 2010 does not use storage groups, and functionality associated with storage groups has been moved to the database level. Because of these changes, Exchange databases have a single, dedicated log stream, which is represented by a series of sequentially named log files. Each log file is 1 megabyte (MB) in size.

In addition to log files, databases have several other types of files associated with them. As Table 9-1 shows, these files include one or more checkpoint files, a temporary working file, and one or more transaction log files. Depending on the state of Exchange Server, you might see other working files as well. When you create a database, you can specify separate folder locations to use for database files and transaction logs. Each database has content-indexing files associated with it as well. These files are generated by the full-text search services running on mailbox servers.

TABLE 9-1 Data and Log Files Used by Databases

TYPE OF FILE	FILE NAME	DESCRIPTION
DATA FILES		
Database file	*DatabaseName*.edb	Primary database file that contains mailbox data
Temporary data	Tmp.edb	Temporary workspace for processing transactions
Checkpoint file	E##.chk	Checkpoint file that tracks the point up to which the transactions in the log file have been committed
TRANSACTION LOG FILES		
Primary log file	E##.log	Primary log file that contains a record of all changes that have yet to be committed

TABLE 9-1 Data and Log Files Used by Databases

TYPE OF FILE	FILE NAME	DESCRIPTION
Secondary log files	E##00000001.log, E##00000002.log, ...	Additional log files used as needed
Reserve log files	E##Res00001.jrs, E##Res00002.jrs, ...	Files used to reserve space for additional log files if the primary log file becomes full
FULL-TEXT INDEXING FILES		
Content index-related files	.ci, .wid, .dir, .000, .001, .002	Files used for full-text indexing of mailbox data

You use Exchange databases to ease the administrative burden that comes with managing large installations. For example, instead of having a single 10-terabyte (TB) database for the entire organization, you can create ten 1-TB databases that you can manage more easily.

TIP As a best practice, 2 TB is the largest recommended size for Exchange Server 2010 databases when you have two or more mailbox database copies. This large size is made possible by the significant core improvements in Exchange Server 2010. You'll also find that large databases make it easier to support the large mailboxes that might be required by your organization's managers and executives. Still, most mailboxes should be limited to between 2 GB and 10 GB in size.

When you create a mailbox or public folder database, you specify the name for the database, and this name sets the name of the primary database file as well. For example, if you create a mailbox database called MarketingDept, the primary database file is set as MarketingDept.edb. With Exchange Server 2010, the default location for database files is the same as the log folder. If you want a database to be in a different location, you can specify the location you want to use. Separating database files and log files from the same database and putting them on different volumes backed by different physical disks can help you scale your organization while ensuring high performance and recoverability.

TIP Recoverability is the primary reason for separating database files and log files. For example, in the case of a failure on a drive where a database is stored, the transaction logs needed for complete recovery would then be on a different (and probably functioning) drive. Whether you want to use this approach depends on the size and configuration of your Exchange Mailbox servers as well as the service level agreements you need to comply with.

The many files associated with databases provide granular control over Exchange Server, and if you configure the data files properly, they can help you scale your

Exchange organization efficiently while ensuring optimal performance. In a small implementation of Exchange, you might want to place all the data files on the same drive. As you scale from a small organization to a larger organization, you'll generally want to organize data according to databases, placing all the data for each database on separate drives. You can't always do this, however, in a small-to-medium-size organization with limited resources. For example, if you have ten 1-TB databases and only five data drives, you might want to have the five data drives configured as follows:

- Drive 1 with Database 1 and Database 2 and all related data files.
- Drive 2 with Database 3 and Database 4 and all related data files.
- Drive 3 with Database 5 and Database 6 and all related data files.
- Drive 4 with Database 7 and Database 8 and all related data files.
- Drive 5 with Database 9 and Database 10 and all related data files.

In a storage area network (SAN) implementation where you are using logical unit numbers (LUNs) and don't know about the underlying disk structure, placing the databases on separate LUNs should be sufficient. To protect the data, you might want to consider using hardware RAID (Redundant Array Of Inexpensive Disks), which is likely already implemented if you are using a SAN. However, if you configure a database availability group with multiple member servers that each have one or more copies of mailbox databases, you likely don't need to use any type of RAID—you likely won't need daily backups either. Just remember that Microsoft recommends having at least three database copies in addition to the active copy.

REAL WORLD If the idea of not needing RAID seems like a radical concept, the idea of not needing to perform backups of your Exchange data might seem revolutionary. However, when you have multiple copies of your data on separate servers, you really might not need to create daily backups of your Exchange data. This doesn't mean that you won't need to create backups ever—it just means you might not need daily backups of Exchange data. You will probably still want to create regular backups of your Exchange servers and still create periodic full backups of all server and Exchange data to rotate to off-site storage as a safeguard against catastrophe.

Database available groups can also make you rethink your use of SANs. Rather than having a single, massive (and likely very expensive) storage device, you might want to rely on a server's internal drives or multiple smaller (and likely less expensive) storage devices. One reason to use internal drives is that reliable, multiple-TB hard drives are becoming increasingly available, and several servers with multiple, large internal hard drives will likely cost a fraction of the price of a single massive SAN. If you use SANs, you might find that multiple smaller storage devices are better than a single, massive storage device because you'll then be protected against a single source of failure (the storage device) causing an outage on all your mailbox servers. I know, I know...the SAN should never go down, but it can (and does) happen.

Improving Availability

Exchange 2010 allows you to protect mailbox databases and the data they contain by configuring your mailbox databases for high availability automatically when you use database availability groups. Database availability groups allow you to group databases logically according to the servers that host a set of databases. Each mailbox server can have multiple databases, and each database can have as many as 16 copies. A single database availability group can have up to 16 Mailbox servers that host databases and provide automatic database-level recovery from failures that affect individual databases. Any server in a database availability group can host a copy of a mailbox database from any other server in the database availability group.

Servers in a database availability group can host other Exchange roles. Member servers must be in the same Active Directory domain.

Unlike Exchange 2007, where achieving a high level of uptime could require a high level of administrator intervention, Exchange 2010 integrates high availability and messaging resilience into the core architecture, providing a simple unified framework for both high availability and disaster recovery. This new approach reduces the cost and complexity of deploying a highly available solution. How does this work? Exchange 2010 has enhanced continuous replication and has replaced clustering features in Exchange 2007 with a more robust solution that doesn't require expensive hardware and also requires less maintenance.

In previous versions of Exchange, Exchange was a clustered application that used the cluster resource management model for high availability. Exchange 2010 is not a clustered application and does not use the cluster resource model for high availability. Instead, Exchange 2010 uses its own internal high-availability model. Although some components of Windows Failover Clustering are still used, these components are now managed exclusively by Exchange 2010.

To support continuous replication, Exchange 2007 offered several approaches, including Local Continuous Replication (LCR), Cluster Continuous Replication (CCR), and Standby Continuous Replication (SCR). LCR was a single-server solution for asynchronous log shipping, replay, and recovery. CCR combined the asynchronous log shipping, replay, and recovery features with the failover and management features of the Cluster service, and it was designed for configurations in which you had clustered mailbox servers with dedicated active and passive nodes. SCR was an extension of LCR and CCR that used the same log shipping, replay, and recovery features of LCR and CCR but was designed for configurations in which you used or enabled the use of standby recovery servers.

Exchange 2010 includes some aspects of the continuous replication technology previously found in CCR and SCR, but the technology has changed substantially. Because storage groups have been removed from Exchange 2010, continuous replication operates at the database level. Exchange 2010 still uses an Extensible

Storage Engine (ESE) database that produces transaction logs that are replicated and replayed into copies of mailbox databases. Because each mailbox database can have as many as 16 copies, you can have one or more database copies on up to 16 different servers.

Instead of using Server Message Block (SMB) for data transfer during log shipping and seeding, continuous replication uses a single administrator-defined TCP port for data transfer, and there are built-in options for network encryption and compression for the data stream. In Exchange 2007, Microsoft Exchange Replication service was responsible for replaying logs into passive database copies. When the passive copy was activated, the database cache was lost when the Microsoft Exchange Information Store service mounted the database. Exchange 2010 does not use the Microsoft Exchange Replication service for this purpose. Instead, the Exchange Replication service periodically monitors the health of all mounted databases and the ESE. If the service detects a failure, it notifies Active Manager, and Active Manager then handles the failure. (See "Introducing Active Manager" later in this chapter for more information.)

Microsoft moved the passive copy replay functionality into the Microsoft Exchange Information Store service. Because active databases and passive database copies are all managed by the same service, the database cache is available for use after a failover or switchover has occurred and no data loss occurs. Having one service manage both active and passive databases has other benefits as well. For example, while failover of a clustered mailbox server in a CCR environment for Exchange 2007 took about 2 minutes to complete, failover of a mailbox database for Exchange 2010 is completed in about 30 seconds (most of the time).

Like SCR, the concepts of replay lag time and truncation lag time apply to database copies. Database copies can be backed up using Exchange-aware, Volume Shadow Copy Service (VSS)–based backup applications.

In Exchange 2010, databases are defined at the organization level rather than at the server level. When an administrator establishes a database copy as the active mailbox database, this process is known as a switchover. When a failure affecting a database occurs and a new database becomes the active copy, this process is known as a failover. Failover and switchover occur at the database level for individual databases and at the server level for all active databases hosted by a server. When either a switchover or failover occurs, other Exchange 2010 server roles become aware of the switchover almost immediately and redirect client and messaging traffic automatically as appropriate.

Although you can perform most management tasks for availability groups in the Exchange Management Console, you have additional options when you work with the Exchange Management Shell. Table 9-2 provides an overview of commands you can use to manage availability groups and their various features.

TABLE 9-2 Cmdlets for Working with Database Availability Groups

MANAGEMENT AREA	RELATED COMMANDS
Database availability group management	Get-DatabaseAvailabilityGroup New-DatabaseAvailabilityGroup Remove-DatabaseAvailabilityGroup Set-DatabaseAvailabilityGroup
Database copy management	Add-MailboxDatabaseCopy Get-MailboxDatabaseCopyStatus Remove-MailboxDatabaseCopy Resume-MailboxDatabaseCopy Set-MailboxDatabaseCopy Suspend-MailboxDatabaseCopy Update-MailboxDatabaseCopy
Database management	Clean-MailboxDatabase Dismount-Database Get-MailboxDatabase Move-DatabasePath New-MailboxDatabase Remove-MailboxDatabase Set-MailboxDatabase
Network configuration	Get-DatabaseAvailabilityGroupNetwork New-DatabaseAvailabilityGroupNetwork Remove-DatabaseAvailabilityGroupNetwork Set-DatabaseAvailabilityGroupNetwork
Switchover management	Move-ActiveMailboxDatabase Start-DatabaseAvailabilityGroup Stop-DatabaseAvailabilityGroup Restore-DatabaseAvailabilityGroup
Server membership	Add-DatabaseAvailabilityGroupServer Remove-DatabaseAvailabilityGroupServer

As part of database availability group planning, keep in mind that you can create database copies only on Mailbox servers in the same database availability group that do not host the active copy of a database. An active copy differs from a passive copy in that it is in use and being accessed by users rather than offline. You cannot create two copies of the same database on the same server. Other things to keep in mind when working with database copies include the following:

- Exchange 2010 mailbox databases can be replicated only to other Exchange 2010 Mailbox servers and the servers must be in the same database availability group. You cannot replicate a database outside a database availability group, nor can you replicate an Exchange 2010 mailbox database to a server running Exchange 2007.

- All copies of a database use the same path on each server containing a copy. The database and log file paths for a database copy on each Mailbox server must not conflict with any other database paths.

- All Mailbox servers in a database availability group must be in the same Active Directory domain. Database copies can be created in the same or different Active Directory sites and on the same or different network subnets. However, database copies are not supported between Mailbox servers with roundtrip network latency greater than 250 milliseconds (by default).

NOTE Database copies are for mailbox databases only. For redundancy and high availability of public folder databases, you should use public folder replication. Unlike when you used CCR with Exchange 2007, you can use public folder replication to replicate multiple public folder databases between servers in a database availability group. Because database availability groups can be stretched across sites, it is possible for a mailbox database to be moved between sites.

Introducing Active Manager

In Exchange 2010, Active Manager provides the resource model and failover management features previously provided by the Cluster service. When you create your first database availability group in an Exchange organization, a Windows Failover Cluster is created by Exchange, but there are no cluster groups for Exchange and no storage resources in the cluster. Therefore, as shown in Figure 9-1, Failover Cluster Manager shows only basic information about the cluster, which includes the cluster name, the cluster networks, and the quorum configuration. Cluster nodes and networks will also exist, and their status can be checked in Failover Cluster Manager. However, all cluster resources, including nodes and networks, are managed for you by Exchange. Exchange makes use of the cluster's node and network management functions, and you can check the node and network status in Exchange Management Console.

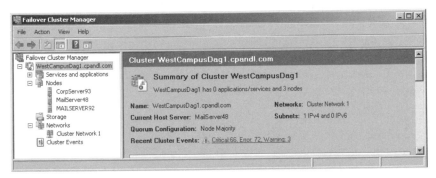

FIGURE 9-1 Check the status of clustering in Failover Cluster Manager.

REAL WORLD Failover Cluster Manager is the primary management tool for working with the Cluster service. Although you need to use the Exchange Management tools to view and manage database availability groups and related features, Failover Cluster Manager does show the status of clustering.

- By selecting the cluster name in the left pane, you get a quick overview of the cluster configuration, including the current quorum configuration, which can be either Node Majority or Node and File Share Majority depending on the number of nodes in the database availability group.

- By selecting the Nodes entry in the left pane, you can quickly check the status of all the nodes in the database availability group.

- By expanding the Networks entry in the left pane and then selecting available cluster networks, you can check the status of the network as well as individual network connections.

- By selecting the cluster name in the left pane and then clicking the link for Recent Cluster Events, you can check the event logs on all cluster nodes for errors and warnings.

Active Manager runs on all Mailbox servers that are members of a database availability group. Active Manager operates as either the primary role holder or a standby secondary role holder with respect to a particular database. The primary role holder, referred to as the Primary Active Manager, decides which database copies will be active and which copies to activate. It also receives topology change notifications and reacts to server failures. Only one copy of a database can be active at any given time, and that copy can be mounted or dismounted.

The group member that holds the primary role is always the member that currently owns the cluster quorum resource and the default cluster group. If the server that owns the cluster quorum resource fails, the primary role automatically moves to another server in the group and that server takes ownership of the default cluster group. Before you take the server that hosts the cluster quorum resource offline for maintenance or an upgrade, you must first move the primary role to another server in the group.

Secondary role holders, referred to as Standby Active Managers, provide information about which server hosts the active copy of a mailbox database to other Exchange components, such as the RPC Client Access service or Hub Transport service. The secondary role holder detects failures of replicated, local databases and the local information store, and it issues failure notifications to the primary role holder and asks the primary role holder to initiate a failover. The secondary role holder does not determine which server takes over, nor does it update the database location state with the primary role holder. With respect to its local system, the primary role holder also performs the functions of the secondary role by detecting local database and local information store failures and issuing related notifications.

Active Manager determines which database copy should be activated by attempting to locate a mailbox database that has characteristics similar to the following:

- The database has a status of Healthy, DisconnectedAndHealthy, or DisconnectedAndResynchronizing.
- The database has a content index with a status of Healthy.
- The database has a copy queue length that is less than 10 log files.
- The database has a replay queue length of less than 50 log files.

If no database copy meets all of these criteria, Active Manager continues looking for the best choice by lowering the selection requirements through successive iterations.

Creating and Managing Database Availability Groups

Database availability groups are a container in Active Directory and a logical layer on top of Windows Clustering. You can create and manage database availability groups in a variety of ways. Establishing a database availability group and making it operational requires the following at a minimum:

1. Creating a database availability group.
2. Adding member servers to the group.
3. Designating a witness server.
4. Creating an availability group network.

These tasks and general management tasks for database availability groups are discussed in the sections that follow.

Creating Database Availability Groups

A database availability group defines a set of servers that provide automatic database-level recovery from database failures. Only members of the Organization Management group can create database availability groups.

When you create a database availability group, you can specify a witness server or let Exchange choose one for you. The witness server's role is to help maintain the state of the group. It does this by maintaining the quorum when there is an even number of members in the group. On the witness server, you can designate a directory, called the witness directory, for use by the database availability group, or you can let Exchange create a default directory for you. Exchange creates and secures the directory automatically as part of configuring the witness server for use. The directory should not be used for any purpose other than for the database availability group witness server. The requirements for the witness server are as follows:

- The witness server cannot be a member of the database availability group.
- The witness server must be in the same forest as the database availability group.
- The witness server must be running Windows Server 2003 or Windows Server 2008 or later.

To be sure that Exchange administrators are aware of the availability of the witness server and that the server remains under the control of an Exchange administrator, Microsoft recommends using an Exchange 2010 server to host the witness directory. Using an Exchange 2010 server as the witness also ensures that Exchange has sufficient permissions to remotely create and share the witness directory. The preferred witness server is a Hub Transport server in the same Active Directory site as the majority of the members of the database availability group.

A single server can serve as a witness for multiple database availability groups. However, every database availability group must have a separate witness directory.

To set up the database availability group, Exchange creates an msExchMDB-AvailabilityGroup object and related objects in Active Directory. These represent the database availability group, its members, networks, and attributes. The msExchMDBAvailabilityGroup directory object is used to store information about the database availability group, such as server membership information. Information about the included databases is stored in the cluster database. When you add the first server to a database availability group, a failover cluster is automatically created for the database availability group and failover monitoring is initiated. The failover cluster heartbeat mechanism and cluster database are then used to track and manage information about the database availability group.

After a database availability group has been created, you can add servers to or remove existing servers from the database availability group. When the first Mailbox server is added to a database availability group, the following occurs:

- The Windows Failover Clustering component and related management tools are installed, if they are not already installed.

  TIP Windows Failover Clustering is available only on Exchange 2010 Enterprise Edition Mailbox servers that are running Windows Server 2008 SP2 Enterprise or later or Windows Server 2008 R2 or later. In addition, each Mailbox server in the database availability group must have at least two network interface cards in order to have separate replication and messaging networks.

- A failover cluster is created using the name of the database availability group. For the purposes of authentication and access permissions, the cluster is represented by a computer account that is created in the default container for computers. This computer account is referred to as the cluster virtual network name account or the cluster network object.

- The server is added to the msExchMDBAvailabilityGroup object in Active Directory.

- When you create a database availability group, an IP address is assigned to the group. When you add the first server to the group, the name and IP address of the database availability group are registered in Domain Name System (DNS) using a Host (A) record. The name must be no longer than 15 characters and must be unique within the Active Directory forest.

  NOTE A database availability group can have multiple IP addresses. If so, only the one that comes online is registered in DNS.

- The cluster database is updated with information about the databases that are mounted on the server.
- Exchange examines the current network configuration, as presented by the cluster. If the server has a properly configured network card, the configuration of that network card is used to create the replication network. If the server has two network cards, the configuration of those network cards are used to create separate replication and messaging networks.
- The witness directory and witness file share are created. Permissions are set so that the network name account representing the cluster has full control.

When you add the second and subsequent servers to the DAG, the following occurs:

- The server is joined to the failover cluster for the DAG.
- The server is added to the msExchMDBAvailabilityGroup object in Active Directory.
- The cluster database is updated with information about the databases that are mounted on the server.

When a database availability group has a single member server, the failover cluster initially uses the Node Majority quorum mode. When you add the second Mailbox server to the database availability group, Exchange changes the cluster quorum to the Node and File Share Majority quorum model and begins using the Universal Naming Convention (UNC) path and directory for the cluster quorum. If the witness directory does not exist, Exchange automatically creates it at this point and configures its security with full control permissions for local administrators and the cluster network computer account for the database availability group.

REAL WORLD   Every failover cluster has a resource that is responsible for main-taining the witness logs. This resource is called the quorum or witness resource. The quorum resource writes information about all cluster database changes to the witness logs, ensuring that the cluster configuration and state data can be recovered. When you create a database availability group, Exchange automatically determines the appropriate quorum configuration for your cluster based on the number of member servers. When a DAG has an odd number of members, Exchange uses the Node Major-ity quorum model. When a DAG has an even number of members, Exchange uses a Node and File Share Majority quorum model. In a Node Majority cluster configuration, servers have a local quorum device. This device stores the cluster configuration infor-mation. In a Node and File Share Majority cluster configuration, servers use a witness file share rather than a quorum (witness) device. Otherwise, the Node and File Share Majority configuration works like the Node Majority configuration.

You can create a database availability group by completing the following steps:

1. In the Exchange Management Console, expand the Organization Configura-tion node. Next, select and then right-click the related Mailbox node. On the shortcut menu, select New Database Availability Group. You should now see the New Database Availability Group Wizard, as shown in Figure 9-2.

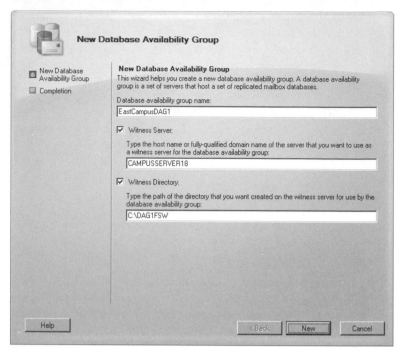

FIGURE 9-2 Set the database availability group name and file locations.

2. In the Database Availability Group Name text box, type a name of up to 15 characters for the database availability group. The name must be unique in the Active Directory forest and cannot contain spaces or other special characters.

3. Optionally, select the Witness Server check box, and then provide the name of a server in the same Active Directory forest as the DAG to act as the witness server. Click OK. Because this server cannot be a member of the database availability group, be sure that you don't select servers that will be members of the database availability group you are configuring.

    NOTE The server you select as the witness server can be a member of a different database availability group. Also note that if you leave the Witness Server check box cleared, Exchange attempts to automatically select a witness server by looking in the same Active Directory site as the majority of the DAG members for a Hub Transport server that does not have the Mailbox role installed.

4. Select the Witness Directory check box, and then provide the local folder path for a directory that will be used to store witness data, such as C:\WitnessDir. If the directory does not exist, Exchange attempts to create it for you on the witness server. If you don't specify a witness directory,

Exchange attempts to create a directory named relative to the database availability group on the witness server's system drive.

NOTE Exchange must have appropriate permissions on the server to create and then share the witness directory. Although you can set the local directory path, the share name is set automatically in the form DAGName.DomainName, such as WestCampusDag1.CPANDL.COM. This share is configured so that the failover cluster's virtual name account has full control.

TIP As long as the witness server is an Exchange server in the same forest, Exchange should be able to create and share the directory. If Exchange is unable to create and share the directory, you'll see an error message and need to take appropriate corrective actions. You can use the Set-DatabaseAvailabilityGroup with the –WitnessDirectory parameter to specify a new directory to use at any time. You also can set a new directory by double-clicking the DAG in the Exchange Management Console, entering a new directory path in the Witness Directory field, and then clicking OK.

If the witness server is not an Exchange 2010 server, you have to add the Exchange Trusted Subsystem security group to the local Administrators group on the witness server.

5. Click New to create the database availability group, and then click Finish. On the Completion page, the Summary states whether the operation was successful. If an error occurred, you need to take the appropriate corrective action. Otherwise, you can now add databases to the database availability group as appropriate.

In the Exchange Management Shell, you can create database availability groups using the New-DatabaseAvailabilityGroup cmdlet. Sample 9-1 provides the syntax and usage. The Exchange Management Console limits you to 15 characters for the group name because the same name is used as the computer name for the cluster network object that represents the group.

NOTE Don't confuse the local witness directory with the witness file share. The local witness directory has a local file path on the witness server, such as C:\WitnessShare. When you specify the witness directory, Exchange creates the directory and then creates the file share as appropriate.

SAMPLE 9-1 New-DatabaseAvailabilityGroup cmdlet syntax and usage

Syntax

```
New-DatabaseAvailabilityGroup -Name DAGName
[-DatabaseAvailabilityGroupIp Addresses]
[-WitnessServer ServerName]
[-WitnessDirectory LocalDirOnWitnessServer]
[-DomainController FullyQualifiedName]
[-ThirdPartyReplication <Disabled | Enabled>]
```

Usage

```
New-DatabaseAvailabilityGroup -Name "EastCampusDAG1"
-WitnessServer "MailServer25"
-WitnessDirectory "C:\EastCampusDAG1"

New-DatabaseAvailabilityGroup -Name "WestCampusDAG1"
-WitnessServer "MailServer25"
-WitnessDirectory "C:\WestCampusDAG1"
-DatabaseAvailabilityGroupIp 192.168.10.52,192.168.11.18
```

Managing Availability Group Membership

When you add a server to a database availability group, the server works with the other servers in the group to provide automatic, database-level recovery from database, server, and network failures. To be included in a database availability group, a server must be running Windows Server 2008 SP2 Enterprise or later or Windows Server 2008 R2 or later and must have at least two network interface cards. Each network interface card must be on a different subnet.

> **NOTE** Each server that you want to add to the database availability group must have two network adapter cards. The first network adapter, referred to as the *replication adapter*, handles replication traffic, and the second adapter, referred to as the *messaging adapter*, handles MAPI network traffic and other traffic originating outside the replication network.

Keep the following in mind when planning database availability group membership:

- If you created the availability group using the Exchange Management Console and want to add servers to the group by using the Exchange Management Console, at least one of the server's network cards must be configured to use Dynamic Host Configuration Protocol (DHCP). When you add the first Mailbox server to the database availability group, the group must be assigned an IP address. By default, Exchange uses DHCP to obtain an IP address for the group. This IP address becomes the IP address for the group. Alternatively, you can create the group by using the Exchange Management Shell. Use New-DatabaseAvailabilityGroup and set the IP address using the –DatabaseAvailabilityGroupIp parameter.

- If you no longer want a server to be a member of a group, you can remove it from the group and the server will no longer be automatically protected from failures. Keep in mind that you must remove all replicated database copies from a server before you can remove it from a database availability group.

- If you didn't create the group and set its IP address by using Exchange Management Shell and DHCP is not available in your organization, or if you want to use a static IP address for an availability group, you can use the –DatabaseAvailablityGroupIpAddresses parameter of the Set-Database-AvailabilityGroup cmdlet to specify a static IP address for the group prior to adding servers. The IP address is needed prior to adding the first Mailbox server to the group.

You can add a Mailbox server to or remove a Mailbox server from a database availability group by completing the following steps:

1. In the Exchange Management Console, expand the Organization Configuration node and then select the related Mailbox node. In the results pane, select the Database Availability Group tab to view existing availability groups, as shown in Figure 9-3.

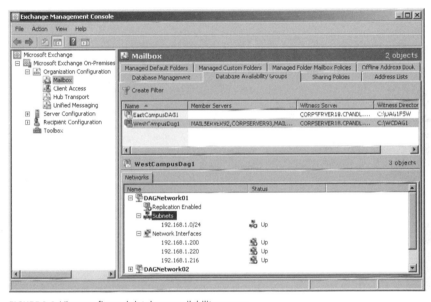

FIGURE 9-3 View configured database availability groups.

2. Right-click the database availability group you want to work with and then select Manage Database Availability Group Membership. On the Manage Database Availability Group Membership page, shown in Figure 9-4, you can

   • Click Add to add a server to the database availability group. In the Select Mailbox Server dialog box, select one or more servers and then click OK.

   • Select a server from the list of current members, and click the red X to remove the server from the database availability group.

3. Click Manage to apply your changes. On the Completion page, the Summary states whether the operation was successful. If an error occurred, you need to take the appropriate corrective action. Otherwise, click Finish.

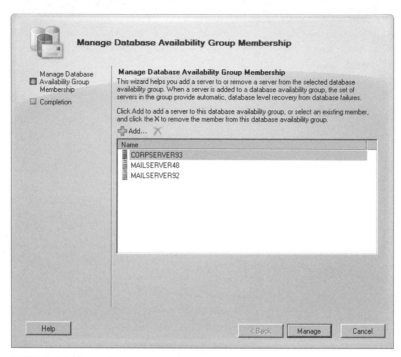

FIGURE 9-4 Add or remove group members.

In the Exchange Management Shell, you can list database availability groups using Get-DatabaseAvailabilityGroup. If you enter Get-DatabaseAvailabilityGroup without additional parameters, you'll see a list of all availability groups in the current Active Directory forest as well as the member servers and operational servers for those groups, as shown in the following example and sample output:

```
Get-DatabaseAvailabilityGroup

Name              Member Servers                  Operational Servers
----              --------------                  -------------------
EastCampusDAG1    MailServer25, CorpServer27      MailServer25, CorpServer27
WestCampusDAG1    MailServer44, MailServer18      MailServer44, MailServer18
```

Use the –Identity parameter to specify the name of the database availability group to query. Add –Status to any query to include real-time status information.

You add or remove group members using Add-DatabaseAvailabilityGroupServer and Remove-DatabaseAvailabilityGroupServer. Samples 9-2 and 9-3 provide the syntax and usage.

Syntax

```
Add-DatabaseAvailabilityGroupServer -Identity DAGName
-MailboxServer ServerToAdd
[-DomainController FullyQualifiedName]
```

Usage

```
Add-DatabaseAvailabilityGroupServer -Identity "EastCampusDAG1"
-MailboxServer "MailServer62"
```

SAMPLE 9-3 Remove-DatabaseAvailabilityGroupServer cmdlet syntax and usage

Syntax

```
Remove-DatabaseAvailabilityGroupServer -Identity DAGName
-MailboxServer ServerToAdd
[-ConfigurationOnly <$true | $false>]
[-DomainController FullyQualifiedName]
```

Usage

```
Remove-DatabaseAvailabilityGroupServer -Identity "EastCampusDAG1"
-MailboxServer "MailServer62"
```

If a Mailbox server has failed and cannot be recovered, you can recover operations in one of two ways:

- You can use the Remove-DatabaseAvailabilityGroupServer cmdlet to remove the configuration settings for the Mailbox server from the database availability group. After you remove the configuration settings, all settings associated with the Mailbox server are gone.

- You can install Exchange on a server that has the same name and domain membership as the old server and use Exchange Server 2010 Setup with the /m:RecoverServer switch. Running Setup with the /m:RecoverServer switch causes Setup to read the failed server's configuration information from Active Directory. After Setup gathers the server's configuration information from Active Directory, Setup installs the original Exchange files and services on the server, restoring the roles and settings that were stored in Active Directory.

Managing Database Availability Group Networks

Each database availability group must have a minimum of two networks: one for replication traffic, referred to as the group's *replication network*, and one for MAPI and other traffic, referred to as the group's *messaging network*. While you should have only one messaging network, you can create additional replication networks in a database availability group and configure them using the Exchange Management tools.

Adding or Removing Availability Group Networks

Each database availability group network must have a unique name of up to 128 characters, one or more subnet associations, and an optional description of up to 256 characters. When you configure the network, you can dedicate the network to replication traffic or dedicate the network to MAPI traffic.

NOTE Disabling replication does not guarantee that Exchange will not use a network for replication. If all configured replication networks are offline, failed, or otherwise unavailable, and only a nonreplication network remains, Exchange will use that network for replication until a replication-enabled network becomes available.

REAL WORLD Every network address has a network identifier that identifies the network and a host identifier that identifies the individual host on the network. The network ID is seen as the prefix of an IPv4 or IPv6 address, and the host ID is the suffix. When you define an availability group network, you need to identify the network and then specify the number of bits in the network number that are part of the network ID (and the remaining bits are understood to be part of the host ID). To write a block of IPv4 addresses and specify which bits are used for the network ID, you write the network number followed by a forward slash and the number of bits in the network ID, as follows:

`NetworkNumber/# of bits in the network ID`

The slash and the number of bits in the network ID are referred to as the network prefix. By default, Class A IPv4 networks have 8 bits in the network ID, Class B IPv4 networks have 16 bits, and Class C IPv4 networks have 24 bits.

IPv6 doesn't use subnet masks to identify which bits belong to the network ID and which bits belong to the host ID. Instead, each IPv6 address is assigned a subnet prefix length that specifies how the bits in the network ID are used. The subnet prefix length is represented in decimal form. If 48 bits in the network ID are used, the subnet prefix length is written as FEC0:1234:5678::/48 to represent the IPv6 addresses FEC0:1234:5678:: through FEC0:1234:5678::FFFF:FFFF:FFFF:FFFF. You can create a network for a database availability group by completing the following steps:

1. In the Exchange Management Console, expand the Organization Configuration node and then select the related Mailbox node. On the Database Availability Group tab, the bottom panel shows the networks currently associated with the selected availability group.

2. Right-click the database availability group you want to work with and then select New Database Availability Group Network.

3. On the New Database Availability Group Network page, shown in Figure 9-5, enter a unique name for the database availability group network of up to 128 characters and then provide an optional description for the database availability group network of up to 256 characters.

4. Under Network Subnets, click Add to add a network subnet to the database availability group network. Subnets should be entered using a format of *IPv4Address/Bitmask,* such as 192.168.15.0/24, or *IPv6Address/Network-SubnetPrefix,* such as FEC0:1234:5678::/48. If you add a subnet that is currently associated with another database availability group network, the subnet is removed from the other database availability group network and associated with the network being created.

5. To establish the network as the replication network for the group, leave the Enable Replication check box selected. Otherwise, clear the check box to use the network as the messaging network for the group.

6. Click New to create the database availability group network. On the Completion page, the Summary states whether the operation was success-ful. If an error occurred, you need to take the appropriate corrective action. Otherwise, click Finish.

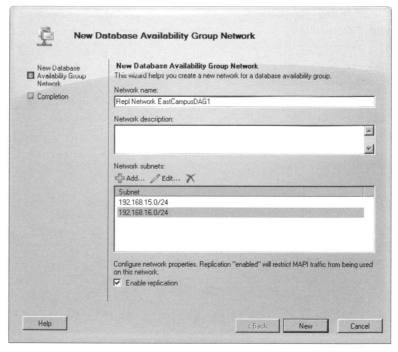

FIGURE 9-5 Create a network for the availability group.

You can remove a network from a database availability group by completing the following steps:

1. In the Exchange Management Console, expand the Organization Configu-ration node and then select the related Mailbox node. On the Database

Availability Group tab, the bottom panel shows the networks currently associated with the selected availability group.

2. Right-click the database availability group network you want to remove, and then click Remove.

In the Exchange Management Shell, you can list availability group networks using Get-DatabaseAvailabilityGroupNetwork. If you enter Get-DatabaseAvailability-GroupNetwork without additional parameters, you see a list of all configured networks for all availability groups. Use the –Identity parameter to specify the name of the network to query. Use the –Server parameter to obtain health information for the network from a specific Mailbox server. The following example lists detailed information for all the networks associated with EastCampusDAG1:

```
Get-DatabaseAvailabilityGroupNetwork -Identity EastCampusDAG1 |
format-list
```

The following example lists detailed information for the Repl network associated with EastCampusDAG1:

```
Get-DatabaseAvailabilityGroupNetwork -Identity EastCampusDAG1\Repl |
format-list
```

You create or remove group networks using New-DatabaseAvailabilityGroup-Network and Remove-DatabaseAvailabilityGroupNetwork. Samples 9-4 and 9-5 provide the syntax and usage.

SAMPLE 9-4 New-DatabaseAvailabilityGroupNetwork cmdlet syntax and usage

Syntax

```
New-DatabaseAvailabilityGroupNetwork -Name NetworkName
-DatabaseAvailabilityGroup DAGName
[-Description Description] [-DomainController FullyQualifiedName]
[-IgnoreNetwork <$true | $false>] [-ReplicationEnabled <$true | $false>]
[-Subnets SubnetIds]
```

Usage

```
New-DatabaseAvailabilityGroupNetwork -DatabaseAvailabilityGroup
"EastCampusDAG1" -Name "Primary DAG Network" -Description ""
-Subnets "{192.168.10.0/24, 192.168.15.0/24}" -ReplicationEnabled $true
```

SAMPLE 9-5 Remove-DatabaseAvailabilityGroupNetwork cmdlet syntax and usage

Syntax

```
Remove-DatabaseAvailabilityGroupNetwork -Identity NetworkName
[-DomainController FullyQualifiedName]
```

```
Remove-DatabaseAvailabilityGroupNetwork
-Identity "EastCampusDAG1\Primary DAG Network"
```

Changing Availability Group Network Settings

Database availability group networks have several properties that you can configure, including the network name, description, associated subnets, and replication status. The replication status determines whether the network is used as the replication network for the group or the messaging network for the group. When replication is enabled, the network is used as the replication network for the group. When replication is disabled, the network is used as the messaging network for the group.

You can manage the settings for a group network by completing the following steps:

1. In the Exchange Management Console, expand the Organization Configuration node and then select the related Mailbox node. On the Database Availability Groups tab, the bottom panel shows the networks currently associated with the selected availability group.

2. Right-click the network you want to work with and then select Properties.

3. On the General tab, the top field shows the name of the network. You can enter a new name if desired and optionally change the network description.

4. Each network must contain at least one subnet. Subnets must be added using a format of *IPAddress/Bitmask*, such as 192.168.15.0/24 , or *IPv6Address/ NetworkSubnetPrefix*, such as FEC0:1234:5678::/48. Use the options provided to add, edit, or remove subnets for the network.

5. To establish the network as the replication network for the group, select the Enable Replication check box. Otherwise, clear the check box to use the network as the messaging network for the group.

6. Click OK to save your settings.

You can use Set-DatabaseAvailabilityGroupNetwork to configure basic settings for availability group networks. Sample 9-6 provides the syntax and usage for Set-DatabaseAvailabilityGroupNetwork.

SAMPLE 9-6 Set-DatabaseAvailabilityGroupNetwork cmdlet syntax and usage

```
Set-DatabaseAvailabilityGroupNetwork -Identity NetworkName
[-Description Description] [-DomainController FullyQualifiedName]
[-IgnoreNetwork <$true | $false>] [-Name NewName] [-ReplicationEnabled
<$true | $false>] [-Subnets Subnets]
```

```
Set-DatabaseAvailabilityGroupNetwork
-Identity "EastCampusDAG1\Primary DAG Network"
-ReplicationEnabled $False
```

Advanced options for the networks associated with availability groups are set at the group level. Advanced options you can configure include encryption, compression, and the TCP port used for replication. Database availability groups support data encryption using the built-in encryption capabilities of the Windows Server operating system. When you enable encryption, database availability groups use Kerberos authentication between Exchange servers to encrypt and decrypt messages. Encryption helps maintain the integrity of the data. Network encryption is a property of the database availability group and not a property of a database availability group network.

You can configure database availability group network encryption by using the –NetworkEncryption parameter of the Set-DatabaseAvailabilityGroup cmdlet in the Exchange Management Shell. The possible encryption settings are as follows:

- **Disabled**   Network encryption is not used for any database availability group networks.
- **Enabled**   Network encryption is used on all database availability group networks for replication and seeding.
- **InterSubnetOnly**   Network encryption is used only with database availability group networks on the same subnet.
- **SeedOnly**   Network encryption is used on all database availability group networks for seeding only.

Database availability groups also support built-in compression. You configure network compression by using the –NetworkCompression parameter of the Set-DatabaseAvailabilityGroup cmdlet in the Exchange Management Shell. The possible compression settings are as follows:

- **Disabled**   Network compression is not used for any database availability group networks.
- **Enabled**   Network compression is used on all database availability group networks for replication and seeding.
- **InterSubnetOnly**   Network compression is used only with database availability group networks on the same subnet.
- **SeedOnly**   Network compression is used on all database availability group networks for seeding only.

You can specify the TCP port to use for replication by using the –ReplicationPort parameter of the Set-DatabaseAvailabilityGroup cmdlet in the Exchange Management Shell.

Configuring Database Availability Group Properties

You can use the Exchange Management Console or the Exchange Management Shell to configure the properties of a database availability group, including the witness server and witness directory used by the database availability group. Using the Exchange Management Shell, you can configure additional properties, such as encryption and compression settings, network discovery, the TCP port used for replication, alternate file share witness settings, and data center activation coordination mode.

To view or modify the properties of an availability group, complete the following steps:

1. In the Exchange Management Console, expand the Organization Configuration node and then select the related Mailbox node. In the results pane, select the Database Availability Group tab to view existing availability groups.

2. Right-click the database availability group you want to work with and then select properties.

3. In the Properties dialog box, shown in Figure 9-6, you'll see a list of member servers, the witness server's fully qualified domain name, and the location of the witness directory on the witness server.

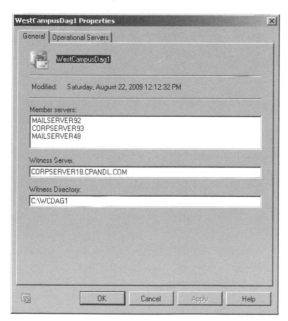

FIGURE 9-6 View or modify properties of the availability group.

4. Using the Witness Server text box, you can specify a new witness server by entering the fully qualified domain name of the new witness server. This

server should be in the same Active Directory forest as the member servers and cannot be a current or future member of the database availability group.

5. Using the Witness Directory text box, you can specify a new witness directory on the witness server. If the directory does not exist, it will be created on the witness server.

6. Click OK.

In the Exchange Management Shell, you can configure properties of database availability groups using the Set-DatabaseAvailabilityGroup cmdlet. Sample 9-7 provides the syntax and usage.

SAMPLE 9-7 Set-DatabaseAvailabilityGroup cmdlet syntax and usage

Syntax

```
Set-DatabaseAvailabilityGroup -Identity DAGName
[-DatabaseAvailabilityGroupIpAddresses IPAddresses]
[-DatacenterActivationMode {"Off"|"DagOnly"}]
[-DiscoverNetworks] [-DomainController FullyQualifiedName]
[-NetworkCompression {"Disabled"|"Enabled"|"InterSubnetOnly"|"SeedOnly"}
[-NetworkEncryption {"Disabled"|"Enabled"|"InterSubnetOnly"|"SeedOnly"}
[-ReplicationPort TCPPort] [-AlternateWitnessServer ServerName]
[-AlternateWitnessServerDirectory DirectoryPath]
[-WitnessServer ServerName] [-WitnessServerDirectory DirectoryPath]
```

Usage

```
Set-DatabaseAvailability -Identity "EastCampusDAG1"
-NetworkCompression "Enabled" -NetworkEncryption "Enabled"
-ReplicationPort 33898 -DatacenterActivationMode "Off"
```

Options for working with encryption, compression, and replication ports were discussed previously in "Changing Availability Group Network Settings." Options that weren't discussed include the datacenter activation coordinator mode, the alternate witness server, and alternate witness server directory. These options can be used as part of a datacenter switchover process. The alternate witness server must not be a part of the database availability group.

The data-center coordinator mode should be set for all database availability groups with three or more members that are extended to two or more physical locations. This mode cannot be enabled for groups with less than three members. When the datacenter coordinator is enabled, you can start, stop, and restore member servers in an availability group individually or collectively using the following:

- **Start-DatabaseAvailabilityGroup** Activates member Mailbox servers in a recovered data center after a data-center switchover, as part of the failback process to the recovered data center. This command sets the configuration and state so that the servers are incorporated into the operating database availability group and joined to the group's cluster. You use the –MailboxServer parameter to start a specific member server or the –ActiveDirectorySite parameter to start all members in a particular site.

```
Start-DatabaseAvailabilityGroup -Identity DAGName
[-MailboxServer ServerName | -ActiveDirectorySite SiteName]
[-ConfigurationOnly <$true | $false>]
[-DomainController FullyQualifiedName]
```

NOTE You can also reactivate servers from a previously failed datacenter that has been restored to service. Before you can reactivate member Mailbox servers in a primary data center, the servers must first be integrated back into the operational database availability group. You reintegrate servers by running the Start-Database-AvailabilityGroup cmdlet and then using the Move-ActiveMailboxDatabase cmdlet to activate databases in the primary data center.

- **Stop-DatabaseAvailabilityGroup** Deactivates member Mailbox servers after a datacenter switchover. You use the –MailboxServer parameter to deactivate a specific member server or the –ActiveDirectorySite parameter to deactivate all members in a particular site.

```
Stop-DatabaseAvailabilityGroup -Identity DAGName
[-MailboxServer ServerName | -ActiveDirectorySite SiteName]
[-ConfigurationOnly <$true | $false>]
[-DomainController FullyQualifiedName]
```

- **Restore-DatabaseAvailabilityGroup** Activates member Mailbox servers in a standby data center. Typically, this process is performed after the failure or deactivation of the active member servers in a primary data center. You use the –ActiveDirectorySite parameter to activate all members in a particular site.

```
Restore-DatabaseAvailabilityGroup -Identity DAGName
[-ActiveDirectorySite SiteName]
[-AlternateWitnessServer ServerName]
[-AlternateWitnessDirectory DirectoryPath]
[-DomainController FullyQualifiedName]
```

Removing Servers from a Database Availability Group

Before you can remove a server from a database availability group, you must also remove all database copies from the server. To remove member servers from a DAG, right-click the DAG, and then click Manage Database Availability Group Membership. On the Manage Database Availability Group Membership page, select each server on the list of current members, and then click the red X to remove the servers from the database availability group. Click Manage, and then click Finish. After you remove the member servers, you can remove the database availability group by right-clicking it and selecting Remove. When prompted to confirm, click Yes.

Removing Database Availability Groups

You can remove a database availability group only if it has no member servers. Therefore, before you can remove a database availability group, you must first remove any member servers from the group.

You can remove an empty availability group by completing the following steps:

1. In the Exchange Management Console, expand the Organization Configuration node and then select the related Mailbox node.

2. On the Database Availability Group tab, right-click the database availability group you want to remove and then select Remove.

3. When prompted to confirm the action, click Yes.

In the Exchange Management Shell, you can remove database availability groups using the Remove-DatabaseAvailabilityGroup cmdlet. Sample 9-8 provides the syntax and usage.

SAMPLE 9-8 Remove-DatabaseAvailabilityGroup cmdlet syntax and usage

Syntax

```
Remove-DatabaseAvailabilityGroup -Identity DAGName
[-DomainController FullyQualifiedName]
```

Usage

```
Remove-DatabaseAvailabilityGroup -Identity "EastCampusDAG1"
```

Switching over Servers and Databases

The Microsoft Exchange Information Store service manages the active and passive databases configured on a Mailbox server. To improve performance, the service running on each server maintains a database cache of changes to active databases that haven't been applied to passive copies. In the event of a failover or switchover, the service can apply the changes in the cache to a passive copy and then make the passive copy the active copy. Most of the time, failover completes in about 30 seconds.

The difference between failover and switchover is important. When Exchange detects a failure of an active database, regardless of whether it is from database failure, server failure, or network failure, Exchange uses failover processes to mark the active database as inactive and dismount it and then mount and mark a passive database copy as the active copy. Prior to performing maintenance on a server or for testing or troubleshooting, you might want Exchange to switch from one database to another by marking an active database as inactive and then marking a passive database copy as the active copy.

Failover and switchover occur at the database level for individual databases and at the server level for all active databases hosted by a server. When either a switchover or failover occurs, other Exchange 2010 server roles become aware of the switchover almost immediately and redirect client and messaging traffic automatically as appropriate.

You can switch over all active databases on a server by completing the following steps:

1. In the Exchange Management Console, expand the Server Configuration node and then select the related Mailbox node.

2. In the main pane, right-click the server that you are performing maintenance on, testing, or troubleshooting and then select Switchover Server.

3. In the Activate Database Copy dialog box, shown in Figure 9-7, the default option is to allow Exchange to handle the switchover and select a server to take over the databases from the source server automatically. To accept the default, click OK. Otherwise, click Use The Specified Target Server and then click Browse. In the Select Mailbox Server dialog box, select the server to take over, click OK, and then click OK again to close the Switchover Server Database Copies dialog box. Keep in mind that you can select only a server that is already a member of the database availability group. You can't have copies outside the group either.

4. When prompted to confirm the action, click Yes.

FIGURE 9-7 Switch over the active databases.

You can perform a switchover of an individual database by completing the following steps:

1. In the Exchange Management Console, expand the Organization Configuration node and then select the related Mailbox node. In the main pane, select the Database Management tab.

2. In the upper pane, click the database you want to work with. In the lower pane, you see the available database copies. The database copies are listed according to their copy status. Only the active copy will have a status of Mounted. All other database copies will display the current status of replication for the database copy.

3. Right-click the passive copy you want to activate, and then click Activate Database Copy.

4. Every mailbox server has a database automount setting and the default is Best Availability. If you want to use the default automount setting, accept the default value of None in the Activate Database Copy dialog box and

then click OK. Otherwise, override the default database mount settings by selecting a value other than None on the Override Mount Dial list and then clicking OK. Values you can select to control the database mount behavior include:

- **Lossless** The database does not automatically mount until all logs that were generated on the original source server have been copied to the target node.

- **Good Availability** The database automatically mounts if the copy queue length is less than or equal to 6. If the queue length is greater than 6, Exchange attempts to replicate the remaining logs to the target server and mounts the databases once the queue length is less than or equal to 6.

- **Best Availability** The database automatically mounts if the copy queue length is less than or equal to 12. The copy queue length is the number of logs that need to be replicated. If the queue length is greater than 12, Exchange attempts to replicate the remaining logs to the target server and mounts the databases once the queue length is less than or equal to 12.

REAL WORLD You can set the default database automount setting for a mailbox server using the –AutoDatabaseMountDail parameter of the Set-MailboxServer cmdlet. If you specify either Best Availability or Good Availability and all of the data has not been replicated to the target server, you might lose some mailbox data. However, the transport dumpster feature (which is enabled by default) helps protect against data loss by resubmitting messages that are in the transport dumpster queue. Because of latency problems or other issues, specifying one of these values can result in a database not being mounted, and you might need to use the -AcceptDataLoss parameter with Mount-Database to force the database to mount after a specified amount of time.

5. When you click OK, Exchange will dismount the current active mailbox database, and establish the previously selected database copy as the active mailbox database.

When you are working with the Exchange Management Shell, you can initiate switchover using Move-ActiveMailboxDatabase. Sample 9-9 shows the syntax and usage.

SAMPLE 9-9 Move-ActiveMailboxDatabase cmdlet syntax and usage

Syntax

```
Move-ActiveMailboxDatabase -Identity DatabaseName
[-SkipClientExperienceChecks <$true | $false>] [-SkipHealthChecks
<$true | $false>] [SkipLagChecks <$true | $false>] {AddtlParams}

Move-ActiveMailboxDatabase -Server ServerName {AddtlParams}
```

```
{AddtlParams}
[-ActivateOnServer ServerOnWhichToActivate] [-MountDialOverride
{"Lossless" | "GoodAvailability" | "BestAvailability"
| "None"} [-DomainController FullyQualifiedName]
[-TerminateOnWarning <$true | $false>]
```

Usage

```
Move-ActiveMailboxDatabase -Identity "Engineering Primary Database"
-ActivateOnServer "MailServer86" -MountDialOverride "Lossless"
```

Content Indexing

Content indexing is a built-in Exchange feature. Every Exchange server in your organization supports and uses some type of indexing. To manage indexing more effectively, use the techniques discussed in this section.

Understanding Indexing

Content indexing enables fast searches and lookups through server-stored mailboxes and public folders. Exchange Server supports two types of indexing:

- Standard indexing with Exchange Search
- Full-text indexing with Exchange Store Search

The Exchange Server storage engine automatically implements and manages Exchange Search. Exchange Search is used with searches for common key fields, such as message subjects. Users take advantage of Exchange Search every time they use the Find feature in Microsoft Office Outlook. With server-based mail folders, Exchange Search is used to quickly search To, From, Cc, and Subject fields. With public folders, Exchange Search is used to quickly search From and Subject fields.

As you probably know, users can perform advanced searches in Office Outlook as well. In Office Outlook 2010, all users need to do is click in the Search box or press Ctrl+E to access the Search tools, click Search Options, and then click Advanced Find. In the Advanced Find dialog box, users can enter their search parameters and then click Find Now. When Exchange Server receives an advanced query without Exchange Store Search, it searches through every message in every folder. This means that as Exchange mailboxes and public folders grow, so does the time it takes to complete an advanced search. With standard searching, Exchange Server is unable to search through message attachments.

With Exchange Store Search, Exchange Server builds an index of all searchable text in a particular mailbox or public folder database before users try to search. The index can then be updated or rebuilt at a predefined interval. Then, when users perform advanced searches, they can quickly find any text within a document or attachment.

NOTE Full-text indexes work only with server-based data. If users have personal folders, Exchange Server doesn't index the data in these folders.

A drawback of Exchange Store Search is that it's resource-intensive. As with any database, creating and maintaining indexes requires CPU time and system memory, which can affect Exchange performance. Full-text indexes also use disk space. A newly created index uses approximately 10 to 20 percent of the total size of the Exchange database (and is directly related to what's in the database's mailboxes). This means that a 1-TB database would have an index of about 100 to 200 GB.

Each time you update an index, the file space that the index uses increases. Don't worry—only changes in the database are stored in the index updates. This means that the additional disk space usage is incremental. For example, if the original 1-TB database grew by 1 GB, the index could use up to 201 GB of disk space (up to 200 GB for the original index and 1 GB for the update).

Managing Exchange Store Search

Exchange Server 2010 doesn't allow administrators to configure how indexing works. With Exchange Server 2010, the Microsoft Search (Exchange) service provides the Exchange Store Search of databases, and Microsoft Exchange Search provides search services. These services provide automated Exchange Store Search.

Full-text indexes are stored as part of the Exchange data files. Because of this, whatever folder location you use for Exchange data files will have a CatalogData-<GUID> subfolder for each database, which contains all the Exchange Store Search data for the related database and all its related databases. By default, you'll find full-text index files for a database in the %SystemDrive%\Program Files\Microsoft\ Exchange Server\V14\Mailbox*DatabaseName*\CatalogData-<GUID> folder.

NOTE Exchange maintains full-text indexes as part of the database maintenance schedule. See the "Setting the Maintenance Interval" section of Chapter 10 for more information.

Each database has an index. If you make a database copy, you are also making an index copy. There's often no need to rebuild an index. That said, as part of the recovery process for a mailbox or public folder database, you might want to rebuild the related full-text index catalog to ensure it is current. You might also want to rebuild the full-text index after you've made substantial changes to a database or if you suspect the full-text index is corrupted.

You can rebuild an index manually at any time. Exchange Server rebuilds an index by re-creating it. This means that Exchange Server takes a new snapshot of the database and uses this snapshot to build the index from scratch. To manually rebuild an index, follow these steps:

1. Log on to the Exchange server using an account with administrator privileges.

2. Open an administrator command prompt.

3. At the command prompt, stop the Microsoft Exchange Search service by typing **net stop MsExchangeSearch**.

4. Use Windows Explorer to delete the CatalogData-*<GUID>* subfolder, which contains the full-text index for the database.

5. At the command prompt, start the Microsoft Exchange Search service by typing **net start MsExchangeSearch.**

TIP Alternatively, you can use the ResetSearchIndex.ps1 script. This PowerShell script accepts the name of the database you want to work with as an input parameter. To get started, enter cd $env:ExchangeInstallPath\Scripts, then run the script by entering .\ResetSearchIndex.ps1 followed by the name of the database, such as .\ResetSearch-Index.ps1 EngineeringMailboxDb.

Exchange Discovery relies on Exchange Store Search for databases and mailboxes within databases. You can enable or disable indexing for individual databases by setting the -IndexEnabled parameter of the Set-MailboxDatabase cmdlet to $true or $false, respectively. The following example disables indexing of the Engineering database:

```
Set-MailboxDatabase "Engineering Database" -IndexEnabled $false
```

When you disable indexing of a database, you also prevent the Exchange 2010 Discovery feature from returning messages from the database or server.

You can disable indexing for all databases on a server by stopping and disabling the Microsoft Exchange Search service. Here's an example using the Exchange Management Shell where you stop and disable the Exchange Search service on a remote server named Server18:

```
Stop-Service MSExchangeSearch -ComputerName Server18

Set-Service MSExchangeSearch -StartupType Disabled -ComputerName Server18
```

You can enable indexing for all databases on a server by enabling the Microsoft Exchange Search service for automatic startup and starting the service. An example using the Exchange Management Shell follows:

```
Set-Service MSExchangeSearch -StartupType Automatic
-ComputerName Server18

Start-Service MSExchangeSearch -ComputerName Server18
```

When you disable indexing on a server, you also prevent Exchange Discovery for all databases on the server.

CHAPTER 10

Mailbox and Public Folder Database Administration

- Working with Active Mailbox Databases **311**
- Working with Mailbox Database Copies **323**
- Using Public Folder Databases **338**
- Managing Mailbox and Public Folder Databases **348**

Databases are containers for information. Microsoft Exchange Server 2010 uses two types of databases to maintain user data: *mailbox databases*, which store a server's mailboxes, and *public folder databases*, which store a server's public folders. The information in a particular database isn't exclusive to either mailboxes or public folders and their associated user data—Exchange Server maintains related information within databases as well. Within mailbox databases, you'll find information about Exchange logons and mailbox usage. Within public folder databases, you'll find information about Exchange logons, public folder instances, and replication. Exchange also maintains information about full-text indexing, although the actual content indexes are stored in separate files. Understanding how to manage databases and the information they contain is the subject of this chapter.

Working with Active Mailbox Databases

Each Mailbox server installed in the organization has an information store. The information store operates as a service and manages the server's databases. Each mailbox database has a database file associated with it. This file is stored in a location that you specify when you create or modify the mailbox database.

Mailbox databases can be either active databases or passive copies of databases. Active databases are the ones users access to get their mailbox data and are the subject of this section. Passive copies of databases are not actively being used and the subject of the section "Working with Mailbox Database Copies" later

311

in this chapter. You create passive copies of databases as part of a high-availability configuration as discussed in Chapter 9, "Managing Data and Database Availability Groups."

Understanding Mailbox Databases

Mailboxes are the normal delivery location for messages coming into an organization. They contain messages, message attachments, and other types of information that the user might have placed in the mailbox. Mailboxes, in turn, are stored in mailbox databases.

When you are installing a Mailbox server, Setup prompts you to specify whether you want to create the default mailbox database. If you decide to create one, you can also specify its name and location. The default mailbox database is meant to be a starting point, and most Exchange organizations can benefit from having additional mailbox databases, especially as the number of users in the organization grows. There are many reasons for creating additional mailbox databases, but the key reasons are the following:

- **To provide a smaller unit of management** Additionally, when you establish database availability groups and create copies of a database, the entire database must be replicated from the source database to the database copies. The larger the database, the longer the initial update process takes. During recovery, you can restore individual databases without affecting the performance or uptime of other databases on the system.

- **To impose a different set of mailbox rules on different sets of users** Each additional mailbox database can have its own property settings for maintenance, storage limits, deleted item retention, indexing, security, and policies. By placing a user's mailbox in one mailbox database instead of another, you can apply a different set of rules.

- **To optimize Exchange performance** Each mailbox database can have its own storage location. By placing the mailbox databases on different drives, you can improve the performance of Exchange Server 2010.

- **To create separate mailbox databases for different purposes** For example, you might want to create a mailbox database called General In-Out to handle all general-purpose mailboxes being used throughout the organization. These general-purpose mailboxes could be set up as shared mailboxes for Postmaster, Webmaster, Technical Support, Customer Support, and other key functions.

When you create a mailbox database, you can specify the following information:

- What the name of the database should be
- Where the database file is to be located
- When maintenance on the database should occur

- Any limitations on mailbox size
- Whether deleted items and mailboxes should be retained

Each mailbox database has a default offline address book (OAB). If you are using public folders, there's also a default public folder database associated with the OAB. Microsoft Outlook 2003 clients access the OAB as part of the public folder data by using Messaging Application Programming Interface (MAPI). Office Outlook 2007 and later clients access the default OAB and default public folder hierarchy on your organization's Client Access servers using Hypertext Transfer Protocol (HTTP) or Secure HTTP (HTTPS). By default, clients inside the corporate network access the OAB using HTTP, and clients outside the corporate network access the OAB using HTTPS.

Exchange 2010 uses the mailbox provisioning load balancer to automatically select a database to use when you create a new mailbox and do not explicitly specify the mailbox database to use. As the name implies, the purpose of the load balancer is to try to balance the workload across mailbox databases in the organization. Although the load balancer uses multiple criteria to try to determine where a mailbox should be created, the selection criteria does not take into account the proximity of the Mailbox server on which a database is stored to the computer or computers used by the user. In a large organization with multiple Active Directory sites, you typically will want a user's mailbox to be located on a Mailbox server in the same site or in an adjacent well-connected site.

Creating Mailbox Databases

You can create mailbox databases using the New Mailbox Database Wizard. The default database file path and default log folder path are set automatically to be the same as those used for other Exchange data.

Any new mailbox databases you create using the Exchange Management Console are configured to use the mailbox provisioning load balancer by default. When you create mailbox databases using the Exchange Management Shell, you can use the –IsExcludedFromProvisioning parameter to specify that the database should not be considered by the mailbox provisioning load balancer. Excluding a database from provisioning means no new mailboxes are automatically added to this database. Rather than excluding a database from provisioning, you can use the –IsSuspendedFromProvisioning parameter to specify that a database be temporarily not considered by the mailbox provisioning load balancer.

To create a mailbox database, complete the following steps:

1. In the Exchange Management Console, expand the Organization Configuration node, and then select the related Mailbox node.

2. In the details pane, the Database Management tab is selected by default. You should see a list of active databases that are available in the Exchange organization.

3. In the left pane, right-click the Mailbox node, and then select New Mailbox Database from the shortcut menu. You should now see the New Mailbox Database Wizard, shown in Figure 10-1.

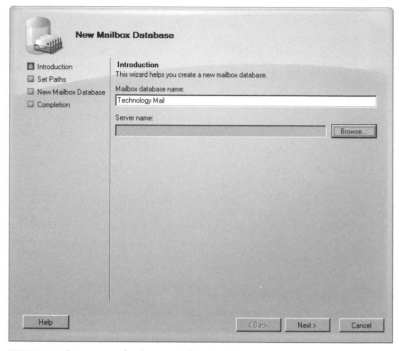

FIGURE 10-1 Enter a name for the new mailbox database.

4. In the Mailbox Database Name text box, type a name for the mailbox database.

5. Click Browse to the right of the Server Name text box. Select the Mailbox server that will host the mailbox database, and then click OK. (See Figure 10-2.) Only Mailbox servers in the Active Directory forest to which you are connected are available. Click Next.

6. On the Set Paths page, shown in Figure 10-3, the database file path and log folder path are set to the default location for Exchange data on the selected server. If you don't want to use the default locations, enter the paths you want to use for the database file and the related logs in the text boxes provided. Select the Mount This Database check box if you want to mount this database. Mounting a database puts it online, making it available for use. Click Next.

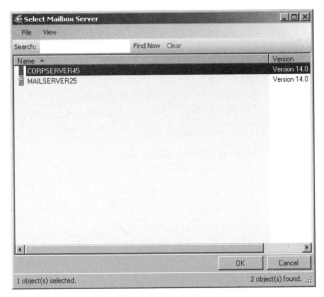

FIGURE 10-2 Select a Mailbox server.

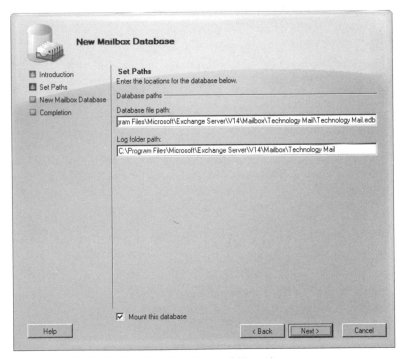

FIGURE 10-3 Set the database file path and the log folder path

NOTE The wizard creates any required folders on the server if they do not exist.

7. Click New to create the mailbox database, and then click Finish. On the Completion page, the Summary states whether the operation was successful. If an error occurred, you need to take the appropriate corrective action. Otherwise, you can now modify the properties of the mailbox database as necessary.

In the Exchange Management Shell, you can create mailbox databases using the New-MailboxDatabase cmdlet. Sample 10-1 provides the syntax and usage.

NOTE You use a separate cmdlet to mount the database. See the section "Mounting and Dismounting Databases" later in this chapter for details.

SAMPLE 10-1 New-MailboxDatabase cmdlet syntax and usage

Syntax

```
New-MailboxDatabase -Name DatabaseName -Server ServerName
[-EdbFilePath DbFilePath] [-LogFolderPath FolderPath] {AddtlParams}

{AddtlParams}
[-DomainController FullyQualifiedName][-IsExcludedFromProvisioning <$true
| $false}] [-IsSuspendedFromProvisioning <$true | $false>]
[-OfflineAddressBook OfflineAddressBook]
[-PublicFolderDatabase DatabaseName]


New-MailboxDatabase -MailboxDatabaseToRecover DatabaseName
-Recovery <$true | $false> -Server ServerName
[-DomainController FullyQualifiedName] [-EdbFilePath DbFilePath]
[-LogFolderPath FolderPath]
```

Usage

```
New-MailboxDatabase -Server "CorpServer88" -Name "Accounting Database"
-EdbFilePath "C:\Databases\Accounting\AccountingMail.edb"
-LogFolderPath "D:\DatabaseLogs\Accounting"
```

Setting the Default Public Folder Database and Default Offline Address Book

Mailbox databases can have different types of information associated with them, including a default public folder database and a default OAB. You set related options for mailbox databases using the Client Settings tab of the related Properties dialog box. To view this dialog box and update the messaging options, follow these steps:

1. In the Exchange Management Console, right-click the mailbox database, and then select Properties.

2. In the Properties dialog box, click the Client Settings tab.

   NOTE If you can't update the text boxes on the Client Settings tab, it means that a policy has been applied to the mailbox database. You must directly edit or remove the policy and then make the necessary changes.

3. The Default Public Folder Database text box shows the full path to the public folder database that the mailbox database is using. If you've recently created public folder databases, this field will be blank, and you should specify the default public folder database to use. You may also want to change the current default. In either case, click Browse, select the public folder database that points to the public folder tree that you want to use, and then click OK.

4. The Offline Address Book text box shows the OAB for the mailbox database. OABs contain information regarding mail-enabled users, contacts, and groups in the organization, and they are used when users aren't connected to the network. If you've created additional OABs beyond the global default, you can specify one of these additional OABs as the default for the mailbox database. Click Browse, select the OAB you want to use, and then click OK. Click OK again to apply the changes.

In the Exchange Management Shell, you can set the default public folder database and default OAB for mailbox databases using the Set-MailboxDatabase cmdlet. Sample 10-2 provides the syntax and usage.

SAMPLE 10-2 Using the Set-MailboxDatabase cmdlet to set defaults

Syntax

```
Set-MailboxDatabase –Identity MailboxDatabase
[ -OfflineAddressBook OABIdentity]
[ -PublicFolderDatabase PublicFolderIdentity]
```

Usage

```
Set-MailboxDatabase –Identity "Accounting Mail"
-OfflineAddressBook "\US Corporate"
-PublicFolderDatabase "CORPSVR127\PublicFolderDB"
```

Setting Mailbox Database Limits and Deletion Retention

Mailbox database limits are designed to control the amount of information that users can store in their mailboxes. Users who exceed the designated limits might receive warning messages and might be subject to certain restrictions, such as the inability to send messages. Deleted item retention is designed to ensure that messages and mailboxes that might be needed in the future aren't deleted inadvertently. If retention is turned on, you can retain deleted messages and mailboxes for a specified period before they are permanently deleted and are nonrecoverable.

An average retention period for messages is about 14 days. The minimum retention period for mailboxes should be about seven days. In most cases, you'll want deleted messages to be maintained for a minimum of five to seven days and deleted mailboxes to be maintained for a minimum of three to four weeks. An interval of five to seven days is used for messages because users usually realize within a few days that they shouldn't have deleted a message. A three-week to four-week interval is used for mailboxes because several weeks can (and often do) pass before users realize that they need a deleted mailbox. To understand why, consider the following scenario.

Sally leaves the company. A coworker is given permission to delete Sally's user account and mailbox. Three weeks later, Sally's boss realizes that she was the only person who received and archived the monthly reports e-mailed from corporate headquarters. The only way to get reports for previous years is to recover Sally's mailbox, and you can do this if you've set a sufficiently long retention period.

NOTE As discussed in Chapter 6, "Mailbox Administration," and in Chapter 8 "Implementing Exchange Server 2010 Security," Exchange has several features to ensure that mailbox items are retained according to policies set forth by an organization for legal reasons, including automatic archiving of old messages and retention policies. Deletion settings on the Limits tab control the minimum length of time deleted items are retained if no retention tags specifically apply to deleted items.

To view or set limits and deletion retention for a mailbox database, follow these steps:

1. In the Exchange Management Console, right-click the mailbox database, and then select Properties.

2. In the Properties dialog box, on the Limits tab (shown in Figure 10-4), use the following options to set storage limits and deleted item retention:

   - **Issue Warning At (KB)** Sets the size limit, in kilobytes, that a mailbox can reach before Exchange Server issues a warning to the user. The warning tells the user to clear out the mailbox.

   - **Prohibit Send At (KB)** Sets the size limit, in kilobytes, that a mailbox can reach before the user is prohibited from sending any new mail. The restriction ends when the user clears out the mailbox and the total mailbox size is under the limit.

   - **Prohibit Send And Receive At (KB)** Sets the size limit, in kilobytes, that a mailbox can reach before the user is prohibited from sending and receiving mail. The restriction ends when the user clears out the mailbox and the total mailbox size is under the limit.

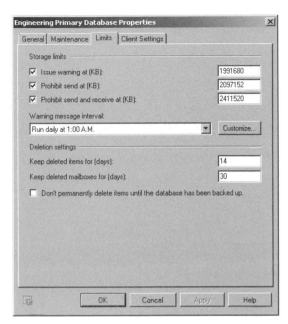

FIGURE 10-4 Use the Limits tab to set storage limits and deleted item retention for individual mailboxes and entire mailbox databases.

CAUTION Prohibiting send and receive might cause users to lose e-mail. When a user sends a message to a user who is prohibited from receiving messages, a nondelivery report (NDR) is generated and delivered to the sender. The recipient never sees the e-mail. Because of this, you should prohibit send and receive only in very rare circumstances. Your organizational policy will likely spell out those circumstances. To remove this restriction, clear the Prohibit Send And Receive At check box.

- **Warning Message Interval**   Sets the interval for sending warning messages to users whose mailboxes exceed the designated limits. The default interval is daily at 1 A.M.

- **Keep Deleted Items For (Days)**   Sets the number of days to retain deleted items. An average retention period is 14 days. If you set the retention period to 0, deleted messages aren't retained, and you can't recover them in the same way you could if retention was enabled.

- **Keep Deleted Mailboxes For (Days)**   Sets the number of days to retain deleted mailboxes. The default setting is 30 days. You'll want to keep most deleted mailboxes for at least seven days to allow the administrators to extract any data that might be needed. If you set the retention period to 0, deleted mailboxes are retained only if you select the next option, and then only until the database has been backed up. If a mailbox is backed up, you can recover it only by restoring it from backups.

- **Do Not Permanently Delete Mailboxes And Items Until The Database Has Been Backed Up** Ensures that deleted mailboxes and items are archived into at least one backup set before they are removed.

3. Click OK to save the settings.

In the Exchange Management Shell, you can set limits for mailbox databases using the Set-MailboxDatabase cmdlet. Sample 10-3 provides the syntax and usage.

NOTE Use the following format for single-event schedules: Startday.Hour:Minute [AM/PM]-End.Hour:Minute [AM/PM]. You can enter names of weekdays in full or abbreviate them. You can also use a 24-hour clock, and if you do this, you must omit the AM/PM designator. Here's an example with the AM/PM designator: **Mon.5:00 AM-Fri.7:00 PM**. And here's an example without the AM/PM designator: **Mon.05:00-Fri.19:00**.

SAMPLE 10-3 Using the Set-MailboxDatabase cmdlet to set limits

---

Syntax

```
Set-MailboxDatabase [-Identity MailboxDatabase]
[-AllowFileRestore <$true | $false>] [-BackgroundDatabaseMaintenence
<$true | $false>] [-CircularLoggingEnabled <$true | $false>]
[-DataMoveReplicationConstraint <None | SecondyCopy | SecondDatacenter |
AllDatacenters | AllCopies>] [-DeletedItemRetention NumberDays]
[-DomainController DCName] [-EventHistoryRetentionPeriod NumberDays]
[-IndexEnabled <$true | $false>] [-IsExcludedFromProvisioning <$true |
$false>] [-IssueWarningQuota Limit] [-JournalRecipient RecipientId]
[-MailboxRetention NumberDays] [-MaintenanceSchedule Schedule]
[-MountAtStartup <$true | $false>] [-Name Name] [-OfflineAddressBook OABId]
[-ProhibitSendQuota Limit] [-ProhibitSendReceiveQuota Limit]
[-PublicFolderDatabase DatabaseId] [-QuotaNotificationSchedule Schedule]
[-RecoverableItemsQuota Limit] [-RecoverableItemsWarningQuota Limit]
[-RetainDeletedItemsUntilBackup <$true | $false>]
[-RcpClientAccessServer ClientAccessServerOrArrayId]
```

Usage

```
Set-MailboxDatabase -Identity "Accounting Mail"
 -IssueWarningQuota 1991680
 -DeletedItemRetention 14
 -MailboxRetention 30
 -ProhibitSendQuota 2097152
 -ProhibitSendReceiveQuota 2411520
 -QuotaNotificationSchedule "Sun.01:00-Sat.23:00"
 -RetainDeletedItemsUntilBackup $true
```

Recovering Deleted Mailboxes

Tasks related to deleting mailboxes are covered in Chapter 5, "User and Contact Administration," in the "Deleting Mailboxes from User Accounts" and "Deleting User Accounts and Their Mailboxes" sections. When you delete a mailbox from a user account, the mailbox is retained as a disconnected mailbox according to the mailbox retention setting. You can reconnect the mailbox to the original user account or another user account if necessary. When you delete a user account and the related mailbox, the mailbox is retained as a disconnected mailbox according to the mailbox retention setting. You can connect the mailbox to an existing user account if necessary.

To recover a deleted mailbox, complete the following steps:

1. In the Exchange Management Console, expand the Recipient Configuration node, and then select the related Disconnected Mailbox node.

2. Deleted mailboxes are listed by the mailbox user's display name and mailbox database. Right-click the deleted mailbox you want to recover, and then click Connect. This starts the Connect Mailbox Wizard.

   NOTE Deleted mailboxes aren't necessarily marked as such immediately. It can take 15 minutes to an hour before the mailbox is marked as deleted and listed accordingly.

3. On the Introduction page, select the type of mailbox you are recovering and then click Next. The available options are User Mailbox, Room Mailbox, Equipment Mailbox, and Linked Mailbox.

4. On the Mailbox Settings page, select Existing User and then click Browse. Use the Select User dialog box to select the user account to which you want to connect the mailbox, and then click OK. You can connect a disconnected mailbox to a user account only if the account doesn't already have a mailbox associated with it.

   NOTE If you previously removed the mailbox rather than disabling it, the user account associated with the mailbox was deleted as well. Because each user account has a unique security identifier associated with it, you can't simply re-create the user account to get back the same set of permissions and privileges. That said, if you want to connect the mailbox to a user account with the same name, you can do this by recovering the deleted account from Active Directory before garbage collection has occurred or by re-creating the account in Active Directory Users And Computers. The account will then be available when you select Existing User and click Browse.

5. The Exchange alias is blank by default. You can change this value by entering a new alias. The Exchange alias is used to set the user's e-mail address.

6. Click Next, and then click Connect.

You can use the Connect-Mailbox cmdlet to perform the same task following the syntax shown in Sample 10-4.

SAMPLE 10-4 Connect-Mailbox cmdlet syntax and usage

Syntax

```
Connect-Mailbox -Identity OrigMailboxIdentity
-Database DatabaseIdentity
-User NewUserIdentity
[-ActiveSyncMailboxPolicy PolicyId] [-Alias Alias]
[-DomainController DCName] [-ManagedFolderMailboxPolicy PolicyId]
[-ManagedFolderMailboxPolicyAllowed <$true | $false>]
[-Archive <$true | $false>] [-Equipment <$true | $false>]
[-Room <$true | $false>] [-Shared <$true | $false>]
[-ValidateOnly <$true | $false>]

[-LinkedCredential Credential] [-LinkedDomainController DCName]
[-LinkedMasterAccount UserId]
```

Usage

```
Connect-Mailbox -Identity "Per Reitzel"
-Database "Accounting Mail" -User "CPANDL\perr" -Alias "perr"

Connect-Mailbox -Identity "Per Reitzel"
-Database "Accounting Mail" –LinkedDomainController CorpServer72
-LinkedMasterAccount "CPANDL\perr"
```

Recovering Deleted Items from Mailbox Databases

You can recover deleted items from mailbox databases as long as you've either set a deleted item retention period for the database from which the items were deleted and the retention period hasn't expired, or you have specified that Exchange should not permanently delete items from mailboxes until the database has been backed up and Exchange hasn't been backed up yet. If either of these conditions are met, you can recover deleted items from mailbox databases.

To use Outlook 2010 for recovery, complete the following steps:

1. Log on as the user who deleted the message, and then start Outlook.

2. Click the Folders pane, and then select Recover Deleted Items.

3. The Recover Deleted Items From dialog box appears. Select the items you want to recover, and then click the Recover Selected Items button.

4. Items you've recovered are copied to the Deleted Items folder. In the left pane, click Deleted Items.

5. In the Deleted Items folder, right-click items you want to keep, select Move, and then click Other Folder.

6. In the Move Items dialog box, select the folder to which the item should be moved, and then click OK.

NOTE The steps are similar for Outlook 2007, except that you start by clicking Recover Deleted Items on the Tools Menu.

To use Outlook Web App (OWA) for recovery, complete these steps:

1. In a Web browser, type *https://servername.yourdomain.com/owa*, where *servername* is a placeholder for the HTTP virtual server hosted by Exchange Server 2010 and *yourdomain.com* is a placeholder for your external domain name, such as https://mail.cpandl.com/owa.

2. Next, log on as the user (or have the user log on). At the security prompt, specify whether the user is using a public or shared computer or a private computer. Type the user name in *domain\username* format, such as **cpandl\ bertk**, or *user@domain* format, such as **berk@cpandl.com**. Type the password, and then click Log On.

3. In the left pane, right-click Deleted Items and then select Recover Deleted Items.

4. In the Recover Deleted Items list, you'll see a list of recoverable items. Select the items you want to recover, and then click the Recover Selected Items button.

5. In the Recover To Folder dialog box, click the folder you want the items recovered to, and then click Recover. You also have the option of creating a new folder and putting the items in that folder.

Working with Mailbox Database Copies

When your Exchange organization uses database availability groups, Exchange replicates transaction logs from an active mailbox database on a source Mailbox server to other Mailbox servers in the database availability group that have passive copies of the database. On these servers, Exchange replays the transaction logs into the passive copy of the mailbox database. You can monitor the health and status of replication and database copies using the Exchange Management tools. Using the Exchange Management tools, you can also perform related management tasks.

The Mailbox server that hosts the active copy of a database is referred to as the *mailbox database primary* for that database. A Mailbox server that hosts a passive copy of a database is referred to as a *mailbox database secondary* for that database. You can move the active database to another Mailbox server in the database availability group by using the switchover process discussed in "Switching over Servers and Databases" in Chapter 9. In a switchover, the active copy of a database is dismounted on the current Mailbox server and a passive copy of the database is activated and mounted on a another Mailbox server in the database availability group.

TIP You can quickly distinguish between an active mailbox database and a passive copy of a database by reviewing the Copy Status column under the Database Copies tab in the Exchange Management Console. Only the active database will have a status of Mounted or Dismounted. For passive database copies, you'll see the current status of replication for the database copy.

Creating Mailbox Database Copies

After you create a database availability group and add Mailbox servers to the group, you can create copies of mailbox databases to initiate replication. Within the group, replication occurs between the active mailbox database on a source Mailbox server and other Mailbox servers that host copies of the database. You cannot replicate a database outside of a database availability group, nor can you replicate an Exchange 2010 mailbox database to a server running Exchange 2007 (or vice versa).

Each database availability group can have up to 16 member servers, and you can create up to 16 instances of a database, including one active instance and 15 passive instances. You can create mailbox database copies only on Mailbox servers that do not host the active copy of a mailbox database, and you cannot create two copies of the same database on the same server.

Because all copies of a database use the same path on each server containing a copy, the database and log file paths for a database copy on each Mailbox server must not conflict with any other database paths. You need to ensure the database and log file paths for the database copy can be created in the same location as all other copies and that the paths do not conflict with any other database paths on the target server.

With respect to Active Directory, the member servers in an availability group must all be in the same Active Directory domain. You can create database copies on Mailbox servers in the same or different Active Directory Sites, and on the same or different network subnets. However, database copies are not supported between Mailbox servers with roundtrip network latency greater than 250 milliseconds (by default). Database copies are automatically assigned an identity in the format *DatabaseName\HostMailboxServerName*, such as Engineering Primary Database\ MailServer36.

To create a copy of a mailbox database, complete the following steps:

1. In the Exchange Management Console, expand the Organization Configuration node, and then select the related Mailbox node.

2. In the details pane, the Database Management tab is selected by default. You should see a list of active databases that are available in the Exchange organization. Select the mailbox database that you want to copy to see a list of all copies of that database in the lower pane.

3. In the upper pane on the Database Management tab, right-click the mailbox database that you want to copy, and select Add Mailbox Database Copy. This starts the Add Mailbox Database Copy Wizard.

4. The wizard shows you which servers already have a copy of the database and sets the activation preference number to the next value for the next database instance, as shown in Figure 10-5. You can set a lower preference value if desired.

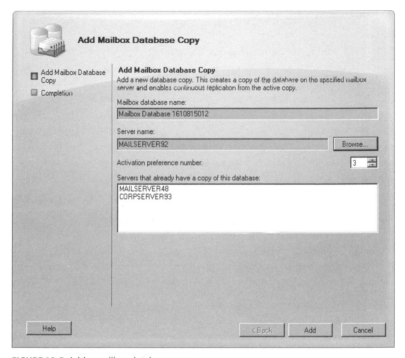

FIGURE 10-5 Add a mailbox database copy.

5. Click Browse. Select the Mailbox server that will host the mailbox database copy and then click OK. Although servers outside the database availability group and Exchange 2007 servers may be listed, you'll only want to select an Exchange 2010 Mailbox server in the same database availability group that doesn't have a copy of the database already. Each Mailbox server in a database availability group can host only one copy of a database.

6. Optionally, in the Activation Preference Number text box, specify the preference value for the database copy. The activation preference number represents the order of activation preference of a database copy after a failure or outage of the active copy. The preference value is a number equal to or greater than 1, where 1 has the highest preference. The preference value cannot be larger than the total number of database copies.

NOTE Active Manager uses the preference value only to break ties in the best-copy selection process. If two or more database copies are seen as the best choice for activation, the database copy with the highest preference is selected. Following this, when there is a tie, a database copy with a preference value of 3 would be selected before a database copy with a preference value of 4. For more information on Active Manager, see "Introducing Active Manager" in Chapter 9.

7. Click Add to create the mailbox database copy, and then click Finish. On the Completion page, the Summary states whether the operation was successful. If an error occurred, you need to take the appropriate corrective action. Otherwise, you can now work with the database copy.

In the Exchange Management Shell, you can create mailbox database copies using the Add-MailboxDatabaseCopy cmdlet. Sample 10-5 provides the syntax and usage. Use the –ReplayLagTime parameter to specify how long the Exchange Replication Service should wait before replaying log files. Use the –TruncationLagTime parameter to specify how long the Exchange Replication Service should wait before truncating logs that have been replayed.

TIP Different database copies can have different lag times. If you want logs to be replayed immediately, set a relatively short replay lag time or none at all. If you want a cushion for protection against inadvertent changes, set a longer replay lag time. As an example, if you have three database copies, you might want two copies to have short replay lag times and one copy to have a long replay lag time.

NOTE The new database copy will remain in a Suspended state if you use the –SeedingPostponed parameter. When the database copy status is set to Suspended, the SuspendMessage is set to "Replication is suspended for database copy '<Name>' because database needs to be seeded." You can seed the database as discussed in the "Updating Mailbox Database Copies" section.

SAMPLE 10-5 Add-MailboxDatabaseCopy cmdlet syntax and usage

Syntax

```
Add-MailboxDatabaseCopy -Identity SourceDatabase
-MailboxServer TargetServer [-ActivationPreference PrefValue]
[-ReplayLagTime Days.Hours:Minutes:Seconds]
[-SeedingPostponed <$true | $false>]
[-TruncationLagTime Days.Hours:Minutes:Seconds]
[-DomainController FullyQualifiedName]
```

Usage

```
Add-MailboxDatabaseCopy -Identity "Engineering Primary Database"
-MailboxServer "MailServer36" -ReplayLagTime 00:03:00
-TruncationLagTime 00:10:00 -ActivationPreference 2
```

Setting Replay, Truncation, and Preference Values for Database Copies

Replay and truncation values are designed to let you fine-tune the way replication works for each database copy. Replay lag time is the amount of time to delay log replay. Truncation lag time is the amount of time that you want to delay log truncation after a log has been successfully replayed. You can also set a relative preference value for database copies. The preferred list sequence number sets the order of activation preference after a failure or outage affecting the active database. As discussed previously, Active Manager uses the preference value in the case of a tie during the best-copy selection process.

To set preference values for a database copy, complete the following steps:

1. In the Exchange Management Console, expand the Organization Configuration node, and then select the related Mailbox node.

2. In the details pane, the Database Management tab is selected by default. Select the mailbox database with the copy that you want to manage.

3. In the lower pane, right-click the database copy you want to modify and then click Properties.

4. On the General tab, the current activation preference number is listed. Change the value as necessary, and then click OK.

In the Exchange Management Shell, you can set replay, truncation, and preference values for mailbox database copies by using the Set-MailboxDatabaseCopy cmdlet. Sample 10-6 provides the syntax and usage.

SAMPLE 10-6 Set-MailboxDatabaseCopy cmdlet syntax and usage

Syntax

```
Set-MailboxDatabaseCopy -Identity Database\Server
[-ActivationPreference PrefValue]
[-ReplayLagTime Days.Hours:Minutes:Seconds]
[-TruncationLagTime Days.Hours:Minutes:Seconds]
[-DomainController FullyQualifiedName]
```

Usage

```
Set-MailboxDatabaseCopy -Identity "Tech Mail Database\MailServer36"
-ReplayLagTime 00:02:00 -TruncationLagTime 00:05:00
-ActivationPreference 6
```

Suspending and Resuming Replication

As part of planned maintenance or for other reasons, it might be necessary to temporarily suspend replication activity for a database copy. In addition, prior to performing some administrative tasks, you need to suspend replication activity before you can complete the task—for example, before performing seeding. You can suspend and resume database copy activity by completing the following steps:

1. In the Exchange Management Console, expand the Organization Configuration node, and then select the related Mailbox node.

2. In the details pane, the Database Management tab is selected by default. Select the mailbox database with the copy that you want to manage.

3. In the lower pane, only the active mailbox database has a Copy Status of Mounted or Dismounted. For all passive database copies, the Copy Status entry shows the current status of replication for the database copy.

4. Right-click the passive database copy (not an active database) for which you want to suspend replication and then click Suspend Database Copy.

5. Optionally, enter a comment as to why you are suspending replication.

6. Click Yes to suspend continuous replication.

To resume replication later, right-click the database copy and then click Resume Database Copy. If a suspend comment was provided, you can read the comment. Click Yes to resume continuous replication.

In the Exchange Management Shell, you can suspend and resume replication using Suspend-MailboxDatabaseCopy and Resume-MailboxDatabaseCopy, respectively. Samples 10-7 and 10-8 provide the syntax and usage. If you use the –ActivationOnly parameter to suspend activation only, the database cannot be activated until you resume replication without specifying the –ReplicationOnly parameter. The –ReplicationOnly parameter resumes replication without affecting the activation setting. For example, if the –ActivationSuspended parameter was set to $True, the parameter remains set to $True.

SAMPLE 10-7 Suspend-MailboxDatabaseCopy cmdlet syntax and usage

Syntax

```
Suspend-MailboxDatabaseCopy -Identity Database\Server
[-ActivationOnly <$true | $false>]
[-DomainController FullyQualifiedName]
[-SuspendComment Comment]
```

Usage

```
Suspend-MailboxDatabaseCopy -Identity "Tech Mail Database\MailServer36"
-ActivationOnly
```

SAMPLE 10-8 Resume-MailboxDatabaseCopy cmdlet syntax and usage

Syntax

```
Resume-MailboxDatabaseCopy -Identity Database\Server
[-ReplicationOnly <$true | $false>]
[-DomainController FullyQualifiedName]
```

```
Resume-MailboxDatabaseCopy -Identity "Tech Mail Database\MailServer36"
```

Updating Mailbox Database Copies

Seeding is the process of initially replicating an active or passive database into a database copy. This creates a baseline passive copy of a database. Normally, seeding occurs automatically, and the length of time required to completely seed a database depends on the size of the source database, the available bandwidth on the network, and the level of activity on the servers involved. However, automatic seeding can fail, and in this case, you then need to manually initiate seeding.

REAL WORLD An automatic seed produces a copy of an active or passive database on a target Mailbox server. Automatic seeding occurs only during the creation of a new database or for a database that has never been backed up.

You can identify a problem with seeding by checking the state of the database copy. When you create a database copy, the database should enter the Initializing state and then the Seeding state. When seeding is complete, the database copy should be in the Healthy state. If the database remains in a Suspended state and does not complete initialization or seeding, there is a problem. Note also that if you are seeding when creating the copy, the task will not complete successfully until the seed is completed. So, you simply watch the task progress and do not need to check copy status.

You can reseed a mailbox database copy anytime you suspect divergence has occurred. However, divergence isn't necessarily a problem because incremental reseed version 2 (incremental resync) takes care of resolving the divergence, which means that you don't need to do a full reseed except in circumstances in which resync isn't possible—for example, when there is no overlap in log files between diverged copies or when you've done something you shouldn't have, like an offline defragmentation of a copy that causes uncorrectable divergence.

When you reseed a database, Exchange empties the database copy and replicates a new passive database copy. Typically, you won't need to reseed database copies after the initial seeding has occurred. However, in some situations you might need to reseed a database copy. One state you can check for is the FailedAndSuspended state. In this state, Exchange has detected a failure and suspended replication replay because resolution of the failure explicitly requires administrator intervention. For example, if Exchange detects that there is an unrecoverable divergence between the active mailbox database and a database copy, Exchange marks the database copy as FailedAndSuspended. If an incremental resync doesn't eventually resolve the problem, you need to resolve the underlying cause of the failure before the database copy can be transitioned to a healthy state, which includes reseeding the database.

Before you can seed or reseed a database, you must suspend replication. For very large databases—that is, those that are multiple terabytes (TB) in size—the preferred technique for seeding the initial passive copy of the database, if service level agreements allow or such an outage is acceptable, is to dismount the active copy of the database and copy the database file to the same location on the target Mailbox server in the same database availability group. Rather than copying the database over the network, which could take several days for a multiterabyte database, you should consider the following:

- Copying the database to one or more disk drives, preferably hot-swappable drives that can be moved between the source and target servers

- Copying the database to one or more logical unit numbers (LUNs) in your storage array that can be assigned to or is assigned to the target server

With this approach, the database will be unavailable until seeding is completed and you can mount the database. Alternatively, you can leave the active database online and use the Exchange Management tools to initiate the seeding process. Once you've created at least one baseline passive copy of a database, you can seed new passive copies from the baseline passive copy at anytime using an online or offline approach.

The size of the database, the available network bandwidth, network latency, and the activity levels on the source and target servers determine how long an over-the-network transfer or update takes. After the seeding process has started, don't close the Exchange Management Console or Exchange Management Shell until the process has completed. If you do, the seeding operation will be terminated and will need to be restarted.

Keep the following in mind when you are considering updating database copies:

- When you seed a database using the Exchange Management Console, both the database copy and the content index catalog are seeded. In the Exchange Management Shell, you can specify that only the database copy should be seeded using the –DatabaseOnly parameter or that only the context index catalog should be seeded using the –CatalogOnly parameter.

- Before you seed the database copy, you should manually remove existing files on the server that hosts the database copy. In the Exchange Management Console, you can specify that existing files should be deleted by selecting Delete Any Existing Files In Target Path. You can delete existing files in the Exchange Management Shell using the –DeleteExistingFiles parameter. However, these options remove only the files Exchange checks for and might fail if other files are present.

- When seeding is complete, Exchange automatically resumes replication. If you want to resume replication manually instead, you can specify the Manually Resume Replication To The Database Copy option in the Exchange Management Console or use the –ManualResume parameter in the Exchange Management Shell.

- By default, seeding data is transferred over the replication network for the database availability group, unless you are seeding to a remote site, in which case it will default to the messaging network. You can override the defaults by using the –Network parameter. The network compression and encryption settings are used and determine whether the transferred data is compressed, encrypted, or both. You specify the networks to use by name in both management tools. In the Exchange Management Shell, you can override the network compression and encryption settings using –NetworkCompression-Override and –NetworkEncryptionOverride, respectively.

You can seed a database manually by completing the following steps:

1. In the Exchange Management Console, expand the Organization Configuration node, and then select the related Mailbox node.

2. In the details pane, the Database Management tab is selected by default. Select the mailbox database with the copy that you want to manage.

3. In the lower pane, only the active mailbox database copy has a Copy Status of Mounted or Dismounted. For all other database copies, the Copy Status entry shows the current status of replication for the database copy.

4. Right-click the passive database copy that you want to update, and then click Update Database Copy. This starts the Update Database Copy Wizard (see Figure 10-6).

TIP The Exchange Management Console won't let you reseed a database that's in a healthy or other normal state. However, you can force a reseed by suspending database copying and then updating the database copy.

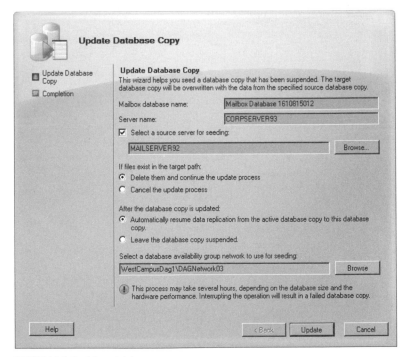

FIGURE 10-6 Update a database copy.

5. By default, Exchange will seed the database from the active copy of the database. If you want to use a passive copy for seeding, choose Select A Source Server For Seeding and then click Browse. In the Select Mailbox Server dialog box, select the source server hosting the passive copy you want to use and then click OK.

6. To remove existing files, select Delete Them And Continue The Update Process. Existing files must be removed for seeding to be successful. Otherwise, the update will be canceled.

7. By default, after the seeding has completed, Exchange automatically resumes continuous replication for the database. If you don't want replication to automatically resume, select Leave The Database Copy Suspended.

8. By default, Exchange selects a network to use for seeding. If the source and target are on the same subnet and you've configured a Replication network that includes the subnet, then the Replication network will be used. If the source and target are on different subnets or in different datacenters, the MAPI network will be used for seeding. To specify which network should be used for seeding, click the Browse button to the right of the Select A Database Availability Group Network text box. In the Select Database Availability Group Network dialog box, click the network to use and then click OK.

9. After you have configured the available options, click Update to begin seeding. When the seeding completes, the Summary states whether the operation was successful. If an error occurred, you need to take the appropriate corrective action. Click Finish.

To seed a database copy in the Exchange Management Shell, you use the Update-MailboxDatabaseCopy cmdlet. Sample 10-9 provides the syntax and usage. Use the –Force parameter when seeding programmatically, and you will not be prompted for administrative input.

SAMPLE 10-9 Update-MailboxDatabaseCopy cmdlet syntax and usage

Syntax

```
Update-MailboxDatabaseCopy -Identity Database\Server
-SourceServer ServerName
[-CatalogOnly <$true | $false>]
[-DatabaseOnly <$true | $false>]
[-DeleteExistingFiles <$true | $false>]
[-DomainController FullyQualifiedName]
[-Force <$true | $false>]
[-ManualResume <$true | $false>]
[-Network NetworkID]
[-NetworkCompressionOverride {"UseDAGDefault"|"Off"|"On"}]
[-NetworkEncryptionOverride {"UseDAGDefault"|"Off"|"On"}]
```

```
Update-MailboxDatabaseCopy -Identity "CS Mail\MailServer25"
-CatalogOnly -Force

Update-MailboxDatabaseCopy -Identity "CS Mail\MailServer25"
-DatabaseOnly

Update-MailboxDatabaseCopy -Identity "CS Mail\MailServer25"
-Network "EastCampusDAG1\Primary DAG Network"
-NetworkCompressionOverride "On" -NetworkEncryptionOverride "Off"
```

Monitoring Database Replication Status

As an Exchange administrator, you need to monitor the health and status of database copies to ensure that they are available when needed. You can view key health and status information for a database copy by completing the following steps:

1. In the Exchange Management Console, expand the Organization Configuration node, and then select the related Mailbox node.

2. In the details pane, the Database Management tab is selected by default. Select the mailbox database with the copy that you want to manage.

3. In the lower pane, you'll see the current status of each database copy. Table 10-1 lists the possible values for the Copy Status and any corrective action that might be required.

4. Right-click the database copy and then select Properties. This opens a Properties dialog box.

5. Use the information provided on the General tab to view the status of the mailbox database copy. The information provided includes

   - **Database**   Displays the name of the selected database

   - **Mailbox Server**   Displays the name of the Mailbox server that hosts the database copy.

   - **Status**   Displays the current health and status of replication for the database copy

   - **Copy Queue Length (Logs)**   Shows the number of log files waiting to be copied and checked

   - **Replay Queue Length (Logs)**   Shows the number of log files waiting to be replayed into this copy of the database

   - **Activation Preference Number**   Shows the activation preference value for the database copy

6. Use the information provided on the Status tab to view additional details about the health and status of replication for the database copy. The information provided includes

   - **Seeding**   Specifies whether a seeding operation is currently in progress

- **Latest Available Log Time**   Shows the time associated with the latest available log generated by the active database copy
- **Last Inspected Log Time**   Shows the modification time of the last log that was successfully validated by the Mailbox server hosting the database copy
- **Last Copied Log Time**   Shows the modification time of the last log that was successfully copied
- **Last Replayed Log Time**   Shows the modification time of the last log that was successfully replayed by the Mailbox server hosting the database copy

7. If any failures have occurred, click the View Errors button to view messages about conditions that triggered the failure.

TABLE 10-1 Copy Status Values

COPY STATUS	STATUS OF THE MAILBOX DATABASE COPY	CORRECTIVE ACTION
ActivationSuspended	Has been manually blocked from activation by an administrator.	Allow activation, if appropriate.
Disconnected-AndHealthy	Has been disconnected, and was in the Healthy state when the loss of connection occurred.	This state can be reported during network failures between the active copy and the database copy.
Disconnected-AndResynchronizing	Is no longer connected to the active database copy, and was in the Resynchronizing state when the loss of connection occurred.	This state can be reported during network failures between the active copy and the database copy.
Dismounted	Is offline and not accepting client connections. Applies only to the active mailbox database.	Mount the database if maintenance is complete.
Dismounting	Is going offline and terminating client connections. Applies only to the active mailbox database.	N/A

TABLE 10-1 Copy Status Values

COPY STATUS	STATUS OF THE MAILBOX DATABASE COPY	CORRECTIVE ACTION
Failed	Is in a failed state because it is not suspended, and is not able to copy or replay log files.	Exchange periodically checks to see whether the problem that caused the copy status to change to Failed has been resolved. If so, and barring no other issues, the copy status automatically changes to Healthy.
FailedAndSuspended	Is in the Failed And Suspended state because a failure was detected and because resolution of the failure explicitly requires administrator intervention.	Take corrective action as appropriate. Exchange does not periodically check to see whether the problem has been resolved and does not automatically recover.
Healthy	Is successfully copying and replaying log files, or has successfully copied and replayed all available log files.	N/A
Initializing	Is being created. Or the Microsoft Exchange Replication service is starting up or has just been started. Or the Mailbox Database copy is transitioning to another state.	While the copy is in this state, Exchange is verifying that the database and log stream are in a consistent state. It should generally not be in this state for longer than 30 seconds.
Mounted	Is online and accepting client connections. Applies only to active mailbox database.	N/A
Mounting	Is coming online and not yet accepting client connections. Applies only to active mailbox database.	N/A

TABLE 10-1 Copy Status Values

COPY STATUS	STATUS OF THE MAILBOX DATABASE COPY	CORRECTIVE ACTION
Resynchronizing	Is being checked for any divergence between the active copy and this passive copy.	The copy status remains in this state until any divergence is detected and resolved.
Seeding	Is being seeded, the related content index is being seeded, or both.	Upon successful completion of seeding, the copy status should change to Initializing.
ServiceDown	Cannot connect to the replication service.	Start or restart the Microsoft Exchange Replication service on the server that hosts the mailbox database copy.
SinglePageRestore	Had a single page error, and this error is being corrected automatically.	N/A
Suspended	Is in a suspended state as a result of an administrator manually suspending the database copy.	Resume replication if appropriate

In the Exchange Management Shell, you can check the health and status of replication using the Get-MailboxDatabaseCopyStatus cmdlet. Sample 10-10 provides the syntax and usage.

SAMPLE 10-10 Get-MailboxDatabaseCopyStatus cmdlet syntax and usage

```
Syntax

Get-MailboxDatabaseCopyStatus -Server ServerName {AddtlParams}

Get-MailboxDatabaseCopyStatus [-Identity LocalDatabaseName]
[-Active <$true | $false>] [-Local <$true | $false>]] {AddtlParams}

{AddtlParams}
[-ConnectionStatus <$true | $false>]
[-DomainController FullyQualifiedName]
[-ExtendedErrorInfo <$true | $false>]]
```

```
Get-MailboxDatabaseCopyStatus -Server "MailServer35"
-ConnectionStatus -ExtendedErrorInfo


Get-MailboxDatabaseCopyStatus


Get-MailboxDatabaseCopyStatus -Identity "Accounting Mail"
```

Removing Database Copies

You can remove a passive database copy at any time by using the Exchange Management tools. After removing a database copy, you need to manually delete any database and transaction log files from the server.

NOTE You cannot use these procedures to remove the active copy of a mailbox database. To remove a database that is an active copy, you must first switch the database over to a new active copy. Alternatively, if you no longer want a database and its copies, you need to remove all passive copies before you can remove the active copy, and then you need to remove all mailboxes from the active database before you can delete it.

TIP You can remove mailbox database copies only from a database availability group with a Healthy status. If the database availability group doesn't have a Healthy status, you won't be able to remove any mailbox database copies.

To remove a database copy, complete the following steps:

1. In the Exchange Management Console, expand the Organization Configuration node, and then select the related Mailbox node.

2. In the details pane, the Database Management tab is selected by default. Select the mailbox database with the copy that you want to manage.

3. In the lower pane, only the active mailbox database has a Copy Status of Mounted or Dismounted. For passive database copies, the Copy Status entry shows the current status of replication for the database copy.

4. Right-click the passive database copy that you want to remove and then click Remove.

5. When prompted to confirm, click Yes.

In the Exchange Management Shell, you can remove a database copy using the Remove-MailboxDatabaseCopy cmdlet. Sample 10-11 provides the syntax and usage.

SAMPLE 10-11 Remove-MailboxDatabaseCopy cmdlet syntax and usage

```
Remove-MailboxDatabaseCopy -Identity DatabaseName\ServerName]
[-DomainController FullyQualifiedName]
```

Using Public Folder Databases

This section explains how to create public folder databases and set basic public folder database properties. It doesn't go into detail about managing the many facets of public folders. That topic is covered in Chapter 11, "Accessing and Managing Public Folders."

Understanding Public Folder Databases

Public folders are used to share messages and files in an organization. You manage public folder databases much differently than you do mailbox databases, but there are many similarities with respect to internal structure and management. And when it comes down to it, a public folder database is really nothing more than a special type of mailbox that Exchange replicates to other public folder databases.

Public folder databases must have a public folder tree associated with them. This public folder tree must be unique and can be assigned to a single public folder database only. Users access items that are stored in public folders through the public folder tree.

Each Mailbox server in your Exchange organization can have a maximum of one public folder database, and this is the default public folder database associated with the mailbox databases configured on that server (assuming that a default database was created during setup). Exchange doesn't support creating multiple public folder databases on a Mailbox server. One of the primary reasons for this is that MAPI mail clients, such as Microsoft Office Outlook 2003, can access only their default public folder tree.

You can replicate public folder databases from one Mailbox server to another. Replication allows mailbox users to access public data, regardless of which Mailbox server they are using. Having multiple Mailbox servers, each with a public folder database that is replicated, helps to distribute the workload. When an Exchange organization has two or more public folder databases, each on separate servers, replication occurs automatically between the public folder databases on those servers using public folder replication. If a replica of the requested content exists on the Exchange server that serves the request, the client application accesses the local replica. If the replica does not exist on the local server, Exchange attempts to locate a replica in the same Active Directory site.

Creating Public Folder Databases

You can create public folder databases using the New Public Folder Database Wizard. The default database file path and default copy file path are set automatically to be the same as those used for system files and backup system files, respectively.

To create a public folder database, complete the following steps:

1. In the Exchange Management Console, expand the Organization Configuration node, and then select the related Mailbox node.

2. In the details pane, the Database Management tab is selected by default. You should see a list of databases that are available in the Exchange organization.

3. In the left pane, right-click the Mailbox node, and then select New Public Folder Database from the shortcut menu. You should now see the New Public Folder Database Wizard, as shown in Figure 10-7.

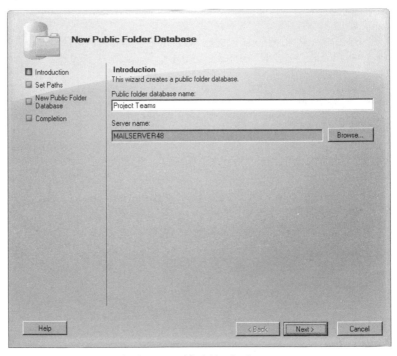

FIGURE 10-7 Enter a name for the new public folder database.

4. In the Public Folder Database Name text box, type a name for the public folder database.

5. Click Browse to the right of the Server Name text box. Select the Mailbox server that will host the mailbox database and then click OK. Only Mailbox servers in the Active Directory forest to which you are connected are available. Click Next.

6. On the Set Paths page, the database file path and log folder path are set to the default location for Exchange data on the selected server. If you don't want to use the default locations, enter the desired paths for the database file and the related logs using the text boxes provided. Leave the

Mount This Database check box selected if you want to mount this database. Mounting a database puts it online, making it accessible to users with permissions. Click Next.

NOTE The wizard creates any required folders on the server if they do not exist.

7. Click New to create the public folder database, and then click Finish. On the Completion page, the Summary states whether the operation was successful. If an error occurred, you need to take the appropriate corrective action. Otherwise, you can now modify the properties of the public folder database as necessary.

In the Exchange Management Shell, you can create public folder databases using the New-PublicFolderDatabase cmdlet. Sample 10-12 provides the syntax and usage.

NOTE A separate cmdlet is used to mount the database. See the section "Mounting and Dismounting Databases" later in this chapter for details.

SAMPLE 10-12 New-PublicFolderDatabase cmdlet syntax and usage

Syntax

```
New-PublicFolderDatabase -Server ServerName -Name DatabaseName
[-DomainController DCName]
[-EdbFilePath EdbFilePath]
[-LogFolderPath LogFolderPath]
```

Usage

```
New-PublicFolderDatabase -Server "MAILSERVER25" -Name "Project Teams"
-EdbFilePath "C:\Project Teams\Project Teams.edb"
-LogFolderPath "C:\Logs\Project Teams"
```

Setting Public Folder Database Limits

Storage limits are designed to control the amount of information that users can post to public folders. As with mailbox databases, users who exceed the designated limits might receive warning messages and might be subject to certain restrictions, such as the inability to post messages.

Because public folders help users share messages, documents, and ideas, they're an important part of any Exchange organization. Over time, however, public folders can become cluttered, which reduces their usefulness. To minimize clutter, you can set an age limit on items that are posted to public folders. Items that reach the age limit expire and Exchange Server removes them permanently from the public folder.

When you set the age limit, keep in mind the type of information stored in the related public folders. For example, if you have a public folder database for general discussion and file sharing, you might want the age limit to be a few weeks. However, if you have a public folder database for projects, you might want the age limit to extend throughout the life of the project, which could be months or years.

The age limit and the deleted item retention are two separate values. Deleted item retention is designed to ensure that postings and documents that could be needed in the future aren't prematurely deleted. When retention is turned on, deleted items are retained for a specified period before they are permanently deleted and might also need to be backed up before being permanently deleted, depending on the settings you've used. If you have backups, you can recover deleted items from backups.

The age limit applies to deleted items as well. If a deleted item reaches the age limit, it's permanently deleted along with other items that have reached their age limit.

To set the storage limits, age limits, and deleted item retention for a public folder database, follow these steps:

1. In the Exchange Management Console, right-click the public folder database, and then select Properties.

2. In the Properties dialog box, click the Limits tab, as shown in Figure 10-8. Use the following options to set the limits:

   - **Issue Warning At (KB)** Sets the size, in kilobytes, of the data that a user can post to the public folder database before a warning is issued. The warning tells the user to clean out the public folder database.

   - **Prohibit Post At (KB)** Sets the maximum size, in kilobytes, of the data that a user can post to the public folder database. The restriction ends when the total size of the user's data is under the limit.

   - **Maximum Item Size (KB)** Sets the maximum size, in kilobytes, for postings to the database.

   - **Warning Message Interval** Sets the interval for sending warning messages to users whose total data size exceeds the designated limits. The default interval is daily at 1 A.M.

   - **Keep Deleted Items For (Days)** Sets the number of days to retain deleted items. An average retention period is 14 days. If you set the retention period to 0, deleted postings are retained only if you select the next option and then retention is only until the database has been backed up. If a database is backed up, you can recover postings only by restoring them from backups.

   - **Don't Permanently Delete Items Until The Database Has Been Backed Up** Ensures that deleted items are archived into at least one backup set before they are removed.

   - **Age Limit For All Folders In This Public Folder Database (Days)** Sets the number of days to retain postings in the database. Postings older than the limit are automatically deleted.

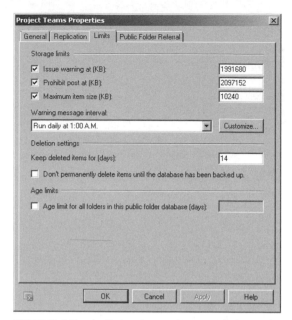

FIGURE 10-8 Use the Limits tab to set the storage limits, age limits, and deleted item retention for a public folder database.

CAUTION If you set an age limit, be sure that all users who post to the public folder know about it. Otherwise, they'll be surprised when data is removed, and they could lose important work.

3. Click OK to save the settings.

In the Exchange Management Shell, you can set limits for public folder databases using the Set-PublicFolderDatabase cmdlet. Sample 10-13 provides the syntax and usage. You can enable or disable database maintenance using the –BackgroundDatabaseMaintenance parameter.

SAMPLE 10-13 Using Set-PublicFolderDatabase to set limits

```
Syntax

Set-PublicFolderDatabase –Identity PublicFolderDatabaseIdentity
[-AllowFileRestore <$true | $false>]
[-BackgroundDatabaseMaintenance <$true | $false>]
[-CircularLoggingEnabled <$true | $false>]
[-CustomReferralServerList ReferralCost]
[-DeletedItemRetention NumberDays]
[-DomainController DCName]
[-EventHistoryRetentionPeriod TimeSpan]
[-IssueWarningQuota Limit]
```

```
[-ItemRetentionPeriod TimeSpan]
[-MaintenanceSchedule Schedule]
[-MaxItemSize Limit]
[-MountAtStartup <$true | $false>]
[-Name Name]
[-ProhibitPostQuota Limit]
[-QuotaNotificationSchedule Schedule]
[-ReplicationMessageSize Size]
[-ReplicationPeriod Interval]
[-ReplicationSchedule Schedule]
[-RetainDeletedItemsUntilBackup <$true | $false>]
[-UseCustomReferralServerList <$true | $false>]
```

Usage

```
Set-PublicFolderDatabase
-Identity "Public DB"
 -IssueWarningQuota 1991680
 -DeletedItemRetention 14
 -MaxItemSize 10240
 -ItemRetentionPeriod "Unlimited"
 -ProhibitPostQuota 2097152
 -QuotaNotificationSchedule "Mon.5:00 AM-Fri.7:00 PM"
 -RetainDeletedItemsUntilBackup $true
```

Configuring Public Folder Replication

With Exchange Server 2010, the public folder hierarchy is replicated automatically
when there are two or more public folder databases. Because each Mailbox server
can have only one public folder database, you must install and configure at least
two Mailbox servers in your Exchange organization for automatic public folder
hierarchy replication to occur. If you want to replicate public folder data between
Mailbox servers, you must create replicas.

To configure basic replication options, follow these steps:

1. In the Exchange Management Console, right-click the public folder database,
   and then select Properties.

2. In the Properties dialog box, on the Replication tab (shown in Figure 10-9),
   use the following options to configure replication:

   - **Replication Interval** Determines when changes to public folders are
     replicated. Select a specific time (Always Run, Run Every Hour, Run Every 2
     Hours, Run Every 4 Hours, or Never Run), or select Use Custom Schedule
     and then click Customize to define the schedule.

   - **Replication Interval For "Always Run" (Minutes)** Sets the interval
     (in minutes) that's used when you select Always Run as the replication
     option. The default is 15 minutes.

- **Replication Message Size Limit (KB)** Sets the size limit (in kilobytes) for messages that are sent between public folder databases to replicate content. The default size limit is 300 kilobytes (KB). This setting does not affect the size of messages posted to a public folder.

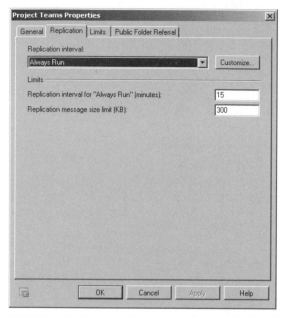

FIGURE 10-9 Use the Replication tab to configure replication of public folder data.

3. Click OK to save the settings.

In the Exchange Management Shell, you can control replication of public folder data using the Set-PublicFolderDatabase cmdlet. Sample 10-14 provides the syntax and usage.

SAMPLE 10-14 Using Set-PublicFolderDatabase to control replication

Syntax

```
Set-PublicFolderDatabase -Identity PublicFolderDatabaseIdentity
[-AllowFileRestore <$true | $false>]
[-BackgroundDatabaseMaintenence <$true | $false>]
[-CustomReferralServerList ServerList]
[-DeletedItemRetention Interval]
[-DomainController FullyQualifiedName]
[-EventHistoryRetentionPeriod Interval]
[-IssueWarningQuota Limit]
[-ItemRetentionPeriod Limit]
[-MaintenenceSchedule Schedule]
```

```
[-MaxItemSize Limit]
[-MountAtStartup <$true | $false>]
[-Name NewName]
[-ProhibitPostQuota Limit]
[-QuotaNotificationSchedule Schedule]
[-ReplicationMessageSize Limit]
[-ReplicationPeriod Interval]
[-ReplicationSchedule Schedule]
[-RetainDeletedItemsUntilBackup <$true | $false>]
[-UseCustomReferralServerList <$true | $false>]
```

Usage

```
Set-PublicFolderDatabase -Identity "Public DB"
 -ReplicationMessageSize "3MB"
 -ReplicationPeriod 15
 -ReplicationSchedule "Always"
```

Configuring Public Folder Referrals

In a large organization with multiple public folder replicas in multiple locations, you need to consider how clients access public folder data. By default, when a user accesses a public folder using Outlook or another client, his or her default public folder database determines which public folder replica the client should access. If the content exists on the Exchange server that handles the client request, the client accesses the local replica. Otherwise, Exchange redirects the client through a referral process to another public folder database that has a copy of the requested content.

The request and referral process works like this:

1. Outlook requests content in a public folder. If the content exists in the user's default public folder database, Exchange connects Outlook to that replica and Outlook retrieves the content. Otherwise, Exchange returns a replica list to Outlook sorted by relative priority.

2. Outlook attempts to access each replica in the list, starting with the replica with the highest relative priority. If that replica contains the desired content, Outlook retrieves the content. Otherwise, Outlook continues through the replica list until it has tried to access all replicas in the list. If Outlook fails to find a replica with the requested content, it displays an error to the user.

By default, Exchange and Outlook use the infrastructure provided by Active Directory to determine relative priority of replicas. In Active Directory, you use subnets to represent the physical structures of a network. Links between sites, referred to as *site links*, have an associated cost, which sets the relative priority of the link. Active Directory uses this relative priority to route requests and data across site links. Typically, the site link or set of site links with the lowest cost is used.

NOTE A good resource for learning more about site-based routing is *Windows Server 2008 Inside Out* (Microsoft Press, 2008). See Chapter 32, "Configuring Active Directory Sites and Replication," and Chapter 37, "Active Directory Site Administration."

Ideally, if you are having problems with replica referrals, you should work with a Windows administrator to resolve the problem. Explain the problems you are seeing—or that users are experiencing—to help the administrator resolve the problem by better optimizing the way site links are used. Keep in mind that site link costs primarily are used for routing Active Directory replication traffic and communications, and it might not be possible to make changes to improve performance for public folder referrals.

NOTE In mixed environments where you have Exchange Server 2010 and supported earlier releases of Exchange, Microsoft recommends assigning users a default public folder database on a server running Exchange Server 2010. When a client is referred to a server running Exchange 2003 Server, Exchange and Outlook manage public folder referrals using routing group connectors and the related configuration settings.

An alternative to using Active Directory site link costs is to create a custom list that assigns a server referral cost. However, Microsoft recommends using a custom list of referrals only in a limited number of situations, such as when you have specific requirements that cannot be resolved using Active Directory site link costs.

When you create a custom list of referrals, you set the referral cost of each server with a public folder database. The referral cost is a value between 1 and 100. The server with the lowest referral cost is first on the referral list, the server with the second lowest referral cost is listed second on the referral list, and so on. Because each public folder database has its own custom list, the user's default public folder database settings determine which custom list of referrals is used. It is important to note that even if you set the maximum referral value of 100, the server may still be used for referrals.

To view and manage the public folder referral configuration of a particular public folder database, follow these steps:

1. In the Exchange Management Console, right-click the public folder database, and then select Properties.

2. In the Properties dialog box, on the Public Folder Referral tab, you'll see the current referral configuration and any custom list that has been created (if applicable).

3. If you want the database to use Active Directory site link costs for referrals, accept the default selection of Use Active Directory Site Costs and then click OK.

4. If you want the database to use a custom list for referrals, select Use Custom List and then add referral servers to the list by clicking Add, specifying a referral server, assigning a referral cost, and then clicking OK.

You can configure custom referrals using the Set-PublicFolderDatabase cmdlet in the Exchange Management Shell. Sample 10-15 provides the syntax and usage. When you set –UseCustomReferralServerList to $false, Exchange stops using and clears out the custom referral lists.

SAMPLE 10-15 Using Set-PublicFolderDatabase to configure custom referrals

Syntax

```
Set-PublicFolderDatabase -Identity PublicFolderDatabaseIdentity
[-UseCustomReferralServerList <$true | $false>]
[-CustomReferralServerList ServerA:Cost, ServerB:Cost, ...]
```

Usage for enabling custom referrals

```
Set-PublicFolderDatabase
-Identity "CORPSVR127\Fourth Storage Group\Public DB"
-UseCustomReferralServerList $true
-CustomReferralServerList "MailServer27:10","MailServer72:20"
```

Usage for disabling custom referrals

```
Set-PublicFolderDatabase
-Identity "CORPSVR127\Fourth Storage Group\Public DB"
-UseCustomReferralServerList $false
```

Recovering Deleted Items from Public Folder Databases

You can recover deleted items from public folder databases without restoring from backup as long as you've set a deleted item retention period for the public folder database from which the items were deleted and the retention period for this database hasn't expired. If both of these conditions are met, you can recover deleted items by completing the following steps:

1. Log on to the domain using either an account with administrative privileges in the domain or an account with full control over the public folder from which you need to recover items.

   TIP Outlook displays public folders only when you fully expand the folder list in the left pane. In Outlook 2007 and later, you'll find a Folder List button in the lower right corner of the left pane. Click this button to expand the folder list. You also can press Ctrl+6 to display the expanded folder list in Outlook 2010.

2. After starting Outlook, access the Public Folders node, and then select the public folder from which you need to recover an item.

3. On the Tools menu or on the Folder pane, select Recover Deleted Items. The Recover Deleted Items From dialog box appears.

4. Select the items you want to recover, and then click the Recover Selected Items button.

Managing Mailbox and Public Folder Databases

Now that you know how to create and use databases, let's look at some general techniques you'll use to manage databases.

NOTE These techniques apply only to active mailbox databases and to public folder databases. Passive copies of mailbox databases are managed as discussed in the "Working with Mailbox Database Copies" section earlier in this chapter.

Mounting and Dismounting Databases

You can access only databases that are mounted. If a database isn't mounted, the database isn't available for use. This means that an administrator has probably dismounted the database or that the drive on which the database is located isn't on-line. It could also mean that the Exchange Information Store service is not running or that the drive, log drive, or both are online but out of disk space.

REAL WORLD A dismounted database can also indicate that there are problems with the database, transaction log, and system files used by the database. During startup, Exchange Server 2010 obtains a list of database files registered in Active Directory and then checks for the related files before mounting each database. If files are missing or corrupted, Exchange Server 2010 will be unable to mount the database. Exchange Server 2010 then generates an error and logs it in the application event log on the Exchange server. A common error is Event ID 9547. An example of this error follows:

```
The Active Directory indicates that the database file
D:\Exchsrvr\mdbdata\Marketing.edb exists for the Microsoft Exchange
Database; however, no such files exist on the disk.
```

This error tells you that the Exchange database (Marketing.edb) is registered in Active Directory but Exchange Server 2010 is unable to find the file on the disk. When Exchange Server 2010 attempts to start the corrupted mailbox database, you'll see an additional error as well. The most common error is Event ID 9519. An example of this error follows:

```
Error 0xfffffb4d starting database Marketing on the Microsoft
Exchange Information Store.
```

This error tells you that Exchange Server 2010 couldn't start the Marketing database. To recover the mailbox database, you should try restoring the database as discussed in Chapter 15, "Backing Up and Restoring Exchange Server 2010," in the section "Recovering Exchange Server." If you are unable to restore the database file, you can create a copy of all database files and store them elsewhere and then re-create the database structures in the Exchange Management Console by mounting the database. When you mount the database, Exchange Server 2010 creates a new database file. As a result, the data in the original database files (and not the copies) is lost and cannot be recovered. Exchange Server 2010 displays a warning before mounting the database and re-creating the database file. Click Yes only when you are absolutely certain that you cannot recover the database.

Be sure you don't overwrite the database files containing the data you want to try to recover. You can still work on the database while users access the newly created empty database. This is effectively a dial-tone database that you are creating. Then, take the damaged database file elsewhere, run repair, make the database consistent, and then use it to complete the dial-tone recovery process.

If you can't restore or repair a database and you need as much of the data as you can get back, you might have clients in cached or offline mode with viable copies of the data that can be exported and imported.

Determining the Status of Databases

Mailbox and public folder databases have several associated states, including

- Mounted
- Dismounted
- Backup In Progress
- Online Maintenance In Progress
- Replication In Progress

You can determine the status of a database by following these steps:

1. In the Exchange Management Console, expand the Organization Configuration node, and then select the related Mailbox node.

2. On the Database Management tab, you should see a list of available databases. The icon to the left of the database name indicates the mount status. If the icon shows a gray down arrow, the database isn't mounted. If the icon shows a question mark, the database is in an unknown state. If the database shows a mailbox or folder, the database is mounted.

3. To determine the status of the database, right-click the database, and then select Properties. In the Properties dialog box, the status is listed on the General tab.

In the Exchange Management Shell, you can determine the status of all databases or specific databases using the Get-MailboxDatabase and Get-PublicFolder-Database cmdlets. Sample 10-16 provides the syntax and usage for these cmdlets. To see status details, you can specify the status flags associated with each state you want to see as part of the formatted output. In the example, the Mounted, Dismounted, Backup In Progress, Online Maintenance In Progress, and Replication In Progress status values are then listed as True or False.

SAMPLE 10-16 Getting database status details

```
Get-MailboxDatabase [-Identity MailboxDatabase | -Server Server]
[-DomainController DCName]
[-DumpsterStatistics <$true | $false>]
[-IncludePreExchange2010 <$true | $false>]
[-Status <$true | $false>] | format-table Name, Mounted,
BackupInProgress, OnlineMaintenanceInProgress

Get-PublicFolderDatabase [-Identity PublicFolderDatabase |
-Server Server] [-DomainController DCName ]
[-IncludePreExchange2010 <$true | $false>]
[-Status <$true | $false>] |
format-table Name, Mounted, BackupInProgress,
OnlineMaintenanceInProgress, ReplicationInProgress
```

Usage for specific database and server

```
Get-MailboxDatabase -Identity "Eng DB"
 -Status | format-table Name,
 Mounted, BackupInProgress, OnlineMaintenanceInProgress
```

Usage for all databases on a server

```
Get-MailboxDatabase -Server "CORPSVR127" -Status | format-table
 Name, Mounted, BackupInProgress, OnlineMaintenanceInProgress
```

Usage for all databases

```
Get-MailboxDatabase -Status | format-table Name,
 Mounted, BackupInProgress, OnlineMaintenanceInProgress
```

Dismounting and Mounting Databases

Before you perform maintenance on a Mailbox server in a database availability group, you should perform a server switchover so that the server's active databases are transitioned and made active on one or more other servers in the group. You might also want to suspend replication or block activation of passive copies on the server being maintained. For public folder databases or mailbox databases that are not part of an availability group, you should rarely dismount an active database, but if you need to do so, follow these steps:

1. In the Exchange Management Console, expand the Organization Configuration node, and then select the related Mailbox node.

2. On the Database Management tab, you should see a list of available databases. The icon to the left of the database name indicates the mount

status. If the icon shows a gray down arrow, the database is already dismounted.

3. Right-click the database you want to dismount, select Dismount Database, and then confirm the action by clicking Yes. Exchange Server dismounts the database. Users will no longer be able to access the database and work with their server-based folders.

After you've dismounted a database and performed maintenance, recovery, or other procedures as necessary, you can remount the database by right-clicking the database in the Exchange Management Console and then selecting Mount Database.

In the Exchange Management Shell, you can dismount and mount databases using the Dismount-Database and Mount-Database cmdlets, respectively. Sample 10-17 provides the syntax and usage for these cmdlets.

SAMPLE 10-17 Dismounting and mounting databases

Syntax

```
Dismount-Database –Identity DatabaseIdentity
[-DomainController FullyQualifiedName]

Mount-Database –Identity DatabaseIdentity
[-AcceptDataLoss <$true | $false>] [-DomainController FullyQualifiedName]
[-Force <$true | $false>]
```

Usage for dismounting a database

```
Dismount-Database –Identity "Eng DB"
```

Usage for mounting a database

```
Mount-Database –Identity "Eng DB"
```

Specifying Whether a Database Should Be Automatically Mounted

Normally, Exchange Server automatically mounts databases on startup. You can, however, change this behavior. For example, if you're recovering an Exchange server from a complete failure, you might not want to mount databases until you've completed recovery. In this case, you can disable automatic mounting of databases.

To enable or disable automatic mounting of a database, complete the following steps:

1. In the Exchange Management Console, expand the Organization Configuration node, and then select the related Mailbox node.

2. On the Database Management tab, right-click the database you want to work with, and then select Properties.

3. On the Maintenance tab, do one of the following and then click OK:

    a. To ensure that a database isn't mounted on startup, select the Don't Mount This Database At Startup check box.

    b. To mount the database on startup, clear the Don't Mount This Database At Startup check box.

In the Exchange Management Shell, you can enable or disable automatic mounting at startup using the Set-MailboxDatabase and Set-PublicFolderDatabase cmdlets. Sample 10-18 provides the syntax and usage for controlling automatic mounting.

SAMPLE 10-18 Controlling automatic mounting

Syntax

```
Set-MailboxDatabase –Identity DatabaseIdentity
 –MountAtStartup <$true | $false>

Set-PublicFolderDatabase –Identity DatabaseIdentity
 –MountAtStartup <$true | $false>
```

Usage

```
Set-MailboxDatabase –Identity "Eng DB"
 –MountAtStartup $false
```

Setting the Maintenance Interval

You should run maintenance routines against databases on a daily basis. The maintenance routines organize the databases, clear out extra space, and perform other essential housekeeping tasks. By default, the automatic background maintenance does some of this work, and Exchange Server runs extended, foreground maintenance tasks daily from 1:00 A.M. to 5:00 A.M. If this conflicts with other activities on the Exchange server, you can change the maintenance settings by following these steps:

1. In the Exchange Management Console, right-click the database you want to work with, and then select Properties.

2. On the Maintenance tab in the Properties dialog box, use the Maintenance Schedule list to set a new maintenance time. Select a time (such as Run Daily From 11:00 P.M. To 3:00 A.M.).

    If you want to set a custom schedule, select Use Custom Schedule, and then click Customize. You can now set the times when maintenance should occur.

3. By default, Exchange performs background maintenance tasks by scanning the ESE 24 hours a day, 7 days a week. Select or clear the related check box as appropriate. Note that if you change this setting, you must dismount and then remount the database for the change to take effect. Click OK.

TIP If you want to set a custom schedule, select Use Custom Schedule, and then click Customize. You can now set the times when maintenance should occur.

In the Exchange Management Shell, you can configure the maintenance schedule for a database by using the Set-MailboxDatabase and Set-PublicFolderDatabase cmdlets. Sample 10-19 provides the syntax and usage. In the example, replication is configured to occur between Friday at 9:00 P.M. and Monday at 1:00 A.M.

SAMPLE 10-19 Setting the maintenance schedule

Syntax

```
Set-MailboxDatabase -Identity DatabaseIdentity
[-MaintenanceSchedule Schedule]
[-BackgroundDatabaseMaintenance <$true | $false>]

Set-PublicFolderDatabase -Identity DatabaseIdentity
 -MaintenanceSchedule Schedule
```

Usage

```
Set-MailboxDatabase -Identity "Eng DB"
 -MaintenanceSchedule "Fri.9:00 PM-Mon.1:00 AM"
```

Moving Databases

As discussed earlier, each database has a database file associated with it, and the location of this file has an important role in managing Exchange Server performance. You can change the database file and log locations by completing the following steps:

1. In the Exchange Management Console, expand the Organization Configuration node, and then select the related Mailbox node.

2. On the Database Management tab, right-click the database you want to move, and then select Move Database Path from the shortcut menu. You should now see the Move Database Path Wizard, as shown in Figure 10-10.

3. On the Move Database Path page, the current database file path and log folder path are shown. Enter the desired paths for the database file and the related logs using the text boxes provided.

    NOTE The wizard creates any required folders on the server if they do not exist.

4. Click Move. Exchange validates the paths you've provided and then moves the files. Click Finish when this process completes.

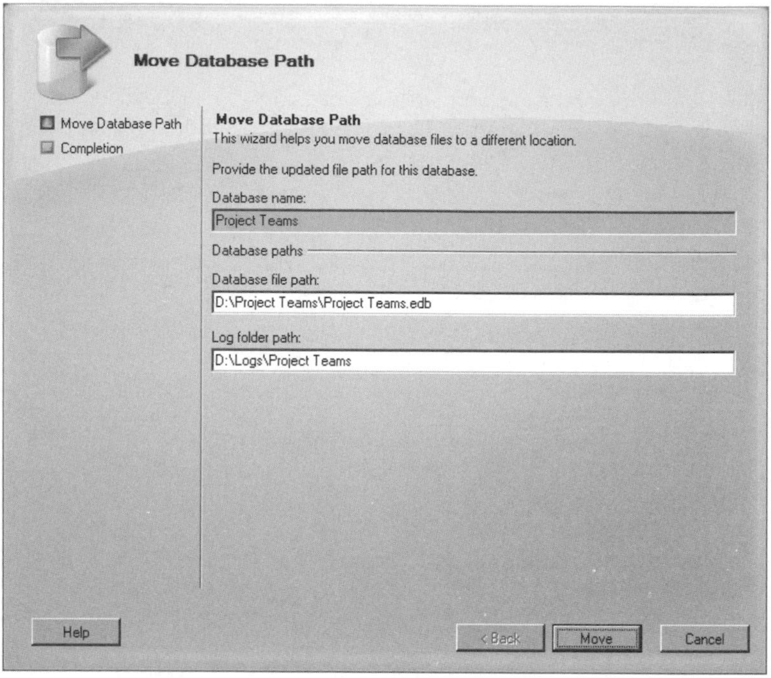

FIGURE 10-10 Move the database and its backup to new locations.

NOTE You cannot move a database that is being backed up or a replicated mailbox database. To move a replicated mailbox database, you must first remove all replicated copies and then perform the move operation. After the move is complete, you can add copies of the mailbox database.

If the specified database is mounted, the database is automatically dismounted and then remounted, and it is unavailable to users while it's dismounted. Whether you are using the Exchange Management Console or the Exchange Management Shell, you can perform a database move only while logged on to the affected Mailbox server, with one exception. If you are performing a configuration-only move, you can perform the configuration-only move from your management computer.

In the Exchange Management Shell, you can move databases using the Move-DatabasePath cmdlet. Sample 10-20 provides the syntax and usage.

SAMPLE 10-20 Move-DatabasePath cmdlet syntax and usage

Syntax

```
Move-DatabasePath -Identity DatabaseIdentity
[-ConfigurationOnly <$true | $false>] [-EdbFilePath EdbFilePath]
[-DomainController DCName] [-Force <$true | $false>]
[-LogFolderPath FolderPath]
```

```
Move-DatabasePath -Identity "Sales Projects"
-EdbFilePath "K:\Databases\SalesProjects.edb"
```

Renaming Databases

To rename a database, follow these steps:

1. In the Exchange Management Console, right-click the database, and then select Properties.
2. In the Properties dialog box, type the new name for the database. Click OK.

NOTE All objects in Active Directory are located by a unique identifier. This identifier uses the directory namespace and works through each element in the directory hierarchy to a particular object. When you change the name of a database, you change the namespace for all the objects in the database.

In the Exchange Management Shell, you can rename databases using the –Name parameter of the Set-MailboxDatabase and Set-PublicFolderDatabase cmdlets. Sample 10-21 provides the syntax and usage.

SAMPLE 10-21 Renaming a database

Syntax

```
Set-MailboxDatabase -Identity DatabaseIdentity
 -Name NewName

Set-PublicFolderDatabase -Identity DatabaseIdentity
 -Name NewName
```

Usage

```
Set-MailboxDatabase -Identity "Eng DB"
 -Name "Engineering Mail Database"
```

Deleting Databases

Before deleting a mailbox database, you must delete or move the mailboxes it contains. After you do this, you can delete the database. You move mailboxes as described in Chapter 6 in the section "Moving Mailboxes." With public folders, public folder data is replicated between or among the public folder databases automatically once you set up replicas. As long as all data has been replicated and you've verified this, you can remove a public folder database from a Mailbox server without losing data. However, because each Mailbox server can have only one public folder database, you need to create a new public folder database if you want to ensure that users with mailboxes on the server can access the local public folder replica.

After you've moved items that you might need, you can delete the database by completing the following steps:

1. In the Exchange Management Console, right-click the database you want to delete, and then select Remove from the shortcut menu.

2. When prompted, confirm the action by clicking Yes.

3. After removing the database, you need to delete any database and transaction log files from the server.

In the Exchange Management Shell, you can delete databases by using the Remove-MailboxDatabase and Remove-PublicFolderDatabase cmdlets. Sample 10-22 provides the syntax and usage.

SAMPLE 10-22 Removing databases

Syntax

```
Remove-MailboxDatabase -Identity DatabaseIdentity
[-DomainController FullyQualifiedName]

Remove-PublicFolderDatabase -Identity DatabaseIdentity
[-DomainController FullyQualifiedName]
[-RemoveLastAllowed <$true | $false>]
```

Usage

```
Remove-MailboxDatabase -Identity "Eng DB"
```

CHAPTER 11

Accessing and Managing Public Folders

- Accessing Public Folders   **357**
- Creating and Working with Public Folders   **363**
- Managing Public Folder Settings   **372**

Y ou use public folders to share messaging content and documents within an organization. Public folders are stored in a hierarchical structure referred to as a *public folder tree*. There is a direct correspondence between public folder databases and public folder trees. Each Mailbox server in a Microsoft Exchange 2010 organization can have one public folder database, and all Mailbox servers share the same public folder tree. Exchange 2010 does not support any alternate public folder trees. If you want users to have access to alternate public folder trees, you must retain a computer running Exchange Server 2003 in your Exchange 2010 organization.

Accessing Public Folders

A public folder server is a Mailbox server with a public folder database. When your Exchange 2010 organization has more than one public folder database, public folder servers replicate the public folder hierarchy automatically between and among these databases. If you want to replicate public folder data between Mailbox servers, you must create replicas. Replicas provide redundancy in case of server failure and help to distribute the user load. All replicas of a public folder are equal. There is no master replica. This means that you can directly modify replicas of public folders. The public folder server with which you are working replicates the folder changes automatically to other servers.

Public folder trees define the structure of an organization's public folders. The public folder tree has two subtrees:

- Default public folders, the IPM_Subtree, also referred to as the *default public folder tree*

- System public folders, the Non_IPM_Subtree, also referred to as the *system public folder tree*

The default public folder tree has its own hierarchy, which is separate from the system public folder tree. You can make the default public folder tree accessible to users based on criteria you set, and then users can create folders and manage their content. All clients, whether using HTTPS or MAPI, connect to the RPC Client Access service running on the Client Access server. This service handles incoming connections for all hosted features, including public folders.

To maintain security, each public folder in the default public folder tree can have specific access permissions. For example, you can create public folders called CompanyWide, Marketing, and Engineering. Whereas you would typically make the CompanyWide folder accessible to all users, you would make the Marketing folder accessible only to users in the marketing department and the Engineering folder accessible only to users in the engineering department.

In contrast, users cannot directly access or create folders in the system public folder tree. Exchange uses the folders in the system public folder tree to store and share specific types of system data stored in the public folder tree, including data for legacy clients, such as offline address books, Schedule+ free/busy information, and organizational forms. Thus, although legacy client applications can use system folders to store and retrieve certain types of data, such as an offline address book, client applications do not have a direct management interface, such as is available with the default public folder tree. Current clients use Web services for these features.

Accessing Public Folders in Mail Clients

You can access public folders from Microsoft Office Outlook clients, including Outlook Web App and Outlook 2003 or later. When you configure Outlook 2007 or later for Exchange Server, users have direct access to the default public folders tree. When you configure Outlook 2007 or later for Internet-only use, users can access public folders using only Internet Message Access Protocol version 4 (IMAP4) and you must have retained a computer running Exchange Server 2003 in your Exchange 2010 organization.

If Outlook is configured properly, users can access public folders by completing the following steps:

1. Start Outlook. If the Folder list isn't displayed and you are using Outlook 2007, click Go, and then select Folder List. If the Folder list isn't displayed and you are using Outlook 2010, click the Folder List button in the lower-right corner of the Navigation pane or press Ctrl+6.

2. In the Folder list, expand Public Folders, and then expand All Public Folders to get a complete view of the available top-level folders. A top-level folder is simply a folder at the next level below the tree root.

NOTE Chapter 16, "Managing Exchange Server 2010 Clients," discusses techniques you can use to configure Outlook. Refer to the section of that chapter titled "Configuring Mail Support for Outlook and Windows Live Mail."

Accessing Public Folders Through the Information Store

As an administrator, you can access public folders through the Exchange information store using either the Public Folder Management Console or the Exchange
Management Shell. The Public Folder Management Console provides access to both
the default public folders and the system public folders. In the Exchange Management Console, you can start the Public Folder Management Console by selecting the Toolbox node in the left pane and then double-clicking the Public Folder
Management Console entry in the main pane.

> **TIP** Like the Exchange Management Console, the Public Folder Management Console
> uses Windows PowerShell to view and work with Exchange. To access the PowerShell
> log, click View Exchange Management Shell Command Log on the View menu. To start
> tracking the PowerShell commands that are used, click Start Command Logging on the
> Action menu.

The Public Folder Management Console allows you to manage public folders on
one server at a time. To connect to a specific server or set a default server, complete
the following steps:

1. In the Public Folder Management Console, with the Public Folders node
    selected in the console tree, click Connect To Server on the Action menu or
    in the Actions pane.

2. In the Connect To Server dialog box, click Browse. In the Select Public Folder
    Servers dialog box, only Mailbox servers with public folder databases are
    available for selection. Select the server to use, and then click OK.

3. If you want the currently selected server to be the default server whenever
    you use the Public Folder Management Console, select the Set As Default
    Server check box.

4. Click Connect to connect to the server. If you set the server as the default,
    this setting is saved for the user account on the computer that is running
    the console. If you start the console on another computer or use a different
    account, the default server might be different.

After you've accessed the Public Folder Management Console and connected
to a server, you can work with the default public folder tree and the system public
folder tree. As shown in Figure 11-1, both trees are accessible in the left pane. By
double-clicking expandable nodes, you can navigate through successive levels of
the public folder hierarchy. The interface doesn't display individual items stored in
folders; the interface displays only public folders and subfolders.

When you select a folder containing subfolders in the left pane, the console
displays details regarding the subfolders in the main pane. By default, the console
displays only the subfolder name and parent path. You can display additional details
by clicking Add/Remove Columns on the View menu, selecting columns to display in
the Available Columns list, and then clicking Add. Additional details you can display
include the age limit in days, the hidden from address list flag, the local replica age
limit in days, the mail-enabled flag, and a list of replicas.

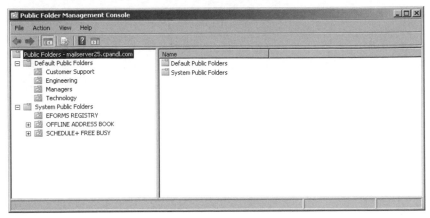

FIGURE 11-1 View and work with the public folder tree in the Public Folder Management Console.

At the Exchange Management Shell prompt, you can get information about the public folder database by using the Get-PublicFolder cmdlet. When you are working with this cmdlet, you use the –Identity parameter to identify the folder with which you want to work:

- \ represents the root of the default public folder tree (also known as the IPM_Subtree).
- \FolderName represents a specific named folder.
- \NON_IPM_SUBTREE represents the root of the hidden system public folder tree.

Sample 11-1 provides the syntax and usage for getting information about a folder. As the sample output shows, the Exchange Management Shell returns configuration details for the folder identity. If you want to examine subfolders of a folder, add the –Recurse parameter.

SAMPLE 11-1 Getting information about a public folder

Syntax

```
Get-PublicFolder -Identity FolderIdentity | fl
```

Usage

```
Get-PublicFolder -Identity "\" | fl
```

Output

```
RunspaceId       :
AgeLimit         :
EntryId          :
HasSubFolders    : True
```

```
HiddenFromAddressListsEnabled  : False
IssueWarningQuota              :
LocalReplicaAgeLimit           :
MailEnabled                    : False
MaxItemSize                    : 102040 KB
Name                           : IPM_SUBTREE
ParentPath                     :
PerUserReadStateEnabled        : True
ProhibitPostQuota              :
Replicas                       : {}
ReplicationSchedule            : {}
RetainDeletedItemsFor          : 90 days
UseDatabaseAgeDefaults         : True
UseDatabaseQuotaDefaults       : True
UseDatabaseReplicationSchedule : False
UseDatabaseRetentionDefaults   : True
FolderType                     :
HasRules                       : False
HasModerator                   : False
Identity                       : \
MapiIdentity                   : \
OriginatingServer              : mailserver25.cpandl.com
IsValid                        : True
```

You can use the –Recurse parameter to examine recursively the folder and its subfolders. When you use this parameter, you should redirect the output through the Format-List command and name the folder details that you want to examine. You can examine any of the properties previously listed in Sample 11-1 by specifying the property names to return in a comma-separated list. For example, if you want to return a list of all subfolders of the public folder root formatted by the Name and MailEnabled properties, you can use the following command:

```
Get-PublicFolder –Identity "\" –Recurse | Format-List Name,MailEnabled
```

The output looks similar to the following:

```
Name        : IPM_SUBTREE
MailEnabled : False

Name        : Projects
MailEnabled : False

Name        : SavedData
MailEnabled : False

Name        : Teams
MailEnabled : False
```

If you suspect a replication problem with public folders, you can compare the configuration details for public folders on your Mailbox servers using the Get-PublicFolder cmdlet. Just specify the –Server parameter and the identity of the server you want to work with, such as the following:

```
Get-PublicFolder -Server "CorpSvr272" -Recurse | fl

Get-PublicFolder -Server "CorpSvr185" -Recurse | fl
```

To get information about a specific public folder on a server, you can use the –Server parameter to identify the server with which you want to work and the –Identity parameter to identify the public folder to examine.

```
Get-PublicFolder -Identity "\Managers" -Server "CorpSvr272" | fl
```

Table 11-1 provides an overview of cmdlets available for working with public folders. On your Exchange servers, in the %ExchangeInstallPath%\Scripts directory, you'll find a number of handy scripts for performing common public folder administration tasks.

TABLE 11-1 Cmdlets for Public Folders

MANAGEMENT TASK	RELATED CMDLETS
Active Directory permissions	Add-ADPermission Get-ADPermission Remove-ADPermission
Administrative permissions	Add-PublicFolderAdministrativePermission Get-PublicFolderAdministrativePermission Remove-PublicFolderAdministrativePermission
Client permissions	Add-PublicFolderClientPermission Remove-PublicFolderClientPermission Get-PublicFolderClientPermission
General management	Get-PublicFolder New-PublicFolder Set-PublicFolder Remove-PublicFolder
Mail-enabling	Get-MailPublicFolder Enable-MailPublicFolder Disable-MailPublicFolder Set-MailPublicFolder

TABLE 11-1 Cmdlets for Public Folders

MANAGEMENT TASK	RELATED CMDLETS
Replication	Resume-PublicFolderReplication Suspend-PublicFolderReplication Update-PublicFolder Update-PublicFolderHierarchy
Statistics	Get-PublicFolderItemStatistics Get-PublicFolderStatistics

Creating and Working with Public Folders

The following sections examine techniques you can use to create and work with public folders. Both users and administrators can create and work with public folders using Outlook. Administrators can also create and work with public folders using the Public Folder Management Console or the Exchange Management Shell.

Creating Public Folders in Microsoft Outlook

Both administrators and authorized users can use Outlook to create public folders in the default public folder tree. To do this, complete the following steps:

1. Start Outlook. If the Folder list isn't displayed and you are using Outlook 2007, click Go, and then select Folder List. If the Folder list isn't displayed and you are using Outlook 2010, click the Folder List button in the lower-right corner of the Navigation pane or press Ctrl+6.

2. Expand Public Folders in the Folder list, and then right-click All Public Folders.

3. Select New Folder. You'll see the Create New Folder dialog box, as shown in Figure 11-2.

4. Enter a name for the public folder, and then use the Folder Contains list box to choose the type of item you want to place in the folder. Public folders can contain the following:

   - Calendar Items
   - Contact Items
   - InfoPath Form Items
   - Journal Items
   - Mail And Post Items
   - Note Items
   - Task Items

FIGURE 11-2 Create a new public folder in the default public folder tree.

5. Select where to place the folder. To create the folder as a top-level folder, select All Public Folders. Otherwise, expand All Public Folders, and then select the folder in which you want to place the public folder.

6. Click OK. Complete, as necessary, the following tasks, as explained in the section of this chapter titled "Managing Public Folder Settings."

   - Control replication and set messaging limits.
   - Set client permissions.
   - Propagate public folder settings.

Creating Public Folders Using the Public Folder Management Console

As an administrator, you can use the Public Folder Management Console to create public folders by completing the following steps:

1. In the Exchange Management Console, start the Public Folder Management Console by selecting the Toolbox node in the left pane and then double-clicking the Public Folder Management Console entry in the main pane.

2. In the left pane, you have access to default public folders and system public folders. Navigate through successive levels of the public folder hierarchy by double-clicking expandable nodes until you get to the folder in which you want to create your folder.

3. Right-click the folder in which you want to create a folder, and then select New Public Folder. This starts the New Public Folder Wizard.

4. On the New Public Folder page, shown in Figure 11-3, type the display name for the public folder. The Path box shows the path to the folder you are creating in the public folder hierarchy. If the path is a backslash ("\"), you are

creating a new top-level folder. Otherwise, you are creating a subfolder of an existing folder.

5. Click New to create the public folder, and then click Finish.

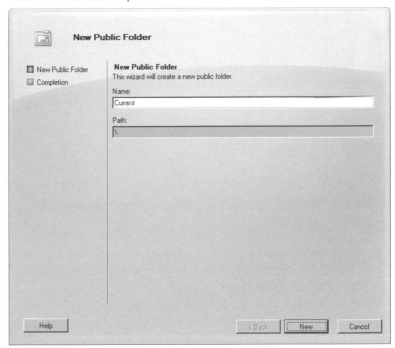

FIGURE 11-3 Create a public folder for the organization.

Creating Public Folders Using the Exchange Management Shell

As an administrator, you can create public folders within the default public folder tree by using the New-PublicFolder cmdlet. Use the –Name parameter to set the name of the public folder and the –Path parameter to create the folder under a particular folder. If you omit the –Path parameter, Exchange creates the folder as a top-level folder under the default public folders root. Sample 11-2 provides the syntax and usage for the New-PublicFolder cmdlet.

SAMPLE 11-2 New-PublicFolder cmdlet syntax and usage

Syntax

```
New-PublicFolder -Name FolderName [-Path ParentFolderName]
[-Server Server] [-DomainController FullyQualifiedDomainName]
```

Usage

```
New-PublicFolder -Name "Projects" -Path \
```

Determining Public Folder Size, Item Count, and Last Access Time

In Outlook, you can determine the size in kilobytes (KBs) of a public folder by completing the following steps:

1. Start Outlook. If the Folder list isn't displayed and you are using Outlook 2007, click Go, and then select Folder List. If the Folder list isn't displayed and you are using Outlook 2010, click the Folder List button in the lower-right corner of the Navigation pane or press Ctrl+6.

2. Expand Public Folders in the Folder list, and then expand All Public Folders.

3. Right-click the public folder with which you want to work, and then select Properties.

4. On the General tab of the Public Folder Properties dialog box, click Folder Size. The Folder Size dialog box lists the total size of the selected public folder, including all subfolders and the individual size of each subfolder.

Using the Public Folder Management Console, you can determine the size, item count, and last access time of a top-level public folder by completing the following steps:

1. In the Public Folder Management Console, select the Default Public Folders node or the System Public Folders node as appropriate for the type of public folder you want to work with.

2. In the left pane, select the top-level folder you want to work with, such as Default Public Folders.

3. In the main pane, right-click the folder you want to examine and then select Properties.

4. On the General tab of the Properties dialog box, you'll see the key details for the selected public folder, as shown in Figure 11-4.

In the Exchange Management Shell, you can view the total number of items contained in and the last access time of public folders using the Get-PublicFolder-Statistics cmdlet as shown in the following example:

```
Get-PublicFolderStatistics
```

The output will be similar to the following:

```
Name            ItemCount           LastAccessTime
----            ---------           --------------
Projects        19292               03/17/2010 5:41:42 AM
SavedData       791                 03/23/2010 7:36:19 AM
Teams           895                 02/14/2010 4:33:21 AM
```

If you use the –Identity parameter to examine a specific public folder and format the output as a list, you can see additional details, including total item size and deleted item size. Sample 11-3 shows the syntax, usage, and sample output. Keep in mind that if you omit the –Identity parameter, you'll view details for all public folders.

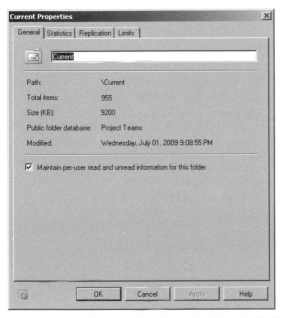

FIGURE 11-4 Get information about the public folder using the Properties dialog box.

SAMPLE 11-3 Getting usage statistics for public folders

Syntax

```
Get-PublicFolderStatistics [-Identity FolderIdentity]
[-Server Server] [-DomainController FullyQualifiedDomainName]
```

Usage

```
Get-PublicFolderStatistics –Identity "\Projects" | fl
```

Output

```
AdminDisplayName      : Customer Support
AssociatedItemCount   : 4
ContactCount          : 52
CreationTime          : 1/22/2010 3:15:22 PM
DeletedItemCount      : 24
EntryId               : 000000001A447390AA6611CD9BC800AA002FC45A030
                        164D2419EE9E7A08CCB68910001907875400000
ExpiryTime            :
FolderPath            : Customer Support
```

```
IsDeletePending          : False
ItemCount                : 789
LastAccessTime           : 2/8/2010 11:42:31 AM
LastModificationTime     : 2/8/2010 7:15:03 AM
LastUserModificationTime  : 2/8/2010 7:17:00 AM
LastUserAccessTime       : 2/8/2010 7:17:01 AM
Name                     : Customer Support
OwnerCount               : 12
TotalAssociatedItemSize  : 9823B
TotalDeletedItemSize     : 1281904B
TotalItemSize            : 397719508223B
ServerName               : MAILSERVER25
DatabaseName             : Public Folder Database
Identity                 : 000000001A447390AA6611CD9BC800AA002FC45A030
MapiIdentity               164D2419EE9E7A08CCB6891000190787540000
OriginatingServer        : mailserver25.cpandl.com
IsValid                  : True
```

Adding Items to Public Folders Using Outlook

Exchange 2010 supports standard public folders and mail-enabled public folders. Authorized users can post items to public folders through Outlook Web App and Outlook 2003 or later. Let's briefly look at how you can use Outlook to post items to public folders.

In Outlook, authorized users can post items to public folders by completing these steps:

1. Start Outlook. If the Folder list isn't displayed, click Go, and then select Folder List.

2. Expand Public Folders and then All Public Folders in the Folder list. Then select the folder you want to use.

3. Click New, or press Ctrl+Shift+S. Notice that when a public folder is selected, the New button automatically changes to public folder post mode.

4. Type a subject for the message, and then type your message text. Add any necessary attachments.

5. Click Post.

Mail-Enabling Public Folders

Public folders are not mail-enabled by default. If you want authorized users to be able to submit items using standard e-mail, you can mail-enable a public folder using the Enable-MailPublicFolder cmdlet. If you later want to disable sending mail to a public folder, you can use the Disable-MailPublicFolder cmdlet. Samples 11-4 and 11-5 provide the syntax and usage for these cmdlets. Use the –Server parameter to specify the Mailbox server with a public folder database on which to perform the procedure.

Syntax

```
Enable-MailPublicFolder -Identity FolderIdentity
 [-HiddenFromAddressListsEnabled <$true|$false>]
 [-Server Server] [-DomainController FullyQualifiedDomainName]
```

Usage

```
Enable-MailPublicFolder -Identity "\Projects"
```

SAMPLE 11-5 Disable-MailPublicFolder cmdlet syntax and usage

Syntax

```
Disable-MailPublicFolder -Identity FolderIdentity
 [-Server 'Server'] [-DomainController FullyQualifiedDomainName]
```

Usage

```
Disable-MailPublicFolder -Identity "\Projects"
```

In the Public Folder Management Console, you can mail enable a public folder by selecting the folder's parent in the left pane, clicking the folder in the main pane, and then clicking Mail Enable. Conversely, to disable sending mail to a public folder, select the folder's parent in the left pane, click the folder in the main pane, and then click Mail Disable. When prompted to confirm that you want to disable sending mail to the public folder, click Yes.

After you've mail-enabled a public folder, users simply address an e-mail to the public folder, and the public folder receives the message as a posting. The default e-mail address is the same as the folder name, with any spaces converted to under-score characters ("_"). For example, if the public folder name is Current Projects and Cpandl.com is the e-mail domain, the e-mail address of the public folder is current_ projects@cpandl.com.

In the Public Folder Management Console, you can view or set a public folder's e-mail–related properties by double-clicking the public folder in the main pane and using the additional tabs provided. As Figure 11-5 shows, Properties dialog boxes for mail-enabled public folders have the following additional tabs:

- **Exchange General** Allows you to view or set general Exchange settings that include the Exchange alias, standard display name, and simple display name. You can also hide the public folder from the address list and add custom attributes using the options on this tab.

- **E-Mail Addresses** Allows you to view or set the e-mail address or addresses associated with the public folder. The related procedures for public folders are similar to those for mailbox users. For more information, see "Adding, Changing, and Removing E-Mail Addresses" in Chapter 5.

- **Mail Flow Settings** Allows you to view and set delivery options, message size restrictions, and message delivery restrictions for the public folder. The related procedures for public folders are similar to those for mailbox users. For more information, see "Configuring Mailbox Delivery Restrictions, Permissions, and Storage Limits" in Chapter 6.

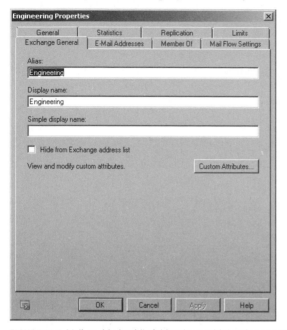

FIGURE 11-5 Mail-enabled public folders have additional properties and option tabs.

You can view information about mail-enabled public folders using the Get-MailPublicFolder cmdlet, and you can set any of the related properties using the Set-MailPublicFolder cmdlet. You can set almost all of the parameters displayed as output for the Get-MailPublicFolder cmdlet by using their parameter names with the Set-MailPublicFolder cmdlet. Samples 11-6 and 11-7 provide the syntax and usage for these cmdlets.

SAMPLE 11-6 Set-MailPublicFolder cmdlet syntax and usage

Syntax

```
Set-MailPublicFolder -Identity FolderIdentity
[-AcceptMessagesOnlyFrom RecipientIds]
[-AcceptMessagesOnlyFromDLMembers RecipientIds]
[-AcceptMessagesOnlyFromSendersOrMembers <$true|$false>]
[-ArbitrationMailbox MailBox]
[-BypassModerationFromSendersOrMembers <$true|$false>]
[-Contacts Contacts]
```

```
[-CreateDTMFMap <$true|$false>]
[-CustomAttributeN Attribute]
[-DeliverToMailboxAndForward <$true|$false>]
[-DisplayName Name]
[-DomainController DCName]
[-EmailAddresses ProxyEmailAddresses]
[-EmailAddressPolicyEnabled <$true|$false>]
[-ForwardingAddress EmailAddress]
[-GrantSendOnBehalfTo Mailboxes]
[-HiddenFromAddressListsEnabled <$true|$false>]
[-IgnoreDefaultScope <$true|$false>]
[-MailTip MailTip]
[-MailTipTranslations <$true|$false>]
[-MaxReceiveSize Size]
[-MaxSendSize Size]
[-ModeratedBy Moderator]
[-ModerationEnabled <$true|$false>]
[-Name Name]
[-PhoneticDisplayName Name]
[-PrimarySmtpAddress SmtpAddress]
[-PublicFolderType {GeneralPurpose|MAPI|NNTP|NotSpecified}]
[-RejectMessagesFrom RejectList]
[-RejectMessagesFromDLMembers ListMembers]
[-RejectMessagesFromSendersOrMembers <$true|$false>]
[-RequireSenderAuthenticationEnabled <$true|$false>]
[-SendModerationNotifications <Never | Internal | Always>]
[-Server ServerName]
[-SimpleDisplayName Name]
[-UMDtmfMap <$true|$false>]
[-WindowsEmailAddress EmailAddress]
```

Usage

```
Set-MailPublicFolder -Identity "\Projects" –Alias "Projects"
```

SAMPLE 11-7 Get-MailPublicFolder cmdlet syntax and usage

Syntax

```
Get-MailPublicFolder -Identity FolderIdentity | fl

Get-MailPublicFolder -Identity FolderIdentity [-Credential Credential]
[-DomainController DCName] [-Filter String] [-IgnoreDefaultScope
<$true|$false>] [-ReadFromDomainController <$true|$false>]
[-ResultSize Limit] [-Server ServerId] [-SortBy String]
```

Usage

```
Get-MailPublicFolder -Identity "\Projects" | fl
```

Managing Public Folder Settings

You should actively manage public folders. If you don't, you won't get optimal performance, and users might encounter problems when reading from or posting to the folders. Each folder in a public folder tree has its own settings, and each time a folder is created, you should review and modify the following settings:

- Replication, messaging limits, deleted item retention, and quotas
- Client and Send As permissions

You might also want to designate folder administrators and propagate the changes you've made. This section of the chapter explains these and other public folder administration tasks. Don't forget that in the Public Folder Management Console you can view or set a public folder's e-mail–related properties by using the related Properties dialog box. As discussed previously in the "Mail-Enabling Public Folders" section, the related procedures are similar to those for mailbox users.

Controlling Folder Replication, Messaging Limits, Quotas, and Deleted Item Retention

Public folders inherit the replication, messaging limit, quota, and deleted item retention settings of the public folder database. The best way to control these settings for public folders is to set the appropriate options for the entire public folder database rather than for individual public folders, as discussed in the "Using Public Folder Databases" section of Chapter 10, "Mailbox and Public Folder Database Administration." That said, the Exchange Management Shell includes the Set-Public-Folder cmdlet for configuring these options for individual public folders.

Sample 11-8 provides the syntax and usage for this cmdlet. To override database settings for replication, messaging limits, quota, deleted item retention settings, or any combination thereof, you must first set the related "Use" parameter to $false as shown in the first usage example, and then set any desired default values as shown in the second usage example.

SAMPLE 11-8 Using Set-PublicFolder to set limits

Syntax

```
Set-PublicFolder -Identity PublicFolderIdentity
[-AgeLimit LimitKB] [-DomainController DCName]
[-LocalReplicaAgeLimit Limit]
[-HiddenFromAddressListsEnabled <$true|$false>]
[-IssueWarningQuota Limit]


[-LocalReplicaAgeLimit TimeSpan]
[-MaxItemSize Limit]
[-Name Name]
[-PerUserReadStateEnabled <$true|$false>]
```

```
[-ProhibitPostQuota Limit]
[-Replicas DatabaseID1, DatabaseID2, ...]
[-ReplicationSchedule Schedule]
[-RetainDeletedItemsFor NumberDays]
[-Server Server]
[-UseDatabaseAgeDefaults <$true|$false>]
[-UseDatabaseQuotaDefaults <$true|$false>]
[-UseDatabaseReplicationSchedule <$true|$false>]
[-UseDatabaseRetentionDefaults <$true|$false>]
```

Usage

```
Set-PublicFolder -Identity "\Projects"
 -UseDatabaseRetentionDefaults $false

Set-PublicFolder -Identity "\Projects"
 -RetainDeletedItemsFor 120
```

You can also configure these values using the Public Folder Management Console. When you display a public folder's Properties dialog box by double-clicking the public folder in the console's main pane, you can use the options on the Replication and Limits tabs to set related values. To override default settings for the related public folder database, use the following techniques:

- On the Replication tab, clear the Use Public Folder Database Replication Schedule check box and then specify the replication schedule.
- On the Limits tab, clear the Use Database Quota Defaults check box and then specify quota values.
- On the Limits tab, clear the Use Database Retention Defaults check box and then set the retention value.
- On the Limits tab, clear the Use Database Age Defaults check box and then set the age limit for replicas.

You can restore the default settings for the related public folder database simply by selecting the related check box or check boxes on the Replication tab, the Limits tab, or both. The default setting on the Replication tab is to use the public folder replication schedule. The default settings on the Limits tab are to use database quota defaults, database retention defaults, and database age defaults.

Setting Client Permissions

You use client permissions to specify which users can access a particular public folder. By default, all users (except those accessing the folder anonymously over the Web) have permission to access the folder, read items in the folder, create items in the folder, and edit and delete items they've created. Anyone accessing the folder anonymously can create items but has no other permissions for viewing or editing items.

To change permissions for anonymous and authenticated users, you need to set a new permission level for the special users Anonymous and Default, respectively. Initially, anonymous users have the role of Contributor and authenticated users have the role of Author. These and other client-permission levels are defined as follows:

- **Owner**   Grants all permissions in the folder. Users with this role can create, read, modify, and delete all items in the folder. They can create subfolders and change permissions on folders as well.

- **Publishing Editor**   Grants permission to create, read, modify, and delete all items in the folder. Users with this role can create subfolders as well.

- **Editor**   Grants permission to create, read, modify, and delete all items in the folder.

- **Publishing Author**   Grants permission to create and read items in the folder, to modify and delete items the user created, and to create subfolders.

- **Author**   Grants permission to create and read items in the folder, as well as to modify and delete items that the user created.

- **Nonediting Author**   Grants permission to create and read items in the folder.

- **Reviewer**   Grants read-only permission.

- **Contributor**   Grants permission to create items but not to view the contents of the folder.

- **None**   Grants no permission in the folder.

To set new roles for users or to modify existing client permissions, complete the following steps:

1. Start Outlook. If the Folder list isn't displayed, click Go, and then select Folder List.

2. Expand Public Folders in the Folder list, and then expand All Public Folders.

3. Right-click the folder with which you want to work, and then select Properties.

4. On the Permissions tab (shown in Figure 11-6), the Name and Permission Level lists display account names and their permissions on the folder. If you want to grant users permissions that are different from the default permission, click Add.

5. In the Add Users dialog box, select the name of a user who needs access to the mailbox. Then click Add to put the name in the Add Users list. Repeat this step as necessary for other users. Click OK when you're finished.

6. In the Name and Permission Level lists, select one or more users whose permissions you want to modify. Then use the Permission Level list to assign a role or select individual permission items. When you're finished granting permissions, click OK.

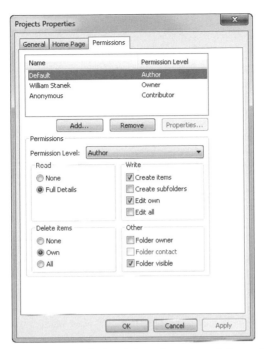

FIGURE 11-6 Use the Permissions tab to set permissions and assign roles for users. The role controls the actions the user can perform.

In the Exchange Management Shell, you can work with permissions using the Get-PublicFolderClientPermission, Add-PublicFolderClientPermission, and Remove-PublicFolderClientPermission cmdlets. Samples 11-9 through 11-11 provide the syntax and usage for these cmdlets. Values for the –AccessRights parameter can be set to the name of the permission level you want. Specify the exact name, as listed previously, without spaces. If you want to create modified permission levels, you can add or remove individual access rights. Use the names exactly as shown on the Permissions tab, without spaces.

SAMPLE 11-9 Get-PublicFolderClientPermission syntax and usage

Syntax

```
Get-PublicFolderClientPermission –Identity PublicFolderIdentity
 [-Server Server]
 [-User UserIdentity]
```

Usage

```
Get-PublicFolderClientPermission –Identity "\Projects"
 -User "William Stanek"
```

SAMPLE 11-10 Add-PublicFolderClientPermission syntax and usage

Syntax

```
Add-PublicFolderClientPermission -Identity PublicFolderIdentity
-AccessRights PermLevelOrAccessRight
-User UserIdentity
[-DomainController DCName] [-Server Server]
```

Usage

```
Add-PublicFolderClientPermission -Identity "\Projects"
-AccessRights "PublishingEditor"
-User "William Stanek"

Add-PublicFolderClientPermission -Identity "\Projects"
-AccessRights "CreateItems"
-User "JimWilson"
```

SAMPLE 11-11 Remove-PublicFolderClientPermission syntax and usage

Syntax

```
Remove-PublicFolderClientPermission -Identity PublicFolderIdentity
-AccessRights PermLevelOrAccessRight
-User UserIdentity
[-DomainController DCName] [-Server Server]
```

Usage

```
Remove-PublicFolderClientPermission -Identity "\Projects"
-AccessRights "PublishingEditor"
-User "William Stanek"

Remove-PublicFolderClientPermission -Identity "\Projects"
-AccessRights "CreateItems"
-User "Jim Wilson"
```

Granting and Revoking Send As Permissions for Public Folders

If you want to allow a user to send messages on behalf of the public folder, you can do this using the Manage Send As Permission Wizard. In the Public Folder Management Console, select the folder's parent in the left pane, click the folder in the main pane, and then click Manage Send As Permission on the Action menu or in the Action pane. In the Manage Send As Permission Wizard, click Add, and then use the Select User or Group dialog box to choose the user or users who should have Send As permission on the public folder. To revoke Send As permission, select an existing user name in the Security Principal list box, and then click the Remove button. Click Manage to set the desired access permissions.

In the Exchange Management Shell, you can use the Add-ADPermission and Remove-ADPermission cmdlets to manage Send As permissions. Samples 11-12 and 11-13 show examples using these cmdlets. Here, the ExtendedRights parameter is set to Send-As to indicate that you are setting Send As permissions on the mailbox.

SAMPLE 11-12 Adding Send As permissions for public folders

Syntax

```
Add-ADPermission –Identity PublicFolderIdentity
–User UserBeingGrantedPermission –ExtendedRights Send-As
```

Usage

```
Add-ADPermission
–Identity "CN=Managers,CN=Microsoft Exchange System Objects,
DC=cpandl,DC=com" –User "CPANDL\andyc" –ExtendedRights "Send-As"
```

SAMPLE 11-13 Removing Send As permissions for public folders

Syntax

```
Remove-ADPermission –Identity PublicFolderIdentity
–User UserBeingRevokedPermission –ExtendedRights Send-As
–InheritanceType All –ChildObjectTypes $null
–InheritedObjectTypes $null
–Properties $null
```

Usage

```
Remove-ADPermission
–Identity "CN=Managers,CN=Microsoft Exchange System Objects,
DC=cpandl,DC=com" –User "CPANDL\andyc" –ExtendedRights "Send-As"
–InheritanceType "All" –ChildObjectTypes $null
–InheritedObjectTypes $null
–Properties $null
```

Propagating Public Folder Settings and Data

Any property changes you make to public folders aren't automatically applied to subfolders or replicated to other Mailbox servers hosting public folder replicas. You must either wait for the maintenance/replication interval to begin or manually propagate setting changes by using the Update Hierarchy feature in the Public Folder Management Console or the Update-PublicFolderHierarchy cmdlet.

In the Public Folder Management Console, you can update the entire public folder hierarchy by selecting the Public Folders node in the left pane and then clicking Update Hierarchy on the Action menu or in the Action pane. Sample 11-14 provides the syntax and usage for the Update-PublicFolderHierarchy cmdlet.

SAMPLE 11-14 Update-PublicFolderHierarchy syntax and usage

Syntax

```
Update-PublicFolderHierarchy -Server Server
```

Usage

```
Update-PublicFolderHierarchy -Server "CorpSvr257"
```

Similarly, changes users make to individual public folders aren't automatically replicated to other Mailbox servers hosting replicas. You must either wait for replication to begin or manually replicate data changes by using the Update Content feature in the Public Folder Management Console or the Update-Public-Folder cmdlet.

In the Public Folder Management Console, you can update an individual public folder and its subfolders by selecting the parent folder in the left pane, clicking the folder in the main pane, and then clicking Update Content on the Action menu or in the Action pane. Sample 11-15 provides the syntax and usage for the Update-PublicFolder cmdlet.

SAMPLE 11-15 Update-PublicFolder syntax and usage

Syntax

```
Update-PublicFolder -Identity PublicFolderIdentity
 -Server Server [-DomainController DCName]
```

Usage

```
Update-PublicFolder -Identity "\Projects"
 -Server "CorpSvr257"
```

You can suspend and resume public folder replication by using Suspend-Public-FolderReplication and Resume-PublicFolderReplication, respectively. Simply enter the cmdlet name in the Exchange Management Shell.

Manipulating, Renaming, and Recovering Public Folders

Public folders are represented as objects in Active Directory. However, the actual data in public folders is stored in public folder databases. You can manipulate public folders by using standard techniques such as cut, copy, and paste. Follow the procedures outlined in this section to manipulate, rename, and recover public folders.

Renaming Public Folders

To rename a public folder using Outlook, follow these steps:

1. In Outlook, right-click the public folder you want to rename.
2. Select Rename Folder, type a new name, and then press Enter.

To rename a public folder using the Public Folder Management Console, follow these steps:

1. In the Public Folder Management Console, select the parent folder in the left pane and then double-click the folder in the main pane.
2. On the General tab of the Properties dialog box, type a new name in the text box provided and then click OK.

NOTE For mail-enabled public folders, you set the Exchange alias, the standard display name, and the simple display name on the Exchange General tab.

Copying and Moving Public Folders

You can copy and move public folders only within the same public folder tree. You can't copy or move a public folder to a different tree. To create a copy of a public folder, follow these steps:

1. In Outlook, right-click the public folder with which you want to work, and then select Copy.
2. Right-click the folder into which you want to copy the folder, and then select Paste.

To move a public folder to a new location in the same tree, follow these steps:

1. In Outlook, right-click the public folder with which you want to work, and then select Cut.
2. Right-click the folder into which you want to move the folder, and then select Paste.

Deleting Public Folders

When you delete a public folder, you remove its contents, any subfolders it contains, and the contents of its subfolders. Before you delete a folder, however, you should ensure that any existing data that the folder contains is no longer needed and that you make a backup of the folder contents just in case.

Using Outlook, you delete public folders and their subfolders by completing the following steps:

1. In Outlook, right-click the public folder you want to remove, and then select Delete.
2. You'll be asked to confirm that you want to delete the folder and all subfolders. Click Yes.

Using the Public Folder Management Console, you delete public folders and their subfolders by completing the following steps:

1. In the Public Folder Management Console, select the parent folder in the left pane and then select the folder that you want to delete in the main pane.
2. On the Action menu or in the Action pane, click Remove.
3. You'll be asked to confirm that you want to delete the folder and all subfolders. Click Yes.

Recovering Public Folders

You can recover deleted folders from public folder databases, provided that you've set a deleted item retention period for the public folder database from which the folders were deleted and the retention period hasn't expired. If both of these conditions are met, you can recover deleted folders by completing the following steps:

1. Log on to the domain using an account with administrative privileges in the domain or by using an account with full control over the public folders you need to recover.
2. After starting Outlook, access the Public Folders node, and then select the parent node that contained the public folders. For example, with a top-level folder, you select the All Public Folders node, but with a subfolder of a top-level folder, you select the node for the top-level folder.
3. On the Tools menu, select Recover Deleted Items. The Recover Deleted Items From dialog box appears.
4. Select the folders you want to recover, and then click the Recover Selected Items button.
5. Each folder restored by the recovery operation has "(Recovered)" appended to the folder name. After you verify the contents of the folder, you can complete the recovery operation by doing the following:

   - **Restoring the original folder name**   Right-click the folder, select Rename, type a new name, and then press Enter.

   - **Restoring the folder's e-mail addresses**   Right-click the folder, and then select Properties. In the Properties dialog box, click the E-Mail Addresses tab. Edit each e-mail address so that it's restored to its original value.

CHAPTER 12

Managing Hub Transport and Edge Transport Servers

You can configure your Microsoft Exchange Server 2010 organization with only Hub Transport servers for message routing and delivery, or you can configure it with Hub Transport servers and Edge Transport servers. When you use only Hub Transport servers, these servers are responsible for

- Messaging routing and delivery within the organization
- Receiving messages from outside the organization and delivering them to Mailbox servers within the organization
- Receiving messages from Mailbox servers within the organization and routing them to destinations outside the organization

When you use Hub Transport and Edge Transport servers, message routing and delivery works like this:

- Hub Transport servers handle message routing and delivery within the organization.
- Edge Transport servers receive messages from outside the organization and route them to Hub Transport servers within the organization that, in turn, deliver them to your Mailbox servers.
- Hub Transport servers receive messages from Mailbox servers within the organization and route them to Edge Transport servers, which, in turn, route them to destinations outside the organization.

The primary mail protocol used by Exchange Server 2010 is Simple Mail Transfer Protocol (SMTP). This chapter discusses how transport servers use SMTP for routing and delivery, as well as how you can view and manage transport server configurations.

REAL WORLD Microsoft recommends that you install the Edge Transport server role on a computer that is not part of the internal Active Directory domain. The server can be part of an external Active Directory domain. This configuration isolates the computer and is the most secure implementation. Although you can install the Edge Transport server on a domain-joined computer, the Edge Transport server role will always use the Active Directory Lightweight Directory Services (AD LDS) directory service to store recipient and configuration information for the Edge stack, and the underlying Windows stack will use Active Directory Domain Services (AD DS). To send and receive messages from your organization to the Internet, Edge Transport servers use Send connectors and Receive connectors.

Prior to installing the Edge Transport role, you need to set the Domain Name System (DNS) suffix for the server and install the AD LDS role. Generally, you'll want to use a DNS suffix for your organization's primary domain. To install the AD LDS role, use the Add Roles Wizard in the Server Manager. You also can use ServerManagerCmd in Windows Server 2008 SP2 or Add-WindowsFeature in Windows Server 2008 R2. Accept the default settings during installation with one exception: you do not need to create an application partition. AD LDS will be configured for the Edge Transport server role when you install the role and the required application partition also will be created at that time.

Working with SMTP Connectors, Sites, and Links

SMTP connectors, Active Directory sites, and Active Directory links all have important roles to play in determining how Exchange routes and delivers messages in your organization. You can work with connectors, sites, and links in a variety of ways, but first you need a strong understanding of how connectors are used.

Connecting Source and Destination Servers

Exchange Server 2010 uses SMTP connectors to represent logically the connection between a source server and a destination server. How you configure an SMTP connector determines how Exchange Server transports messages using that connection. Because each SMTP connector represents a one-way connection, Exchange Server uses both Send and Receive connectors.

A Send connector is a logical gateway through which transport servers send all outgoing messages. When you create a Send connector, it is stored in Active Directory or in Active Directory Lightweight Directory Services (AD LDS) as a connector object. Send connectors are not scoped to a single server. Multiple servers can use a single Send connector for sending messages. Send connectors deliver mail by looking up a mail exchanger (MX) record on a DNS server, by looking up an Address (A) record, or by using a smart host as a destination. With DNS records, the DNS server settings you configure on the Transport server are used for name resolution. You can configure different settings for internal and external DNS lookups if necessary. See the "Configuring Send Connector DNS Lookups" section of this chapter.

A Receive connector is a logical gateway through which all incoming messages are received. When you create a Receive connector, it is stored in Active Directory or in AD LDS as a connector object. Unlike Send connectors, Receive connectors are scoped to a single server and determine how that server listens for connections. The permissions on a Receive connector determine from whom the connector will accept connections. The authentication mechanisms you configure for a Receive connector determine whether anonymous connections are allowed and the types of authentication that are permitted.

Exchange Server creates the Send and Receive connectors required for mail flow when you install your Hub Transport servers. If your organization also uses Edge Transport servers, Exchange creates the additional Send and Receive connectors required during the Edge Subscription process. You can also explicitly create Send and Receive connectors or automatically compute them from the organization topology using Active Directory sites and site-link information.

Viewing and Managing Active Directory Site Details

By default, Hub Transport servers use Active Directory sites and the costs that are assigned to the Active Directory Internet Protocol (IP) site links to determine the least-cost routing path to other Hub Transport servers in the organization. You can override the Active Directory costs with Exchange costs.

After a Hub Transport server determines the least-cost routing path, the server routes messages over the link or links in this path, and in this way, a source Hub Transport server relays messages to target Hub Transport servers. By default, when there are multiple Active Directory sites between the source and destination server, the Hub Transport servers that are located in Active Directory sites along the path between the source server and the target server don't process or relay the messages in any way—with several exceptions:

- If you want messages to be processed en route, you can configure an Active Directory site as a hub site so that Exchange routes messages to the hub site to be processed by the site's Hub Transport servers before being relayed to a target server. The hub site must exist along the least-cost routing path between source and destination Hub Transport servers.

- If a message cannot be delivered to the target site, the Hub Transport server in the closest reachable site along the least-cost routing path of the target site queues the message for relay. The message is then relayed when the destination Hub Transport server becomes available.

TIP To determine which Active Directory and global catalog servers a Hub Transport server is using, click the System Settings tab in the server's Properties dialog box. Expand the Server Configuration node, and then select the Hub Transport node. Right-click the entry for the transport server, and then select Properties. In the Properties dialog box, click the System Settings tab.

You can use the Get-AdSite cmdlet to display the configuration details of an Active Directory site. If you do not provide an identity with this cmdlet, configuration information for all Active Directory sites is displayed.

Sample 12-1 provides the syntax and usage, as well as sample output, for the Get-AdSite cmdlet. Note that the output specifies whether the site is enabled as a hub site.

SAMPLE 12-1 Get-AdSite cmdlet syntax and usage

Syntax

```
Get-AdSite [-Identity 'SiteIdentity']
    [-DomainController 'DCName']
```

Usage

```
Get-AdSite -Identity 'First-Seattle-Site' | fl
```

Output

```
Runspaceid        :
HubSiteEnabled    : False
Partnerid         : -1
Name              : First-Seattle-Site
AdminDisplayName  :
ExchangeVersion   : 0.0 (6.5.6500.0)
DistinguishedName : CN=First-Seattle-Site,
                    CN=Sites,CN=Configuration,DC=cpandl,DC=com
Identity          : cpandl.com/Configuration/Sites/First-Seattle-Site
Guid              : dda814f3-2173-4943-bdd9-5ba8d6b6e5d7
ObjectCategory    : cpandl.com/Configuration/Schema/Site
ObjectClass       : {top, site}
WhenChanged       : 12/17/2009 8:27:00 PM
WhenCreated       : 12/17/2009 8:27:00 PM
WhenChangedUTC    : 12/17/2009 3:27:00 AM
WhenCreatedUTC    : 12/17/2009 3:27:00 AM
OrganizationId    :
OriginatingServer : MAILSERVER25.cpandl.com
IsValid           : True
```

You can use the Set-AdSite cmdlet to configure an Active Directory site as a hub site to override the default message routing behavior. When a hub site exists along the least-cost routing path between source and destination Hub Transport servers, messages are routed to the hub site for processing before they are relayed to the destination server.

Sample 12-2 provides the syntax and usage, as well as sample output, for the Set-AdSite cmdlet. To enable a site as a hub site, set the –HubSiteEnabled parameter to $true. To disable a site as a hub site, set the –HubSiteEnabled parameter to $false. You must have Enterprise Administrator rights to use the –Name parameter to change a site's name.

SAMPLE 12-2 Set-AdSite cmdlet syntax and usage

Syntax

```
Set-AdSite -Identity 'SiteIdentity'
[-HubSiteEnabled <$true | $false>]
[-DomainController 'DCName']
[-Name 'NewSiteName']
```

Usage

```
Set-AdSite -Identity 'First-Seattle-Site' –HubSiteEnabled $true
```

Viewing and Managing Active Directory Site Link Details

You can use the Get-AdSiteLink cmdlet to view the configuration information about an Active Directory IP site link. This configuration information includes the value of the Exchange-specific cost, the cost assigned to the Active Directory IP site link, and a list of the sites in the IP site link.

> **NOTE** A good resource to learn more about Active Directory sites and site links is *Windows Server 2008 Inside Out Second Edition* (Microsoft Press, 2010). See Chapter 32, "Configuring Active Directory Sites and Replication," and Chapter 37, "Active Directory Site Administration."

Sample 12-3 provides the syntax and usage, as well as sample output, for the Get-AdSiteLink cmdlet. Use the –Identity parameter to retrieve the configuration information about a specific IP site link. If you do not provide an identity, the configuration information about all IP site links is returned.

SAMPLE 12-3 Get-AdSiteLink cmdlet syntax and usage

Syntax

```
Get-AdSiteLink [-Identity 'SiteIdentity']
[-DomainController 'DCName']
```

```
Get-AdSiteLink -Identity 'PORTLANDSEATTLELINK' | fl
```

```
Runspaceid        :
Cost              : 100
ADCost            : 100
ExchangeCost      :
MaxMessageSize    : unlimited
Sites             : {First-Seattle-Site}
AdminDisplayName  :
ExchangeVersion   : 0.0 (6.5.6500.0)
Name              : PORTLANDSEATTLELINK
DistinguishedName : CN=PORTLANDSEATTLELINK,CN=IP,
                    CN=Inter-Site Transports,CN=Sites,
                    CN=Configuration,DC=cpandl,DC=com
Identity          : cpandl.com/Configuration/Sites/
                    Inter-Site Transports/IP/PORTLANDSEATTLELINK
Guid              : b304910a-4a2e-47af-8755-ac0e72653f9f
ObjectCategory    : cpandl.com/Configuration/Schema/Site-Link
ObjectClass       : {top, siteLink}
WhenChanged       : 12/17/2009 8:36:00 PM
WhenCreated       : 12/17/2009 8:36:00 PM
WhenChangedUTC    : 12/17/2009 3:36:00 AM
WhenCreatedUTC    : 12/17/2009 3:36:00 AM
OrganizationId    :
OriginatingServer : MAILSERVER25.cpandl.com
IsValid           : True
```

By default, Exchange Server 2010 determines the least-cost routing path by using the cost that is assigned to the Active Directory IP site links. You can change this behavior by using the Set-AdSiteLink cmdlet to configure an Exchange-specific cost for Active Directory IP site links. After you configure it, the Exchange-specific cost is used instead of the Active Directory–assigned cost to determine the Exchange routing path.

Sample 12-4 provides the syntax and usage, as well as sample output, for the Set-AdSiteLink cmdlet. When there are multiple wide area network (WAN) paths between sites, you can set a higher site-link cost if you want to reduce the likelihood that a link will be used. You can set a lower site-link cost if you want to increase the likelihood that a link will be used. You must have Enterprise Administrator rights to use the –Name parameter to change the name of a site link.

You can use the –MaxMessageSize parameter to set the maximum size for messages that are relayed across a specified link. The default value is "unlimited," which allows messages of any size to be relayed. You can specify the units for values using B for bytes, KB for kilobytes, MB for megabytes, or GB for gigabytes. The valid range for maximum size is from 64 KB to the largest value in bytes that can be set using a 64-bit integer (9,223,372,036,854,775,807).

SAMPLE 12-4 Set-AdSiteLink cmdlet syntax and usage

Syntax

```
Set-AdSiteLink -Identity 'SiteIdentity'
[-DomainController 'DCName']
[-ExchangeCost Cost]
[-MaxMessageSize <'Size' | 'Unlimited'>]
[-Name 'NewSiteLinkName']
```

Usage

```
Set-AdSiteLink -Identity 'PORTLANDSEATTLELINK'
-ExchangeCost 20

Set-AdSiteLink -Identity 'LASACRAMENTOLINK'
-MaxMessageSize 'Unlimited'

Set-AdSiteLink -Identity 'LASACRAMENTOLINK'
-MaxMessageSize '24MB'
```

Creating Send Connectors

Send connectors are the gateways through which transport servers send messages. Exchange automatically creates the Send connectors required for internal mail flow but does not create the Send connectors required for mail flow to the Internet. As an administrator, you can explicitly create Send connectors for Internet mail flow and other Send connectors that are needed, and then manage the configuration of these explicitly created Send connectors as necessary. You cannot, however, manage the configuration of Send connectors created implicitly by Exchange to enable mail flow. The key reasons for creating Send connectors are when you want to

- Control explicitly how message routing works within domains or between domains.
- Control explicitly the hosts used as destinations or the way messages are routed over the Internet.
- Send mail to systems that are not Exchange servers.

When you create Send connectors, you can encrypt message traffic sent over the link and require strict authentication. You can transmit messages to a designated internal server—called a *smart host*—or you can use DNS records to route messages. If you use a smart host, Exchange Server 2010 transfers messages directly to the smart host, which then sends out messages over an established link. The smart host allows you to route messages on a per-domain basis. If you use DNS records, Exchange Server 2010 performs a DNS lookup for each address to which the connector sends mail.

When you create a Send connector, you must either define the address space for the connector or link it to a specific Receive connector. The address space determines when the Send connector is used and the domain names to which the connector sends messages. For example, if you want to connect two domains in the same Exchange organization—dev.cpandl.com and corp.cpandl.com—you can create a Send connector in dev.cpandl.com, and then add an SMTP address type for the e-mail domain corp.cpandl.com.

Send connectors can be used by multiple Transport servers. When you create a Send connector within an Exchange organization, you can select the Hub Transport servers that are permitted to use the Send connector. When you create a Send connector on an Edge Transport server, the Send connector is configured for only that server.

To create a Send connector, complete the following steps:

1. Start the Exchange Management Console. On an Edge Transport server, select Edge Transport and then in the main pane click the Edge Transport server that you want to work with. On a Hub Transport server, expand the Organization Configuration node, and then select Hub Transport.

2. On the Send Connectors tab in the details pane, right-click an open area, and then select New Send Connector. This starts the New Send Connector Wizard, shown in Figure 12-1.

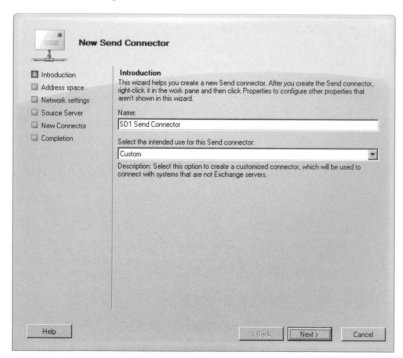

FIGURE 12-1 Create a new SMTP Send connector.

3. In the Name text box, type a descriptive name for the connector, and then set the connector type. The available options are as follows:

- **Custom** Creates a customized Send connector for connecting with systems that are not Exchange servers.

- **Internal** Creates a Send connector for sending mail to another transport server in the organization, and sets the default permissions so that the connector can be used by Exchange servers. This connector will be configured to route mail using smart hosts.

- **Internet** Creates a Send connector that sends mail to external users over the Internet. This connector will be configured to use DNS records to route mail.

- **Partner** Creates a Send connector that sends mail to partner domains. Partner domains cannot be configured as smart hosts. Only connections that authenticate with Transport Layer Security (TLS) certificates are allowed by default. Partner domains must also be listed on the TLS Send Domain Secure list, which can be set using the –TLSSendDomain-SecureList parameter of the Set-TransportConfig command.

4. Click Next. On the Address Space page, click Add. In the SMTP Address Space dialog box, enter the domain name to which this connector will send mail. To use this connector to send e-mail to all subdomains of the address space, select the Include All Subdomains check box. Click OK to close the SMTP Address Space dialog box. Repeat as necessary to add more address spaces to this connector. If you make a mistake, select the address space and then click Remove.

> **NOTE** If you enter Adatum.com as the address and then select the Include All Subdomains check box, the address entry is created as *.adatum.com. You can enter the wildcard character (*) directly in the address space as defined in RFC 1035. For example, you can enter * for all domains, *.com for all .com domains, or *.adatum.com for the adatum.com domain and all subdomains of adatum.com.

5. If you'd like to scope the Send connector to the current site, select the Scoped Send Connector check box. When a Send connector is scoped, only Hub Transport servers in the same Active Directory site as the Send connector's source servers consider that Send connector in routing decisions. Click Next to continue.

6. On the Network Settings page, select how you want to send e-mail with the Send connector. If you select Use Domain Name System (DNS) "MX" Records To Route Mail Automatically, the Send connector uses the DNS client service on the Transport server to query a DNS server and resolve the destination address. Skip steps 7–10.

7. If you select Route Mail Through The Following Smart Hosts, you have to specify the smart hosts to which mail should be forwarded for processing. Click Add.

8. In the Add Smart Host dialog box, select either IP Address or Fully Qualified Domain Name (FQDN) to specify how to locate the smart host. If you select IP Address, enter the IP address of the smart host. If you select Fully Qualified Domain Name (FQDN), enter the full domain name of the smart host. The Transport server must be able to resolve the FQDN.

9. Click OK to close the Add Smart Host dialog box. Repeat steps 7–9 as necessary to add more smart hosts to this connector. If you make a mistake, select the smart host, and then click Edit or Remove as appropriate. When you are finished, click Next to continue.

10. After you've configured smart hosts, you'll see the Configure Smart Host Authentication Settings page next. On this page, select the method that you want to use to authenticate your servers to the smart host. Choose one of the following options, and then click Next:

- **None** No authentication. Use this option only if the smart host is configured to accept anonymous connections.

- **Basic Authentication** Standard authentication with wide compatibility. With basic authentication, the user name and password specified are passed as cleartext to the remote domain.

- **Basic Authentication Over TLS** Transport Layer Security (TLS) authentication is combined with basic authentication to allow encrypted authentication for servers with smart cards or X.509 certificates.

- **Exchange Server Authentication** Secure authentication for Exchange servers. With Exchange Server authentication, credentials are passed securely.

- **Externally Secured** Secure authentication for Exchange servers. With externally secured authentication, credentials are passed securely using an external security protocol for which the server has been separately configured, such as Internet Protocol security (IPsec).

NOTE With the Basic Authentication or Basic Authentication Over TLS option, you must provide the name and password for the account authorized to establish connectors to the designated smart hosts. All smart hosts must use the same user name and password.

11. When you are working with a Hub Transport server, you see the Source Server page next. If you are logged on to a Hub Transport server, this server is added as the source server automatically. Click Add to associate the connector with Hub Transport servers and Edge subscriptions. In the Select Hub Transport And Subscribed Edge Transport Servers dialog box, select the Hub Transport server or the Edge subscription that will be used as the source server for sending messages to the address space that you previously specified and then click OK. Repeat as necessary to add more Transport servers. If you make a mistake, select the server and then click Remove. When you are finished, click Next to continue.

12. On the New Connector page, review the configuration summary for the connector. To modify the settings, click Back. To create the Send connector, click New. On the Completion page, click Finish.

In the Exchange Management Shell, you can create Send connectors using the New-SendConnector cmdlet. The –Usage parameter sets the Send connector type as Custom, Internal, Internet, or Legacy. The –AddressSpaces parameter sets the address spaces for the Send connector by FQDN or IP address. The –DNSRoutingEnabled parameter determines whether DNS records are used for lookups or smart hosts are used. To use DNS records, set DNSRoutingEnabled to $true. To use smart hosts, set DNSRoutingEnabled to $false, and then use the –SmartHosts parameter to designate the smart hosts.

Sample 12-5 provides the syntax and usage for the New-SendConnector cmdlet. With Basic Authentication or Basic Authentication Over TLS, you will be prompted to provide credentials. To scope the Send connector to the current Active Directory site, set the –IsScopedConnector parameter to $true.

SAMPLE 12-5 New-SendConnector cmdlet syntax and usage

Syntax

```
New-SendConnector –Name Name
 [-AddressSpaces Addresses]
 [-AuthenticationCredential Credentials]
 [-Comment Comment]
 [-ConnectionInactivityTimeout TimeSpan]
 [-Custom <$true | $false>]
 [-DNSRoutingEnabled <$true | $false>]
 [-DomainController DCName]
 [-DomainSecureEnabled <$true | $false>]
 [-Enabled <$true | $false>]
 [-Force <$true | $false>]
 [-ForceHELO <$true | $false>]
 [-Fqdn FQDN]
 [-IgnoreStartTLS <$true | $false>]
 [-Internal <$true | $false>]
 [-Internet <$true | $false>]
 [-IsScopedConnector <$true | $false>]
 [-LinkedReceiveConnector ReceiveConnectorIdentity]
 [-MaxMessageSize <Size | Unlimited>]
 [-Partner <$true | $false>]
 [-Port PortNumber]
 [-ProtocolLoggingLevel <None | Verbose>]
 [-RequireTLS <$true | $false>]
 [-SmartHostAuthMechanism <None|BasicAuth|BasicAuthRequireTls
                           |ExchangeServer|ExternalAuthoritative>]
 [-SmartHosts SmartHosts]
 [SmtpMaxMessagesPerConnection MaxMessages]
 [-SourceIPAddress IPAddress]
```

```
[-SourceTransportServers TranportServers]
[-Usage <Custom|Internal|Internet|Partner>]
[-UseExternalDNSServersEnabled <$true | $false>]
```

Usage for DNS MX records

```
New-SendConnector -Name "Adatum.com Send Connector"
 -Usage "Custom"
 -AddressSpaces "smtp:*.adatum.com;1"
 -IsScopedConnector $true
 -DNSRoutingEnabled $true
 -UseExternalDNSServersEnabled $false
 -SourceTransportServers "CORPSVR127"
```

Usage for smart hosts

```
New-SendConnector -Name "Cohovineyards.com"
 -Usage "Custom"
 -AddressSpaces "smtp:*.cohovineyards.com;1"
 -IsScopedConnector $false
 -DNSRoutingEnabled $false
 -SmartHosts "[192.168.10.52]"
 -SmartHostAuthMechanism "ExternalAuthoritative"
 -UseExternalDNSServersEnabled $false
 -SourceTransportServers "CORPSVR127"
```

Viewing and Managing Send Connectors

The Exchange Management tools provide access only to the Send connectors you've explicitly created. On Hub Transport servers, Send connectors created by Exchange Server are not displayed or configurable. On Edge Transport servers, you can view and manage the internal Send connector used to connect to the Hub Transport servers in your Exchange organization.

To view the Send connectors and manage their configuration, start the Exchange Management Console. On an Edge Transport server, select Edge Transport, click the server you want to work with, and then click the Send Connectors tab in the details pane. On a Hub Transport server, expand the Organization Configuration node, select Hub Transport, and then click the Send Connectors tab in the details pane. Send connectors you've created are listed by name and status. You can now do the following:

- **Change a connector's properties** To change a connector's properties, right-click the connector, and then select Properties. Use the Properties dialog box to manage the connector's properties. You'll also be able to specify the maximum message size and protocol logging level. By default, the maximum message size is set to 10,240 KB and the protocol logging level is set to None.

- **Enable a connector**   To enable a connector, right-click it, and then select Enable.

- **Disable a connector**   To disable a connector, right-click it, and then select Disable.

- **Remove a connector**   To remove a connector, right-click it, and then select Remove.

In the Exchange Management Shell, you can view, update, or remove Send connectors using the Get-SendConnector, Set-SendConnector, or Remove-SendConnector cmdlets, respectively. Samples 12-6 through 12-8 provide the syntax and usage. With Get-SendConnector, if you don't specify an identity, the cmdlet returns a list of all administrator-configured Send connectors.

SAMPLE 12-6 Get-SendConnector cmdlet syntax and usage

Syntax

```
Get-SendConnector

Get-SendConnector -Identity ConnectorIdentity
[-DomainController DCName]
```

Usage

```
Get-SendConnector -Identity "Adatum.com Send Connector"
```

SAMPLE 12-7 Set-SendConnector cmdlet syntax and usage

Syntax

```
Set-SendConnector -Identity ConnectorIdentity
[-Name NewName]
[-AddressSpaces Addresses]
[-AuthenticationCredential Credentials]
[-Comment Comment]
[-ConnectionInactivityTimeout TimeSpan]
[-DNSRoutingEnabled <$true | $false>]
[-DomainController DCName]
[-DomainSecureEnabled <$true | $false>]
[-Enabled <$true | $false>]
[-Force <$true | $false>]
[-ForceHELO <$true | $false>]
[-Fqdn FQDN]
[-IgnoreStartTLS <$true | $false>]
[-IsScopedConnector <$true | $false>]
[-LinkedReceiveConnector ReceiveConnectorIdentity]
[-MaxMessageSize <Size | Unlimited>]
[-Port PortNumber]
[-ProtocolLoggingLevel <None | Verbose>]
[-RequireTLS <$true | $false>]
```

```
[-SmartHostAuthMechanism <None|BasicAuth|BasicAuthRequireTls
                         |ExchangeServer|ExternalAuthoritative>]
[-SmartHosts SmartHosts]
[-SourceIPAddress IPAddress]
[-SourceTransportServers TranportServers]
[SmtpMaxMessagesPerConnection MaxMessages]
[-UseExternalDNSServersEnabled <$true | $false>]
```

Usage

```
Set-SendConnector -Name "Adatum.com Send Connector"
 -AddressSpaces "smtp:*.adatum.com;1"
 -DNSRoutingEnabled $true -SmartHosts 10.10.2.205
 -SmartHostAuthMechanism "None"
 -SourceTransportServers "CORPSVR127"
```

SAMPLE 12-8 Remove-SendConnector cmdlet syntax and usage

Syntax

```
Remove-SendConnector -Identity ConnectorIdentity
 [-Confirm <$true | $false>] [-DomainController DCName]
```

Usage

```
Remove-SendConnector -Identity "Adatum.com Send Connector"
```

Configuring Send Connector DNS Lookups

You can configure different settings for internal and external DNS lookups by configuring a Transport server's External DNS Lookups and Internal DNS Lookups properties. External DNS Lookup servers are used to resolve the IP addresses of servers outside your organization. Internal DNS Lookup servers are used to resolve IP addresses of servers inside the organization.

To configure DNS Lookup servers, complete these steps:

1. Start the Exchange Management Console. On an Edge Transport server, select Edge Transport. On a Hub Transport server, expand the Server Configuration node, and then select the Hub Transport node.

2. In the details pane, right-click the server and then select Properties.

3. On the External DNS Lookups tab, shown in Figure 12-2, specify how external lookups should be performed:

   - To use DNS settings from the server's network card or cards for external lookups, select Use Network Card DNS Settings, and then choose either All Available to use all configured settings or a specific network card to use the configured settings of that card.

- To use a specific DNS server for external lookups, click Use These DNS Servers. Then type the IP address of a DNS server to use for external lookups, and then click Add. Repeat this process to specify multiple servers.

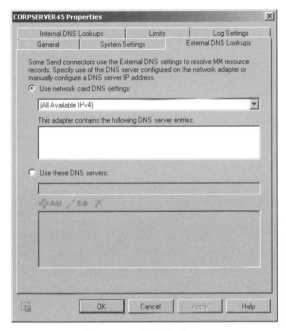

FIGURE 12-2 Configure external DNS lookups

4. On the Internal DNS Lookups tab, specify how internal lookups should be performed:

    - To use DNS settings from the server's network card or cards for internal lookups, select Use Network Card DNS Settings and then choose either All Available to use all configured settings or a specific network card to use the configured settings of that card.

    - To use a specific DNS server for internal lookups, click Use These DNS Servers. Then type the IP address of a DNS server to use for internal lookups, and then click Add. Repeat this process to specify multiple servers.

5. Click OK to save your settings.

Setting Send Connector Limits

Send connector limits determine how mail is delivered after a connection has been established and the receiving computer has acknowledged that it's ready to receive the data transfer. After a connection has been established and the receiving computer has acknowledged that it's ready to receive the data transfer, Exchange Server attempts to deliver messages queued for delivery to the computer. If a message can't be delivered on the first attempt, Exchange Server tries to send the message again after a specified time. Exchange Server keeps trying to send the message at the intervals you've specified until the expiration time-out is reached. When the time limit is reached, the message is returned to the sender with a nondelivery report (NDR). The default expiration time-out is two days.

After multiple failed attempts to deliver a message, Exchange Server generates a delay notification and queues it for delivery to the sender of the message. Notification doesn't occur immediately after failure. Instead, Exchange Server sends the delay notification message only after the notification delay interval and then only if the message hasn't already been delivered. The default delay notification is 4 hours.

With SMTP, you have much more control over outgoing connections than you do over incoming connections. You can limit the number of simultaneous connections and the number of connections per domain. These limits set the maximum number of simultaneous outbound connections. By default, the maximum number of connections is 1,000 and the maximum number of connections per domain is 20.

You can view or change the Send connector limits by completing the following steps:

1. Start the Exchange Management Console. On an Edge Transport server, select Edge Transport. On a Hub Transport server, expand the Server Configuration node, and then select the Hub Transport node.

2. In the details pane, right-click the server and then select Properties.

3. On the Limits tab, shown in Figure 12-3, use the following options for retrying unsuccessful outbound connections:

   - **Outbound Connection Failure Retry Interval (Minutes)**   Sets the retry interval for subsequent connection attempts to a remote server where previous connections have failed. The default is 10 minutes.

   - **Transient Failure Retry Interval (Seconds)**   Sets the interval at which the server immediately retries when it encounters a connection failure with a remote server. The default is 300 seconds.

   - **Transient Failure Retry Attempts**   Sets the maximum number of times that the server immediately retries when it encounters a connection failure with a remote server. The default is six. If you enter 0 as the number of retry attempts or the maximum number of attempts has been reached, the server no longer immediately retries a connection and instead waits according to the outbound connection failure retry interval.

4. When messages that cannot be delivered reach the Maximum Time Since Submission value, they expire, and Exchange Server generates a nondelivery report. To set the expiration time-out for messages, enter the desired message expiration value in the Maximum Time Since Submission (Days) text box. The default expiration time-out for messages is two days.

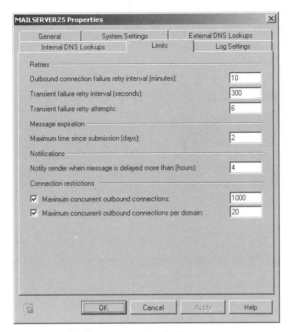

FIGURE 12-3 Configure connection limits.

5. When messages are delayed longer than the allowed delay interval, Exchange Server sends a delay notification to the sender. To set the amount of time to wait before notifying senders of a delay, enter the desired wait time in the Notify Sender When Message Is Delayed More Than (Hours) text box. The default wait time is four hours.

6. To remove outgoing connection limits, clear the Maximum Concurrent Outbound Connections check box. To set an outgoing connection limit, select the Maximum Concurrent Outbound Connections check box, and then type the limit value. The default limit is 1,000 outbound connections.

7. To remove outgoing connection limits per domain, clear the Maximum Concurrent Outbound Connections Per Domain check box. To set an outgoing connection limit per domain, select the Maximum Concurrent Outbound Connections Per Domain check box, and then type the limit value. The default limit is 20 outbound connections per domain.

8. Click OK to save your settings.

Creating Receive Connectors

Receive connectors are the gateways through which Transport servers receive messages. Exchange creates the Receive connectors required for mail flow automatically. The receive permissions on a Receive connector determine who is allowed to send mail through the connector.

As an administrator, you can explicitly create Receive connectors and then manage the configuration of those explicitly created Receive connectors as necessary. You cannot, however, manage the configuration of connectors created implicitly by Exchange to enable mail flow. The key reasons for creating SMTP connectors are when you want to

- Control explicitly how messages are received within domains or between domains.
- Control explicitly the permitted incoming connections.
- Receive mail from systems that are not Exchange servers.

Unlike Send connectors, Receive connectors are used by only a single, designated Transport server. When you create a Receive connector within an Exchange organization, you can select the Hub Transport or Edge Transport server with which the connector should be associated and configure the specific binding for that connector. A binding is a combination of local IP addresses, ports, and remote IP address ranges for the Receive connector. You cannot create a Receive connector that duplicates the bindings of existing Receive connectors. Each Receive connector must have a unique binding.

NOTE Exchange Server 2010 uses standard SMTP or Extended SMTP (ESMTP) to deliver mail. Because the ESMTP standard is more efficient and secure than SMTP, SMTP connectors always try to initiate ESMTP sessions before trying to initiate standard SMTP sessions. SMTP connectors initiate ESMTP sessions with other mail servers by issuing an EHLO start command. SMTP connectors initiate SMTP sessions with other mail servers by issuing the HELO start command.

To create a Receive connector, complete the following steps:

1. Start the Exchange Management Console. On an Edge Transport server, select Edge Transport. On a Hub Transport server, expand the Server Configuration node, and then select the Hub Transport node. On the Receive Connectors tab in the details pane, select the server on which you want to create the receive connection and then click the server's Receive Connectors tab.

2. Click the server you want to work with in the main pane. In the details pane, below Receive Connectors, right-click an open area, and then select New Receive Connector. This starts the New Receive Connector Wizard, shown in Figure 12-4.

3. In the Name text box, type a descriptive name for the connector and then set the connector type. The available options are as follows:

   - **Custom** Creates a Receive connector bound to a specific port or IP address on a server with multiple receive ports or IP addresses. It can also be used to specify a remote IP address from which the connector receives messages. A custom Receive connector is used to connect with systems that are not Exchange servers.

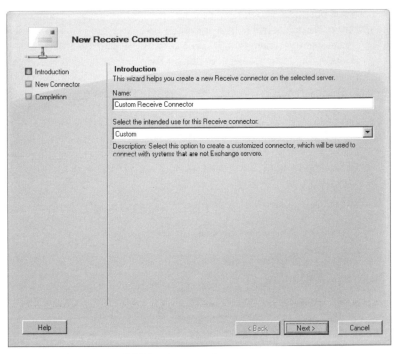

FIGURE 12-4 Create a new SMTP Receive connector.

- **Internal** Creates a Receive connector to receive messages from another Transport server in the organization. For Edge Transport servers, it sets the default permissions so that the connector can be used by Exchange servers. For Hub Transport servers, it sets the default permissions so that the connector is configured to accept connections from Exchange servers.

- **Internet** Creates a Receive connector that accepts incoming connections from the Internet. This connector accepts connections from anonymous users.

- **Client** Creates a Receive connector used to receive mail from Exchange users. Only connections from authenticated Microsoft Exchange users are accepted by default.

- **Partner** Creates a Receive connector used to receive mail from partner domains. Partner domains cannot be configured as smart hosts. Only connections that authenticate with Transport Layer Security (TLS) are allowed by default. Partner domains must also be listed on the TLS Receive Domain Secure list, which can be set using the –TLSReceive-DomainSecureList parameter of the Set-TransportConfig command.

4. Click Next. For Custom, Partner, and Internet Receive connectors, you can specify the local IP addresses and the port on which mail can be received.

(See Figure 12-5.) By default, Custom and Internet Receive connectors are configured to receive mail over port 25 on all available IPv4 addresses configured for the server. Port 25 is the default TCP port for SMTP. To use a different configuration, select the default entry on the Local Network Settings page and then click Remove. You can now create new entries by clicking Add. In the Add Receive Connector Binding dialog box, select Use All Available IP Addresses to have the connector listen for connections on all the IP addresses that are assigned to the network adapters on the local server. Select Specify An IP Address if you want to type an IP address that is assigned to a network adapter on the local server and have the connector listen for connections only on this IP address. As necessary, modify the listen port value. Click OK.

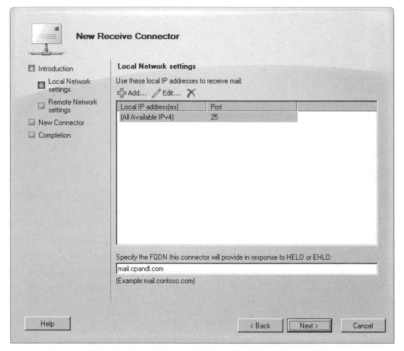

FIGURE 12-5 Specify the local IP addresses and ports for receiving e-mail.

5. For Custom, Partner, and Internet Receive connectors, you can specify the FQDN the Transport server provides in response to HELO or EHLO messages on the Local Network Settings page. In the Specify The FQDN This Connector Will Provide In Response To HELO Or EHLO text box, type the name that the server advertises, such as **mail.cpandl.com.** Click Next.

NOTE If you don't specify the FQDN, the wizard uses the name of the server.

6. On the Remote Network Settings page, shown in Figure 12-6, you can specify the remote IP addresses from which the server can receive mail. By default, Receive connectors are configured to accept mail from all remote IP addresses, which is why the IP address range 0.0.0.0–255.255.255.255 is set as the default entry. You'll only want to change this behavior if you want to limit the servers that are permitted to send mail to the Transport server. To use a different configuration, select the default entry on the Remote Network Settings page and then click Remove. To specify the remote servers by a range of IP addresses, click the small arrow next to Add and then select IP Range. In the Add Remote Servers—IP Address Range dialog box, enter a start IP address and an end IP address for the first acceptable range of IP addresses, and then click OK. Repeat this process as necessary to configure other acceptable IP address ranges. Click Next.

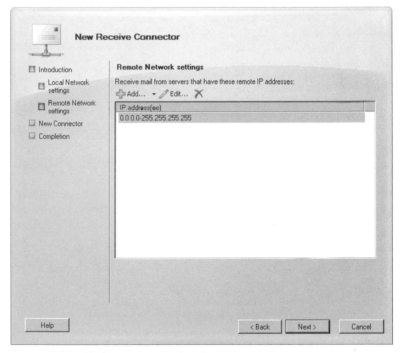

FIGURE 12-6 Specify the remote network settings.

7. On the New Connector page, review the configuration summary for the connector. If you want to modify the settings, click Back. To create the Receive connector by using the settings in the configuration summary, click New.

8. On the Completion page, click Finish.

In the Exchange Management Shell, you can create Receive connectors using the New-ReceiveConnector cmdlet. The –Usage parameter sets the Receive connector type as Custom, Internal, Internet, or Legacy. The –Bindings parameter sets the internal IP addresses and ports on which to listen. The –FQDN parameter sets the FQDN to advertise in response to HELO or EHLO messages. The –RemoteIPRanges parameter provides a comma-separated list of acceptable IP address ranges. The –Server parameter specifies the server on which to create the Receive connector.

As Sample 12-9 shows, the required parameters for the New-ReceiveConnector cmdlet depend on the type of Receive connector you are creating. After you provide the required parameters, the remaining parameters can be used in the same way regardless of which type of Receive connector you are creating. You use –AuthMechanism to specify the authentication type. With Basic Authentication or Basic Authentication Over TLS, you will be prompted to provide credentials.

SAMPLE 12-9 New-ReceiveConnector cmdlet syntax and usage

Syntax

```
New-ReceiveConnector -Name Name
-Usage <Custom | Internet | Internal | Client | Partner> {AddtlParams}

New-ReceiveConnector -Name Name -Bindings Bindings
-RemoteIPRanges IPRange1, IPRange2, . . . {AddtlParams}

New-ReceiveConnector -Name Name -Bindings Bindings
-Internet <$true | $false > {AddtlParams}

New-ReceiveConnector -Name Name -Client <$true | $false >
-RemoteIPRanges IPRange1, IPRange2, . . . {AddtlParams}

New-ReceiveConnector -Name Name -Internal <$true | $false >
-RemoteIPRanges IPRange1, IPRange2, . . . {AddtlParams}

New-ReceiveConnector -Name <String> -Bindings Bindings
-Partner <$true | $false > -RemoteIPRanges IPRange1, IPRange2, . . .
{AddtlParams}

{AddtlParams}
[-AdvertiseClientSettings <$true | $false>]
[-AuthMechanism <None | Tls | Integrated | BasicAuth |
BasicAuthRequireTLS | ExchangeServer | ExternalAuthoritative>]
[-Banner Banner]
[-BinaryMimeEnabled <$true | $false>]
[-Bindings Bindings]
[-ChunkingEnabled <$true | $false >]
[-Comment Comment]
[-Confirm <$true | $false >]
[-ConnectionInactivityTimeout TimeSpan]
[-ConnectionTimeout TimeSpan]
[-Custom <$true | $false >]
[-DefaultDomain DefaultDomain]
[-DeliveryStatusNotificationEnabled <$true | $false>]
```

```
[-DomainController DCName]
[-DomainSecureEnabled <$true | $false>]
[-EightBitMimeEnabled <$true | $false>]
[-EnableAuthGSSAPI <$true | $false>]
[-Enabled <$true | $false>]
[-EnhancedStatusCodesEnabled <$true | $false>]
[-Fqdn FQDN]
[-LongAddressesEnabled <$true | $false>]
[-LiveCredentialEnabled <$true | $false>]
[-MaxAcknowledgementDelay MaxDelay]
[-MaxHeaderSize MaxHeaderBytes]
[-MaxHopCount MaxHops]
[-MaxInboundConnection <MaxConn | Unlimited>]
[-MaxInboundConnectionPercentagePerSource MaxPercentage]
[-MaxInboundConnectionPerSource <MaxConnPerSource | Unlimited>]
[-MaxLocalHopCount MaxHops]
[-MaxLogonFailures MaxLogonFailures]
[-MaxMessageSize MaxMessageSize]
[-MaxProtocolErrors <MaxErrors | Unlimited>]
[-MaxRecipientsPerMessage MaxRecipients]
[-MessageRateLimit <RateLimit | Unlimited>]
[-MessageRateSource <User | IPAddress | Both>]
[-OrarEnabled <$true | $false>]
[-PermissionGroups <None | AnonymousUsers | ExchangeUsers |
ExchangeServers | ExchangeLegacyServers | Partners | Custom >]
[-PipeliningEnabled < $true | $false>]
[-ProtocolLoggingLevel <None | Verbose>]
[-RemoteIPRanges IPRange1, IPRange2, . . .]
[-RequireEHLODomain <$true | $false>]
[-RequireTLS < $true | $false>]
[-Server Server]
[-SizeEnabled <Disabled | Enabled | EnabledWithoutValue>]
[-SuppressXAnonymousTls < $true | $false>]
[-TarpitInterval TimeSpan]
```

Usage

```
New-ReceiveConnector -Name "Custom Receive Connector"
-Usage "Custom"  -Bindings "0.0.0.0:425"
 -Fqdn "mailserver85.cpandl.com"
 -RemoteIPRanges "0.0.0.0-255.255.255.255"
 -Server "CORPSVR127"
```

Viewing and Managing Receive Connectors

To view all available Receive connectors for a server, do one of the following in the
Exchange Management Console:

- On a Hub Transport server, expand the Server Configuration node and then
  click the server you want to work with in the main pane.

- On an Edge Transport server, select Edge Transport and then click the server you want to work with.

On the Receive Connectors tab in the details pane, Receive connectors are listed by name and status. You can now

- **Change a connector's properties** To change a connector's properties, right-click the connector, and then select Properties. Use the Properties dialog box to manage the connector's properties.
- **Enable a connector** To enable a connector, right-click it, and then select Enable.
- **Disable a connector** To disable a connector, right-click it, and then select Disable.
- **Remove a connector** To remove a connector, right-click it, and then select Remove.

When configuring Receive connector properties, you can specify the security mechanisms that can be used for incoming connections on the Authentication tab. Use any combination of the following:

- **Transport Layer Security** Allows encrypted authentications with TLS for servers with smart cards or X.509 certificates.
- **Enable Domain Security (Mutual Auth TLS)** When TLS is enabled, you can also enable domain security to require mutual authentication.
- **Basic Authentication** Allows basic authentication. With basic authentication, the user name and password specified are passed as base64-encoded text to the remote domain.
- **Offer Basic Authentication Only After Starting TLS** Allows basic authentication only within an encrypted TLS session.
- **Exchange Server Authentication** Allows secure authentication for Exchange servers. With Exchange Server authentication, credentials are passed securely.
- **Integrated Windows Authentication** Allows secure authentication using NT LAN Manager (NTLM) or Kerberos.
- **Externally Secured** Allows secure external authentication. With externally secured authentication, credentials are passed securely using an external security protocol for which the server has been separately configured, such as IPsec.

Also when configuring Receive connector properties, you can specify the security group that is allowed to connect on the Permission Groups tab. Use any combination of the following:

- **Anonymous Users** Allows unauthenticated, anonymous users to connect to the Receive connector.
- **Exchange Users** Allows connections by authenticated users who are valid recipients in the organization (Hub Transport servers only).

- **Exchange Servers** Allows connections by authenticated servers that are members of the Exchange Server Administrator group.
- **Legacy Exchange Servers** Allows connections by authenticated servers that are members of the ExchangeLegacyInterop group (Hub Transport servers only).
- **Partners** Allows connections by authenticated servers that are members of partner domains, as listed on the TLS Receive Domain Secure list.

In the Exchange Management Shell, you can view, update, or remove Receive connectors using the Get-ReceiveConnector, Set-ReceiveConnector, or Remove ReceiveConnector cmdlets, respectively. Samples 12-10 through 12-12 provide the syntax and usage. With Get-ReceiveConnector, you can return a list of all available Receive connectors if you don't specify an identity or server. If you want to see only the Receive connectors configured on a particular server, use the –Server parameter.

SAMPLE 12-10 Get-ReceiveConnector cmdlet syntax and usage

Syntax

```
Get-ReceiveConnector [-Identity Server\ConnectorIdentity]
[-Server Server] [-DomainController DCName]
```

Usage

```
Get-ReceiveConnector

Get-ReceiveConnector -Identity "Corpsvr127\Adatum.com Receive Connector"

Get-ReceiveConnector -Server "Corpsvr127"
```

SAMPLE 12-11 Set-ReceiveConnector cmdlet syntax and usage

Syntax

```
Set-ReceiveConnector -Identity Identity
[-AdvertiseClientSettings <$true | $false>]
[-AuthMechanism <None | Tls | Integrated | BasicAuth |
BasicAuthRequireTLS | ExchangeServer | ExternalAuthoritative>]
[-Banner Banner]
[-BinaryMimeEnabled <$true | $false>]
[-Bindings Bindings]
[-ChunkingEnabled <$true | $false >]
[-Comment Comment]
[-Confirm <$true | $false >]
[-ConnectionInactivityTimeout TimeSpan]
[-ConnectionTimeout TimeSpan]
[-DefaultDomain DefaultDomain]
[-DeliveryStatusNotificationEnabled <$true | $false>]
[-DomainController DCName]
```

```
[-DomainSecureEnabled <$true | $false>]
[-EightBitMimeEnabled  <$true | $false>]
[-EnableAuthGSSAPI <$true | $false>]
[-Enabled <$true | $false>]
[-EnhancedStatusCodesEnabled <$true | $false>]
[-Fqdn FQDN]
[-LongAddressesEnabled <$true | $false>]
[-LiveCredentialEnabled <$true | $false>]
[-MaxAcknowledgementDelay MaxDelay]
[-MaxHeaderSize MaxHeaderBytes]
[-MaxHopCount MaxHops]
[-MaxInboundConnection <MaxConn | Unlimited>]
[-MaxInboundConnectionPercentagePerSource MaxPercentage]
[-MaxInboundConnectionPerSource <MaxConnPerSource | Unlimited>]
[-MaxLocalHopCount MaxHops]
[-MaxLogonFailures MaxLogonFailures]
[-MaxMessageSize MaxMessageSize]
[-MaxProtocolErrors <MaxErrors | Unlimited>]
[-MaxRecipientsPerMessage MaxRecipients]
[-MessageRateLimit <RateLimit | Unlimited>]
[-MessageRateSource <None | User | IPAddress | All>]
[-Name Name]
[-OrarEnabled <$true | $false>]
[-PermissionGroups <None | AnonymousUsers | ExchangeUsers |
ExchangeServers | ExchangeLegacyServers | Partners | Custom>]
[-PipeliningEnabled < $true | $false>]
[-ProtocolLoggingLevel <None | Verbose>]
[-RemoteIPRanges IPRange1, IPRange2, . . .]
[-RequireEHLODomain <$true | $false>]
[-RequireTLS < $true | $false>]
[-Server Server]
[-SizeEnabled <Disabled | Enabled | EnabledWithoutValue>]
[-SuppressXAnonymousTls < $true | $false>]
[-TarpitInterval TimeSpan]
```

Usage

```
Set-ReceiveConnector -Identity "Corpsvr127\Custom Receive Connector"
-Bindings "0.0.0.0:425"
-Fqdn "mailserver85.cpandl.com"
-RemoteIPRanges "0.0.0.0-255.255.255.255"
```

SAMPLE 12-12 Remove-ReceiveConnector cmdlet syntax and usage

Syntax

```
Remove-ReceiveConnector -Identity ConnectorIdentity
[-Confirm <$true | $false >]
[-DomainController DCName]
```

```
Remove-ReceiveConnector -Identity "CorpSvr127\Adatum.com Receive
Connector"
```

Connecting to Exchange 2003 Routing Groups

Although Exchange 2010 doesn't use routing groups, you must create routing group connectors to route messages between Exchange Server 2010 Hub Transport servers and Exchange Server 2003 routing groups. You can manage routing group connectors only by using the Exchange Management Shell.

You can view, create, update, or remove routing group connectors using the Get-RoutingGroupConnector, New-RoutingGroupConnector, Set-RoutingGroupConnector, or Remove-RoutingGroupConnector cmdlet, respectively. With Get-RoutingGroupConnector, you can return a list of all available routing group connectors if you don't specify an identity or server. If you want to see only the routing group connectors configured on a particular server, use the –Server parameter.

When you are creating or updating a routing group connector using New-RoutingGroupConnector or Set-RoutingGroupConnector, you specify source and target servers. The source and target servers must be Exchange 2010 Hub Transport servers or Exchange Server 2003 bridgehead servers. By using the –Bidirectional parameter, you can specify whether the connector is used for one-way or two-way mail flow. If you specify a two-way connector, a reciprocal connector is created in the target routing group.

Samples 12-13 through 12-16 provide the syntax and usage for the Get-RoutingGroupConnector, New-RoutingGroupConnector, Set-RoutingGroupConnector, and Remove-RoutingGroupConnector cmdlets. With the Set-RoutingGroupConnector cmdlet, you can use the –MaxMessageSize parameter to set the maximum size for messages that are relayed between Exchange 2010 Hub Transport servers and Exchange 2003 bridgehead servers.

SAMPLE 12-13 Get-RoutingGroupConnector cmdlet syntax and usage

Syntax

```
Get-RoutingGroupConnector [-Identity RoutingGroup\ConnectorIdentity]
  [-DomainController DCName]
```

Usage

```
Get-RoutingGroupConnector

Get-RoutingGroupConnector -Identity "Exchange Administrator Group\
Exchange 2003 Interop"
```

SAMPLE 12-14 New-RoutingGroupConnector cmdlet syntax and usage

Syntax

```
New-RoutingGroupConnector -Name Name
 -SourceTransportServers SourceServer1, SourceServer2,...
 -TargetTransportServers TransportServer1, TransportServer2,...
 [-BiDirectional <$true | $false>]
 [-Cost ConnectorCost] [-DomainController DCName]
 [-PublicFolderReferralsEnabled <$true | $false>]
```

Usage

```
New-RoutingGroupConnector -Name "Exchange 2003 Interop"
 -SourceTransportServers "Exchange2010Server12.cpandl.com"
 -TargetTransportServers "Exchange2003Server08.cpandl.com"
 -Cost 100
 -BiDirectional $true
```

SAMPLE 12-15 Set-RoutingGroupConnector cmdlet syntax and usage

Syntax

```
Set-RoutingGroupConnector -Identity Group\Connector Identity
 [-Cost ConnectorCost] [-DomainController DCName]
 [-MaxMessageSize <Size | Unlimited>] [-Name Name]
 [-PublicFolderReferralsEnabled <$true | $false>]
 [-SourceTransportServers SourceServer1, SourceServer2,...]
 [-TargetTransportServers TransportServer1, TransportServer2,...]
```

Usage

```
Set-RoutingGroupConnector -Identity "Exchange Administrator
Group\Exchange 2003 Interop" -Name "Exchange 2003 Interop"
 -SourceTransportServers "Exchange2010Server12.cpandl.com"
 -TargetTransportServers "Exchange2003Server08.cpandl.com"
 -Cost 100
 -BiDirectional $true
```

SAMPLE 12-16 Remove-RoutingGroupConnector cmdlet syntax and usage

Syntax

```
Remove-RoutingGroupConnector [-Identity RoutingGroup\ConnectorIdentity]
[-DomainController DCName]
```

Usage

```
Remove-RoutingGroupConnector -Identity "Exchange Administrator Group\
Exchange 2003 Interop"
```

Completing Transport Server Setup

After you install Transport servers running Exchange Server 2010, you need to finalize the configuration by creating and configuring a postmaster mailbox and performing any other necessary tasks. For Exchange organizations with only Hub Transport servers, you should enable anti-spam features. For Exchange organizations with Edge Transport servers, you need to subscribe the Edge Transport servers to your Exchange organization. For either type of Exchange organization, you might also want to configure journal and transport rules on your Hub Transport servers.

Configuring the Postmaster Address and Mailbox

Every organization that sends and receives mail should have a postmaster address. This is the e-mail address listed on nondelivery reports and other delivery status notification reports created by Exchange Server. The postmaster address is not set by default. You must manually set the postmaster address.

To view your Exchange organization's postmaster address, enter the following command at the Exchange Management Shell prompt:

```
Get-TransportConfig | Format-List Name,ExternalPostMasterAddress
```

This command lists the postmaster address for the organization, as shown in this sample output:

```
Name: Transport Settings
ExternalPostmasterAddress : postmaster@cpand1.com
```

If you don't set the postmaster address, the address typically is set to $null, except when you have an Edge Transport server that hasn't been through the Edge Sync process. To change the postmaster address, you can use the –ExternalPostMasterAddress parameter of the Set-TransportServer cmdlet, as shown in this example:

```
Set-TransportConfig -ExternalPostMasterAddress "nondelivery@cpand1.com"
```

If you want the postmaster address to be able to receive mail, you must either create a mailbox and associate it with the postmaster address or assign the postmaster address as a secondary e-mail address for an existing mailbox. See Chapter 6, "Mailbox Administration," for more information.

You also can view or change the organization's postmaster address by completing the following steps:

1. In the Exchange Management Console, expand the Organization Configuration node, and then select the Hub Transport node.

2. In the main pane, select the Global Settings node and then double-click Transport Settings. This displays the Transport Settings Properties dialog box.

3. On the General tab, the current postmaster e-mail address is listed. If you want to change the postmaster address, enter the address you want to use, and then click OK.

Configuring Transport Limits

Exchange Server 2010 automatically places receive size, send size, and number of recipient limits on messages being routed through an Exchange organization. By default, the maximum message size that can be received by or sent by recipients in the organization is 10,240 KB and messages can have no more than 5,000 recipients. You configure maximum message size limits on individual Receive and Send connectors as discussed previously.

You can view or change the default limits for the Exchange organization by completing the following steps:

1. In the Exchange Management Console, expand the Organization Configuration node, and then select the Hub Transport node.

2. In the main pane, select the Global Settings tab and then double-click Transport Settings. This displays the Transport Settings Properties dialog box with the General tab selected by default, as shown in Figure 12-7.

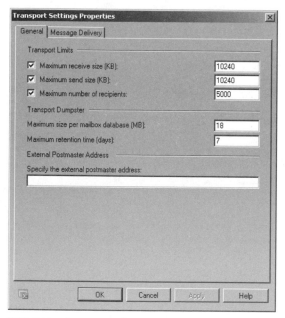

FIGURE 12-7 Set transport limits for the Exchange organization.

3. To set a maximum receive size limit, select the Maximum Receive Size check box and then type the desired receive limit in the related text box. The valid input range is 0 to 2,097,151 KB. If you clear the check box or use a value of

0, no limit is imposed on the message size that can be received by recipients in the organization.

4. To set a maximum send size limit, select the Maximum Send Size check box and then type the desired send limit in the related text box. The valid input range is 0 to 2,097,151 KB. If you clear the check box or use a value of 0, no limit is imposed on the message size that can be sent by senders in the organization.

5. To set a maximum number of recipients limit, select the Maximum Number Of Recipients check box and then type the desired limit in the related text box. The valid input range is 0 to 2,147,483,647. If you clear the check box or use a value of 0, no limit is imposed on the number of recipients in a message. Note that Exchange handles an unexpanded distribution group as one recipient.

6. Click OK to apply your settings.

In the Exchange Management Shell, you assign the desired transport limits using the Set-TransportConfig cmdlet, as shown in Sample 12-17. The –MaxReceiveSize and –MaxSendSize parameters set the maximum receive size and maximum send size, respectively. MaxRecipientEnvelopeLimit sets the maximum number of recipients in a message. When you use the –MaxReceiveSize and –MaxSendSize parameters, you must specify the units for values using KB for kilobytes, MB for megabytes, or GB for gigabytes. Your changes are made at the organization level and apply to the entire Exchange Server 2010 organization.

SAMPLE 12-17 Setting transport limits

Syntax

```
Set-TransportConfig [-Identity OrgId] [-DomainController DCName]
[-MaxReceiveSize <'MaxSize' | 'Unlimited'>]
[-MaxSendSize <'MaxSize' | 'Unlimited'>]
[-MaxRecipientEnvelopeLimit <'MaxRecipients' | 'Unlimited'>]
```

Usage

```
Set-TransportConfig -MaxReceiveSize '15MB' -MaxSendSize '15MB'
 -MaxRecipientEnvelopeLimit '1000'
```

Configuring the Transport Dumpster

When your organization has replicated mailbox databases, your Hub Transport servers use the transport dumpster to maintain a queue of messages that were recently delivered to recipients on a replicated mailbox database. During a database or server failover, the Mailbox server on which replicated mailbox databases become active requests redelivery of messages from the transport dumpster for every Hub Transport server in the originating Active Directory site. In addition, if the mailbox database copy becomes active in a different Active Directory site, the Mailbox server makes the same request to Hub Transport servers in the other site.

Exchange Server 2010 also supports transport dumpster truncation based on log copy status. This feature ensures that messages replicated successfully to all mailbox databases are removed from the transport dumpster. Thus, the transport dumpster will contain only nonreplicated data.

You can view or change the transport dumpster configuration by completing the following steps:

1. In the Exchange Management Console, expand the Organization Configuration node, and then select the Hub Transport node.

2. In the main pane, select the Global Settings tab and then double-click Transport Settings. This displays the Transport Settings Properties dialog box with the General tab selected by default.

3. The Maximum Size Per Mailbox Database text box specifies the maximum size of the transport dumpster for each replicated mailbox database. Size this setting to accommodate all messages being sent in the recovery period— the period of time from failure to failover and full recovery (which could be calculated according to the formula RecoveryWindowSizeInMinutes * MessagesPerMinute * AverageMessageSize). The valid input range for this parameter is 0 to 2,147,483,647 KB. The default value is 18 MB.

4. The Maximum Retention Time text box specifies how long an e-mail message should remain in the transport dumpster. When continuous replication is used, transport servers should retain messages in the queue for a period of time that is long enough to allow messages to be recovered. The default retention period is 7 days. The valid input range is 0 to 24,855 days. If you set the retention period to 0 days, you disable the transport dumpster completely.

5. Click OK to apply your settings.

In the Exchange Management Shell, you configure the transport dumpster using the Set-TransportConfig cmdlet, as shown in Sample 12-18. The –MaxDumpsterSizePerDatabase and –MaxDumpsterTime parameters set the maximum size and maximum retention time for the transport dumpster, respectively. When you use the –MaxDumpsterSizePerDatabase parameter, you must specify the units for values using KB for kilobytes, MB for megabytes, GB for gigabytes, or TB for terabytes. When you use the –MaxDumpsterTime parameter, you set the time span in the following format: DD.HH:MM:SS. The example sets the maximum dumpster time to 3 days, 12 hours.

SAMPLE 12-18 Setting transport dumpster options

Syntax

```
Set-TransportConfig [-Identity OrgId] [-DomainController DCName]
[-MaxDumpsterSizePerDatabase MaxSize] [-MaxDumpsterTime <TimeSpan>]
```

```
Set-TransportConfig -MaxDumpsterSizePerDatabase "5GB"
-MaxDumpsterTime "3.12:00:00"
```

Configuring Shadow Redundancy

Shadow redundancy ensures that messages are protected from loss the entire time they are in transit. It does this by delaying the deletion of a message from a transport database until the transport server verifies that the message has been successfully delivered to all of the next hops in the delivery route. If any transport server along the route fails to report a successful delivery, Exchange resubmits the message for delivery, and this ensures the message continues through to its destination.

Thanks to shadow redundancy, as long as you have multiple Hub Transports and multiple Edge Transports, you can remove any transport server that fails and not have to worry about emptying its queues or losing messages. If you have multiple Hub Transports and multiple Edge Transports, you also can upgrade or replace a Hub Transport or Edge Transport server at any time without the risk of losing messages. If you have a single Hub Transport, you should drain all SMTP queues on the server before performing maintenance. The same is true if you have a single Edge Transport. This ensures that there is no risk of message loss, even without shadow redundancy. Keep in mind that if you have a single transport server, and it fails and must be replaced, you've likely lost data if you can't restore the mail.que file.

When you work with shadow redundancy, a key concept to understand is that the primary transport server has ownership of the messages in its shadow queue. The first primary owner is always the server on which the message originates. As the message travels through the transport pipeline, different transport servers may become the primary owner of a message. In addition, if a primary owner fails, another server can take over as the primary.

In the Exchange Management Shell, you configure shadow redundancy using the Set-TransportConfig cmdlet, as shown in Sample 12-19. The related parameters are used as follows:

- **ShadowHeartbeatRetryCount**   Sets the number of timeouts a transport server waits for before deciding that the primary server has failed and assuming ownership of messages in the shadow queue for that server. The default value is 3. Set this value according to the size of your Exchange implementation and the relative amount of latency on the network. For example, a large global organization might want to set a higher retry count, while the default may suffice for a smaller organization.

- **ShadowHeartbeatTimeoutInterval**   Sets the amount of time a transport server waits before establishing a connection to the primary server to check the discard status of shadow messages. The default value is 300 seconds. Set this value according to the size of your Exchange implementation, the level of messaging traffic, and the relative latency on the network. For example, in a large global organization where transport servers handle an extremely high volume of messages, you might want to set a longer timeout interval, while the default may suffice for a smaller organization.

- **ShadowMessageAutoDiscardInterval** Sets the amount of time a server retains discard events for shadow messages. Primary servers queue discard events until they are checked by another server or until the discard interval has elapsed, whichever comes first. The default value is 2 days. Set the value according to the size of your Exchange implementation, the level of messaging traffic, and the relative reliability of your network. For example, in a large global organization where transport servers handle an extremely high volume of messages on a highly reliable network, you might want to set a shorter discard interval, while the default may suffice for a smaller organization.

- **ShadowRedundancyEnabled** Enables or disables shadow redundancy. If you don't use shadow redundancy, you can use this parameter to disable the feature. Ideally, you'd only disable the feature temporarily or in situations where you are have a single Exchange server implementation and are experiencing problems related to this feature.

SAMPLE 12-19 Setting shadow queue options

Syntax

```
Set-TransportConfig [-Identity OrgId] [-DomainController DCName]
[-ShadowHeartbeatRetryCount Count] [-ShadowHeartbeatTimeoutInterval
<TimeSpan>] [-ShadowMessageAutoDiscardInterval <TimeSpan>]
[-ShadowRedundancyEnabled <$true | $false>]
```

Usage

```
Set-TransportConfig -ShadowHeartbeatRetryCount 5
-ShadowHeartbeatTimeoutInterval "0.00:10:00"
-ShadowMessageAutoDiscardInterval "3.00:00:00"
```

Enabling Anti-Spam Features

By default, Edge Transport servers have anti-spam features enabled and Hub Transport servers do not. In an Exchange organization with Edge Transport servers, this is the desired configuration: you want your Edge Transport servers to run anti-spam filters on messages before they are routed into the Exchange organization. After Edge Transport servers have filtered messages, you don't need to filter them again—which is why Hub Transport servers have this feature disabled.

If your organization doesn't use Edge Transport servers and has only Hub Transport servers, you should enable the anti-spam features on Hub Transport servers that receive messages from the Internet. In this way, you can filter incoming messages for spam. You can enable or disable anti-spam features on Hub Transport servers using the Set-TransportServer cmdlet. To enable these features, set the –AntispamAgentsEnabled parameter to $true. To disable these features, set the –AntispamAgentsEnabled parameter to $false.

The following example shows how you can enable anti-spam features on a Hub Transport server named CorpSvr127:

```
Set-TransportServer –Identity 'CorpSvr127' –AntispamAgentsEnabled $true
```

You then need to restart the Microsoft Exchange Transport service on the server. If you exit and restart the Exchange Management Console, you'll then see the Antispam tab in the details pane. (Expand the Server Configuration node, and then select the Hub Transport node.)

You can now configure the transport server's anti-spam features as discussed in the "Configuring Anti-Spam and Message Filtering Options" section later in this chapter. When you turn on anti-spam features, a transport server can automatically get updates for spam signatures, IP reputation, and anti-spam definitions through automatic updates, provided that you've done the following:

- Conformed to Microsoft's licensing requirements
- Enabled Automatic Updates for use on the server
- Specifically enabled and configured anti-spam updates

To obtain anti-spam updates through automatic updates, Microsoft requires an Exchange Enterprise Client Access License (CAL) for each mailbox user or the purchase of Microsoft Forefront Protection for Exchange Server 2010. You can configure automatic updates by using the Windows Update utility in Control Panel. Click Start, click Control Panel\Security, and then click Windows Update to start this utility. You can also configure Automatic Updates through Group Policy. After you've ensured that automatic updates are enabled, you can check a transport server's anti-spam update configuration by completing the following steps:

1. Start the Exchange Management Console. On an Edge Transport server, select Edge Transport. On a Hub Transport server, expand the Server Configuration node, and then select the Hub Transport node.

2. Right-click the transport server for which you are configuring anti-spam updates and then select Enable Anti-Spam Updates. This starts the Enable Anti-Spam Updates Wizard, shown in Figure 12-8.

3. Under Update Mode, select Automatic to ensure the server automatically retrieves and applies available updates.

4. Generally, you'll want a server to retrieve updates for both spam signatures and IP reputation. However, if you don't use IP allow or block lists or other features that use IP reputation details, you might not want to retrieve this information.

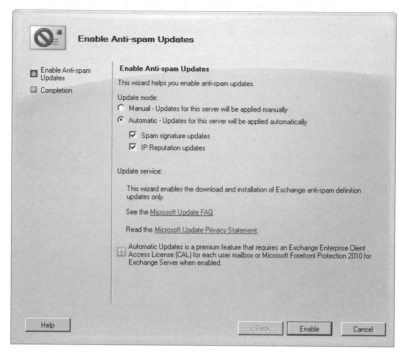

FIGURE 12-8 Configure anti-spam updates.

5. The wizard enables the server to download and install anti-spam definition updates using Microsoft Update.

6. Click Enable and then click Finish.

In the Exchange Management Shell, you can use the Get-AntispamUpdates, Enable-AntispamUpdates, and Disable-AntispamUpdates cmdlets to view settings or enable or disable anti-spam updates.

Subscribing Edge Transport Servers

When your Exchange organization uses Edge Transport servers and you want to use the Edge Synchronization feature, you must subscribe the Edge Transport server to your Exchange organization prior to performing other configuration tasks on the Edge Transport server. Creating a subscription allows the Microsoft Exchange EdgeSync service running on designated Hub Transport servers to establish one-way replication of recipient and configuration information from your internal Active Directory database to the AD LDS database on an Edge Transport server. After you create an Edge subscription, synchronization is automatic. If problems occur, however, you can force synchronization or remove the Edge subscription.

Creating an Edge Subscription

A subscribed Edge Transport server receives the following from the EdgeSync service:

- Send connector configurations
- Accepted domain configurations
- Remote domain configurations
- Safe Senders lists
- Recipients

Any manually configured accepted domains, message classifications, remote domains, and Send connectors are deleted as part of the subscription process, and the related Exchange management interfaces are locked out as well. To manage these features after a subscription is created, you must do so within the Exchange organization and have the EdgeSync service update the Edge Transport server.

Also as part of the subscription process, you must select an Active Directory site for the subscription. The Hub Transport server or servers in the site are the servers responsible for replicating Active Directory information to the Edge Transport server.

You can create a subscription for an Edge Transport server by completing the following steps:

1. Log on to the Edge Transport server for which you are creating a subscription using an administrator account.

2. At the Exchange Management Shell prompt, type the following command:

   `New-EdgeSubscription -filename "C:\EdgeSubscriptionExport.xml"`

3. When prompted, confirm that it is okay to delete any manually configured accepted domains, message classifications, remote domains, and Send connectors by pressing A (which answers Yes to all deletion prompts).

4. Copy the EdgeSubscriptionExport.xml file to a Hub Transport server in your Exchange organization.

5. Log on to a Hub Transport server in your Exchange organization using an account with Exchange administration privileges.

6. On the Hub Transport server, start the Exchange Management Console. Expand the Organization Configuration node, and then select the Hub Transport node.

7. In the details pane, the Edge Subscriptions tab lists existing subscriptions by Edge Transport server name and associated Active Directory site.

8. Right-click an open area of the details pane, and then select New Edge Subscription. This starts the New Edge Subscription Wizard, as shown in Figure 12-9.

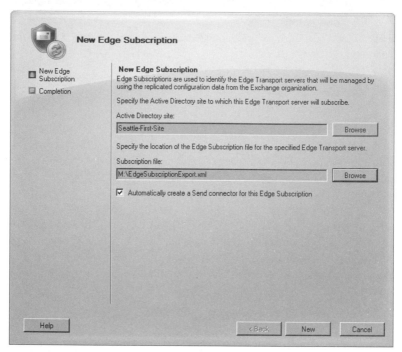

FIGURE 12-9 Create a new Edge subscription.

9. On the New Edge Subscription page, click Browse to the right of the Active Directory Site text box. In the Select Active Directory Site dialog box, choose the Active Directory site for replication and then click OK.

   REAL WORLD Hub Transport servers in the Active Directory site you select must be able to resolve the IP addresses for the Edge Transport server. You need to ensure that subnets have been created in Active Directory Sites And Services and that DNS is configured to resolve the fully qualified domain name of the Edge Transport server. Hub Transport servers in the site must also be able to connect to the Edge Transport server over TCP port 50636.

10. Click Browse to the right of the Subscription File text box. In the Open dialog box, locate and then select the Edge Subscription file to import. Click Open.

11. On the New Edge Subscription page, if you don't want to create the required Send connectors now, clear Automatically Create A Send Connector For This Edge Subscription, and then click New to begin the subscription process. If you want to create Send connectors now, just click New to begin the subscription process.

12. On the Completion page, click Finish. Initial synchronization will begin, as discussed in "Synchronizing Edge Subscriptions."

After you've completed steps 1–5, you can use the New-EdgeSubscription cmdlet to start a subscription. Sample 12-20 provides the syntax and usage. By default, the –CreateInboundSendConnector parameter is set to $true, which ensures that a Send connector from the Edge Transport server to Hub Transport servers is created. By default, the –CreateInternetSendConnector parameter is set to true, which ensures that a Send connector to the Internet is created.

SAMPLE 12-20 New-EdgeSubscription cmdlet syntax and usage

Syntax

```
New-EdgeSubscription -FileName FilePath
 -Site SiteName [-AccountExpiryDuration <TimeSpan>]
[-CreateInboundSendConnector <$true | $false>]
[-CreateInternetSendConnector <$true | $false>]
[-DomainController DCName] [-FileData ByteStr] [-Force <$true | $false>]
```

Usage

```
New-EdgeSubscription -FileName "Z:\EdgeSubscriptionExport.xml"
-Site "Default-First-Site-Name"
-CreateInboundSendConnector $true
-CreateInternetSendConnector $true
```

Getting Edge Subscription Details

In the Exchange Management Console, you can view Edge subscriptions by expanding the Organization Configuration node, selecting the Hub Transport node, and then clicking the Edge Subscriptions tab. Each Edge subscription is listed by Edge Transport server name and associated Active Directory site as shown in Figure 12-10.

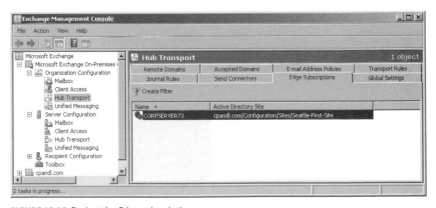

FIGURE 12-10 Review the Edge subscriptions.

As Sample 12-21 shows, you can use the Get-EdgeSubscription cmdlet to get information about Edge subscriptions as well. If you do not provide an identity with this cmdlet, configuration information for all Edge Subscriptions is returned.

SAMPLE 12-21 Get-EdgeSubscription cmdlet syntax and usage

Syntax

```
Get-EdgeSubscription -Identity EdgeTransportServerName
[-DomainController DCName]
```

Usage

```
Get-EdgeSubscription -Identity "EdgeSvr04"
```

Synchronizing Edge Subscriptions

During the configuration of an Edge subscription, you specified an Active Directory site to associate with the subscription. Hub Transport servers in this site run the EdgeSync service and are responsible for synchronizing configuration data between Active Directory Domain Services and AD LDS on the Edge Transport server. By default, the EdgeSync service synchronizes configuration data hourly and recipient data every four hours.

If you've just created a new subscription and synchronization has occurred, you should verify that replication is taking place as expected by completing the following steps:

1. On the Edge Transport server, start the Exchange Management Shell.

2. Verify that a Send connector was created to send Internet mail by typing the command **get-sendconnector.** As shown in the following example and sample output, you should see an Inbound connector and an Internet connector for EdgeSync:

```
get-sendconnector


Identity                            AddressSpaces          Enabled
--------                            -------------          -------
Primary Send Connector              {SMTP:*.cpandl.com;1}  True
SD1 Send Connector                  {SMTP:*.adatum.com;1}  True
EdgeSync - Seattle-First-Site to Int {smtp:*;100}          True
EdgeSync - Inbound to Seattle-First- {smtp:--;100}         True
```

3. Verify that there is at least one entry for accepted domains by typing get-accepteddomain as shown in the following example and sample output:

```
get-accepteddomain

Name              DomainName        DomainType        Default
----              ----------        ----------        -------
cpandl.com        cpandl.com        Authoritative     True
```

If you suspect there is a problem with synchronization and you want to start immediate synchronization of configuration data for all Edge subscriptions, complete the following steps:

1. Start the Exchange Management Shell.

2. At the prompt, type the following command

   ```
   start-edgesynchronization -Server ServerName
   ```

   where *ServerName* is the name of the Hub Transport server on which you want to run the command, such as:

   ```
   start-edgesynchronization -Server mailserver25
   ```

If you are running the command on the Hub Transport server, you can omit the –Server parameter.

Verifying Edge Subscriptions

The easiest way to verify the subscription status of Edge Transport servers is to run the Test-EdgeSynchronization cmdlet. This cmdlet provides a report of the synchronization status, and you also can use it to verify that a specific recipient has been synchronized to the Active Directory Lightweight Directory Service on an Edge Transport server.

Sample 12-22 provides the syntax and usage for the Test-EdgeSynchronization cmdlet. By default, the cmdlet verifies configuration objects and recipient objects. To have the cmdlet verify only configuration data, set –ExcludeRecipientTest to $true. Use the –VerifyRecipient parameter to specify the e-mail address of a recipient to verify.

SAMPLE 12-22 Test-EdgeSynchronization cmdlet syntax and usage

Syntax

```
Test-EdgeSynchronization [-ExcludeRecipientTest <$true | $false>]
[-DomainController DCName] [-FullCompareMode <$true | $false>]
[-MaxReportSize <MaxNumberofObjectsToCheck | Unlimited>]
[-MonitoringContext <$true | $false>] [-TargetServer EdgeServer]

Test-EdgeSynchronization -VerifyRecipient RecipientEmailAddress
[-DomainController DCName]
```

```
Test-EdgeSynchronization -ExcludeRecipientTest

Test-EdgeSynchronization -MaxReportSize 500

Test-EdgeSynchronization -VerifyRecipient "williams@cpandl.com"

Test-EdgeSynchronization -TargetServer CorpServer73.cpandl.com
```

Example and sample output

```
test-edgesynchronization
```

```
RunspaceId                      : 9654f021-e26d-4428-83ba-50cb75c645fe
UtcNow                          : 12/12/2009 9:12:31 PM
Name                            : CORPSERVER73
LeaseHolder                     : CN=MAILSERVER25,CN=Servers,CN=Exchange
Administrative Group (FYDIBOHF23SPDLT),CN=Administrative Groups,
CN=First Organization,CN=Microsoft Exchange,CN=Services,CN=Configuration,
DC=cpandl,DC=com
LeaseType                       : Option
ConnectionResult                : Succeeded
FailureDetail                   :
LeaseExpiryUtc                  : 12/12/2009 10:11:50 PM
LastSynchronizedUtc             : 12/12/2009 9:11:50 PM
CredentialStatus                : Synchronized
TransportServerStatus           : Synchronized
TransportConfigStatus           : Synchronized
AcceptedDomainStatus            : Synchronized
RemoteDomainStatus              : Synchronized
SendConnectorStatus             : Synchronized
MessageClassificationStatus     : Synchronized
RecipientStatus                 : Synchronized
CredentialRecords               : Number of credentials 62
CookieRecords                   : Number of cookies 25
```

Removing Edge Subscriptions

If you replace or decommission an Edge Transport server, you no longer need the related Edge subscription and can remove it. Removing an Edge subscription

- Stops synchronization of information from the Active Directory Domain Service to AD LDS.
- Removes all the accounts that are stored in AD LDS.
- Removes the Edge Transport server from the source server list of any Send connector.

You can remove an Edge subscription by completing the following steps:

1. Log on to a Hub Transport server using an account with Exchange administrator privileges.

2. In the Exchange Management Console, expand the Organization Configuration node, and then select the Hub Transport node.

3. In the details pane, on the Edge Subscriptions tab, right-click the subscription that you no longer need, and then select Remove.

4. When prompted to confirm, click Yes.

In the Exchange Management Shell, you can remove an Edge Subscription by passing the identity of the subscription to remove to the Remove-EdgeSubscription cmdlet. Sample 12-23 provides the syntax and usage.

SAMPLE 12-23 Remove-EdgeSubscription cmdlet syntax and usage

Syntax

```
Remove-EdgeSubscription -Identity EdgeTransportServerName
[-DomainController DCName] [-Force <$true | $false>]
```

Usage

```
Remove-EdgeSubscription -Identity "EdgeSvr04"
```

Configuring Journal Rules

As discussed in Chapter 8, "Implementing Exchange Server 2010 Security," journaling allows you to forward copies of messaging items and related reports automatically to an alternate location. You can use journaling to verify compliance with policies implemented in your organization and to help ensure that your organization can meet its legal and regulatory requirements. One way to implement journaling is to do so through managed folder settings. You can also enable journaling for the entire organization using journal rules.

Creating Journal Rules

You can target journal rules for

- **Internal messaging items** Tracks messaging items sent and received by recipients inside your Exchange organization.

- **External messaging items** Tracks messaging items sent to recipients or from senders outside your Exchange organization.

- **Global messaging items** Tracks all messaging items, including those already processed by journal rules that track only internal or external messaging items.

When you enable journal rules for one or more of these scopes, the rules are executed on your organization's Hub Transport servers. Journal rules can be targeted to all recipients or to specific recipients. For example, you can create a rule to journal all messages sent to the AllEmployees distribution group.

You can create a journal rule by completing the following steps:

1. In the Exchange Management Console, expand the Organization Configuration node, and select the Hub Transport node.

2. On the Journal Rules tab, right-click an open area of the details pane, and then select New Journal Rule. This starts the New Journal Rule Wizard (shown in Figure 12-11).

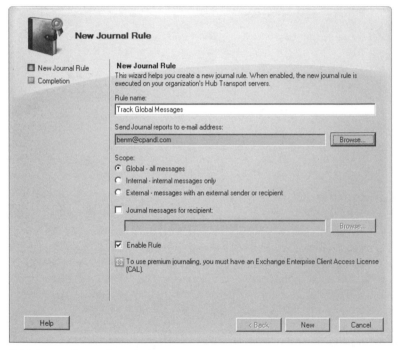

FIGURE 12-11 Create a journal rule.

3. In the Rule Name text box, type a descriptive name for the rule.

4. You now need to provide the journal e-mail address. Click Browse. In the Select Recipient dialog box, select the recipient to which Exchange Server should forward journal reports.

5. Use the Scope options to set the scope as Global, Internal, or External.

6. If you want the rule to apply to a specific recipient rather than to all recipients, select the Journal Messages For Recipient check box and then click Browse. In the Select Recipient dialog box, select the recipient for which journal reports should be created and then click OK.

7. By default, journal rules are enabled. If you want to create the rule but not enable it, clear the Enable Rule check box.

8. Click New to create the rule. On the Completion page, click Finish.

Managing Journal Rules

To manage journal rules, you can right-click and then select one of the following options:

- **Disable Rule**   Disables the journal rule so that it is no longer applied.
- **Remove**   Removes the journal rule.
- **Properties**   Allows you to edit the properties of the journal rule.

In the Exchange Management Shell, you can manage journal rules using the following cmdlets: New-JournalRule, Set-JournalRule, Get-JournalRule, and Remove-JournalRule.

Configuring Transport Rules

Transport rules allow you to screen messaging items and apply actions to those that meet specific conditions. When you enable transport rules, all Hub Transport servers in your Exchange organization screen messages according to the rules you've defined.

Understanding Transport Rules

Transport rules have conditions, actions, and exceptions that you can apply. Conditions you can screen for include

- **From People**   Allows you to screen messages from a specific recipient
- **From A Member Of A Distribution List**   Allows you to screen messages from a member of a distribution list
- **Sent To People**   Allows you to screen messages sent to a specific recipient
- **Sent To A Member Of A Distribution List**   Allows you to screen messages sent to a member of a distribution list
- **Sent To Users Inside Or Outside The Corporation**   Allows you to screen messages sent by users inside the organization or received from users outside the organization
- **When Any Of The Recipients In The To Field Is People**   Allows you to screen messages sent to specific recipients
- **When Any Of The Recipients In The Cc Field Is People**   Allows you to screen messages copied to specific recipients
- **When Any Of The Recipients In The From Field Is People**   Allows you to screen messages sent by specific recipients
- **When The Subject Field Contains Specific Words**   Allows you to screen messages that have specific words in their subject line

- **When The Subject Field Or The Message Body Contains Specific Words** Allows you to screen messages that have specific words in their subject line or message body
- **With A Spam Confidence Level (SCL) Rating That Is Greater Than Or Equal To Limit** Allows you to screen messages that have a spam confidence level (SCL) rating that is greater than or equal to a limit that you set
- **When The Size Of Any Attachment Is Greater Than Or Equal To Limit** Allows you to screen messages with attachments that are greater than or equal to the size limit that you set

When a message meets all of the conditions you specify in a transport rule, the message is handled according to the actions you've defined. Actions you can apply to messages that meet your transport rule conditions include

- **Log An Event With Message** Logs an event in the application logs with the message you specify
- **Prepend The Subject With String** Inserts a string you specify into the message subject
- **Apply Message Classification** Applies a message classification, such as Privileged, Confidential, Company Internal, or Attachment Removed
- **Append Disclaimer Text** Appends disclaimer text to the message
- **Add A Recipient To The To Field Addresses** Adds the recipients you specify to the To field of the message
- **Copy The Message To Addresses** Adds the recipients you specify to the Cc field of the message
- **Blind Carbon Copy (Bcc) The Message To Addresses** Adds the recipients you specify to the Bcc field of the message
- **Redirect The Message To Addresses** Redirects the message to the recipients you specify
- **Send Bounce Message** Drops the message, and sends a bounce message to the sender
- **Silently Drop The Message** Drops the message, and provides no notification of this action

Transport rules can also have exceptions. Exception criteria are similar to condition criteria. For example, you can exclude messages from certain people or from certain members of distribution lists. You can also exclude messages sent to certain people or to particular members of a distribution list.

Creating Transport Rules

You can create a transport rule by completing the following steps:

1. In the Exchange Management Console, expand the Organization Configuration node, and select the Hub Transport node.

2. On the Transport Rules tab, right-click an open area of the details pane, and then select New Transport Rule. This starts the New Transport Rule Wizard. (See Figure 12-12.)

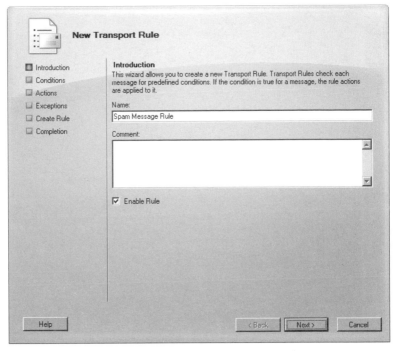

FIGURE 12-12 Create a transport rule.

3. In the Name text box, type a descriptive name for the rule and optionally enter a descriptive comment.

4. By default, transport rules are enabled. If you want to create the rule but not enable it, clear the Enable Rule check box.

5. Click Next. You now need to specify the conditions for the rule. When you select a condition's check box, as shown in Figure 12-13, you must then edit the rule description by clicking the link or links provided and specifying any required value. For example, to configure the From People condition, you select the From People check box and then click the People link under Edit

The Rule Description (Click An Underlying Value). In the Select Senders dialog box, you then click Add to display the Select Recipient dialog box. You use the Select Recipient dialog box to select the recipient to which the condition should apply, and then click OK.

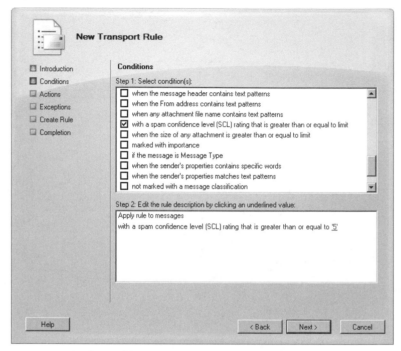

FIGURE 12-13 Set the conditions.

6. Click Next. You now need to specify the actions to take when a message meets the conditions you specified. When you select the check box for an action, as shown in Figure 12-14, you must then edit the rule description by clicking the link or links provided and specifying any required value.

7. Click Next. You now need to specify any exceptions. When you select the check box for an exception, you must then edit the rule description by clicking the link or links provided and specifying any required value.

8. Click Next, and then click New to create the rule. On the Completion page, click Finish.

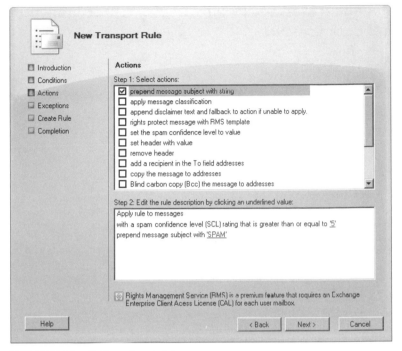

FIGURE 12-14 Specify the actions to take.

Managing Transport Rules

You can manage transport rules in several different ways. You can edit their properties or disable them. When you've created multiple rules, you can also change their
priority to determine the precedence order for application in case there are conflicts
between rules. When multiple rules apply to a message, the rule with the highest
priority is the one that your Hub Transport server applies.

To manage transport rules, you can right-click and then select one of the following options:

- **Change Priority**   Allows you to set the priority of the rule. The valid range
  for priorities depends on the number of rules you've configured.
- **Disable Rule**   Disables the transport rule so that it is no longer applied.
- **Remove**   Removes the transport rule.
- **Edit Rule**   Allows you to edit the properties of the transport rule.

In the Exchange Management Shell, you can manage transport rules using the
following cmdlets: New-TransportRule, Set-TransportRule, Get-TransportRule, and
Remove-TransportRule.

Managing Message Pickup, Replay, Throttling, and Back Pressure

To support message routing and delivery, Hub Transport and Edge Transport servers maintain a few special directories:

- **Pickup** A folder to which users and applications can manually create and submit new messages for delivery
- **Replay** A folder for messages bound for or received from non-SMTP mail connectors

The sections that follow discuss how the Pickup and Replay directories are used and configured and also look at the related concepts of message throttling and back pressure.

Understanding Message Pickup and Replay

When a Hub Transport or an Edge Transport server receives incoming mail from a server using a non-SMTP connector, it stores the message in the Replay directory and then resubmits it for delivery using SMTP. When a Hub Transport or an Edge Transport server has messages to deliver to a non-SMTP connector, it stores the message in the Replay directory and then resubmits it for delivery to the foreign connector. In this way, messages received from non-SMTP connectors are processed and routed, and messages to non-SMTP connectors are delivered.

Your Transport servers automatically process any correctly formatted .eml message file copied into the Pickup directory. Exchange considers a message file that is copied into the Pickup directory to be correctly formatted if it meets the following conditions:

- Is a text file that complies with the basic SMTP message format and can also use Multipurpose Internet Mail Extensions (MIME) header fields and content
- Has an .eml file name extension, zero or one e-mail address in the Sender field, and one or more e-mail addresses in the From field
- Has at least one e-mail address in the To, Cc, or Bcc fields and a blank line between the header fields and the message body

Transport servers check the Pickup directory for new message files every five seconds. Although you can't modify this polling interval, you can adjust the rate of message file processing by using the –PickupDirectoryMaxMessagesPerMinute parameter on the Set-TransportServer cmdlet. The default value is 100 messages per minute. When a transport server picks up a message, it checks the message against the maximum message size, the maximum header size, the maximum number of recipients, and other messaging limits. By default, the maximum message size is 10 megabytes (MB), the maximum header size is 64 kilobytes (KB), and the maximum number of recipients is 100. You change these limits using the Set-TransportServer cmdlet. If a message file doesn't exceed any assigned limits, the Transport server renames the message file using a .tmp extension and then converts the .tmp file to an e-mail message. After the message is successfully queued for delivery, the Transport server issues a "close" command and deletes the .tmp file from the Pickup directory.

Your Transport servers automatically process any correctly formatted .eml message file copied into the Replay directory. Exchange considers a message file that is copied into the Replay directory to be correctly formatted if it meets the following conditions:

- Is a text file that complies with the basic SMTP message format and can also use MIME header fields and content
- Has an .eml file name extension and its X-Header fields occur before all regular header fields
- Has a blank line between the header fields and the message body

Transport servers check the Replay directory for new message files every five seconds. Although you can't modify this polling interval, you can adjust the rate of message file processing. To do this, use the –PickupDirectoryMaxMessagesPerMinute parameter of the Set-TransportServer cmdlet. This parameter controls the rate of processing for both the Pickup directory and the Replay directory. The Transport server renames the message file using a .tmp extension and then converts the .tmp file to an e-mail message. After the message is successfully queued for delivery, the server issues a "close" command and deletes the .tmp file from the Replay directory.

Exchange considers any improperly formatted e-mail messages received in the Pickup or Replay directory to be undeliverable and renames them from the standard message name (*MessageName*.eml) to a bad message name (*MessageName*.bad). Because this is considered a type of message-processing failure, a related error is generated as well in the event logs. In addition, if you restart the Microsoft Exchange Transport service when there are .tmp files in the Pickup directory, Replay directory, or both directories, all .tmp files are renamed as .eml files and are reprocessed. This can lead to duplicate message transmissions.

Configuring and Moving the Pickup and Replay Directories

Because of the way message pickup and replay works, Transport servers do not perform any security checks on messages submitted through these directories. This means that if you've configured anti-spam, antivirus, sender filtering, or recipient filtering actions on a Send connector, those checks are not performed on the Pickup or Replay directory. To ensure that the Pickup and Replay directories are not compromised by malicious users, specific security permissions are applied, which must be tightly controlled.

For the Pickup and Replay directories, you must configure the following permissions:

- Full Control for Administrator
- Full Control for Local System
- Read, Write, and Delete Subfolders and Files for Network Service

As might be necessary for balancing the load across a server's disk drives or ensuring ample free space for messages, you can move the Pickup and Replay directories to new locations. You move the location of the Pickup directory by using the –PickupDirectoryPath parameter on the Set-TransportServer cmdlet. You move the location of the Replay directory by using the –ReplayDirectoryPath parameter on the Set-TransportServer cmdlet. With either parameter, successfully changing the directory location depends on the rights that are granted to the Network Service account on the new directory location and whether the new directory already exists. Keep the following in mind:

- If the new directory does not already exist and the Network Service account has the rights to create folders and apply permissions at the new location, the new directory is created and the correct permissions are applied to it.

- If the new directory already exists, the existing folder permissions are not checked or changed. Exchange assumes you've already set the appropriate permissions.

Sample 12-24 provides the syntax and usage for moving the Pickup and Replay directories. If you want to move both the Pickup and Replay directories, you should do this in two separate commands.

SAMPLE 12-24 Changing the Pickup directory

Syntax

```
Set-TransportServer -Identity ServerIdentity
[-PickupDirectoryPath LocalFolderPath]
[-ReplayDirectoryPath LocalFolderPath]
```

Usage

```
Set-TransportServer -Identity "CorpSvr127"
-PickupDirectoryPath "g:\Pickup"
```

Changing the Message Processing Speed

By default, Transport servers simultaneously and separately process the Pickup and Replay directories. Transport servers scan the Pickup and Replay directories for new message files once every 5 seconds (or 12 times per minute), and they process messages copied to either directory at a rate of 100 messages per minute, per directory. Because the polling interval is not configurable, this means the maximum number of messages that can be processed in either the Pickup or Replay directory during each polling interval, by default, is approximately 8 (100 messages per minute divided by 12 messages processed per minute).

Although the polling interval is not configurable, the maximum number of messages that can be processed during each polling interval is configurable. You assign the desired processing rate using the –PickupDirectoryMaxMessagesPerMinute parameter, because this processing speed is used with both the Pickup and Replay directories. You might want to adjust the message processing rate in these situations:

- If the server is unable to keep up with message processing, you might want to decrease the number of messages processed per minute to reduce processor and memory utilization.

- If the server is handling message transport for a large organization and you are seeing delays in message transport because of an abundance of messages in the Pickup directory, Replay directory, or both directories, you might want to increase the number of messages processed per minute, providing that the server can handle the additional workload.

You assign the desired processing rate using the –PickupDirectoryMaxMessages-PerMinute parameter of the Set-TransportServer cmdlet, as shown in Sample 12-25, and this processing speed is used with both the Pickup and Replay directories. Your Transport server then attempts to process messages in each directory independently at the rate specified. You can use a per-minute message processing value between 1 and 20,000.

SAMPLE 12-25 Changing the message processing speed

Syntax

```
Set-TransportServer -Identity ServerIdentity
[-PickupDirectoryMaxMessagesPerMinute Speed]
```

Usage

```
Set-TransportServer -Identity "CorpSvr127"
-PickupDirectoryMaxMessagesPerMinute "500"
```

Configuring Messaging Limits for the Pickup Directory

You can set messaging limits for the Pickup directory for message header sizes and maximum recipients per message. The default message header size is 64 KB. To change this setting, you can set the –PickupDirectoryMaxHeaderSize parameter of the Set-TransportServer cmdlet to the desired size. The valid input range for this parameter is 32,768 to 2,147,483,647 bytes. When you specify a value, you must qualify the units for that value by ending with one of the following suffixes:

- B for bytes
- KB for kilobytes
- MB for megabytes
- GB for gigabytes

The following example sets the maximum header size to 256 KB:

```
Set-TransportServer -Identity MailServer48
-PickupDirectoryMaxHeaderSize "256KB"
```

The default maximum recipients per message is 100. To change this setting, you can set the –PickupDirectoryMaxRecipientsPerMessage parameter of the Set-TransportServer cmdlet to the desired size. The valid input range for this parameter is 1 to 10,000. The following example sets the maximum recipients to 500:

```
Set-TransportServer -Identity MailServer48
-PickupDirectoryMaxRecipientsPerMessage "500"
```

Configuring Message Throttling

Message throttling sets limits on the number of messages and connections that can be processed by a Hub or an Edge Transport server. These limits are designed to prevent the accidental or intentional inundation of transport servers and help ensure that transport servers can process messages and connections in an orderly and timely manner. Throttling works in conjunction with size limits on messages that apply to header sizes, attachment sizes, and number of recipients.

On Hub and Edge Transport servers, you can set some message throttling options in the Exchange Management Console. You do this by using the options on the Limits tab in the transport server's Properties dialog box. In the Exchange Management Shell, you can configure all message throttling options by using Set-TransportServer and related parameters.

- **MaxConcurrentMailboxDeliveries**   Sets the maximum number of delivery threads that can be open at the same time to deliver messages to mailboxes. The default value is 30.

- **MaxConcurrentMailboxSubmissions**   Sets the maximum number of delivery threads that can be open at the same time to accept messages from mailboxes. The default value is 30.

- **MaxConnectionRatePerMinute**   Sets the maximum rate at which new inbound connections can be opened to any Receive connectors that exist on the server. The default value is 1,200 connections per minute.

- **MaxOutboundConnections**   Sets the maximum number of concurrent outbound connections that can be open at the same time for Send connectors. The default value is 1,000.

- **MaxPerDomainOutboundConnections**   Sets the maximum number of connections that can be open to any single remote domain for any available Send connectors. The default value is 20.

With Set-SendConnector, you can configure throttling by using Connection-InactivityTimeOut. This parameter sets the maximum idle time before an open SMTP connection is closed. The default value is 10 minutes.

With Set-ReceiveConnector, you can configure throttling using the following parameters:

- **ConnectionInactivityTimeOut**   Sets the maximum idle time before an open SMTP connection is closed. The default value is 5 minutes for a Hub Transport and 1 minute for an Edge Transport.

- **ConnectionTimeOut**   Sets the maximum time that an SMTP connection can remain open, even if it is active. The default value is 10 minutes for a Hub Transport and 5 minute for an Edge Transport. ConnectionTimeout must be longer than ConnectionInactivityTimeout.

- **MaxInboundConnection**   Sets the maximum number of simultaneous inbound SMTP connections. The default value is 5,000.

- **MaxInboundConnectionPercentagePerSource**   Sets the maximum number of simultaneous inbound SMTP connections from a single source server. The value is expressed as the percentage of available remaining connections on a Receive connector (as defined by the –MaxInboundConnection parameter). The default value is 2 percent.

- **MaxInboundConnectionPerSource**   Sets the maximum number of simultaneous inbound SMTP connections from a single source messaging server. The default value is 100.

- **MaxProtocolErrors**   Sets the maximum number of SMTP protocol errors allowed before a Receive connector closes a connection with a source messaging server. The default value is 5.

- **TarpitInterval**   Sets artificial delay in SMTP responses where unwelcome messages are being received from anonymous connections. The default value is 5 seconds.

Understanding Back Pressure

Back pressure limits overutilization of system resource on a Hub Transport or an Edge Transport server. Transport servers monitor key system resources to determine usage levels. If usage levels exceed a specified limit, the server stops accepting new connections and messages. This prevents server resources from being completely overwhelmed and enables the server to deliver the existing messages. When usage of system resources returns to a normal level, the server accepts new connections and messages. Resources monitored as part of the back pressure feature include:

- Free space on hard disk drives that store the message queue database transaction logs.

- Free space on the hard disk drives that store the message queue database.

- The amount of memory used by all processes.

- The amount of memory used by the Edgetransport.exe process.

- The number of uncommitted message queue database transactions that exist in memory.

Levels of usage are defined as normal, medium, or high. With the normal level, the resource is not overused, and the server accepts new connections and messages. With the medium level, the resource is slightly overused, and limited back pressure is applied, allowing mail from senders in the authoritative domain to continue being sent while the server rejects new connections and messages from other sources. With the high level, the resource is severely overused and full back pressure is applied, meaning message flow stops and the server rejects all new connections and messages.

You have limited control over how back pressure is applied. Some related settings can be configured in the Edgetransport.exe.config file on Edge Transport servers. However, Microsoft recommends that you don't change the default settings.

Creating and Managing Accepted Domains

An accepted domain is any SMTP namespace for which an Exchange organization sends or receives e-mail. Accepted domains include domains for which the Exchange organization is authoritative, as well as domains for which the Exchange organization relays mail.

Understanding Accepted Domains, Authoritative Domains, and Relay Domains

An organization can have more than one SMTP domain. The set of e-mail domains your organization uses are its authoritative domains. An accepted domain is considered authoritative when the Exchange organization hosts mailboxes for recipients in this SMTP domain. Transport servers should always accept e-mail that is addressed to any of the organization's authoritative domains. By default, when you install the first Hub Transport server, one accepted domain is configured as authoritative for the Exchange organization, and this default accepted domain is based on the FQDN of your forest root domain.

In many cases, an organization's internal domain name might differ from its external domain name. You must create an accepted domain to match your external domain name. You must also create an e-mail address policy that assigns your external domain name to user e-mail addresses. For example, your internal domain name might be cpandl.local, while your external domain name is cpandl.com. When you configure DNS, the DNS MX records for your organization will reference cpandl.com, and you will want to assign this SMTP namespace to users by creating an e-mail address policy.

When e-mail is received from the Internet by a Transport server and the recipient of the message is not a part of your organization's authoritative domains, the sending server is trying to relay messages through your Transport servers. To prevent abuse of your servers, Transport servers reject all e-mail that is not addressed to a recipient in your organization's authoritative domains. However, at times you might need to relay e-mail from another domain, such as e-mail from a partner or subsidiary. In this case, you can configure accepted domains as relay domains. When your Transport servers receive the e-mail for a configured relay domain, they will relay the messages to an e-mail server in that domain.

You can configure a relay domain as an internal relay domain or as an external relay domain. You configure an internal relay domain when there are contacts from the relay domain in the global address list. If your organization contains more than one forest and has configured global address list synchronization, the SMTP domain for one forest can be configured as an internal relay domain in a second forest. Messages from the Internet that are addressed to recipients in internal relay domains are received and processed by your Edge Transport servers. They are then relayed to your Hub Transport servers, which, in turn, route the messages to the Hub Transport servers in the recipient forest. Configuring an SMTP domain as an internal relay domain ensures that all e-mail addressed to the relay domain is accepted by your Exchange organization.

You configure an external relay domain when you want to relay messages to an e-mail server that is both outside your Exchange organization and outside the boundaries of your organization's network perimeter. For this configuration to work, your DNS servers must have an MX record for the external relay domain that references a public IP address for the relaying Exchange organization. When your Edge Transport servers receive the messages for recipients in the external relay domain, they route the messages to the mail server for the external relay domain. You must also configure a Send connector from the Edge Transport server to the external relay domain. The external relay domain can also be using your organization's Edge Transport server as a smart host for outgoing mail.

Viewing Accepted Domains

You can view the accepted domains configured for your organization by completing the following steps:

1. In the Exchange Management Console, expand the Organization Configuration node, and then select the Hub Transport node.

2. On the Accepted Domains tab, accepted domains are listed by name, SMTP domain name, and domain type. The domain type is listed as Authoritative, External Relay, or Internal Relay as shown in Figure 12-15.

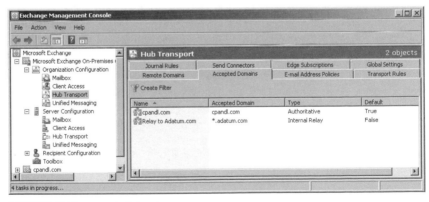

FIGURE 12-15 View accepted domains.

You can use the Get-AcceptedDomain cmdlet to list accepted domains or to get information on a particular accepted domain as well. If you do not provide an identity with this cmdlet, configuration information for all accepted domains is displayed. Sample 12-26 provides the syntax and usage, as well as sample output, for the Get-AcceptedDomain cmdlet.

SAMPLE 12-26 Get-AcceptedDomain cmdlet syntax and usage

Syntax

```
Get-AcceptedDomain [-Identity DomainIdentity]
[-DomainController DCName] [-Organization OrganizationId]
```

Usage

```
Get-AcceptedDomain -Identity "cpandl.com"
```

Output

Name	DomainName	DomainType	Default
cpandl	cpandl.com	Authoritative	True
cohowinery	*.cohowinery.com	ExternalRelay	False

Creating Accepted Domains

You can create accepted domains for your organization by completing the following steps:

1. In the Exchange Management Console, expand the Organization Configuration node, and select the Hub Transport node.

2. On the Accepted Domains tab, right-click an open area of the details pane, and then select New Accepted Domain. This starts the New Accepted Domain Wizard, as shown in Figure 12-16.

3. On the New Accepted Domain page, use the Name text box to identify the accepted domain. You can use a descriptive name that identifies the purpose of the accepted domain or simply enter the actual SMTP domain name.

4. In the Accepted Domain text box, type the SMTP domain name for which the Exchange organization will accept e-mail messages. If you want to accept e-mail for the specified domain only, enter the full domain name, such as **adatum.com.** If you want to accept e-mail for the specified domain and child domains, type * (a wildcard character), then a period, and then the domain name, such as ***.adatum.com.**

    NOTE Only domain names you specify can be used as part of an e-mail address policy. Because of this, if you want to use a subdomain as part of an e-mail address policy, you must either explicitly configure the subdomain as an accepted domain or use a wildcard character to include the parent domain and all related subdomains.

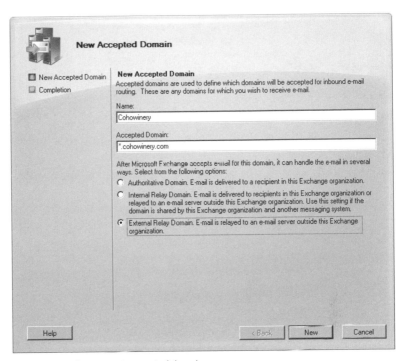

FIGURE 12-16 Create a new accepted domain.

5. Select one of the following options to set the accepted domain type:

   - **Authoritative Domain**   E-Mail Is Delivered To A Recipient In This Exchange Organization
   - **Internal Relay Domain**   E-Mail Is Relayed To An E-Mail Server In Another Active Directory Forest In The Organization
   - **External Relay Domain**   E-Mail Is Relayed To An E-Mail Server Outside The Organization By The Edge Transport Server

6. Click New to create the accepted domain.

7. On the Completion page, click Finish.

In the Exchange Management Shell, you can use the New-AcceptedDomain cmdlet to create accepted domains. Sample 12-27 provides the syntax and usage.

SAMPLE 12-27 New-AcceptedDomain cmdlet syntax and usage

Syntax

```
New-AcceptedDomain -Name Name
 -DomainName DomainName
 -DomainType <Authoritative|InternalRelay|ExternalRelay>
[-Organization OrganizationId]
```

```
new-AcceptedDomain -Name "Relay to Cohowinery.com"
-DomainName "*.cohowinery.com"
-DomainType "ExternalRelay"
```

Changing the Accepted Domain Type and Identifier

You can change an accepted domain's type and identifier by completing the follow-ing steps:

1. In the Exchange Management Console, expand the Organization Configura-tion node, and select the Hub Transport node.

2. On the Accepted Domains tab, right-click the accepted domain you want to change, and then select Properties.

3. In the Properties dialog box, shown in Figure 12-17, enter a new identifier, use the options provided to change the accepted domain type as necessary, and then click OK.

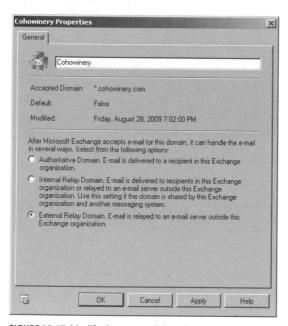

FIGURE 12-17 Modify the accepted domain.

In the Exchange Management Shell, you can use the Set-AcceptedDomain cmdlet to modify accepted domains. Sample 12-28 provides the syntax and usage. Use the –AddressBookEnabled parameter to enable recipient filtering for this accepted domain. You should set this parameter to $true only if all the recipients in this accepted domain are replicated to the AD LDS database on the Edge Transport servers. For authoritative domains and internal relay domains, the default value is $true. For external relay domains, the default value is $false.

SAMPLE 12-28 Set-AcceptedDomain cmdlet syntax and usage

Syntax

```
Set-AcceptedDomain -Identity AcceptedDomainIdentity
[-AddressBookEnabled <$true | $false>] [-DomainController DCName]
[-DomainType <Authoritative|InternalRelay|ExternalRelay>]
[-MakeDefault <$true | $false>] [-Name Name]
```

Usage

```
Set-AcceptedDomain -Identity "Relay to Cohowinery.com"
-DomainType "ExternalRelay"
```

Removing Accepted Domains

You can remove an accepted domain that is no longer needed by completing the following steps:

1. In the Exchange Management Console, expand the Organization Configuration node, and select the Hub Transport node.
2. On the Accepted Domains tab, right-click the accepted domain you want to remove, and then select Remove.
3. When prompted to confirm, click Yes.

In the Exchange Management Shell, you can use the Remove-AcceptedDomain cmdlet to remove accepted domains. Sample 12-29 provides the syntax and usage.

SAMPLE 12-29 Remove-AcceptedDomain cmdlet syntax and usage

Syntax

```
Remove-AcceptedDomain -Identity AcceptedDomainIdentity
[-DomainController DCName]
```

Usage

```
Remove-AcceptedDomain -Identity "Relay to Cohowinery.com"
```

Creating and Managing E-Mail Address Policies

E-mail address policies allow you to generate or rewrite e-mail addresses automatically for each recipient in your organization based on specific criteria you set. Exchange Server uses e-mail address policies in two key ways:

- Whenever you create a new recipient, Exchange Server sets the recipient's default e-mail address based on the applicable e-mail address policy.

- Whenever you apply an e-mail address policy, Exchange Server automatically rewrites the e-mail addresses for recipients to which the policy applies.

Every Exchange organization has a default e-mail address policy, which is required to create e-mail addresses for recipients. You can create additional e-mail address policies as well—for example, if your organization's internal domain name is different from its external domain name. You must create an accepted domain to match your external domain name and an e-mail address policy that assigns your external domain name to user e-mail addresses.

Viewing E-Mail Address Policies

You can view the e-mail address policies configured for your organization by completing the following steps:

1. In the Exchange Management Console, expand the Organization Configuration node, and then select the Hub Transport node.

2. On the E-Mail Address Policies tab, shown in Figure 12-18, e-mail address policies are listed by name, priority, last modified time, and applied status. The applied status is listed as True for a policy that has been applied to recipients and False for a policy that has not been applied to recipients.

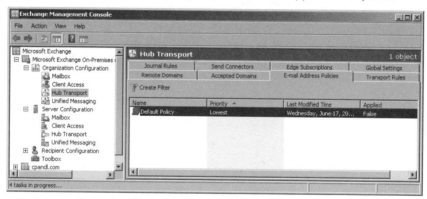

FIGURE 12-18 View the e-mail address policies.

You can use the Get-EmailAddressPolicy cmdlet to list e-mail address policies or to get information on a particular e-mail address policy. If you do not provide an identity with this cmdlet, configuration information for all e-mail address policies is displayed. Sample 12-30 provides the syntax and usage, as well as sample output, for the Get-EmailAddressPolicy cmdlet.

SAMPLE 12-30 Get-EmailAddressPolicy cmdlet syntax and usage

Syntax

```
Get-EmailAddressPolicy [-Identity PolicyIdentity]
[-DomainController DCName] [-IncludeMailboxSettingOnlyPolicy <$true |
$false>] [-Organization OrgId]
```

Usage

```
Get-EmailAddressPolicy

Get-EmailAddressPolicy -Identity "Default Policy"
```

Output

Name	Priority	RecipientFilter
----	--------	---------------
Default Policy	Lowest	Alias -ne $null
Cohowinery	1	Alias -ne $null

Creating E-Mail Address Policies

You can create e-mail address policies for your organization by completing the following steps:

1. In the Exchange Management Console, expand the Organization Configuration node, and select the Hub Transport node.

2. On the E-Mail Address Policies tab, right-click an open area of the details pane, and then select New E-Mail Address Policy. This starts the New E-Mail Address Policy Wizard, as shown in Figure 12-19.

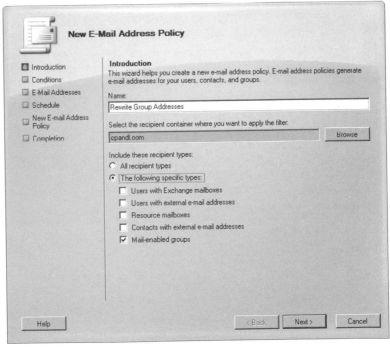

FIGURE 12-19 Create a new e-mail address policy.

3. On the Introduction page, use the Name text box to identify the e-mail address policy. You can use a descriptive name that identifies the purpose of the e-mail address policy or simply enter the actual SMTP domain name to which it applies.

4. Use the Include These Recipient Types options to specify the types of recipients to include in the policy. Select All Recipient Types, or select The Following Specific Types and then select the check boxes for the types of recipients to which you want to apply the policy.

5. Click Next. On the Conditions page, you can now set the filter conditions. The following types of conditions are available:

- **Recipient Is In A State Or Province** Filters recipients based on the value of the State/Province field on the Address And Phone tab in the related Properties dialog box. Click the related In The Specified State Or Province link. In the Specify State Or Province dialog box, type a state or province to use as a filter condition and then press Enter or click Add. Repeat as necessary, and then click OK.

- **Recipient Is In A Department** Filters recipients based on the value of the Department field on the Organization tab in the related Properties dialog box. Click the related In The Specified Department(s) link. In the Specify Department dialog box, type a department to use as a filter condition and then press Enter or click Add. Repeat as necessary, and then click OK.

- **Recipient Is In A Company** Filters recipients based on the value of the Company field on the Organization tab in the related Properties dialog box. Click the related In The Specified Company link. In the Specify Company dialog box, type a company name to use as a filter condition and then press Enter or click Add. Repeat as necessary, and then click OK.

6. Click Next. On the E-Mail Address page, click the small arrow to the right of Add, and then select SMTP Address. The SMTP E-Mail Address dialog box appears, as shown in Figure 12-20.

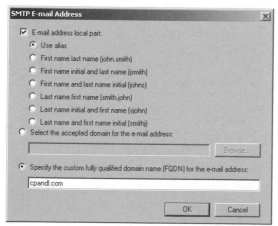

FIGURE 12-20 Select options to generate e-mail addresses.

7. Use the E-Mail Address Local Part options to specify how to generate or rewrite e-mail addresses automatically for each recipient to which the policy applies. You can use the Exchange alias or parts of the user name in various orders.

8. Use the Select The Accepted Domain For The E-Mail Address drop-down list to select the e-mail address domain, and then click OK.

9. Click Next. If you want to create and apply the policy immediately, select Immediately. To schedule the policy application, select At The Following Time, and then set the date and time to apply the policy.

10. Click Next, and then click New to create and apply the policy or schedule the policy to be applied. After the policy is applied, e-mail addresses for recipients to which the policy applies will be rewritten.

11. On the Completion page, click Finish.

In the Exchange Management Shell, you create and apply e-mail address policies using separate tasks. You can create e-mail address policies using the New-EmailAddressPolicy cmdlet. Once you create a policy, you apply it using the Update-EmailAddressPolicy cmdlet. Samples 12-31 and 12-32 provide the syntax and usage for these cmdlets.

NOTE Any time you receive an error regarding missing aliases, you should run the Update-EmailAddressPolicy cmdlet with the –FixMissingAlias parameter set to $true. This tells Exchange to generate an alias for recipients who do not have an alias.

SAMPLE 12-31 New-EmailAddressPolicy cmdlet syntax and usage

Syntax

```
New-EmailAddressPolicy -Name PolicyName
-EnabledPrimarySMTPAddressTemplate Template
-IncludedRecipients RecipientTypes {AddtlParams} {ConditionalParams}

New-EmailAddressPolicy -Name PolicyName
-EnabledEmailAddressTemplates Templates -RecipientFilter Filter
[-DisabledEmailAddressTemplates Templates] {AddtlParams}

New-EmailAddressPolicy -Name PolicyName
-EnabledPrimarySMTPAddressTemplate Template
-RecipientFilter Filter {AddtlParams}

New-EmailAddressPolicy -Name PolicyName
-EnabledEmailAddressTemplates Templates
-IncludedRecipients RecipientTypes
[-DisabledEmailAddressTemplates Templates]
{AddtlParams} {ConditionalParams}

{AddtlParams}
[-DomainController DCName] [-Organization OrgId]
[-Priority Priority] [-RecipientContainer OUId]
```

```
{ConditionalParams}
[-ConditionalCompany CompanyNameFilter1, CompanyNameFilter2,... ]
[-ConditionalCustomAttributeN Value1, Value2, ...]
[-ConditionalDepartment DeptNameFilter1, DeptNameFilter2, ... ]
[-ConditionalStateOrProvince StateNameFilter1, StateNameFilter2, ... ]
```

Usage

```
New-EmailAddressPolicy -Name "Primary E-Mail Address Policy"
-IncludedRecipients "MailboxUsers, MailContacts, MailGroups"
 -ConditionalCompany "City Power & Light"
 -ConditionalDepartment "Sales","Marketing"
 -ConditionalStateOrProvince "Washington","Idaho","Oregon"
 -Priority "Lowest"
 -EnabledEmailAddressTemplates "SMTP:%g.%s@cpandl.com"
```

SAMPLE 12-32 Update-EmailAddressPolicy cmdlet syntax and usage

Syntax

```
Update-EmailAddressPolicy -Identity PolicyIdentity
[-DomainController DCName] [-FixMissingAlias <$true | $false>]
```

Usage

```
Update-EmailAddressPolicy -Identity "Primary E-Mail Address Policy"

Update-EmailAddressPolicy -Identity "Primary E-Mail Address Policy"
 -FixMissingAlias
```

Editing and Applying E-Mail Address Policies

You can manage e-mail address policies in several different ways. You can edit their properties or apply them to rewrite e-mail addresses automatically for each recipient to which the policy applies. You can also change their priority to determine the precedence order for application in case there are conflicts between policies. When multiple policies apply to a recipient, the policy with the highest priority is the one that applies.

You can change the way e-mail address policies work by completing the following steps:

1. In the Exchange Management Console, expand the Organization Configuration node, and select the Hub Transport node.

2. On the E-Mail Address Policies tab, right-click the e-mail address policy you want to change, and then select Edit. This starts the Edit E-Mail Address Policy Wizard.

3. Follow steps 3–11 in the "Creating E-Mail Address Policies" section.

You can change the priority of an e-mail address policy by completing the following steps:

1. In the Exchange Management Console, right-click the policy, and then select Change Priority.

2. In the Change E-Mail Address Policy Priority dialog box, type the desired priority and then click OK.

NOTE The valid range for priorities depends on the number of policies you've configured.

You can apply an e-mail address policy immediately or at a scheduled time by completing the following steps:

1. In the Exchange Management Console, right-click the policy, and then select Apply. This starts the Apply E-Mail Address Policy Wizard.

2. If you want to create and apply the policy immediately, select Immediately. To schedule the policy application, select At The Following Time and then set the date and time to apply the policy.

3. Click Next, and then click Apply.

4. On the Completion page, click Finish.

In the Exchange Management Shell, you can use the Set-EmailAddressPolicy cmdlet to modify e-mail address policies, as shown in Sample 12-33. The Update-EmailAddressPolicy cmdlet, used to apply policies, was discussed previously.

SAMPLE 12-33 Set-EmailAddressPolicy cmdlet syntax and usage

Syntax

```
Set-EmailAddressPolicy -Identity PolicyIdentity
[-ConditionalCompany CompanyNameFilter1, CompanyNameFilter2,... ]
[-ConditionalCustomAttributeN Value1, Value2, ...]
[-ConditionalDepartment DeptNameFilter1, DeptNameFilter2, ... ]
[-ConditionalStateOrProvince StateNameFilter1, StateNameFilter2, ... ]
[-DisbledEmailAddressTemplates Templates] [-DomainController DCName]
[-EnabledEmailAddressTemplates Templates]
[-EnabledPrimarySMTPAddressTemplate Template]
[-ForceUpgrade <$true | $false>] [-IncludedRecipients RecipientTypes]
[-Name PolicyName] [-Priority Priority]
[-RecipientContainer OUId] [-RecipientFilter Filter]
```

Usage

```
Set-EmailAddressPolicy  -Identity "Primary E-Mail Address Policy"
 -Name "Cpandl.com E-Mail Address Policy"
 -IncludedRecipients "MailboxUsers"
 -ConditionalCompany "City Power & Light"
 -ConditionalDepartment "Sales"
 -ConditionalStateOrProvince "Washington"
 -Priority "2"
 -EnabledEmailAddressTemplates "SMTP:%g.%s@cpandl.com"
```

Removing E-Mail Address Policies

You can remove an e-mail address policy that is no longer needed by completing the following steps:

1. In the Exchange Management Console, expand the Organization Configuration node, and select the Hub Transport node.

2. On the E-Mail Address Policies tab, right-click the e-mail address policy you want to remove, and then select Remove.

3. When prompted to confirm, click Yes.

In the Exchange Management Shell, you can use the Remove-EmailAddressPolicy cmdlet to remove e-mail address policies. Sample 12-34 provides the syntax and usage.

SAMPLE 12-34 Remove-EmailAddressPolicy cmdlet syntax and usage

Syntax

```
Remove-EmailAddressPolicy -Identity EmailAddressPolicyIdentity
[-DomainController DCName]
```

Usage

```
Remove-EmailAddressPolicy -Identity "Cpandl.com
E-Mail Address Policy"
```

Creating and Managing Remote Domains

Remote domain settings help you manage mail flow for most types of automated messages, including out-of-office messages, automatic replies, automatic forwarding, delivery reports, and nondelivery reports. Remote domain settings also control some automated message-formatting options, such as whether to display a sender's name on a message or only the sender's e-mail address. Your Exchange organization has a default remote domain policy that sets the global defaults. You can create additional policies to create managed connections for specific remote domains as well.

Viewing Remote Domains

You can view the remote domains configured for your organization by completing the following steps:

1. In the Exchange Management Console, expand the Organization Configuration node, and then select the Hub Transport node.

2. On the Remote Domains tab, shown in Figure 12-21, remote domains are listed by name and the domain to which they apply. The Default remote domain applies to all remote domains, unless you override it with specific settings.

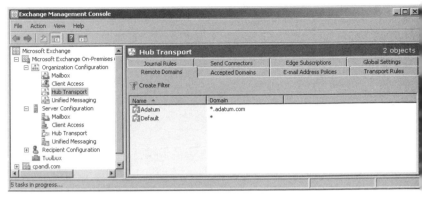

FIGURE 12-21 View remote domains.

You can use the Get-RemoteDomain cmdlet to list remote domains or to get information on a particular remote domain. If you do not provide an identity with this cmdlet, configuration information for all remote domains is displayed. Sample 12-35 provides the syntax and usage, as well as sample output, for the Get-RemoteDomain cmdlet.

SAMPLE 12-35 Get-RemoteDomain cmdlet syntax and usage

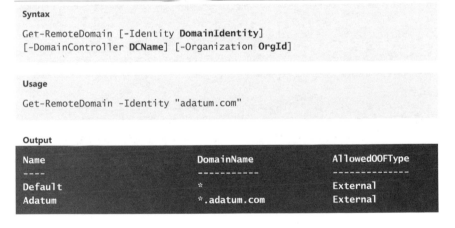

Syntax

```
Get-RemoteDomain [-Identity DomainIdentity]
[-DomainController DCName] [-Organization OrgId]
```

Usage

```
Get-RemoteDomain -Identity "adatum.com"
```

Output

Name	DomainName	AllowedOOFType
Default	*	External
Adatum	*.adatum.com	External

Creating Remote Domains

You can create remote domains for your organization by completing the following steps:

1. In the Exchange Management Console, expand the Organization Configuration node, and select the Hub Transport node.

2. On the Remote Domains tab, right-click an open area of the details pane, and then select New Remote Domain. This starts the New Remote Domain Wizard, as shown in Figure 12-22.

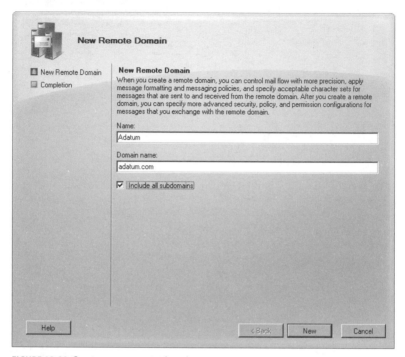

FIGURE 12-22 Create a new remote domain.

3. On the New Remote Domain page, use the Name text box to identify the remote domain. You can use a descriptive name that identifies the purpose of the remote domain or simply enter the actual SMTP domain name.

4. In the Domain Name text box, type the SMTP domain name for which you want to manage connections. If you want to manage connections for the specified domain and its child domains, select the Include All Subdomains check box.

5. Click New to create the remote domain.

6. On the Completion page, click Finish.

In the Exchange Management Shell, you can use the New-RemoteDomain cmdlet to create remote domains. Sample 12-36 provides the syntax and usage. The way you set the –DomainName parameter determines whether the remote domain includes subdomains. You insert an asterisk and a period before the domain name to include child domains.

Syntax

```
New-RemoteDomain -Name Name  -DomainName DomainName
[-DomainController DCName] [-Organization OrgId]
```

Usage for parent domain only

```
New-RemoteDomain -Name "Cohowinery Managed Connection"
 -DomainName "cohowinery.com"
```

Usage for parent domain and child domains

```
New-RemoteDomain -Name "Cohowinery Managed Connection"
 -DomainName "*.cohowinery.com"
```

Configuring Messaging Options for Remote Domains

Remote domains are used to control how automated messages are used and to specify some types of messaging format options. To change the default configuration for a remote domain, follow these steps:

1. In the Exchange Management Console, expand the Organization Configuration node, and select the Hub Transport node.

2. On the Remote Domains tab, right-click the remote domain you want to change, and then select Properties.

3. On the General tab, specify whether and how out-of-office messages are sent to the remote domain. The options are

   - **Allow None** Blocks all out-of-office messages.

   - **Allow External Out-Of-Office Messages Only** Allows out-of-office messages to be received by the Exchange organization, but does not allow the organization's out-of-office messages to be sent

   - **Allow External Out-Of-Office Messages And Legacy Out-Of-Office Messages** Allows out-of-office messages to be received by the Exchange organization and receipt of out-of-office messages generated by Microsoft Outlook 2003, Exchange 2003, or earlier

   - **Allow Internal Out-Of-Office Messages And Legacy Out-Of-Office Messages** Allows out-of-office messages to be sent from the Exchange organization and the sending of out-of-office messages generated by Outlook 2003, Exchange 2003, or earlier

4. On the Message Format tab, specify how Exchange should format messages. Allow messaging options by selecting the related check boxes, or disallow messaging options by clearing the related check boxes. The options available are

   - **Allow Automatic Replies** Allows the sender to be notified that the message was received

- **Allow Automatic Forward**   Allows Exchange Server to forward or deliver a duplicate message to a new recipient
- **Allow Delivery Reports**   Allows Exchange Server to return delivery confirmation reports to the sender
- **Allow Non-Delivery Reports**   Allows Exchange Server to return nondelivery confirmation reports to the sender
- **Display Sender's Name On Messages**   Allows both the sender's name and e-mail address to appear on outbound e-mail messages

5. By default, text word-wrapping is disabled, which means that Exchange enforces no maximum line length. If you'd like message text to wrap at a specific line length, you can enable text word-wrapping at a specific column position, such as 72 characters. Select the Use Message Text Line Wrap At Column check box, and then enter the column position for text line wrap.

6. If you want to send Transport Neutral Encapsulation Format (TNEF) message data to the remote domain rather than Exchange Rich-Text format, select Never Use under Exchange Rich-Text Format.

7. To set a specific MIME and non-MIME character set, enter the character set code in the text boxes provided. Click OK to save your settings.

In the Exchange Management Shell, you can use the Set-RemoteDomain cmdlet to configure remote domains. Sample 12-37 provides the syntax and usage.

SAMPLE 12-37 Set-RemoteDomain cmdlet syntax and usage

Syntax

```
Set-RemoteDomain -Identity "RemoteDomainIdentity"
[-AllowedOOFType <"External"|"InternalLegacy"|"ExternalLegacy"|"None">]
[-AutoForwardEnabled <$true | $false>]
[-AutoReplyEnabled <$true | $false>]
[-CharacterSet "CharacterSet"]
[-ContentType <"MimeHtmlText"|"MimeText"|"MimeHtml">]
[-DeliveryReportEnabled <$true | $false>]
[-DisplaySenderName <$true | $false>]
[-DomainController DCName]
[-LineWrapSize "Size"]
[-MeetingForwardNotificationEnabled <$true | $false>]
[-Name "Name"]
[-NDREnabled <$true | $false>]
[-NonMimeCharacterSet "CharacterSet"]
[-TNEFEnabled <$true | $false>]
```

Usage

```
Set-RemoteDomain -Identity "Cohowinery"
 -DeliveryReportEnabled $false
```

Removing Remote Domains

You can remove a remote domain that is no longer needed by completing the following steps:

1. In the Exchange Management Console, expand the Organization Configuration node, and select the Hub Transport node.

2. On the Remote Domains tab, right-click the remote domain you want to remove, and then select Remove.

3. When prompted to confirm, click Yes.

In the Exchange Management Shell, you can use the Remove-RemoteDomain cmdlet to remove remote domains. Sample 12-38 provides the syntax and usage.

SAMPLE 12-38 Remove-RemoteDomain cmdlet syntax and usage

Syntax

```
Remove-RemoteDomain -Identity RemoteDomainIdentity
[-DomainController DCName]
```

Usage

```
Remove-RemoteDomain -Identity "Cohowinery"
```

Configuring Anti-Spam and Message Filtering Options

Every minute users spend dealing with unsolicited commercial e-mail (spam) or other unwanted e-mail is a minute they cannot do their work and deal with other issues. To try to deter spammers and other senders from whom users don't want to receive messages, you can use message filtering to block these people from sending messages to your organization. Not only can you filter messages that claim to be from a particular sender or that are sent to a particular receiver, you can also establish connection filtering rules based on IP block lists. The sections that follow discuss these and other anti-spam options.

As you configure message filtering, keep in mind that while Exchange Server 2010 is designed to combat most spammer techniques, no system can block all of them. Like the techniques of those who create viruses, the techniques of those who send spam frequently change, and you won't be able to prevent all unwanted e-mail from going through. You should, however, be able to substantially reduce the flow of spam into your organization.

Filtering Spam and Other Unwanted E-Mail by Sender

Sometimes, when you are filtering spam or other unwanted e-mail, you'll know specific e-mail addresses or e-mail domains from which you don't want to accept messages. In this case, you can block messages from these senders or e-mail domains by configuring sender filtering. Another sender from which you probably don't want to accept messages is a blank sender. If the sender is blank, it means the From field of the e-mail message wasn't filled in and the message is probably from a spammer.

Sender filtering is enabled by default. To configure filtering according to the sender of the message, follow these steps:

1. Start the Exchange Management Console. On an Edge Transport server, select Edge Transport, click the server you want to work with, and then click the Anti-Spam tab in the details pane. On a Hub Transport server for which you've enabled spam filtering, expand the Organization Configuration node, select Hub Transport, and then click the Anti-Spam tab in the details pane.

2. Right-click Sender Filtering, and then select Properties. The Sender Filtering Properties dialog box appears.

3. On the Blocked Senders tab (shown in Figure 12-23), the Senders list box shows the current sender filters, if any.

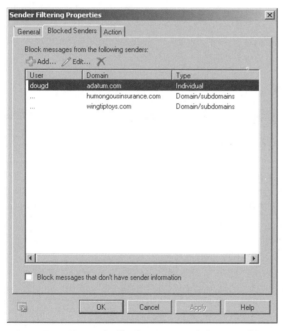

FIGURE 12-23 Use sender filtering to set restrictions on addresses and domains that can send mail to your organization.

4. You can add a sender filter by clicking Add. In the Add Blocked Senders dialog box, select Individual E-mail Address if the filter is for a specific e-mail address, or select Domain if you want to filter all e-mail sent from a particular

domain. Type the e-mail address or domain name, as appropriate, and then click OK.

5. You can remove a filter by selecting it and then clicking Remove.

6. To edit a filter, double-click the filter entry, enter a new value, and then click OK.

7. On the Blocked Senders tab, you can also filter messages that don't have an e-mail address in the From field. To do this, select the Block Messages That Don't Have Sender Information check box.

8. On the Action tab, specify how messages from blocked senders are to be handled. If you want to ensure that Exchange doesn't waste processing power and other resources dealing with messages from filtered senders, select the Reject Message option. If you want to mark messages as being from a blocked sender and continue processing them, select Stamp Message With Blocked Sender And Continue Processing. Click OK.

Filtering Spam and Other Unwanted E-Mail by Recipient

In any organization, you'll have users whose e-mail addresses change, perhaps because they request it, leave the company, or change office locations. Although you might be able to forward e-mail to these users for a time, you probably won't want to forward e-mail indefinitely. At some point, you, or someone else in the organization, will decide it's time to delete the user's account, mailbox, or both. If the user is subscribed to mailing lists or other services that deliver automated e-mail, the automated messages continue to come in, unless you manually unsubscribe the user or reply to each e-mail that you don't want to receive the messages. That's a measure that wastes time, but Exchange administrators often find themselves doing this. It's much easier to add the old or invalid e-mail address to a recipient filter list and specify that Exchange shouldn't accept messages for users who aren't in the Exchange directory. Once you do this, Exchange won't attempt to deliver messages for filtered or invalid recipients, and you won't see related nondelivery reports (NDRs), either.

Recipient filtering is enabled by default. To configure filtering according to the message recipient, follow these steps:

1. Start the Exchange Management Console. On an Edge Transport server, select Edge Transport, click the server you want to work with and then click the Anti-Spam tab in the details pane. On a Hub Transport server for which you've enabled spam filtering, expand the Organization Configuration node, select Hub Transport, and then click the Anti-Spam tab in the details pane.

2. Right-click Recipient Filtering, and then select Properties. The Recipient Filtering Properties dialog box appears.

3. On the Blocked Recipients tab (shown in Figure 12-24), the Recipients list box shows the current recipient filters, if any.

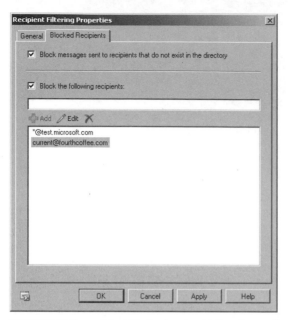

FIGURE 12-24 Use recipient filtering to set restrictions for specific or invalid recipients.

4. You can filter messages that are sent to recipients who don't have e-mail addresses and aren't listed as recipients in your Exchange organization. To do this, select the Block Messages Sent To Recipients That Do Not Exist In The Directory check box.

5. Before you can add other recipient filters, you must select the Block Messages Sent To The Following Recipients check box. You can then add a recipient filter by typing the address you'd like to filter and then clicking Add. Addresses can refer to a specific e-mail address, such as walter@blueyonderairlines.com, or a group of e-mail addresses designated with the wildcard character (*), such as *@blueyonderairlines.com to filter all e-mail addresses from blueyonderairlines.com, or *@*.blueyonderairlines.com, to filter all e-mail addresses from child domains of blueyonderairlines.com.

6. You can remove a filter by selecting it and then clicking Remove.

7. To edit a filter, double-click the filter entry, enter a new value, and then press Enter. Click OK.

Filtering Connections with IP Block Lists

If you find that sender and recipient filtering isn't enough to stem the flow of spam into your organization, you might want to consider subscribing to an IP block list service. Here's how this works:

- You subscribe to an IP block list service. Although there are free services available, you might have to pay a monthly service fee. In return, the service lets you query its servers for known sources of unsolicited e-mail and known relay servers.

- The service provides you with domains you can use for validation and a list of status codes to watch for. You configure Exchange to use the specified domains and enter connection filtering rules to match the return codes. Then you configure any exceptions for recipient e-mail addresses or sender IP addresses.

- Each time an incoming connection is made, Exchange performs a lookup of the source IP address in the block list domain. A "host not found" error is returned to indicate the IP address is not on the block list and that there is no match. If there is a match, the block list service returns a status code that indicates the suspected activity. For example, a status code of 127.0.0.3 might mean that the IP address is from a known source of unsolicited e-mail.

- If there is a match between the status code returned and the filtering rules you've configured, Exchange returns an error message to the user or server attempting to make the connection. The default error message says that the IP address has been blocked by a connection filter rule, but you can specify a custom error message to return instead.

The sections that follow discuss applying IP block lists, setting provider priority, defining custom error messages to return, and configuring block list exceptions. These are all tasks you'll perform when you work with IP block lists.

Applying IP Block Lists

Before you get started, you need to know the domain of the block list service provider, and you should also consider how you want to handle the status codes the provider returns. Exchange allows you to specify that any return status code is a match, that only a specific code matched to a bit mask is a match, or that any of several status codes that you designate can match.

Table 12-1 shows a list of typical status codes that might be returned by a provider service. Rather than filter all return codes, in most cases, you'll want to be as specific as possible about the types of status codes that match. This ensures that you don't accidentally filter valid e-mail. For example, based on the list of status codes of the provider, you might decide that you want to filter known sources of unsolicited e-mail and known relay servers but not filter known sources of dial-up user accounts, which might or might not be sources of unsolicited e-mail.

TABLE 12-1 Typical Status Codes Returned by Block List Provider Services

RETURN STATUS CODE	CODE DESCRIPTION	CODE BIT MASK
127.0.0.1	Trusted nonspam (on the "white" list)	0.0.0.1
127.0.0.2	Known source of unsolicited e-mail/spam (on the "black" list)	0.0.0.2

RETURN STATUS CODE	CODE DESCRIPTION	CODE BIT MASK
127.0.0.3	Possible spam, like a mix of spam and nonspam (on the "yellow" list)	0.0.0.3
127.0.0.4	Known source of unsolicited e-mail/spam, but not yet blocked (on the "brown" list)	0.0.0.4
127.0.0.5	Not a spam-only source, and not on the "black" list	0.0.0.5

You can filter connections using IP block lists by completing the following steps:

1. Start the Exchange Management Console. On an Edge Transport server, select Edge Transport, click the server you want to work with and then click the Anti-Spam tab in the details pane. On a Hub Transport server for which you've enabled spam filtering, expand the Organization Configuration node, select Hub Transport, and then click the Anti-Spam tab in the details pane.

2. Right-click IP Block List Providers, and then select Properties. The IP Block List Providers Properties dialog box appears.

3. Click the Providers tab. The Block List Providers list box shows the current Block List providers, if any.

4. Click Add to add a Block List provider. The Add IP Block List Provider dialog box appears, shown in Figure 12-25.

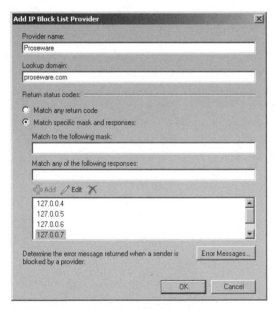

FIGURE 12-25 Configure the Block List provider.

5. Type the name of the provider in the Provider Name text box.

6. In the Lookup Domain text box, type the domain name of the block list provider service, such as proseware.com.

7. Under Return Status Codes, select Match Any Return Code to match any return code (other than an error) received from the provider service or select one or more of the following options:

   - **Match Specific Mask And Responses** Select this option to match a specific mask and return codes from the provider service.

   - **Match To The Following Mask** Select this option to match a specific return code from the provider service. For example, if the return code for a known relay server is 127.0.0.4 and you want to match this specific code, you type the mask 0.0.0.4.

   - **Match Any Of The Following Responses** Select this option to match specific values in the return status codes. Type a return status code to match, and then click Add. Repeat as necessary for each return code that you want to add.

8. Click OK to start using IP block lists from the block list provider.

Setting Priority and Enabling Block List Providers

You can configure multiple block list providers. Each provider is listed in priority order, and if Exchange makes a match using a particular provider, the other providers are not checked for possible matches. In addition to being prioritized, providers can also be enabled or disabled. If you disable a provider, it is ignored when looking for possible status code matches.

You can set block list provider priority and enable or disable providers by completing the following steps:

1. Start the Exchange Management Console. On an Edge Transport server, select Edge Transport, click the server you want to work with and then click the Anti-Spam tab in the details pane. On a Hub Transport server for which you've enabled spam filtering, expand the Organization Configuration node, select Hub Transport, and then click the Anti-Spam tab in the details pane.

2. Right-click IP Block List Providers, and then select Properties. The IP Block List Providers Properties dialog box appears.

3. Click the Providers tab. The Block List Providers list box shows the current block list providers in priority order.

4. To change the priority of a provider, select it and then click the Move Up or Move Down button to change its order in the list.

5. To disable a provider, select it and then click Disable.

6. To enable a provider, select it and then click Enable. Click OK to close the Properties dialog box.

Specifying Custom Error Messages to Return

When a match is made between the status code returned and the filtering rules you've configured for block list providers, Exchange returns an error message to the user or server attempting to make the connection. The default error message says that the IP address has been blocked by a connection filter rule. If you want to override the default error message, you can specify a custom error message to return on a per-rule basis. The error message can contain the following substitution values:

- %0 to insert the connecting IP address
- %1 to insert the name of the connection filter rule
- %2 to insert the domain name of the block list provider service

Some examples of custom error messages include the following:

- The IP address (%0) was blocked and not allowed to connect.
- %0 was rejected by %2 as a potential source of unsolicited e-mail.

Using the substitution values, you can create a custom error message for each block list provider by following these steps:

1. Start the Exchange Management Console. On an Edge Transport server, select Edge Transport, click the server you want to work with and then click the Anti-Spam tab in the details pane. On a Hub Transport server for which you've enabled spam filtering, expand the Organization Configuration node, select Hub Transport, and then click the Anti-Spam tab in the details pane.

2. Right-click IP Block List Providers, and then select Properties. The IP Block List Providers Properties dialog box appears.

3. On the Providers tab, the Block List Providers list box shows the current Block List providers in priority order. Select the block list provider for which you want to create a custom error message, and then click Edit.

4. In the Edit IP Block List Provider dialog box, click Error Messages.

5. In the IP Block List Provider Error Message dialog box, select Custom Error Message, and then type the error message to return. Click OK twice.

Defining Block List Exceptions and Global Allow/Block Lists

Sometimes, you'll find that an IP address, a network, or an e-mail address shows up incorrectly on a block list. The easiest way to correct this problem is to create a block list exception that indicates that the specific IP address, network, or e-mail address shouldn't be filtered.

Creating or Removing Connection Filter Exceptions for E-Mail Addresses

You can define connection filter exceptions for e-mail addresses by completing the following steps:

1. Start the Exchange Management Console. On an Edge Transport server, select Edge Transport, click the server you want to work with, and then click

the Anti-Spam tab in the details pane. On a Hub Transport server for which you've enabled spam filtering, expand the Organization Configuration node, select Hub Transport, and then click the Anti-Spam tab in the details pane.

2. Right-click IP Block List Providers, and then select Properties. The IP Block List Providers Properties dialog box appears.

3. On the Exceptions tab, any current exceptions are listed by e-mail address. Type the e-mail address to add as an exception, such as **abuse@adatum.com**, and then click Add.

4. To delete an exception, select an existing e-mail address and then click Remove.

5. Click OK to save your settings.

Creating or Removing Global Allowed Lists for IP Addresses and Networks

Exchange will accept e-mail from any IP address or network on the global allowed list. Before you can define allowed entries for IP addresses and networks you must be sure that the IP Allow List is enabled. To do this, complete the following steps:

1. Start the Exchange Management Console. On an Edge Transport server, select Edge Transport, click the server you want to work with, and then click the Anti-Spam tab in the details pane. On a Hub Transport server, expand the Organization Configuration node, select Hub Transport, and then click the Anti-Spam tab in the details pane.

2. Check the status of IP Allow List. If the feature is not enabled, right-click IP Allow List, and then select Enabled.

You use Add-IPAllowListEntry to add an IP address or IP address range to the IP Allow list configured on a Hub or an Edge Transport server. Sample 12-39 provides the syntax and usage.

SAMPLE 12-39 Add-IPAllowListEntry cmdlet syntax and usage

Syntax

```
Add-IPAllowListEntry -IPAddress IPAddress {AddtlParams}

Add-IPAllowListEntry -IPRange IPRange {AddtlParams}

{AddtlParams}
[-Comment Comment] [-ExpirationTime DateTime] [-Server ServerId]
```

Usage

```
Add-IPAllowListEntry -IPAddress 192.168.10.45

Add-IPAllowListEntry -IPRange 192.168.10.0/24
Add-IPAllowListEntry -IPRange 192.168.10.1-192.168.10.254
```

You use Get-IPAllowListEntry to list IP Allow List entries and Remove-IPAllow-ListEntry to remove IP Allow List entries. Samples 12-40 and 12-41 provide the syntax and usage.

SAMPLE 12-40 Get-IPAllowListEntry cmdlet syntax and usage

Syntax

```
Get-IPAllowListEntry [-Identity IPListEntryId] {AddtlParams}

Get-IPAllowListEntry -IPAddress IPAddress {AddtlParams}

{AddtlParams}
[-ResultSize Size] [-Server ServerId]
```

Usage

```
Get-IPAllowListEntry
Get-IPAllowListEntry -IPAddress 192.168.10.45
```

SAMPLE 12-41 Remove-IPAllowListEntry cmdlet syntax and usage

Syntax

```
Remove-IPAllowListEntry -Identity IPListEntryId
[-Server ServerId]
```

Usage

```
Get-IPAllowListEntry | Where {$_.IPRange -eq '192.168.10.45'} |
Remove-IPAllowListEntry

Get-IPAllowListEntry | Where {$_.IPRange -eq '192.168.10.0/24'} |
Remove-IPAllowListEntry
```

Creating or Removing Global Block Lists for IP Addresses and Networks

Exchange will reject e-mail from any IP address or network on the block list. Before you can define blocked entries for IP addresses and networks, you must ensure that the IP block list is enabled. To do this, complete the following steps:

1. Start the Exchange Management Console. On an Edge Transport server, select Edge Transport, click the server you want to work with, and then click the Anti-Spam tab in the details pane. On a Hub Transport server, expand the Organization Configuration node, select Hub Transport, and then click the Anti-Spam tab in the details pane.

2. Check the status of the IP block list. If the feature is not enabled, right-click IP Block List, and then click Enabled.

You use Add-IPBlockListEntry to add an IP address or IP address range to the IP block list configured on a Hub or an Edge Transport server. Sample 12-42 provides the syntax and usage.

SAMPLE 12-42 Add-IPBlockListEntry cmdlet syntax and usage

Syntax

```
Add-IPBlockListEntry -IPAddress IPAddress {AddtlParams}

Add-IPBlockListEntry -IPRange IPRange {AddtlParams}

{AddtlParams}
[-Comment Comment] [-ExpirationTime DateTime] [-Server ServerId]
```

Usage

```
Add-IPBlockListEntry -IPAddress 192.168.10.45

Add-IPBlockListEntry -IPRange 192.168.10.0/24
Add-IPBlockListEntry -IPRange 192.168.10.1-192.168.10.254
```

You use Get-IPBlockListEntry to list IP block list entries and Remove IPBlockList-Entry to remove IP block list entries. Samples 12-43 and 12-44 provide the syntax and usage.

SAMPLE 12-43 Get-IPBlockListEntry cmdlet syntax and usage

Syntax

```
Get-IPBlockListEntry [-Identity IPListEntryId] {AddtlParams}

Get-IPBlockListEntry -IPAddress IPAddress {AddtlParams}

{AddtlParams}
[-ResultSize Size] [-Server ServerId]
```

Usage

```
Get-IPBlockListEntry
Get-IPBlockListEntry -IPAddress 192.168.10.45
```

SAMPLE 12-44 Remove-IPBlockListEntry cmdlet syntax and usage

Syntax

```
Remove-IPBlockListEntry -Identity IPListEntryId
[-Server ServerId]
```

```
Get-IPBlockListEntry | Where {$_.IPRange -eq '192.168.10.45'} |
Remove-IPBlockListEntry

Get-IPBlockListEntry | Where {$_.IPRange -eq '192.168.10.0/24'} |
Remove-IPBlockListEntry
```

Preventing Internal Servers from Being Filtered

Typically, you don't want Exchange to apply Sender ID or connection filters to servers on your organization's network or to internal SMTP servers deployed in a perimeter zone. One way to ensure this is to configure message delivery options for your organization's transport servers so that they don't apply filters to IP addresses from internal servers and your perimeter network.

You can configure which IP addresses to ignore by completing the following steps:

1. In the Exchange Management Console, expand the Organization Configuration node, and then select the Hub Transport node.

2. In the main pane, select the Global Settings node and then double-click Transport Settings. This displays the Transport Settings Properties dialog box with the General tab selected by default.

3. On the Message Delivery tab, shown in Figure 12-26, you'll see a list of any existing IP addresses that are being ignored.

4. You can enter IP addresses and IP address ranges in the Internet Protocol Version 4 (IPv4) format, Internet Protocol Version 6 (IPv6) format, or both formats. Click the option button to the right of the Add button and then do one of the following:

   - Select IP Address to enter the IP address of a server or a network that should not be filtered. In the dialog box provided, type a server IP address or network address and then click OK.

   - Select IP Address And Mask to enter the IP address and subnet mask of a server that should not be filtered. In the dialog box provided, type the server's IP address and subnet mask, and then click OK.

   - Select IP Address Range to enter a range of IP addresses on your organization's network that should not be filtered. In the dialog box provided, type a start IP address and an end IP address for the range of addresses, and then click OK.

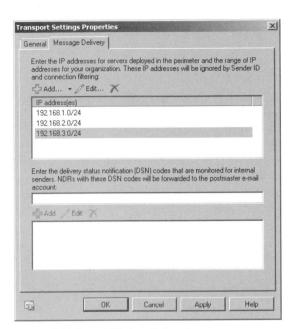

FIGURE 12-26 Prevent filtering of internal servers.

5. Repeat step 4 as necessary. To modify a previous entry, select the entry and then click Edit. To remove an existing entry, select the entry and then click the Remove button.

6. Click OK to save your settings.

CHAPTER 13

Managing Client Access Servers

- Managing Web and Mobile Access   **467**

- Configuring POP3 and IMAP4   **488**

- Deploying Outlook Anywhere   **497**

- Managing Exchange Server Features for Mobile Devices   **503**

Microsoft Outlook Web App, Exchange ActiveSync, and Outlook Anywhere are essential technologies for enabling users to access Microsoft Exchange anywhere at any time. As you know from previous chapters, Outlook Web App (OWA) lets users access Exchange over the Internet or over a wireless network using a standard Web browser; Exchange ActiveSync lets users access Exchange through a wireless carrier using mobile devices, such as smart phones; and Outlook Anywhere lets users access Exchange mailboxes using Microsoft Office Outlook from the Internet via remote procedure call (RPC) over Hypertext Transfer Protocol (HTTP). When users access Exchange mail and public folders over the Internet or a wireless network, virtual directories and Web applications hosted by Client Access servers are working behind the scenes to grant access and transfer files. As you'll learn in this chapter, managing mobile access, virtual directories, and Web applications is a bit different from other tasks you'll perform as an Exchange administrator—and not only because you use the Microsoft Internet Information Services (IIS) Manager snap-in to perform many of the management tasks.

Managing Web and Mobile Access

When you install the Client Access server role on an Exchange server, Outlook Web App and Exchange ActiveSync are automatically configured for use. This makes them fairly easy to manage, but there are some essential concepts you need to know to manage these implementations more effectively. This section explains these concepts.

NOTE Before you can install the Client Access server role on an Exchange server, you must install and configure Internet Information Services (IIS). Microsoft has released several different versions of IIS. IIS 7.0 and IIS 7.5 are the versions discussed in this chapter.

Using Outlook Web App and Exchange ActiveSync with IIS

IIS handles incoming requests to a Web site within the context of a Web application. A Web application is a software program that delivers content to users over HTTP or HTTPS. Each Web site has a default Web application and one or more additional Web applications associated with it. The default Web application handles incoming requests that you haven't assigned to other Web applications. Additional Web applications handle incoming requests that specifically reference the application.

When you install a Client Access server, virtual directories and Web applications are installed to support various Exchange services. Each Web application must have a root virtual directory associated with it. The root virtual directory sets the application's name and maps the application to the physical directory that contains the application's content. Typically, the default Web application is associated with the root virtual directory of the Web site and any additional virtual directories you've created but haven't mapped to other applications.

In the default configuration, the default application handles an incoming request for the / directory of a Web site as well as other named virtual directories. IIS maps references to / and other virtual directories to the physical directory that contains the related content. For the / directory of the default Web site, the default physical directory is %SystemRoot%/inetpub/wwwroot.

In most cases, you only need to open port 443 on your organization's firewall to allow users to access Exchange data hosted by IIS. Then you simply tell users the Uniform Resource Locator (URL) that they need to type in their browser's Address field or in their smart phone's browser. Users can then access Outlook Web App or Exchange ActiveSync when they're off-site. The URLs for Outlook Web App and Exchange ActiveSync are different. The Outlook Web App URL is *https://yourserver .yourdomain.com/owa*, and the Exchange ActiveSync URL is *https://yourserver .yourdomain.com/Microsoft-Server-ActiveSync*. Generally, however, the address users enter for both matches the OWA address.

You can configure Outlook Web App and Exchange ActiveSync for single-server and multi-server environments. In a single-server environment, you use one Client Access server for all your Web and mobile access needs. In a multiple server environment, you could instruct users to access different URLs to access different Client Access servers, or you could use a technique such as Round Robin Domain Name System (DNS) to load-balance between multiple servers automatically while giving all users the same access URLs. However, for optimal scalability and availability, you should configure a Client Access server (CAS) array and then use a software or hardware load balancer.

You can use Outlook Web App and Exchange ActiveSync with firewalls. You configure your network to use a perimeter network with firewalls in front of the designated Client Access servers and then open port 443 to your Client Access servers or to the URL for the CAS array.

Working with Virtual Directories and Web Applications

When you install a Client Access server, Exchange Setup installs and configures virtual directories and Web applications for use. The virtual directories and Web applications allow authenticated users to access their messaging data from the Web. In the Exchange Management Shell, you can use the Get-OWAVirtualDirectory cmdlet to view information about OWA virtual directories, the New-OWAVirtual-Directory cmdlet to create an OWA directory if one does not exist, the Remove-OWAVirtualDirectory cmdlet to remove an OWA directory, and the Test-OWA-Connectivity cmdlet to test OWA connectivity. There are similar sets of commands for ActiveSync, Autodiscover, ECP, OAB, Windows PowerShell, and Web services. If you examine the virtual directory structure for the default Web site, you'll find several important virtual directories and Web applications, including

- **Autodiscover** Autodiscover is used to provide the Autodiscover service for all clients. By default, this directory is configured for anonymous authentication and integrated Windows authentication.

- **ECP** The Exchange Control Panel (ECP) is used for Web-based administration of Exchange and end-user self-service. By default, this directory is configured for anonymous authentication and basic authentication.

- **EWS** Exchange Web Services (EWS) is used to enable applications to interact with Exchange mailboxes and messaging items using HTTPS. By default, this directory is configured for anonymous authentication and basic authentication.

- **Microsoft-Server-ActiveSync** Microsoft-Server-ActiveSync is the directory to which Exchange ActiveSync users connect to access their Exchange data. By default, this virtual directory is configured for Basic authentication.

- **OAB** OAB is the directory that provides the offline address book (OAB) to clients. By default, this directory is configured for integrated Windows authentication .

- **OWA** OWA is the directory to which users connect with their Web browsers to start an Outlook Web App session. By default, this directory is configured for basic authentication.

- **PowerShell** PowerShell is the directory to which the Exchange Management tools connect for remote administration. By default, this directory is configured for anonymous authentication.

- **Public** Public is the directory to which users connect to access the default Public Folders tree. By default, this directory is configured for both basic and integrated Windows authentication, with the default domain set to the pre–Windows 2000 domain name, such as ADATUM.

This section examines key tasks that you use to manage IIS, virtual directories, and Web applications.

Enabling and Disabling Outlook Web App Features

Microsoft uses the term *segmentation* to refer to your ability to enable and disable the various features within Outlook Web App. Segmentation settings applied to the OWA virtual directory on Client Access servers control the features available to users. If a server has multiple OWA virtual directories or you have multiple Client Access servers, you must configure each directory and server separately. Table 13-1 provides a summary of the segmentation features that are enabled by default for use with Outlook Web App.

TABLE 13-1 An Overview of Segmentation Features

FEATURE	WHEN THIS FEATURE IS ENABLED, USERS CAN
All Address Lists	View all the available address lists. When this feature is disabled, users can view only the default global address list.
Calendar	Access their calendars in Outlook Web App.
Change Password	Change their passwords in Outlook Web App.
Contacts	Access their contacts in Outlook Web App.
E-Mail Signature	Customize their signatures and include a signature in outgoing messages.
Exchange ActiveSync Integration	Remove mobile devices, initiate mobile wipe, view their device passwords, and review their mobile access logs.
Instant Messaging	Access Instant Messaging in Outlook Web App.
Journal	Access their journals in Outlook Web App.
Junk E-Mail Filtering	Filter junk e-mail using Outlook Web App.
Notes	Access their notes in Outlook Web App.
Premium Client	Use Premium features if users have a Premium access license. Otherwise, a client can use only OWA light.
Public Folders	Browse and read items in public folders using Outlook Web App.
Recover Deleted Items	View items that have been deleted from Deleted Items and choose whether to recover them.
Reminders And Notifications	Receive new e-mail notifications, task reminders, calendar reminders, and automatic folder updates.
Rules	Customize rules in Outlook Web App.

TABLE 13-1 An Overview of Segmentation Features

FEATURE	WHEN THIS FEATURE IS ENABLED, USERS CAN
S/MIME	Download the S/MIME control and use it to read and compose signed and encrypted messages (Internet Explorer only).
Search Folders	Access their Search folders in Outlook Web App.
Spelling Checker	Access the spelling checker in Outlook Web App.
Tasks	Access their tasks in Outlook Web App.
Text Messaging	Send and receive text messages in Outlook Web App.
Theme Selection	Change the color scheme in Outlook Web App.
Unified Messaging Integration	Access their voice mail and faxes in Outlook Web App. They can also configure voice mail options.

You can enable or disable segmentation features by completing the following steps:

1. In the Exchange Management Console, expand the Server Configuration node, and then select the Client Access node.

2. In the upper portion of the details pane, you'll see a list of your organization's Client Access servers. Select the server you want to configure, as shown in Figure 13-1.

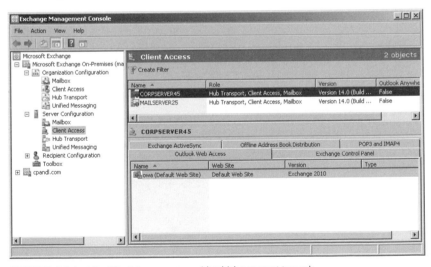

FIGURE 13-1 Select the Client Access server with which you want to work.

3. In the lower portion of the details pane, you'll see a list of option tabs for the selected server. On the Outlook Web App tab, right-click the virtual directory for which you want to implement segmentation, and then select Properties.

Typically, you'll want to configure the OWA virtual directory on the Default Web Site, as this directory is used by default for Outlook Web App.

4. On the Segmentation tab, select a feature you want to enable or disable. Click Enable to enable the feature. Click Disable to disable the feature. Click OK.

In the Exchange Management Shell, you can enable or disable segmentation features using the Set-OWAVirtualDirectory cmdlet. To enable or disable these features for individual users, use the Set-CASMailbox cmdlet.

Configuring Ports, IP Addresses, and Host Names Used by Web Sites

Each Web site hosted by IIS has one or more bindings. A binding is a unique combination of ports, IP addresses, and host names that identifies a Web site. For unsecure connections, the default port is TCP port 80. For secure connections, the default port is TCP port 443. The default IP address setting is to use any available IP address. The default host name is the Client Access server's DNS name.

Normally, you won't want to multihome a Client Access server. However, when the server is multihomed, or when you use it to provide Outlook Web App or Exchange ActiveSync services for multiple domains, the default configuration isn't ideal. On a multihomed server, you'll usually want messaging protocols to respond only on a specific IP address. To do this, you need to change the default settings. On a server that provides Outlook Web App and Exchange ActiveSync services for multiple domains, you'll usually want to specify an additional host name for each domain.

When you are working with IIS 7.0 or IIS 7.5, you can change the identity of a Web site by completing the following steps:

1. If you want the Web site to use a new IP address, you must configure the IP address before trying to specify it on the Web site.

2. Start IIS Manager. Click Start, point to Programs or All Programs as appropriate, point to Administrative Tools, and select Internet Information Services (IIS) Manager.

   NOTE By default, IIS Manager connects to the services running on the local computer. If you want to connect to a different server, select the Start Page node in the left pane and then click the Connect to a Server link. This starts the Connect To Server Wizard. Follow the prompts to connect to the remote server.

3. In IIS Manager, double-click the entry for the server with which you want to work, and then double-click Sites.

4. In the left pane, select the Web site that you want to manage, and then select Bindings on the Actions pane.

5. As Figure 13-2 shows, you can now use the Site Bindings dialog box to configure multiple bindings for the Web site.

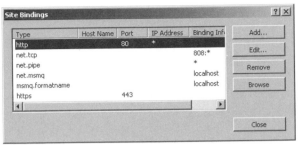

FIGURE 13-2 You can use the Site Bindings dialog box to configure multiple bindings for the Web site.

6. Use the Site Bindings dialog box to manage the site's bindings by using the following settings:
   - **Add** Adds a new identity. To add a new identity, click Add. In the Add Site Binding dialog box, select the binding type, IP address, and TCP port to use. Optionally, type a host header name or select an Secure Sockets Layer (SSL) certificate as appropriate for the binding type. Click OK when you have finished.
   - **Edit** Allows you to edit the currently selected identity. To edit an identity, click the identity, and then click Edit. In the Edit Site Binding dialog box, select an IP address and TCP port to use. Optionally, type a host header name or select an SSL certificate as appropriate for the binding type. Click OK when you have finished.
   - **Remove** Allows you to remove the currently selected identity. To remove an identity, click the identity, and then click Remove. When prompted to confirm, click Yes.
   - **Browse** Allows you to test an identity. To test an identity, click the identity, and then click Browse. IIS Manager then opens a browser window and connects to the selected binding.

7. Click OK twice.

Enabling SSL on Web Sites

SSL is a protocol for encrypting data that is transferred between a client and a server. Without SSL, servers pass data in readable, unencrypted text to clients, which could be a security risk in an enterprise environment. With SSL, servers pass data encoded using 128-bit encryption.

Although Web sites are configured to use SSL on port 443 automatically, the server won't use SSL unless you've created and installed a valid X.509 certificate. When you install the Client Access server role on your Exchange server, a default X.509 certificate is created for Exchange Server 2010 and registered with IIS. In IIS

Manager, you can view the default X.509 certificate by completing the following steps:

1. Log on locally to the Client Access server. Start IIS Manager. Click Start, point to Programs or All Programs as appropriate, point to Administrative Tools, and then select Internet Information Services (IIS) Manager.

2. In IIS Manager, select the server node and then double-click the Server Certificates feature.

3. On the Server Certificates page, you'll see a list of certificates the Web server can use. The default X.509 certificate for Exchange Server has the name Microsoft Exchange and is issued to the Exchange server configured with the Client Access server role. Click the certificate entry, and then click View in the Actions pane to view detailed information regarding the certificate. By default, this certificate is valid for one year from the date you install the Client Access server role.

For a long-term solution, you need to create a permanent certificate for the Client Access server. This certificate can be a certificate assigned by your organization's certificate authority (CA) or a third-party certificate. To create a certificate for use with Exchange and IIS, use the features provided by the Exchange management tools. In the Exchange Management Console, you can view available certificates for each server by selecting the Server Configuration node in the left pane and then selecting the server you want to work with in the right pane. In the lower panel of the details pane, you'll see a list of available certificates. You can then work with the available certificates in a variety of ways:

- Right-click a certificate and then select Open to view the certificate.
- Right-click a certificate and then select Assign Services To Certificate to view the services the certificate is registered with and to assign services (if permitted).

To create a certificate, complete the following steps:

1. In the Exchange Management Console, select the Server Configuration node in the left pane, and then select the server you want to work with in the right pane.

2. Right-click in the lower panel, and then select New Exchange Certificate. This starts the New Exchange Certificate Wizard. Use the wizard to create a certificate request file.

3. Send the certificate request file to a third-party certificate authority or your organization's CA as appropriate. When you receive the certificate back from the CA, import the certificate. In the Exchange Management Console, select the Server Configuration node in the left pane, and then select the server you want to work with in the right pane.

4. Right-click in the lower panel, and then select Import Exchange Certificate. This starts the Import Exchange Certificate Wizard. Use the wizard to import the certificate file.

After you've installed the certificate, you should test the certificate with an external client by accessing OWA from a remote computer. Clients won't automatically trust self-signed certificates or certificates issued by your CA. Because of this, you might see an error stating that there is a problem with the Web site's security certificate. In this case, follow these steps to have the client trust the certificate:

1. Click the Continue To This Website link. When you continue to the site, a Certificate Error option appears to the right of the address field.

2. Click the Certificate Error option to display a related error dialog box, and then click View Certificates to display the Certificate dialog box.

3. On the General tab of the Certificate dialog box, you'll see an error stating the CA Root Certificate isn't trusted. To enable trust, click Install Certificate. This starts the Certificate Import Wizard.

4. Accept the default settings by clicking Next twice and then clicking Finish. Click OK twice. The browser will now trust the certificate, and you shouldn't see the certificate error again for this client.

You also can test OWA connectivity by using the Remote Connectivity Analyzer. In Exchange Management Console, select the Toolbox node and then double-click the Remote Connectivity Analyzer entry. Select the tests you want to run, click Next, and then follow the prompts. Cmdlets for testing connectivity are listed in Chapter 14, "Exchange Server 2010 Maintenance, Monitoring, and Queuing."

Restricting Incoming Connections and Setting Time-Out Values

You control incoming connections to a Web site in several ways: you can set a maximum limit on the bandwidth used, you can set a limit on the number of simultaneous connections, and you can set a connection time-out value. However, typically you wouldn't want to do any of this for a Client Access server or OWA. OWA has its own timers based on whether the end user is on a public/shared or a private computer. These values are fixed and not affected by any restrictions or settings discussed in this section.

Normally, Web sites have no maximum bandwidth limits and accept an unlimited number of connections, and this is an optimal setting in most environments. However, when you're trying to prevent the underlying server hardware from becoming overloaded or you want to ensure other Web sites on the same computer have enough bandwidth, you might want to limit the bandwidth available to the site and the number of simultaneous connections. When either limit is reached, no other clients are permitted to access the server. The clients must wait until the connection load on the server decreases.

The connection time-out value determines when idle user sessions are disconnected. With the default Web site, sessions time out after they've been idle for 120 seconds (2 minutes). It's a sound security practice to disconnect idle sessions and force users to log back on to the server. If you don't disconnect idle sessions within a reasonable amount of time, unauthorized persons could gain access to your messaging system through a browser window left unattended on a remote terminal.

You can modify connection limits and time-outs by completing the following steps:

1. Start IIS Manager. Click Start, point to Programs or All Programs as appropriate, point to Administrative Tools, and then select Internet Information Services (IIS) Manager.

2. In IIS Manager, double-click the entry for the server with which you want to work, and then double-click Sites.

3. In the left pane, select the Web site that you want to manage, and then click Limits in the Actions pane. This displays the Edit Web Site Limits dialog box, as shown in Figure 13-3.

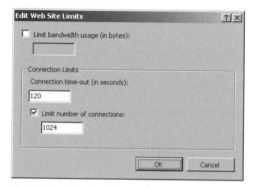

FIGURE 13-3 Use the Edit Web Site Limits dialog box to limit connections and set time-out values for each Web site.

4. To remove maximum bandwidth limits, clear the Limit Bandwidth Usage check box. To set a maximum bandwidth limit, select the Limit Bandwidth Usage check box and then set the desired limit in bytes.

5. The Connection Time-Out field controls how long idle user sessions remain connected to the server. The default value is 120 seconds. Type a new value to change the current time-out value.

6. To remove connection limits, clear the Limit Number Of Connections check box. To set a connection limit, select the Limit Number Of Connections check box, and then type a limit.

7. Click OK.

Redirecting Users to Alternate URLs

Sometimes, you might find that you want to redirect users to alternate URLs. For example, you might want users to type **http://mail.cpandl.com** and get redirected to *https://mail.cpandl.com/owa*.

You can redirect users from one URL to another by completing the following steps:

1. Start IIS Manager. Click Start, point to Programs or All Programs as appropriate, point to Administrative Tools, and then select Internet Information Services (IIS) Manager.

2. In IIS Manager, navigate to the level you want to manage. You manage redirection for an entire site at the site level. You manage redirection for a directory at the directory level.

3. In the main pane, double-click the HTTP Redirect feature. This displays the HTTP Redirect page.

   NOTE With IIS 7.0 and IIS 7.5, HTTP redirection is an optional role service. Therefore, if the HTTP Redirect feature is not available, you need to install the related role service by using Server Manager's Add Role Services Wizard.

4. On the HTTP Redirect page, select Redirect Requests To This Destination.

5. In the Redirect Requests To This Destination text box, type the Uniform Resource Locator (URL) to which the user should be redirected. To redirect the user to a different server, type the full path, starting with **http://** or **https://**, such as **https://mailer2.cpandl.com/owa**. To redirect the user to a virtual directory on the same server, type a slash mark (/) followed by the directory name, such as **/owa**. Click Apply to save your settings.

Controlling Access to the HTTP Server

IIS supports several authentication methods, including

- **Anonymous authentication**   With anonymous authentication, IIS automatically logs users on with an anonymous or guest account. This allows users to access resources without being prompted for user name and password information.

- **ASP.NET Impersonation**   With ASP.NET Impersonation, a managed code application can run either as the user authenticated by IIS or as a designated account that you specify when configuring this mode.

- **Basic authentication**   With basic authentication, users are prompted for logon information. When entered, this information is transmitted unencrypted (base64-encoded) across the network. If you've configured secure communications on the server, as described in the section of this chapter titled "Enabling SSL on Web Sites," you can require that clients use SSL. When you use SSL with basic authentication, the logon information is encrypted before transmission.

- **Windows authentication**   With Windows authentication, IIS uses kernel-mode Windows security to validate the user's identity. Instead of prompting for a user name and password, clients relay the logon credentials that users supply when they log on to Windows. These credentials are fully encrypted without the need for SSL, and they include the user name and password needed to log on to the network.

- **Digest authentication** With digest authentication, user credentials are transmitted securely between clients and servers. Digest authentication is a feature of HTTP 1.1 and uses a technique that can't be easily intercepted and decrypted.

- **Forms authentication** With Forms authentication, you manage client registration and authentication at the application level instead of relying on the authentication mechanisms in IIS. As the mode name implies, users register and provide their credentials using a logon form. By default, this information is passed as cleartext. To avoid this, you should use SSL encryption for the logon page and other internal application pages.

When you install IIS 7.0 or IIS 7.5 on a Client Access server, you are required to enable basic authentication, digest authentication, and Windows authentication. These authentication methods, along with anonymous authentication, are used to control access to the server's virtual directories. A virtual directory is simply a folder path that is accessible by a URL. For example, you could create a virtual directory called Data that is physically located on C:\CorpData\Data and accessible using the URL *https://myserver.mydomain.com/Data*.

Table 13-2 summarizes the default authentication settings for each directory. You should rarely change the default settings. However, if your organization has special needs, you can change the authentication settings at the virtual directory level.

TABLE 13-2 Default Authentication Settings for Virtual Directories

VIRTUAL DIRECTORY	ANONYMOUS AUTHENTICATION	BASIC AUTHENTICATION	DIGEST AUTHENTICATION	WINDOWS AUTHENTICATION
Autodiscover	Yes	Yes	No	Yes
ECP	Yes	Yes	No	No
EWS	Yes	No	No	Yes
Microsoft-Server-ActiveSync	No	Yes	No	No
OAB	No	No	No	Yes
OWA	No	Yes	No	No
PowerShell	Yes	No	No	No
Public	No	Yes	No	Yes

As the table shows, the default public folder tree is accessible through basic and Windows authentication. If you want to grant public access to this folder tree or restrict the tree so that only Windows authentication is allowed, you can do so by editing the individual security settings on the related virtual directory.

The authentication settings on virtual directories are different from authentication settings on the Web site itself. By default, the Web site allows anonymous access. This means that anyone can access the server's home page without authenticating themselves. If you disable anonymous access at the server level and enable some other type of authentication, users need to authenticate themselves twice: once for the server and once for the virtual directory they want to access.

The preferred way to manage authentication settings is to use the appropriate cmdlet in the Exchange Management Shell:

- For ActiveSync, use Set-ActiveSyncVirtualDirectory.
- For Autodiscover, use Set-AutodiscoverVirtualDirectory.
- For ECP, use Set-EcpVirtualDirectory.
- For OAB, use Set-OabVirtualDirectory.
- For OWA, use Set-OwaVirtualDirectory.
- For PowerShell, use Set-PowerShellVirtualDirectory.
- For Exchange Web Services, use Set-WebServicesVirtualDirectory.

As an example, to disable basic authentication on the default ActiveSync directory, you would enter:

```
Set-ActiveSyncVirtualDirectory -Identity "cpandl\microsoft-server-
activesync" -BasicAuthEnabled $false
```

You can change the authentication settings for an entire site or for a particular virtual directory by completing the following steps:

1. Start IIS Manager. Click Start, point to Programs or All Programs as appropriate, point to Administrative Tools, and then select Internet Information Services (IIS) Manager.

2. In IIS Manager, navigate to the level you want to manage and then double-click the Authentication feature. On the Authentication page, shown in Figure 13-4, you should see the available authentication modes. If a mode you want to use is not available, you need to install and enable the related role service using Server Manager's Add Role Services Wizard.

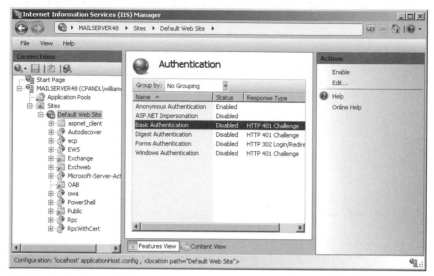

FIGURE 13-4 Use the Authentication page to set access control on virtual directories. Virtual directories can have different authentication settings than the Web site.

3. To enable or disable anonymous access, select Anonymous Authentication and then click Enable or Disable as appropriate.

> **NOTE** With anonymous access, IIS uses an anonymous user account for access to the server. The anonymous user account is named IUSR_ServerName, such as IUSR_Mailer1. If you use this account, you don't need to set a password. Instead, let IIS manage the password. If you want to use a different account, click Edit, and then click Set to specify the user name and password for a different account to use for anonymous access.

4. To configure other authentication methods, select the authentication method and then click Enable or Disable as appropriate. Keep the following in mind:

- Disabling basic authentication might prevent some clients from accessing resources remotely. Clients can log on only when you enable an authentication method that they support.

- A default domain isn't set automatically. If you enable Basic authentication, you can choose to set a default domain that should be used when no domain information is supplied during the logon process. Setting the default domain is useful when you want to ensure that clients authenticate properly.

- With Basic and Digest authentication, you can optionally specify the realm that can be accessed. Essentially, a *realm* is the DNS domain name or Web address that will use the credentials that have been authenticated against the default domain. If the default domain and realm are set to the same value, the internal Windows domain name might be exposed to external users during the user name and password challenge/response.

- If you enable ASP.NET Impersonation, you can specify the identity to impersonate. By default, IIS uses pass-through authentication, and the identity of the authenticated user is impersonated. You can also specify a particular user if necessary.

- If you enable Forms authentication, you can set the logon URL and cookies settings used for authentication.

Throttling Client Access

Every Client Access server in your organization is subject to the default client throttling policy. Client throttling policies are designed to ensure users aren't intentionally or unintentionally overloading Exchange. Exchange tracks the resources that each user consumes and applies throttling policy to enforce connection bandwidth limits as necessary.

The default policy is set in place when you install your first Exchange 2010 Client Access server. In Exchange 2010, there is a single default throttling policy for the organization. You can customize the default policy or add additional policies as necessary.

To manage throttling policy, you use Exchange Management Shell and the Get-ThrottlingPolicy, Set-ThrottlingPolicy, New-ThrottlingPolicy, and Remove-ThrottlingPolicy cmdlets. Throttling policy applies to:

- Exchange Web Services (EWS)
- IMAP
- Microsoft Exchange ActiveSync (EAS)
- Outlook Web App (OWA)
- POP
- PowerShell

With all of these features except PowerShell, you can specify separate settings for

- Maximum concurrency controls the maximum number of connections a user can have at one time. The valid range is 0 to 100, with $null removing the limit. There are EASMaxConcurrency, EWSMaxConcurrency, IMAPMaxConcurrency, OWAMaxConcurrency, POPMaxConcurrency, and PowerShellMaxConcurrency parameters.

- PercentTimeInCAS, PercentTimeInAD, and PercentTimeInMailboxRPC control the maximum percentage of a minute that can be spent executing CAS code requests, LDAP requests and mailbox RPC requests respectively. The valid range is any percent value. To remove the limit use a value of $null. There are EASPercentTimeInCAS, EASPercentTimeInAD, and EASPercentTimeInMailboxRPC parameters, as well as similar parameters for other services.

NOTE LDAP and mailbox RPC requests are a subset of CAS code requests. Here, a value of 100 indicates that for every one minute window, the caller can spend 60 seconds on that request. With concurrent requests, each request has a separate window, so two requests that spend 60 seconds each result in 120 seconds being used in a 60 second window. If this was the maximum allowed, you'd set the percent time to 200.

Unified Messaging users have the throttling settings of Exchange Web Services. You also can specify the CPU start percent. This value sets the per-process CPU usage percentage at which users governed by this policy will be throttled. Valid values are from 0 through 100. Use $null to turn off CPU percentage-based throttling for a policy.

With PowerShell you can specify:

- Maximum number of concurrent Remote PowerShell sessions per user using PowerShellMaxConcurrency
- Maximum number of cmdlets that a user can run in a given interval using PowerShellMaxCmdlets
- The time period for determining whether the maximum number of cmdlets has been exceeded using PowerShellMaxCmdletsTimePeriod
- The maximum number of operations per user with the PowerShellMaxCmdletQueueDepth

NOTE Maximum concurrency controls the number of user sessions. Maximum cmdlets controls the number of cmdlets in each user session. The two values together are affected by the maximum queue depth allowed. For example, if five user sessions are allowed, and each can run four cmdlets in a given interval, the maximum queue depth to allow this is 20 (5 user session x 4 cmdlets each = 20). Any value less than 20 restricts the number of operations that can be performed in this scenario.

You can get the default throttling policy by entering: **Get-ThrottlingPolicy default*** or **Get-ThrottlingPolicy | where-object {$_.IsDefault -eq $true}**. You can get the throttling policy applied to a particular user by entering **(Get-Mailbox UserAlias).ThrottlingPolicy** where UserAlias is the alias for a user, such as:

```
(Get-Mailbox jimj).ThrottlingPolicy | Get-ThrottlingPolicy
```

You can create a nondefault throttling policy using the New-ThrottlingPolicy cmdlet. You can then assign the policy to a mailbox using the -ThrottlingPolicy parameter of the Set-Mailbox and New-Mailbox cmdlets. In the following example, you apply TempUserThrottlingPolicy to AmyG:

```
Set-Mailbox -Identity amyg -ThrottlingPolicy (Get-ThrottlingPolicy
TempUserThrottlingPolicy)
```

You can modify default and nondefault throttling policies using Set-Throttling-Policy. To have a user go back to the default policy, set the -ThrottlingPolicy parameter to $null as shown in this example:

```
Set-Mailbox -Identity amyg -ThrottlingPolicy $null
```

You can find all user mailboxes that currently have a particular policy applied using Get-Mailbox with a where-object filter. In the following example, you look for all user mailboxes that have the TempUserThrottlingPolicy:

```
$p = Get-ThrottlingPolicy TempUserThrottlingPolicy
Get-Mailbox | where-object {$_.ThrottlingPolicy -eq $p.Identity}
```

To switch multiple users from one policy to another, you can do the following:

```
$op = Get-ThrottlingPolicy TempUserThrottlingPolicy
$ms = Get-Mailbox | where-object {$_.ThrottlingPolicy -eq $op.Identity}
$np = Get-ThrottlingPolicy RestrictedUserThrottlingPolicy
foreach ($m in $ms) {Set-Mailbox $m.Identity -ThrottlingPolicy $np;}
```

You can remove nondefault policies that aren't currently being applied using Remove-ThrottlingPolicy. Simply enter Remove-ThrottlingPolicy followed by the name of the policy as shown in this example:

```
Remove-ThrottlingPolicy TempUserThrottlingPolicy
```

Starting, Stopping, and Restarting Web Sites

Web sites run under a server process that you can start, stop, and pause, much like other server processes. For example, if you're changing the configuration of a Web site or performing other maintenance tasks, you might need to stop the Web site, make the changes, and then restart it. When a Web site is stopped, it doesn't accept connections from users and can't be used to deliver or retrieve mail.

The master process for all Web sites is the World Wide Web Publishing Service. Stopping this service stops all Web sites using the process, and all connections are disconnected immediately. Starting this service restarts all Web sites that were running when you stopped the World Wide Web Publishing Service.

You can start, stop, or restart a Web site by completing the following steps:

1. Start IIS Manager. Click Start, point to Programs or All Programs as appropriate, point to Administrative Tools, and then select Internet Information Services (IIS) Manager.

2. In IIS Manager, double-click the entry for the server you want to work with, and then double-click Sites.

3. Select the Web site you want to manage. Using the options in the Actions pane, you can now do the following:

 • Select Start to start the Web site.

 • Select Stop to stop the Web site.

 • Select Restart to stop and then start the Web site.

If you suspect there's a problem with the World Wide Web Publishing Service or other related IIS services, you can use the following technique to restart all IIS services:

1. Start IIS Manager. Click Start, point to Programs or All Programs as appropriate, point to Administrative Tools, and then select Internet Information Services (IIS) Manager.

2. Select the entry for the server you want to work with, and then select Restart in the Actions Pane.

Configuring URLs and Authentication for the OAB

Outlook 2007 and later clients can retrieve the offline address book (OAB) from a Web distribution point. The default distribution point is the OAB virtual directory on the Default Web Site. Each distribution point has three associated properties:

 ■ **PollInterval** The time interval during which the Microsoft Exchange File Distribution service should poll the generation server for new updates (in minutes)

 ■ **ExternalUrl** The URL from which Outlook clients outside the corporate network can access the OAB

 ■ **InternalUrl** The URL from which Outlook clients inside the corporate network can access the OAB

You can configure Web distribution points by completing the following steps:

1. In the Exchange Management Console, expand the Server Configuration node, and then select the Client Access node.

2. In the upper portion of the details pane, you'll see a list of your organization's Client Access servers. Select the server with which you want to work.

3. In the lower portion of the details pane, on the Offline Address Book Distribution tab, you'll see an entry for each OAB Web distribution point configured on the server.

4. Right-click the distribution point you want to configure and then select Properties. This opens the Properties dialog box as shown in Figure 13-5.

5. On the General tab, set the desired polling interval using the Polling Interval text box. The default interval is 480 minutes.

6. On the URLs tab, the current internal and external URLs are listed. If you want to change the current settings, enter the desired internal and external URLs in the text boxes provided. Click OK.

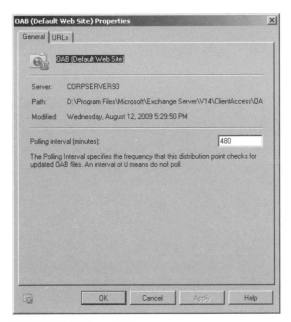

FIGURE 13-5 Configure OAB.

Configuring Urls and Authentication for OWA

When you install a Client Access server, the server is configured with a Default Web Site and the virtual directories discussed previously. Through the OWA virtual directory, you can set the base URL for these directories so that different URLs are used for internal access and external access. You can also configure different authentication mechanisms for each directory.

You can configure OWA virtual directory URLs and authentication by completing the following steps:

1. In the Exchange Management Console, expand the Server Configuration node, and then select the Client Access node.

2. In the upper portion of the details pane, you'll see a list of your organization's Client Access servers. Select the server with which you want to work.

3. In the lower portion of the details pane, on the Outlook Web App tab, you'll see an entry for the OWA virtual directory used by Exchange Server.

4. Right-click the OWA virtual directory and then select Properties. This opens the Properties dialog box. Two of its tabs are shown in Figure 13-6.

5. On the General tab, the current internal and external URLs are listed. If you want to change the current settings, enter the internal and external URLs you want to use in the text boxes provided.

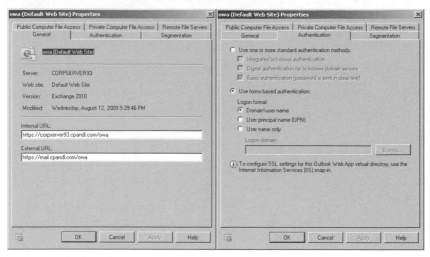

FIGURE 13-6 Configure OWA.

6. On the Authentication tab, forms-based authentication is configured by default with the logon format set to Domain\User Name. Change this configuration only if you have specific requirements that necessitate a change.

7. Click OK to save your settings.

Configuring URLs and Authentication for Exchange ActiveSync

When you install a Client Access server, the server is configured with a Default Web Site that has a virtual directory for Exchange ActiveSync. The URL for this directory can be set so that different URLs are used for internal access and external access and so that different authentication mechanisms can be used.

You can configure the Exchange ActiveSync URLs and authentication by completing the following steps:

1. In the Exchange Management Console, expand the Server Configuration node, and then select the Client Access node.

2. In the upper portion of the details pane, you'll see a list of your organization's Client Access servers. Select the server with which you want to work.

3. In the lower portion of the details pane, on the Exchange ActiveSync tab, you'll see an entry for each virtual directory used by Exchange Server for ActiveSync.

4. Right-click the virtual directory you want to configure and then select Properties. This opens the Properties dialog box. Two of its tabs are shown in Figure 13-7.

5. On the General tab, the current internal and external URLs are listed. If you want to change the current settings, enter the internal and external URLs you want to use in the text boxes provided.

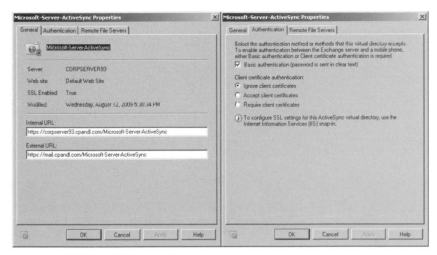

FIGURE 13-7 Configure Exchange ActiveSync.

6. On the Authentication tab, by default, basic authentication is enabled and client certificates are ignored. If your organization uses client certificates, you can clear the Basic Authentication check box and then select either Accept Client Certificates or Require Client Certificates as appropriate.

7. Click OK to save your settings.

Configuring URLs and Authentication for ECP

When you install a Client Access server, the server is configured with a Default Web Site and the virtual directories discussed previously. Through the ECP virtual directory, you can set the base URL for these directories so that different URLs are used for internal access and external access. You can also configure different authentication mechanisms for each directory.

You can configure ECP virtual directory URLs and authentication by completing the following steps:

1. In the Exchange Management Console, expand the Server Configuration node, and then select the Client Access node.

2. In the upper portion of the details pane, you'll see a list of your organization's Client Access servers. Select the server with which you want to work.

3. In the lower portion of the details pane, on the Exchange Control Panel tab, you'll see an entry for the ECP virtual directory used by Exchange Server. The current internal and external URLs are listed. If you want to change the

current settings, enter the internal and external URLs you want to use in the text boxes provided.

4. Right-click the ECP virtual directory and then select Properties. This opens the Properties dialog box. Two of its tabs are shown in Figure 13-8.

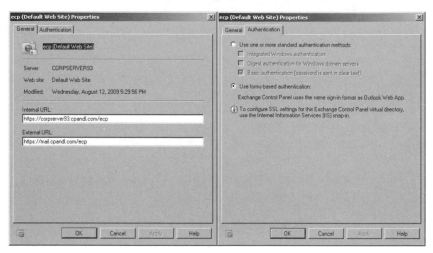

FIGURE 13-8 Configure ECP.

Configuring POP3 and IMAP4

Exchange Server 2010 supports Internet Message Access Protocol 4 (IMAP4) and Post Office Protocol 3 (POP3). IMAP4 is a protocol for reading mail and accessing public and private folders on remote servers. Clients can log on to an Exchange server and use IMAP4 to download message headers and then read messages individually while online. POP3 is a protocol for retrieving mail on remote servers. Clients can log on to an Exchange server and then use POP3 to download their mail for offline use.

By default, POP3 (version 3) and IMAP4 (rev 1) are configured for manual startup. Because Outlook Web App, Exchange ActiveSync, and Outlook Anywhere offer so much more than POP and IMAP, they are the preferred way for users to access Exchange Server. If you still have users who want to use POP3 and IMAP4 to access Exchange Server, you can configure this, but you should try to move these users to Outlook Web App, Exchange ActiveSync, or Outlook Anywhere.

Enabling the Exchange POP3 and IMAP4 Services

Clients that retrieve mail using POP3 or IMAP4 send mail using Simple Mail Transfer Protocol (SMTP). SMTP is the default mail transport in Exchange Server 2010. To enable POP3 and IMAP4, you must first start the POP3 and IMAP4 services on the Client Access servers that will provide these services. You must then configure these services to start automatically in the future. You should also review the related settings for each service and make changes as necessary to optimize the way these services are used in your Exchange organization.

You can enable and configure POP3 for automatic startup by completing these steps:

1. Start the Services utility by clicking Start, selecting Administrative Tools, and then selecting Services.

2. Right-click Microsoft Exchange POP3, and then select Properties

3. On the General tab, under Startup Type, select Automatic and then click Apply.

4. Under Service Status, click Start, and then click OK.

You can enable and configure IMAP4 for automatic startup by completing these steps:

1. Start the Services utility by clicking Start, clicking Administrative Tools, and then selecting Services.

2. Right-click Microsoft Exchange IMAP4, and then click Properties.

3. On the General tab, under Startup Type, select Automatic and then click Apply.

4. Under Service Status, click Start, and then click OK.

You can use Set-Service to enable and configure POP3 and IMAP4 as well. Use the –StartupType parameter to set the startup type as Automatic, Manual, or Disabled. Use the –Status parameter to set the status as Running, Paused, or Stopped. The following examples enable POP3 and IMAP4 for automatic startup and then start the services:

```
Set-Service –Name MSExchangePop3 –StartupType Automatic –Status Running

Set-Service –Name MSExchangeImap4 –StartupType Automatic –Status Running
```

POP3 and IMAP4 have related IP address and TCP port configuration settings. The default IP address setting is to use any available IP address. On a multihomed server, however, you'll usually want messaging protocols to respond on a specific IP address. To do this, you need to change the default setting.

The default port setting depends on the messaging protocol being used and whether SSL is enabled or disabled. For users to be able to retrieve mail using POP3 and IMAP4, you must open the related messaging ports on your organization's fire-walls. Table 13-3 shows the default port settings for key protocols used by Exchange Server 2010.

TABLE 13-3 Standard and Secure Port Settings for Messaging Protocols

PROTOCOL	DEFAULT PORT	DEFAULT SECURE PORT
SMTP	25	587
HTTP	80	443
IMAP4	143	993
POP3	110	995

In the Exchange Management Shell, you can manage POP3 and IMAP4 by using the following cmdlets:

- **Get-POPSettings** Lists POP3 configuration settings
- **Set-POPSettings** Configures POP3 settings
- **Test-POPConnectivity** Tests the POP3 configuration
- **Get-IMAPSettings** Lists IMAP4 configuration settings
- **Set-IMAPSettings** Configures IMAP4 settings
- **Test-IMAPConnectivity** Tests the IMAP4 configuration

Configuring POP3 and IMAP4 Bindings

The bindings for POP3 and IMAP4 use a unique combination of an IP address and a TCP port. To change the IP address or port number for POP3 or IMAP4, complete the following steps:

1. In the Exchange Management Console, expand the Server Configuration node, and then select the Client Access node.

2. In the upper portion of the details pane, you'll see a list of your organiza-tion's Client Access servers. Select the server with which you want to work.

3. In the lower portion of the details pane, on the POP3 And IMAP4 tab, you'll see separate entries for POP3 and IMAP4.

4. Right-click POP3 or IMAP4 as appropriate for the protocol you want to work with, and then select Properties. (See Figure 13-9.)

   - On the General tab, you'll see the last modification date for the protocol settings as well as the status of the related Exchange service.

   - On the Binding tab, you'll see the currently assigned IP addresses and ports used for TLS or unencrypted connections and SSL connections. The default configuration is as follows: POP3 and IMAP4 are configured to use all available IPv4 and IPv6 addresses, POP3 uses port 110 for TLS or unencrypted connections and port 995 for SSL connections, and IMAP4 uses port 143 for TLS or unencrypted connections and port 993 for SSL connections.

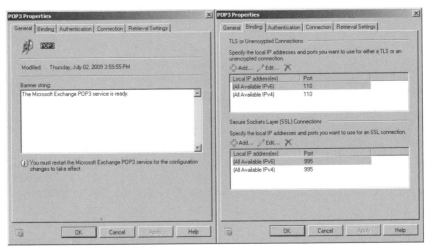

FIGURE 13-9 View settings and bindings.

5. Select the Binding tab. To configure IP addresses and ports for TLS or unencrypted connections, use the following options on the TLS Or Unencrypted Connections panel:

- **Add** Adds a TCP port on a per-IP address basis or all unassigned IP address basis. Click Add, and then specify the IP address and port you want to use.

- **Edit** Allows you to edit the IP address and port settings for the currently selected entry in the Address list box.

- **Remove** Allows you to remove the IP address and port settings for the currently selected entry in the Address list box.

NOTE The IP address/TCP port combination must be unique. You can assign the same port as long as the protocol is configured to use a different IP address. You can also assign the same IP address and use a different port.

6. To configure IP addresses and ports for secure connections, use the following options on the Secure Sockets Layer (SSL) Connections panel:

- **Add** Adds a TCP port on a per-IP address basis or an all-unassigned IP address basis. Click Add, and then specify the IP address and port you want to use.

- **Edit** Allows you to edit the IP address and port settings for the currently selected entry in the Address list box.

- **Remove** Allows you to remove the IP address and port settings for the currently selected entry in the Address list box.

7. Click OK to save your settings. When you add new ports, you must open the related messaging ports on your organization's firewalls.

8. Use the Services utility to restart the Exchange POP3 or IMAP4 service. Restarting the service applies the new settings.

Configuring POP3 and IMAP4 Authentication

By default, POP3 and IMAP4 clients pass connection information and message data through an insecure connection. If corporate security is a high priority, however, your information security team might require mail clients to connect over secure communication channels. You have several options for configuring secure communications, including plain-text authentication, logon using integrated Windows authentication, and a fully secure logon using TLS.

You configure communications using plain-text authentication logon with or without integrated Windows authentication by completing the following steps:

1. In the Exchange Management Console, expand the Server Configuration node, and then select the Client Access node.

2. In the upper portion of the details pane, you'll see a list of your organization's Client Access servers. Select the server with which you want to work.

3. In the lower portion of the details pane, on the POP3 And IMAP4 tab, you'll see separate entries for POP3 and IMAP4.

4. Right-click POP3 or IMAP4 as appropriate for the protocol you want to work with and then select Properties.

5. On the Authentication tab, shown in Figure 13-10, do one of the following and then click OK:

- Select Plain Text Logon (Basic Authentication) to use unsecure plain text for communications.

- Select Plain Text Authentication Logon (Integrated Windows Authentication) to use secure communications with Windows authentication.

6. Use the Services utility to restart the Exchange POP3 or IMAP4 service. Restarting the service applies the new settings.

You configure secure TLS communications by completing the following steps:

1. Ensure that an X.509 certificate is installed on your organization's Client Access servers as discussed in "Enabling SSL on Web Sites" earlier in this chapter.

2. Configure the server to require secure TLS communications as follows:

   a. In the Exchange Management Console, expand the Server Configuration node, and then select the Client Access node.

   b. In the upper portion of the details pane, you'll see a list of your organization's Client Access servers. Select the server with which you want to work.

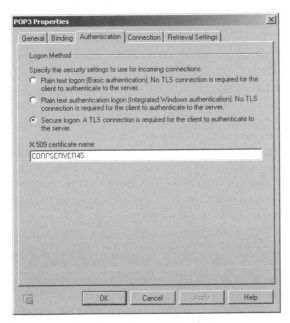

POP3 Properties

General | Binding | Authentication | Connection | Retrieval Settings |

Logon Method

Specify the security settings to use for incoming connections.

○ Plain text logon (Basic authentication). No TLS connection is required for the
client to authenticate to the server.

○ Plain text authentication logon (Integrated Windows authentication). No TLS
connection is required for the client to authenticate to the server.

◉ Secure logon. A TLS connection is required for the client to authenticate to
the server.

X.509 certificate name:

CONMSERVER45

OK   Cancel   Apply   Help

FIGURE 13-10 Configure authentication settings.

   c. In the lower portion of the details pane, on the POP3 And IMAP4 tab, you'll see separate entries for POP3 and IMAP4.

   d. Right-click POP3 or IMAP4 as appropriate for the protocol you want to work with, and then select Properties.

   e. On the Authentication tab, select the Secure Logon option and ensure that the certificate name in the X.509 Certificate Name text box is the correct one to use for TLS connections. If not, enter the name of the appropriate certificate. Click OK.

3. Use the Services utility to restart the Exchange POP3 or IMAP4 service. Restarting the service applies the new settings.

4. You can configure an Outlook client to use TLS by completing the following steps:

   a. In Office Outlook 2007, select Account Settings on the Tools menu. In Office 2010, click the Office button, click Account Settings, and then select the Account Settings option.

   b. In the Account Settings dialog box, select the POP3/IMAP4 account, and then click Change.

   c. In the Change E-Mail Account dialog box, click More Settings.

   d. On the Advanced tab in the Internet E-Mail Settings dialog box, select TLS or Auto as the type of encrypted connection.

   e. Click OK. Click Next and then click Finish. Click Close.

Configuring Connection Settings for POP3 and IMAP4

You can control incoming connections to POP3 and IMAP4 in two ways. You can set a limit on the number of simultaneous connections, and you can set a connection time-out value.

POP3 and IMAP4 normally accept a maximum of 2,000 connections each and a maximum of 16 connections from a single user, and in most environments these are acceptable settings. However, when you're trying to prevent the underlying server hardware from becoming overloaded or you want to ensure resources are available for other features, you might want to restrict the number of simultaneous connections even further. When the limit is reached, no other clients are permitted to access the server. The clients must wait until the connection load on the server decreases.

The connection time-out value determines when idle connections are disconnected. Normally, unauthenticated connections time out after they've been idle for 60 seconds and authenticated connections time out after they've been idle for 1,800 seconds (30 minutes). In most situations, these time-out values are sufficient. Still, at times you'll want to increase the time-out values, and this primarily relates to clients who get disconnected when downloading large files. If you discover that clients are being disconnected during large downloads, the time-out values are one area to examine. You'll also want to look at the maximum command size. By default, the maximum command size is restricted to 45 bytes.

You can modify connection limits and time-outs by completing the following steps:

1. In the Exchange Management Console, expand the Server Configuration node, and then select the Client Access node.

2. In the upper portion of the details pane, you'll see a list of your organization's Client Access servers. Select the server with which you want to work.

3. In the lower portion of the details pane, on the POP3 And IMAP4 tab, you'll see separate entries for POP3 and IMAP4.

4. Right-click POP3 or IMAP4 as appropriate for the protocol you want to work with and then select Properties. In the Properties dialog box, click the Connection tab. (See Figure 13-11.)

5. To set time-out values for authenticated and unauthenticated connections, enter the desired values in the Authenticated Time-Out and Unauthenticated Time-Out text boxes, respectively. The valid range for authenticated connections is from 30 to 86,400 seconds. The valid range for unauthenticated connections is from 10 to 3,600 seconds.

6. To set connection limits, enter the desired limits in the text boxes on the Connection Limits panel. The valid input range for maximum connections is from 1 to 25,000. The valid input range for maximum connections from a single IP address is from 1 to 1,000. The valid input range for maximum connections from a single user is from 1 to 1,000. The valid input range for maximum command size is from 40 to 1,024 bytes.

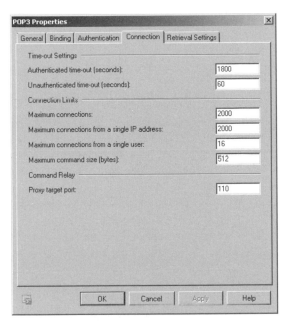

FIGURE 13-11 Configure connection settings.

7. Click OK to save your settings. Use the Services utility to restart the Exchange POP3 or IMAP4 service. Restarting the service applies the new settings.

Configuring Message Retrieval Settings for POP3 and IMAP4

Message retrieval settings for POP3 and IMAP4 control the following options:

- **Message formatting** Message format options allow you to set rules that POP3 and IMAP4 use to format messages before clients read them. By default, when POP3 or IMAP4 clients retrieve messages, the message body is converted to the best format for the client and message attachments are identified with a Multipurpose Internet Mail Extensions (MIME) content type based on the attachment's file extension. You can change this behavior by applying new message MIME formatting rules. Message MIME formatting rules determine the formatting for elements in the body of a message. Message bodies can be formatted as plain text, HTML, HTML and alternative text, enriched text, or enriched text and alternative text.

- **Message sort order** Message sort order options allow you to control the time sorting of messages during new message retrieval. By default, POP3 and IMAP4 sort messages in descending order according to the time/date stamp. This ensures that the most recent messages are listed first. You can also sort messages by ascending order, which places newer messages lower in the message list.

- **Calendar Retrieval** Calendar retrieval settings control the technique used for retrieval of calendar items. By default, IMAP4 uses the iCalendar standard for retrieval of calendar items. Alternatively, you can specify an internal or external URL with which users can access their calendar information, or you can specify a custom URL for the organization's OWA server.

You can modify message retrieval settings by completing the following steps:

1. In the Exchange Management Console, expand the Server Configuration node, and then select the Client Access node.

2. In the upper portion of the details pane, you'll see a list of your organization's Client Access servers. Select the server with which you want to work.

3. In the lower portion of the details pane, on the POP3 And IMAP4 tab, you'll see separate entries for POP3 and IMAP4.

4. Right-click POP3 or IMAP4 as appropriate for the protocol you want to work with and then select Properties. In the Properties dialog box, click the Retrieval Settings tab. (See Figure 13-12, which shows this tab for POP3 and for IMAP4.)

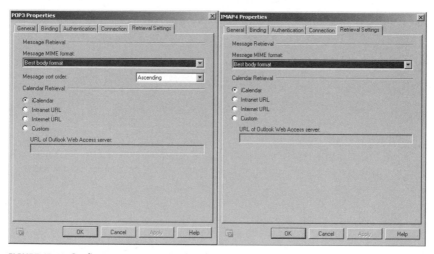

FIGURE 13-12 Configure message retrieval settings.

5. Use the Message MIME Format list to choose the desired body format for messages. As discussed previously, the options are Text, HTML, HTML And Alternative Text, Enriched Text, Enriched Text And Alternative Text, or Best Body Format.

6. If you are working with POP3, use the Message Sort Order list to specify the default sort order for message retrieval. Select Descending for descending sort order during message retrieval or Ascending for ascending sort order.

7. Use the Calendar Retrieval options to specify the technique to use for retrieving calendar items. As discussed previously, the options are iCalendar, Intranet URL, Internet URL, or Custom. If you select Custom, specify the URL of the organization's OWA server in the additional text box provided.

8. Click OK to save your settings. Use the Services utility to restart the Exchange POP3 or IMAP4 service. Restarting the service applies the new settings.

Deploying Outlook Anywhere

Outlook Anywhere provides secure Internet-based access to Exchange Server. When you enable and configure this feature, users can use HTTPS to connect to their Exchange mailboxes, eliminating the need for virtual private network (VPN) connections. Because Outlook Anywhere uses the same URLs and namespaces that you use for Exchange ActiveSync and Outlook Web App, no additional configuration is required beyond the initial setup. Outlook Anywhere is secure, so unauthenticated requests from Outlook clients are blocked from accessing Exchange Server.

You can deploy Outlook Anywhere by performing the following procedures:

1. Install a valid public SSL certificate on the Exchange Server.

2. Install RPC Over HTTP Proxy Windows networking (if this isn't installed already).

3. Enable Outlook Anywhere.

These procedures are discussed in the sections that follow.

Installing an SSL Certificate on the Exchange Server

For Outlook Anywhere to work, a default SSL certificate is created for Exchange Server during installation of a Client Access server. This certificate is meant to help you get started and is not designed for long-term client use. Because of this, you'll likely want to use one issued by your organization's certificate authority (CA) or a third-party certificate service. The first time users access Exchange Server using Outlook Web App, they may need to specify that they trust the server certificate. See "Enabling SSL on Web sites" earlier in this chapter.

Because Outlook Anywhere requests use HTTPS, you must allow port 443 through your firewall. If you already use Outlook Web App with SSL or Exchange ActiveSync with SSL, port 443 should already be open and you do not have to open any additional ports.

Installing the RPC Over HTTP Proxy

For Outlook Anywhere to work, you should install the RPC Over HTTP Proxy Windows networking component on the Exchange Server during installation of a Client Access server. If for some reason this component was not installed, was uninstalled, or becomes corrupted, you must reinstall it.

With Windows Server 2008, you install this component by completing the following steps:

1. Start Server Manager. Click Start, point to Programs or All Programs as appropriate, point to Administrative Tools, and then select Server Manager. Or click the Server Manager button on the Quick Launch toolbar.

2. In Server Manager, select the Features node in the left pane and then click Add Features. This starts the Add Features Wizard.

3. On the Select Features page, select RPC Over HTTP Proxy (as shown in Figure 13-13). If you see a prompt about additional required services, click Add Required Role Services to ensure that these additional services are installed.

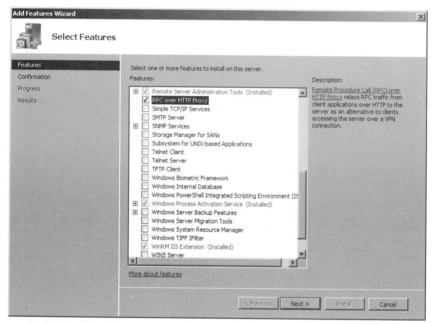

FIGURE 13-13 Install the RPC Over HTTP proxy.

4. Click Next and then click Install. When the Add Features Wizard finishes the installation, click Close.

Determining Whether Outlook Anywhere Is Enabled

In the Exchange Management Console, you can determine whether Outlook Anywhere is enabled by expanding the Server Configuration node and then selecting the Client Access node. In the upper portion of the details pane, Client Access servers are listed by default by name, role, Exchange version, and Outlook Anywhere Enabled status.

You can use the Get-OutlookAnywhere cmdlet to list similar information about Outlook Anywhere for all Client Access servers in your organization. If you use the –Server parameter, you can limit the results to a specific server. If you use the –Identity parameter, you can examine a particular virtual directory on a server. Sample 13-1 provides the syntax, usage, and sample output.

SAMPLE 13-1 Get-OutlookAnywhere cmdlet syntax and usage

Syntax

```
Get-OutlookAnywhere [-Server ServerName] [-DomainController DCName]

Get-OutlookAnywhere [-Identity VirtualDirId] [-DomainController DCName]
```

Usage

```
Get-OutlookAnywhere

Get-OutlookAnywhere -Server "CorpSvr127"

Get-OutlookAnywhere -Identity "CorpSvr127\Rpc (Default Web Site)"
```

Output

```
ServerName                  : MAILSERVER25
SSLOffloading               : False
ExternalHostname            : mailserver25.cpandl.com
ClientAuthenticationMethod  : Basic
IISAuthenticationMethods    : {Basic}
MetabasePath                : IIS://MAILSERVER25.cpandl.com/W3SVC/1/
                              ROOT/Rpc
Path                        : C:\Windows\System32\RpcProxy
Server                      : MAILSERVER25
AdminDisplayName            :
ExchangeVersion             : 0.1 (8.0.535.0)
Name                        : Rpc (Default Web Site)
DistinguishedName           : CN=Rpc (Default Web
Site),CN=HTTP,CN=Protocols,CN=MAILSERVER25,CN=Servers,CN=Exchange
AdministrativeGroup (FYDIBOHF23SPDLT),CN=Administrative Groups,CN=First
Organization,CN=Microsoft Exchange,CN=Services,CN=Configuration,
DC=cpandl,DC=com
Identity                    : MAILSERVER25\Rpc (Default Web Site)
Guid                        : e7333d25-8ad7-47ce-8120-f65ccc2279c8
ObjectCategory              : cpandl.com/Configuration/Schema/ms-Exch-Rpc-
Http-Virtual-Directory
ObjectClass                 : {top, msExchVirtualDirectory,
msExchRpcHttpVirtualDirectory}
WhenChanged                 : 1/22/2008 5:02:32 PM
WhenCreated                 : 1/22/2008 5:02:32 PM
OriginatingServer           : MAILSERVER25.cpandl.com
IsValid                     : True
```

Enabling and Modifying Outlook Anywhere

You can deploy Outlook Anywhere by enabling the feature on at least one Client Access server in each site of your Exchange organizations. To enable Outlook Anywhere, complete the following steps:

1. In the Exchange Management Console, expand the Server Configuration node, and then select the Client Access node.

2. In the upper portion of the details pane, you'll see a list of your organization's Client Access servers. Right-click the server on which you want to enable Outlook Anywhere, and select Enable Outlook Anywhere.

3. In the Enable Outlook Anywhere Wizard, shown in Figure 13-14, type the external host name for the Client Access server, such as **mailer1.cpandl.com**.

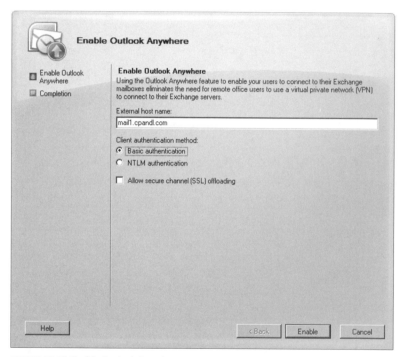

FIGURE 13-14 Enable Outlook Anywhere.

4. Select an available external authentication method. You can select Basic Authentication or NTLM Authentication. NT LAN Manager (NTLM) authentication is more secure than basic authentication.

5. Select the Allow Secure Channel (SSL) Offloading check box only if you have configured an advanced firewall server to work with Exchange 2010 and handle your SSL processing.

6. Click Enable to apply your settings and enable Outlook Anywhere, and then click Finish.

In the Exchange Management Shell, you can enable Outlook Anywhere by using the Enable-OutlookAnywhere cmdlet. Sample 13-2 provides the syntax and usage. The –IISAuthenticationMethods parameter sets the authentication method for the /rpc virtual directory as either Basic or NTLM and disables all other methods. The authentication methods the –DefaultAuthenticationMethod and –ClientAuthenticationMethod parameters use include the following:

- Basic for Basic Authentication
- NTLM for NTLM Authentication
- Digest for Digest Authentication
- Fba for Forms-based Authentication
- WindowsIntegrated for Integrated Windows Authentication
- LiveIdFba for Live ID Forms-based Authentication
- LiveIdBasic for Windows Live ID Basic Authentication
- WSSecurity for Windows SharePoint Security
- Certificate for SSL Certificate Authentication
- NegoEx for Negotiable Exchange

SAMPLE 13-2 Enable-OutlookAnywhere cmdlet syntax and usage

Syntax

```
Enable-OutlookAnywhere -DefaultAuthenticationMethod {AuthMethod}
-ExternalHostName ExternalHostName -SSLOffloading <$true|$false>
[-Server ServerName] [-DomainController DCName]

Enable-OutlookAnywhere [-ClientAuthenticationMethod {AuthMethod}
[-IISAuthenticationMethods <Basic | NTLM>]
-ExternalHostName ExternalHostName -SSLOffloading <$true|$false>
[-Server ServerName] [-DomainController DCName]

{AuthMethod}
<Basic | Digest | NTLM | Fba | WindowsIntegrated | LiveIdFba |
LiveIdBasic | WSSecurity | Certificate | NegoEx | MaxValidValue |
Misconfigured>
```

Usage

```
Enable-OutlookAnywhere -Server "CAServer21"
-ExternalHostName "mailer1.cpandl.com"
-DefaultAuthenticationMethod "Basic"
-SSLOffloading $false
```

If you want to modify the Outlook Anywhere configuration, you can use the Set-OutlookAnywhere cmdlet to do this. Sample 13-3 provides the syntax and usage.

Syntax

```
Set-OutlookAnywhere -Identity VirtualDirId
  [-ClientAuthenticationMethod {AuthMethod}]
  [-DefaultAuthenticationMethod {AuthMethod}]
  [-ExternalHostName ExternalHostName]
  [-IISAuthenticationMethods <Basic | NTLM>]
  [-Name Name]
  [-SSLOffloading <$true | $false>]

{AuthMethod}
<Basic | Digest | NTLM | Fba | WindowsIntegrated | LiveIdFba |
LiveIdBasic | WSSecurity | Certificate | NegoEx | MaxValidValue |
Misconfigured>
```

Usage

```
Set-OutlookAnywhere -Identity "CorpSvr127\Rpc (Default Web Site)"
  -ExternalHostName "mailer1.cpandl.com"
  -ExternalAuthenticationMethod "NTLM"
  -SSLOffloading $true
```

Disabling Outlook Anywhere

If you no longer want a particular Client Access server to allow Outlook clients to use Outlook Anywhere, you can disable this feature by completing the following steps:

1. In the Exchange Management Console, expand the Server Configuration node, and then select the Client Access node.

2. In the upper portion of the details pane, you'll see a list of your organization's Client Access servers. Right-click the server on which you want to enable Outlook Anywhere, and select Disable Outlook Anywhere.

3. When prompted to confirm, click Yes.

In the Exchange Management Shell, you can disable Outlook Anywhere using the Disable-OutlookAnywhere cmdlet. Sample 13-4 provides the syntax and usage.

SAMPLE 13-4 Disable-OutlookAnywhere cmdlet syntax and usage

Syntax

```
Disable-OutlookAnywhere [-Server ServerName | -Identity VirtualDirID]
  [-DomainController DCName]
```

Usage

```
Disable-OutlookAnywhere -Server "CAServer21"
```

Managing Exchange Server Features for Mobile Devices

Mobile access to Exchange Server is supported on any device running Windows Mobile software, including Windows Mobile 5.0 and higher. Devices running Windows Mobile 5.0 with Messaging & Security Feature Pack (MSFP) and later versions of Windows Mobile software include extensions for cellular phones that permit the use of additional features, including

- Autodiscover (Windows Mobile 6.0 or higher only)
- Direct Push
- Exchange ActiveSync Mailbox Policy
- Remote Device Wipe
- Password Recovery
- Direct File Access (Windows Mobile 6.0 or higher only)
- Remote File Access (Windows Mobile 6.0 or higher only)

In Exchange Server, these features are all enabled by default. The sections that follow discuss how these features work and how related options are configured.

Understanding and Using Autodiscover

The Autodiscover service simplifies the provisioning process for mobile devices and for Outlook 2007 and later clients by returning the required Exchange settings after a user enters his or her e-mail address and password. This eliminates the need to configure mobile carriers in Exchange Server, as well as the need to download and install the carriers list on mobile devices.

Autodiscover is enabled by default, and the Default Web Site associated with a particular Web site has an associated Autodiscover virtual directory through which devices can be provisioned.

You can manage Autodiscover using the Exchange Management Shell. To get detailed information about the Autodiscover configuration, type the following command:

```
Get-AutodiscoverVirtualDirectory –Server MyServer
```

where *MyServer* is the name of the Client Access server you want to examine. Included in the detailed information is the identity of the Autodiscover virtual directory, which you can use with related cmdlets.

By default, Autodiscover is configured to use Anonymous, Basic, and Windows authentication. Using the Set-AutodiscoverVirtualDirectory cmdlet, you can enable or disable these authentication methods, as well as digest authentication. You can also set the internal and external URLs for Autodiscover. Neither URL is set by default.

To disable Autodiscover, type the following command:

```
Remove-AutodiscoverVirtualDirectory -Server MyServer
```

where *MyServer* is the name of the Client Access server on which this feature should be disabled.

If you later want to enable Autodiscover, you can type the following command:

```
New-AutodiscoverVirtualDirectory -Server MyServer
```

where *MyServer* is the name of the Client Access server on which this feature should be enabled for the Default Web Site.

Samples 13-5 to 13-8 provide the full syntax and usage for the Get-AutodiscoverVirtualDirectory, New-AutodiscoverVirtualDirectory, Set-AutodiscoverVirtualDirectory and Remove-AutodiscoverVirtualDirectory cmdlets, respectively.

SAMPLE 13-5 Get-AutodiscoverVirtualDirectory cmdlet syntax and usage

Syntax

```
Get-AutodiscoverVirtualDirectory [-Server ServerName | -Identity
VirtualDirID] [-DomainController DCName]
```

Usage

```
Get-AutodiscoverVirtualDirectory
-Identity "CorpMailSvr25\Autodiscover(Default Web Site)"
```

SAMPLE 13-6 New-AutodiscoverVirtualDirectory cmdlet syntax and usage

Syntax

```
New-AutodiscoverVirtualDirectory [-ApplicationRoot RootPath]
[-AppPoolId AppPoolIdentity]
[-BasicAuthentication <$true | $false>]
[-DigestAuthentication <$true | $false>]
[-DomainController DCName]
[-ExternalURL ExternalURL]
[-InternalURL InternalURL]
[-Path FileSystemPath]
[-WebSiteName SiteName]
[-WebSiteName WebSiteName]
[-WindowsAuthentication <$true | $false>]
[-WSSecurityAuthentication <$true | $false>]
```

Usage

```
New-AutodiscoverVirtualDirectory -WebSiteName "Default Web Site"
 -BasicAuthentication $true -DigestAuthentication $false
 -WindowsAuthentication $true
```

Syntax

```
Set-AutodiscoverVirtualDirectory -Identity DirectoryIdentity
[-ExternalURL ExternalURL]
[-InternalURL InternalURL]
[-BasicAuthentication <$true | $false>]
[-DigestAuthentication <$true | $false>]
[-LiveIdBasicAuthentication <$true | $false>]
[-LiveIdSpNegoAuthentication <$true | $false>]
[-DomainController DCName]
[-WindowsAuthentication <$true | $false>]
[-WSSecurityAuthentication <$true | $false>]
```

Usage

```
Set-AutodiscoverVirtualDirectory
-Identity "CorpMailSvr25\Autodiscover(Default Web Site)"
-BasicAuthentication $false -DigestAuthentication $false
-WindowsAuthentication $true
```

Syntax

```
Remove-AutodiscoverVirtualDirectory -Identity DirectoryIdentity
```

Usage

```
Remove-AutodiscoverVirtualDirectory
-Identity "CorpMailSvr25\Autodiscover(Default Web Site)"
```

Understanding and Using Direct Push

Direct Push automates the synchronization process, enabling a mobile device to make requests to keep itself up to date. When the Web site used with Exchange ActiveSync has SSL enabled, Direct Push allows a mobile device to issue long-lived Hypertext Transfer Protocol Secure (HTTPS) monitoring requests to Exchange Server. Exchange Server monitors activity in the related user's mailbox. If new mail arrives or other changes are made to the mailbox—such as modifications to calendar or contact items—Exchange sends a response to the mobile device, stating that changes have occurred and that the device should initiate synchronization with Exchange Server. The device then issues a synchronization request. When synchronization is complete, the device issues another long-lived HTTPS monitoring request.

Port 443 is the default TCP port used with SSL. For Direct Push to work, port 443 must be opened between the Internet and the organization's Internet-facing

Client Access server or servers. You do not need to open port 443 on your external firewalls to all of your Client Access servers—only those to which users can establish connections. The Client Access server receiving the request automatically proxies the request so that it can be handled appropriately. If necessary, this can also mean proxying requests between the mobile device and the Client Access server in the user's home site. A user's home site is the Active Directory site where the mailbox server hosting his or her mailbox is located.

TIP Microsoft recommends increasing the maximum time-out value for connections to 30 minutes.

Understanding and Using Exchange ActiveSync Mailbox Policy

Exchange ActiveSync Mailbox Policy makes it possible to enhance the security of mobile devices used to access your Exchange servers. For example, you can use policy to require a password of a specific length and to configure devices to automatically prompt for a password after a period of inactivity.

Each mailbox policy you create has a name and a specific set of rules with which it is associated. Because you can apply policies separately to mailboxes when you create or modify them, you can create different policies for different groups of users. For example, you can have one policy for users and another policy for managers. You can also create separate policies for departments within the organization. For example, you can have separate policies for Marketing, Customer Support, and Technology.

Viewing Existing Exchange Active Sync Mailbox Policies

When the Client Access server role is installed on an Exchange server, the setup process creates a default Exchange ActiveSync policy. This default policy allows ActiveSync to be used without restrictions or password requirements. All users with mailboxes have this policy applied by default. You can modify the settings of this policy to change the settings for all users or create new policies for specific groups of users.

In the Exchange Management Console, you can view the currently configured Exchange ActiveSync Mailbox policies by expanding the Organization Configuration node, selecting the Client Access node, and then selecting the Exchange ActiveSync Mailbox Policies node. In the details pane, you'll see a list of current policies.

In the Exchange Management Shell, you can list policies using the Get-ActiveSyncMailboxPolicy cmdlet. Sample 13-9 provides the syntax, usage, and sample output. If you do not provide an identity with this cmdlet, all available Exchange ActiveSync Mailbox policies are listed.

Syntax

```
Get-ActiveSyncMailboxPolicy [-Identity PolicyIdentity]
[-DomainController DCName] [-Organization OrgId]
```

Usage

```
Get-ActiveSyncMailboxPolicy

Get-ActiveSyncMailboxPolicy
-Identity "Primary ActiveSync Mailbox Policy"
```

Output

```
RunspaceId                            :
AllowNonProvisionableDevices          : True
AlphanumericDevicePasswordRequired    : False
AttachmentsEnabled                    : True
DeviceEncryptionEnabled               : False
RequireStorageCardEncryption          : False
DevicePasswordEnabled                 : False
PasswordRecoveryEnabled               : False
DevicePolicyRefreshInterval           : unlimited
AllowSimpleDevicePassword             : True
MaxAttachmentSize                     : unlimited
WSSAccessEnabled                      : True
UNCAccessEnabled                      : True
MinDevicePasswordLength               : 4
MaxInactivityTimeDeviceLock           : 00:15:00
MaxDevicePasswordFailedAttempts       : 8
DevicePasswordExpiration              : unlimited
DevicePasswordHistory                 : 0
IsDefaultPolicy                       : True
AllowStorageCard                      : True
AllowCamera                           : True
RequireDeviceEncryption               : False
AllowUnsignedApplications             : True
AllowUnsignedInstallationPackages     : True
AllowWiFi                             : True
AllowTextMessaging                    : True
AllowPOPIMAPEmail                     : True
AllowIrDA                             : True
RequireManualSyncWhenRoaming          : False
AllowDesktopSync                      : True
AllowHTMLEmail                        : True
RequireSignedSMIMEMessages            : False
RequireEncryptedSMIMEMessages         : False
AllowSMIMESoftCerts                   : True
AllowBrowser                          : True
```

```
AllowConsumerEmail                           : True
AllowRemoteDesktop                           : True
AllowInternetSharing                         : True
AllowBluetooth                               : Allow
MaxCalendarAgeFilter                         : All
MaxEmailAgeFilter                            : All
RequireSignedSMIMEAlgorithm                  : SHA1
RequireEncryptionSMIMEAlgorithm              : TripleDES
AllowSMIMEEncryptionAlgorithmNegotiation     : AllowAnyAlgorithmNegotiation
MinDevicePasswordComplexCharacters           : 3
MaxEmailBodyTruncationSize                   : unlimited
MaxEmailHTMLBodyTruncationSize               : unlimited
UnapprovedInROMApplicationList               : {}
ApprovedApplicationList                      : {}
AllowExternalDeviceManagement                : False
MobileOTAUpdateMode                          : MinorVersionUpdates
AllowMobileOTAUpdate                         : False
AdminDisplayName                             :
ExchangeVersion                              : 0.1 (8.0.535.0)
Name                                         : Default
DistinguishedName                            : CN=Default,CN=Mobile Mailbox
Policies,CN=First Organization,CN=Microsoft Exchange,CN=Services,
CN=Configuration,DC=cpandl,DC=com
Identity                                     : Default
Guid                                         :
ObjectCategory                               : cpandl.com/Configuration/
Schema/ms-Exch-Mobile-Mailbox-Policy
ObjectClass                                  : {top, msExchRecipientTemplate,
msExchMobileMailboxPolicy}
WhenChanged                                  : 12/17/2009 10:21:15 PM
WhenCreated                                  : 12/17/2009 10:21:15 PM
WhenChangedUTC                               : 12/18/2009 5:21:15 AM
WhenCreatedUTC                               : 12/18/2009 5:21:15 AM
OrganizationId                               :
OriginatingServer                            : CORPSERVER45.cpandl.com
IsValid                                      : True
```

Creating Exchange ActiveSync Mailbox Policies

The Exchange ActiveSync Mailbox policies you create apply to your entire organization. You apply policies separately after you create them, as discussed in the
"Assigning Exchange ActiveSync Mailbox Policies" section of this chapter.

You can create a new policy by completing the following steps:

1. Start the Exchange Management Console. Expand the Organization Configu-
    ration node, and then select Client Access.

2. In the details pane, select the Exchange ActiveSync Mailbox Policies tab.
    Right-click an open area of the details pane, and select New Exchange
    ActiveSync Mailbox Policy.

3. As shown in Figure 13-15, type a descriptive name for the policy, and then use the following options to configure the policy:

- **Allow Non-Provisionable Devices** Nonprovisionable devices are older devices that do not support all policy settings. If you select this option, these older devices can connect to Exchange 2010 by using Exchange ActiveSync.

- **Allow Attachments To Be Downloaded To Device** Enables attachments to be downloaded to mobile devices. If you do not select this option, message attachments are not downloaded with user messages.

- **Require Alphanumeric Passwords** Requires that a password contain numeric and alphanumeric characters. If you do not select this option, users can use simple passwords, which might not be as secure.

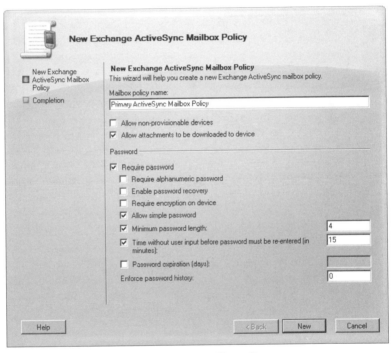

FIGURE 13-15 Create the Exchange ActiveSync Mailbox policy.

- **Enable Password Recovery** Enables the device password to be recovered from the server. If you do not select this option and the user forgets his or her password, you will not be able to reset the device password and the user will be unable to access his or her mailbox using the device.

- **Require Encryption On Device** Requires mobile devices to use encryption. Because encrypted data cannot be accessed without the appropriate password, this helps to protect the data on the device. If you select this option, Exchange allows devices to download data only if they use encryption.

- **Allow Simple Password** Allows the user to use a noncomplex password instead of a password that meets the minimum complexity requirements.

- **Minimum Password Length** Allows you to set a minimum password length. You must select the related check box to set the minimum password length, such as eight characters. The longer the password, the more secure it is. A good minimum password length is between 8 and 12 characters. This length is sufficient in most cases.

- **Time Without User Input Before Password Must Be Re-Entered (in minutes)** Allows you to specify the length of time that a device can go without user input before it locks. You must select the related check box to set the time interval, such as 15.

- **Password Expiration (days)** Allows you to specify the maximum length of time users can keep a password before they have to change it. You can use this option to require users to change their passwords periodically. A good password expiration value is between 30 and 90 days. This period is sufficient to allow use of the password without requiring overly frequent changes.

- **Enforce Password History** Allows you to specify how frequently old passwords can be reused. You can use this option to discourage users from changing back and forth between a common set of passwords. To disable this option, set the size of the password history to zero. To enable this option, set the desired size of the password history. A good value is between 3 and 6. This helps to deter users from switching between a small list of common passwords.

4. Click New to create the policy, and then click Finish. Optimize the configuration, as discussed in "Optimizing Exchange ActiveSync Mailbox Policies."

In the Exchange Management Shell, you can create new Exchange ActiveSync Mailbox policies using the New-ActiveSyncMailboxPolicy cmdlet. Sample 13-10 provides the syntax and usage. There are additional policy settings you can access in the shell that you cannot access in the Exchange Management Console. Some of the policy settings are available only with an enterprise client access license.

SAMPLE 13-10 New-ActiveSyncMailboxPolicy cmdlet syntax and usage

Syntax

```
New-ActiveSyncMailboxPolicy -Name Name
[-AllowBluetooth <Disable | HandsfreeOnly | Allow>]
[-AllowBrowser <$true | $false>]
[-AllowCamera <$true | $false>]
[-AllowConsumerEmail <$true | $false>]
[-AllowDesktopSync <$true | $false>]
[-AllowExternalDeviceManagement <$true | $false>]
[-AllowHTMLEmail <$true | $false>]
```

```
[-AllowInternetSharing <$true | $false>]
[-AllowIrDA <$true | $false>]
[-AllowMobileOTAUpdate <$true | $false>]
[-AllowNonProvisionableDevices <$true | $false>]
[-AllowPOPIMAPEmail <$true | $false>]
[-AllowRemoteDesktop <$true | $false>]
[-AllowSimpleDevicePassword <$true | $false>]
[-AllowSMIMEEncryptionAlgorithmNegotiation <BlockNegotiation |
OnlyStrongAlgorithmNegotiation | AllowAnyAlgorithmNegotiation>]
[-AllowSMIMESoftCerts <$true | $false>]
[-AllowStorageCard <$true | $false>]
[-AllowTextMessaging <$true | $false>]
[-AllowUnsignedApplications <$true | $false>]
[-AllowUnsignedInstallationPackages <$true | $false>]
[-AllowWiFi <$true | $false>]
[-AlphanumericDevicePasswordRequired < $true | $false>]
[-ApprovedApplicationList AppList]
[-AttachmentsEnabled <$true | $false>]
[-DeviceEncryptionEnabled <$true | $false>]
[-DevicePasswordEnabled <$true | $false>]
[-DevicePasswordExpiration <dd.hh.mm:ss | Unlimited>]
[-DevicePasswordHistory NumPasswords]
[-DomainController <Fqdn>]
[-IsDefaultPolicy <$true | $false>]
[-MaxAttachmentSize <SizeKB | Unlimited>]
[-MaxCalendarAgeFilter <All | TwoWeeks | OneMonth | ThreeMonths
| SixMonths>]
[-MaxDevicePasswordFailedAttempts <Unlimited>]
[-MaxEmailAgeFilter <All | OneDay | ThreeDays | OneWeek | TwoWeeks
| OneMonth>]
[-MaxEmailBodyTruncationSize <Unlimited>]
[-MaxEmailHTMLBodyTruncationSize <MaxSizeKB | Unlimited>]
[-MaxInactivityTimeDeviceLock <hh.mm:ss | Unlimited>]
[-MinDevicePasswordComplexCharacters MinNumberOfComplexCharacters]
[-MinDevicePasswordLength MinPasswordLength]
[-MobileOTAUpdateMode <MajorVersionUpdates | MinorVersionUpdates |
BetaVersionUpdates>] [-Organization OrganizationId]
[-PasswordRecoveryEnabled <$true | $false>]
[-RequireDeviceEncryption <$true | $false>]
[-RequireEncryptedSMIMEMessages <$true | $false>]
[-RequireEncryptionSMIMEAlgorithm <TripleDES | DES | RC2128bit
| RC264bit | RC240bit>]
[-RequireManualSyncWhenRoaming <$true | $false>]
[-RequireSignedSMIMEAlgorithm <SHA1 | MD5>]
[-RequireSignedSMIMEMessages <$true | $false>]
[-RequireStorageCardEncryption <$true | $false>]
[-TemplateInstance Instance]
[-UnapprovedInROMApplicationList AppList]
[-UNCAccessEnabled <$true | $false>]
[-WSSAccessEnabled <$true | $false>]
```

```
New-ActiveSyncMailboxPolicy -Name "Primary ActiveSync Mailbox Policy"
-AllowNonProvisionableDevices $true
-DevicePasswordEnabled $true
-AlphanumericDevicePasswordRequired $true
-MaxInactivityTimeDeviceLock "00.15:00"
-MinDevicePasswordLength "8"
-PasswordRecoveryEnabled $true
-DeviceEncryptionEnabled $true
-AttachmentsEnabled $true
```

Optimizing Exchange ActiveSync Mailbox Policies

When you create an Exchange ActiveSync Mailbox policy, some additional settings are configured automatically. By default, access to both Windows file shares and Microsoft Windows SharePoint Services is allowed. If you specified that passwords are required, by default, the number of failed attempts allowed is eight. If the policy allows devices to download attachments, there is no default limit on the attachment size. You can modify these and other policy settings by completing the following steps:

1. In the Exchange Management Console, right-click the policy, and select Properties.

2. On the General tab, shown on the left in Figure 13-16, use the options to configure whether nonprovisionable devices are allowed and optionally, set a refresh interval.

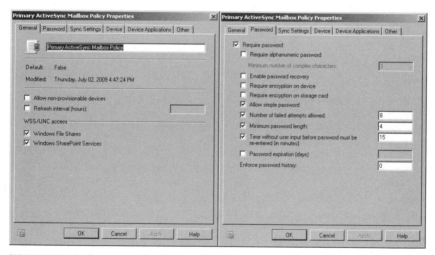

FIGURE 13-16 Configure general and password options.

3. On the Password tab, also shown in Figure 13-16, you must select the Require Password check box to set controls for device passwords. The options

available are the same as when you are creating a policy, with one addition: Number Of Failed Attempts Allowed. To limit the number of failed password attempts that can be made before a user's account is locked, select this check box and then set the allowed limit.

4. On the Sync Settings tab, shown on the left in Figure 13-17, you can configure general device sync options. For past calendar and e-mail items, you can specify whether all items should be synced or only items from a specific period of time, such as the last two weeks. If you want to limit message size, select the Limit E-Mail Size To check box and then enter the size limit in kilobytes (KB), such as 512. If you allow attachments and you want to limit the size of attachments that users can download, select the Maximum Attachment Size (KB) check box and then enter the size limit in kilobytes (KB), such as 900.

5. On the Device tab, shown on the right in Figure 13-17, you can configure device-specific settings. To allow the use of a device-specific setting, select the related Allow check box. To prevent the uses of a device-specific setting, clear the related Allow check box. You can:

   - Allow or disallow the device to access removable storage, such as memory cards.
   - Allow or disallow the device's built-in camera.
   - Allow or disallow the device to connect to a wireless network.
   - Allow or disallow the device to connect to other devices using infrared.
   - Allow or disallow another device to share the device's Internet connection.
   - Allow or disallow remote desktop connections.
   - Allow or disallow the device to connect to and synchronize with a desktop computer.

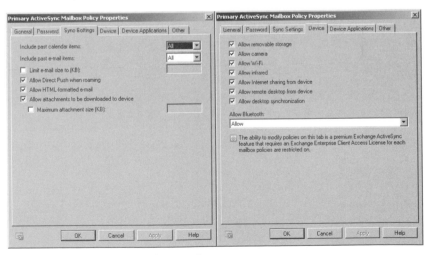

FIGURE 13-17 Configure sync and device settings.

6. Using the Allow Bluetooth list, you can specify whether and how the device can use Bluetooth. To allow the device to use Bluetooth, select Allow. To allow the device to use Bluetooth only in hands-free mode, select Handsfree Only. To prevent the device from using Bluetooth, select Disable.

7. On the Device Applications tab, shown on the left in Figure 13-18, you can configure allowed or blocked applications. To enable features of the mobile device, you can:

   - Select Allow Browser to allow the device to use Pocket Internet Explorer.

   - Select Allow Consumer Mail to allow the device to access e-mail accounts other than Microsoft Exchange.

   - Select Allow Unsigned Applications to allow the device to execute unsigned applications.

   - Select Allow Unsigned Installation Packages to allow the device to install unsigned applications.

8. On the Other tab, shown on the left in Figure 13-18, identify allowed or blocked applications using the options provided.

9. Click OK to apply your settings.

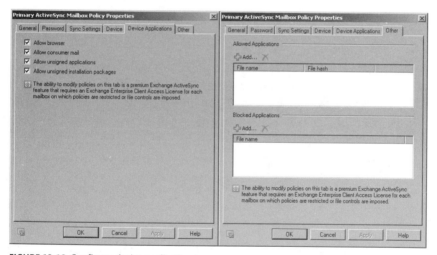

FIGURE 13-18 Configure device applications.

In the Exchange Management Shell, you can modify Exchange ActiveSync Mailbox policies using the Set-ActiveSyncMailboxPolicy cmdlet. Sample 13-11 provides the syntax and usage.

Syntax

```
Set-ActiveSyncMailboxPolicy -Identity Name
[-AllowBluetooth <Disable | HandsfreeOnly | Allow>]
[-AllowBrowser <$true | $false>]
[-AllowCamera <$true | $false>]
[-AllowConsumerEmail <$true | $false>]
[-AllowDesktopSync <$true | $false>]
[-AllowExternalDeviceManagement <$true | $false>]
[-AllowHTMLEmail <$true | $false>]
[-AllowInternetSharing <$true | $false>]
[-AllowIrDA <$true | $false>]
[-AllowMobileOTAUpdate <$true | $false>]
[-AllowNonProvisionableDevices <$true | $false>]
[-AllowPOPIMAPEmail <$true | $false>]
[-AllowRemoteDesktop <$true | $false>]
[-AllowSimpleDevicePassword <$true | $false>]
[-AllowSMIMEEncryptionAlgorithmNegotiation <BlockNegotiation |
OnlyStrongAlgorithmNegotiation | AllowAnyAlgorithmNegotiation>]
[-AllowSMIMESoftCerts <$true | $false>]
[-AllowStorageCard <$true | $false>]
[-AllowTextMessaging <$true | $false>]
[-AllowUnsignedApplications <$true | $false>]
[-AllowUnsignedInstallationPackages <$true | $false>]
[-AllowWiFi <$true | $false>]
[-AlphanumericDevicePasswordRequired < $true | $false>]
[-ApprovedApplicationList AppList]
[-AttachmentsEnabled <$true | $false>]
[-DeviceEncryptionEnabled <$true | $false>]
[-DevicePasswordEnabled <$true | $false>]
[-DevicePasswordExpiration <dd.hh.mm:ss | Unlimited>]
[-DevicePasswordHistory NumPasswords]
[-DomainController DCName]
[-IsDefaultPolicy <$true | $false>]
[-MaxAttachmentSize <SizeKB | Unlimited>]
[-MaxCalendarAgeFilter <All | TwoWeeks | OneMonth | ThreeMonths
| SixMonths>]
[-MaxDevicePasswordFailedAttempts <Unlimited>]
[-MaxEmailAgeFilter <All | OneDay | ThreeDays | OneWeek | TwoWeeks
| OneMonth>]
[-MaxEmailBodyTruncationSize <Unlimited>]
[-MaxEmailHTMLBodyTruncationSize <MaxSizeKB | Unlimited>]
[-MaxInactivityTimeDeviceLock <hh.mm:ss | Unlimited>]
[-MinDevicePasswordComplexCharacters MinNumberOfComplexCharacters]
[-MinDevicePasswordLength MinPasswordLength]
[-MobileOTAUpdateMode <MajorVersionUpdates | MinorVersionUpdates |
BetaVersionUpdates>] [-Organization OrganizationId]
[-Name Name]
[-PasswordRecoveryEnabled <$true | $false>]
```

```
[-RequireDeviceEncryption <$true | $false>]
[-RequireEncryptedSMIMEMessages <$true | $false>]
[-RequireEncryptionSMIMEAlgorithm <TripleDES | DES | RC2128bit
| RC264bit | RC240bit>]
[-RequireManualSyncWhenRoaming <$true | $false>]
[-RequireSignedSMIMEAlgorithm <SHA1 | MD5>]
[-RequireSignedSMIMEMessages <$true | $false>]
[-RequireStorageCardEncryption <$true | $false>]
[-TemplateInstance Instance]
[-UnapprovedInROMApplicationList AppList]
[-UNCAccessEnabled <$true | $false>]
[-WSSAccessEnabled <$true | $false>]
```

Usage

```
Set-ActiveSyncMailboxPolicy -Identity "Primary ActiveSync Mailbox Policy"
 -AllowNonProvisionableDevices $false
 -DevicePasswordEnabled $true
 -AlphanumericDevicePasswordRequired $true
 -MaxInactivityTimeDeviceLock "00:08:00"
 -MinDevicePasswordLength "6"
 -MaxDevicePasswordFailedAttempts "5"
```

Assigning Exchange ActiveSync Mailbox Policies

Mailbox servers automatically apply the default Exchange ActiveSync Mailbox policy through implicit inheritance when you create a new mailbox. Any mailbox that has implicitly inherited policy automatically applies the current default policy and its settings. When you modify the default policy or configure a new default policy, you change the Exchange ActiveSync settings for all mailbox users that implicitly inherit the default policy.

To set a new default policy and have it automatically applied through inheritance, follow these steps:

1. Start the Exchange Management Console. Expand the Organization Configuration node, and then select the Client Access node.

2. On the Exchange ActiveSync Mailbox Policies tab, you'll see a list of current policies. The current default policy has the value True in the Default column. To make another policy the default and apply this policy to all users in the Exchange organization, right-click the policy and then select Set As Default.

To prevent a mailbox from implicitly inheriting the default policy and its settings, you can explicitly assign a policy to the mailbox by completing the following steps:

1. In the Exchange Management Console, expand the Recipient Configuration node, and then select the Mailbox node.

2. Right-click the mailbox with which you want to work, and then select Properties.

3. On the Mailbox Features tab, select Exchange ActiveSync and then click Properties.

4. Click Browse. In the Select ActiveSync Mailbox Policy dialog box, select the policy you want to assign and then click OK. Click OK twice to apply your settings.

NOTE When you explicitly assign an Exchange ActiveSync policy, the mailbox applies only the settings from that policy and is not affected by the default policy. However, if you delete the Exchange ActiveSync policy being applied to the mailbox, the default policy will once again be inherited implicitly and applied.

In Exchange Management Shell, you can assign an Exchange ActiveSync Mailbox policy to a mailbox using the –ActiveSyncMailboxPolicy parameter of the Set-CAS-Mailbox cmdlet. Sample 13-12 provides the syntax and usage.

SAMPLE 13-12 Assigning an Exchange ActiveSync Mailbox policy to a mailbox

Syntax

```
Set-CASMailbox -Identity MailboxIdentity
-ActiveSyncMailboxPolicy PolicyIdentity
```

Usage

```
Set-CASMailbox -Identity "markh@cpandl.com"
-ActiveSyncMailboxPolicy "Primary ActiveSync Mailbox Policy"
```

Removing Exchange ActiveSync Mailbox Policies

When you no longer need an Exchange ActiveSync Mailbox policy, you can remove it, provided that it isn't the current default policy. In the Exchange Management Console, right-click the policy, and select Remove. When prompted to confirm, click Yes to delete the policy. If users are assigned to the policy, they will stop using the policy and implicitly inherit the current default policy.

In the Exchange Management Shell, you can remove an Exchange ActiveSync Mailbox policy using the Remove-ActiveSyncMailboxPolicy cmdlet. Sample 13-13 provides the syntax and usage.

SAMPLE 13-13 Remove-ActiveSyncMailboxPolicy cmdlet syntax and usage

Syntax

```
Remove-ActiveSyncMailboxPolicy -Identity Name [-DomainController DCName]
[-Force <$true | $false>]
```

Usage

```
Remove-ActiveSyncMailboxPolicy -Identity "Primary ActiveSync
Mailbox Policy"
```

Understanding and Using Remote Device Wipe

Although passwords help to protect mobile devices, they don't prevent access to the device. Malicious individuals could still gain access to data. In the event that a device is lost or stolen, you can use Remote Device Wipe to instruct a mobile device to delete all its data.

Remotely Wiping a Device

An administrator or the owner of the device can prevent the compromising of sensitive data by initiating a remote device wipe. After you initiate a remote device wipe and the device receives the request, the device confirms the remote wipe request by sending a confirmation message and then removes all its data the next time it connects to Exchange Server. Not only does this return the device to its factory default condition, but it also removes any data stored on any storage card inserted into the device. Wiping the data should prevent it from being compromised.

The easiest way to wipe a device remotely is to have the device owner initiate the wipe using Outlook Web App. When the device acknowledges the request, the user will get a confirmation e-mail. Alternatively, an administrator can log on to Outlook Web App as the device owner and initiate the remote wipe. To do this, follow these steps:

1. Open your Web browser. In the Address field, type the Outlook Web App URL, such as **https://mail.cpandl.com/owa**, and then press Enter to access this page.
2. When prompted, provide the logon credentials of the user whose device you want to wipe. Do not provide your administrator credentials.
3. On the Outlook Web App toolbar, click Options.
4. The left pane of the Options view provides a list of options. Click Phone.
5. The user's mobile devices are listed in the details pane. Select the device you want to wipe, and then click Wipe Device.
6. Confirm the action when prompted.
7. Click Remove Device From List.

NOTE You can use Outlook Web App for remote device wiping only if the user has used the device previously to access Exchange Server and if you have enabled the Segmentation feature of Exchange Active Directory Integration (which is the default configuration).

CAUTION Because wiping a device causes complete data loss, you should do this only when you've contacted the user directly (preferably in person) and confirmed that the mobile device has been lost and that he or she understands the consequences of wiping the device. If your organization has a formal policy regarding the wiping of lost devices that might contain sensitive company data, be sure you follow this policy and get any necessary approvals. Keep in mind that while a remote wipe makes it very difficult to retrieve any data from the device, in theory this is possible with sophisticated data recovery tools.

In the Exchange Management Shell, you can list the mobile devices registered as partners for a user's mailbox using the Get-MobileDeviceStatistics cmdlet. The device identity you want is the DeviceId string. If the user has multiple mobile devices, also be sure to consult the DeviceModel and DeviceOperatorNetwork values.

After you know the mobile device identity, you can issue a remote device wipe command using the Clear-ActiveSyncDevice cmdlet. You then need to confirm that you want to wipe the device when prompted by pressing the Y key. Samples 13-14 and 13-15 provide the syntax and usage for Get-MobileDeviceStatistics and Clear-ActiveSyncDevice cmdlets, respectively. With Get-MobileDeviceStatistics, you can specify either the unique identity of the remote device or the user mailbox you want to work with. The –GetMailboxLog parameter retrieves mailbox logs and usage information. Use the –OutputPath parameter to direct the statistics to a specific folder path or the –NotificationEmailAddresses parameter to e-mail the statistics to specified e-mail addresses.

NOTE If you determine that you've made a mistake in issuing a remote wipe, you should immediately issue a cancellation request using the Clear-ActiveSyncDevice cmdlet. Here, set the –Cancel parameter to $true. The remove device processes the cancellation request only if the remote wipe has not yet been initiated.

SAMPLE 13-14 Get-MobileDeviceStatistics cmdlet syntax and usage

Syntax

```
Get-MobileDeviceStatistics -Identity DeviceIdentity

Get-MobileDeviceStatistics -Mailbox MailboxIdentity
[-GetMailboxLog <$true | $false>]
[-NotificationEmailAddresses EmailAddress1, EmailAddress2, . . .]
[-OutputPath Path] [-ShowRecoveryPassword <$true | $false>]
```

Usage

```
Get-MobileDeviceStatistics -Mailbox "David Pelton"
```

SAMPLE 13-15 Clear-ActiveSyncDevice cmdlet syntax and usage

Syntax

```
Clear-ActiveSyncDevice -Identity MobileDeviceIdentity
[-Cancel <$true | $false>] [-DomainController DCName]
[-NotificationEmailAddresses EmailAddress1, EmailAddress2, . . .]
```

Usage

```
Clear-ActiveSyncDevice -Identity "Mobile_DavidP"

Clear-ActiveSyncDevice -Identity "Mobile_DavidP" -Cancel $true
```

Reviewing the Remote Wipe Status

When you initiate a remote wipe, the mobile device removes all its data the next time it connects to Exchange Server. You can review the remote wipe status using an alternate syntax for the Get-MobileDeviceStatistics cmdlet. Instead of passing the cmdlet the –Mailbox parameter, use the Identity parameter to specify the DeviceId string of the device you wiped. The statistics returned will include these output parameters:

- **DeviceWipeRequestTime**   The time you request a remote wipe
- **DeviceWipeSentTime**   The time the server sent the remote wipe command to the device
- **DeviceWipeAckTime**   The time when the device acknowledged receipt of the remote wipe command

If there is a DeviceWipeSentTime timestamp, the device has connected to Exchange Server and Exchange Server sent the device the remote wipe command. If there is a DeviceWipeAckTime timestamp, the device acknowledged receipt of the remote wipe and has started to wipe its data.

Understanding and Using Password Recovery

Users can create passwords for their mobile devices. If a user forgets his or her password, you can obtain a recovery password that unlocks the device and lets the user create a new password. The user can also recover his or her device password by using Outlook Web App.

To use Outlook Web App to recover a user's device password, complete the following steps:

1. Open a Web browser. In the Address field, type the Outlook Web App URL, such as **https://mail.cpandl.com/owa**, and then press Enter to access this page.

2. When prompted, provide the user's logon credentials. Do not provide your administrator credentials.

3. On the Outlook Web App toolbar, click Options.

4. The left pane of the Options view provides a list of options. Click Phone.

5. The user's mobile devices are listed in the details pane. Select the device for which you are recovering the password.

6. Click Display Recovery Password.

You also can display the device recovery password by completing the following steps:

1. In the Exchange Management Console, expand the Recipient Configuration node, and then select the Mailbox node.

2. Right-click the user's mailbox, and then select Manage Mobile Device. The device recovery password is displayed in the Manage Mobile Device dialog box.

In the Exchange Management Shell, you can display the device recovery password using the –ShowRecoveryPassword parameter of the Get-ActiveSyncDevice-Statistics cmdlet. Sample 13-16 provides the syntax and usage.

SAMPLE 13-16 Recovering a device password

Syntax

```
Get-ActiveSyncDeviceStatistics -Mailbox MailboxIdentity
 -ShowRecoveryPassword $true {AddtlParams}


Get-ActiveSyncDeviceStatistics -Identity ActiveSyncDeviceIdentity
 -ShowRecoveryPassword $true {AddtlParams}


{AddtlParams}
[-GetMailboxLog <$true | $false>] [-DomainController DCName]
[-NotificationEmailAddresses AliasOrEmail1, AliasOrEmail2, . . . ]
```

Usage

```
Get-ActiveSyncDeviceStatistics -Mailbox "HelenB@cpandl.com"
 -ShowRecoveryPassword $true
```

Understanding and Configuring Direct File Access

By default, Exchange Server 2010 allows users to access files directly through Outlook, Outlook Web App, and related services. This means that users will be able to access files attached to e-mail messages. You can configure how users interact with files using one of three options in the Exchange Management Console:

- **Allow**   Allows users to access files of the specified types, and sends the users' browser information that allows the files to be displayed or opened in the proper applications
- **Block**   Prevents users from accessing files of the specified types
- **Force Save**   Forces users to save files of the specified types prior to opening them

Table 13-4 lists the default file extensions and default Multipurpose Internet Mail Extensions (MIME) values that Exchange Server allows, blocks, or sets to force save by default. These settings are applied to the OWA virtual directory on Client Access servers. If a server has multiple OWA virtual directories or you have multiple Client Access servers, you must configure each directory and server separately.

NOTE   If there are conflicts between the allow, block, and force save lists, the allow list takes precedence. This means that the allow list settings override the block list and the force save list. As updates are applied to Exchange Server, the default lists can change. Be sure to check the currently applied defaults.

TABLE 13-4 Default File Extensions and Default MIME Values for Direct File Access

OPTION	DEFAULT FILE NAME EXTENSIONS	DEFAULT MIME VALUES
Allow	.avi, .bmp, .doc, .docm, .docx, .gif, .jpg, .mp3, .one, .pdf, .png, .ppsm, .ppsx, .ppt, .pub, .rpmsg, .rtf, .tif, .tiff, .txt, .vsd, .wav, .wma, .wmv, .xls, .xlsb, .xlsm, .xlsx, .zip	image/jpeg, image/png, image/gif, image/bmp
Block	.ade, .adp, .asx, .app, .asp, .aspx, .asx, .asx, .bas, .bat, .cer, .chm, .cmd, .com, .cpl, .crt, .csh, .der, .exe, .fxp, .gadget, .hlp, .hta, .htc, .inf, .ins, .isp, .its, .js, .jse, .ksh, .lnk, .mad, .maf, .mag, .mam, .maq, .mar, .mas, .mat, .mau, .mav, .maw, .mda, .mdb, .mde, .mdt, .mdw, .mdz, .mht, .mhtml, .msc, .msh, .msh1, .mshxml, .msh1xml, .msi, .msp, .mst, .ops, .pcd, .pif, .plg, .prf, .prg, .ps1, .ps2, .psc1, .psc2, .ps1xml, .ps2xml, .pst, .reg, .scf, .scr, .sct, .shb, .shs, .spl, .swf, .tmp, .url, .vb, .vbe, .vbs, .vsmacros, .vss, .vst, .vsw, .ws, .wsc, .wsf, .wsh, .xml	application/hta, application/javascript, application/msaccess, application/prg, application/x-javascript, application/xml, text/javascript, text/scriptlet, text/xml, x-internet-signup
Force Save	.vsmacros, .mshxml, .aspx, .xml, .wsh, .wsf, .wsc, .vsw, .vst, .vss, .vbs, .vbe, .url, .tmp, .swf, .spl, . shs, .shb, .sct, .scr, .scf, .reg, .pst, .prg, .prf, .plg, .pif, .pcd, .ops, .mst, .msp, .msi, .msh, .msc, .mdz, .mdw, .mdt, .mde, .mdb, .mda, .maw, .mav, .mau, .mat, .mas, .mar, .maq, .mam, .mag, .maf, .mad, .lnk, .ksh, .jse, .its, .isp, .ins, .inf, .hta, .hlp, .fxp, .exe, .dir, .dcr, .csh, .crt, .cpl, .com, .cmd, .chm, .cer, .bat, .bas, .asx, .asp, .app, .adp, .ade, .ws, .vb, .js	Application/x-shockwave-flash, Application/octet-stream, Application/futuresplash, Application/x-director

Exchange Server considers all file extensions and MIME types not listed on the allow, block, or force save list to be unknown files and file types. The default setting for unknown file types is force save.

Based on the user's selection, the configuration of his or her network settings, or both, Exchange divides all client connections into one of two classes:

- **Public or shared computer** A public computer is a computer being used on a public network or a computer shared by multiple people.

- **Private computer** A private computer is a computer on a private network that is used by one person.

You can enable or disable direct access to files separately for public computers and private computers. However, the allow, block, and force save settings for both types of computers are shared and applied to both public and private computers in the same way.

You can configure direct file access by completing the following steps:

1. In the Exchange Management Console, expand the Server Configuration node, and then select the Client Access node.

2. In the upper portion of the details pane, you'll see a list of your organization's Client Access servers. Select the server you want to configure.

3. In the lower portion of the details pane, you'll see a list of option tabs for the selected server. On the Outlook Web App tab, right-click the virtual directory for which you are configuring direct file access, and then select Properties. Typically, you'll want to configure the OWA virtual directory on the Default Web Site because this directory is used by default for Outlook Web App.

4. To enable or disable direct file access for public computers, on the Public Computer File Access tab, select or clear the Enable Direct File Access check box, as appropriate. (See Figure 13-19.)

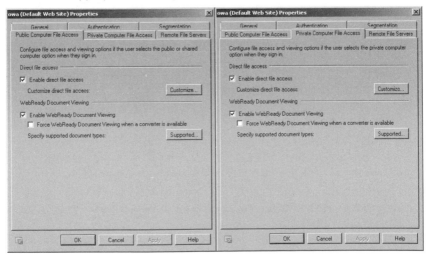

FIGURE 13-19 Enable or disable direct file access for public computers.

5. To enable or disable direct file access for private computers, on the Private Computer File Access tab (shown on the right in Figure 13-19), select or clear the Enable Direct File Access check box, as appropriate.

6. On either the Public Computer File Access tab or Private Computer File Access tab, click the Customize button on the Direct File Access panel. The Direct File Access Settings dialog box appears, as shown in Figure 13-20.

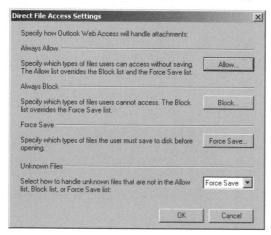

FIGURE 13-20 Configure the direct file access settings.

7. In the Direct File Access Settings dialog box, you can configure allowed files by clicking Allow. The Allow List dialog box appears, as shown in Figure 13-21. Use the following techniques to configure allowed files, and then click OK:

   • To allow a new file extension, type it in the text box provided. Be sure to include the period, such as **.xhtml**, and then press Enter or click Add.

   • To allow a new MIME type, enter it in the text box provided. Be sure to include the full MIME type designator, such as **text/xhtml**, and then press Enter or click Add.

   • To stop allowing a file extension or MIME type, select it and then click the Remove button. This button shows an X.

8. In the Direct File Access Settings dialog box, you can configure blocked files by clicking Block. The Block List dialog box appears. Use the following techniques to configure blocked files, and then click OK:

   • To block a new file extension, type it in the text box provided. Be sure to include the period, such as **.src**, and then press Enter or click Add.

   • To block a new MIME type, enter it in the text box provided. Be sure to include the full MIME type designator, such as **application/src**, and then press Enter or click Add.

   • To stop blocking a file extension or MIME type, select it, and then click the Remove button.

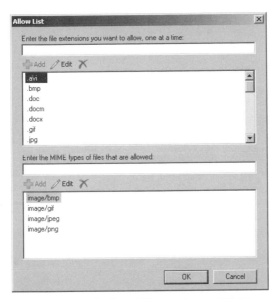

FIGURE 13-21 Specify allowed file extensions and MIME types.

9. In the Direct File Access Settings dialog box, you can configure allowed files by clicking Force Save. The Force Save List dialog box appears. Use the following techniques to configure force-saved files, and then click OK:

   - To force save a new file extension, type it in the text box provided. Be sure to include the period, such as **.aap**, and then press Enter or click Add.

   - To force save a new MIME type, enter it in the text box provided. Be sure to include the full MIME type designator, such as **application/stream**, and then press Enter or click Add.

   - To stop force saving a file extension or MIME type, select it, and then click the Remove button. This button shows an X.

10. In the Direct File Access Settings dialog box, you can configure allowed files using the selection list on the Unknown Files panel. Set the desired action to Allow, Block, or Force Save. Click OK to save your settings, and then click OK to close the Properties dialog box for the virtual directory you selected.

In the Exchange Management Shell, you can use the Set-OWAVirtualDirectory cmdlet to manage the direct file-access configuration. Set the –Identity parameter to the identity of the virtual directory on the server with which you want to work, such as:

```
Set-OWAVirtualDirectory –Identity "Corpsvr127\owa (Default Web Site)"
 –DirectFileAccessOnPublicComputersEnabled $false
 –DirectFileAccessOnPrivateComputersEnabled $true
```

If you are unsure of the virtual directory identity value, use the Get-OWAVirtual-Directory cmdlet to retrieve a list of available virtual directories on a named server, as shown in the following example:

```
Get-OWAVirtualDirectory -Server "Corpsvr127"
```

Understanding and Configuring Remote File Access

By default, Exchange Server 2010 allows users to access files remotely through Outlook Web App as long as they have a Premium Client Access License. This means users will be able to access Windows SharePoint Services and Universal Naming Convention (UNC) file shares on SharePoint sites. SharePoint sites consist of Web Parts and Windows ASP.NET–based components that allow users to share documents, tasks, contacts, events, and other information. When you configure UNC file shares on SharePoint sites, you enable users to share folders and files.

To configure remote file access, complete the following steps:

1. In the Exchange Management Console, expand the Server Configuration node, and then select the Client Access node.

2. In the upper portion of the details pane, you'll see a list of your organiza-tion's Client Access servers. Select the server you want to configure.

3. In the lower portion of the details pane, you'll see a list of option tabs for the selected server. On the Outlook Web App tab, right-click the virtual directory for which you are configuring remote file access, and then select Properties. Typically, you'll want to configure the OWA virtual directory on the Default Web Site because this directory is used by default for Outlook Web App.

4. To configure remote file access for private computers, on the Private Computer File Access tab, select or clear the Windows File Shares and Windows SharePoint Services check boxes, as appropriate.

5. On the Remote File Servers tab (shown in Figure 13-22), you can specify the host names of servers from which clients are denied or allowed access using block and allow lists, respectively. If there is a conflict between the block list and the allow list, the block list takes precedence.

6. To configure the block list, click Block. Use the following techniques to configure the block list, and then click OK:

   • To add a server to the block list, type the fully qualified domain name of the server, such as **mailsvr83.cpandl.com**, and then press Enter or click Add.

   • To remove a server from the block list, select the host entry, and then click the Remove button.

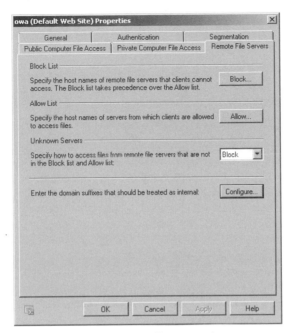

FIGURE 13-22 Configure remote file server options.

7. To configure the allow list, click Allow. Use the following techniques to configure the allow list, and then click OK:

   - To add a server to the allow list, type the fully qualified domain name of the server, such as **mailsvr83.cpandl.com**, and then press Enter or click Add.
   - To remove a server from the allow list, select the host entry and then click the Remove button.

8. Servers that are not listed on either the allow list or the block list are considered to be unknown servers. By default, access to unknown servers is allowed. On the Remote File Servers tab, use the Unknown Servers selection list to allow or block unknown servers.

9. Users have access only to shares hosted on internal servers. For a server to be considered an internal server, you must tell Exchange about the domain suffixes that should be handled as internal. On the Remote File Servers tab, click the Configure button. Use the following techniques to configure your internal domain suffixes, and then click OK:

   - To add a domain suffix, type the fully qualified domain name of the suffix, such as **cpandl.com**, and then press Enter or click Add.
   - To remove a domain suffix, select the suffix entry and then click the Remove button.

In the Exchange Management Shell, you can use the Set-OWAVirtualDirectory cmdlet to manage the direct file access configuration. Set the –Identity parameter to the identity of the virtual directory on the server you want to work with, such as:

```
Set-OWAVirtualDirectory -Identity "Corpsvr127\owa (Default Web Site)"
-UNCAccessOnPublicComputersEnabled $false
-UNCAccessOnPrivateComputersEnabled $true
-WSSAccessOnPublicComputersEnabled $false
-WSSAccessOnPrivateComputersEnabled $true
```

If you are unsure of the virtual directory identity value, use the Get-OWAVirtual-Directory cmdlet to retrieve a list of available virtual directories on a named server, as shown in the following example:

```
Get-OWAVirtualDirectory -Server "Corpsvr127"
```

Understanding and Using WebReady Document Viewing

WebReady Document Viewing allows users to view common file types in Outlook Web App without having the applications associated with those file types installed on their computer. This allows users to view the following files:

- Adobe PDF documents with the .pdf extension
- Microsoft Office Excel spreadsheets with the.xls and .xlsx extensions
- Text and Microsoft Office Word documents with the .doc, .docx, .dot, .rtf, and .txt extensions
- Microsoft Office PowerPoint presentations with the .pps, .ppt, and .pptx extensions

For attachments, the following related MIME types are supported, as well as related open XML formats for presentations, spreadsheets, and word processing documents:

- application/msword
- application/pdf
- application/vnd.ms-excel
- application/vnd.ms-powerpoint
- application/x-msexcel
- application/x-mspowerpoint

NOTE WebReady Document Viewing works by converting documents in supported formats to HTML so that they can be viewed as a Web page in Outlook Web App. Thus, when an e-mail message has an attachment in a supported format, WebReady Document Viewing allows the document to be viewed without having to first download the document to the user's computer or open a helper application.

When there are conflicting settings between the direct file, remote file, and WebReady Document Viewing settings, you can force clients to use WebReady Document Viewing first, if you want. This means that the documents will be opened within Internet Explorer rather than in a related application, such as Microsoft Office Word.

You can enable or disable WebReady Document Viewing separately for public computers and private computers. However, supported document settings for both types of computers are shared and applied to both public and private computers in the same way.

To configure WebReady Document Viewing, complete the following steps:

1. In the Exchange Management Console, expand the Server Configuration node, and then select the Client Access node.

2. In the upper portion of the details pane, you'll see a list of your organization's Client Access servers. Select the server you want to configure.

3. In the lower portion of the details pane, you'll see a list of option tabs for the selected server. On the Outlook Web App tab, right-click the virtual directory for which you are configuring WebReady Document Viewing, and then select Properties. Typically, you'll want to configure the OWA virtual directory on the Default Web Site because this directory is used by default for Outlook Web App.

4. On the Public Computer Files Access tab, use the following techniques to configure WebReady Document Viewing from public computers:

   - Enable WebReady Document Viewing by selecting the Enable WebReady Document Viewing check box.
   - Disable WebReady Document Viewing by clearing the Enable WebReady Document Viewing check box.
   - Force the use of WebReady Document Viewing first by selecting the Force WebReady Document Viewing First check box.
   - Allow documents with supported WebReady Document Viewing formats to be opened in related applications by clearing the Force WebReady Document Viewing First check box.

5. To configure WebReady Document Viewing for private computers, on the Private Computer File Access tab, select or clear the Enable WebReady Document Viewing and Force WebReady Document Viewing First check boxes, as appropriate.

6. On either the Public Computer File Access tab or Private Computer File Access tab, click the Supported button on the WebReady Document Viewing panel. The WebReady Document Viewing Settings dialog box appears, as shown in Figure 13-23.

7. To allow all supported document types to be used with WebReady Document Viewing, select All Supported Document Types and then click OK.

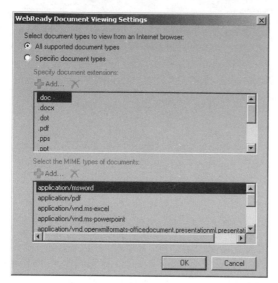

FIGURE 13-23 Configure WebReady Document Viewing.

8. To customize the supported document types, click Specific Document Types. Use the following techniques to configure supported document types:

- To stop allowing a document extension or MIME type, select it and then click the Remove button.

- To restore a previously removed document extension, under Specify Document Extensions, click the Add button, select the document extension to add, and then click OK.

- To restore a previously removed MIME type, under Specify The MIME Types Of Documents, click the Add button, select the MIME type to add, and then click OK.

9. Click OK to close the Properties dialog box for the virtual directory.

In the Exchange Management Shell, you can use the Set-OWAVirtualDirectory cmdlet to manage the WebReady Document Viewing configuration. Set the –Identity parameter to the identity of the virtual directory on the server with which you want to work, such as:

```
Set-OWAVirtualDirectory –Identity "Corpsvr127\owa (Default Web Site)"
 -WebReadyDocumentViewingAccessOnPublicComputersEnabled $false
 -WebReadyDocumentViewingOnPrivateComputersEnabled $true
```

If you are unsure of the virtual directory identity value, use the Get-OWAVirtual-Directory cmdlet to retrieve a list of available virtual directories on a named server, as shown in the following example:

```
Get-OWAVirtualDirectory –Server "Corpsvr127"
```

CHAPTER 14

Exchange Server 2010 Maintenance, Monitoring, and Queuing

Few administration tasks are more important than maintenance, monitoring, and queue tracking. You must maintain Microsoft Exchange Server 2010 to ensure proper flow and recoverability of message data. You need to monitor Exchange Server to ensure that services and processes are functioning normally, and you need to track Exchange Server queues to ensure that messages are being processed.

Understanding Troubleshooting Basics

In the Exchange Management Console, you'll find several tools in the toolbox to help you troubleshoot messaging problems. These tools include

- **Mailflow Troubleshooter**   Can help you troubleshoot message delivery delays, unexpected nondelivery reports, and problems with Edge Transport server synchronization. It can also help you find lost messages.

- **Performance Troubleshooter**   Can help you troubleshoot performance issues related to delays while using Microsoft Office Outlook, frequent Remote Procedure Call (RPC) dialog box display in Outlook, and higher-than-expected RPC operations.

Using the troubleshooting tools is straightforward, and you can follow these steps to get started:

1. In the Exchange Management Console, access the Toolbox node.
2. Double-click the troubleshooter with which you want to work.

> **NOTE** The first time you start the troubleshooter, you need to specify your update and error reporting options. You can configure the troubleshooter either to check for updates automatically on startup or to not check for updates. If you want to send Microsoft anonymous information about your server hardware and how you use Exchange Server, join the customer experience improvement program. Otherwise, specify that you don't want to join the program.

3. After the troubleshooter checks for updates or you manually check for updates by clicking Check For Updates Now, click Go To The Welcome Screen.
4. Enter an identifying label for the analysis data. For the performance troubleshooter, select Troubleshoot New Performance Issue, click Next, use the selection list provided to specify the symptoms you are seeing, and then click Next again. For the mailflow troubleshooter, use the selection list provided to specify the symptoms you are seeing and then click Next.
5. Follow the prompts, and select the appropriate options to perform troubleshooting tasks.

As part of your standard operating procedure, you should track changes in the configuration of your Exchange servers. The Exchange Management Shell provides the following cmdlets for obtaining detailed information on the current configuration of your Exchange servers:

- **Get-ExchangeServer** Displays the general configuration details for Exchange servers
- **Get-TransportServer** Displays configuration details for servers with the Hub Transport Server or Edge Transport server role
- **Get-MailboxServer** Displays configuration details for servers with the Mailbox server role
- **Get-ClientAccessServer** Displays configuration details for servers with the Client Access server role
- **Get-UMServer** Displays configuration details for servers with the Unified Messaging server role

To get related details for a specific server, you pass a cmdlet the identity of the server, as shown in the following example:

```
Get-TransportServer mailserver25 | fl
```

To get related details for all servers, omit the –Identity parameter, as shown in the following example:

```
Get-TransportServer | fl
```

When you finalize the configuration of your Exchange servers, you should use these cmdlets to store the configuration details for each server role. To store the configuration details in a file, redirect the output to a file, as shown in the following example:

```
Get-TransportServer mailserver25 | fl >
c:\SavedConfigs\transport2010-0418.txt
```

If you then store the revised configuration on a per-role basis any time you make significant changes, you can use this information during troubleshooting to help resolve problems that might be related to configuration changes. To compare two configuration files, you can use the file compare command, fc, at an elevated, administrator command prompt. When you use the following syntax with the fc command, the output is the difference between two files:

```
fc FilePath1 FilePath2
```

where *FilePath1* is the full file path to the first file and *FilePath2* is the full file path to the second file. Here is an example:

```
fc c:\SavedConfigs\transport2010-0418.txt c:\SavedConfigs\
transport2010-0521.txt
```

Because the files contain configuration details for specific dates, the changes shown in the output represent the configuration changes that you've made to the server.

To take the idea of gathering and checking configuration information a step further, you can use the Exchange Best Practices Analyzer (Exchange BPA). Exchange BPA is designed to gather organizational configuration for you and then perform various types of scans, including:

- **Organizational health check**   Exchange BPA performs a full scan of the organization, checking for errors, warnings, nondefault configurations, recent changes, and other configuration details.

- **Permissions check**   Exchange BPA performs a health check and then samples the performance for over a 2-hour period.

- **Connectivity tests**   Exchange BPA tests network connections and permissions on each Exchange server.

- **Baseline configuration checks**   Exchange BPA checks for configuration settings that deviate from baseline values. This allows you to compare the settings on a baseline server with settings on other servers and report the differences.

You can follow these steps to get started with Exchange BPA:

1. In the Exchange Management Console, access the Toolbox node, and then double-click Best Practices Analyzer.

2. After Exchange BPA checks for updates or you manually check for updates by clicking Check For Updates Now, click Go To The Welcome Screen.

3. Do one of the following:

- To start a new scan, click Select Options For A New Scan. Follow the prompts, and select the appropriate options to perform a scan.

- To view the results of a scan, click Select A Best Practices Scan To View. Click a scan to review, and then click View A Report Of This Scan.

In the Exchange Management Console, you can generate basic organizational health reports as well. To do this, select the organization node in the left pane, and then select the Click Here To Access The Latest Data link on the Organizational Health tab. When the Collect Organizational Health Data Wizard starts, click Next, and then click Collect. When the wizard finishes gathering information, click Finish. You can then see current summary information for the Exchange organization, Exchange servers, and Exchange recipients. You can use Get-OrganizationConfig to get summary information about your Exchange organization. Here is an example:

```
$s=Get-OrganizationConfig; $os=$s.organizationsummary;$os|ft key,value
```

Other useful cmdlets for checking the Exchange organization include:

- **Test-ActiveSyncConnectivity**   Performs a full synchronization against a specified mailbox to test the configuration of Exchange ActiveSync.

- **Test-EcpConnectivity**   Verifies that the Exchange Control Panel is running as expected.

- **Test-EdgeSynchronization**   Verifies that the subscribed Edge Transport servers have a current and accurate synchronization status.

- **Test-ExchangeSearch**   Verifies that Exchange Search is currently enabled and is indexing new e-mail messages in a timely manner.

- **Test-FederationTrust**   Verifies that the federation trust is properly configured and functioning as expected.

- **Test-FederationTrustCertificate**   Verifies the status of certificates used for federation on all Hub Transport and Client Access servers.

- **Test-ImapConnectivity**   Verifies that the IMAP4 service is running as expected.

- **Test-IPAllowListProvider**   Verifies the configuration for a specific IP allow list provider.

- **Test-IPBlockListProvider**   Verifies the configuration for a specific IP block list provider.

- **Test-IRMConfiguration**   Verifies Information Rights Management (IRM) configuration and functionality.

- **Test-Mailflow**   Verifies whether mail can be successfully sent from and delivered to the system mailbox as well as whether e-mail is sent between Mailbox servers within a defined latency threshold.

- **Test-MapiConnectivity**   Verifies server functionality by logging on to the mailbox that you specify.

- **Test-MRSHealth** Verifies the health of an instance of the Microsoft Exchange Mailbox Replication Service.
- **Test-OutlookConnectivity** Verifies end-to-end Microsoft Outlook client connectivity and also tests for Outlook Anywhere (RPC/HTTP) and TCP-based connections.
- **Test-OutlookWebServices** Verifies the Autodiscover service settings for Outlook.
- **Test-OwaConnectivity** Verifies that Outlook Web App is running as expected.
- **Test-PopConnectivity** Verifies that the POP3 service is running as expected.
- **Test-PowerShellConnectivity** Verifies whether Windows PowerShell remoting on the target Client Access server is functioning correctly.
- **Test-ReplicationHealth** Verifies all aspects of the replication and replay status for a Mailbox server in a database availability group.
- **Test-SenderId** Verifies whether a specified IP address is the legitimate sending address for a specified SMTP address.
- **Test-ServiceHealth** Verifies whether all the Windows services that Exchange requires on a server have started.
- **Test-SystemHealth** Collects data about your Exchange system and analyzes it.
- **Test-UMConnectivity** Verifies the operation of a computer that has the Unified Messaging server role installed.
- **Test-WebServicesConnectivity** Verifies the functionality of Exchange Web Services.

Performing Tracking and Logging Activities in an Organization

This section examines message tracking, protocol logging, and diagnostic logging. You use these features to monitor Exchange Server and to troubleshoot messaging problems.

Using Message Tracking

You use message tracking to monitor the flow of messages into and out of an organization and within it. With message tracking enabled, Exchange Server maintains daily log files, with a running history of all messages transferred within an organization. You use the logs to determine the status of a message, such as whether a message has been sent, has been received, or is waiting in the queue to be delivered. Because Exchange Server handles postings to public folders in much the same way as e-mail messages, you can also use message tracking to monitor public folder usage.

TIP Tracking logs can really save the day when you're trying to troubleshoot delivery and routing problems. The logs are also useful in fending off problem users who blame e-mail for their woes. Generally speaking, users can't claim they didn't receive e-mails if you can find the messages in the logs. That said, if you use third-party applications that integrate with Outlook, those applications could potentially delete messages before the user sees them.

Configuring Message Tracking

By default, all Hub Transport, Edge Transport and Mailbox servers perform message tracking. You can enable or disable message tracking on a per-server basis by setting the –MessageTrackingLogEnabled parameter of the Set-TransportServer cmdlet to $true or $false, as appropriate. The following example disables message tracking on MailServer16:

```
Set-TransportServer -Identity "MailServer16"
-MessageTrackingLogEnabled $false
```

TIP You can configure basic message tracking options in the Exchange Management Console. Expand the Server Configuration node and then select the Hub Transport node. In the main pane, double-click the server you want to configure to display the related Properties dialog box. On the Log Settings tab, select or clear the Enable Message Tracking Log check box. If you enable message tracking, you can enter the desired directory path for logging as well or accept the default setting.

Each Transport and Mailbox server in your organization can have different message tracking settings that control

- Where logs are stored
- How logging is performed
- The maximum log size and maximum log directory size
- How long logs are retained

By default, message tracking logs are stored in the %ExchangeInstallPath%\TransportRoles\Logs\MessageTracking directory. Generally, message tracking does not have high enough input/output activity to warrant a dedicated disk. However, in some high usage situations, you might want to move the tracking logs to a separate disk. Before you do this, however, you should create the directory you want to use and set the following required permissions:

- Full Control For Administrator
- Full Control For Local System
- Read, Write, And Delete Subfolders And Files For Network Service

After you've created the directory and set the required permissions, you can change the location of the tracking logs to any local directory by setting the –MessageTrackingLogPath parameter of the Set-TransportServer cmdlet to the desired local directory. The following example sets the message tracking directory as G:\Tracking on MailServer16:

```
Set-TransportServer -Identity "MailServer16"
-MessageTrackingLogPath "G:\Tracking"
```

NOTE When you change the location of the message tracking directory, Exchange Server does not copy any existing tracking logs from the old directory to the new one. You must manually copy the old logs to the new location if you want all the logs to be in the same location.

By default, all Hub Transport, Edge Transport, and Mailbox servers perform extended message tracking, which allows you to perform searches based on message subject lines, header information, sender, and recipient. If you don't want to collect information on potentially sensitive subject lines, you can disable subject line tracking by setting the –MessageTrackingLogSubjectLoggingEnabled parameter of the Set-TransportServer cmdlet to $false, as shown in the following example:

```
Set-TransportServer -Identity "MailServer16"
-MessageTrackingLogSubjectLoggingEnabled $false
```

Exchange Server continues to write to message tracking logs until a log grows to a specified maximum size, at which point Exchange Server creates a new log and then uses this log to track current messages. By default, the maximum log file size is 10 megabytes (MB). You can change this behavior by setting the –Message TrackingLogMaxFileSize parameter to the desired maximum file size. You must qualify the desired file size using B for bytes, KB for kilobytes, MB for megabytes, or GB for gigabytes. The following example sets the message log file size to 50 MB:

```
Set-TransportServer -Identity "MailServer16"
-MessageTrackingLogMaxFileSize "50MB"
```

Exchange Server overwrites the oldest message tracking logs automatically when tracking logs reach a maximum age or when the maximum log directory size is reached. By default, the maximum age is 30 days and the maximum log directory size is 250 MB. You can use the –MessageTrackingLogMaxAge parameter to set the maximum allowed age in the following format:

```
DD.HH:MM:SS
```

where DD is the number of days, HH is the number of hours, MM is the number of minutes, and SS is the number of seconds. The following example sets the maximum age for logs to 90 days:

```
Set-TransportServer -Identity "MailServer16"
-MessageTrackingLogMaxAge "90.00:00:00"
```

You can set the maximum log directory size using the –MessageTrackingLogMax-DirectorySize parameter. As with the maximum log file size, the qualifiers are B, KB, MB, and GB. The following example sets the maximum log directory size to 2 GB:

```
Set-TransportServer -Identity "MailServer16"
 -MessageTrackingLogMaxDirectorySize "2GB"
```

Searching Through the Tracking Logs

The tracking logs are useful in troubleshooting problems with routing and delivery. In the Exchange Management Shell, you use Get-MessageTrackingLog to search through the message tracking logs. The related syntax is:

```
Get-MessageTrackingLog [-Start DateTime] [-Server ServerId]
[-End DateTime] {AddtlParams}

{AddtlParams}
[-DomainController DCName] [-EventId {"BadMail" | "Defer" | "Deliver" |
"DSN" | "Expand" | "Fail" | "PoisonMessage" | "Receive" | "Redirect" |
"Resolve" | "Send" | "Submit" | "Transfer"} ] [-InternalMessageId
MessageTrackingLogId] [-MessageId MessageId] [-MessageSubject
Subject] [-Recipients SMTPemailAddress1, SMTPemailAddress2,...]
[-Reference ReferenceField] [-ResultSize NumEntriesToReturn]
[-Sender SMTPemailAddress]
```

These parameters allow you to search the message tracking logs in several ways:

- By message ID
- By sender
- By recipients
- By server that processed the messages
- By event ID
- By date
- By message subject

To begin a search, you must specify one or more of the previously listed identifiers as the search criteria. You must also identify a server in the organization that has processed the message in some way. This server can be the sender's server, the recipient's server, or a server that relayed the message.

You set the search criteria using the following parameters:

- **–End**   Sets the end date and time for the search.
- **–EventID**   Specifies the ID of the event for which you want to search, such as a RECEIVE, SEND, or FAIL event.
- **–InternalMessageID**   Specifies the ID of the message tracking log entries for which you want to search.
- **–MessageID**   Specifies the ID of the message for which you want to search.

- **–MessageSubject** Specifies the subject of the message for which you want to search.
- **–Recipients** Sets recipient's SMTP e-mail address or addresses to return
- **–Reference** Specifies the reference field value within the message for which you want to search.
- **–Sender** Sets the sender's SMTP e-mail address (listed in the From field of the message) to return.
- **–Server** Sets the name of the Transport or Mailbox server that contains the message tracking logs to be searched.
- **–Start** Sets the start date and time for the search.

Using the –Start and –End parameters, you can search for messages from a starting date and time to an ending date and time. Using the –Server parameter, you specify the server to search. Consider the following example:

```
Get-MessageTrackingLog -Start "05/25/2010 5:30AM"
-End "05/30/2010 7:30PM" -Server MailServer18 -Sender daved@cpandl.com
```

In this example, you search for a messages sent by DaveD@Cpandl.com between 5:30 A.M. May 25, 2010 and 7:30 P.M. May 30, 2010.

> **NOTE** Keep in mind that only messages that match all of the search criteria you've specified are displayed. If you want to perform a broader search, specify a limited number of parameters. If you want to focus the search precisely, specify multiple parameters.

Reviewing Message Tracking Logs Manually

Exchange Server creates message tracking logs daily and stores them by default in the %ExchangeInstallPath%\TransportRoles\Logs\MessageTracking directory. For US-English, each log file is named by the date on which it was created, using one of these formats:

- MSGTRKYYYYMMDD-N.log, such as MSGTRK20100325-1.log for the first log created on March 25, 2010.
- MSGTRKMYYYYMMDD-N.log, such as MSGTRKM20100325-1.log for the first log created on March 25, 2010.

The message tracking log stores each message event on a single line. The information on a particular line is organized by comma-separated fields. Logs begin with a header that shows the following information:

- A statement that identifies the file as a message tracking log file
- The version of the Exchange Server that created the file
- The date on which the log file was created
- A comma-delimited list of fields contained in the body of the log file

Table 14-1 summarizes message event fields and their meaning. Not all of the fields are tracked for all message events.

TABLE 14-1 Message Tracking Log Fields

LOG FIELD	DESCRIPTION
Client-hostname	The hostname of the client making the request
Client-ip	The IP address of the client making the request
Connector-id	The identity of the connector used
Custom-Data	Optional custom data that was logged
Date-Time	The connection date and time
Directionality	An indication of the source of the message
Event-id	The type of event being logged, such as Submit
Internal-message-id	The internal identifier used by Exchange to track the message
Message-id	The message identifier
Message-info	Any related additional information on the message
Message-subject	The subject of the message
Original-client-ip	The IP address for the original client
Original-server-ip	The IP address for the original server
Recipient-address	The e-mail addresses of the message recipients
Recipient-count	The total number of recipients
Recipient-status	The status of the recipient e-mail address
Reference	The references, if any
Related-recipient-address	The e-mail addresses of any related recipients
Return-path	The return path on the message
Sender-address	The distinguished name of the sender's e-mail address
Server-hostname	The server on which the log entry was generated
Server-ip	The IP address of the server on which the log entry was generated
Source	The messaging component for which the event is being logged, such as StoreDriver
Source-context	The context of the event source
Tenant-id	A tenant identifier
Total-bytes	The total size of the message in bytes

You can view the message tracking log files with any standard text editor, such as Microsoft Notepad. You can also import the message tracking log files into a spreadsheet or a database. Follow these steps to import a message tracking log file into Microsoft Office Excel:

1. Start Excel 2007 or Excel 2010. Click the Microsoft Office button and then click Open. Use the Open dialog box to select the message tracking log file you want to open. Set the file type as All Files (*.*), select the log file, and then click Open.

2. The Text Import Wizard starts automatically. Click Next. On the Delimiters list, choose Comma. Click Next and then click Finish.

3. The log file should now be imported. You can view, search, and print the message tracking log as you would any other spreadsheet.

Using Protocol Logging

Protocol logging allows you to track Simple Mail Transfer Protocol (SMTP) communications that occur between servers as part of message routing and delivery. These communications could include both Exchange servers and non-Exchange servers. When non-Exchange servers send messages to an Exchange server, Exchange does the protocol logging of the communications.

You use protocol logging to troubleshoot problems with the Send and Receive connectors that are configured on Hub Transport and Edge Transport servers. However, you shouldn't use protocol logging to monitor Exchange activity. This is primarily because protocol logging can be processor intensive and resource intensive, which means that an Exchange server may have to perform a lot of work to log protocol activity. The overhead required for protocol logging depends on the level of messaging activity on the Exchange server.

Configuring Protocol Logging

By default, Hub Transport and Edge Transport servers do not perform protocol logging. As long as you know the identity of the connector with which you want to work, you can configure protocol logging for a specified connector. To retrieve a list of available Send and Receive connectors for a server, use the Get-SendConnector and Get-ReceiveConnector cmdlets, respectively. If you run either cmdlet without specifying additional parameters, a list of all available Send or Receive connectors is returned.

You enable or disable protocol logging on a per-connector basis. For Send connectors, you use the Set-SendConnector cmdlet to enable protocol logging. For Receive connectors, you use the Set-ReceiveConnector cmdlet to enable protocol logging. Both cmdlets have a –ProtocolLoggingLevel parameter that you can set to Verbose to enable protocol logging or to None to disable protocol logging. Here is an example:

```
Set-ReceiveConnector -Identity "Corpsvr127\Custom Receive Connector"
  -ProtocolLoggingLevel 'Verbose'
```

Although you enable protocol logging on a per-connector basis, you configure the other protocol logging parameters on a per-server basis for either all Send connectors or all Receive connectors using the Set-TransportServer cmdlet. As it does with message tracking logs, Exchange Server overwrites the oldest protocol logs automatically when tracking logs reach a maximum age or when the maximum log directory size is reached. If you decide to move the protocol log directories, you should create the directories you want to use and then set the following required permissions:

- Full Control For Administrator
- Full Control For Local System
- Read, Write, And Delete Subfolders And Files For Network Service

Because the parameters are similar to those for message tracking, I'll summarize the available parameters. Table 14-2 shows the Send connector parameters for configuring protocol logging. Table 14-3 shows the Receive connector parameters for configuring protocol logging.

TIP You can configure send and receive protocol log paths in the Exchange Management Console. Expand the Server Configuration node, and then select the Hub Transport node. In the main pane, double-click the server you want to configure to display the related Properties dialog box. On the Log Settings tab, the Protocol log panel shows the current send and receive protocol log paths. You can specify the log file path by entering the desired directory path for logging or accept the default setting.

TABLE 14-2 Send Connector Parameters for Protocol Logging

PARAMETER	DESCRIPTION	DEFAULT
SendProtocolLogPath	Sets the local file path for protocol logging of Send connectors	%Exchange-InstallPath%\ TransportRoles\ Logs\ProtocolLog\ SmtpSend
SendProtocolLogMaxFileSize	Sets the maximum size for Send connector protocol logs	10 MB
SendProtocolLogMax-DirectorySize	Sets the maximum size for the Send connector protocol log directory	250 MB
SendProtocolLogMaxAge	Sets the maximum age for Send connector protocol logs	30.00:00:00

TABLE 14-3 Receive Connector Parameters for Protocol Logging

PARAMETER	DESCRIPTION	DEFAULT
ReceiveProtocolLogPath	Sets the local file path for protocol logging of Receive connectors	%Exchange-InstallPath%\ TransportRoles\ Logs\ProtocolLog\ SmtpReceive
ReceiveProtocol-LogMaxFileSize	Sets the maximum size for Receive connector protocol logs	10 MB
ReceiveProtocol-LogMaxDirectorySize	Sets the maximum size for the Receive connector protocol log directory	250 MB
ReceiveProtocolLogMaxAge	Sets the maximum age for Receive connector protocol logs	30.00:00:00

Working with Protocol Logging Properties and Fields

When protocol logging is enabled, a Mailbox server or a transport server creates protocol logs daily. Mailbox and transport servers store logs in either the %ExchangeInstallPath%\TransportRoles\Logs\ProtocolLog\SmtpSend or %ExchangeInstallPath%\TransportRoles\Logs\ProtocolLog\SmtpReceive directory as appropriate for the type of connector being logged. For POP, IMAP, and Hotmail content aggregation, related logs are in the %ExchangeInstallPath%\TransportRoles\ Logs\ProtocolLog\HTTPClient directory. Each log file is named by the date on which it was created, using the format SENDYYYYMMDD-N.log or RECVYYYYMMDD-N. log, such as SEND20100925-1.log for the first Send connector log created on September 25, 2010. Additional protocol logs are found in subdirectories of the %ExchangeInstallPath%\Logging directory. In the AddressBook Service subdirectory, you'll find logs for the Address Book service. In the RPC Client Access subdirectory, you'll find logs for Remote Procedure Calls for Client Access services.

The protocol log stores each SMTP protocol event on a single line. The information on a particular line is organized by comma-separated fields. Logs begin with a header that shows the following information:

- A statement that identifies the file as either a Send connector protocol log or a Receive connector protocol log
- The date on which the log file was created
- The version of the Exchange Server that created the file
- A comma-delimited list of fields contained in the body of the log file

Table 14-4 summarizes SMTP event fields and their meanings. Not all of the fields are tracked for all protocol events. You can view the protocol log files with any standard text editor, such as Notepad. You can also import the protocol log files into a spreadsheet or a database.

TABLE 14-4 Protocol Log Fields

LOG FIELD	DESCRIPTION
Date-time	The date and time of the protocol event in a locale-specific format. For U.S. English, the format is *YYYY-MM-DDTHH:MM:SSZ*, such as 2010-03-21T23:30:59Z.
Connector-id	The distinguished name of the connector associated with the event.
Session-id	The globally unique identifier of the SMTP session. Each event for a particular session has the same identifier.
Sequence-number	The number of the event within an SMTP session. The first event has a sequence number of 0.
Local-endpoint	The local endpoint of the SMTP session, identified by the Internet Protocol (IP) address and Transmission Control Protocol (TCP) port.
Remote-endpoint	The remote endpoint of the SMTP session, identified by the IP address and TCP port.
Event	The type of protocol event: + for Connect, – for Disconnect, > for Send, < for Receive, and * for Information.
Data	The data associated with the SMTP event.
Context	The context for the SMTP event.

Enabling Protocol Logging for HTTP

Client Access servers have Web-based applications and virtual directories that use Microsoft Internet Information Services (IIS) to provide the related services. In IIS 7.0 or IIS 7.5, protocol logging for HTTP is a feature is available when HTTP Logging module is installed and logging is enabled. By default, this module is installed with IIS and enabled. The default configuration is to use one log file per Web site per day.

You can view and manage the logging settings by completing the following steps:

1. Start Internet Information Services (IIS) Manager. Click Start, point to Programs or All Programs as appropriate, point to Administrative Tools, and select Internet Information Services (IIS) Manager.

   NOTE By default, IIS Manager connects to the services running on the local computer. If you want to connect to a different server, select the Start Page node in the left pane and then click the Connect To A Server link. This starts the Connect To Server Wizard. Follow the prompts to connect to the remote server. Keep in mind that with IIS 7.0 and IIS 7.5, the Windows Remote Management Service must be configured and running on the remote server.

2. When you install Exchange Server, the default Web site is created (or updated) to include the virtual directories and Web-based applications used to provide Web-based services for Exchange Server. In IIS Manager, double-click the entry for the server with which you want to work, and then double-click Sites.

3. In the left pane, select the Web site that you want to manage, and then double-click Logging in the main pane to open the Logging feature as shown in Figure 14-1.

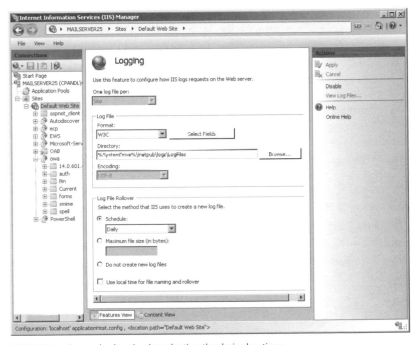

FIGURE 14-1 Customize logging by selecting the desired options.

4. If all logging options are dimmed and the server is configured for per-site logging, you can click Enable in the Actions pane to enable logging for this site. Otherwise, if logging is configured per server, you need to configure logging at the server level rather than at the site level; the procedure is similar.

5. Use the Format selection list to choose one of the following log formats:

   ■ **W3C Extended Log File Format**   Writes the log in ASCII text following the World Wide Web Consortium (W3C) extended log file format. Fields are space-delimited, and each entry is written on a new line. This style is the default. Using this option allows you to include extensive information about clients, servers, and connections.

- **Microsoft IIS Log File Format**   Writes the log in ASCII text following the IIS log file format. Fields are tab-delimited, and each entry is written on a new line. Using this option allows you to collect basic information about clients, servers, and connections.

- **NCSA Common Log File Format**   Writes the log in ASCII text following the National Center for Supercomputing Applications (NCSA) common log file format. Fields are space-delimited, and each entry is written on a new line. When you use this option, log entries are small because only basic information is recorded.

TIP   W3C Extended Log File Format is the preferred logging format because you can record detailed information. Unless you're certain that another format meets your needs, you should use this format.

6. On the Log File panel, use the Directory text box to set the main folder for log files. By default, log files are written to a subdirectory of %SystemDrive%\inetpub\logs\LogFiles.

7. On the Log File Rollover panel, select Schedule and then use the related selection list to choose a logging time period. In most cases, you'll want to create daily or weekly logs, so select either Daily or Weekly.

8. If you selected W3C, click Select Fields, and then choose the fields that should be recorded in the logs. Click Apply.

Working with HTTP Protocol Logs

On Client Access servers, HTTP protocol log files can help you detect and trace problems with HTTP, Outlook Web App, Exchange ActiveSync, and Outlook Anywhere. By default, Exchange Server writes protocol log files to a subdirectory of %SystemDrive%\inetpub\logs\LogFiles. You can use the logs to determine the following:

- Whether a client was able to connect to a specified server and, if not, what problem occurred

- Whether a client was able to send or receive protocol commands and, if not, what error occurred

- Whether a client was able to send or receive data

- How long it took to establish a connection

- How long it took to send or receive protocol commands

- How long it took to send or receive data

- Whether server errors are occurring and, if so, what types of errors are occurring

- Whether server errors are related to Windows or to the protocol itself
- Whether a user is connecting to the server using the proper logon information

Most protocol log files are written as ASCII text. This means you can view them in Notepad or another text editor. You can import these protocol log files into Office Excel 2007 in much the same way as you import tracking logs.

Log files, written as space-delimited or tab-delimited text, begin with a header that shows the following information:

- A statement that identifies the protocol or service used to create the file
- The protocol, service, or software version
- A date and timestamp
- A space-delimited or tab-delimited list of fields contained in the body of the log file

Using Connectivity Logging

Connectivity logging allows you to track the connection activity of outgoing mes-sage delivery queues. You use connectivity logging on transport servers to trouble-shoot problems with messages reaching their designated destination Mailbox server or recipient.

Configuring Connectivity Logging

By default, Hub Transport and Edge Transport servers do not perform connectivity logging. You can enable or disable connectivity logging on a per-server basis by setting the –ConnectivityLogEnabled parameter of the Set-TransportServer cmdlet to $true or $false, as appropriate. The following example enables connectivity log-ging on MailServer16:

```
Set-TransportServer -Identity "MailServer16"
-ConnectivityLogEnabled $false
```

TIP You can configure basic connectivity logging options in the Exchange Management Console. Expand the Server Configuration node and then select the Hub Transport node. In the main pane, double-click the server you want to configure to display the related Properties dialog box. On the Log Settings tab, select or clear the Enable Connectivity Logging check box. If you enable connectivity logging, you can specify the log file path and then click OK.

Each transport server in your organization can have different connectivity logging settings:

- Use the –ConnectivityLogPath parameter to move the log directory to a new location. The default location is %ExchangeInstallPath%\TransportRoles\Logs\ Connectivity directory.

- Use the –ConnectivityLogMaxFileSize parameter to set the maximum log file size. The default maximum log file size is 10 MB.
- Use the –ConnectivityLogMaxDirectorySize parameter to set the maximum log directory size. The default maximum log directory size is 250 MB.
- Use the –ConnectivityLogMaxAge parameter to set the maximum log file age. The default maximum age is 30.00:00:00.

As it does with other logs, Exchange Server overwrites the oldest connectivity logs automatically when tracking logs reach a maximum age or when the maximum log directory size is reached. If you decide to move the protocol log directories, you should create the directories you want to use and set the following required permissions:

- Full Control For Administrator
- Full Control For Local System
- Read, Write, And Delete Subfolders And Files For Network Service

Working with Connectivity Log Properties and Fields

Exchange Server creates connectivity logs daily and stores them in the %ExchangeInstallPath%\TransportRoles\Logs\Connectivity directory. Each log file is named by the date on which it was created, using the format CONNECTLOGYYYY-MMDD-N.log, such as CONNECTLOG20100325-1.log for the first connectivity log created on March 25, 2010.

The connectivity log stores outgoing queue connection events on a single line. The information on a particular line is organized by comma-separated fields. Logs begin with a header that shows the following information:

- A statement that identifies the file as a connectivity log
- The date on which the log file was created
- The version of Exchange Server that created the file
- A comma-delimited list of fields contained in the body of the log file

Table 14-5 summarizes connectivity logging fields and their meanings. Not all of the fields are tracked for all outgoing queue connection events. You can view the connectivity log files with any standard text editor, such as Notepad. You can also import the connectivity log files into a spreadsheet or a database, as discussed previously.

TABLE 14-5 Connectivity Log Fields

LOG FIELD	DESCRIPTION
Date-time	The date and time of the outgoing queue connection event.
Session	The globally unique identifier of the SMTP session. Each event for a particular session has the same identifier. For Messaging Application Programming Interface (MAPI) sessions, this field is blank.

TABLE 14-5 Connectivity Log Fields

LOG FIELD	DESCRIPTION
Destination	The name of the destination Mailbox server, smart host, or domain.
Direction	The direction of the event: + for Connect, – for Disconnect, > for Send, and < for Receive.
Description	The data associated with the event, including the number and size of messages transmitted, Domain Name Server (DNS) name resolution information, connection success messages, and connection failure messages.

Monitoring Events, Services, Servers, and Resource Usage

As an Exchange administrator, you should routinely monitor event logs, services, servers, and resource usage. These elements are the keys to ensuring that the Exchange organization is running smoothly. Because you can't be on-site 24 hours a day, you can set alerts to notify you when problems occur.

Viewing Events

System and application events generated by Exchange Server are recorded in the Windows event logs. The primary log that you'll want to check is the application log. In this log, you'll find the key events recorded by Exchange Server services. Keep in mind that related events might be recorded in other logs, including the directory service, DNS server, security, and system logs. For example, if the server is having problems with a network card and this card is causing message delivery failures, you'll have to use the system log to pinpoint the problem.

You access the application log by completing the following steps:

1. Click Start, point to All Programs, point to Administrative Tools, and then select Event Viewer.

2. If you want to view the logs on another computer, in the console tree, right-click the Event Viewer entry, and choose Connect To Another Computer from the shortcut menu. You can now choose the server for which you want to manage logs.

3. Double-click the Windows Logs node. You should now see a list of logs.

4. Select the Application log, as shown in Figure 14-2.

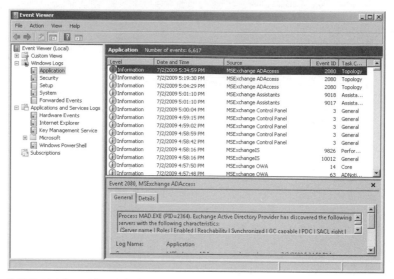

FIGURE 14-2 Event Viewer displays events for the selected log.

Entries in the main panel of Event Viewer provide an overview of when, where, and how an event occurred. To obtain detailed information on an event, select its entry. The event level precedes the date and time of the event. Event levels include the following:

- **Information** An informational event, generally related to a successful action

- **Warning** Details for warnings are often useful in preventing future system problems

- **Error** An error such as the failure of a service to start

In addition to level, date, and time, the summary and detailed event entries provide the following information:

- **Source** The application, service, or component that logged the event.
- **Event ID** An identifier for the specific event.
- **Task Category** The category of the event, which is sometimes used to further describe the related action.
- **User** The user account that was logged on when the event occurred.
- **Computer** The name of the computer on which the event occurred.
- **Description** In the detailed entries, this provides a text description of the event.
- **Data** In the detailed entries, this provides any data or error code output created by the event.

Use the event entries to detect and diagnose Exchange performance problems. Exchange-related event sources include the following:

- **Microsoft Forefront Protection** Helps you track activities related to Microsoft Forefront Protection and licensed anti-spam/antivirus engines. Watch for errors related to signature file updates for the anti-spam and antivirus engines. If you've improperly configured Microsoft Forefront Protection, or if Microsoft Forefront Protection is unable to access the Internet to retrieve updates, you'll see update errors. You'll see additional errors from the GetEngineFiles source because there are no updates to process. Additional related sources for Microsoft Forefront Protection include FSCController, FSCMonitor, FSCRealtimeScanner, FSCStatisticsService, FSCTransportScanner, FSEIMC, and FSEMailPickup.

- **MSExchangeIS, MSExchangeIS Mailbox Store, MSExchangeIS Public Store** Help you track activities related to the Microsoft Exchange Information Store service, mailbox databases, and public folder databases. If a user is having problems logging on to Exchange, you might see multiple logon errors. You might also see lots of logon errors if someone is trying to hack into an Exchange mailbox.

- **ESE** Helps you track activities related to the Extensible Storage Engine (ESE) used by Exchange Server 2010. Watch for logging and recovery errors, which might indicate a problem with the database engine. If you want to track the status of online defragmentation, look for Event ID 703.

- **MSExchangeADAccess** Helps you track activities related to the Exchange Active Directory Provider, which is used for retrieving information for Active Directory and performing the DNS lookups that Exchange uses to locate domain controllers and global catalog servers. Watch for topology discovery failures and DNS lookup failures, which can indicate problems with the DNS configuration as well as with the Active Directory site configuration.

- **MSExchange Anti-Spam Update** Helps you track activities related to Windows Update. When you've configured Microsoft Exchange to use Microsoft Update to retrieve anti-spam updates, watch for errors regarding update failure. You might need to change the Microsoft Update configuration or the way updates are retrieved.

- **MSExchange Assistants, MSExchangeMailboxAssistants** Help you track activities related to the Microsoft Exchange Mailbox Assistants service. The Microsoft Exchange Mailbox Assistants service performs background processing of mailboxes and public folder data. Watch for processing errors, which can indicate database structure problems. Additional related sources include MSExchangeMailboxAssistants and MSExchangeSA.

- **MSExchange EdgeSync, MSExchangeEdgeSync** Help you track activities related to the Edge Synchronization processes. The Microsoft Exchange EdgeSync service uses the Exchange Active Directory Provider to obtain information about the Active Directory topology. If the service cannot locate a suitable domain controller, the service fails to initialize and edge synchronization fails as well.

- **MSExchange Messaging Policies** Helps you track activities related to messaging policies, including transport rules, journal rules, and address rewrite. Watch for load failures, which can indicate a configuration problem that needs to be resolved.

- **MSExchangeIMAP4, MSExchange IMAP4 service, MSExchange IMAP4, MSExchangePOP3, MSExchange POP3 service, MSExchange POP3, MS Exchange OWA** Help you track activities related to IMAP4, POP3, and Outlook Web App (OWA), respectively. Keep in mind Outlook Anywhere requires the RPC Over HTTP Proxy component. If you enable Outlook Anywhere but don't install this component, you'll see errors for the MSExchange RPC Over HTTP Autoconfig source stating that this component is not installed or is not configured correctly. Additional related sources include MSExchange IMAP4 service and MSExchange POP3 service.

- **MSExchange TransportService, MSExchange Unified Messaging** Help you track activities related to the Microsoft Exchange Transport service and the Microsoft Exchange Unified Messaging service, respectively. Watch for errors that can indicate configuration issues. For example, if you haven't created a dial plan, you'll see errors for the MSExchange Unified Messaging service. Additional related sources include MSExchangeTransport, MSExchangeServiceHost, and MSExchangeMailSubmission.

- **MSExchangeFDS, MSExchange OAB Maintenance** Help you track activities related to the Microsoft Exchange File Distribution service. This service is responsible for synchronizing offline address books (OABs) and generating related files for distribution. Watch for errors regarding synchronization and directory generation. The Microsoft Exchange File Distribution service generates OAB data in a subfolder of the OAB Distribution share. By default, this share is located under %SystemDrive%\Program Files\Microsoft\Exchange Server\ExchangeOAB. The Exchange Servers group must have read access to the share, the directory, and subdirectories of the directory. If for some reason the automatically generated directory is not created, you should create the required directory. The related error message provides the expected directory name.

Managing Essential Services

Most of Exchange Server's key components run as system services. If an essential service stops, its related functionality will not be available and Exchange Server won't work as expected. When you are troubleshooting Exchange Server problems, you'll want to check to ensure that essential services are running as expected early in your troubleshooting process. To manage system services, you'll use the Services node in the Computer Management console. You can start Computer Management and access the Services entry by completing the following steps:

1. Select Computer Management in the Administrative Tools folder.

2. If you want to manage the services on another computer, right-click the Computer Management entry in the console tree, and select Connect To Another Computer on the shortcut menu. You can now choose the system whose services you want to manage.

3. Expand the Services And Applications node, and then select Services.

As Figure 14-3 shows, you'll now see the available services. Services are listed by

- **Name**   The name of the service.

- **Description**   A short description of the service and its purpose.

- **Status**   The status of the service. If the entry is blank, the service is stopped.

- **Startup Type**   The startup setting for the service.

- **Log On As**   The account the service logs on as. The default in most cases is the local system account.

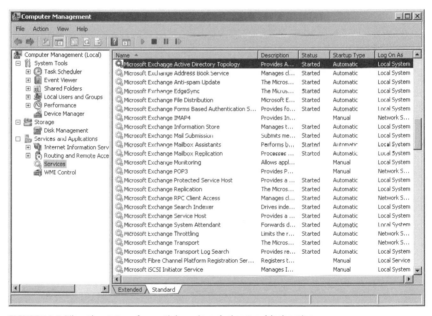

FIGURE 14-3 View the status of essential services during troubleshooting.

TIP Any service that has a startup type of Automatic should have a status of Started. If a service has a startup type of Automatic and the status is blank, the service is not running and you should start it (unless another administrator has stopped it to perform maintenance or troubleshooting).

If a service is stopped and it should be started, you need to restart it. If you suspect a problem with a service, you might want to stop and then restart it. To start, stop, or restart a service, complete the following steps:

1. Access the Services node in the Computer Management console.
2. Right-click the service you want to manage, and then select Start, Stop, or Restart, as appropriate.

After you start or restart a service, you should check the event logs to see if there are errors related to the service. Any related errors you find might help you identify why the service wasn't running.

Monitoring Exchange Messaging Components

When you are troubleshooting or optimizing a server for performance, you can use performance monitoring to track the activities of Exchange messaging components. Performance Monitor graphically displays statistics for the set of performance parameters you've selected for display. These performance parameters are referred to as *counters*. Performance Monitor displays information for only the counters you're tracking. Thousands of counters are available, and these counters are organized into groupings called *performance objects*.

When you install Exchange Server 2010 on a computer, Performance Monitor is updated with a set of objects and counters for tracking Exchange performance. These objects and counters are registered during setup in the Win32 performance subsystem and the Windows registry. You'll find dozens of related performance objects for everything from the Microsoft Exchange Availability Service to the Microsoft Exchange Journaling Agent to Microsoft Exchange Outlook Web App.

You can select which counters you want to monitor by completing the following steps:

1. In the Exchange Management Console, select the Toolbox node, and then double-click Performance Monitor. This opens the Exchange Server Performance Monitor, which is a custom console with several preselected objects and counters. You also can start Performance Monitor by selecting the related option on the Administrative Tools menu.
2. Select the System Monitor entry in the left pane, as shown in Figure 14-4.
3. The Performance Monitor tool has several views and view types. Ensure that you are viewing current activity by clicking View Current Activity on the toolbar or pressing Ctrl+T. You can switch between the view types (Line, Histogram Bar, and Report) by clicking the Change Graph Type button or pressing Ctrl+G.
4. To add counters, click Add on the toolbar. This displays the Add Counters dialog box shown in Figure 14-5.

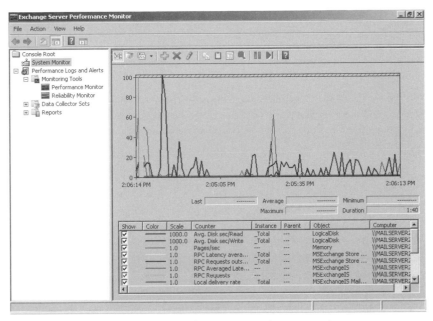

FIGURE 14-4 Track performance objects and counters to monitor server performance.

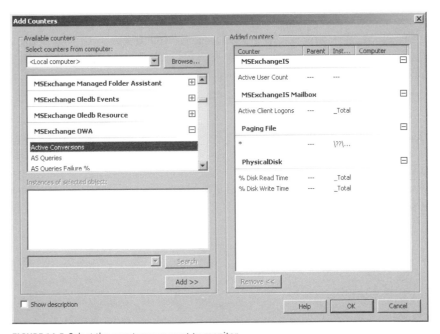

FIGURE 14-5 Select the counters you want to monitor.

5. In the Select Counters From Computer combo box, enter the Universal Naming Convention (UNC) name of the Exchange server you want to work with,
   such as **\\MailServer18**, or leave it at the default setting of <Local computer>
   to work with the local computer.

   NOTE You need to be at least a member of the Performance Monitor Users group
   in the domain or the local computer to perform remote monitoring. When you use
   performance logging, you need to be at least a member of the Performance Log
   Users group in the domain or the local computer to work with performance logs on
   remote computers.

6. In the Available Counters panel, Performance Objects are listed alphabeti-
   cally. If you select an object entry by clicking it, all related counters are
   selected. If you expand an object entry, you can see all the related counters
   and you can then select individual counters by clicking them. For example,
   you can expand the entry for the MSExchangeIS object and then select the
   Active User Count, Client RPCs Attempted/Sec, Connection Count, and RPC
   Operations/Sec counters.

7. When you select an object or any of its counters, you see the related instances,
   if any. Choose All Instances to select all counter instances for monitoring.
   Or select one or more counter instances to monitor. For example, you can
   select the Exchange ActiveSync or Exchange Content Indexing instances of
   MSExchangeIS Client.

8. When you've selected an object or a group of counters for an object as well
   as the object instances, click Add to add the counters to the graph. Repeat
   steps 5 through 8 to add other performance parameters.

9. Click OK when you're finished adding counters. You can delete counters later
   by clicking their entry in the lower portion of the Performance window and
   then clicking Delete.

Using Performance Alerting

In Windows Server 2008, Data Collector Sets are used to collect performance data.
When you configure Data Collector Sets to alert you when specific criteria are met,
you are using performance alerting. Windows performance alerting provides a fully
automated method for monitoring server performance and reporting when certain
performance thresholds are reached. You can use performance alerting to track the
following:

- Memory usage
- CPU utilization
- Disk usage
- Messaging components

Using notifications, you can then provide automatic notification when a server
exceeds a threshold value.

Tracking Memory Usage

Physical and virtual memory is critical to normal system operation. When a server runs low on memory, system performance can suffer and message processing can grind to a halt. To counter this problem, you should configure performance alerting to watch memory usage. You can then increase the amount of virtual memory available on the server or add more random access memory (RAM) as needed.

You configure a memory alert by completing the following steps:

1. In the Exchange Management Console, click the Toolbox node, and then double-click Performance Monitor. This opens the Exchange Server Performance Monitor.

2. Expand the Performance Logs And Alerts and the Data Collector Sets nodes, and then select User Defined. You should see a list of current alerts (if any) in the right pane.

3. Right-click the User-Defined node in the left pane, point to New, and then choose Data Collector Set.

4. In the Create New Data Collector Set Wizard, type a name for the Data Collector Set, such as **Memory Usage Alert**. Select the Create Manually option and then click Next.

5. On the What Type Of Data Do You Want To Include page, the Create Data Logs option is selected by default. Select the Performance Counter Alert option and then click Next.

6. On the Which Performance Counters Would You Like To Monitor page, click Add. This displays the Add Counter dialog box. Because you are configuring memory alerts, expand the Memory object in the Performance Object list. Select Available Mbytes by clicking it, and then click Add.

7. Expand the Paging File object in the Performance Object list. Click %Usage. In the Instances Of Selected Object panel, select _Total, and then click Add. Click OK.

8. On the Which Performance Counters Would You Like To Monitor page, you'll see the counters you've added. In the Performance Counters panel, select Available Mbytes (as shown in Figure 14-6), set the Alert When list to Below, and then enter a Limit value that is approximately 5 percent of the total physical memory (RAM) on the server for which you are configuring alerting. For example, if the server has 2 GB of RAM, you set the value to 100 MB to alert you when the server is running low on available memory.

9. In the Performance Counters panel, select %Usage. Set the Alert When list to Above, and then type **98** as the Limit value. This ensures that you are alerted when more than 98 percent of the paging file is being used.

10. Click Next and then click Finish. This saves the Data Collector Set and closes the wizard.

11. In the left pane, select the related Data Collector Set and then double-click the data collector for the alert in the main pane. This displays the data collector Properties dialog box.

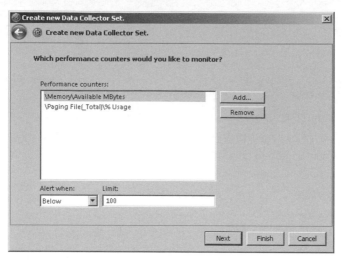

FIGURE 14-6 Configure the alert threshold.

12. On the Alerts tab, use the Sample Interval options to set a sample interval. (See Figure 14-7.) The sample interval specifies when new data is collected. Don't sample too frequently, however, because you'll use system resources and might cause the server to seem unresponsive. By default, Performance Monitor checks the values of the configured counters every 15 seconds. A better value might be once every 10 to 30 minutes. Generally, you'll want to track performance periodically over several hours at a minimum and during a variety of usage conditions.

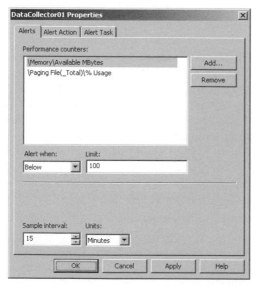

FIGURE 14-7 Set the sample interval.

13. If you want to log an event rather than be alerted every time an alert limit is reached, on the Alert Action tab, select the Log An Entry In The Application Event Log check box. Selecting this option ensures that an event is logged when the alert occurs but does not alert you via the console.

14. Click OK to close the Properties dialog box. By default, alerting is configured to start manually. To start alerting, select the User Defined node in the left pane, click the alert in the main pane to select it, and then click the Start button on the toolbar.

To manage an alert, select the User Defined node in the left pane, right-click the alert in the main pane, and then select one of the following options:

- **Delete** Deletes the alert
- **Properties** Displays the alert's Properties dialog box
- **Start** Activates alerting
- **Stop** Halts alerting

Tracking CPU Utilization

You can use a CPU utilization alert to track the usage of a server's CPUs. When CPU utilization is too high, Exchange Server can't effectively process messages or manage other critical functions. As a result, performance can suffer greatly. For example, CPU utilization at 100 percent for an extended period of time can be an indicator of serious problems on a server. To recover, you might need to use Task Manager to end the process or processes with high CPU utilization, or you might need to take other corrective actions to resolve the problem, such as closing applications you are running while logged on to the server.

You'll also want to closely track process threads that are waiting to execute. A relatively high number of waiting threads can be an indicator that a server's processors need to be upgraded.

You configure a CPU utilization alert by completing the following steps:

1. In the Exchange Management Console, click the Toolbox node, and then double click Performance Monitor. This opens the Exchange Server Performance Monitor.

2. Expand the Performance Logs And Alerts and Data Collector Sets nodes, and then select User Defined. You should see a list of current alerts (if any) in the right pane.

3. Right-click the User-Defined node in the left pane, point to New, and then choose Data Collector Set.

4. In the Create New Data Collector Set Wizard, type a name for the Data Collector Set, such as **CPU Utilization Alert**. Select the Create Manually option and then click Next.

5. On the What Type Of Data Do You Want To Include page, the Create Data Logs option is selected by default. Select the Performance Counter Alert option and then click Next.

6. On the Which Performance Counters Would You Like To Monitor page, click Add. This displays the Add Counter dialog box. Because you are configuring CPU alerts, expand the Processor object in the Performance Object list. Click % Processor Time. In the Instances Of Selected Object panel, select _Total and then click Add.

7. Expand the System object in the Performance Object list. Click Processor Queue Length, and then click Add. Click OK.

8. On the Which Performance Counters Would You Like To Monitor page, you'll see the counters you've added. Select % Processor Time. Then set the Alert When list to Above, and type **98** as the Limit value. This ensures that you are alerted when processor utilization is more than 98 percent.

9. In the Performance Counters panel, select Processor Queue Length. Then set the Alert When list to Above, and type **3** as the Limit value. This ensures that you are alerted when more than three processes are waiting to execute, which can be an indicator that a server's processors need to be upgraded.

10. Click Next and then click Finish. This saves the Data Collector Set and closes the wizard.

11. Finish configuring the alert by following steps 11 through 14 under "Tracking Memory Usage."

Tracking Disk Usage

Exchange Server uses disk space for data storage, logging, tracking, and virtual memory. To ensure there is always ample disk space available, Exchange Server monitors free disk space. If free disk space drops below specific thresholds, Exchange will gracefully shut itself down. When Exchange is in this state, it is likely that data could get lost. To prevent serious problems, you should monitor free disk space closely on all drives used by Exchange Server.

You'll also want to track closely the number of system requests that are waiting for disk access. A relatively high value for a particular disk can affect server performance and is also a good indicator that a disk is being overutilized or that there may be some problem with the disk. To resolve this problem, you'll want to try to shift part of the disk's workload to other disks, such as by moving databases, logs or both.

You configure disk usage alerting by completing the following steps:

1. In the Exchange Management Console, click the Toolbox node, and then double-click Performance Monitor. This opens the Exchange Server Performance Monitor.

2. Expand the Performance Logs And Alerts and Data Collector Sets nodes, and then select User Defined. You should see a list of current alerts (if any) in the right pane.

3. Right-click the User-Defined node in the left pane, point to New, and then choose Data Collector Set.

4. In the Create New Data Collector Set Wizard, type a name for the Data Collector Set, such as **Disk Usage Alert**. Select the Create Manually option and then click Next.

5. On the What Type Of Data Do You Want To Include page, the Create Data Logs option is selected by default. Select the Performance Counter Alert option and then click Next.

6. On the Which Performance Counters Would You Like To Monitor page, click Add. This displays the Add Counter dialog box. Because you are configuring disk alerts, expand the LogicalDisk object in the Performance Object list. Click % Free Space. In the Instances Of Selected Object panel, select all individual logical disk instances except _Total and then click Add.

7. Expand the PhysicalDisk object in the Performance Object list. Click Current Disk Queue Length. In the Instances Of Selected Object panel, select all individual physical disk instances except _Total and then click Add. Click OK.

8. On the Which Performance Counters Would You Like To Monitor page, you'll see the counters you've added. Select the first logical disk instance, set the Alert When list to Below, and then type **5** as the Limit value. This ensures that you are alerted when available free space is less than 5 percent. Repeat this procedure for each logical disk.

9. In the Performance Counters panel, select the first physical disk instance, set the Alert When list to Above, and then type **2** as the Limit value. This ensures that you are alerted when more than two system requests are waiting for disk access. Repeat this procedure for each physical disk.

10. Click Next and then click Finish. This saves the Data Collector Set and closes the wizard.

11. Finish configuring the alert by following steps 11 through 14 under "Tracking Memory Usage."

Working with Queues

As an Exchange administrator, it's your responsibility to monitor Exchange queues regularly. Hub Transport and Edge Transport servers use queues to hold messages while they are processing them for routing and delivery. If messages remain in a queue for an extended period, there could be a problem. For example, if an Exchange server is unable to connect to the network, you'll find that messages aren't being cleared out of queues.

Understanding Exchange Queues

As discussed in the "Working with the Exchange Server Message Queues" section of Chapter 3, "Exchange Server 2010 Administration Essentials," queues are temporary holding locations for messages that are waiting to be processed, and

Exchange Server 2010 uses an Extensible Storage Engine (ESE) database for queue storage. Exchange Server 2010 uses the following types of queues:

- **Submission queue** The submission queue is a persistent queue that is used by the Exchange Categorizer (a transport component) to store temporarily all messages that have to be resolved, routed, and processed by transport agents. All messages that are received by a transport server enter processing in the submission queue. Messages are submitted through SMTP-receive, the Pickup directory, or the store driver. Each transport server has only one submission queue. Messages that are in the submission queue cannot be in other queues at the same time.

  Edge Transport servers use the Categorizer to route messages to the appropriate destinations. Hub Transport servers use the Categorizer to expand distribution lists, to identify alternative recipients, and to apply forwarding addresses. After the Categorizer retrieves the necessary information about recipients, it uses that information to apply policies, route the message, and perform content conversion. After categorization, the transport server moves the message to a delivery queue or to the Unreachable queue.

- **Mailbox delivery queue** Mailbox delivery queues hold messages that are being delivered to a Mailbox server by using encrypted Exchange RPC. Only Hub Transport servers have mailbox delivery queues, and they use the queue to store temporarily messages that are being delivered to mailbox recipients whose mailbox data is stored on a Mailbox server that is located in the same site as the Hub Transport server. Hub Transport servers have one mailbox delivery queue for each destination Mailbox server associated with messages currently being routed. After queuing the message, the Hub Transport server delivers the messages to the distinguished name of the mailbox database.

- **Remote delivery queue** Remote delivery queues hold messages that are being delivered to a remote server by using SMTP. Both Hub Transport servers and Edge Transport servers can have remote delivery queues, and they use the queue to store temporarily messages that are being routed to remote destinations. On an Edge Transport server, these destinations are external SMTP domains or SMTP connectors. On a Hub Transport server, these destinations are outside the Active Directory site in which the Hub Transport server is located. Transport servers have one remote delivery queue for each remote destination associated with messages currently being routed. After queuing the message, the transport server delivers it to the appropriate server, smart host, IP address, or Active Directory site.

- **Poison message queue** The poison message queue is used to hold messages that are detected to be potentially harmful to Exchange Server 2010 after a server failure. Messages that contain errors that are potentially fatal to Exchange Server 2010 are delivered to the poison message queue. Each transport server has one poison message queue. Although this queue is persistent, it typically is empty and, as a result, is not displayed in queue viewing interfaces. By default, all messages in the poison message queue are suspended and can be manually deleted.

- **Shadow redundancy queue**   The shadow redundancy queue is used to prevent the loss of messages that are in transit by storing queued messages until the next transport server along the route reports a successful delivery of the message. If the next transport server doesn't report successful delivery, the message is resubmitted for delivery. This queue is nonpersistent. Hub and Edge Transport servers have one for each hop to which the server delivered the primary message.

- **Transport dumpster queue**   The transport dumpster queue is used to hold messages that are being delivered to recipients whose mailboxes are stored in replicated mailbox databases. This queue is nonpersistent. Hub and Edge Transport servers have one queue for each Active Directory site.

- **Unreachable queue**   The unreachable queue contains messages that cannot be routed to their destinations. Each transport server has one unreachable queue. Although this queue is persistent, it typically is empty and, as a result, is not displayed in queue viewing interfaces.

When a transport server receives a message, a transport mail item is created and saved in the appropriate queue within the queue database. Exchange Server assigns each mail item a unique identifier when it stores the mail item in the database. If a mail item is being routed to more than one recipient, the mail item can have more than one destination and, in this case, there is a routed mail item for each destination. A routed mail item is a reference to the transport mail item, and it is the routed mail item that Exchange queues for delivery.

Accessing the Queue Viewer

You access system and link queues by completing the following steps:

1. In the Exchange Management Console, select the Toolbox node, and then double-click Queue Viewer. This opens the Queue Viewer.

2. By default, the Queue Viewer connects to the queuing database on the local server (if applicable). To connect to a different server, on the Action menu, select Connect To Server. In the Connect To Server dialog box, click Browse. Select the Exchange Server with which you want to work, and then click OK. Click Connect.

3. As shown in Figure 14-8, the Queue Viewer provides an overview of the status of each active queue, including the following information:

   - A folder icon indicates an active state.
   - A folder icon with a green check mark indicates the queue has a ready status.
   - A folder icon with a blue button and a small down arrow indicates a retry state.
   - A folder icon with a red exclamation point indicates a warning state, such as Not Available or Error.

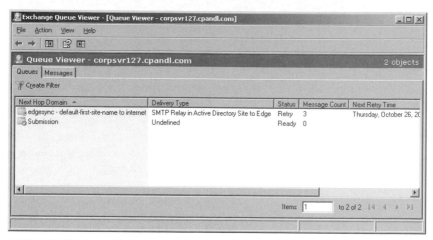

FIGURE 14-8 The Queue Viewer provides an overview of the status of each active queue.

Managing Queues

You usually won't see messages in queues because they're processed and routed quickly. Messages come into a queue, Exchange Server performs a lookup or establishes a connection, and then Exchange Server either moves the message to a new queue or delivers it to its destination.

Understanding Queue Summaries and Queue States

Messages remain in a queue when there's a problem or if they have been suspended by an administrator. To check for problem messages, use the Queue Viewer to examine the number of messages in the queues. If you see a queue with a consistent or growing number of messages, there might be a problem. Again, normally, messages should come into a queue and then be processed quickly. Because of this, the number of messages in a queue should gradually decrease over time as the messages are processed, provided no new messages come into the queue.

Whenever you click the Queues tab in the Queue Viewer, you get a summary of the currently available queues for the selected server. Although queue summaries provide important details for troubleshooting message flow problems, you do have to know what to look for. The connection status is the key information to look at first. This value tells you the state of the queue. States you'll see include these:

- **Active** An active queue has messages that are being transported.
- **Ready** A ready queue is needed to allow messages to be transported. When queues are ready, they can have a connection allocated to them.
- **Retry** A connection attempt has failed and the server is waiting to retry.

- **Suspended**   The queue is suspended, and none of its messages can be processed for routing. Messages can enter the queue, however, as long as the Exchange Categorizer is running. You must resume the queue to resume normal queue operations.

Administrators can choose to enable or disable connections to a queue by right-clicking the queue and selecting Suspend. If a queue is suspended, it is unable to route and deliver messages.

You can change the queue state to Ready by right-clicking the queue and selecting Resume. When you do this, Exchange Server should immediately enable the queue, which allows messages to be routed and delivered from it. If a queue is in the retry state, you can force an immediate retry using the Retry command.

Other summary information that you might find useful in troubleshooting includes

- **Delivery Type**   Tells you for what type of recipient messages are being queued for delivery.

- **Next Hop Domain**   Tells you the next destination of a delivery queue. For mailbox delivery and remote delivery queues, this field tells you the next hop domain. Messages queued for delivery to an EdgeSync server list the associated site and destination, such as EdgeSync—Default-First-Site To Internet.

- **Message Count**   Tells you the total number of messages waiting in the queue. If you see a large number, you might have a connectivity or routing problem.

- **Next Retry Time**   When the connection state is Retry, this column tells you when another connection attempt will be made. You can click the Retry command to attempt a connection immediately.

- **Last Retry Time**   When the connection state is Retry, this column tells you when the last retry attempt was made.

- **Last Error**   Tells you the error code and details of the last error to occur in a particular queue. This information can help you determine why a queue is having delivery problems.

Refreshing the Queue View

Use the queue summaries and queue state information to help you find queuing problems, as discussed in the "Understanding Queue Summaries and Queue States" section earlier in this chapter. By default, the queue view is refreshed every 30 seconds and the maximum number of message items that can be listed on each page is 1,000.

To change the viewing options, follow these steps:

1. In the Queue Viewer, on the View menu, click Options.
2. To turn off automatic refresh, clear the Auto-Refresh Screen check box. Otherwise, enable automatic refresh by selecting the Auto-Refresh Screen check box.

3. In the Refresh Interval text box, type a specific refresh rate in seconds.

4. Type the desired maximum number of messaging items to be displayed per page in the Number Of Items To Display text box. Click OK.

Working with Messages in Queues

To manage queues, you must enumerate messages. This process allows you to examine queue contents and perform management tasks on messages within a particular queue.

The easiest way to enumerate messages is to do so in sets of 1,000. To display the first 1,000 messages in a queue, follow these steps:

1. On the Queues tab in the Queue Viewer, you should see a list of available queues. Double-click a queue to enumerate the first 1,000 messages, as shown in Figure 14-9.

2. After you enumerate messages in a queue, you can examine message details by double-clicking the entries for individual messages.

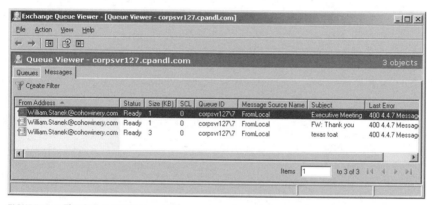

FIGURE 14-9 The Queue Viewer provides a summary for each message in a queue.

You can also create a filter to search for specific types of messages. To do this, follow these steps:

1. Double-click the queue with which you want to work. This enumerates the first 1,000 messages in the queue, as discussed previously.

2. If you haven't previously created a filter, click Create Filter.

3. Use the first selection list to specify the field you want to use for filtering messages. You can filter messages by the following criteria: Date Received, Expiration Time, From Address, Internet Message ID, Last Error, Message Source Name, Queue ID, SCL, Size (KB), Source IP, Status, and Subject.

4. Use the second selection list to specify the filter criteria. The available filter criteria depend on the filter field and include Equals, Does Not Equal, Contains, Does Not Contain, Greater Than, and Less Than.

5. Use the text box provided to specify the exact criteria to match. For example, if you are filtering messages using the Status field, you might want to see all messages where the Status field equals Retry. Your filter is automatically applied, and you can examine message details by double-clicking the entries for individual messages.

6. To stop filtering, click the Remove Expression button.

Forcing Connections to Queues

In many cases, you can change the queue state to Ready by forcing a connection. Simply right-click the queue, and then select Retry. When you do this, Exchange Server should immediately enable connections to the queue, and this should allow messages to be routed to and delivered from it.

Suspending and Resuming Queues

When you suspend a queue, all new message transfer activity out of that queue stops and only messages being processed will be delivered. This means that messages can continue to enter the queue, but no new messages will leave it. To restore normal operations, you must resume the queue.

You suspend and resume a queue by completing the following steps:

1. On the Queues tab in the Queue Viewer, you should see a list of available queues. Right-click a queue, and then select Suspend.

2. When you're done troubleshooting, right-click the queue, and then select Resume.

Another way to suspend messages in a queue is to do so selectively. In this way, you can control the transport of a single message or several messages that might be causing problems on the server. For example, if a large message is delaying the delivery of other messages, you can suspend that message until other messages have left the queue. Afterward, you can resume the message to resume normal delivery.

To suspend and then resume individual messages, complete the following steps:

1. On the Queues tab in the Queue Viewer, you should see a list of available queues. Double-click the queue with which you want to work.

2. Right-click the message you want to suspend, and then select Suspend. You can select multiple messages using Shift and Ctrl.

3. When you're ready to resume delivery of the message, right-click the suspended message, and then select Resume.

Deleting Messages from Queues

You can remove messages from queues if necessary. To do this, follow these steps:

1. On the Queues tab in the Queue Viewer, you should see a list of available queues. Double-click the queue with which you want to work.

2. Right-click the message you want to remove. You can select multiple messages using Shift and Ctrl, and then right-click. Select one of the following options from the shortcut menu:

- **Remove (With NDR)**   Deletes the selected messages from the queue, and notifies the sender with a nondelivery report (NDR)
- **Remove (Without Sending NDR)**   Deletes the message or messages from the queue without sending an NDR to the sender

3. When prompted, click Yes to confirm the deletion.

Deleting messages from a queue removes them from the messaging system permanently. You can't recover the deleted messages.

CHAPTER 15

Backing Up and Restoring Exchange Server 2010

- Understanding the Essentials of Exchange Server Availability and Recovery **569**
- Performing Backup and Recovery on Windows Server 2008 **579**
- Performing Additional Backup and Recovery Tasks **590**

Microsoft Exchange Server 2010 is critically important to your organization. If a Mailbox server crashes and you haven't planned for this possibility, you are faced with the possibility of every user on that server losing days, weeks, or even months of work. If your primary Client Access server crashes and you don't have any alternates, users won't be able to remotely access messages, calendars, address lists, and more. If your primary transport server crashes and you don't have any alternates, messages will not be properly routed and delivered. To ensure access to Exchange Server and protect your users' data, you need to extend your Exchange organization to meet availability expectations and implement a recovery plan.

Understanding the Essentials of Exchange Server Availability and Recovery

Designing your Exchange organization for availability and recovery scenarios can protect against database corruption, hardware failures, accidental loss of user messages, and even natural disasters. As an administrator, your job is to make sure that servers are available and that data can be recovered.

Ensuring Data Availability

With Exchange Server 2010, it is easier than ever to design a highly available (HA) solution that ensures the availability of most messaging services. Simply by deploying multiple Hub Transport, Edge Transport, and Client Access servers and placing the additional servers within the appropriate Active Directory sites, you can ensure availability of key messaging services if a primary Hub Transport, Edge Transport, or Client Access server fails.

When it comes to Mailbox servers, you can use several techniques to improve availability and avoid having to restore from backups:

- **Database copies** Each member server in a database availability group (DAG) can have one copy of a database that is hosted and active on another member server. Exchange uses continuous replication to create and maintain copies of databases.

- **Deleted item retention** Deleted item retention allows users to restore a single item or an entire folder in Microsoft Office Outlook.

- **Deleted mailbox retention** Deleted mailbox retention allows administrators to restore deleted mailboxes without having to restore the mailboxes from backups.

- **Archive mailboxes** Archive mailboxes are used to store users' old messages, such as may be required to comply with company policy, government regulations, or legal requirements.

- **Retention policy** Retention policy is applied to enforce message retention settings. When messages reach a retention limit, they are processed by Exchange based on the actions defined in retention tags that have been applied. This allows messages to be archived, deleted, or flagged for user attention.

- **Multiple mailbox databases** By using multiple mailbox databases, configuring storage appropriately, and distributing users across these databases, you can reduce significantly the impact of the loss of a single database and allow for faster restores when needed.

With all of these features in place and configured appropriately, you might not need traditional point-in-time backups of Mailbox servers or long-term data storage on tape. Keep the following in mind:

- For high availability, Microsoft recommends having at least three highly available database copies, which means one active copy and at least two highly available passive copies. A highly available copy is a copy that does not have a replay lag time and is not blocked for activation by an administrator. This means you'll need at least three Mailbox servers in each highly available DAG.

- For disaster recovery, I recommend having at least four database copies, which means one active copy, at least two highly available passive copies, and at least one lagged copy. A lagged copy is a copy that has a replay lag time. This means you'll need at least four Mailbox servers in each DAG optimized for disaster recovery.

As part of your Exchange organization planning, you should have at least one Mailbox server in each Active Directory site. Because any database availability group can be extended to multiple sites, you don't necessarily need to have multiple Mailbox servers in each site, and having multiple site locations for Mailbox servers can help protect you against data center failures. For example, if Site A goes offline but Site B remains available, users who normally access their mailboxes in Site A would be redirected automatically to the appropriate Mailbox server in Site B, as long as you've configured your database copies appropriately.

To eliminate the need for point-in-time backups, you need at least two highly available copies in addition to the active copy. I also recommend having a lagged copy of a database. Having a lagged database copy can help safeguard against data corruption that is replicated to the databases in a group, resulting in a need to return to a previous point in time. Keep in mind that deleted item retention and hold policy are your first line of defense in case of accidental deletion of mailboxes and mailbox data.

If you have multiple copies of an active database, you'll likely want one of these copies to have a long lag time. What is sufficiently long is subject to interpretation and the needs of your organization. Ideally, the lag time would be sufficient to allow someone to identify a problem and for an administrator to begin recovery. In a 24x7 environment, where administrators are always available, a sufficient lag time may be 12, 24, or 48 hours, depending on your needs. In other environments, a sufficient lag time likely would be measured in multiple days.

REAL WORLD Lagged copies are designed for disaster recovery purposes and specifically to protect against store logical corruption. The combination of mailbox database copies, hold policy, and Extensible Storage Engine's (ESE) single page restore leaves only the extremely rare but catastrophic store logical corruption case to deal with. The decision on whether to use a lagged copy should depend primarily on which third-party applications you use and your organization's history with store logical corruption.

Some examples of strategies for small, medium, and large organizations are shown in Table 15-1. When you create or configure database copies using Add-MailboxDatabaseCopy or Set-MailboxDatabaseCopy, respectively, you can use the −ReplayLagTime parameter to specify how long the Exchange Information Store service should wait before replaying log files, and use the −TruncationLagTime parameter to specify how long Exchange Replication service should wait before truncating logs that have been inspected on all copies. The maximum replay lag time is 14 days, as is the maximum truncation lag time.

TABLE 15-1 Database Copy Strategies for Small, Medium, and Large Organizations

ORGANIZATION SIZE	RECOVERY NEEDS	RECOMMENDATION
SMALL	Low	At least 2 HA database copies.
	High	At least 2 HA database copies with at least one lagged copy (3 to 7 days).
MEDIUM	Low	At least 2 HA database copies with at least one lagged copy (3 to 7 days).
	High	At least 2 HA database copies with at least one lagged copy (24 to 72 hours).
LARGE	Low	At least 2 HA database copies with at least one lagged copy (3 to 7 days).
	High	At least 3 HA database copies with at least one lagged copy (24 to 72 hours).

While database copies may be able to eliminate the need for point-in-time database snapshots, database copies alone won't eliminate the need for long-term storage of backups. To reduce the need for long-term storage of backups, you must properly implement deleted item retention and deleted mailbox retention. In most cases, you'll want deleted items and mailboxes to be retained for at least 30, 60, or 90 days. In addition, you'll want to apply retention policy to enforce message retention settings and configure archiving as appropriate for your organization. If you want to eliminate the need for long-term storage of backups, you'll want to supplement these strategies with database copies written to Mailbox servers in multiple geographic locations. For example, if you have offices in Los Angeles and Sacramento, your Los Angeles office could act as the failsafe recovery location for your Sacramento office and vice versa. As such, each office location would have a Mailbox server with a copy of each active mailbox database. If your organization doesn't have multiple geographic locations, you'll likely want to continue to create archival backups and rotate them to offsite storage as appropriate.

Backing Up Exchange Server: The Basics

To create a complete backup of an Exchange server, you must back up the following:

- Exchange user data, which includes Exchange mailbox databases, public folder databases, and transaction logs. If you want to be able to recover mailbox and public folder databases from backups, you must back up this data. User data doesn't contain Exchange configuration settings.
- Folders and drives that contain Windows and Exchange files. Normally, this means backing up the root drive C, which includes the special partition for Exchange Server.

- System state data for the operating system, which includes essential system files needed to recover the local system. All computers have System State data, which you must back up in addition to other files to restore a complete working system. To be clear, system state data is needed for Windows recovery but is not needed for Exchange recovery.

Because Exchange Server 2010 supports only VSS-based backups, volumes are the units of backup. You back up a volume and then you restore the data, get the portion of the data you want to work with, and recover that. Although you can recover an individual database from backup, you should know about some fundamental issues before you try to do so. These issues pertain to transactions, transaction logs, and transaction logging modes.

The Exchange Information Store service creates transaction logs. Exchange Server uses transactions to record database changes. You can think of a transaction as a logical unit of work that contains one or more operations that affect the Exchange store. If Exchange Server executes all of the operations in a transaction successfully, it marks the transaction as successful and permanently commits the changes. If one or more of the operations in a transaction fails to complete, Exchange Server marks the transaction as failed and removes any changes that the transaction created. The process of removing changes is referred to as *rolling back* the transaction.

Transaction logs are units of storage for transactions. Exchange Server writes each transaction to a log file and maintains the log files according to the logging mode. With standard logging, Exchange Server reserves 1 megabyte (MB) of disk space for the active transaction log. Exchange Server commits or rolls back transactions based on their success or failure. When the contents of the log reach 1 MB, Exchange Server creates a new log file. Because Exchange Server maintains the transaction logs until the next full backup, you can recover Exchange Server to the last transaction (as long Exchange is using standard logging).

NOTE The active transaction log is named E##.log, where ## is the unique identifier for the database. Additional transaction logs are named E##00000001.log, E##00000002.log, and so on.

Exchange can use standard logging or circular logging. With standard logging, each database transaction is written to a log file and then to the database. When a log file reaches 1 megabyte (MB) in size, the Exchange Information Store service renames the log and creates a new log file. If Exchange stops unexpectedly, you can recover databases to the last transaction. You do this by replaying the data from the log files into the database.

In Exchange 2010, circular logging is disabled by default. With circular logging, Exchange overwrites and reuses the first log file after the data it contains has been written to the database. This saves disk space but is not a recommended best practice. Why? One of the reasons is that when circular logging is enabled, you can recover data only up until the last full backup.

Creating a Disaster Recovery Plan Based on Exchange Roles

With Exchange Server 2010, you need to tailor your recovery plan to the roles installed on your Exchange servers. Because most configuration data for Exchange Server 2010 is stored in Active Directory, you can fully restore some server roles by running the Exchange Setup program with the /mode:recoverserver command on a server. With other roles, running this command restores the Exchange configuration, but you need to recover the critical Exchange data from backup.

NOTE Recoverserver mode is only for recovering a server or moving a server to new hardware while maintaining the same server name. When you run Setup in this mode, Setup reads configuration data from Active Directory for a server with the same name as the server from which you are running Setup. This mode doesn't recover custom settings stored locally or in databases; it recovers only settings stored in Active Directory.

Use the following guidelines for your recovery planning:

- **Mailbox servers** You can fully restore the Mailbox server role by running the Exchange Setup program with the /mode:recoverserver command. However, you can't recover databases with this mode. You can restore mailbox data from a backup that includes the necessary mailbox data. Mailbox servers store Exchange database files, including both mailbox and public folder databases, and Exchange transaction log files specific to each database. You can rebuild database copies by re-creating them. You can also rebuild replicated public folder data through the normal replication process if there are available replicas. Mailbox servers also store full-text indexing information specific to each mailbox database. You do not need to back up full-text indexes, because you'll need to rebuild them, as discussed in the "Content Indexing" section of Chapter 9, "Managing Data and Database Availability Groups." Other types of Exchange databases on mailbox servers include free/busy information and the offline address book (OAB). This information can be rebuilt by automated maintenance and then replicated.

- **Hub Transport servers** You can restore the Hub Transport server role and make it fully functional by running Exchange Setup with the /mode:recoverserver command. Hub Transport servers store all essential configuration data in Active Directory. In addition to configuration data, Hub Transport servers store queues in database files and any logs you've enabled, including message tracking, protocol, and connectivity logs. Queues store messages actively being processed, and logs are primarily used for historical reference and troubleshooting. Queues and logs are not essential to restoring Hub Transport server functionality. Because of shadow redundancy, any queued messages are automatically resent and do not need to be recovered (unless you have only one Hub Transport server).

- **Edge Transport servers** The Edge Transport server role is designed for perimeter network deployment. You can restore the Edge Transport server role and make it fully functional by using a cloned configuration. Edge Transport servers store configuration data, queues, replicated data from Active Directory, and any logs you've enabled, including message tracking, protocol, and connectivity logs. Replicated data from Active Directory is stored in Active Directory Lightweight Directory Service (AD LDS). Queues store messages actively being processed, and logs are primarily used for historical reference and troubleshooting. Replicated data, queues, and logs are not essential to restoring Edge Transport server functionality. Replicated data can be resynchronized as necessary, and both queues and logs are created automatically as necessary. If you've applied custom settings to an Edge Transport server, such as those for content filtering, you can create a backup of the configuration, as discussed in the "Cloning Edge Transport Server Configurations" section of this chapter.

- **Client Access servers**   You can restore the Client Access server role to its initial default state by running Exchange Setup with the /mode:recoverserver command. However, any custom changes you've made to Web sites running on a Client Access server are not restored. Changes to Web sites are stored in the Internet Information Services (IIS) configuration data. Although you can restore the IIS configuration data from backup to recover the custom settings, this is not recommended because you might experience errors on the Client Access server if the IIS configuration data and the recovered Active Directory settings aren't exactly in sync. To restore a Client Access server, you can build a new server with a new name by running Exchange Setup, or you can restore the old server with the same name by running Exchange Setup with the /mode:recoverserver command. When Setup finishes, you then need to apply the same customizations that you had on the server before, re-creating additional Web sites and virtual directories as necessary. To apply the setting changes, you should restart IIS.

- **Unified Messaging servers**   The Unified Messaging server role stores all of its essential configuration data in Active Directory, and you can restore a server to its initial default state by running the Exchange Setup program with the /mode:recoverserver command. In addition, you can restore any custom audio files used for prompts automatically through replication if you have other UM servers in the organization.

Finalizing Your Exchange Server Disaster Recovery Plan

As you've seen, creating a disaster recovery plan for Exchange Server 2010 requires forethought on your part. As part of your planning, you also need take a close look at the overall architecture of your Exchange organization and make any changes required to ensure that the architecture meets the availability and recoverability expectations of your bosses. You need to review

- **The number of Exchange servers to use in your organization.**   Do you need multiple servers to ensure high availability? Do you need multiple servers to improve performance? Do you need multiple servers because the organization spans several geographic areas?

- **The number of databases for each Exchange server, as well as how database availability groups are organized.** Do you need to create databases for each department or division in the organization? Do you need to create databases for different business functions? Do you need to create separate databases for public folders and other types of data?

After you've reviewed the architecture of the Exchange organization and implemented any necessary changes, you can create an availability and disaster recovery plan to support that organization. If your plan includes point-in-time backups, archival backups, or both, you need to figure out what data you need to back up, how often you should back up the data, and more. To help you create a plan, consider the following:

- **How important is the mailbox or public folder database you're backing up?** The importance of the data can go a long way in helping you determine when and how you should back up the database. For critical data, such as a department's mailbox database, you'll want to have redundant backup sets that extend back for several backup periods. For less important data, such as public folders for nonessential documents, you won't need such an elaborate backup plan, but you'll need to back up the data regularly and ensure that you can recover the data easily.

- **How available does the data need to be or how quickly do you need to recover the data?** Time is an important factor in creating a backup plan. You might need to get critical data, such as the primary mailbox database, back online swiftly. To do this, you might need to alter your recovery plan. For example, you might need to create multiple mailbox databases and then create a copy of each on multiple servers in a database availability group. You can then recover individual databases or individual servers as the situation warrants.

- **Do you have the equipment to perform backups?** If you don't have backup hardware, you can't perform backups. To perform timely backups, you might need several backup devices and several sets of backup media. Backup hardware includes tape drives, tape library systems, storage arrays, and removable disk drives.

- **Who will be responsible for the recovery plan?** Ideally, someone should be the primary contact for the Exchange recovery plan. This person might also be responsible for performing the actual backup and recovery of Exchange Server.

- **What is the best time to schedule backups?** Scheduling backups when system use is as low as possible may speed up the backup process. However, because you can't always schedule backups for off-peak hours, you need to carefully plan when you back up data. For example, you may want to back up a passive copy of a database rather than the active copy.

- **Do you need to store backups off-site?** Storing copies of backup tapes off-site is essential to recovering Exchange Server in a variety of situations, especially in the case of a natural disaster. In your off-site storage location, you should also include copies of all the software you might need to recover Exchange Server and change management records so that you can re-create custom settings after recovery.

Choosing Backup and Recovery Options

As you'll find when you work with Exchange backup and recovery, there are many techniques for backing up data. The techniques you use depend on the type of data you're backing up, how convenient you want the recovery process to be, and other factors.

To back up Exchange, you must use an Exchange-aware Volume Shadow Copy Service (VSS)–based backup program with Exchange. You cannot use streaming Extensible Storage Engine–based backup programs with Exchange.

Exchange Server includes a plug-in for Windows Server Backup that makes it possible for you to create VSS-based backups of Exchange data. This plug-in runs as a service named Microsoft Exchange Server Extension for Windows Server Backup and is configured by default for manual startup. To use the plug-in, you must install the Windows Server Backup feature on Exchange servers you want to back up. The related command-line tools are not compatible with Exchange Server 2010, however, and you should not install them.

Windows Server Backups should be performed at the volume level. To back up a database and its transaction logs, you must back up the entire volume containing the database and logs. You cannot back up only the data. Although you can create a backup on a local drive or a remote network share, you must be logged on to the server to perform backups. You can log on locally at the keyboard or via a remote desktop connection.

When you are using Windows Server Backup to back up Exchange Server, you can perform only full or copy backups. Both approaches back up all Exchange data that has been selected, including the related databases and the current transaction logs. However, only a full backup tells Exchange Server you've performed a complete backup, which allows Exchange Server to clear out the transaction logs.

In your backup plan, you'll probably want to perform full or copy backups on a weekly basis. You might also want to create an extended backup set for monthly and quarterly backups that you rotate to off-site storage. This will ensure that you have recent data for recovery as well as older data for recovery.

When you restore data, you can restore only Exchange data. The Exchange data can be restored to its original location or an alternate location. Keep the following in mind:

- If you restore Exchange data to its original location, Windows Server Backup and the backup plug-in automatically handle the recovery process. This means they dismount any existing databases, replay logs into recovered databases, and mount databases for you. All backed-up databases must be restored together. You cannot restore a single database.

- If you restore Exchange data to an alternate location, Windows Server Backup and the backup plug-in do not handle the recovery process. This means you need to manually work with the data and restore it. While this requires more work, you can restore a single database as well as individual mailboxes.

You can move manually restored data from the alternate location to a recovery database (rdb). A recovery database is a special-purpose database that allows you to mount a restored mailbox database and select data for recovery. You create a recovery database using New-MailboxDatabase with the –Recovery parameter. You use Restore-Mailbox to extract data from a restored database.

Restore-Mailbox works only with disconnected mailboxes. The disconnected mailboxes are specified as the recovery sources, and the recovery targets are connected mailboxes in an active mailbox database. Thus, you extract data from a disconnected source mailbox and move it to a connected target mailbox. The source and target mailboxes must be in the same Active Directory forest.

A recovery database is completely disconnected. As a result, a recovery database:

- Applies only to mailbox databases and does not apply to public folder databases.
- Does not have system or mailbox management policies.
- Is not enabled for logging or maintenance.
- Cannot be accessed by or connected to by users.

A recovery database enables the following recovery scenarios:

- Recovering or repairing a database. One recovery approach is to create a new empty database, called a dial-tone database, to replace the failed database. This allows users to continue sending and receiving mail while you are recovering a database. You can then merge the recovery database with the dial-tone database.

- Recovering a database to a different server. One recovery approach is to restore a database on a server other than the original server for that database. As necessary, you can then merge the recovered data back to the original database on the original server.

- Recovering deleted mailboxes or deleted items after the retention period has expired. One recovery approach is to restore the database in an alternate location. Then you would extract the required data and merge it into the existing data.

Only one recovery database can be mounted on a Mailbox server at one time. The recovery database does not count toward the maximum number of allowed databases per Mailbox server.

Performing Backup and Recovery on Windows Server 2008

Windows Server 2008 and Windows Server 2008 Release 2 provide different tools for performing backup and recovery procedures. The one common tool on both is Windows Server Backup.

Getting Started with Windows Server Backup

You'll use Windows Server Backup for creating backups and for recovery using backups. You can install Windows Server Backup by following these steps:

1. In Server Manager, select the Features node in the left pane and then click Add Features. This starts the Add Features Wizard.

2. On the Select Features page, expand the Windows Server Backup Features node, and then select the Windows Server Backup option. Do not select the Command-line Tools option. Click Next.

3. Click Install. When the wizard finishes installing the selected features, click Close. From now on, Windows Server Backup will be available as an option on the Administrative Tools menu and as an option under the Storage node in Server Manager.

When you start Windows Server Backup the first time, you'll see a warning that no backup has been configured for the computer. You clear this warning by creating a backup using the Backup Once feature or by scheduling backups to run automatically by using the Backup Schedule feature. Only members of the Administrators and Backup Operators groups have full authority to back up and restore any type of file, regardless of who owns the file and the permissions set on it.

Windows Server Backup provides extensions for working with System State and application data. All computers have system state data, which must be backed up in addition to other files to restore a complete working system. Windows Server Backup creates block-level backups of application data using VSS.

When you start Windows Server Backup, the utility connects to the local computer by default. This allows you to easily manage backups on the local computer. The Exchange plug-in for Windows Server Backup does not support backups on a remote computer.

When you use Windows Server Backup, you'll always want to create a full or copy backup rather than an incremental or differential backup. These basic types of backups are used as follows:

- **Full backups**   Backs up all Exchange data that has been selected, including the related databases and the current transaction logs. A full backup tells Exchange Server you've performed a complete backup, which allows Exchange Server to clear out the transaction logs.

- **Copy backups**   Backs up all Exchange data that has been selected, including the related databases and the current transaction logs. Unlike a full backup, a copy backup doesn't tell Exchange Server you've performed a complete backup and, as a result, the backup does not clear the log files. This allows you to perform other types of Exchange backups later.

- **Differential backups (not supported)**   Designed to create backup copies of all data that has changed since the last full backup. Backs up only transaction log files and not the actual databases. Does not clear the log files

- **Incremental backups (not supported)**   Designed to create backups of data that has changed since the most recent full or incremental backup. Backs up only transaction log files and not the actual databases. Clears the log files after the incremental backup completes.

You can start a backup by selecting Backup Once on the Action menu or in the Action pane. You can configure a backup schedule by clicking Backup Schedule on the Action menu or in the Action pane.

The available backup options differ somewhat between Windows Server 2008 and Windows Server 2008 Release 2. Keep the following in mind:

- The Exchange plug-in for Windows Server Backup only supports full backups. You must ensure you only perform full backups.

- Whether Windows Server Backup subsequently performs full or incremental backup depends on the default performance settings that you configure. In Windows Server Backup, click the Configure Performance Settings option to ensure full backups are the default setting.

- Whether Windows Server Backup performs full or copy backups depends on the default VSS settings that you configure. Copy backups are the default. To use full backups, you must specify this when creating the backup.

Backing Up Exchange Server on Windows Server 2008

As part of your planning for each server you plan to back up, you should consider which volumes you want to back up and whether backups will include system state recovery data, application data, or both. You can create backups manually or according to a schedule, or you can use both methods. After you configure a disk for scheduled backups, Windows Server Backup automatically manages the disk usage and automatically overwrites older backups when creating new backups. After you schedule backups, you need to check periodically to ensure that backups are being performed as expected and that the backup schedule meets current needs.

When you create or schedule backups, you need to specify the volumes that you want to include, and this affects the ways you can recover your servers and your data. As part of the backup process, you also need to specify a storage location for backups. Keep the following in mind when you are choosing storage locations:

- When you use an internal hard disk for storing backups, you are limited in how you can recover your system. You can recover the data from a volume, but you cannot rebuild the entire disk structure.

- When you use an external hard disk for storing backups, the disk will be dedicated for storing your backups and will not be visible in Windows Explorer. Choosing this option formats the selected disk or disks, removing any existing data.

- When you use a remote shared folder for storing backups, your backup will be overwritten each time you create a new backup. Do not choose this option if you want to store multiple backups for each server.

- When you use removable media or DVDs for storing manually created backups, you can recover only entire volumes, not applications or individual files. The media you use must be at least 1 GB in size.

You can schedule automated backups for a server by following these steps:

1. In Windows Server Backup, click Backup Schedule on the Action menu or in the Action pane. This starts the Backup Schedule Wizard. Click Next.

2. On the Select Backup Type page, note the backup size listed under the Full Server option. This is the storage space required to back up the server data, applications, and system state. Volumes that contain operating system files or applications are included in the backup by default and cannot be excluded. To back up all volumes on the server, select the Full Server option and then click Next. To back up selected volumes on the server, click Custom and then click Next.

3. If you selected Custom, the Select Backup Items page is displayed. With Windows Server 2008, select the check boxes for the volumes you want to back up, and clear the check boxes for the volumes you want to exclude. With Windows Server 2008 R2, you must click Add Items to select the items to back up. Click Advanced Settings. Use the options on the VSS Settings tab to specify whether you want to perform a VSS copy backup or a VSS full backup. Click OK.

   After you've selected items, click Next to continue.

4. On the Specify Backup Time page, you can specify how often and when you want to run backups. To perform backups daily at a specific time, choose Once A Day and then select the time to start running the daily backup. To perform backups multiple times each day, choose More Than Once A Day. Next, click a start time under Available Time, and then click Add to move the time to the Scheduled Time list. Repeat this step for each start time that you want to add. Click Next when you are ready to continue.

5. With Windows Server 2008, select the external disk you want to use for scheduled backups. If the disk you want to use is not listed, click Show All Available Disks. Then select the check box next to the disk you want to use to store the backups. Each external disk can store up to 512 backups, depending on the amount of data contained in each backup. You can select multiple disks. If you do so, Windows Server Backup rotates among them.

   When you click Next, you'll see a warning prompt informing you that the selected disk will be formatted and any existing data will be deleted. Click Yes. On the Label Destination Disk page, the disk that you selected is listed.

A label that includes the disk type, the server name, the current date, the current time, and a disk size is assigned to the disk. Be sure to record this information because you need it to identify the disk if you need to recover data from the backup stored on the disk. With external disks, you might want to attach a printed label containing this information.

6. With Windows Server 2008 Release 2, you have these options:

- **Backup To A Hard Disk That Is Dedicated For Backups** Allows you to specify a dedicated hard disk for backups. Although you can use multiple disks for backups, any disk that you select will be formatted and then dedicated only to backups. This option is recommended because you get the best performance. If you select this option, click Next, select the disk or disks to use, and then click Next again.

- **Backup To A Volume** Allows you to write backups to individual volumes on a hard disk. Because any volume you select is not dedicated to backups, it can be used for other purposes. However, the performance of any selected volumes will be reduced while backups are being written. If you select this option, click Next, use the Add and Remove options to select the volumes to use, and then click Next again.

- **Backup To A Shared Network Folder** Allows you to specify a shared network folder for backups. With this option, you can have only one backup at a time, because each new backup overwrites the previous backup. If you select this option, click Next. When prompted, click OK. Type the UNC path to the network share, such as \\FileServer25\Backups\ Exchange. If you want the backup to be accessible to everyone who has access to the shared folder, select Inherit under Access Control. If you want to restrict access to the shared folder to the current user, administrators, and backup operators, select Do Not Inherit under Access Control. Click Next. When prompted to provide access credentials, type the user name and password for an account authorized to access and write to the shared folder.

7. On the Confirmation page, review the details and then click Finish. The wizard will then format the disk. The formatting process might take several minutes or considerably longer depending on the size of the disk.

8. On the Summary page, click Close. Your backups are now scheduled for the selected server.

You can manually back up servers by following these steps:

1. In Windows Server Backup, click Backup Once on the Action menu or in the Action pane. This starts the Backup Once Wizard. Ensure that Different Options is selected, and then click Next again.

2. Note the backup size listed under the Full Server option. This is the storage space required to back up the server data, applications, and system state. To back up all volumes on the server, select the Full Server option and then click Next. To back up selected volumes on the server, click Custom and then click Next.

3. If you selected Custom, the Select Backup Items page is displayed. With Windows Server 2008, select the check boxes for the volumes you want to back up, and clear the check boxes for the volumes you want to exclude. With Windows Server 2008 R2, you must click Add Items to select the items to back up. Click Advanced Settings. Use the options on the VSS Settings tab to specify whether you want to perform a VSS copy backup or a VSS full back up. Click OK.

   After you've selected items, click Next to continue.

4. On the Specify Destination Type page, do one of the following:

   - If you want to back up to local drives, select Local Drives and then click Next. On the Backup Destination page, select the internal or external disc or DVD drive to use as the backup target. Backups are compressed when stored on a DVD. As a result, the size of the backup on a DVD might be smaller than the volume on the server. With Windows Server 2008, if the backup target is a removable media drive, the backup is verified automatically after the wizard writes the backup data. Clear the Verify After Writing check box if you do not want to verify the backup. Click Next.

   - If you want to back up to a remote shared folder, select Remote Shared Folder and then click Next. On the Specify Remote Folder page, type the UNC path to the remote folder, such as **\\BackupServer18\backups**. If you want the backup to be accessible to everyone who has access to the shared folder, select Inherit under Access Control. If you want to restrict access to the shared folder to the current user, administrators, and backup operators, select Do Not Inherit under Access Control. Click Next. When prompted to provide access credentials, type the user name and password for an account authorized to access and write to the shared folder.

5. With Windows Server 2008, specify whether you want to perform a copy backup or a VSS full backup. Choose Copy Backup if you are using a separate backup utility to backup application data. Otherwise, choose VSS Full Backup to fully back up the selected volumes, including all application data.

6. Click Next and then click Backup. The Backup Progress dialog box shows you the progress of the backup process. If you click Close, the backup will continue to run in the background.

Performing a Full Server Recovery

Often, you may find that the fastest and easiest way to recover an Exchange server is to start from scratch, install a fresh operating system, and then run Exchange Setup in recoverserver mode. That said, both Windows Server 2008 and Windows Server 2008 Release 2 include startup repair features that can recover a server in case of corrupted or missing system files. The startup repair process can also recover from some types of boot failures involving the boot manager. If these processes fail and the boot manager is the reason you cannot start the server, you can use the installation disc or a recovery partition to restore the boot manager and enable startup.

If Startup Repair fails and you are not able to start the server, you can attempt to recover the server using the recovery tools. When you install Windows Server 2008 R2, the Setup program automatically installs additional components that can be used for recovery and troubleshooting startup in this partition. Because of this, the Windows recovery tools are always available on computers running Windows Server 2008 R2. These tools include:

- **System Image Recovery**   Performs a full recovery of the computer using a system image created previously. If your other troubleshooting techniques fail to restore the computer and you have a system image for recovery, you can use this feature to restore the server from a system image.

- **Windows Memory Diagnostics**   Performs diagnostics on the server's memory. If memory hardware errors are causing startup or other problems with the server, you can use this tool to identify the problem.

- **Command Prompt**   Allows you to work with any command-line tools that are available, including DiskPart.

As an administrator, you can use these tools to recover computers. You can boot the server and initiate recovery by following these steps:

1. During startup, press F8 to access the Advanced Boot Options screen. If the computer has multiple operating systems, you'll see the Windows Boot Manager screen. Select the operating system to work with, and then press F8.

2. On the Advanced Boot Options menu, use the arrow keys to select Repair Your Computer, and then press Enter.

3. The computer will load the recovery options. In the System Recovery Options dialog box, select a language and keyboard layout, and then click Next.

4. To access recovery options, you need to log on using a local administrator account. Select the local administrator to log on as, type the password for this account, and then click OK.

5. In the System Recovery Options dialog box, note the location of the operating system, and then choose the appropriate repair option. If you want to perform a system image recovery, select the related option, and then perform steps 5 to 8 of the next procedure.

If Startup Repair fails and you are not able to start the server, you can attempt to recover the server from a system image by following these steps:

1. Insert the Windows disc into the DVD drive, and turn on the computer. If needed, press the required key to boot from the disc. After Windows loads files, the Install Windows Wizard should appear.

2. Specify the language settings to use, and then click Next.

3. Click Repair Your Computer. Setup searches the hard disk drives for an existing Windows installation and then displays the results in the System Recovery Options Wizard. If you are recovering the operating system onto new hardware, the list should be empty and there should be no operating system on the computer. Click Next.

4. With Windows Server 2008, click Windows Complete PC Restore to start the Windows Complete PC Restore Wizard. With R2, the Restore Your Computer option is selected by default, and you can click Next to continue.

5. Click Use The Latest Available ... (Recommended) and then click Next. Or click the alternative option, and then click Next.

6. If you chose to restore a different backup, on the Select The Location Of The Backup... page, do one of the following:

   - Click the computer that contains the backup you want to use, and then click Next. On the Select The Backup To Restore page, select the backup you want to use and then click Next.

   - To browse for a system image on the network, click Advanced, and then click Search For A System Image On The Network. When you are prompted to confirm that you want to connect to the network, click Yes. In the Network Folder text box, specify the location of the server and shared folder in which the system image is stored, such as \\Server21\Images\ Exchange, and then click OK.

   - To install a driver for a backup device that doesn't show up in the location list, click Advanced, and then click Install A Driver. Insert the installation media for the device, and then click OK. After Windows installs the device driver, the backup device should be listed in the location list.

7. On the Choose How To Restore The Backup page, perform the following optional tasks and then click Next:

   - Select the Format And Repartition Disks check box to delete existing partitions and reformat the destination disks to be the same as the backup.

   - Click the Exclude Disks button and then select the check boxes associated with any disks you want to exclude from being formatted and partitioned. The disk that contains the backup you are using is automatically excluded.

   - Click Install Drivers to install device drivers for the hardware to which you are recovering.

   - Click Advanced to specify whether the computer is restarted and whether the disks are checked for errors immediately after the recovery operation is completed.

8. On the Confirmation page, review the details for the restoration and then click Finish. The Wizard then restores the operating system or the full server as appropriate for the options you've selected.

Recovering Exchange Server

In cases where you only need to recover Exchange data, you don't need to initiate a full server recovery. Instead, you can recover an Exchange database to the point of failure by restoring the most recent full backup.

With this in mind, you can recover Exchange data by following these steps:

1. Start Windows Server Backup. In the Action pane or on the Action menu, click Recover. This starts the Recovery Wizard.

2. On the Getting Started page, specify whether you will recover data from the local computer or another computer/location and then click Next.

3. If you are recovering data from another location, specify whether the backup you want to restore is on a local drive or a remote shared folder, click Next, and then specify location-specific settings. When you are recovering from a local drive, on the Select Backup Location page, select the location of the backup from the drop-down list. When you are recovering from a remote shared folder, on the Specify Remote Folder page, type the path to the folder that contains the backup. In the remote folder, the backup should be stored at *BackupServer*\WindowsImageBackup*ComputerName*.

4. If you are recovering from the local computer and there are multiple back-ups, on the Select Backup Location page, select the location of the backup on the drop-down list.

5. On the Select Backup Date page, select the date and time of the backup you want to restore using the calendar and the time list. Backups are available for dates shown in bold. Click Next.

6. On the Select Recovery Type page, select Files And Folders and then click Next. On the Select Items To Recover page, under Available items, click the plus sign (+) to expand the list until the Exchange folder you want is visible. Click a folder to display the contents of the folder in the adjacent pane, select each item that you want to restore, and then click Next.

7. On the Specify Recovery Options page, under Recovery Destination, specify whether you want to restore data to its original location (non–system files only) or an alternate location. For an alternate location, type the path to the desired restore location or click Browse to select it.

8. Next, choose a recovery technique to apply when files and folders already exist in the recovery location. You can create copies so that you have both versions of the file or folder, overwrite existing files with recovered files, or not recover items that already exist.

9. On the Confirmation page, review the details and then click Recover to restore the specified items. Keep the following in mind:

   • If you restore Exchange data to its original location, Windows Server Backup and the backup plug-in automatically handle the recovery process. This means they dismount any existing databases, replay logs into recovered databases, and mount databases for you. All backed up databases must be restored together. You cannot restore a single database.

   • If you restore Exchange data to an alternate location, Windows Server Backup and the backup plug-in do not handle the recovery process. This means you need to manually work with the data and restore it. While this requires more work, you can restore a single database as well as individual mailboxes.

Recovering data from an alternate location is a multipart process that requires the following:

1. Use Windows Server Backup to recover a mailbox database.

2. At the Exchange Management Shell prompt, create a recovery database using New-MailboxDatabase with the –Recovery parameter.

3. Use Restore-Mailbox to extract data from the recovered database and restore it to its original database.

Each Mailbox server can have only one recovery database. To create the recovery database, use New-MailboxDatabase with the –Recovery parameter. You can create a recovery database named RecoveryDB on MailServer28 as shown in this example:

```
New-MailboxDatabase –Recovery –Name RecoveryDB –Server MailServer28
```

Here, the database files and log files are created in the default Exchange path. You also can set these paths using –EdbFilePath and –LogFolderPath as shown in this example:

```
New-MailboxDatabase –Recovery –Name RecoveryDB –Server MailServer28
-EdbFilePath 'D:\Exchange\database\recovery.edb'
–LogFolderPath 'D:\Exchange\database'
```

You use Restore-Mailbox to extract data from a restored database. Restore-Mailbox works only with disconnected mailboxes. The disconnected mailboxes are specified as the recovery sources, and the recovery targets are connected mailboxes in an active mailbox database. Thus, you extract data from a disconnected source mailbox and move it to a connected target mailbox. The source and target mailboxes must be in the same Active Directory forest.

Sample 15-1 provides the syntax and usage for Restore-Mailbox, and Table 15-2 provides an overview of how the related parameters are used. Many of the parameters act as filters. Keep the following in mind:

- With –AllContentKeywords, you can search the subject, message body, and attachment content for the keyword or keywords you specify. For example, you could search the subject, message body, and attachment content for the keywords "Dataset" or "Shareholder" using **–AllContentKeywords "Dataset", "Shareholder"**.

- With other filters like –AttachmentFilenames, –ContentKeywords, –RecipientKeywords, –SenderKeywords, and –SubjectKeywords, you look at a specific part of mail items for a matching keyword or keywords. For example, you could use –ContentKeywords to search the message body and attachments of mail items for the keyword "Report" or "Inventory" using **-ContentKeywords "Report", "Inventory"**.

- Multiple filters restrict the search. For example, you could look for message subjects containing the keyword "Analysis" that also have the keyword "Report" in the message body or attachments using **–SubjectKeywords "Analysis" –ContentKeywords "Report"**.

- With –ExcludeFolders and –IncludeFolders, the MAPI folder paths are locale specific. The English folder paths are \Inbox, \Drafts, \SentItems, \Notes, \JunkEmail, \DeletedItems, and \Archive.

- With –StartDate and –EndDate, the start date for the search must be before the end date. Specify the date to use in short date format mm/dd/yyyy, such as 05/01/2010 to specify May 1, 2010.

SAMPLE 15-1 Recovering mailbox data

Syntax

```
Restore-Mailbox -Identity MailboxId -RecoveryDatabase DatabaseId
{AddtlParams}

Restore-Mailbox -Identity MailboxId -RecoveryDatabase DatabaseId
-RecoveryMailbox MailboxId -TargetFolder FolderName {AddtlParams}


{AddtlParams}
[-AllContentKeywords Keywords] [-AttachmentFilenames FileNames]
[-BadItemLimit Limit] [-ContentKeywords Keywords] [-EndDate DateTime]
[-ExcludeFolders MapiFolderPaths] [-GlobalCatalog GCServer]
[-IncludeFolders MapiFolderPaths] [-Locale LocaleCode] [-MaxThreads
NumThreads] [-RecipientKeywords Recipients] [-SenderKeywords Senders]
[-StartDate DateTime] [-SubjectKeywords Subjects]
[-ValidateOnly <$true | $false>]
```

Usage

```
'Restores TonyG's mailbox from the recovery database
Restore-Mailbox -Identity TonyG -RecoveryDatabase RecoveryDb

'Restores LisaN's mailbox to the Restored folder in TonyG's mailbox
Restore-Mailbox -Identity LisaN -RecoveryDatabase RecoveryDb
-RecoveryMailbox TonyG -TargetFolder Restored

'Restores items with the subject keyword Report, and with the message
'location either in the Inbox or Calendar folder.
Restore-Mailbox -Identity DonH -RecoveryDatabase RecoveryDb
-SubjectKeywords "Report" -IncludeFolders \Inbox,\Calendar

'Restores all the mailboxes in the EngDatabase mailbox database from
'RecoveryDB, if they are present.
Get-Mailbox -Database EngDatabase | Restore-Mailbox –RecoveryDatabase
RecoveryDb
```

TABLE 15-2 Parameters Used with Restore-Mailbox

PARAMETER	USAGE
AllContentKeywords	Specifies the filters for the subject, message body, and attachment content. If your search criteria are part of the subject, message body, or attachment content, results are returned.
AttachmentFilenames	Specifies the filter for the attachment file name. You can use wildcard characters in the string, such as *.doc, to export items that have a .doc extension.
/BadItemLimit	Specifies the number of corrupted items in a mailbox to skip before the export operation fails.
/ContentKeywords	Specifies the keyword filters for the message body and attachment content in the source mailbox.
EndDate	Specifies the end date for filtering content that will be exported from the source mailbox. Use the short date format mm/dd/yyyy, such as 05/15/2010 to specify May 15, 2010.
ExcludeFolders	Specifies the list of folders to exclude during the export, such as Calendar. Folders aren't localized and must be excluded for each included locale.
GlobalCatalog	Specifies the global catalog to use to search for the target mailbox.
Identity	Specifies the identity of the target mailbox. You can use the mailbox name or GUID.
IncludeFolders	Specifies the list of folders to include during the export. Folders aren't localized and must be excluded for each included locale.
Locale	Specifies the locale setting on a message to restore. Only messages with the specified locale setting are extracted.
MaxThreads	Specifies the maximum number of threads to use for the export.
RecipientKeywords	Specifies the keyword filters for recipients of items in the source mailbox. Finds the search string even if it's part of a word.
RecoveryDatabase	Specifies the recovery database from which you're restoring the mailbox. You can use the database name, GUID, or server name\database name.

TABLE 15-2 Parameters Used with Restore-Mailbox

PARAMETER	USAGE
RecoveryMailbox	Specifies the mailbox to be used as the source mailbox. Required if the source mailbox is different from the target mailbox.
SenderKeywords	Specifies the keyword filters for senders of items in the source mailbox. Finds the search string even if it's part of a word.
StartDate	Specifies the start date for filtering content that will be exported from the source mailbox. Use the short date format mm/dd/yyyy, such as 05/01/2010 to specify May 1, 2010.
SubjectKeywords	Specifies the keyword filters for subjects in the source mailbox. Finds the search string even if it's part of a word.
TargetFolder	Specifies the mailbox folder that's created on the mailbox specified. Required if the mailbox being restored is different from the target mailbox.
ValidateOnly	Evaluates the conditions and requirements necessary to perform the operation and then reports whether the operation will succeed or fail. No changes are made.

Performing Additional Backup and Recovery Tasks

You might want to perform several additional backup and recovery tasks. These include

- Recovering a server using Setup/mode:recoverserver
- Cloning Edge Transport server configurations
- Troubleshooting database mount problems
- Mounting databases on alternate servers

These tasks are discussed in the sections that follow.

Using the Recover Server Mode

You use Setup with the /mode:recoverserver switch to recover a server that was once fully functional or to move a server to new hardware and maintain the same name. You cannot use this as a repair tool, to recover from a failed install, to recover from a failed uninstall, or to reconfigure a server. In addition, this recovery process does not restore customized settings that were stored on the server or in Exchange databases.

Running Setup with the /m:RecoverServer switch causes Setup to read the server's configuration information from Active Directory. Once the server's configuration information is read from Active Directory, the original Exchange files and services are then installed on the server, and the roles and settings that were stored in Active Directory are then applied to the server.

When you use the /mode:recoverserver command with Exchange Setup, the new server needs to have the same name as the server that it will be replacing and have a matching drive configuration for drives that had Exchange data on them. With this in mind, you can recover all roles (except for Mailbox servers that are part of a database availability group) by completing the following steps:

1. Reset the domain computer account for the lost server. In Active Directory Users And Computers, right-click the computer name, and then click Reset Account.

2. Install the new server, making sure you give it the same name as the old server and a matching drive configuration for drives that had Exchange data on them.

3. Join the server to the domain, and restart the server if necessary.

4. If you are using installation media, insert the Exchange Server 2010 disc in the DVD-ROM drive. At a command prompt, change to the Exchange source directory containing the Exchange Setup program.

5. At the command prompt, type **Setup /mode:recoverserver**. This tells Setup to read the configuration information from Active Directory for a server with the same name as the server from which you are running Setup. Setup then installs the Exchange roles and files on the new server using the settings that were stored in Active Directory.

For Mailbox servers that are part of a database availability group, you can perform a server recovery operation by completing the following steps:

1. Reset the domain computer account for the lost server. In Active Directory Users And Computers, right-click the computer name, and then click Reset Account.

2. Install the new server, making sure you give it the same name as the old server and a matching drive configuration for drives that had Exchange data on them.

3. Join the server to the domain.

4. Remove any mailbox database copies that exist on the server being recovered by using the Remove-MailboxDatabaseCopy cmdlet. Here is an example:

```
Remove-MailboxDatabaseCopy -Identity EngDB1\MailServer48
```

TIP Before removing copies, you should capture any lag settings for the copies so that when you add the copies again, you use the same lag settings. You can use the Get-MailboxDatabase and Set-MailboxDatabaseCopy cmdlets in the Exchange Management Shell to view and configure replay lag time, truncation lag time, and activation preference order (as well as other settings).

5. Remove the failed server's configuration from the database availability group by using the Remove-DatabaseAvailabilityGroupServer cmdlet. Here is an example:

```
Remove-DatabaseAvailabilityGroupServer -Identity EastCampusDag1
-MailboxServer MailServer48
```

6. If you are using installation media, insert the Exchange Server 2010 disc in the DVD-ROM drive. At a command prompt, change to the Exchange source directory containing the Exchange Setup program.

7. At the command prompt, type **Setup /mode:recoverserver**. This tells Setup to read the configuration information from Active Directory for a server with the same name as the server from which you are running Setup. Setup then installs the Exchange roles and files on the new server using the settings that were stored in Active Directory.

8. When the Setup recovery process is finished, add the server being recovered to the database availability group by using the Add-DatabaseAvailability-GroupServer cmdlet. Here is an example:

```
Add-DatabaseAvailabilityGroupServer -Identity EastCampusDag1
-MailboxServer MailServer48
```

9. Once the server has been added back to the database availability group, you can add the appropriate database copies to the server by using the Add-MailboxDatabaseCopy cmdlet. Here is an example:

```
Add-MailboxDatabaseCopy -Identity EngDb1
-MailboxServer MailServer48
```

Cloning Edge Transport Server Configurations

Most Edge Transport server settings are set by default, either because they are updated from the Web, such as with anti-spam data, or because they are replicated from Active Directory through the EdgeSync process. If you haven't modified the settings or created custom settings, no Edge Transport server data needs to be backed up, and you can fully recover Edge Transport services simply by setting up a new Edge Transport server. If you've modified or customized the settings, you can clone the configuration to capture any settings you've changed.

On an Edge Transport server, you'll find two scripts in the C:\Program Files\ Microsoft\Exchange Server\V14\Scripts directory. If you run the first script, ExportEdgeConfig.ps1, Exchange exports all user-configured settings and stores the data in an .xml file. If you copy the .xml file or a backup of the .xml file to a new Edge Transport server and run the second script, ImportEdgeConfig.ps1, Exchange imports all user-configured settings in the .xml file.

Mounting Mailbox Databases on Alternate Servers

Database portability in Exchange Server 2010 allows mailbox databases to be moved to and mounted on any other Exchange 2010 Mailbox server in the organization. Because Exchange Server 2010 can run on both Windows Server 2008 and Windows Server 2008 Release 2, the way the move operation works depends on the operating system running on the source and target server.

Thanks to the database portability feature in Exchange Server 2010, you can mount a mailbox database on a server other than the server on which you created the database. Database portability is not supported for public folder databases.

You can move a mailbox database to a new server by completing the following steps:

1. Your first step in moving a database to a new server is to commit any uncommitted transaction log files to the database by running the following command at a command prompt:

   eseutil /r ENN

   where ENN specifies the log file prefix for the database into which you intend to replay into the database.

   NOTE If there are no transaction logs to commit, you can skip step 1.

2. Your next step is to create a new Mailbox database on the new server, as discussed in the "Creating Mailbox Databases" section of Chapter 10, "Mailbox and Public Folder Database Administration." Do not mount the database. The new database must have the same name as the name configured on the previous Exchange server. You can use the Get-MailboxDatabase cmdlet to obtain the required database name. Set the –Identity parameter to the identity of the original server, such as:

   get-mailboxdatabase -Identity 'CORPSVR127'

3. After you create the database, you must enable the database to be overwritten by a restore operation. You can do this by setting the –AllowFileRestore parameter of the Set-MailboxDatabase cmdlet to $true, as shown in the following example:

   Set-MailboxDatabase -Identity 'Accounting DB'
     -AllowFileRestore $true

4. Move the database files (.edb files, log files, and content indexing catalog) to the appropriate location on the new server. You must put the files in the exact locations the new server expects these files to be in. You set these locations when you created the database.

5. Mount the database using the Mount-Database cmdlet, as shown in the following example:

```
Mount-Database -Identity 'Accounting DB'
```

6. After you mount the database, you must modify the user account settings with Set-Mailbox so that the accounts point to the mailbox on the new mailbox server. To use Set-Mailbox to move all of the users from the old database to the new database, run the following command:

```
Get-Mailbox -Database 'OldDatabaseIdentity' | where {$_.ObjectClass
-NotMatch '(SystemAttendantMailbox|ExOleDbSystemMailbox)'}|
Set-Mailbox -Database 'NewDatabaseIdentity'
```

where *OldDatabaseIdentity* is the name of the source database and *NewDatabaseIdentity* is the name of the target database, such as:

```
Get-Mailbox -Database 'Mailbox DB 1105' | where {$_.ObjectClass
-NotMatch '(SystemAttendantMailbox|ExOleDbSystemMailbox)'}|
Set-Mailbox -Database 'Accounting DB'
```

Most mailbox users will be redirected to the new mailbox location automatically when Active Directory replication has completed. If the server name has changed, however, Outlook 2003 and earlier clients need to be manually configured to point to the new server.

CHAPTER 16

Managing Exchange
Server 2010 Clients

- Configuring Mail Support for Outlook and Windows Live Mail **597**
- Leaving Mail on the Server with POP3 **608**
- Checking Private and Public Folders with IMAP4 and UNIX Mail Servers **610**
- Managing the Exchange Server Configuration in Outlook **612**
- Using Mail Profiles to Customize the Mail Environment **620**

A s a Microsoft Exchange administrator, you need to know how to configure
and maintain Exchange clients. With Microsoft Exchange Server 2010, you can
use any mail client that supports standard mail protocols. For ease of administration, however, you'll want to choose specific clients for on-site users as a standard
and supplement these with specific clients for off-site or mobile users. The on-site
and off-site clients can be the same. I recommend focusing on Microsoft Office
Outlook 2007 or Outlook 2010 for on-site users, and Outlook Web App (OWA)
for off-site users. Depending on your needs, you might also want to consider
Windows Mail or Windows Live Mail. Each client supports a slightly different
set of features and messaging protocols, and each client has its advantages and
disadvantages, including the following:

- With Outlook 2007 and Outlook 2010, you get a full-featured client that
  on-site, off-site, and mobile users can use. Outlook 2007 is part of the 2007
  Microsoft Office system of applications, and Outlook 2010 is part of the
  2010 Microsoft Office system of applications. They are the only mail clients
  spotlighted here that support the latest messaging features in Exchange
  Server. Corporate and workgroup users often need their rich support for
  calendars, scheduling, voice mail, and e-mail management. Of the two, only
  Outlook 2010 supports calendar sharing and other enhancements available
  with Exchange Server 2010.

595

- With Windows Mail in Windows Vista and Windows Live Mail in Windows 7, you get lightweight clients that are best suited for off-site or mobile users.
  - Windows Mail is the replacement for Outlook Express and is installed by default with Windows Vista. Although Windows Mail supports standard messaging protocols for Post Office Protocol version 3 (POP3) and Internet Message Access Protocol version 4 (IMAP4), the client doesn't support HTTP mail, calendars, scheduling, voice mail, or key messaging features of Exchange Server. Windows Mail is, however, easy to configure.
  - Windows Live Mail is the replacement for Windows Mail and can be installed as part of the Windows Live application suite available for free download from *http://download.live.com/wlmail*. Windows Live Mail supports standard messaging protocols for POP3 and IMAP4 as well as HTTP mail, calendars, scheduling, and contacts. Windows Live Mail doesn't support voice mail or key messaging features of Exchange Server. Windows Live Mail is, however, easy to configure.
- With Outlook Web App, you get a mail client that you can access securely through a standard Web browser. With Microsoft Internet Explorer 7.0, Internet Explorer 8.0, Firefox 3.0.1 or later, and Safari 3.1 or later, Outlook Web App supports many of the features found in Outlook 2007 and Outlook 2010, including calendars, scheduling, and voice mail. With other browsers, the client functionality remains the same, but some features, such as S/MIME, might not be supported. You don't need to configure Outlook Web App on the client, and it's ideal for users who want to access e-mail while away from the office.

Outlook 2007 and Outlook 2010 are the most common Exchange clients for corporate and workgroup environments. With the Outlook Anywhere feature of Exchange, which eliminates the need for a virtual private network (VPN) to securely access Exchange Server over the Internet by using a remote procedure call (RPC) over Secure Hypertext Transfer Protocol (HTTPS) connection, Outlook 2007 and Outlook 2010 might also be your clients of choice for off-site and mobile users. The catch with Outlook Anywhere is that the feature is not enabled by default and requires additional components.

Windows Mail and Windows Live Mail, on the other hand, aren't designed for corporate users and are really meant for personal use. That said, both Windows Mail and Windows Live Mail are easy to configure and require relatively little back-end configuration. In fact, you can quickly and easily configure Exchange Server to work with both clients.

This chapter shows you how to manage Outlook 2007, Outlook 2010, and Windows Live Mail. For ease of reference, I will refer to Outlook 2007 and Outlook 2010 simply as Outlook, unless I need to differentiate between them. Chapter 17, "Managing Mobile Messaging Users," describes using Outlook Web App and other options for mobile users.

Configuring Mail Support for Outlook and Windows Live Mail

You can install both Outlook and Windows Live Mail as clients on a user's computer. The following sections look at these topics:

- Understanding Offline Address Books and Autodiscover
- Configuring Outlook and Windows Live Mail for the first time
- Adding Internet mail accounts to Outlook and Windows Live Mail
- Reconfiguring Outlook mail support

Understanding Offline Address Books and Autodiscover

Although Exchange Server 2010 continues to support public folders, public folders are no longer required for access to the global address list or the offline address book (OAB). Exchange now provides these features through a Web-based distribution point. Microsoft Office Outlook 2007 and later clients use the Web-based distribution point for the global address list and the offline address book automatically.

Every Exchange organization has a default OAB and one or more additional custom OABs. Each OAB has a designated Mailbox server, referred to as the *generation server*, responsible for creating and updating that particular OAB. The Microsoft Exchange File Distribution service running on a Client Access server is responsible for gathering the OAB data and keeping the content synchronized with the content on the Mailbox server.

The OAB virtual directory is the Web-based distribution point for the OAB. By default, when you install a Client Access server, this directory is created on the default Web site in Internet Information Services (IIS) and configured for internal access. You can specify an external URL as well.

Outlook 2007, Outlook 2010, and some mobile devices use the Autodiscover service to automatically configure themselves for access to Exchange. The Autodiscover service runs on a Client Access server as well and returns the correct OAB URL for a particular client connection.

When you install a Client Access server, an Autodiscover virtual directory is created on the default Web site in Internet Information Services (IIS) and an internal URL is set up for automatic discovery and other features, such as the OAB (which can be automatically discovered as well).

For external users who are running Outlook 2007 or later clients, for Outlook Anywhere to be automatically configured by using the Autodiscover service you must install a valid Secure Sockets Layer (SSL) certificate on your Internet-facing Client Access server that includes both the common name, such as mail.cpandl.com, and a Subject Alternative name for the Autodiscover service, such as autodiscover.cpandl.com. You also need to configure the external URLs for the offline address book, Exchange Web Services, and Outlook Anywhere.

To configure the external URL for the OAB, you can use the –ExternalUrl parameter of the Set-OABVirtualDirectory cmdlet. In the following example, you set the
OAB external URL and configure it for use with SSL:

```
Set-OABVirtualDirectory -identity "CASServer01\OAB (Default Web Site)"
-externalurl https://mail.cpandl.com/OAB -RequireSSL:$true
```

To configure the external URL for Exchange Web Services, you can use the
–ExternalUrl parameter of the Set-WebServicesVirtualDirectory cmdlet. In the
following example, you set the Exchange Web Services external URL and configure it
for use with basic authentication:

```
Set-WebServicesVirtualDirectory -identity "CASServer01\EWS (Default Web
Site)" -externalurl https://mail.cpandl.com/EWS/Exchange.asmx
-BasicAuthentication:$True
```

To configure the external host name for Outlook Anywhere, you can use the
–ExternalHostname parameter of Enable-OutlookAnywhere. In the following
example, you set the external host name and configure Outlook Anywhere for basic
authentication:

```
Enable-OutlookAnywhere -Server CASServer01 -ExternalHostname
"mail.cpandl.com" -ExternalAuthenticationMethod "Basic"
-SSLOffloading:$False
```

Once you've configured the Autodiscover service and the required URLs, you can
test Autodiscover by using Test-OutlookWebServices. Here is an example:

```
Test-OutlookWebServices -ClientAccessServer "CASServer01"
```

Configuring Outlook for the First Time

You can install Outlook as a standalone product or as part of Microsoft Office.
Outlook can be used to connect to the following types of e-mail servers:

- **Microsoft Exchange Server**   Connects directly to Exchange Server; best
  for users who are connected to the organization's network. Users will have
  full access to Exchange Server. If users plan to connect to Exchange Server
  using Outlook Anywhere, this is the option to choose as well. With Exchange
  Server, users can check mail on an e-mail server and access any private or
  public folders to which they have been granted permissions. If you define a
  personal folder and specify that new e-mail messages should be delivered to
  the personal folder, e-mail messages can be delivered to a personal folder on
  a user's computer.

- **POP3**   Connects to Exchange or another POP3 e-mail server through the
  Internet; best for users who are connecting from a remote location, such as

a home or a remote office, using dial-up or broadband Internet access. With POP3, users can check mail on an e-mail server and download it to their inboxes. Users can't, however, synchronize mailbox folders or access private or public folders on the server. By using advanced configuration settings, the user can elect to download the mail and leave it on the server for future use. By leaving the mail on the server, the user can check mail on a home computer and still download it to an office computer later.

- **IMAP4** Connects to Exchange or another IMAP4 e-mail server through the Internet; best for users who are connecting from a remote location, such as a home or a remote office, using dial-up or broadband Internet access. Also well suited for users who have a single computer, such as a laptop, that they use to check mail both at the office and away from it. With IMAP4, users can check mail on an e-mail server and synchronize mailbox folders. Users can also download only message headers and then access each e-mail individually to download it. Unlike POP3, IMAP4 has no option to leave mail on the server. IMAP4 also lets users access public and private folders on an Exchange server.

- **HTTP** Connects to an HTTP e-mail server, such as MSN Hotmail, through the Internet; best as an additional e-mail configuration option. Here, users can have an external e-mail account with a Web-based e-mail service that they can check in addition to corporate e-mail.

- **Additional Server Types** Connects to a third-party mail server or other services, such as Outlook Mobile Text Messaging. If your organization has multiple types of mail servers, including Exchange Server, you'll probably want to configure a connection to Exchange Server first and then add more e-mail account configurations later.

To begin, log on to the computer as the user whose e-mail you are configuring or have the user log on themselves. If the computer is part of a domain, you should log on using the user's domain account. If you are configuring e-mail for use with a direct Exchange Server connection rather than a POP3, IMAP4, or HTTP connection, you should ensure that the user's mailbox has been created. If the user's mailbox has not been created, auto-setup will fail, as will the rest of the account configuration.

NOTE You can configure both Outlook and Windows Live Mail on the same computer. If you configure Windows Live Mail after configuring Outlook, Windows Live Mail assumes you might be migrating from Outlook to Windows Live Mail and offers to import Outlook mail after you complete the initial e-mail setup. If you configure Outlook after configuring Windows Live Mail, Outlook assumes you might be migrating from Windows Live Mail and offers to import mail after you complete the initial e-mail setup.

Unlike Outlook 2003 and earlier releases, Outlook 2007 and later releases are easy to configure, especially with Autodiscover. The first time you start Outlook, the application runs the Outlook Startup Wizard. You can use the Startup Wizard to configure e-mail for Exchange Server, POP3, IMAP4, and HTTP mail servers, as discussed in the sections that follow.

First-Time Configuration: Connecting to Exchange Server

You can use the Startup Wizard to configure e-mail for Exchange Server in Outlook by completing the following steps:

1. Start Outlook and click Next on the Welcome page.

    NOTE If you've previously configured Outlook Express or Windows Live Mail, you'll see the E-Mail Upgrade Options page. You can then elect to upgrade from or not upgrade from Outlook Express or Windows Live Mail. If you elect to upgrade, Outlook attempts to import e-mail messages, address books, and settings from the e-mail programs detected during initial setup.

2. When prompted as to whether you would like to configure an e-mail account, verify that Yes is selected and then click Next.

3. The next page of the wizard varies depending on the computer's current configuration:

    - For computers that are part of a domain and for users that have an existing Exchange Server mailbox, the Startup Wizard uses the Autodiscover feature to automatically discover the required account information, as shown in Figure 16-1.

    - For computers that are part of a domain and for users for which you have not created an Exchange mailbox, leave the wizard open, create the user's Exchange mailbox, and then proceed with the wizard once the mailbox is automatically discovered.

    - For computers that are part of a workgroup or for which you are logged on locally, Outlook assumes you want to configure the user to use an Internet e-mail account. You must next enter the user's account name, e-mail address, and password. Then type and confirm the user's password.

4. When you click Next, the Startup Wizard, taking advantage of the new Auto Account Setup feature, attempts to automatically discover the rest of the information needed to configure the account and then uses the settings to log on to the server. If the auto-configuration and server logon are successful, click Finish and skip the remaining steps in this procedure. The wizard then sets up the user's Exchange mailbox on the computer as appropriate.

5. If auto-configuration is not successful, click Next so that the wizard can attempt to establish an unencrypted connection to the server. If the auto-configuration and server logon are successful this time, click Finish and then skip the remaining steps in this procedure.

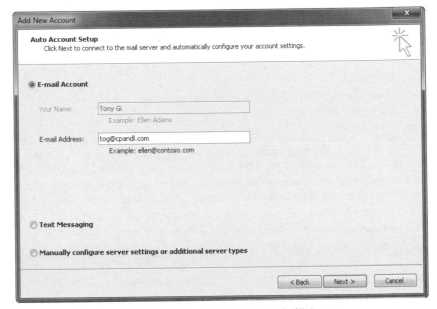

FIGURE 16-1 The Microsoft Outlook Startup Wizard automatically fills in your account information when you are logged on to a domain.

6. If auto-configuration fails twice, you'll see a prompt to confirm the user's e-mail address. If the e-mail address is incorrect, change it to the correct one and then click Retry. If the auto-configuration and server logon are successful this time, click Finish and then skip the remaining steps in this procedure.

7. If all attempts at auto-configuration fail, you can try to configure settings manually. The wizard automatically selects the Manually Configure Server Settings check box. Click Next. On the Choose E-Mail Service page, select Internet E-Mail or, Microsoft Exchange. Click Next. On the next wizard page, complete the necessary information for the type of e-mail service you selected. If necessary, click More Settings, and then use the Properties dialog box provided to configure the additional required settings. When you are finished, click OK to close the Properties dialog box. Click Next and then click Finish to complete the mail configuration.

First-Time Configuration: Connecting to Internet E-Mail Servers

When a user is logged on to a domain, Outlook automatically attempts to configure itself for use with the user's Exchange mailbox as part of its initial configuration. This configuration works for internal users but not for remote users who need to or prefer to access Exchange using POP3 or IMAP4 (rather than Outlook Anywhere).

For these users, you can complete the first-time configuration of Outlook by following these steps:

1. In the Startup Wizard, when you are prompted as to whether you would like to configure an e-mail account, verify that Yes is selected and then click Next.

2. Select the Manually Configure Server Settings Or Additional Server Types check box, and then click Next.

3. On the Choose E-Mail Service page, select Internet E-Mail and then click Next.

4. In the Your Name text box, type the name that will appear in the From field of outgoing messages for this user, such as **William Stanek**.

5. In the E-Mail Address text box, type the e-mail address of the user. Be sure to type the e-mail user name as well as the domain name, such as **williams@cpandl.com**.

6. From the Account Type list, select the type of protocol to use for the incoming mail server as POP3 or IMAP4. The advantages and disadvantages of these protocols are as follows:

    *   POP3 is used to check mail on an e-mail server and download it to the user's inbox. The user can't access private or public folders on the server. By using advanced configuration settings, the user can elect to download the mail and leave it on the server for future use. By leaving the mail on the server, the user can check mail on a home computer and still download it to an office computer later.

    *   IMAP4 is used to check mail on an e-mail server and download message headers. The user can then access each e-mail individually and download it. Unlike POP3, IMAP4 has no option to leave mail on the server. IMAP4 also lets users access public and private folders on an Exchange server. It is best suited for users who have a single computer, such as a laptop, that they use to check mail both at the office and away from it.

7. Enter the fully qualified domain name (FQDN) for the incoming and outgoing mail servers. Although these entries are often the same, some organizations have different incoming and outgoing mail servers. If you are not certain of your mail servers' fully qualified domain names, contact your network administrator.

    NOTE If you're connecting to Exchange with POP3 or IMAP4, you should enter the fully qualified domain name for the Exchange server rather than just the host name. For example, you would use MailServer.cpandl.com instead of MailServer. This ensures Outlook will be able to find the Exchange server.

8. Under Logon Information, type the user's logon name and password. If the mail server requires secure logon, select the Require Logon Using Security Password Authentication check box.

9. To verify the settings, click Test Account Settings. Outlook then sends a test message to the specified mail server. If the test fails, note the errors and make corrections as necessary.

10. If necessary, click More Settings, and then use the Properties dialog box provided to configure the additional required settings and then click OK. When you are ready to continue, click Next, and then click Finish to complete the configuration.

Configuring Windows Live Mail for the First Time

You can install Windows Live Mail as part of the Windows Live applications. It runs the Add An E-Mail Account Wizard the first time you start the application. You also can access this wizard at any time to configure additional accounts by clicking the Add E-Mail Account link while working with the Mail view.

You configure Windows Live Mail by completing the following steps:

1. Type the e-mail address and password of the user. Be sure to type the e-mail user name as well as the domain name, such as **williams@cpandl.com**.

2. In the Display Name text box, type the name that will appear in the From field of outgoing messages for this user, such as **William Stanek**. Click Next.

3. If you are configuring e-mail for Hotmail, Yahoo, or another online service, Windows Live Mail automatically configures itself for the service and then attempts to connect to the service to download your mailbox and related folders. In some cases, you might be required to subscribe to a specific service to use Windows Live Mail with the service. If Windows Live Mail successfully connects to the service, you're done and don't need to follow the remaining steps. If Windows Live Mail can't connect to the service, ensure you've entered the correct e-mail address and password, or perform a required procedure, such as upgrading to Yahoo Plus.

4. If you're configuring a connection to mail servers in your organization or other mail servers Windows Live Mail doesn't recognize, you need to manually configure mail. As shown in Figure 16-2, select the type of protocol to use for the incoming mail server as POP3, IMAP4, or HTTP. The advantages and disadvantages of these protocols are as follows:

   - POP3 is used to check mail on an e-mail server and download it to the user's inbox. The user can't access private or public folders on the server. By using advanced configuration settings, the user can elect to download the mail and leave it on the server for future use. By leaving the mail on the server, the user can check mail on a home computer and still download it to an office computer later.

   - IMAP4 is used to check mail on an e-mail server and download message headers. The user can then access each e-mail individually and download it. Unlike POP3, IMAP4 has no option to leave mail on the server. IMAP4 also lets users access public and private folders on an Exchange server. It is best suited for users who have a single computer, such as a laptop, that they use to check mail both at the office and away from it.

- HTTP is used to check mail on a Web-based e-mail server, such as Hotmail or MSN. The user can then access e-mail through Windows Live Mail instead of through a Web browser.

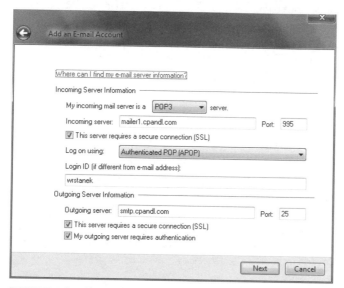

FIGURE 16-2 Specify incoming and outgoing mail server options with the Internet Connection Wizard.

5. If you select POP3 or IMAP4, you must enter the fully qualified domain name for the incoming and outgoing mail servers. Although these entries are often the same, some organizations have different incoming and outgoing mail servers. If you are not certain of your mail servers' fully qualified domain names, contact your network administrator.

   NOTE If you're connecting to Exchange with POP3 or IMAP4, you should enter the fully qualified domain name for the Exchange server instead of the host name. For example, you would use MailServer.cpandl.com instead of MailServer. This ensures Outlook can find the Exchange server.

6. If the incoming server, outgoing server, or both servers require a secure connection, select the related check box to enable Secure Sockets Layer (SSL).

7. Confirm that the login ID is correct. The login ID is usually the same as the e-mail user name. For some mail servers, however, you might need to enter the name of the domain as well. You type this information in the form: *domain\e-mail_alias*, such as **technology\williams**. In some cases, you might need to type this information in the form: *domain/e-mail_alias*, such as **technology/williams**.

8. If the mail server requires a user name and password when a user sends mail in addition to when a user retrieves mail, select the My Outgoing Server Requires Authentication check box.

NOTE To enhance security, most mail servers should require a user name and password for both sending and receiving mail. If a password isn't required for sending mail, the mail server might be vulnerable to exploitation.

9. Click Next, and then click Finish to complete the configuration.

Configuring Outlook for Exchange

If you didn't configure Outlook to use Exchange Server the first time it was started, don't worry: You can change the Outlook configuration to use Exchange. It does take a bit of extra work, however.

To get started, you should close Outlook if it is started, and then follow these steps to configure Outlook to use Exchange:

1. Start the Mail utility. Click Start, and then click Control Panel. In Control Panel, click Small Icons on the View By list and then double-click Mail. If you are using a 64-bit operating system, the Mail utility is listed under the 32-bit Control Panel. In Control Panel, click Small Icons on the View By list, double-click 32-Bit Control Panel, and then double-click Mail.

2. In the Mail Setup–Outlook dialog box, click E-Mail Accounts. The Accounts Settings dialog box appears.

3. In the Account Settings dialog box, the E-Mail tab is selected by default. Click New. This starts the Add New Account wizard.

4. Follow steps 3–7 outlined previously in the "First-Time Configuration: Connecting to Exchange Server" section.

5. When you finish the previous procedure, close all the open dialog boxes, and then start Outlook.

Adding Internet Mail Accounts to Outlook and Windows Live Mail

Through e-mail account configuration, Outlook supports only one Exchange Server account at a time. If you need access to multiple Exchange mailboxes, you must configure access to these mailboxes as discussed in the section "Accessing Multiple Exchange Server Mailboxes" later in the chapter.

Although you can configure only one Exchange e-mail account at a time, both Outlook and Windows Live Mail allow you to retrieve mail from multiple Internet servers. For example, you can configure Outlook to check mail on the corporate Exchange server, a personal account on Earthlink, and a personal account on MSN Hotmail.

Adding Internet Mail Accounts in Outlook

You can add Internet mail accounts to Outlook. In Outlook 2007, complete the following steps:

1. Display the Account Settings dialog box by selecting Tools and then selecting Account Settings.

2. In the Account Settings dialog box, the E-Mail tab is selected by default. Click New.

3. On the Choose E-Mail Service page, select Microsoft Exchange, POP3, IMAP, Or HTTP and then click Next.

4. Follow steps 2–10 outlined previously in the "First-Time Configuration: Connecting to Internet E-Mail Servers" section.

In Outlook 2010, click the Office button, click Account Settings, and then select Add Account. Follow steps 4–10 outlined previously in the "First-Time Configuration: Connecting to Internet E-Mail Servers" section.

Adding Internet Mail Accounts in Windows Live Mail

With Windows Live Mail, you add Internet mail accounts by completing the following steps:

1. On the Views list, click Mail and then click Add E-Mail Account. This starts the Add An E-Mail Account Wizard.

2. Follow the steps outlined previously in the "Configuring Windows Live Mail for the First Time" section.

Repairing and Changing Outlook Mail Accounts

When you first configure Outlook on a computer, you can configure it to connect to an Exchange server, to Internet e-mail, or to another e-mail server. With Exchange Server, Outlook uses MAPI to connect to the RPC Client Access service on the appropriate Client Access server, and the RPC Client Access service connects Outlook to the appropriate Mailbox server for the user by proxying or redirecting the connection as necessary. Outlook clients remain connected to the Client Access server. They use the RPC Client Access service as the MAPI endpoint, and the Address Book service as the Active Directory endpoint. The Client Access server that is proxying or redirecting the connection for them then communicates with the appropriate Mailbox server using MAPI/RPC.

Because of how this connection process works, the underlying infrastructure is transparent to users—they are connected automatically to their mailbox. If a user's mailbox is moved to a different server within the Exchange organization, the user is connected to this server automatically the next time he or she starts Outlook. If, for some reason, a user has a problem connecting to Exchange Server or needs to get updated configuration settings, you can accomplish this with a repair operation. Repairing the user's account restarts the Auto Account Setup feature.

With non-Exchange servers, access to e-mail very much depends on the account and server configuration remaining the same. If the account or server configuration changes, the account configuration in Outlook must be updated. The easiest way to do this is with a repair operation.

To start a repair, follow these steps:

1. Log on as the domain account of the user for which you are repairing e-mail.

2. In Outlook 2007, display the Account Settings dialog box by selecting Tools, and then selecting Account Settings. In Outlook 2010, click the Office button, click the Account Settings button, and then select the Account Settings option.

3. In the Account Settings dialog box, the E-Mail tab lists all currently configured e-mail accounts by name. Select the account to repair and then click Repair.

4. On the Auto Account Setup page, check the account settings. With Exchange accounts for domain users, you cannot change the displayed information. With other accounts, you can modify the user's e-mail address and password, which might be necessary.

5. When you click Next, the Repair E-Mail Account Wizard contacts the mail server and tries to determine the correct account settings. If the auto-configuration and server logon are successful, click Finish. Skip the remaining steps in this procedure.

6. If auto-configuration is not successful, click Next so that the wizard can attempt to establish an unencrypted connection to the server. If the auto-configuration and server logon are successful this time, click Finish and then skip the remaining steps in this procedure.

7. If auto-configuration fails twice, you can try to configure settings manually. Select the Manually Configure Settings check box, and then click Next.

8. Use the fields provided to update the mail account configuration. If you need to configure additional settings beyond the user, server, and logon information, click More Settings, and then use the Properties dialog box provided to configure the additional required settings. When you are finished, click OK to close the Properties dialog box.

9. Check the new settings by clicking Test Account Settings.

10. Click Next, and then click Finish.

In some cases, if you've incorrectly configured Exchange, you might not be able to start Outlook and access the Account Settings dialog box. In this case, you can repair the settings using the following procedure:

1. Start the Mail utility. Click Start, and then click Control Panel. In Control Panel, click Small Icons on the View By list and then double-click Mail. If you are using a 64-bit operating system, the Mail utility is listed under the 32-Bit Control Panel. In Control Panel, click Small Icons on the View By list, double-click 32-Bit Control Panel, and then double-click Mail.

2. In the Mail Setup–Outlook dialog box, click E-Mail Accounts. The Accounts Settings dialog box appears.

3. In the Account Settings dialog box, the E-Mail tab is selected by default. Click the incorrectly configured Exchange account and then do the following:

   - Click Change to modify the Exchange settings using the techniques discussed previously.

   - Click Remove to remove the Exchange settings so that they are no longer used by Outlook.

4. When you are finished, close the Mail Setup–Outlook dialog box, and then start Outlook.

For POP3 or IMAP4, you can change a user's e-mail configuration at any time by completing the following steps:

1. In Outlook 2007, display the Account Settings dialog box by selecting Tools, and then selecting Account Settings. In Outlook 2010, click the Office button, click the Account Settings button, and then select the Account Settings option.

2. In the Account Settings dialog box, the E-Mail tab lists all currently configured e-mail accounts by name. Select the account you want to work with, and then click Change.

3. Use the fields provided to update the mail account configuration. If you need to configure additional settings beyond the user, server, and logon information, click More Settings, and then use the Properties dialog box provided to configure the additional required settings. When you are finished, click OK to close the Properties dialog box.

4. Check the new settings by clicking Test Account Settings.

5. Click Next, and then click Finish.

Leaving Mail on the Server with POP3

If the user connects to an Internet e-mail server, an advantage of POP3 is that it lets the user leave mail on the server. By doing this, the user can check mail on a home computer and still download it to an office computer later.

Leaving Mail on the Server: Outlook

With Outlook, you can configure POP3 accounts to leave mail on the server by completing the following steps:

1. Start Outlook. In Outlook 2007, on the Tools menu, click Account Settings. In Outlook 2010, click the Office button, click the Account Settings button, and then select the Account Settings option.

2. In the Account Settings dialog box, select the POP3 mail account you want to modify and then click Change.

3. Click More Settings to display the Internet E-Mail Settings dialog box.

4. In the Internet E-Mail Settings dialog box, click the Advanced tab, as shown in Figure 16-3.

FIGURE 16-3 Use the Advanced tab to configure how and when mail should be left on the server.

5. Use the options below Delivery to configure how and when mail should be left on the server. To enable this option, select the Leave A Copy Of Messages On The Server check box. The additional options depend on the client configuration. Options you might see include the following:

   - **Remove From Server After *N* Days**   Select this option if you're connecting to an Internet service provider (ISP) and want to delete messages from the server after a specified number of days. By deleting ISP mail periodically, you ensure that your mailbox size doesn't exceed your limit.

   - **Remove From Server When Deleted From "Deleted Items"**   Select this option to delete messages from the server when you delete them from the Deleted Items folder. You'll see this option with Internet-only Outlook configurations.

6. Click OK when you've finished changing the account settings.

7. Click Next, and then click Finish. Click Close to close the Account Settings dialog box.

Leaving Mail on the Server: Windows Live Mail

With Windows Live Mail, you can configure POP3 accounts to leave mail on the server by completing the following steps:

1. Start Windows Live Mail. Then, on the Tools menu, click Accounts.
2. Select the POP3 mail account you want to modify, and then click Properties.
3. In the Properties dialog box, click the Advanced tab.
4. Use the options below Delivery to configure how and when mail should be left on the server. To enable this option, select Leave A Copy Of Messages On The Server. The additional options depend on the client configuration. Options you might see include the following:

   - **Remove From Server After N Days** Select this option if you're connecting to an ISP and want to delete messages from the server after a specified number of days. By deleting ISP mail periodically, you ensure that your mailbox size doesn't exceed your limit.

   - **Remove From Server When Deleted From "Deleted Items"** Select this option to delete messages from the server when you delete them from the Deleted Items folder. You'll see this option with Internet-only Outlook configurations.

5. Click OK, and then click Close.

Checking Private and Public Folders with IMAP4 and UNIX Mail Servers

With IMAP4, you can check public and private folders on a mail server. This option is enabled by default, but the default settings might not work properly with UNIX mail servers.

Checking Folders: Outlook

With Outlook, you can check or change the folder settings used by IMAP4 by completing the following steps:

1. Start Outlook. In Outlook 2007, on the Tools menu, click Account Settings. In Outlook 2010, click the Office button, click the Account Settings button, and then select the Account Settings option.
2. In the Account Settings dialog box, select the IMAP4 mail account you want to modify and then click Change.
3. Click More Settings to display the Internet E-Mail Settings dialog box.
4. In the Internet E-Mail Settings dialog box, click the Advanced tab, as shown in Figure 16-4.
5. If the account connects to a UNIX mail server, enter the path to the mailbox folder on the server, such as **~williams/mail**. Don't end the folder path with a forward slash (/), and then click OK.

6. Click Next, and then click Finish.

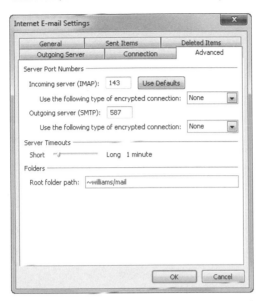

FIGURE 16-4 Use the Advanced tab to configure how folders are used with IMAP4 mail accounts.

Checking Folders: Windows Live Mail

With Windows Live Mail, you can check or change the folder settings used by IMAP4 by completing the following steps:

1. Start Windows Live Mail. Then, on the Views list, click Mail.

2. Right-click the IMAP4 mail account you want to modify, and then click Properties.

3. In the Properties dialog box, select the IMAP4 tab.

4. If the account connects to a UNIX mail server, enter the path to the mailbox folder on the server, such as **~williams/mail**. Don't end the folder path with a forward slash (/).

5. To automatically check for new messages in all public, private, and hidden folders, make sure the Check For New Messages In All Folders check box is selected.

6. To store sent items, draft messages, deleted items, and junk e-mail on the IMAP4 server, select the Store Special Folders On IMAP4 Server check box, and then type the name for these folders. The default names are Sent Items, Drafts, Deleted Items, and Junk E-Mail, respectively.

7. Click OK, and then click Close.

Managing the Exchange Server Configuration in Outlook

Whenever you use Outlook to connect to Exchange Server, you have several options for optimizing the way mail is handled. These options include the following:

- E-mail delivery and processing
- Remote mail
- Scheduled connections
- Multiple mailboxes

Each of these options is examined in the sections that follow.

Managing Delivery and Processing E-Mail Messages

When Outlook uses Exchange Server, you have strict control over how e-mail is delivered and processed. Exchange mail can be delivered in one of two ways:

- Server mailboxes with local copies
- Personal folders

Exchange mail can be processed by any of the information services configured for use in Outlook. These information services include the following:

- Microsoft Exchange
- Internet e-mail

Let's look at how you use each of these delivery and processing options.

Using Server Mailboxes

When you are using Outlook 2007 or Outlook 2010 with Exchange Server 2010, server mailboxes with local copies are the default configuration option. With server mailboxes, new e-mail is delivered to a mailbox on the Exchange server, and users can view or receive new mail only when they're connected to Exchange. When users are connected to Exchange, Outlook retrieves their mail and stores a local copy on their computer in addition to the e-mail stored on Exchange Server.

The local copy of a user's mail is stored in an offline folder .ost file. With Windows Vista and Windows 7, the default location of a .ost file is *%LocalAppData%*
Microsoft\Outlook, where *%LocalAppData%* is a user-specific environment variable that points to a user's local application data. Using server mailboxes offers users protected storage and the ability to have a single point of recovery in case of failure.

Using Personal Folders

An alternative to using server mailboxes is to use personal folders. Personal folders are stored in a .pst file on the user's computer. With personal folders, you can specify that mail should be delivered to the user's inbox and stored on the server or that mail should be delivered only to the user's inbox. Users have personal folders when Outlook is configured to use Internet e-mail or other e-mail servers. Users might also have personal folders if the auto-archive feature is used to archive messages.

REAL WORLD With Windows Vista and Windows 7, the default location of a .pst file is *%LocalAppData%*\Microsoft\Outlook, where *%LocalAppData%* is a user-specific environment variable that points to a user's local application data. Personal folders are best suited for mobile users who check mail through dial-up connections and who might not be able to use a dial-up connection to connect directly to Exchange.

Users with personal folders lose the advantages that server-based folders offer—namely, protected storage and the ability to have a single point of recovery in case of failure. In addition, .pst files have many disadvantages. They get corrupted more frequently and, on these occasions, you must use the Inbox Repair Tool to restore the file. If the hard disk on a user's computer fails, you can recover the mail only if the .pst file has been backed up. Unfortunately, most workstations aren't backed up regularly (if at all), and the onus of backing up the .pst file falls on the user, who might or might not understand how to do this.

DETERMINING THE PRESENCE OF PERSONAL FOLDERS

You can determine the presence of personal folders by following these steps:

1. Start Outlook. On the Tools menu, click Account Settings.
2. In the Account Settings dialog box, click the Data Files tab.
3. The location of the data file associated with each e-mail account is listed. If the file name ends in .pst, the account is using a personal folder.

CREATING NEW OR OPENING EXISTING PERSONAL FOLDERS

If personal folders aren't available and you want to configure them, follow these steps:

1. Start Outlook. On the Tools menu, click Account Settings.
2. In the Account Settings dialog box, click the Data Files tab.
3. Click Add. The New Outlook Data File dialog box appears.
4. Office Outlook Personal Folders File (.pst) should be selected by default. Click OK, and the Create Or Open Outlook Data File dialog box appears, as shown in Figure 16-5.

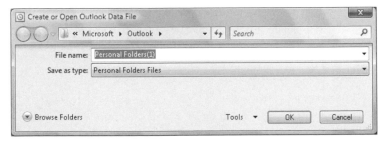

FIGURE 16-5 Use the Create Or Open Outlook Data File dialog box to search for an existing .pst file or to create a new one.

5. You can now create a new .pst file or open an existing .pst file:
   - To create a new .pst file in the default folder, type the file name in the text box provided and then click OK. In the Create Microsoft Personal Folders dialog box, specify a password, verify a password for the .pst file, and click OK.
   - To create a new .pst file in a nondefault folder, click Browse Folders to expand the dialog box. Browse for the folder you want to use, type the file name in the text box provided, and then click OK. In the Create Microsoft Personal Folders dialog box, specify a password, verify a password for the .pst file, and click OK.
   - To open an existing .pst file, click Browse Folders to expand the dialog box. Browse to the folder containing the .pst file. Select the .pst file, and then click OK. In the Personal Folders dialog box, you can use the options provided to change the current password or compact the personal folder, and then click OK.

   NOTE It is important to be aware that Exchange Server does not ship with any password recovery utility for .pst files. If a user sets a password on a .pst file and forgets it, the Exchange administrator has no way to reset it. You might find third-party vendors who make password-cracking or recovery tools, but they are not guaranteed to work and they are not supported by Microsoft.

6. Click Close. The personal folder you've selected or created is displayed in the Outlook folder list. You should see related subfolders as well.

DELIVERING MAIL TO PERSONAL FOLDERS

When you deliver mail to a personal folder, Outlook saves e-mail messages only locally on your computer. As a result, Outlook removes the messages from Exchange Server and you can access the messages only on the currently logged-on computer. If you want mail to be delivered to a personal folder, complete the following steps:

1. Start Outlook. In Outlook 2007, on the Tools menu, click Account Settings. In Outlook 2010, click the Office button, click the Account Settings button, and then select the Account Settings option.
2. In the Account Settings dialog box, click the Data Files tab.
3. Select the .pst file to use in the list of data files provided, and then click Set As Default.
4. When prompted to confirm, click Yes. Click Close.
5. Exit and restart Outlook. Outlook will now use personal folders.

If you want mail to resume using server-stored mail, complete the following steps:

1. Start Outlook. In Outlook 2007, on the Tools menu, click Account Settings. In Outlook 2010, click the Office button, click the Account Settings button, and then select the Account Settings option.

2. In the Account Settings dialog box, click the Data Files tab.

3. Select the .ost file to use in the list of data files provided, and then click Set As Default.

4. When prompted to confirm, click OK. Click Close.

5. Exit and restart Outlook. Outlook will now use personal folders.

BACKING UP PERSONAL FOLDERS

The Personal Folders Backup Tool is available as a free download on the Microsoft Office Online Web site (office.microsoft.com). Be sure to download the appropriate version of the tool for your version of Outlook, and then exit Outlook before installing this tool. After you download and install this backup tool, you can back up a user's personal folders by completing the following steps:

1. Log on as the user, and then start Outlook.

2. In Outlook, on the File menu, click Backup.

3. Click Options. Select the check boxes for the personal folders you want to back up.

4. Click Browse. Navigate to the location where you want to save the backup, and then click Open.

5. To remind users to create personal folder backups, select the Remind Me To Backup Every ... Days check box, specify the reminder interval, and then click OK.

6. Click Save Backup.

7. Exit Outlook so that the backup process can begin.

RESTORING BACKED-UP PERSONAL FOLDER DATA

After you've created a backup of a personal folder, you can recover any backed-up messages or data by following these steps:

1. In Outlook, open the .pst file as discussed previously in the "Creating New or Opening Existing Personal Folders" section.

2. Drag messages or data entries from the backup personal folder to the current personal folder. You'll restore the selected items.

To recover the entire .pst file from backup, follow these steps:

1. In Outlook, on the Tools menu, click Account Settings.

2. In the Account Settings dialog box, click the Data Files tab. Write down the name and folder location of the damaged .pst file.

3. Exit Outlook.

4. In Windows Explorer, rename the damaged .pst file.

5. In Windows Explorer, copy the backup .pst file to the folder containing the original .pst file.

6. In Windows Explorer, give the backup .pst file the original name of the .pst file.

7. Restart Outlook.

Accessing Multiple Exchange Server Mailboxes

Earlier in the chapter, I discussed how users could check multiple Internet mail accounts in Outlook. You might have wondered whether users could check multiple Exchange mailboxes as well—and they can. Users often need to access multiple Exchange mailboxes for many reasons:

- Help desk administrators might need access to the help desk mailbox in addition to their own mailboxes.
- Managers might need temporary access to the mailboxes of subordinates who are on vacation.
- Mailboxes might need to be set up for long-term projects and project members need access to those mailboxes.
- Resource mailboxes might need to be set up for accounts payable, human resources, corporate information, and so on.

Normally, a one-to-one relationship exists between user accounts and Exchange mailboxes. You create a user account and add a mailbox to it; only this user can access the mailbox directly through Exchange. To change this behavior, you must change the permissions on the mailbox. One way to change mailbox access permissions is to do the following:

1. Log on to Exchange as the owner of the mailbox.
2. Delegate access to the mailbox to one or more additional users.
3. Have users with delegated access log on to Exchange and open the mailbox.

The sections that follow examine each of these steps in detail.

Logging On to Exchange as the Mailbox Owner

Logging on to Exchange as the mailbox owner allows you to delegate access to the mailbox. Before you can do this, however, you must complete the following steps:

1. Log on as the user or have the user log on for you. You need to know the account name and password for the domain.
2. Start Outlook. Make sure that mail support is configured to use Exchange Server. If necessary, configure this support, which creates the mail profile for the user.
3. After you configure Outlook to use Exchange Server, you should be able to log on to Exchange Server as the mailbox owner.

> **TIP** With multiple mailbox users, you should configure the mailbox to deliver mail to the server rather than to a personal folder. In this way, the mail is available to be checked by one or more mailbox users.

Delegating Mailbox Access

After you've logged on as the mailbox owner, you can delegate access to the mailbox by completing these steps:

1. Start Outlook. In Outlook 2007, on the Tools menu, click Account Settings. In Outlook 2010, click the Office button, click the Account Settings button, and then select the Account Settings option. On the Delegates tab or in the Delegates dialog box, click Add.

2. The Add Users dialog box appears, as shown in Figure 16-6. To add users, double-click the name of a user who needs access to the mailbox. Repeat this step as necessary for other users, and then click OK when you're finished.

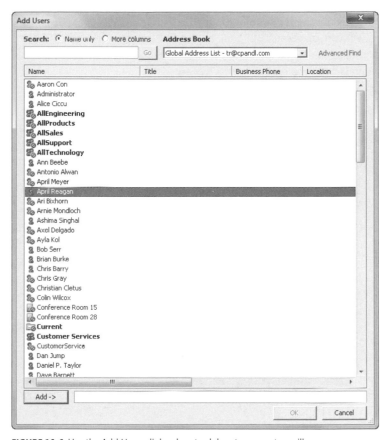

FIGURE 16-6 Use the Add Users dialog box to delegate access to mailboxes.

3. If you are configuring Outlook 2007, in the Delegate Permissions dialog box, assign permissions to the delegates for the Calendar, Tasks, Inbox, Contacts, Notes, and Journal items. The available permissions include

   - **None**   No permissions

   - **Reviewer**   Grants read permission only

   - **Author**   Grants read and create permissions

   - **Editor**   Grants read, create, and modify permissions

NOTE If the user needs total control over the mailbox, you should grant the user Editor permission for all items.

4. If you are configuring Outlook 2010, you'll need to assign additional permissions separately.
5. Click OK twice. These changes take place when the user restarts Outlook.
6. Delegated users can access the mailbox and send mail on behalf of the mailbox owner. To change this behavior, set folder permissions as described later in the "Granting Permission to Access Folders Without Delegating Access" section.

Opening Additional Exchange Mailboxes

The final step is to let Exchange Server know about the additional mailboxes the user wants to open. To do this, follow these steps:

1. Have the user who wants access to additional mailboxes log on and start Outlook.
2. In Outlook 2007, on the Tools menu, click Account Settings. In Outlook 2010, click the Office button, click the Account Settings button, and then select the Account Settings option.
3. Select the Microsoft Exchange Server account, and then click Change.
4. Click More Settings to display the Microsoft Exchange Server dialog box.
5. In the Change E-Mail Account Wizard, click More Settings.
6. In the Microsoft Exchange dialog box, on the Advanced tab, click Add. Then type the name of a mailbox to open. Generally, this is the same as the mail alias for the user or account associated with the mailbox. Click OK. Repeat this step to add other mailboxes.
7. Click Next, and then click Finish.
8. Click Close. The additional mailboxes are displayed in the Outlook folder list.

Granting Permission to Access Folders Without Delegating Access

When a mailbox is stored on the server, you can grant access to individual folders in the mailbox. Granting access in this way allows users to add the mailbox to their mail profiles and work with the folder. Users can perform tasks only for which you've granted permission.

To grant access to folders individually, follow these steps:

1. Right-click the folder for which you want to grant access, and then select Properties. In the Properties dialog box, select the Permissions tab, as shown in Figure 16-7.

FIGURE 16-7 Grant access to a folder through the Permissions tab.

2. The Name and Permission Level lists display account names and their permissions on the folder. Two special names might be listed:

   - **Default** Provides default permissions for all users

   - **Anonymous** Provides permissions for anonymous users, such as those who anonymously access a published public folder through the Web

3. If you want to grant users permission that differs from the default permission, click Add.

4. In the Add Users dialog box, double-click the name of a user who needs access to the mailbox. Click Add to put the name in the Add Users list. Repeat this step as necessary for other users, and click OK when finished.

5. In the Name and Role lists, select one or more users whose permissions you want to modify. Afterward, use the Roles list to assign permissions or select individual permission items. The roles are defined as follows:

   - **Owner** Grants all permissions in the folder. Users with this role can create, read, modify, and delete all items in the folder. They can create subfolders and change permissions on folders as well.

   - **Publishing Editor** Grants permission to create, read, modify, and delete all items in the folder. Users with this role can create subfolders as well.

- **Editor**   Grants permission to create, read, modify, and delete all items in the folder.

- **Publishing Author**   Grants permission to create and read items in the folder, to modify and delete items the user created, and to create subfolders.

- **Author**   Grants permission to create and read items in the folder and to modify and delete items the user created.

- **Nonediting Author**   Grants permission to create and read items in the folder.

- **Reviewer**   Grants read-only permission.

- **Contributor**   Grants permission to create items but not to view the contents of the folder.

- **None**   Grants no permission in the folder.

6. When you're finished granting permissions, click OK.

Using Mail Profiles to Customize the Mail Environment

The mail profile used with Outlook determines which information services are available and how they are configured. A default mail profile is created when you install and configure Outlook for the first time. This mail profile is usually called Outlook.

The active mail profile defines the mail setup for the user who is logged on to the computer. You can define additional profiles for the user as well. You can use these additional profiles to customize the user's mail environment for different situations. Here are two scenarios:

- A manager needs to check the Technical Support and Customer Support mailboxes only on Mondays when she writes summary reports. On other days, the manager doesn't want to see these mailboxes. To solve this problem, you create two mail profiles: Support and Standard. The Support profile displays the manager's mailbox as well as the Technical Support and Customer Support mailboxes. The Standard profile displays only the manager's mailbox. The manager can then switch between these mail profiles as necessary.

- A laptop user wants to check Exchange mail directly while connected to the LAN. When at home, the user wants to use remote mail with scheduled connections. On business trips, the user wants to use Simple Mail Transfer Protocol (SMTP) and POP3. To solve this problem, you create three mail profiles: On-Site, Off-Site, and Home. The On-Site profile uses the Exchange Server service with a standard configuration. The Off-Site profile configures Exchange Server for remote mail and scheduled connections. The Home profile doesn't use the Exchange information service and uses the Internet mail service instead.

Common tasks you'll use to manage mail profiles are examined in the sections that follow.

Creating, Copying, and Removing Mail Profiles

You manage mail profiles through the Mail utility. To access this utility and manage profiles, follow these steps:

1. Start the Mail utility. Click Start, and then click Control Panel. In Control Panel, click Small Icons on the View By list and then double-click Mail. If you are using a 64-bit operating system, the Mail utility is listed under the 32-bit Control Panel. In Control Panel, click Small Icons on the View By list, double-click 32-Bit Control Panel, and then double-click Mail.

2. In the Mail Setup–Outlook dialog box, click Show Profiles.

3. As Figure 16-8 shows, you should see a list of mail profiles for the current user. Mail profiles for other users aren't displayed. You can now perform the following actions:

   - Click Add to create a new mail profile using the Account Settings Wizard.
   - Delete a profile by selecting it and clicking Remove.
   - Copy an existing profile by selecting it and clicking Copy.
   - View a profile by selecting it and clicking Properties.

FIGURE 16-8 To add, remove, or edit mail profiles, click Show Profiles to display this dialog box.

Selecting a Specific Profile to Use on Startup

You can configure Outlook to use a specific profile on startup or to prompt for a profile to use. To start with a specific profile, follow these steps:

1. Start the Mail utility. Click Start, and then click Control Panel. In Control Panel, click Small Icons on the View By list and then double-click Mail. If you are using a 64-bit operating system, the Mail utility is listed under the 32-bit Control Panel. In Control Panel, click Small Icons on the View By list, double-click 32-Bit Control Panel, and then double-click Mail.

2. In the Mail Setup–Outlook dialog box, click Show Profiles.

3. Select Always Use This Profile, and then use the drop-down list to choose the startup profile. Click OK.

To prompt for a profile before starting Outlook, follow these steps:

1. Start the Mail utility. Click Start, and then click Control Panel. In Control Panel, click Small Icons on the View By list and then double-click Mail. If you are using a 64-bit operating system, the Mail utility is listed under the 32-bit Control Panel. In Control Panel, click Small Icons on the View By list, double-click 32-Bit Control Panel, and then double-click Mail.

2. In the Mail Setup–Outlook dialog box, click Show Profiles.

3. Select Prompt For A Profile To Be Used, and then click OK.

The user will be prompted for a profile the next time Outlook is started.

Managing Mobile Messaging Users

I n our increasingly connected world, most users want to be able to access e-mail, calendars, contacts, and scheduled tasks no matter what time it is or where they are. With Microsoft Exchange Server 2010, you can make anywhere, any-time access to Exchange data a real possibility. How? Start by using Exchange's built-in Web and mobile access features to allow users to connect to Exchange over the Internet and from cellular networks. Afterward, configure your network to allow direct dial-up or secure anywhere connections from Microsoft Office Outlook 2007 or Outlook 2010, and then create Microsoft Outlook profiles that use these configurations.

Web access, mobile access, and secure anywhere access are implemented as separate features that are available when you install the Client Access server role for Exchange Server 2010. These features include Exchange ActiveSync, Outlook Web App, and Outlook Anywhere. Although Exchange ActiveSync and Outlook Web App (then called Outlook Web Access) were available in Exchange Server 2003 and earlier releases of Exchange Server, Outlook Anywhere is an enhanced feature that builds on the remote procedure call (RPC) over Hypertext Transfer Protocol (HTTP) feature introduced in the previous Exchange Server release.

Mastering Outlook Web App Essentials

Outlook Web App is a standard Exchange Server 2010 technology that allows users to access their mailboxes using a Web browser. If public folders are hosted by Exchange 2010, users will be able to access public folder data as well. The technology works with standard Internet protocols, including Hypertext Transfer Protocol (HTTP) and Secure HTTP (HTTPS).

When users access mailboxes and public folder data over the Web, a Client Access server is working behind the scenes to grant access and transfer files to the browser. Because you don't need to configure Outlook Web App on the client, it's ideally suited for users who want to access e-mail while away from the office and may also be a good choice for users on the internal network who don't need the full version of Microsoft Outlook. Outlook Web App is automatically configured for use when you install the Client Access server role for Exchange Server 2010. This makes Outlook Web App easy to manage. That said, there are some essential concepts you should know to manage it more effectively, and this section explains these concepts.

NOTE For detailed information on managing the related server components, see Chapter 13, "Managing Client Access Servers." At a minimum, to ensure that proper security procedures are in place, you'll want to configure Exchange ActiveSync Mailbox Policy. You might also want to configure how Outlook Web App is used with public and private computers.

Getting Started with Outlook Web App

Outlook Web App (OWA) is installed automatically when you install the Client Access server role for Exchange Server 2010. In your Exchange organization, you must install at least one Client Access server in each Active Directory site containing an Exchange 2010 Mailbox server. If users will be accessing Outlook Web App over the Internet, then one of the Client Access servers you install must be Internet facing. This server accepts connections from external clients on an external Uniform Resource Locator (URL).

In most cases, you need to open only TCP port 443 on your organization's firewall, as discussed in Chapter 13, to allow users to access mailboxes and public folder data over the Web. After that, you simply tell users the URL path that they need to type into their browser's Address text box. The users can then access Outlook Web App when they're off-site.

Outlook Web App is optimized for screen resolutions of 800 by 600 or higher. Two different versions are available

- **Light** Provides a basic experience with a simplified user interface that supports accessibility for blind and low-vision users. No Standard-only features are available. In addition, calendar options are limited and messages can be composed only as plain text. OWA shortcut menus are not displayed when you right-click. The OWA toolbar has slightly different options, and the Options page itself is simplified as well.

- **Standard** Provides a rich experience with performance that closely approximates Outlook 2007 and Outlook 2010, including a folder hierarchy that you can expand or collapse, drag-and-drop functionality, move and copy functionality, and shortcut menus that you can access by right-clicking. In addition, you can use all of the following features: appearance color schemes, calendar views, file share integration, notifications, personal distribution lists, public folder access, reading pane, recover deleted items, reminders, search, secure signed and encrypted e-mail with Secure Multipurpose Internet Mail Extensions (S/MIME), server-side rules, spelling checker, voice mail options, and WebReady Document viewing. Standard does not, however, support accessibility for blind and low-vision users.

Outlook Web App uses Hypertext Markup Language (HTML) 4.0 and JavaScript [European Computer Manufacturers Association (ECMA)] script. Unlike earlier implementations of OWA, the standard version of Outlook Web App is available on Windows and Linux using Internet Explorer 7, Internet Explorer 8, and Firefox 3.0.1, and on the Mac using Safari 3.1 or later.

Outlook Web App for Exchange Server 2010 has many features and enhancements, including:

- **Instant messaging**   Users can chat with any contact listed in their Contacts list simply by double-clicking a contact's name. (Requires Office Communications Server and some integration DLLs on your Client Access servers.)

- **Inbox rules**   Users can create inbox rules to automatically sort incoming e-mail into folders. Users create rules on the Inbox Rules tab or by right-clicking a message they want to base a rule on and selecting Create Rule.

- **Message attachments**   Users can attach files, meeting requests, and other messages to messages by clicking the attach file icon on the toolbar. Users can even drag and drop attachments into messages if they are using Internet Explorer and install the S/MIME control.

- **Delivery reports**   Users can generate delivery reports to search for delivery information about message they've sent or received during the previous two weeks.

- **Personal groups**   Users can create personal groups that will appear in their address book.

- **Public groups**   Users can create public groups that will appear in the global address book for everyone to use.

When it comes to supported OWA features, Firefox 3.0.1 or later and Safari 3.1 or later have feature parity with Internet Explorer 7.0 and Internet Explorer 8.0. The one exception is support for the S/MIME control, which only Internet Explorer supports.

Connecting to Mailboxes and Public Folder Data over the Web

With Outlook Web App, you can easily access mailboxes and public folder data over the Web and the corporate intranet. To access a user's mailbox, type the Exchange Outlook Web App URL into your browser's Address text box, and then enter the user name and password for the mailbox you want to access. The general steps are as follows:

1.   In a Web browser, type **https://*servername.yourdomain.com*/owa**, where *servername* is a placeholder for the Web server hosted by Exchange

Server 2010 and *yourdomain.com* is a placeholder for your external domain name. For example, if your Client Access server is configured to use *mail* as the external DNS name and your external domain is *cpandl.com,* you type **https://mail.cpandl.com/owa**.

2. At the security prompt, the user needs to specify whether he is using a public or shared computer, or a private computer. If the browser supports the standard version of Outlook Web App, the user can elect to use Outlook Web App Light by selecting the Use Outlook Web App Light check box.

3. Type the user name in domain\username format, such as cpandl\williams, or User Principal Name (UPN) format, such as williams@cpandl.com.

4. Type the password for the previously specified account, and then click the Log On button.

Exchange Server uses the computer type (as specified by the user) to determine the period of inactivity to allow before logging the user off automatically. With a private computer, the user will be allowed a longer period of inactivity before being logged off. With a public or shared computer, Exchange Server will log the user off more quickly to prevent the user's data from being compromised.

NOTE By default, Client Access servers are configured to use Secure HTTP (HTTPS) for Outlook Web App. When you install Exchange Server 2010, a self-signed security certificate is issued for the Client Access server automatically. Because this default certificate is not issued by a trusted certificate authority, users will see a warning that there is a problem with the Web site's security certificate. At the warning prompt, the user can click the Continue To This Website link. The user will see this warning continuously until you install a certificate on the server from a trusted source.

After a user has accessed her mailbox in OWA, she can access public folders data that is available as well as long as the public folders are hosted on Exchange 2010. To access public folders, follow these steps:

1. In the left pane of the OWA window, click Public Folders.

2. Under Public Folders, you'll see a list of the available top levels to which you have access.

3. Select folders to navigate their contents and open items by double-clicking.

Working with Outlook Web App

After you enter the Exchange Outlook Web App URL into Internet Explorer's Address text box and enter the user name and password for the mailbox you want to access, you'll see the view of Outlook Web App compatible with your browser. Figure 17-1 shows the full-featured view of Outlook Web App. Most users with Internet Explorer 7.0 or Internet Explorer 8.0 see this view of Outlook Web App automatically. If their browsers don't support a necessary technology for the full-featured view, or if this technology has been disabled, they might see the Light view instead. If they can right-click and see a shortcut menu, they have the full-featured view.

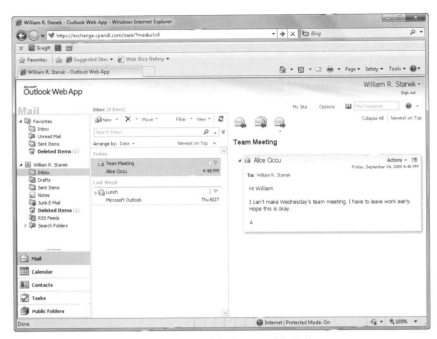

FIGURE 17-1 Outlook Web App has nearly all of the features of Outlook.

As shown in Figure 17-1, the latest version of Outlook Web App has a toolbar that provides quick access to the following key features:

- **Address Book** Displays the Address Book, which provides quick access to address lists and contacts. Any tracked resources, such as conference rooms or projectors, are available as well. If you click a contact or resource in an address list, the e-mail address and availability information are displayed.

- **Address Book Search** Search the Address Book for a specific contact or resource. Simply enter as much of the name as is necessary to uniquely identify the contact or resource, and then press Enter. If multiple matches are found, you'll see a shortcut menu with a list of matches. Clicking a match displays the properties for that item.

- **Options** Takes you to the Exchange Control Panel. Use the Select What To Manage list to choose what you want to manage, including yourself, your organization, or another user's mailbox. When you are managing your own account, you can configure Outlook Web App properties or view current configuration details.

- **Help** Shows the help page, which provides information on setting up e-mail, using instant messaging in OWA, creating rules for managing incoming e-mail, adding attachments and meeting requests to e-mail, and more.

- **Help, About** If you click the options button to the right of the Help button while viewing the mailbox, you can select the About option. This option lists the current configuration being used by the Client Access server and the Outlook Web App client. This information is useful for troubleshooting.

Listing 17-1 shows an example of the details on the About page, which can be helpful for troubleshooting. If a user is having problems with Outlook Web App, you can instruct the user to click Options, scroll through the options, and then select About. If he has a problem that is not related to e-mail and is able to send e-mail, he can click Copy To Clipboard, and then paste the contents of the Clipboard into an e-mail message by pressing Ctrl+V.

LISTING 17-1 Outlook Web App Configuration Details

```
Mailbox owner: William Stanek [williams@cpandl.com]
User-Agent: Mozilla/4.0
(compatible; MSIE 8.0; Windows NT 6.1; WOW64; SLCC2;
.NET CLR 2.0.50727; .NET CLR 3.5.30729; .NET CLR 3.0.30729)
Outlook Web App experience: Standard
User language: English (United States)
User time zone: (GMT-08:00) Pacific Time (US & Canada)
Exchange mailbox address: /o=First Organization/ou=Exchange
Administrative Group (FYDIBOHF23SPDLT)/cn=Recipients/cn=williams
Host address: https://mailserver25.cpandl.com/owa
Version: 14
Host name: mailserver25.cpandl.com
Exchange Client Access server name: MAILSERVER25.cpandl.com
Exchange Client Access server .NET Framework version: 2.0.50727.3521
Client Access server operating system version: Microsoft Windows NT
6.1.7600 Service Pack 1
Client Access server operating system language: en-US
Microsoft Exchange Client Access server version: 14
Client Access server language: en-US
Client Access server time zone: Pacific Standard Time
Client Access server platform: 64bit
Mailbox server name: MAILSERVER25.cpandl.com
Mailbox server Microsoft Exchange version: 14
Other Microsoft Exchange server roles currently installed on the Client
Access server: Mailbox, Hub Transport, Unified Messaging
Authentication type associated with this Outlook Web App session: Basic
Public logon: No
```

In addition to being able to manage their inbox, calendar, contacts, public folders, and mailbox rules, users can set the following Outlook Web App options by clicking Options in the task pane, making whatever changes are desired, and then clicking Save:

- **Account** Allows users to view and edit their general information as well as their contact location and contact numbers in the address book.

- **Organize Email, Inbox Rules** Allows users to create and manage inbox rules.

- **Organize Email, Automatic Replies** Allows users to create and manage automatic replies. Separate messages can be configured for internal recipients and external recipients. With external recipients, you have the option of sending auto-reply messages only to those in your contacts list.

- **Organize Email, Delivery Reports** Allows users to search for messages they've sent or received.

- **Groups** Allows users to create and manage public groups. They can create new public groups that will be available to other users in the address book. They can join or leave groups unless membership restrictions apply.

- **Phone, Mobile Phone** Allows users to manage mobile devices. You can remove mobile devices you are no longer using, display a device password, and retrieve related access logs. If you lose a mobile device, you can start a remote device wipe to protect your information. All data is removed the next time the device connects to Exchange Server, returning the device to its factory default condition. If a user initiates a remote wipe in Outlook Web App, she receives a confirmation e-mail when the device acknowledges the remote wipe request. If an administrator initiates a remote wipe on a user's behalf, the administrator and the user receive a confirmation e-mail when the device acknowledges the remote wipe request.

- **Phone, Text Messaging** Allows users to send e-mail and calendar notifications to their mobile phone as text messages. Before a user can send notifications, he needs to configure calendar settings for text messaging.

- **Settings, Mail** Allows you to set key messaging options. You can edit your e-mail signature, preferred message format, and preferred font to use for messages. The default font is 10-point Tahoma. Read receipts options allow you to specify how to respond to requests for read receipts. Reading pane options allow you to specify whether and how messages are marked as read in the reading pane. There are also settings for the conversation reading pane, message format, and message options.

- **Settings, Spelling** Allows you to set options for the spelling checker, including the dictionary language. The default language is set according to the browser's language setting.

- **Settings, Calendar** Allows you to specify when the first day of the week is and when the work day starts and ends for the purposes of calendar scheduling. Reminder options allow you to enable or disable reminders for calendars and tasks. Automatic processing options specify how meeting requests, notifications, and responses are handled.

- **Settings, General** Allows you to configure e-mail name resolution, and accessibility options. E-mail name resolution options allow you to specify whether the global address list or your personal contacts are checked first when resolving e-mail addresses in messages you are composing. By default, the global address list is checked first. Appearance options allow you to select the color scheme used by Outlook Web App. The default color scheme is blue.

NOTE Under General Settings, accessibility options allow you to optimize Outlook Web App for blind and low-vision users. By selecting Use The Blind And Low Vision Experience, you ensure that Outlook Web App Light is used rather than the standard version of Outlook Web App.

- **Settings, Regional** Allows you to set the language, dates, and time formats to use with Outlook Web App.
- **Settings, Password** Allows users to change their domain passwords. After changing their passwords, users might need to re-enter their credentials and log on again.
- **Settings, S/MIME** Allows users to download the S/MIME control. They can then use this control to encrypt and digitally sign e-mail.
- **Block or Allow** Allows you to filter junk e-mail and manage the Safe Senders and Recipients list as well as the Blocked Senders list.

When you are working with the Options page, you can use the Select What To Manage list to choose what you want to manage. If you choose Myself, you can manage your user mailbox. If you choose My Organization, you can manage Exchange mailboxes, groups, contacts, and roles. If you choose Another User, you can select a mailbox to manage. If you have been granted permission to access another mailbox or delegated permission to access a folder within a mailbox, as discussed in Chapter 16, "Managing Exchange Server 2010 Clients," you can open the mailbox and access any authorized folders by selecting Another User, clicking the mailbox name, and then clicking OK.

The Sign-Out option logs off the current user, and ends the Outlook Web App session. As a recommended best practice, you should advise all users to log off from their Outlook Web App sessions when they are finished.

Enabling and Disabling Web Access for Users

Exchange Server 2010 enables Outlook Web App for each user by default. If necessary, you can disable Outlook Web App for specific users. To do this, complete the following steps:

1. In Exchange Management Console, expand Recipient Configuration and then select Mailbox.

2. You should now see a list of users with Exchange mailboxes in the organization. Double-click the user's name to open the Properties dialog box for the user account.

3. On the Mailbox Features tab, the enabled mailbox features for the user are displayed, as shown in Figure 17-2.

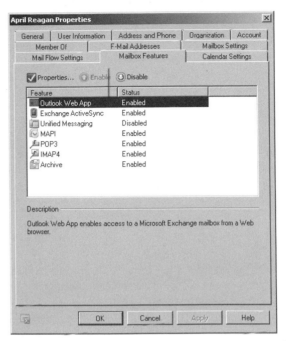

- To disable Outlook Web App for this user, under Feature, select Outlook Web App, and then click Disable.
- To enable Outlook Web App for this user, under Feature, select Outlook Web App, and then click Enable.

4. Click OK.

Mastering Mobile Device and Wireless Access Essentials

Exchange Server 2010 supports wireless access for users with many types of mobile devices. Exchange Server 2010 uses Exchange ActiveSync to provide mobile access functionality. Using Exchange ActiveSync, users with mobile devices can access their e-mail, calendar, contacts, and scheduled tasks.

When you install Exchange Server 2010, Exchange ActiveSync is automatically configured for use. As with Outlook Web App, this makes Exchange ActiveSync easy to manage, but there are still some essential concepts you should know to manage it more effectively. This section explains these concepts.

As an Exchange administrator, you can do many things to fine-tune the mobile access configuration for your organization, as discussed in Chapter 13. At a minimum, you'll want to ensure that the appropriate level of authentication is applied. You'll also want to create and apply Exchange ActiveSync Mailbox Policy.

Using Exchange Server ActiveSync, users whose mobile devices have Windows Mobile 5.0 and the Messaging and Security Feature Pack (MSFP) and later versions of Windows Mobile software can initiate synchronization with Exchange to keep their data up to date and receive notices from Exchange that trigger synchronization through the Direct Push feature. Direct Push is a key feature that you probably want to know a bit more about. It works like this:

1. The user configures her mobile device to synchronize with Exchange, selecting specific Exchange folders that she wants to keep up to date.

2. When a new message arrives in a designated sync folder, a control message is sent to the mobile device.

3. The control message initiates a data synchronization session, and the device performs background synchronization with Exchange.

Users with third-party synchronization software for their mobile devices can also sync with Exchange, provided the software is compatible with Exchange ActiveSync. After they are synchronized, users can then access their data while they are offline. In Exchange Server 2010, Direct Push is either enabled or disabled along with Exchange ActiveSync itself.

Exchange Server 2010 enables ActiveSync for each user by default. If necessary, you can disable ActiveSync for specific users. To do this, complete the following steps:

1. In Exchange Management Console, expand Recipient Configuration and then select Mailbox.

2. You should now see a list of users with Exchange mailboxes in the organization. Double-click the user's name to open the Properties dialog box for the user account.

3. On the Mailbox Features tab, the enabled mobile and Web access features for the user are displayed, as shown previously in Figure 17-2:

    • To disable Exchange ActiveSync for this user, under Feature, select Exchange ActiveSync, and then click Disable.

    • To enable Exchange ActiveSync for this user, under Feature, select Exchange ActiveSync, and then click Enable.

4. Click OK.

REAL WORLD ActiveSync notifications are sent over wireless networks using the Internet. To take advantage of these services, users must subscribe to the Internet services of a wireless carrier. The actual process of receiving synchronization requests and sending synchronization notifications is handled by Exchange. Exchange Active-Sync is, in fact, configured as an ASP.NET application on the Web server. For Exchange

Activesync to work properly, the Web server must be configured properly, as discussed in Chapter 13. If you want to learn more about Internet Information Services (IIS) and ASP.NET, I recommend *Microsoft IIS 7.0 Administrator's Pocket Consultant* (Microsoft Press, 2007).

To define organization-wide security and authentication options, you can use Exchange ActiveSync Mailbox policies. When you install Exchange Server 2010, a default Exchange ActiveSync Mailbox policy is created. Through Exchange ActiveSync Mailbox policy settings, you can precisely control mobile browsing capabilities for all users in the enterprise, including:

- Whether passwords are required and how passwords must be configured
- Synchronization settings to include past calendar and e-mail items
- Permitted devices and device options, such as whether a device can use Wi-Fi, infrared, Bluetooth, or Internet sharing

For more information, see the section "Understanding and Using Exchange ActiveSync Mailbox Policy" in Chapter 13.

Mastering Remote Mail and Outlook Anywhere Essentials

Two additional technologies you can use for mobile access are remote mail and Outlook Anywhere. These technologies require extra configuration for both Outlook clients and Exchange servers. This section discusses Outlook client configuration. See Chapter 13 for a discussion of Exchange server configuration.

Using Remote Mail and Outlook Anywhere

Using remote mail, you can configure Outlook to connect to Exchange Server using a dial-up connection to your organization's modem bank. Remote mail is useful in these scenarios:

- Users at a branch office must connect to Exchange Server by means of dial-up connections.
- Laptop users want to connect to Exchange Server through dial-up connections when out of the office. (Here, you might want to configure on-site and off-site mail profiles for the user. See the section in Chapter 16 titled "Using Mail Profiles to Customize the Mail Environment.")
- Users working at home need to connect to Exchange Server by means of dial-up connections.

Outlook Anywhere is a technology that allows users to access Exchange Server over the Internet using Outlook. With Outlook Anywhere, you don't need to use a virtual private network (VPN) to securely connect Outlook to Exchange Server. Instead of relying on VPN for security, Outlook Anywhere takes advantage of security features of Microsoft Windows, Microsoft Outlook, and Exchange Server 2010 to ensure that communications are secure.

Outlook Anywhere builds on the RPC over HTTP feature introduced with Exchange Server 2003 and Outlook 2003. It provides additional, more dynamic communication protocols for remotely accessing Exchange Server using RPC over HTTP, with or without SSL encryption: With RPC over HTTP, remote procedure calls (RPCs) are nested within HTTP packets, which can either be encrypted with SSL or not encrypted with SSL, and then transmitted. By adding encryption to either technique, you ensure that data transmitted between Outlook and Exchange Server is encrypted and, therefore, protected.

Outlook Anywhere is useful in these scenarios:

- Users at a branch office must connect to Exchange Server over a broadband connection, such as a digital subscriber line (DSL) or a cable modem, and you don't have a VPN, or you want to simplify the connection process by eliminating the need for a VPN.

- Laptop users want to connect to Exchange Server through broadband or T1 connections when out of the office without having to use VPNs. (Here, you might want to configure on-site and off-site mail profiles for the user. See the section in Chapter 16 titled "Using Mail Profiles to Customize the Mail Environment.")

- Users working at home need to connect to Exchange Server by means of broadband connections without having to use a VPN.

Enabling remote mail and Outlook Anywhere requires separate client and server configurations. As discussed in "Creating Outlook Profiles for Dial-Up Connections to Corporate Networks" and "Configuring Outlook Profiles for Outlook Anywhere" later in this chapter, configuring Outlook for use with remote mail or Outlook Anywhere is easy—all you need to do is properly configure a related mail profile. What isn't so easy is implementing the required back-end server configuration.

Remote mail requires a fairly complex server implementation on the back end to enable the technology for users, the discussion of which is beyond the scope of this book. You can deploy Outlook Anywhere by following the procedure discussed in Chapter 13.

Creating Outlook Profiles for Dial-Up Connections to Corporate Networks

You configure dial-up connections for Outlook (also called remote mail) by creating an Outlook profile that can be used for dial-up connections to the corporate network. Before you can create this profile, you must also configure the area code and dialing options to use with the computer's modem.

To configure the area code and dialing options for Windows 7, follow these steps:

1. Click Start, and then click Control Panel. In Control Panel, click Small Icons on the View By list. Finally, click Phone And Modem Options.

2. Using the selection list provided, specify the country or region you are located in, such as the United States.

3. Enter your area code, such as **212**.

4. Optionally, enter carrier codes, the number needed to dial in an outside line, or both.

5. Select either Tone Dialing or Pulse Dialing.

6. When you click OK, the Phone And Modem Options dialog box appears with the Dialing Rules tab selected. Review the configuration, and then click OK when you are finished.

To create the Outlook profile for remote mail, follow these steps:

1. Exit Outlook. Start the Mail utility. (Click Start, and then click Control Panel. In Control Panel, click User Accounts, and then click Mail.)

2. In the Mail Setup–Outlook dialog box, click Show Profiles. Then, in the Mail window, click Add.

3. Type the name of the profile, such as **Remote Exchange**, and then click OK. This starts the Add New E-Mail Account Wizard.

4. You need to manually configure settings. Select the Manually Configure Server Settings check box, and then click Next.

5. Select Microsoft Exchange, and then click Next.

6. In the Microsoft Exchange Server text box, type the host name of the mail server, such as **mailer1**. You can also enter the fully qualified domain name (FQDN) of the mail server, such as **mailer1.cpandl.com**. Using the fully qualified domain name can help ensure a successful connection when the mail server is in a different domain or forest.

7. In the User Name text box, enter the user's domain logon name or domain user name, such as **Williams** or **William Stanek**. Click Check Name to confirm that you've entered the correct user name for the mailbox. You'll want to store a local copy of the user's e-mail on his computer, so ensure that the Use Cached Exchange Mode check box is selected.

8. Click More Settings. This displays the Microsoft Exchange Server dialog box.

9. With remote mail connections, you'll usually want to work offline and dial up only as necessary. Select Manually Control Connection State, and then select Work Offline And Use Dial-Up Networking, as shown in Figure 17-3.

10. If you want the user to be prompted for the connection type, select the Choose The Connection Type When Starting check box.

11. By default, data sent between Outlook and Exchange is encrypted. If you don't want to encrypt message traffic, click the Security tab. Under Encryption, clear the Encrypt Data Between Microsoft Office Outlook And Microsoft Exchange check box.

12. On the Connection tab, choose Connect Using My Phone Line. Then, under Use The Following Dial-Up Networking Connection, choose an existing

connection to use for remote mail, as shown in Figure 17-4. If no connection is available, click Add, and create a connection.

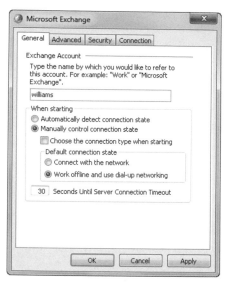

FIGURE 17-3 Use manual connection settings for working offline and dial-up networking.

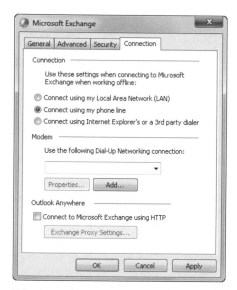

FIGURE 17-4 Connect using a phone line, and then specify the dial-up networking connection to use.

13. Click OK. In the Add New E-mail Account Wizard, click Next, and then click Finish.

14. In the Mail dialog box, select Prompt For A Profile To Be Used and then click OK.

Configuring Outlook Profiles for Outlook Anywhere

You configure Outlook to use Outlook Anywhere by completing the following steps:

1. Exit Outlook. Start the Mail utility. Click Start, and then click Control Panel. In Control Panel, click User Accounts, and then click Mail.

2. In the Mail Setup–Outlook dialog box, click Show Profiles. Then, in the Mail window, click Add.

3. Type the name of the profile, such as **Outlook Anywhere**, and then click OK. This starts the Add New E-mail Account Wizard.

4. If you've properly configured the Autodiscover service, Autodiscover will automatically configure the client for you, and you can skip the rest of this procedure. Otherwise, you need to manually configure settings. Select the Manually Configure Server Settings check box, and then click Next.

5. Select Microsoft Exchange, and then click Next.

6. In the Microsoft Exchange Server text box, type the host name of the mail server, such as **mailer1**. You can also enter the FQDN of the mail server, such as **mailer1.cpandl.com**. Using the fully qualified domain name can help ensure a successful connection when the mail server is in a different domain or forest.

7. In the User Name text box, enter the user's domain logon name or domain user name, such as **Williams** or **William Stanek**. Click Check Name to confirm that you've entered the correct user name for the mailbox. You'll want to store a local copy of the user's e-mail on his computer, so ensure that the Use Cached Exchange Mode check box is selected.

8. Click More Settings. This displays the Microsoft Exchange dialog box.

9. With Outlook Anywhere connections, you'll usually want to manually control the connection state and connect to Exchange only when there is an active connection (meaning when you are online as opposed to when you are offline). On the General tab, select both Manually Control Connection State and Connect With The Network options.

10. If you want the user to be prompted for a connection type, select the Choose Connection Type When Starting check box.

11. By default, data sent between Outlook and Exchange is encrypted. If you don't want to encrypt message traffic, on the Security tab, under Encryption, clear the Encrypt Data Between Microsoft Office Outlook And Microsoft Exchange.

12. On the Connection tab, select Connect Using Internet Explorer's Or A Third Party Dialer.

13. Select the Connect To Microsoft Exchange Using HTTP check box.

14. Click the Exchange Proxy Settings button to open the Exchange Proxy Settings dialog box, shown in Figure 17-5.

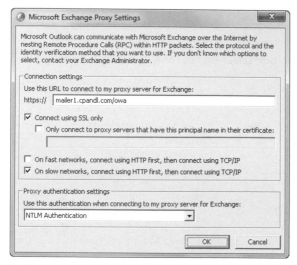

FIGURE 17-5 Connect to the Internet-facing Client Access server.

15. In the Use This URL To Connect To My Proxy Server For Exchange text box, enter the Exchange Outlook Web App URL. Selecting the Connect Using SSL Only check box ensures that the connection to Exchange Server is secure and uses SSL.

16. The On Fast Networks and On Slow Networks check boxes allow you to configure the protocols used by Outlook Anywhere. When configuring these options, keep the following in mind:

- If you select neither check box, Outlook tries to use TCP/IP. Outlook can switch between TCP/IP and Outlook Anywhere. If you are not connected to the corporate LAN either directly or via a VPN, TPC/IP will fail.

- If you select both check boxes, Outlook Anywhere first tries to use RPC over HTTP. If it experiences problems connecting or transmitting, it then tries to use RPC over TCP/IP.

- If you select only the Slow Network check box and Outlook Anywhere detects the user is on a slow network, it first tries to use RPC over HTTP and then tries to use RPC over TCP/IP. The definition of a slow network is configured in Group Policy. By default, a slow network is a network with a connection speed of 256 kilobits per second or less transmission speed.

- If you select only the Fast Network check box and Outlook Anywhere detects the user is on a fast network, it first tries to use RPC over HTTP and then tries to use RPC over TCP/IP.

17. NTLM authentication is the default authentication technique. Using NT LAN Manager (NTLM) authentication ensures that the user's credentials are protected and encrypted when transmitted over the network.

18. After you finish configuring remote mail, click OK. In the Add New E-mail Account Wizard, click Next, and then click Finish.

19. In the Mail dialog box, select Prompt For A Profile To Be Used and then click OK.

Index

Symbols and Numbers

$env:path, 96
$remoteSession, 107
$s session, 112
$sessionOptionsTimeout variable, 107
/mode:recoverserver command, 574
| pipe symbol, 116
32-bit processors
  description of, 4
  I/O performance for Mailbox servers, 31
  management tools for, 53
64-bit processors
  description of, 3–4
  I/O performance for Mailbox servers, 31

A

accepted domains
  changing type and identifier, 440–441
  creating, 438–440
  removing, 441
  understanding, 436–437
  viewing, 437–438
accessibility options, Outlook Web App, 624,
  629–630
active databases, 311
Active Directory
  about, 14
  accounts, disabling, 149
  Client Access servers and, 40
  configuring, 51
  data storage and, 74–75
  Edge Transport server and, 41–42
  Exchange data in, 15–17
  Exchange Server 2010 and, 39–44
  Exchange Server and, 7, 17–19
  global catalogs, 46, 74–75
  Hub Transport servers and, 39–42, 60
  IP subnets, 60
  Mailbox servers and, 41
  mailboxes, 117–118
  multimaster replication, 74
  permissions, 245, 362
  preparing for Exchange Server 2010, 43–44
  remote management tools, 32, 35, 38
  roles, integrating with, 39–42
  site details, 383–385
  site link details, 385–387
  site-based routing, 59–60

  Unified Messaging servers and, 41
  users, 117
Active Directory Lightweight Directory Services
  (AD LDS), 39, 41–42
Active Directory Topology, Microsoft Exchange, 11
Active Directory Users and Computers, 15, 45
active mail profile, 620
Active Manager, 285–287
ActiveSync. *See* Exchange ActiveSync
Add A Recipient To The To Field Addresses
  (transport rules), 426
Add cmdlets
  Add-ADPermission, 362, 377
  Add-Computer, 97, 99
  Add-DatabaseAvailabilityGroupServer, 284,
    294, 592
  Add-DistributionGroupMember, 201–203
  Add-IPAllowListEntry, 461
  Add-IPBlockListEntry, 463
  Add-MailboxDatabaseCopy, 284, 326, 571, 592
  Add-PSSnapin, 111
  Add-PublicFolderAdministrativePermission, 362
  Add-PublicFolderClientPermission, 362, 376
  Add-WindowsFeature, 38
Add/Remove Self As Member permission, 241
Address Book feature (Outlook Web App), 627
Address Book Search feature (Outlook Web
  App), 627
Address Book service, 11
address books, offline. *See* OAB (offline address
  book)
Address Lists role, 245
Address Lists segmentation, 470
address lists, managing. *See also* OAB (offline
  address book)
  configuring clients to use, 222
  creating and applying, 218–221
  custom mailbox attributes, defining, 173
  domainwide configuration and updates,
    222–223
  groups, hiding from, 214
  lists, editing, 223–224
  lists, renaming and deleting, 224–225
  mailboxes, hiding from, 172–173
  overview, 71
  using default lists, 217–218
administration of mailboxes
  mailbox properties, configuring, 182–189
  mailboxes, moving, 173–181
  management essentials, 169–173

recoverserver mode, 574
scheduling, 576, 579, 581–582
storage location for, 580–581, 583
streaming Extensible Storage Engine-based
    backup programs, 577
types of backups, 579–580
VSS-based backups, 577
baseline configuration checks, 533
basic authentication, 109, 477
Best Practices Analyzer, 20, 533
binary files, 6
bindings, 472, 490–492
blind and low-vision users, 624, 629–630
Blind Carbon Copy (Bcc) The Message To Addresses
    (transport rules), 426
block lists. *See* IP block lists
Block setting, 630
Bluetooth functionality, 514
booking resources, 12
bridgehead servers, 16, 236, 407
browsers, 596, 625
built-in accounts, 149
built-in groups, 197

C

CA (certificate authority), 121, 474–475
CAL (Client Access License), 6
calendar
    retrieval settings (POP3 and IMAP4), 496
    segmentation, 470
    settings, 629
    updates, 12
Categorizer, 60, 119–120
CCR (Cluster Continuous Replication), 2, 30, 282
certificate authentication, 109
certificates, public, 128
certification authority (CA), 121, 474–475
Change Password permission, 241
Change Password segmentation, 470
checkpoint file, 77, 81, 279
Checkpoint-Computer cmdlet, 97
CheckServicesStarted, 105
circular transaction logging, 573
Clean-MailboxDatabase cmdlets, 284
Clear cmdlets
    Clear-ActiveSyncDevice, 519
    Clear-EventLog, 98
    Clear-Host, 99
    Clear-Variable, 99
Client Access License (CAL), 6
Client Access Server (CAS) array
    cmdlets, 34–35
    description of, 9
    failover support, 34
    features, 47
    load balancing, 34, 40, 51
    related services, 34

Client Access server role
    about, 9, 26, 28
    configuration, 28
    deploying, 45, 50
    Exchange Server and, 45
    forest organization, 49
    high availability, achieving, 51
    IIS and, 467
    installation of, 35, 54
    migrating, 46
    multiple servers and, 51
    Organization Configuration node and, 67
    security and, 50
    Server Configuration node, 69
    transitioning, 48
Client Access server, Web and mobile access
    configuring, 472–473, 484–488
    controlling access to the HTTP server, 477–481
    enabling SSL on Web sites, 473–475
    redirecting users to alternate URLs, 476–477
    restricting incoming connections, 475–476
    segmentation, 470–472
    setting time-out values, 475–476
    starting, stopping, and restarting Web sites,
        483–484
    throttling Client Access, 481–483
    virtual directories, 469–470, 478
    Web applications, 469–472
Client Access servers
    Active Directory and, 40
    arrays, 34–35
    Availability service, 33
    deploying, 33–35, 55
    deploying Outlook Anywhere, 497–502
    disaster recovery plan for, 575
    Exchange ActiveSync, 55, 468–469, 486–487
    Exchange Server and, 34
    Forefront Protection and, 10
    I/O operations, 33
    IIS (Internet Information Services), 468–469
    installing, 468
    multiple servers and, 51
    Outlook Web App (OWA), 468–469
    site-based routing, 60
Client Access servers protocol (POP3 and IMAP4)
    authentication, 33, 492–493
    bindings, 490–492
    connection settings, 494–495
    enabling services, 488–490
    message retrieval settings, 495–497
    client permissions, 362, 373–376
    clients
        address lists, configuring to use, 222
        offline address lists, configuring to use, 228–229
        Outlook 2003 and, 278
        public folder data, accessing, 345
        public folders, accessing, 358
    cloud service. *See* Exchange Online

Q

quarantine mailbox, 10
query filters, dynamic distribution groups, 209
query-based distribution, 75
queue at point of failure, 61
Queue Viewer
    accessing, 563
    deleting messages, 567–568
    described, 21
    enumerate messages, 565–566
    filtering messages, 566–567
    refreshing, 565–566
    suspending and resuming, 567
queues. See also Queue Viewer
    connections, forcing, 567
    messages, deleting, 567–568
    messages, managing, 565–567
    summaries and states, 564–565
    suspending and resuming, 567
    types of, 559–563
queuing transactions, 81
quick reference administration tools table, 21
quorum resource, 289
quotas, 372–373

R

RAID, 2, 4, 281
Read All Properties permission, 241
Read Permissions permission, 241
Read Value(s) permission, 241
Read-Host cmdlet, 99
Receive As permission, 241
Receive connectors
    configuring, 45
    creating, 397–403
    types of, 119
    viewing and managing, 403–407
Receive Connectors role, 248
Recipient Configuration node
    about, 16, 65
    Disconnected Mailbox subnode, 71
    display maximum, changing, 73
    Distribution Group subnode, 71
    Mail Contact subnode, 71
    Mailbox subnode, 71
    Move Request, 71
    scope, configuring, 72–73
    working with, 70–73
Recipient filtering, 10
Recipient Management Group, 17, 237
Recipient Policies role, 247
recipients
    administration settings, 71–73
    moderated, 167
    overview, 70–71
records management, 275–276

Records Management Group, 17, 237
Recover Deleted Items segmentation, 470
Recover Server Mode, 590–592
Recoverable Items folder, 272
Recoverserver mode, 574
recovery
    automatic, 2
    from alternate location, 587
    from system image, 584–585
    full server, 583–585
    steps for, 585 586
recovery database, 578
Redirect The Message To Addresses (transport
    rules), 426
redirecting cmdlet output, 116
redirecting users to alternate URLs, 476 477
redundant arrays of inexpensive disks (RAID).
    See RAID
regional settings, 630
relay domains, 436–437
Reminders and Notifications segmentation, 470
$remoteSession, 107
Remote Connectivity Analyzer, 21, 475
Remote delivery queue, 79, 562
Remote Device Wipe
    remotely wiping, 518–519
    reviewing status, 520
remote domains
    creating, 449–451
    messaging options, 451–452
    removing, 453
    viewing, 448–449
remote file access, 526–528
remote mail
    Outlook profiles for dial-up connections, creating,
        634–637
    Outlook profiles, configuring, 637–639
    using, 633–634
remote management
    about, 7–9
    one-to-many, 112–113
    tools, 32, 35, 38
Remote Management service. See also Windows
    Remote Management (WinRM)
    customizing, 86–89
    description of, 14
    Exchange Management Console and, 64, 86–89
remote procedure call (RPC), 12
remote shared folder for storing backups, 581, 583
RemoteExchange.ps1 profile file, 104–105
removable media for storing backups, 581
Remove cmdlets
    Remove-AcceptedDomain, 441
    Remove-ActiveSyncMailboxPolicy, 517
    Remove-AddressList, 224–225
    Remove-ADPermission, 362, 377
    Remove-AutodiscoverVirtualDirectory, 504–505
    Remove-ClientAccessArray, 35

Update cmdlets, *continued*
  Update-PublicFolder, 363, 378
  Update-PublicFolderHierarchy, 363, 377–378
user accounts
  contact information, changing, 143
  creating, 15, 120, 139–140
  defined, 117
  deleting account, 148–149
  display names, 142–144
  distribution groups, 123–124
  Exchange alias, 117–118, 143–144
  global settings, 145
  logon names, 128–129, 142–143
  mailbox-enabled, 117, 122–123, 128
  mailboxes, adding, 140–142
  mailboxes, deleting, 148–149
  mail-enabled, 118, 122, 129–133
  passwords, 128, 147–148
  passwords, changing, 147–148
  permissions, assigning, 234–235
  reply-to address, 145
  security certificates, 120–121
user names, 106–107, 128
User objects, 117
User Options role, 248
user scope, 249

V

viewing attachments, 528
View-Only Configuration role, 248
View-Only Organization Management Group,
    17, 238
View-Only Recipients role, 248
virtual directories, 469–470, 478
virtual directory, 108–109
virtual servers, multihomed, 472
voice access responsiveness, 50
Volume Shadow Copy Service (VSS)-based backup
    program, 577

W

Wait-Process cmdlets, 99
Warning Message Interval, 319
Web access. *See* Outlook Web App (OWA)
Web applications, 108–109, 469–472
Web Management Service, 14
WebReady Document Viewing, 528–530
Windows authentication, 109, 477
Windows Installer, 9–10, 52
Windows Live Mail
  advantages/disadvantages, 596
  configuring, 603–605
  folders, checking, 611
  Internet mail accounts, 606
  leaving mail on server, 610
  Outlook and, 599

Windows Mail, 596
Windows Media Player, 37
Windows Memory Diagnostics, 584
Windows PowerShell. *See* PowerShell
Windows Remote Management (WinRM)
  analyze and configure service, command, 9
  description of, 14
  Exchange Server set up and, 7–9, 52
  listeners, 112
  remote management services, customizing, 64,
    86–89
  requirements for, 7
  trusted hosts, adding to, 8
  verify the availability of, 7–8
Windows Server 2008
  backing up Exchange Server, 580–583
  full server recovery, 583–585
  getting started with backup, 579–580
  recovering Exchange server, 585–590
Windows Server 2008 operating system
  Client Access role installation, 35
  domain controllers, 39
  Edge Transport role installation, 39
  global catalog servers, 39
  Hub Transport role installation, 38
  mailbox role installation, 32
  .NET Framework, installation of, 32, 35–36,
    38–39
  roles, add/remove, 56
  unified messaging role installation, 36–37
Windows Server Backup
  about, 577
  application data, 579
  backup options, 582
  installing, 579
  System State data, 579
Windows Vista, 52
Windows, Exchange Server and, 11–17
winrm quickconfig, 112
wireless access, 146, 631–633
witness server, 287–288
Word documents, viewing, 528
workgroups, 8
World Wide Web Publishing Services, 14
Write All Properties permission, 241
Write cmdlets
  Write-EventLog, 98
  Write-Host, 99
  Write-Output, 99
  Write-Warning, 99
Write Value(s) permission, 241
write-back caching controllers, 5
WS-Management protocol, 7

X

X.400, 119, 144, 154
X.500, 117

About the Author

William R. Stanek (*http://www.williamstanek.com/*) has more than 20 years of hands-on experience with advanced programming and development. He is a leading technology expert, an award-winning author, and a pretty-darn-good instructional trainer. Over the years, his practical advice has helped millions of programmers, developers, and network engineers all over the world. He has written more than 100 books. Current or forthcoming books include *Active Directory Administrator's Pocket Consultant*, *Windows Group Policy Administrator's Pocket Consultant*, *Windows PowerShell 2.0 Administrator's Pocket Consultant*, and *Windows Server 2008 Inside Out*.

William has been involved in the commercial Internet community since 1991. His core business and technology experience comes from more than 11 years of military service. He has substantial experience in developing server technology, encryption, and Internet solutions. He has written many technical white papers and training courses on a wide variety of topics. He frequently serves as a subject matter expert and consultant.

William has a BS in computer science, magna cum laude, and an MS with distinction in information systems. He is proud to have served in the Persian Gulf War as a combat crewmember on an electronic warfare aircraft. He flew on numerous combat missions into Iraq and was awarded nine medals for his wartime service, including one of the United States of America's highest flying honors, the Air Force Distinguished Flying Cross. Currently, he resides in the Pacific Northwest with his wife and children.

William recently rediscovered his love of the great outdoors. When he's not writing, teaching, or making presentations, he can be found hiking, biking, backpacking, traveling, or trekking the great outdoors in search of adventure!

Follow William on Twitter at WilliamStanek.

What do you think of this book?

We want to hear from you!

To participate in a brief online survey, please visit:

microsoft.com/learning/booksurvey

Tell us how well this book meets your needs—what works effectively, and what we can do better. Your feedback will help us continually improve our books and learning resources for you.

Thank you in advance for your input!

Microsoft *Press*

Stay in touch!

To subscribe to the *Microsoft Press® Book Connection Newsletter*—for news on upcoming books, events, and special offers—please visit:

microsoft.com/learning/books/newsletter